BARRON'S

TOEIC®

TEST OF ENGLISH FOR INTERNATIONAL COMMUNICATION

7TH EDITION

Lin Lougheed
Ed.D., Teachers College
Columbia University

IMPORTANT
NEW TOEIC

In some countries, there will be a "new" TOEIC. After May 2016, there will be a different TOEIC administered in certain countries. Japan and Korea will be the first countries to administer the new TOEIC. The TOEIC will change in other countries over the next few years. Please visit the ETS TOEIC website (*www.ets.org/toeic*) for dates when the test will change in your country.

The new TOEIC will have the same question types as the old TOEIC plus some new question types. The new question types for each part are discussed in detail at the end of each chapter in this book. Look for the gray bar at the side of the page.

If you are taking the new TOEIC, you should study each chapter AND the pages with gray bars that immediately follow each chapter. There are also two complete TOEIC tests in the new format in this book.

If you are taking the old TOEIC, you only need to study each chapter. However, it would be good practice for you to study everything. You will still be learning English.

AUDIO AND AUDIOSCRIPTS

The MP3 files and audioscripts for all listening segments can be found online at *http://barronsbooks.com/tp/toeic/audio/*

All inquiries should be addressed to:
Barron's Educational Series, Inc.
250 Wireless Boulevard
Hauppauge, New York 11788
www.barronseduc.com

Library of Congress Control No.: 2016942367

ISBN: 978-1-4380-7636-2 (Book with Audio CD Package)

PRINTED IN THE UNITED STATES OF AMERICA
9 8 7 6 5 4 3 2 1

10%
POST-CONSUMER WASTE
Paper contains a minimum of 10% post-consumer waste (PCW). Paper used in this book was derived from certified, sustainable forestlands.

Contents

TOEIC MODEL TESTS

Overview of the TOEIC

There are two sections on the TOEIC: Listening Comprehension and Reading. Specific information about each section is given in detail in this book. The kinds of questions asked and the strategies you'll need to master in order to perform well are provided in the respective chapters. These charts show the differences between the old and new TOEICs.

TOEIC			NEW TOEIC		
Section 1: Listening Comprehension **Time: Approximately 45 minutes**			**Section 1: Listening Comprehension** **Time: Approximately 45 minutes**		
Part	Name	Number of questions	Part	Name	Number of questions
1	Photographs	10	1	Photographs	6
2	Question-Response	30	2	Question-Response	25
3	Conversations (10)	30	3	Conversations (13) with and without a visual image	39
4	Talks (10)	30	4	Talks (10) with and without a visual image	30

TOEIC			NEW TOEIC		
Section 2: Reading **Time: 75 minutes**			**Section 2: Reading** **Time: 75 minutes**		
Part	Name	Number of questions	Part	Name	Number of questions
5	Incomplete Sentences	40	5	Incomplete Sentences	30
6	Text Completion (4)	12	6	Text Completion (4)	16
7	Reading Comprehension ■ Single Passages ■ Double passages	 28 20	7	Reading Comprehension ■ Single Passages ■ Multiple passages	 29 25

TO THE TEACHER

Rationale for a TOEIC Preparation Course

Barron's TOEIC preparation book may be used as either a self-study course or a class course. In a class situation, this text will provide an excellent structure for helping the students improve their English language skills and prepare for the TOEIC.

Adult learners of English are very goal-oriented. For many adults who are required to take the TOEIC, their goal is, obviously enough, a high score. Having a goal that can be easily measured will be very motivating for your students.

Many teachers do not like to "teach to the test." They feel that developing a general knowledge of English will be more useful to the students than reviewing test items. But students want to "study the test." They don't want to "waste their time" learning something that might not be tested.

Both arguments ignore what actually happens during a TOEIC preparation course. General English is used to discuss how the exam is structured, what strategies should be used, and what skills should be developed. General English is used to explain problems and to expand into other areas. By helping students prepare for an exam, you can't help but improve their general knowledge of English.

A TOEIC preparation course gives the students what they want: a streamlined approach to learning what they think they need to know for the exam. The course gives the teachers what they want: a scheme to help them improve the English language ability of their students.

Organization of a TOEIC Preparation Course

TIMETABLE

Every test-preparation course faces the same dilemma: how to squeeze a total review of English into a class timetable. Some of you may have an afternoon TOEIC orientation; others may have a one-week intensive class; some may have a ten-week session. However long your class time, one thing is true: no class is ever long enough to cover everything you want to cover.

As a guideline, you might want to follow this plan and expand it as your time allows.

■ First period:	Study Chapter 1, Introduction. Have students sign the TOEIC Contract.
■ Next period:	Take a Model Test. Evaluate answers; determine the weak areas of the class.
■ Subsequent periods:	Review Listening Comprehension. Take the Mini-Test. Review Reading. Take the Mini-Test. Take additional Model Tests.
■ Last period:	Take a final Model Test and note the improvement in scores.

After students have completed the exercises, the Mini-Tests, or the Model Tests, they can check the Answer Key for quick access to the correct answer or read the Explanatory Answers for reasons why the correct answer is right and the incorrect answers are wrong.

These abbreviations are used in the exercises and Explanatory Answers.

adjective	(adj)	noun	(n)
adverb	(adv)	preposition	(prep)
article	(art)	pronoun	(pron)
auxiliary	(aux)	subject of a sentence	(sub)
conjunction	(conj)	verb	(v)
interjection	(interj)		

The symbol ≁ is also used, to mean "is not the same as," "is different from," and "does not equal."

Teaching Listening Comprehension

The more students hear English, the better their listening comprehension will be. Encourage a lot of discussion about the various strategies mentioned in the Listening Comprehension activities. Have the students work in pairs or small groups to increase the amount of time they will spend listening and speaking.

All tests require the students to choose a correct answer. This means the students must eliminate the incorrect answers. There are common distractors (traps) on an exam that a student can be trained to listen for. And coincidentally, while they are learning to listen for these traps, they are improving their listening comprehension.

The Listening Comprehension activities in this text are a gold mine. You can use them for the stated purpose, which is to help students learn how to analyze photos, answer choices, question types, and language functions. In addition, you can use them for a variety of communicative activities.

PHOTOGRAPH EXERCISES

The photographs can be used to help students develop their vocabulary. There are over 140 photographs in this text. Have the students pick a photograph and, in pairs or small groups, name everything they can see in the picture.

Then, in the same small groups (or individually) have them use those words in a sentence. They can write a short description of the photograph or, even better, they can write a short narrative. The narratives can be extremely imaginative—the more imaginative the better. Have the students describe what happened before the photograph was taken and what might happen afterwards.

Once students have the vocabulary under control, they can make an oral presentation. The other students or groups will then have to retell the narrative. This will help them evaluate their own listening comprehension.

QUESTION-RESPONSE EXERCISES

In this section, there is one short question, followed by an equally short answer. There is sometimes just a statement followed by a short response. This is not the way people communicate. Have the students establish a context for the short question or statement. Where are the speakers? Who are they? What are they talking about? What were they doing before? What will they do next? What did they say before? What will they say next?

Have them create a short skit that a pair of students can act out. Then have others in the class try to summarize the dialogue. Again, you are helping them evaluate their own listening comprehension.

CONVERSATION EXERCISES

The same technique can work here. Actually, it will be easier, because there is more dialogue for the students to use as a basis. This time have the students listen to the skit created by their colleagues and ask "wh" questions. Have them learn to anticipate *who, what, when, where, why,* and *how.*

TALKS EXERCISES

There are a variety of short talks: some are about the weather; others are public service announcements; some are advertisements. Have the students take one of the small talks and rewrite it. If it is a weather announcement, have them take a rainy day and make it sunny; have them change an advertisement for a television into an advertisement for a car.

Then, as with the other activities, have the other students create the "wh" questions. See if they can stump their colleagues. Have them make these talks challenging.

Teaching Reading

Again, the best way for students to improve their reading is to read, read, read. On the TOEIC, even the grammar activities focus on reading. They demand that students understand the whole context of the statement, not just an isolated part. That is why the structure tests are in the Reading section.

As in the Listening Comprehension section, it is as important to know why an answer is wrong as it is to know why an answer is right. Training your students to use the strategies mentioned in these sections will make them more efficient readers.

VOCABULARY EXERCISES

All students want to know words and more words. Remind them that it is important to know how to use them. They will learn more by reading and learning words in context than they will from memorizing word lists.

They can and should create their own personal word lists. Every time they encounter an unfamiliar word, they should write it down in a notebook. They should try to use it in a sentence, or even better, in a dialogue. Have the students create their own skits using the words in their own personal word lists.

If the students insist on lists, show them all the charts of words in the various sections of both the Listening and Reading sections. Have the students use these words to learn how to use words in context.

GRAMMAR EXERCISES

The grammar reviewed in this text covers those areas that are most likely to be found on the TOEIC and that most likely will give students the most problems. You can help students focus their attention by having them analyze their mistakes in the Model Tests.

READING EXERCISES

The strategies emphasized in the Reading review are not only for reading on the TOEIC. They can be, and should be, applied to all reading a student might have to do. Use outside reading materials such as English news magazines and newspapers. Have the students read not only the articles but also the ads, announcements, subscription forms, and tables of contents. In fact, have them scan and read the entire magazine. Everything found in a news magazine, including charts and graphs, is found on the TOEIC.

As the students did in the Listening Comprehension review, have them create "wh" questions for the articles, graphs, tables, and so on that they find. Let them try to stump their colleagues. To make the lesson even more communicative, have the students give an oral presentation of what they have read. Let the "wh" questions be oral, too.

USE A MODEL TEST AS A DIAGNOSTIC

If the students have several errors on questions testing prepositions, you would suggest they concentrate on the problems dealing with prepositions. Lists in the front of Chapter 2 and Chapter 3 provide an easy way for you to find the specific exercises your students need. (See pages 15 and 133.) By focusing on problem areas, they will be able to study more efficiently and effectively.

1 Introduction

What to Look for in This Chapter

- Questions and Answers Concerning the TOEIC
- Study Plan for the TOEIC
- Self-Study Activities
- On Test Day

QUESTIONS AND ANSWERS CONCERNING THE TOEIC

More than 4,500,000 people take the TOEIC each year, and this number is growing. The TOEIC is administered in Europe, Asia, North America, South America, and Central America. Since the test is relatively new (compared to the TOEFL, which was first given in 1963), many test takers are unfamiliar with the TOEIC. The following are some commonly asked questions about the TOEIC.

Online Resources
You can also learn more at the TOEIC website *www.toeic.com* or at my website *www.lougheed.com.*

What Is the Purpose of the TOEIC?

Since 1979, the TOEIC (the Test of English for International Communication) has been used internationally as a standard assessment of English-language proficiency. The TOEIC has been developed by linguists, language experts, and staff at The Chauncey Group International Ltd. to evaluate the English language skills of nonnative speakers of English in the field of business.

What Skills Are Tested on the TOEIC?

The TOEIC consists of two sections: Listening Comprehension (100 multiple-choice questions) and Reading (100 multiple-choice questions). Audio is used to test Listening Comprehension.

The content of the TOEIC is not specialized; the vocabulary and content are familiar to those individuals who use English in daily activities.

Who Uses the TOEIC?

Government agencies, multinational corporations, and international organizations use the TOEIC to ascertain the English-language capabilities of employees and prospective employees. The scores are used as an independent measure of proficiency and can be helpful in identifying personnel capable of handling language-specific responsibilities, in placing personnel in language-training programs, and in promoting personnel to positions where reliable linguistic standards are met.

Language-training programs use the TOEIC to establish language-training goals and to assess students' progress in overall English ability.

Who Takes the TOEIC?

In addition to the staffs of the companies and organizations previously mentioned, individuals take the TOEIC to document their abilities for personal and professional reasons.

What Is the Format of the TOEIC?

The TOEIC consists of two sections:

Listening Comprehension	
Part 1: Photographs	10 questions
Part 2: Question-Response	30 questions
Part 3: Conversations	30 questions
Part 4: Talks	30 questions
Reading	
Part 5: Incomplete Sentences	40 questions
Part 6: Text Completion	12 questions
Part 7: Reading Comprehension	
■ Single passages	28 questions
■ Double passages	20 questions

There are a total of 200 items; total time allowed for the test (including administrative tasks) is approximately 2½ hours. The Listening Comprehension section takes 45 minutes; the Reading section takes 75 minutes.

Why Are TOEIC Questions so Tricky?

TOEIC questions are carefully designed to test your knowledge of English. The questions must be difficult in order to discriminate between test takers of varying abilities. That is, the difficult questions separate those who are more proficient in English from those who are less proficient. A test question and the answer options may use one or more of these tricks to test your language competence:

- Use words with similar sounds.
- Use homonyms.
- Use related words.
- Omit a necessary word.
- Include unnecessary words.
- Alter the correct word order.

How Is the TOEIC Score Determined?

Separate scores are given for Listening Comprehension (5 to 495) and Reading (5 to 495). These two sub-scores are added to arrive at the total score. The TOEIC score is represented on a scale of 10 to 990 and is based on the total number of correct answers.

What Do TOEIC Scores Mean?

There is no established minimum passing score; each institution, through experience, sets up its own acceptable score.

How Are TOEIC Scores Obtained?

TOEIC test takers who are sponsored by companies, institutions, or organizations receive their scores from their sponsors. Those examinees who register individually to take the TOEIC receive their scores directly.

When and Where Can I Take the TOEIC?

The TOEIC is offered worldwide and is generally available upon demand. The dates, times, and locations of the test sites are determined by the local TOEIC representatives. For test fees, test dates, and locations, contact the TOEIC office in your country or contact ETS in the USA. The TOEIC representative offices are listed on ETS website, *www.ets.org*.

TIP

TOEIC representatives keep individual test scores for two years.

How Can I Prepare for the TOEIC?

If you plan to take the TOEIC, make a concerted effort to use English as much as possible, and in many different situations.

The best preparation is using a book/audio combination such as this—a program designed to help you specifically with the TOEIC. Following through with this book will:

- make you aware of certain test-taking skills;
- make you familiar with the format of the test; and
- improve your total score.

Additional suggestions are found in the next section, entitled "Study Plan for the TOEIC."

How Can I Get a Better Score on the TOEIC?

Assuming you have prepared well for the TOEIC, you can maximize your score on the test day by following these suggestions:

- Read the directions carefully.
- Work quickly.
- Do not make notes in the test booklet.
- Guess if you're not sure.
- Mark only one answer.

Additional suggestions are found in the next section, "Study Plan for the TOEIC."

STUDY PLAN FOR THE TOEIC

There is an English expression: "You can lead a horse to water, but you can't make him drink." Similarly, this book can lead you through the TOEIC, but it can't make you think. Learning is a self-motivated activity. Only you can prepare yourself for the TOEIC.

TOEIC Contract

It takes a lot of discipline to learn a foreign language. You need to formalize your commitment by signing a contract with yourself. This contract will obligate you to spend a certain number of hours each week learning English for a certain period of time. You will promise (1) to study *Barron's TOEIC* book and other Barron's TOEIC preparation materials, and (2) to study on your own. Sign the contract below to make your commitment.

- Print your name on line 1.
- Write the time you will spend each week studying English on lines 4–8. Think about how much time you have to study every day and every week and make your schedule realistic.
- Sign your name and date the contract on the last line.
- At the end of each week, add up your hours. Did you meet the requirements of your contract? Did you study both the *Barron's TOEIC* and the self-study activities?

TOEIC STUDY CONTRACT

I, ____________________, promise to study for the TOEIC. I will begin my study with *Barron's TOEIC* and I will also study English on my own.

I understand that to improve my English I need to spend time on English.

I promise to study English ____________________ hours per week.

I will spend ________ hours per week listening to English.

I will spend ________ hours per week writing English.

I will spend ________ hours per week speaking English.

I will spend ________ hours per week reading English.

This is a contract with myself. I promise to fulfill the terms of this contract.

____________________ ____________________

Signed Date

Good TOEIC Preparation Tips

1. **STUDY REGULARLY.** Pick the same time of day to practice. If you don't develop a routine, you won't develop good study habits. Tell yourself that you can't watch television at 7:30 because that is your TOEIC time. If you do miss your scheduled time one day, don't worry. Try to make it up later that day. But don't study at a different time every day. You will never get any studying done.
2. **DO A LITTLE AT A TIME.** Tell yourself that you will study for ten minutes on the train every morning or ten minutes just before you go to bed. It is better to learn one thing very well in a short period of time than to spend long periods trying to study everything.
3. **BUDGET YOUR TIME.** The TOEIC is a timed test, so time your study sessions. Give yourself ten minutes to study and then stop. You must use your time effectively. Learn how to take advantage of short periods of time.
4. **WRITE OUT A STUDY SCHEDULE.** If you put something in writing, you are more likely to do it.
5. **KNOW YOUR GOAL.** Why are you taking the TOEIC? If it's to qualify for a better position in your company, picture yourself in that job. What kind of score will you need? Work for that score (or a higher one).
6. **DEVELOP A POSITIVE ATTITUDE.** Before Olympic athletes compete, many shut their eyes and imagine themselves skiing down the mountain, running around the track, or swimming the fastest and passing the finish line first. They imagine themselves performing perfectly, scoring the best, and winning. This is the power of positive thinking. It is not just for athletes. You can use it, too.

   You must have a positive attitude when you take the TOEIC. Every night just before you fall asleep (when the right side of the brain is most receptive) repeat the following sentence ten times. "I understand English very well, and I will score very high on the TOEIC." The subconscious mind is very powerful. If you convince yourself that you can succeed, you are more likely to succeed.
7. **RELAX.** Don't become anxious about the exam. Get a good night's rest the night before the exam. Don't study that night. Relax and have a good time. Your mind will be more receptive if you are calm. Relax before, during, and especially after the exam.

Using *Barron's TOEIC*

1. **BECOME FAMILIAR WITH THE TOEIC QUESTIONS AND DIRECTIONS.** Read the sections on the TOEIC and the introductions to the Listening Comprehension and Reading chapters carefully. They contain information and advice that will help you raise your score.
2. **TAKE A MODEL TEST.** Use the Explanatory Answers as a guide to help you determine your weaknesses. If you miss more questions about prepositions than about adverbs of frequency, then you should spend your time studying prepositions. Use the skills lists found on pages 15 and 133 to easily find the exercises you need most.
3. **STUDY EFFICIENTLY.** When time is limited, concentrate on what you really need to study. Don't try to do everything if you don't have enough time.

4. **STUDY AND USE THE STRATEGIES.** This book lists many strategies that will help you score well on the exam. A strategy is a technique to use to help you approach a problem. In this case, a strategy will help you comprehend spoken and written English.

5. **STUDY ALL THE POTENTIAL PROBLEMS.** Know what to look for in the Listening Comprehension and Reading sections. You should learn how to recognize an incorrect answer.

6. **DO THE EXERCISES, REVIEW EXERCISES, AND MINI-TESTS.** All of the exercises are designed like those on the TOEIC. You will develop both your English ability and your test-taking skills by studying these exercises.

7. **REVIEW THE EXPLANATORY ANSWERS.** All of the answers for the review exercises, Mini-Tests, and the Model Tests are explained thoroughly at the end of the chapter in which they appear. Studying these explanations will sharpen your ability to analyze a test question. Knowing why you made an error will help you avoid the error the next time.

   Answer Keys are provided. You can use these keys to quickly find out which questions you did not answer correctly. Then, go to the Explanatory Answers to learn where you went wrong. This will help you to focus your studies on the areas in which you need the most practice.

8. **USE OTHER BARRON'S TOEIC PREPARATION MATERIALS.** Improve your TOEIC vocabulary with *Barron's Essential Words for the TOEIC.* Get more test practice with *Barron's TOEIC Practice Exams.* You can order both of these books online at *www.barronseduc.com*

DO A LITTLE EVERY DAY

It is worth repeating this advice. Following a consistent study routine will help you prepare for the TOEIC. You may not have to study everything in this book. Study the types of questions for which you need additional practice. But do it every day!

SELF-STUDY ACTIVITIES

1. **LISTEN TO AS MUCH ENGLISH AS YOU CAN.** The best way to improve your listening comprehension is by listening. As you listen, ask yourself these questions:

   Who is talking?
   Who are they talking to?
   What are they talking about?
   Where are they talking?
   Why are they talking?

   As you answer these questions, you will improve your ability to understand English through context.

2. **READ AS MUCH ENGLISH AS YOU CAN.** It should be no surprise that the best and easiest way to improve your reading comprehension is by reading. Concentrate on weekly news magazines. Look at the tables of contents, the advertisements, the announcements, and the articles. Read anything in English you can find: want ads, train schedules, hotel registration forms, etc. Again, always ask yourself questions as you read.

   Use the PSRA reading strategy technique discussed on pages 196–197. That will help you on the TOEIC and every time you read anything—even reading material in your own language!

3. **WRITE AND SPEAK AS MUCH ENGLISH AS YOU CAN.** Every time you listen and ask yourself who, what, when, where, why, give your answers out loud and then write them down.

4. **KEEP A VOCABULARY NOTEBOOK.** Be on the lookout for new vocabulary. Be aggressive about it. Get on the Internet and start reading websites. Any English website will be useful, but you can get both reading and listening practice on many of them such as CNN and BBC. Many newspapers, magazines, zines, and blogs are on the Internet. Do a search on an area of interest to you. You may be surprised how many sites are available.

   Here are some ways you can practice your listening, reading, speaking, and writing skills in English. You will find many opportunities to practice English in books and magazines as well as on the Internet. Check the ones you plan to try and add some ideas of your own on the blank lines provided.

TIP

Don't bother learning long lists of words. That will not help you as much as learning words in context.

If you like lists, there are lists in Chapter 2, *Listening*, and in Chapter 3, *Reading*. Study the lists and the examples given in context.

Listening

☐ Listen to podcasts on the Internet.
☐ Listen to news websites: CNN, BCC, NBC, ABC, CBS.
☐ Watch movies and television in English.
☐ Find YouTube videos that interest you.
☐ Find videos and movies that interest you at this website: *http://archive.org/details/movies.*
☐ Listen to CNN and BBC on the radio or on the Internet.
☐ Listen to Pandora or other Internet radio applications.
☐ Listen to music in English.
☐ ______________________________
☐ ______________________________

Speaking

☐ Describe what you see and what you do out loud.
☐ Practice having a conversation with a buddy.
☐ Use Skype to talk to English speakers.
☐ ______________________________
☐ ______________________________

Writing

- ☐ Write a daily journal.
- ☐ Write a letter to an English speaker.
- ☐ Make lists of the things that you see every day.
- ☐ Write descriptions of your family and friends.
- ☐ Write e-mails to website contacts.
- ☐ Write a blog.
- ☐ Leave comments on blogs and YouTube.
- ☐ Post messages in a chat room.
- ☐ Use Facebook and MySpace.
- ☐ ______________________________
- ☐ ______________________________

Reading

- ☐ Read newspapers and magazines in English.
- ☐ Read books in English.
- ☐ Read graphic novels in English.
- ☐ Read news and magazine articles online.
- ☐ Do web research on topics that interest you.
- ☐ Follow blogs that interest you.
- ☐ ______________________________
- ☐ ______________________________

Examples of Self-Study Activities

Whether you read an article in a newspaper or on a website, you can use that article in a variety of ways to practice reading, writing, speaking, and listening in English.

- Read about it.
- Paraphrase and write about it.
- Give a talk or presentation about it.
- Record or make a video of your presentation.
- Listen to or watch what you recorded.
- Write down your presentation.
- Correct your mistakes.
- Do it all again.

Here are some specific examples you can do to study on your own.

PLAN A TRIP

Go to *www.cntraveler.com*

Choose a city and a hotel, go to that hotel's website and choose a room, then choose some sites to visit (*reading*). Write a report about the city. Tell why you want to go there. Describe the hotel and the room you will reserve. Tell what sites you plan to visit and when. Where will you eat? How will you get around?

Now write a letter to someone recommending this place (*writing*). Pretend you have to give a lecture on your planned trip (*speaking*). Make a video of yourself talking about this place, and then watch the video and write down what you said. Correct any mistakes you made and record the presentation again. Then choose another city and do this again.

SHOP FOR AN ELECTRONIC PRODUCT

Go to *www.cnet.com*

Choose an electronic product and read about it (*reading*). Write a report about the product. Tell why you want to buy the product. Describe its features.

Now write a letter to someone recommending this product (*writing*). Pretend you have to give a talk about this product (*speaking*). Make a video of yourself talking about this product, and then watch the video and write down what you said. Correct any mistakes you made and record the presentation again. Then choose another product and do this again.

DISCUSS A BOOK OR A CD

Go to *www.amazon.com*

Choose a book, CD, or any product. Read the product's description and reviews (*reading*). Write a report about the product. Tell why you want to buy the product or why it is interesting to you. Describe its features.

Now write a letter to someone recommending this product (*writing*). Pretend you have to give a talk about this product (*speaking*). Make a video of yourself talking about this product, and then watch the video and write down what you said. Correct any mistakes you made and record the presentation again. Then choose another product and do this again.

DISCUSS ANY SUBJECT

Go to *http://simple.wikipedia.org/wiki/Main_Page*

This website is written in simple English. Pick any subject and read the entry (*reading*).

Write a short essay about the topic (*writing*). Give a presentation on the topic (*speaking*). Record the presentation, and then watch the video and write down what you said. Correct any mistakes you made and record the presentation again. Choose another topic and do this again.

DISCUSS ANY EVENT

Go to *http://news.google.com*

Google News has a variety of links. Pick one event and read the articles (*reading*).

Write a short essay about the event (*writing*). Give a presentation about the event (*speaking*). Record the presentation, and then watch the video and write down what you said. Correct any mistakes you made and record the presentation again. Then choose another event and do this again.

REPORT THE NEWS

Listen to an English-language news report on the radio or watch a news program on television (*listening*). Take notes as you listen. Write a summary of what you heard (*writing*).

Pretend you are a news reporter. Use the information from your notes to report the news (*speaking*). Record the presentation, and then watch the video and write down what you said. Correct any mistakes you made and record the presentation again. Then listen to another news program and do this again.

EXPRESS AN OPINION

Read a letter to the editor in the newspaper (*reading*). Write a letter in response in which you say whether or not you agree with the opinion expressed in the first letter. Explain why (*writing*).

Pretend you have to give a talk explaining your opinion (*speaking*). Record yourself giving the talk, and then watch the video and write down what you said. Correct any mistakes you made and record the presentation again. Then read another letter to the editor and do this again.

REVIEW A BOOK OR MOVIE

Read a book (*reading*). Think about your opinion of the book. What did you like about it? What didn't you like about it? Who would you recommend it to and why? Pretend you are a book reviewer for a newspaper. Write a review of the book stating your opinion and recommendations (*writing*).

Give an oral presentation about the book. Explain what the book is about and state your opinion (*speaking*). Record yourself giving the presentation, and then watch the video and write down what you said. Correct any mistakes you made and record the presentation again. Then read another book and do this again.

You can do this same activity after watching a movie (*listening*).

SUMMARIZE A TELEVISION SHOW

Watch a television show in English (*listening*). Take notes as you listen. After watching, write a summary of the show (*writing*).

Use your notes to give an oral summary of the show. Explain the characters, setting, and plot (*speaking*). Record yourself speaking, and then watch the video and write down what you said. Correct any mistakes you made and record the presentation again. Then watch another television show and do this again.

LISTEN TO A LECTURE

Listen to an academic or other type of lecture on the Internet. Go to any of the following or similar sites and look for lectures on topics that are of interest to you:

http://lecturefox.com

http://podcasts.ox.ac.uk

http://freevideolectures.com

www.ted.com/talks

Listen to a lecture and take notes as you listen. Listen again to check and add to your notes (*listening*). Use your notes to write a summary of the lecture (*writing*).

Pretend you have to give a lecture on the same subject. Use your notes to give your lecture (*speaking*). Record yourself as you lecture. Then watch the video and write down what you said. Correct any mistakes you made and record the lecture again. Then listen to another lecture and do this again.

ON TEST DAY

You are well prepared. You studied this book and other Barron's preparation material, and now it is test day. Here are some suggestions that will help you on the day of the test.

1. **BE EARLY.** You should avoid rushing on the test day. Leave yourself plenty of time to get to the testing center.
2. **BE COMFORTABLE.** If you can, choose your own seat; pick one that is away from distractions. You don't want to be near an open door where you can watch people pass outside. On the other hand, you might want to be near a window to get good light. Try, if you can, to sit near the audio player. If you can't hear well, be sure to tell the test administrator.
3. **BRING WHAT YOU NEED.** Your test site may provide pencils with erasers, but to be safe you should bring three or four No. 2 pencils with erasers. You may find a watch useful, too.
4. **LISTEN TO THE DIRECTIONS.** Even though you will know the format after using this book, you should listen to the directions carefully. Listening to the familiar directions will help you relax.

5. **ANSWER ALL QUESTIONS.** Even if you do not know an answer, you should mark your best answer. But try to make it an educated guess. When time is running out, just blacken any letter for the questions you have not answered—even if you didn't have time to read the question. You may be right.

6. **MATCH THE NUMBERS.** Make sure that the number on your answer sheet matches the number in your test book.

7. **MARK ONLY ONE ANSWER PER QUESTION ON THE ANSWER SHEET.** Only one black mark will be counted. If you make a mistake and erase, do it completely. Do not make any other marks on the answer sheet.

8. **ANSWER THE EASY QUESTIONS FIRST.** In the Reading section, you can pace yourself. If you do not immediately know an answer to a question, skip that question and go to one you can answer. At the end of the section, come back and do the more difficult questions. This will give you an opportunity to answer as many questions as you can.

9. **PACE YOURSELF.** The audio player will keep you moving in the Listening Comprehension section. But in the Reading section you will be able to adjust your own pace. You will have less than 45 seconds for each question in the Reading section.

10. **LEAVE TIME AT THE END.** If you can, try to leave a minute at the end to go over your answer sheet and make sure you have filled in every question.

11. **CELEBRATE AFTER THE EXAM.** Go ahead. Have a good time. You deserve it. Congratulations on a job well done.

TOEIC Review

2 Listening

OVERVIEW—CURRENT TOEIC

There are four parts to the Listening Comprehension section of the TOEIC. You will have approximately 45 minutes to complete this section.

Part 1: Photographs	10 Questions
Part 2: Question-Response	30 Questions
Part 3: Conversations	30 Questions
Part 4: Talks	30 Questions

To prepare for the four parts of the Listening Comprehension section, you must develop certain listening and analytical skills. Most of the skills targeted in this chapter are useful for all parts of the Listening Comprehension section.

SKILLS LIST

Part 1: Photographs
Skill
1. Assumptions
2. People
3. Things
4. Actions
5. General Locations
6. Specific Locations

Part 2: Question-Response
Skill
1. Similar Sounds
2. Related Words
3. Homonyms
4. Same Sound/Same Spelling but Different Meaning
5. Suggestions
6. Offers
7. Requests

Part 3: Conversations
Skill
1. Questions About People
2. Questions About Occupations
3. Questions About Place
4. Questions About Time
5. Questions About Activities
6. Questions About Opinions

Part 4: Talks
Skill
1. Questions About Events and Facts
2. Questions About Reasons
3. Questions About Numbers
4. Questions About Main Topics
5. Paraphrases

OVERVIEW—NEW TOEIC

There are four parts to the Listening Comprehension section of the new TOEIC. You will have approximately 45 minutes to complete this section.

Part 1: Photographs	6 Questions
Part 2: Question-Response	25 Questions
Part 3: Conversations	39 Questions
Part 4: Talks	30 Questions

The following skills are directed towards preparing you for the new question types on the Listening Comprehension section of the new TOEIC. You should also study the listening skills for the current TOEIC, as those question types will also appear on the new TOEIC.

SKILLS LIST

Part 3: Conversations
Skill
1. Graphic
2. Implied Meaning
3. Deleted Sounds
4. Incomplete Sentences
5. Multiple Accents

Part 4: Talks
Skill
1. Graphic
2. Implied Meaning
3. Multiple Accents

AUDIO AND AUDIOSCRIPTS

The MP3 files and audioscripts for all listening segments can be found online at ***http://barronsbooks.com/tp/toeic/audio/***

PART 1: PHOTOGRAPHS

Sample Question

> **Directions:** You will see a photograph. You will hear four statements about the photograph. Choose the statement that most closely matches the photograph and fill in the corresponding oval on your answer sheet. The statements will not be printed and will be spoken only once.

You will hear: Look at the photo marked number 1 in your test book.

(A) They're waiting at the bus stop. 

(B) They're leaving the building.

(C) They're selling tickets.

(D) They're getting off the bus.

Statement (D), "They're getting off the bus," best describes what you see in the photo. Therefore, you should choose answer (D).

SKILL

1 Assumptions

You may have to *make assumptions* when you listen to the TOEIC. These assumptions will be based on what you can infer in the photograph. You will have to determine which of the four statements you hear is true or might be true. One statement (answer choice) will be true or will most likely be true. That choice will be the correct answer.

> **TIP** Listen carefully to the whole sentence and determine which one choice best matches the photo.

PHOTO 1

PHOTO 2

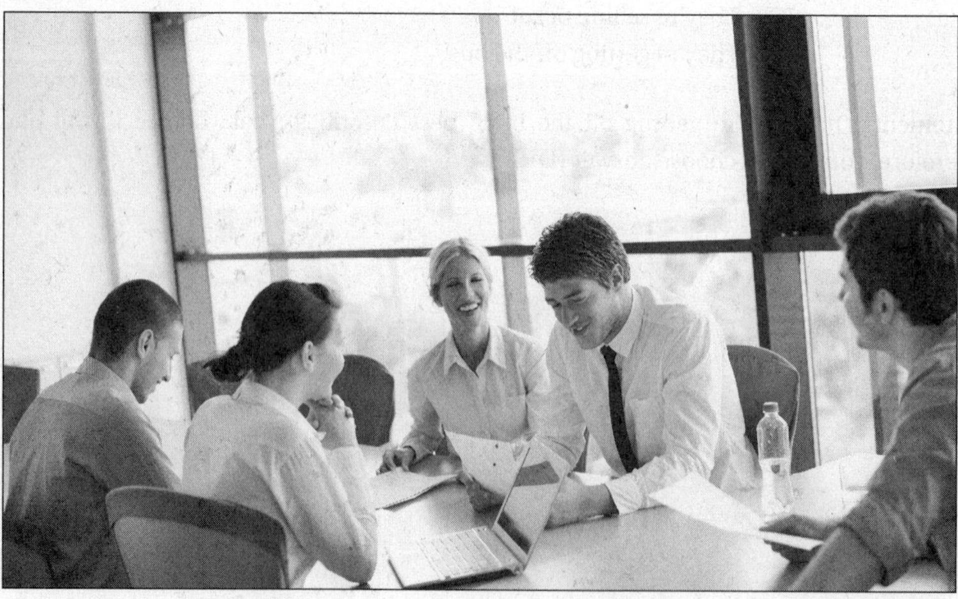

➡ Example

Look at these statements about Photo 1.

These statements are true.

This is a laboratory.

There are bottles on the shelves.

There is equipment on the counter.

The people are wearing protective clothing.

There are at least four people in the lab.

Wires run from the equipment.

These statements are probably true, but you can't tell for sure.

The people are lab technicians.	*They look like technicians, but they could be pharmacists.*
The people are students with a teacher.	*A teacher may be working with a class, or they may all be employees.*
The technicians are doing experiments.	*They might be doing experiments, or they might be producing some chemical compound.*

TIP

If you do not have access to the MP3 files, you can download the audioscripts at *http://barronsbooks.com/tp/toeic/audio/*

PRACTICE

Look at Photo 2 and read the following statements. Mark the statements True (T), Probably True (PT), or False (F).

A. There are five people around the table.
B. It's nighttime.
C. They're business colleagues.
D. They're smiling.
E. There is a bottle on the table.
F. There is water in the bottle.
G. They're drinking coffee.
H. They're eating something.
I. The computer is open.
J. They're reading a report.

Track 2

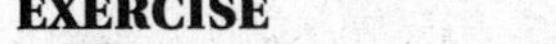

EXERCISE

Choose the statement that best describes what you see in the photos on page 18.

Photo 1 (A) (B) (C) (D)

Photo 2 (A) (B) (C) (D)

TIP

For more practice, look at the other photos in this book and try to make assumptions about what you see.

SKILL

2 People

You may have to *identify the people* in a photograph. You may identify them by number, gender, location, description, activity, or occupation.

> **TIP** Determine the number, gender, location, description, activity, and occupation of the people as best you can.

PHOTO 3

PHOTO 4

➥ Example

Look at these statements about Photo 3.

Number:	There are four people in the photo.
Gender:	There are two men and two women in the photo.
Location:	On the left, there are two men. On the right, there are two women.
Description:	One of the men is wearing glasses. The woman on the right is shorter than the other woman.
Activity:	The group is looking at a map. One woman is pointing to the map. All four people are leaning on the table.
Occupation:	Their profession is unknown. They are looking at and discussing a map. We can assume they are planners of some sort.

You may not be able to answer all questions. You may not know their occupation, for example. However, the more assumptions you can make, the easier it will be to answer the questions.

TIP

For more practice, look at the other photos in this book and try to identify the people you see in the photos.

PRACTICE

Complete the information about the people in Photo 4.

Number: ______________________

Gender: ______________________

Location: ______________________

Description: ______________________

Activity: ______________________

Occupation: ______________________

STRATEGY

Remember, statements must be completely true. Be careful about statements that are partly true, but not totally true. Analyze the photo carefully. Pay attention to the number, gender, or occupation of the people in the photo.

EXERCISE

Choose the statement that best describes what you see in the photos on page 20.

Photo 3 Ⓐ Ⓑ Ⓒ Ⓓ

Photo 4 Ⓐ Ⓑ Ⓒ Ⓓ

SKILL 3

Things

You may have to *identify things* in a photo. When you look at a photo, try to name everything you see. On the TOEIC, you will NOT have to know words, expressions, or idioms that are specific to one particular occupation. For example, in the photo below, you should know the general word "piano." You do not have to know the specific term "grand piano."

TIP Use the context of the photo to help you identify the things.

PHOTO 5

PHOTO 6

➥ Example

Find the following items in the photo. Keep in mind the context of Photo 5: It is a living room in a private home.

Words to Find

window	window shade	curtain
chair	cushion	carpet
floor	wall	fireplace
mantel	plant	plant
piano	piano bench	vase
candle	piano keys	shelf

PRACTICE

Make a list of the items you see in Photo 6.

________________ ________________

________________ ________________

________________ ________________

________________ ________________

________________ ________________

EXERCISE

Choose the statement that best describes what you see in the photos on page 22.

Photo 5 Ⓐ Ⓑ Ⓒ Ⓓ

Photo 6 Ⓐ Ⓑ Ⓒ Ⓓ

TIP

For more vocabulary practice, look at the other photos in this book and try to name as many things as you can.

Actions

You may have to *identify the actions* in a photo. There may be more than one action happening, even if there is only one person in the photo. If there are several people in the photo, they may all be doing the same thing or they may each be doing something different.

> **TIP** Determine what each person in the photo is doing.

PHOTO 7

PHOTO 8

➡ Example

Identify the following actions in Photo 7:

standing in the trench
standing next to the trench
kneeling in the trench
wearing a hard hat
holding the pipe
looking at the pipe
laying the pipe
leaning against the rocks

PRACTICE

Make a list of the actions you see in Photo 8.

______________________ ______________________

______________________ ______________________

______________________ ______________________

______________________ ______________________

______________________ ______________________

TIP

For more practice, look at the other photos in this book and identify past, present, and future actions.

EXERCISE

Choose the statement that best describes what you see in the photos on page 24.

Photo 7 Ⓐ Ⓑ Ⓒ Ⓓ

Photo 8 Ⓐ Ⓑ Ⓒ Ⓓ

SKILL

General Locations

You may have to *identify the general location* of a photograph. When you look at a picture, analyze the clues to determine a location. If you see a car, a mechanic, some tools, and a customer in a photo, you can assume the location is an automobile repair shop. If you see men and women working at desks with computers, you can assume the location is an office. A photo is full of clues to help you identify the general location.

> **TIP** Use the context of the photograph to help you make assumptions about the general location.

PHOTO 9

PHOTO 10

➡ Example

The following is a list of context clues in Photo 9. You may hear these words or variations of these words in Part I. Pay attention—the words may differ on the actual test.

TIP

For more practice, look at the other photos in this book and find the clues that will help you identify the general location.

Context Clues

Security checkpoint	Security officers
Departure information	Man with mobile phone
Gate sign	Airline names
People with baggage	Names of destinations
Porter with luggage cart	Sign about X-ray
Security personnel	Uniformed personnel

PRACTICE

Determine the general location in Photo 10. List the context clues you used.

Location ______________________________

______________________ ______________________

______________________ ______________________

______________________ ______________________

______________________ ______________________

______________________ ______________________

Use context clues to determine where the action is taking place.

EXERCISE

Choose the statement that best describes what you see in the photos on page 26.

Photo 9 Ⓐ Ⓑ Ⓒ Ⓓ

Photo 10 Ⓐ Ⓑ Ⓒ Ⓓ

SKILL 6

Specific Locations

You may have to *identify the specific location* of people and things in a photograph. When you look at a photo, analyze the relationship of the people and things.

TIP Listen for the correct preposition.

PHOTO 11

PHOTO 12

➡ Examples

Prepositions and Phrases of Location

above	beneath	far from	near	over
across	beside	in	next to	to the left of
around	between	in back of	on	to the right of
at	by	in front of	on top of	under
below	close to	inside	outside	underneath

TIP

For more practice, look at the other photos in this book and identify the specific location of each person or thing. You should also study the section on Prepositions in Chapter 3, beginning on page 56.

Look at these sentences about specific locations in Photo 11.

The server is <u>next to</u> the table.
There is a bottle <u>in front of</u> the woman.
The forks are <u>on</u> a plate.
There is a plate <u>in</u> the server's hand.
The man is sitting <u>across from</u> a woman.
A woman is sitting <u>next to</u> the man.

PRACTICE

Write sentences about specific locations in Photo 12 using the prepositions and phrases provided.

A. (on) ______________________________

B. (in front of) ______________________________

C. (over) ______________________________

D. (between) ______________________________

E. (to the left of) ______________________________

F. (on top of) ______________________________

EXERCISE

Choose the statement that best describes what you see in the photos on page 28.

Photo 11 Ⓐ Ⓑ Ⓒ Ⓓ

Photo 12 Ⓐ Ⓑ Ⓒ Ⓓ

NEW TOEIC—PART 1: PHOTOGRAPHS

There are NO changes in Part 1: Photographs in the types of statements. The statements will focus on people, actions, places, or things. The skills and strategies to prepare for Part 1 are the same for both the current and the new TOEIC.

There will be fewer statements. There are only 6 rather than 10 statements.

PRACTICE

Track 8

Directions: You will see a photograph. You will hear four statements about the photograph. Choose the statement that most closely matches the photograph and fill in the corresponding oval on your answer sheet.

TIP

See page 122 for the Answer Key and page 125 for the Explanatory Answers for new TOEIC practice Part 1.

1.

Ⓐ Ⓑ Ⓒ Ⓓ

2.

Ⓐ Ⓑ Ⓒ Ⓓ

NEW TOEIC

3.

Ⓐ Ⓑ Ⓒ Ⓓ

4.

Ⓐ Ⓑ Ⓒ Ⓓ

5.

Ⓐ Ⓑ Ⓒ Ⓓ

6.

Ⓐ Ⓑ Ⓒ Ⓓ

STRATEGY SUMMARY

Strategies for Analyzing Photographs

- **When you look at a photograph, analyze the people. Determine their number, gender, location, and occupation.**
- **Look for context clues in the photo.**
- **Listen for the meaning of the *whole sentence* to determine which choice best matches the photo.**

PART 2: QUESTION-RESPONSE

Sample Question

Directions: You will hear a question and three possible responses. Choose the response that most closely answers the question and fill in the corresponding oval on your answer sheet. The statements will not be printed and will be spoken only once.

You will hear: 1. How can I get to the airport from here?

(A) Take a taxi. It's just a short ride. ● Ⓑ Ⓒ

(B) No, I don't.

(C) You can get on easily.

The best response to the question "How can I get to the airport from here?" is Choice (A), "Take a taxi. It's just a short ride." Therefore, you should choose answer (A).

SKILL 1

Similar Sounds

On the TOEIC, you may have to distinguish between words with *similar sounds.* When you hear the answer choices, pay attention to the meaning. There will be context clues that help you understand the meaning. Do not be confused by words with similar sounds.

TIP Listen carefully to the meaning of the statement or question and determine which answer choice really answers the question.

Examples

Here are examples of similar sounds:

Different Vowel Sounds			
bass	car	deep	gun
base	core	dip	gone
boots	cart	fall	grass
boats	court	full	grease
bus	drug	fun	letter
boss	drag	phone	later
Different Initial Consonant Sounds			
back	core	race	hair
pack	tore	case	fair
rack	sore	place	tear
Different Final Consonant Sounds			
cab	little	nab	think
cap	litter	nap	thing
Two or More Words That Sound Like One Word			
mark it	sent her	letter	in tents
market	center	let her	intense
Words That Have Sounds That Are Part of a Longer Word			
nation	mind	give	intention
imagination	remind	forgive	unintentional

EXERCISE

Choose the best response to each question.

1. Ⓐ Ⓑ Ⓒ
2. Ⓐ Ⓑ Ⓒ
3. Ⓐ Ⓑ Ⓒ

SKILL 2

Related Words

On the TOEIC, you may have to distinguish between *related words.* When you hear the answer choices, pay attention to the meaning. Be careful of words from the same word family or words with associated meanings. An answer choice that contains a word related to the context of the question is not necessarily the correct answer.

> **TIP** Listen for the choice that completely answers the question.

➥ Examples

These are some related words:

Airline				
ticket	pilot	reservation	baggage claim	check-in
seatbelt	flight attendant	ticket counter	crew	turbulence
Hotel				
room	pool	floor	suite	fitness center
front desk	check in/out	bed	lobby	housekeeping
Restaurant				
table	server	menu	tray	waiter/waitress
dish	napkin	meal	dinner	breakfast
lunch	dessert	tip	plate	bill/check
Bank				
cash	deposit	withdrawal	teller	officer
account	loan	savings	receipt	check
Weather				
sunny	cool	rain	drizzle	wind
cold	sleet	rainstorm	mist	breeze
freezing	warm	hot	cloudy	blizzard
snow	humid	smoggy	thunder	tornado
chilly	humidity	fog	lightning	hurricane

EXERCISE

Choose the best response to each question.

1. Ⓐ Ⓑ Ⓒ
2. Ⓐ Ⓑ Ⓒ
3. Ⓐ Ⓑ Ⓒ

Homonyms

On the TOEIC, you may have to determine whether the answer choices contain a word that is a *homonym*. Homonyms are words that are pronounced the same, but have different meanings and different spellings.

> **TIP** Listen for the meaning of the word in the context of the sentence.

➡ Examples

Homonyms

allowed	feet	male	right	tale
aloud	feat	mail	rite	tail
bear	find	meat	write	threw
bare	fined	meet	sail	through
blew	flew	mind	sale	too
blue	flu	mined	seen	two
bough	flour	morning	scene	to
bow	flower	mourning	sight	wait
buy	for	one	site	weight
by	four	won	sowing	week
do	loan	pale	sewing	weak
due	lone	pail	steak	
dew	made	plane	stake	
fare	maid	plain	steel	
fair			steal	

EXERCISE

Choose the best response to each question.

1. Ⓐ Ⓑ Ⓒ
2. Ⓐ Ⓑ Ⓒ
3. Ⓐ Ⓑ Ⓒ

Same Sound/Same Spelling but Different Meaning

On the TOEIC, you may have to distinguish between *words that have the same sound and same spelling but have a different meaning.* When you hear the answer choices, pay attention to the meaning. Be careful of words with the same sounds and same spellings, but with different meanings.

TIP Listen to the context for the word that answers the question.

➡ Examples

Different Meanings for the Same Word

Call:	Animal or bird noise Shout Telephone call	*File:*	Folder Row Tool
Class:	Social position Group of students Level of quality	*Hard:*	Difficult Tough Firm
Court:	Tennis court Court of law Royal court	*Note:*	Musical note Short letter Currency
Date:	Type of fruit Meeting with someone Particular day	*Seat:*	A chair Location of power Membership in a club
Band:	Group of musicians Strip of cloth or other material	*Park:*	Open, grassy area in a city Leave your car in a certain place
Bank:	Financial institution Land along a river	*Right:*	Correct Opposite of *left* Just or fair
Left:	Past tense of *leave* Opposite of *right*		

EXERCISE

Choose the best response to each question.

1. Ⓐ Ⓑ Ⓒ
2. Ⓐ Ⓑ Ⓒ
3. Ⓐ Ⓑ Ⓒ

SKILL

Suggestions

Some of the questions in Part 2 may actually be suggestions. They require a certain type of response.

> **TIP** Listen for words that signal suggestions.

➥ Examples

If you hear these question types, listen for answers about suggestions.

Suggestions

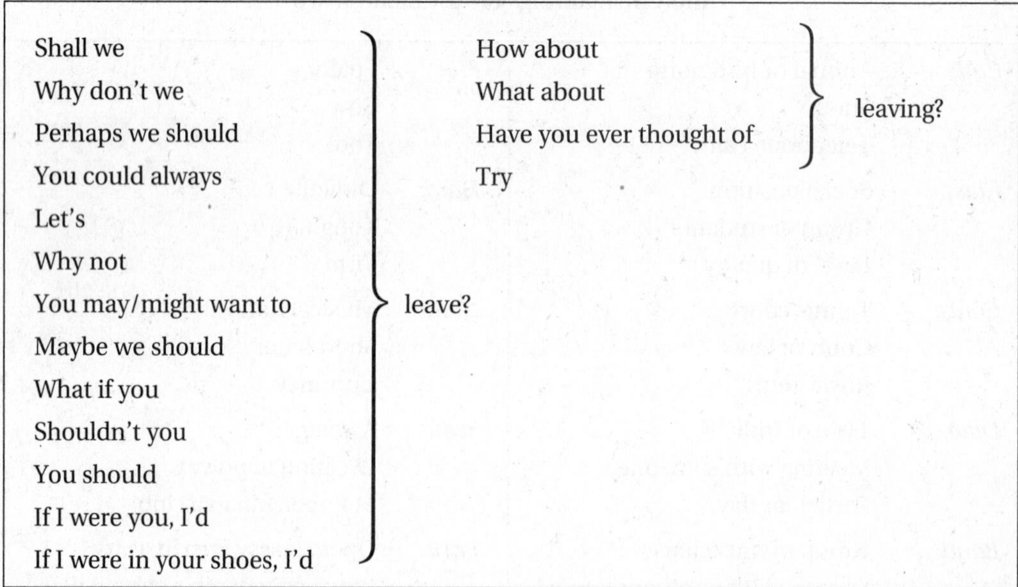

Shall we Why don't we Perhaps we should You could always Let's Why not You may/might want to Maybe we should What if you Shouldn't you You should If I were you, I'd If I were in your shoes, I'd	leave?
How about What about Have you ever thought of Try	leaving?

The answers to those questions are usually responses to a suggestion. The responses can be positive (*let's go*) or negative (*let's not*). If you see or hear answers like these, look or listen for questions that are suggestions.

Answers

Yes, let's.	What a brilliant idea!
That's a good idea.	No, I haven't yet.
Why not?	OK.
Suits me.	Good idea.

EXERCISE

Choose the best response to each question.

1. Ⓐ Ⓑ Ⓒ
2. Ⓐ Ⓑ Ⓒ
3. Ⓐ Ⓑ Ⓒ

SKILL
6

Offers

Some of the questions in Part 2 may actually be offers. Learn to recognize the words, phrases, and suggestions that signal an offer.

TIP Listen for words that signal offers.

➥ Examples

If you hear these question types, which begin with these common offer markers, listen to see what is being offered.

Offers

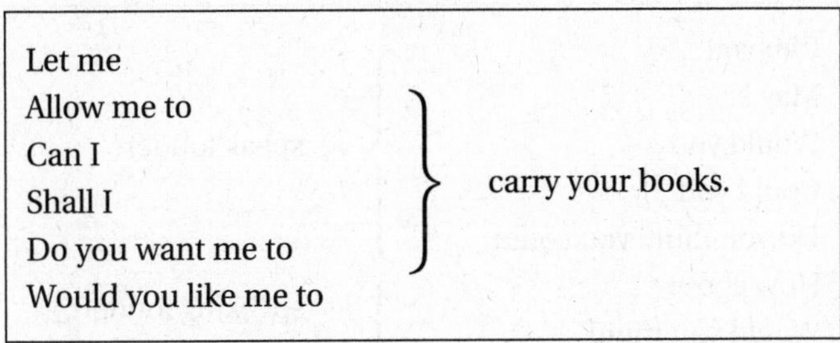

Let me
Allow me to
Can I
Shall I
Do you want me to
Would you like me to
} carry your books.

The answers to those questions are usually polite responses that accept or decline an offer. If you see or hear answers like these, look or listen for questions that make an offer.

Answers

Thank you.	You're too kind.
That's very kind of you.	No, thanks. I can manage.
I'd appreciate that.	

EXERCISE

Choose the best response to each question.

1. Ⓐ Ⓑ Ⓒ
2. Ⓐ Ⓑ Ⓒ
3. Ⓐ Ⓑ Ⓒ

SKILL 7 Requests

A request is a polite way of asking someone to do something. Learn to recognize requests and the information in them.

TIP Listen for words that signal requests.

➡ Examples

If you hear these question types, which begin with these common request markers, listen to see what is being requested.

Requests

Can you May I Would you Could you Do you think you could	speak louder?
How about Would you mind	speaking louder?

The answers to those questions are usually polite responses that acknowledge a request. If you see or hear answers like these, look or listen for questions that make a request.

Answers

Of course.	I'm sorry. I can't.
Is this OK?	Regretfully, no.
No problem.	Not at all. I'd be glad to.
Certainly.	I'd be happy to.

EXERCISE

Choose the best response to each question.

1. Ⓐ Ⓑ Ⓒ
2. Ⓐ Ⓑ Ⓒ
3. Ⓐ Ⓑ Ⓒ

NEW TOEIC—PART 2: QUESTION-RESPONSE

There are NO changes in Part 2: Question-Response in the types of questions. The skills and strategies to prepare for Part 2 are the same for both the current and the new TOEIC.

There will be fewer questions. There are only 25 rather than 30 questions.

TIP

See page 122 for the Answer Key and pages 125–126 for the Explanatory Answers for new TOEIC practice Part 2.

PRACTICE

Directions: You will hear a question and three possible responses. Choose the response that most closely answers the question and fill in the corresponding oval on your answer sheet.

1.	Ⓐ Ⓑ Ⓒ	11.	Ⓐ Ⓑ Ⓒ	21.	Ⓐ Ⓑ Ⓒ
2.	Ⓐ Ⓑ Ⓒ	12.	Ⓐ Ⓑ Ⓒ	22.	Ⓐ Ⓑ Ⓒ
3.	Ⓐ Ⓑ Ⓒ	13.	Ⓐ Ⓑ Ⓒ	23.	Ⓐ Ⓑ Ⓒ
4.	Ⓐ Ⓑ Ⓒ	14.	Ⓐ Ⓑ Ⓒ	24.	Ⓐ Ⓑ Ⓒ
5.	Ⓐ Ⓑ Ⓒ	15.	Ⓐ Ⓑ Ⓒ	25.	Ⓐ Ⓑ Ⓒ
6.	Ⓐ Ⓑ Ⓒ	16.	Ⓐ Ⓑ Ⓒ		
7.	Ⓐ Ⓑ Ⓒ	17.	Ⓐ Ⓑ Ⓒ		
8.	Ⓐ Ⓑ Ⓒ	18.	Ⓐ Ⓑ Ⓒ		
9.	Ⓐ Ⓑ Ⓒ	19.	Ⓐ Ⓑ Ⓒ		
10.	Ⓐ Ⓑ Ⓒ	20.	Ⓐ Ⓑ Ⓒ		

PART 3: CONVERSATIONS

Sample Questions

Directions: You will hear a short conversation between two people. You will see three questions on each conversation and four possible answers. Choose the best answer to each question and fill in the corresponding oval on your answer sheet. The conversations will not be printed and will be spoken only once.

You will hear:

Man: We'll need your medical history so take this form and fill it out, please.

Woman: Will there be a long wait for my appointment?

Man: No, the doctor is seeing patients on schedule.

Woman: That's good news. The last time I was here, I waited almost an hour.

Man: I'd say you won't have to be in the waiting room longer than a few minutes. Certainly not a half an hour. Not even twenty minutes.

Question 1

You will read: Where are the speakers?

(A) At a sidewalk cafe

(B) In a history class
(C) At an airport check-in counter
(D) In a physician's office

The best response to the question "Where are the speakers?" is Choice (D), "In a physician's office." Therefore, you should choose answer (D).

Question 2

You will read: Who is likely talking?

(A) A doctor and a nurse

(B) A clerk and a shopper
(C) A receptionist and a patient
(D) A pilot and a passenger

The best response to the question "Who is likely talking?" is Choice (C), "A receptionist and a patient." Therefore, you should choose answer (C).

Question 3

You will read: How long will the woman have to wait?

(A) A little bit
(B) Twenty minutes
(C) Thirty minutes
(D) Over an hour

● Ⓑ Ⓒ Ⓓ

The best response to the question "How long will the woman have to wait?" is Choice (A), "A little bit." Therefore, you should choose answer (A).

SKILL 1

Questions About People

On the TOEIC, questions about people are common. They ask you to identify the speaker or the performer of an action. Questions about people usually begin with *who,* although some what questions may also be about people.

TIP When you see a *who* question, listen for information about people.

Examples

If you see these question types, listen for answers about people.

Questions

Questions with ***What***	*Questions with* ***Who***
What is your name?	Who is taking part in this conversation?
What is her title?	Who is the man?
	Who is the woman?
	Who are the speakers?

Answers

Proper names	*Identification by activity or role*	*Identification by group*	*Identification by relationship*
Mr. Tanza	A tourist	Business people	His boss
Mrs. Green	A passenger	Family members	Her son
Ms. Hu	A driver	College students	Their teacher
Dr. Shapiro	A jogger		My colleague
			The woman's friend

EXERCISE

Choose the best answer to the question.

1. Who are the speakers?
   (A) Lifeguards at the beach
   (B) Painters
   (C) Salespeople selling coats
   (D) Bartenders

   Ⓐ Ⓑ Ⓒ Ⓓ

2. Who will prepare the wall?
   (A) The man
   (B) The woman
   (C) The boss
   (D) The helper

   Ⓐ Ⓑ Ⓒ Ⓓ

3. Who owns the house?
   (A) The man's father
   (B) The man's mother
   (C) The man's brother
   (D) The man's friend

   Ⓐ Ⓑ Ⓒ Ⓓ

SKILL 2

Questions About Occupations

Questions about a person's occupation are commonly asked on the TOEIC. You should first look at the answer choices to see what four occupations are given. Then you should try to think of words related to those occupations. These words will be clues.

It is important to listen for occupational clues in the conversations and short talks. If a person is an auto mechanic, you might hear references to engines, cars, oil, brakes, gas stations, and so on. If you hear those words, it is likely that the correct answer is *auto mechanic*.

> **TIP** Look for types of occupations in the answer choices BEFORE you hear the audio. Make assumptions about those occupations and listen for the clues.

Examples

If you see these question types, listen for answers about someone's occupation.

Questions

What kind of job does the man have?
What is Mr. Smith's present position?
What type of work does the woman do?
How does this man earn a living?
What is the man's job?
What kind of job is available?
What is the woman's occupation?
Who can benefit from seeing this memo?
What is the man's profession?
Who was interviewed?
What does this woman do?
Who would most likely use the conference hall?

Answers

She's the director.	A dentist
He's a lawyer.	A travel agent
They're accountants.	A hotel clerk
The office manager	A pilot
The personnel director	A flight attendant
The receptionist	A waiter/waitress/server
A computer programmer	A chef

EXERCISE

Choose the best answer to the question.

1. What is the woman's occupation?

   (A) Running coach
   (B) Baseball player
   (C) Telephone operator
   (D) Telephone installer

2. What is the man's job?

   (A) Mailman
   (B) Website designer
   (C) Employment counselor
   (D) Mail order company owner

3. Who is responsible for answering the phone?

   (A) The man only
   (B) The woman only
   (C) Everyone at the company
   (D) Some of the customers

Questions About Place

Most questions about place begin with *where.* These questions are generally answered by locations preceded by *in, on,* or *at.*

TIP When you see a *where* question, listen for information about place.

➥ Examples

If you see these question types, listen for answers about places.

Questions

Where did the conversation probably take place? Where did the conversation likely occur? Where is the man? Where is the woman? Where is the speaker? Where are the man and woman? Where are the speakers? Where is the package?	Where has the man/woman been? Where does the man/woman want to go? Where did the man/woman come from? Where are they going? Where did the man think the woman was? Where should he call? Where did he put his coat?

Answers

Without prepositions	*With prepositions*	
The train station	In the closet	By the door
The store	Under the desk	In the dining room
The office	At the office	At home
The house	Next to the bank	On the bus
	At the train station	At the dentist's
	At the beach	To the airport
	To the store	

EXERCISE

Choose the best answer to the question.

1. Where did he put the letter?

   (A) On the shelf
   (B) Under the books
   (C) On top of the books on the desk
   (D) In the drawer

   Ⓐ Ⓑ Ⓒ Ⓓ

2. Where is the shelf?

   (A) By the door
   (B) By the computer
   (C) By the desk
   (D) By the letterbox

   Ⓐ Ⓑ Ⓒ Ⓓ

3. Where does the woman want the man to put the letter?

   (A) Next to the printer
   (B) In a box
   (C) In a folder
   (D) On top of her computer

   Ⓐ Ⓑ Ⓒ Ⓓ

SKILL

Questions About Time

Most questions about time begin with *when* or *how long.* These questions are generally answered by time of day, days of the week, seasons, and dates. The answers give a specific time or a duration.

> **TIP** Look for clues on time in the answer choices BEFORE you hear the audio. Listen carefully for those clues in the audio.

➡ Examples

If you see these question types, listen for answers about time. Note the questions begin with *when* and *how.*

Questions

Questions with ***When***	*Questions with* ***How***
When did the conversation take place?	How long will the manager live in Tokyo?
When is the man's birthday?	How long will it take to arrive?
When is the woman's vacation date?	How often is the magazine published?
When is the restaurant open?	How many weeks were most people away each year?
When was the meeting?	
When will the increase go into effect?	
When did he join the firm?	

Listen for time questions. They generally begin with *when, how often, how many days,* or *how long.* Make sure that the correct response addresses the question that was asked. Answer a *when* question with a point in time, answer a *how long* question with a length of time, and answer a *how often* question with a frequency expression.

Answers

Points in time	*Lengths of time*	*Frequency*
11:00 A.M.	45 minutes	Every hour
Noon	An hour	Every day
Midnight	Two days	Every other day
At 6:00	A week	Every two weeks
Before 5:30	About a month	Once a month
In the morning	Less than a year	Twice a year
Tomorrow		Three times a week
In the summer		
Next year		
In April		
On January 3rd		

EXERCISE

Choose the best answer to the question.

1. How much longer will the man stay?

   (A) 10 minutes
   (B) 15 minutes
   (C) 30 minutes
   (D) 60 minutes

   Ⓐ Ⓑ Ⓒ Ⓓ

2. When is the man's appointment?

   (A) 8:00
   (B) 8:30
   (C) 9:00
   (D) 9:30

   Ⓐ Ⓑ Ⓒ Ⓓ

3. How long will it take the man to get home?

   (A) twenty minutes
   (B) twenty-five minutes
   (C) forty minutes
   (D) forty-five minutes

   Ⓐ Ⓑ Ⓒ Ⓓ

SKILL 5

Questions About Activities

Most questions about activities begin with *what.* Some questions can begin with *how.* These questions are generally answered by short phrases or complete sentences. You should first look at the answer choices to see what four activities are given. Then you should try to think of words related to those activities. These words will be activity clues.

It is important to listen for activity clues. For example, the activity playing golf might have words such as *golf club, bag, course, fairway, hole,* and *green* in the audio.

TIP Look for types of activities in the answer choices BEFORE you hear the audio. Make assumptions about those activities and listen for the clues.

Examples

If you see these question types, listen for answers about an activity. Note the questions begin with *what* and *how.*

Questions

Questions with ***to Do***	*Questions about an event or occurrence*
What will the man do?	What happened?
What did the woman do?	What occurred?
What has the customer decided to do?	What took place?
	What happened to the woman?
What are they planning to do?	What will happen next?
What does the woman have to do?	
What is the man going to do?	*Questions with* ***How***
What is Mrs. Park supposed to do?	How can the package be sent?
What are they doing?	How will the room be changed?

Answers

Activities in phrases
See a movie
Go out for lunch
Take a Spanish course
Play golf
Attend tonight's lecture
Finish the proposal
Take the day off
Read the fax

Activities in complete sentences
They will go out for dinner.
He will send a fax.
She should call her office.

Events or occurrences
The car stopped.
The conference let out early.
The chemical tanker arrived on schedule.
She was late for the meeting.
The phone lines were out of service.

Method or manner
By overnight mail
By express mail
By messenger
By courier
By moving the desk
By painting the walls
By covering the windows
By adding more light

EXERCISE

Choose the best answer to the question.

1. What are they doing?

   (A) Taking a walk
   (B) Taking a nap
   (C) Buying a map
   (D) Driving a car

2. What did they do earlier?

   (A) Rested
   (B) Played in the snow
   (C) Had dinner
   (D) Rented a movie

3. What will they do next?

   (A) Read
   (B) Go to bed
   (C) See a play
   (D) Go to the movies

SKILL 6

Questions About Opinions

Most questions about opinions begin with *what.* These questions are generally answered by complete sentences that begin with *it* or clauses that begin with *that.*

TIP Look for clues on opinions in the answers BEFORE you hear the audio. Listen carefully for those clues.

Examples

If you see these question types, listen for answers about an opinion.

Questions

What *questions*
What did the man think about the play?
What did the speaker think about the talk?
What did the woman say about the presentation?
What was the matter with the conference?
What do you think about the new manager?

Answers

It's boring.
He's highly qualified.
The room is too dark.
It was too expensive.
She was very helpful.
It wasn't long enough.

EXERCISE

Choose the best answer to the question.

1. What did they like about the speaker?

    (A) His short presentation
    (B) His humor
    (C) His clothes
    (D) His folks

    Ⓐ Ⓑ Ⓒ Ⓓ

2. What is the man's opinion of the hotel?

    (A) The décor is nice.
    (B) The food is great.
    (C) The seats are too hard.
    (D) The room is too big.

    Ⓐ Ⓑ Ⓒ Ⓓ

3. What does the woman think of the hotel?

    (A) It's very expensive.
    (B) It's cheaper than she expected.
    (C) The tables are nice.
    (D) It's uncomfortable.

    Ⓐ Ⓑ Ⓒ Ⓓ

NEW TOEIC—PART 3: CONVERSATIONS

The changes in Part 3: Conversations are outlined below. However, the Part 3 Skills and Strategies on pages 44–55 will help you prepare for both the current and the new TOEIC.

You will need to be familiar with changes in the conversations and the question types.

Changes in the Conversations

- Parts of the conversation may be shorter.
- There may be more than two speakers.
- Conversations may include incomplete sentences.
- Sounds in words may be deleted as in normal speech.

Changes in the Question Types

- Some questions may ask about the relationship between a graphic and the conversation.
- Some questions may ask about implied meaning.
- There are more conversations and questions. There are 13 conversations and 39 questions on the new TOEIC.

Sample Questions

> **Directions:** You will hear a short conversation between two people. You will see three questions on each conversation and four possible answers. Choose the best answer to each question and fill in the corresponding oval on your answer sheet. The conversations will not be printed and will be spoken only once.

You will hear:	Man:	Great conference, right?
	Woman:	I know. After last year's disastrous event I thought I'd never come to this conference again. But I'm glad I did.
	Man:	I know what you mean. You know, that "25 Years of Fashion" workshop this morning was fantastic. It's being repeated this afternoon if you want to go.
	Woman:	I'd love to, but there's also that one on "International Clothing Design" at the same time. That's the one I've decided to go to.
	Man:	Good choice.

Question 1

You will read: Who is the conference most likely for?

(A) People in the fashion industry ● Ⓑ Ⓒ Ⓓ
(B) People in international finance
(C) Magazine editors
(D) Historians

The best response to the question "Who is the conference most likely for?" is Choice (A), "People in the fashion industry." Therefore, you should choose answer (A).

NEW TOEIC

Question 2

You will read: What do the speakers imply about last year's conference?

(A) It was fantastic. 
(B) It was far away.
(C) It was very bad.
(D) It was expensive.

The best response to the question "What do the speakers imply about last year's conference?" is Choice (C), "It was very bad." Therefore, you should choose answer (C).

Question 3

You will read: Look at the graphic. Where will the woman be at 2:00?

(A) Room A  
(B) Room B
(C) Room C
(D) Room D

Afternoon Workshops 2:00–4:00

25 Years of Fashion	Room A
International Clothing Design	Room B
Trends in Footwear	Room C
Styles for the Millennium	Room D

The best response to the question "Where will the woman be at 2:00?" is Choice (B), "Room B." Therefore, you should choose answer (B).

Take note of the short and incomplete sentences:

Great conference, right?
I know.
Good choice.

Note the phrases that may be spoken with deleted sounds as in normal speech.

want to go = wanna go
to go to = t'goda

Graphic

Some of the conversations in Part 3 may include a graphic. The graphic could be a chart, a graph, an agenda, a timetable, or something similar. The speakers could verify the information in the graphic or they could contradict the information.

TIP Scan the questions quickly and look for key words in the visual. Listen for the key words in the conversation.

➡ Examples

Questions about graphics always begin with the sentence *Look at the graphic,* followed by a *wh-* question.

Look at the graphic. Who works on Tuesday?
Look at the graphic. When will the visitor arrive?
Look at the graphic. Where will they sit?

You cannot answer the question only by looking at the graphic. You need to listen to the conversation for clues that will help you know what information to select from the graphic in order to answer the question.

EXERCISE

Listen to the conversation, then choose the best answer to the question.

1. Look at the graphic. When will Sue work at the reception desk?

(A) Monday
(B) Tuesday
(C) Wednesday
(D) Thursday

Ⓐ Ⓑ Ⓒ Ⓓ

Reception Desk Schedule

Monday	Sue
Tuesday	Sam
Wednesday	Bill
Thursday	Jim
Friday	open

2. Look at the graphic. Which printer will the woman buy?

Ⓐ Ⓑ Ⓒ Ⓓ

(A) Model XX
(B) Model XZ
(C) Model Y
(D) Model WY

Printer Model	Price
Model XX	$115
Model XZ	$155
Model Y	$175
Model WY	$225

3. Look at the graphic. When was Mr. Kim hired?

(A) February
(B) March
(C) April
(D) May

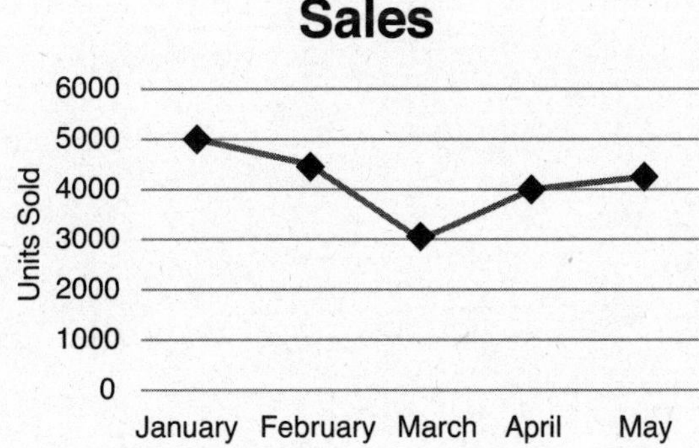

4. Look at the graphic. What topic will be discussed first at the meeting?

Ⓐ Ⓑ Ⓒ Ⓓ

(A) Budget Report
(B) Sales Update
(C) New Ad Campaign
(D) Hiring Update

Staff Meeting
January 12 2:00 P.M.

Budget Report .... Robert Franks
Sales Update .... Maya Lopez
New Ad Campaign ..... Sue Lin
Hiring Update .... Ben Ingram

5. Look at the graphic. Where will they meet for lunch?

(A) Location A
(B) Location B
(C) Location C
(D) Location D

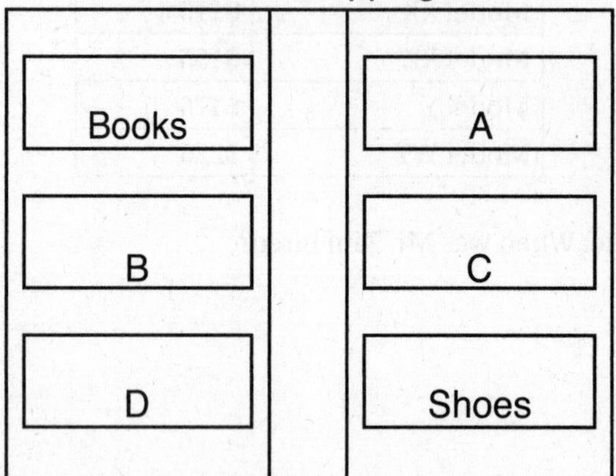

SKILL 2

Implied Meaning

Some of the speakers may not express an idea directly. They may imply something without saying it directly.

> **TIP** The meaning comes from the context of the conversation.

➥ Examples

Statement: It will take you forever to finish if you do it that way.
Implication: Your method is not efficient.

EXERCISE

Choose the implied meaning of the following conversations.

1. Man: Have you looked at the sales report yet?
   Woman: Yes. Finally things are starting to turn around.

   (A) Sales are improving. Ⓐ Ⓑ
   (B) Sales are declining.

2. Woman: How's your job hunt going? I heard it was quite slow for a while.
   Man: Yes, but now things are starting to pick up. I have an interview tomorrow.

   (A) The man got a promotion. Ⓐ Ⓑ
   (B) The man is feeling optimistic.

3. Man: I wonder who chose that new carpet in the front office. I mean, that color!
   Woman: I know. It's certainly not one that would be at the top of my list.

   (A) They like the carpet. Ⓐ Ⓑ
   (B) They don't like the carpet.

4. Woman: I thought that meeting would never end.
   Man: I know what you mean. I almost fell asleep in the middle of it.

   (A) The meeting was boring. Ⓐ Ⓑ
   (B) The meeting was shorter than expected.

5. Man: That report is going to need a lot of editing, and we need it ready for the meeting tomorrow.
   Woman: Don't worry. I'm on top of it.

   (A) The woman is aware of the work schedule. Ⓐ Ⓑ
   (B) The woman is confident she can finish the work on time.

SKILL 3

Deleted Sounds

In normal conversation, the sounds of some words are not pronounced distinctly. Sounds may combine with the sounds before or after or be dropped completely.

TIP Become familiar with the ways words and phrases are commonly pronounced.

➥ Examples

Written: We have got to go.
Spoken: We gotta go.

Written: I want to leave before 5:00.
Spoken: I wanna leave before 5:00.

These sounds are never written as such; they are only spoken.

EXERCISE

Listen to the following phrases and sentences and write the words you hear.

1. ____________________
2. ____________________
3. ____________________
4. ____________________
5. ____________________
6. ____________________
7. ____________________
8. ____________________

SKILL

Incomplete Sentences

In normal conversation, much is understood through context. Speakers do not always use complete sentences.

> **TIP** Use the context to understand the meaning of short, fragmented answers.

➡ Examples

Are you coming to the meeting?
Maybe later.

Maybe later in this case means *Maybe I will come to the meeting later.* The idea *I will come to the meeting* is implied by the context.

I'm going out for lunch. Wanna come?
Sorry. Gotta work.

Wanna come means *Do you want to come*? The *Do* is omitted and *want to come* is shortened in speech only (never in writing) to *Wanna.* Similarly, *Gotta work* means *I have got to work.* The subject *I* and the modal *have to* is shortened in speech only (never in writing) to *Gotta.*

EXERCISE

Choose the correct meaning for the underlined fragments.

1. Woman: So, the meeting day has been changed to Friday?
   Man: <u>Right.</u>

   (A) It's on the right. Ⓐ Ⓑ
   (B) You are correct.

2. Man: Let's take a break now and finish this later.
   Woman: <u>Fine with me.</u>

   (A) I agree with your plan. Ⓐ Ⓑ
   (B) That's a bad idea.

3. Woman: Please make ten copies of this report, leave one on my desk, and send the rest to Mr. Sato.
   Man: <u>Got it.</u>

   (A) I have Mr. Sato's address. Ⓐ Ⓑ
   (B) I understand everything you want me to do.

4. Man: We're having lunch at Café de Oro. Will you join us?
   Woman: Wish I could.

   (A) I would like to join you, but I can't. Ⓐ Ⓑ
   (B) I have always wanted to eat at that café.

5. Woman: Ms. Chang is in a meeting and can't see you now.
   Man: Too bad.

   (A) The meeting is a bad idea. Ⓐ Ⓑ
   (B) I'm sorry she can't see me.

SKILL

Multiple Accents

In the international business world, there are many different varieties of English spoken. On the TOEIC, the speakers could have American, British, Australian, South African, Canadian, or Indian accents. You will not have to identify the accent, but you should be able to understand the meaning of what is being said regardless of the speaker's accent.

> **TIP** Practice listening to speakers with different accents.

Track 25

EXERCISE

Listen to these statements, then write what you hear in the blanks below.

1. ______________________________
2. ______________________________
3. ______________________________
4. ______________________________
5. ______________________________
6. ______________________________
7. ______________________________
8. ______________________________
9. ______________________________
10. ______________________________
11. ______________________________
12. ______________________________
13. ______________________________
14. ______________________________
15. ______________________________
16. ______________________________
17. ______________________________
18. ______________________________
19. ______________________________
20. ______________________________

NEW TOEIC

PART 4: TALKS

Sample Questions

> **Directions:** You will hear a short talk given by a single speaker. You will see three questions on each talk, each with four possible answers. Choose the best answer to each question and fill in the corresponding oval on your answer sheet. The talks will not be printed and will be spoken only once.

You will hear: In five minutes, for one hour only, women's coats and hats go on sale in our fifth-floor Better Fashions department. All merchandise is reduced by twenty-five to forty percent. Not all styles in all sizes, but an outstanding selection nonetheless. You should hurry to the fifth floor now. Last week, we sold out completely in a matter of minutes. We don't want any of you to be disappointed.

Question 1

You will read: 1. When does the sale begin?

(A) In five minutes ● Ⓑ Ⓒ Ⓓ
(B) In one hour
(C) At 2:45
(D) Tomorrow

The best response to the question "When does the sale begin?" is Choice (A), "In five minutes." Therefore, you should choose answer (A).

Question 2

You will read: 2. What is going on sale?

(A) Men's coats Ⓐ ● Ⓒ Ⓓ
(B) Women's hats
(C) Cosmetics
(D) Old merchandise

The best response to the question "What is going on sale?" is Choice (B), "Women's hats." Therefore, you should choose answer (B).

Question 3

You will read: 3. How long will the sale last?

(A) Five minutes Ⓐ Ⓑ ● Ⓓ
(B) Fifteen minutes
(C) Sixty minutes
(D) One week

The best response to the question "How long will the sale last?" is Choice (C), "Sixty minutes." Therefore, you should choose answer (C).

SKILL

Questions About Events and Facts

Most questions about events and facts begin with *what.* These questions are generally answered by phrases or complete sentences. The strategy for these questions is similar to the strategies for the previous questions. Read the answer choices, make some assumptions about the events listed, and listen for the relevant clues.

> **TIP** Look for clues on events or facts in the answer choices BEFORE you hear the audio. Listen carefully for those clues in the audio.

➥ Examples

If you see these question types, listen for answers about an event or fact. Note that the questions begin with *what.*

Questions

What is the conversation about? What are they talking about? What are they discussing?	What happens if they don't like the movie? What is unusual about this event? What was the outcome of the meeting?

Answers

Phrases	*Sentences*
Cost of insurance	It's free.
Shipping fees	They can leave.
Overdue accounts	The companies decided not to merge.
Methods of delivery	

EXERCISE

Choose the best answer to the question.

1. What event will take place this weekend?

   (A) A book fair
   (B) A conference
   (C) A national celebration
   (D) An international dance

   Ⓐ Ⓑ Ⓒ Ⓓ

2. What will happen on Saturday evening?

   (A) A parade
   (B) A food sale
   (C) A concert
   (D) A circus performance

   Ⓐ Ⓑ Ⓒ Ⓓ

3. What will the mayor do on Sunday?

   (A) Sell tickets
   (B) Address the crowds
   (C) Play basketball
   (D) Buy some baskets

   Ⓐ Ⓑ Ⓒ Ⓓ

SKILL

2 Questions About Reasons

Most questions about reasons begin with *why*. Sometimes the question can begin with *what*. These questions are generally answered by complete sentences, but sometimes by short phrases. Use the same strategies that you have been using for the other question types.

TIP Look for clues on reasons in the answer choices BEFORE you hear the audio. Listen carefully for those clues.

➥ Examples

If you see these question types, listen for answers about a reason. Note that most of the questions begin with *why*.

Questions

Why did the man come? Why did the man leave? Why did the woman leave? Why does he need a typewriter? Why does she need a map?	Why is she going by taxi? Why is he going by train? Why is she going by car? What does the man say about the delay? What did she request?

Answers

He wanted to take a tour. She wanted to pick up the package. He didn't have a reservation. He needs to write a letter. She needs directions to the conference.	A taxi is faster than the train. The train goes directly to New York. It will be only ten more minutes. More justification for expenses.

EXERCISE

Choose the best answer to the question.

1. Why is there a delay?

   (A) Workers are staging a work action. Ⓐ Ⓑ Ⓒ Ⓓ
   (B) The weather is bad.
   (C) There are flight control problems.
   (D) Passengers are boarding slowly.

2. Why should passengers get something to eat now?

   (A) The restaurants will close at midnight. Ⓐ Ⓑ Ⓒ Ⓓ
   (B) The restaurants won't be open tomorrow.
   (C) There will be no food served on the flight.
   (D) There are some restaurants close to the gate.

3. Why should passengers pay attention to the announcements?

   (A) To find out which gate their flight will leave from Ⓐ Ⓑ Ⓒ Ⓓ
   (B) To hear which restaurants are open
   (C) To keep from getting bored
   (D) To know when it is time to board the flight

SKILL 3

Questions About Numbers

Questions about numbers are common in the Listening section of the TOEIC. You will have to be able to distinguish different numbers. You will also have to understand some measurements. You will not have to do mathematical calculations, but you will be expected to know equivalencies such as *sixty minutes* and *one hour, a dozen* and *twelve*, or *two weeks* and *fourteen days*.

> **TIP** Listen carefully for numbers and words that indicate a mathematical calculation.

Examples

Look at these words that express measurements and their equivalents. The first part of the list should be part of your *active* vocabulary: memorize and use these terms and concepts. The second part is *passive*—you need only be familiar with these terms.

Common Measurements—Active

Quantity	
1 dozen	12 units
1 half dozen	6 units
Money	
penny	1 cent
nickel	5 cents
dime	10 cents
quarter	25 cents
half dollar	50 cents
dollar	100 cents
Time	
60 seconds	minute
60 minutes	1 hour
24 hours	1 day
noon	12:00 midday
midnight	24:00 in the night
Morning: 6 A.M. to noon	
Afternoon: Noon to 6 P.M.	
Evening: 6 P.M. to 10 P.M.	
Night: 10 P.M. to 6 A.M.	

Common Measurements—Passive

Temperature	
Fahrenheit	Centigrade
32 degrees	0 degrees
212 degrees (water boils)	100 degrees (water boils)
Distance	
foot	meter
1 inch	2.54 centimeters
1 yard	0.9144 meter
1 mile	1.609 kilometers
12 inches	1 foot
3 feet	1 yard
Quantity	
1 ounce	28.350 grams
1 pound	453.59237 grams
1 US ton = 2000 pounds	0.907 metric ton of 907 kilograms
1 British ton = 2240 pounds	0.1016 metric ton or 1016 kilograms
1 cup	8 ounces
2 cups	1 pint
4 cups	1 quart
8 cups	1/2 gallon
16 cups	1 gallon
Fluid Measurement	
1 ounce	29.573 milliliters
1 pint	0.473 liter
1 quart	0.946 liter
1 gallon	3.785 liters
1 imperial gallon	4.55 liters
Dry Measurement	
pint	0.551 liter
quart	8.810 liter
Average Seasonal Weather in the United States	
Spring	March 21 to June 20 (temperate)
Summer	June 21 to September 20 (hot)
Autumn (fall)	September 21 to December 20 (cool)
Winter	December 21 to March 20 (cold)

Look at these words that indicate a mathematical calculation.

Common Mathematical Calculations

twice three times	100 becomes 200 100 becomes 300
half as much twice as much half as much again	100 becomes 50 100 becomes 200 100 becomes 150
half off third off 10% off	100 becomes 50 100 becomes 66.66 100 becomes 90
per hour per day	$100 for 6 hours becomes $600 $100 for 3 days becomes $300

STRATEGY

Although you are not tested on your mathematical ability, you may have to perform simple math calculations. Listen carefully for words that indicate division, multiplication, addition, or subtraction.

You hear: **Bob bought a half-dozen eggs.**
Question: **How many eggs did he buy?**
Answer: **6**

You hear: **The door is 30 inches wide and the window is twice as wide as the door.**
Question: **How wide is the window?**
Answer: **60 inches wide (5 feet wide)**

These two examples test your understanding of the words *half*, *dozen*, and *twice*.

EXERCISE

Choose the best answer to the question.

1. What is the potential discount on an order of $200?

   (A) $10
   (B) $15
   (C) $20
   (D) $25

   Ⓐ Ⓑ Ⓒ Ⓓ

2. During a seasonal sale, what would be the price of an item that normally costs $200?

   (A) $25
   (B) $150
   (C) $160
   (D) $175

   Ⓐ Ⓑ Ⓒ Ⓓ

3. How much sales tax is charged for a $200 purchase?

   (A) $5
   (B) $10
   (C) $25
   (D) $50

   Ⓐ Ⓑ Ⓒ Ⓓ

SKILL

Questions About Main Topics

Answers to questions are often found among details, but sometimes they are about larger ideas. Questions about the main topic require you to understand the general purpose of the talk.

> **TIP** Look for ideas that indicate the general purpose.

➡ Examples

If you see these question types, listen for answers about the main topic. When you see these types of questions, you should look in the answer choices for the overall subject of what you heard. The question might ask about the identity of the speaker, the context of the talk, the purpose of the talk, or the audience.

Questions

Who is this information for? What is the talk about?	What is the purpose of this talk? Where would you hear this talk?

Answers

General categories	*Specific examples*
A role, job title, or group	A client A ticket clerk The woman's colleagues Airline passengers
A kind of place or a situation	In an office At a convention During a banquet At an airport
Any subject	The new machinery Politics Environmental responsibility An advertising campaign
A summary or implication	The supervisor doesn't agree with the idea They need more time to finish the project A change in the regulations Consumers' confidence in the product

EXERCISE

Choose the best answer to the question.

1. What changes are taking place in the company?

   (A) The Board of Directors resigned. Ⓐ Ⓑ Ⓒ Ⓓ
   (B) The Managing Director was fired.
   (C) The workers went on strike.
   (D) All letters will be sent by computer.

2. Who is the speaker addressing?

   (A) Some clients Ⓐ Ⓑ Ⓒ Ⓓ
   (B) His coworkers
   (C) A server
   (D) The director

3. What does the speaker plan to do soon?

   (A) Become a clothes salesman Ⓐ Ⓑ Ⓒ Ⓓ
   (B) Start a business
   (C) Go to college
   (D) Work as a restaurant manager

Strategy for Analyzing Question Types

Read the answer choices before you hear the audio. Make reasonable assumptions about the choices listed and listen for relevant clues.

SKILL

Paraphrases

The answer to a question is often a paraphrase of what you hear in the talk. A paraphrase is a restatement of information using different words.

> **TIP** Pay attention to synonyms and similar phrases that restate the meaning of a statement.

➥ Examples

Answer choices are often paraphrases of statements in the talk. Look at these examples:

Statement:	Temperatures will be high today.
Paraphrase:	It will be a warm day.
Statement:	Please remain seated.
Paraphrase:	Please stay in your seats.
Statement:	Mr. Johnson has written several books.
Paraphrase:	Mr. Johnson is an author.
Statement:	Houses in this neighborhood don't cost a great deal.
Paraphrase:	It isn't expensive to live in this area.

Track 30

EXERCISE

Choose the best answer to the question.

1. What is the purpose of the form?

(A) To make a complaint
(B) To borrow money
(C) To apply for a job
(D) To get a license

Ⓐ Ⓑ Ⓒ Ⓓ

2. How will copies of the form be made?

(A) Carbon paper
(B) Photocopier
(C) Computer
(D) Fax machine

Ⓐ Ⓑ Ⓒ Ⓓ

3. When will the listener be contacted?

(A) In two days
(B) In four days
(C) In ten days
(D) In fourteen days

Ⓐ Ⓑ Ⓒ Ⓓ

NEW TOEIC

NEW TOEIC—PART 4: TALKS

The changes in Part 4: Talks are outlined below. However, the Part 4 Skills and Strategies on pages 68–79 will also help you prepare for both the current and the new TOEIC.

You will need to be familiar with changes in the conversations and the question types.

Changes in the Conversations

- The talk may include incomplete sentences. (*review pages 63–64 in Part 3*)
- Sounds in words may be deleted as in normal speech. (*review page 62 in Part 3*)
- There may be a graphic accompanying the talk.

Changes in the Question Types

- Some questions may ask about the relationship between a graphic and the conversation.
- Some questions may ask about implied meaning.

Sample Questions

> **Directions:** You will hear a short talk given by a single speaker. There may or may not be a graphic accompanying the short talk. You will see three sets of questions on each talk, each with four possible answers. Choose the best answer to the question and fill in the corresponding oval on your answer sheet. The talks will not be printed and will be spoken only once.

You will hear: Good morning and welcome. I am so pleased to see such a great turn out for today's workshop as, frankly, we were uncertain about how much interest there'd be in the topic. I never expected to see the room so filled up. So, we're off to a great start. Before we begin, let me go over a few items. First, we'll take a 15-minute break at around 10:30. Then, we'll break again for lunch at 12:30 and begin the afternoon part of our program at 1:30. And, unfortunately, Lydia Strata won't be able to be with us until after lunch, so we'll have to begin our program with Mr. Rizzo's presentation.

Question 1

You will read: What does the speaker imply about the workshop?

(A) She thought the room would not be comfortable.

(B) She expected many more people would sign up.

(C) She is surprised to have so many participants.

(D) She needed help in choosing the topic.

The best response to the question "What does the speaker imply about the workshop?" is Choice (C), "She is surprised to have so many participants." Therefore, you should choose answer (C).

Question 2

You will read: How many breaks will there be?

(A) 1
(B) 2
(C) 3
(D) 4

Ⓐ ● Ⓒ Ⓓ

The best response to the question "How many breaks will there be?" is Choice (B), "2." Therefore, you should choose answer (B).

Question 3

You will read: Look at the graphic. Which topic will workshop participants hear about first?

(A) Generating Ideas
(B) Using Design Software
(C) Design and Color
(D) Logos and Branding

Ⓐ ● Ⓒ Ⓓ

Creative Design Workshop Program

Session 1
Lydia Strata—Generating Ideas

Session 2
Marco Rizzo—Using Design Software

Session 3
Amalia Jones—Design and Color

Session 4
Lars Andersen—Logos and Branding

The best response to the question "Which topic will workshop participants hear about first?" is Choice (B), "Using Design Software." Therefore, you should choose answer (B).

Note the following phrases that may be spoken with shortened sounds as in normal speech.

off to = offta
have to = hafta

TIP

See page 123 for the Answer Key and page 128 for the Explanatory Answers for new TOEIC practice Part 4.

SKILL 

Graphic

Some of the conversations in Part 4 may include a graphic. The graphic could be a chart, an agenda, a timetable, or something similar. The speaker could verify the information in the graphic or the speaker could contradict the information.

> **TIP** Scan the questions quickly and look for key words in the visual. Listen for the key words from the questions.

➥ Examples

As in Part 3, questions about graphics in Part 4 always begin with the sentence *Look at the graphic*, followed by a *wh-* question.

Look at the graphic. Who will speak first?
Look at the graphic. What will they discuss first?
Look at the graphic. What time will the bus leave?

You cannot answer the question only by looking at the graphic. You need to listen to the talk for clues that will help you know what information to select from the graphic in order to answer the question.

EXERCISE

Listen to the talk, then choose the best answer to the question.

1. Look at the graphic. Which train will Pamela take?

(A) 30
(B) 31
(C) 32
(D) 33

Ⓐ Ⓑ Ⓒ Ⓓ

Timetable

Train No.	Lv. Ardale	Arr. Springfield
30	5:00 A.M.	7:17
31	6:45	9:02
32	8:45	11:02
33	10:30	12:47

2. Look at the graphic. Which part of the budget does the speaker want to reduce first?

(A) Advertising
(B) Salaries
(C) Overhead
(D) Materials

Ⓐ Ⓑ Ⓒ Ⓓ

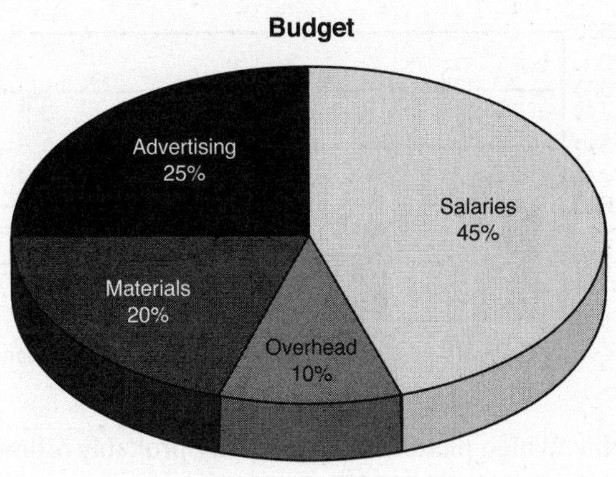

3. Look at the graphic. Where will the group have lunch?

(A) Pine Grove
(B) Butterfly Garden
(C) Rose Garden
(D) Nature Center

Ⓐ Ⓑ Ⓒ Ⓓ

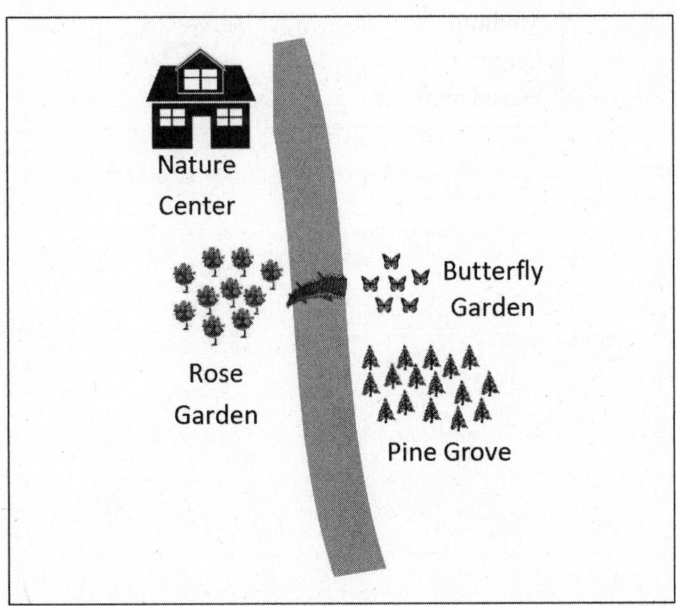

4. Look at the graphic. Which region will the speaker discuss?

(A) Northwest
(B) Southwest
(C) Northeast
(D) Southeast

Ⓐ Ⓑ Ⓒ Ⓓ

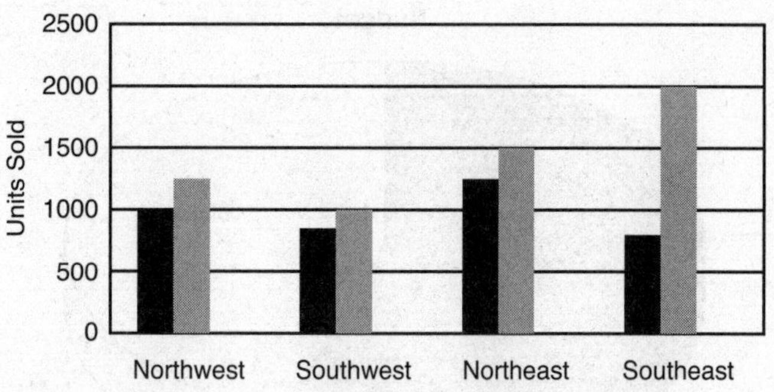

5. Look at the graphic. Which platter will the speaker probably order?

(A) Small
(B) Medium
(C) Large
(D) Extra Large

Ⓐ Ⓑ Ⓒ Ⓓ

Kim's Catering		
Cold Cuts Platter		
Small	....	serves 15
Medium	....	serves 25
Large	....	serves 50
Extra Large	....	serves 75

SKILL 2

Implied Meaning

The speaker may not express an idea directly. The speaker may imply something without saying it directly.

They were a bit disappointed by the turn out.

implies

They expected more people to be there.

TIP The meaning comes from the context of the talk.

EXERCISE

Track 32

Listen to the talks and choose the implied meaning.

1. (A) He has rescheduled this appointment several times already. Ⓐ Ⓑ
   (B) This is the first time he has rescheduled this appointment.

2. (A) She wishes the weather were warmer. Ⓐ Ⓑ
   (B) She thinks the weather is very nice.

3. (A) The ticket machine accepts both cash and credit cards. Ⓐ Ⓑ
   (B) The ticket machine accepts credit cards only.

4. (A) The event is more crowded than it was last year. Ⓐ Ⓑ
   (B) The stadium isn't big enough to hold the crowds.

5. (A) Members get a discount on tickets. Ⓐ Ⓑ
   (B) Tickets are for members only.

SKILL 3

Multiple Accents

In the international business world, there are many different varieties of English spoken. On the TOEIC, the speakers could have American, British, Australian, South African, Canadian, or Indian accents. You will not have to identify the accent, but you should be able to understand the meaning of what is being said regardless of the speaker's accent.

> **TIP** Use the Internet to listen to news broadcasts from cities in the U.S., the U.K., Australia, Canada, New Zealand, and India. Listen to the same news from different sources.

EXERCISE

Listen to these short talks, then write what you hear.

1. ______________________________

   ____

2. ______________________________

   ____

3. ______________________________

   ____

4. ______________________________

   ____

5. ______________________________

   ____

NEW TOEIC

Strategy Summary

Strategies to Improve
Your Listening Comprehension Score

The following strategies are a review of those presented in this Listening Comprehension Review. Using these strategies will improve your score on the TOEIC.

Part 1: Photographs

- **When you look at the photo, analyze the people. Determine their number, gender, location, occupation, and so on.**
- **Look for context clues in the photo.**
- **Listen for the meaning of the *whole sentence* to determine which choice best matches the photo.**
- **Try to analyze every detail in the photograph.**
- **Try to describe these details in English to yourself.**
- **Listen to all answers until you hear the obviously correct one. Once you are sure, don't listen to the rest of the answer options. Start analyzing the next photograph.**
- **If you aren't sure, keep your pencil on the most likely correct answer. If you listen to all options and have no other choice, mark that answer and move on quickly.**

Part 2: Question-Response

- **Listen and look for context clues.**
- **Listen and look for the *meaning* of the statement, question, and answer choices. Do not be confused by words with similar sounds, homonyms, and related words.**
- **Listen for suggestions, offer markers, and request markers.**
- **Listen carefully to the entire question and ALL the answer choices before making a final decision.**

Part 3: Conversations and Part 4: Talks

- **Learn to recognize types of questions. Study the questions and answers presented in this chapter. Remember that questions about people generally begin with *who* or *what*, questions about location generally begin with *where*, questions about time generally begin with *when* or *how long*, etc.**
- **Read the answer choices, make assumptions about the items listed, and listen for relevant clues.**
- **Focus on the question. Read the three questions before you hear the talk. Don't read the answer choices. Try to listen carefully for the answer.**
- **As the conversations and talks start, write your potential answer choices in the exam book.**
- **Focusing on the details of the talk will also help you with inference and main idea questions.**

Many thanks to my readers, especially Jean-Pierre Saint-Aimé, who have provided valuable tips on test-taking strategies.

ANSWER SHEET
Listening Comprehension Mini-Test

Part 1: Photographs

1. Ⓐ Ⓑ Ⓒ Ⓓ	4. Ⓐ Ⓑ Ⓒ Ⓓ	7. Ⓐ Ⓑ Ⓒ Ⓓ	10. Ⓐ Ⓑ Ⓒ Ⓓ
2. Ⓐ Ⓑ Ⓒ Ⓓ	5. Ⓐ Ⓑ Ⓒ Ⓓ	8. Ⓐ Ⓑ Ⓒ Ⓓ	
3. Ⓐ Ⓑ Ⓒ Ⓓ	6. Ⓐ Ⓑ Ⓒ Ⓓ	9. Ⓐ Ⓑ Ⓒ Ⓓ	

Part 2: Question-Response

11. Ⓐ Ⓑ Ⓒ	15. Ⓐ Ⓑ Ⓒ	19. Ⓐ Ⓑ Ⓒ	23. Ⓐ Ⓑ Ⓒ
12. Ⓐ Ⓑ Ⓒ	16. Ⓐ Ⓑ Ⓒ	20. Ⓐ Ⓑ Ⓒ	24. Ⓐ Ⓑ Ⓒ
13. Ⓐ Ⓑ Ⓒ	17. Ⓐ Ⓑ Ⓒ	21. Ⓐ Ⓑ Ⓒ	25. Ⓐ Ⓑ Ⓒ
14. Ⓐ Ⓑ Ⓒ	18. Ⓐ Ⓑ Ⓒ	22. Ⓐ Ⓑ Ⓒ	

Part 3: Conversations

26. Ⓐ Ⓑ Ⓒ Ⓓ	30. Ⓐ Ⓑ Ⓒ Ⓓ	34. Ⓐ Ⓑ Ⓒ Ⓓ	38. Ⓐ Ⓑ Ⓒ Ⓓ
27. Ⓐ Ⓑ Ⓒ Ⓓ	31. Ⓐ Ⓑ Ⓒ Ⓓ	35. Ⓐ Ⓑ Ⓒ Ⓓ	39. Ⓐ Ⓑ Ⓒ Ⓓ
28. Ⓐ Ⓑ Ⓒ Ⓓ	32. Ⓐ Ⓑ Ⓒ Ⓓ	36. Ⓐ Ⓑ Ⓒ Ⓓ	40. Ⓐ Ⓑ Ⓒ Ⓓ
29. Ⓐ Ⓑ Ⓒ Ⓓ	33. Ⓐ Ⓑ Ⓒ Ⓓ	37. Ⓐ Ⓑ Ⓒ Ⓓ	

Part 4: Talks

41. Ⓐ Ⓑ Ⓒ Ⓓ	44. Ⓐ Ⓑ Ⓒ Ⓓ	47. Ⓐ Ⓑ Ⓒ Ⓓ	50. Ⓐ Ⓑ Ⓒ Ⓓ
42. Ⓐ Ⓑ Ⓒ Ⓓ	45. Ⓐ Ⓑ Ⓒ Ⓓ	48. Ⓐ Ⓑ Ⓒ Ⓓ	51. Ⓐ Ⓑ Ⓒ Ⓓ
43. Ⓐ Ⓑ Ⓒ Ⓓ	46. Ⓐ Ⓑ Ⓒ Ⓓ	49. Ⓐ Ⓑ Ⓒ Ⓓ	52. Ⓐ Ⓑ Ⓒ Ⓓ

For Mini-Test for New TOEIC Listening Comprehension go to page 103.

MINI-TEST FOR LISTENING COMPREHENSION

Part 1: Photographs

Track 34

Directions: You will see a photograph. You will hear four statements about the photograph. Choose the statement that most closely matches the photograph and fill in the corresponding oval on your answer sheet.

TIP

See page 112 for the Answer Key and pages 118–121 for the Explanatory Answers for this Mini-Test.

1.

2.

3.

4.

5.

6.

7.

8.

9.

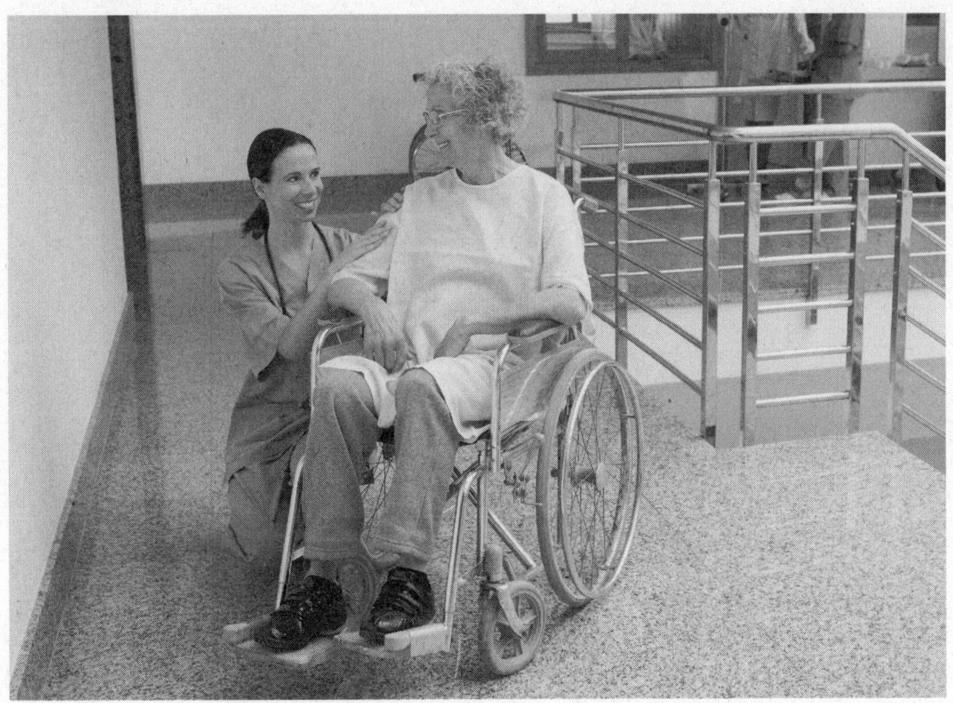

10.

Part 2: Question-Response

Directions: You will hear a question and three possible responses. Choose the response that most closely answers the question and fill in the corresponding oval on your answer sheet.

11. Mark your answer on your answer sheet.
12. Mark your answer on your answer sheet.
13. Mark your answer on your answer sheet.
14. Mark your answer on your answer sheet.
15. Mark your answer on your answer sheet.
16. Mark your answer on your answer sheet.
17. Mark your answer on your answer sheet.
18. Mark your answer on your answer sheet.
19. Mark your answer on your answer sheet.
20. Mark your answer on your answer sheet.
21. Mark your answer on your answer sheet.
22. Mark your answer on your answer sheet.
23. Mark your answer on your answer sheet.
24. Mark your answer on your answer sheet.
25. Mark your answer on your answer sheet.

Part 3: Conversations

Directions: You will hear a conversation between two people. You will see three questions on each conversation and four possible answers. Choose the best answer to each question and fill in the corresponding oval on your answer sheet.

26. What are the speakers going to do?

(A) View some art
(B) Play tennis
(C) Go to the theater
(D) See a movie

27. What time do they have to be there?

(A) 2:00
(B) 5:00
(C) 6:00
(D) 7:00

28. What is the weather?

(A) Sunny
(B) Icy
(C) Rainy
(D) Snowing

---

29. What does the woman want to discuss at the meeting?

(A) Planes
(B) Lunch plans
(C) A conference
(D) Ordering office supplies

30. When will the speakers meet?

(A) Sunday
(B) Monday
(C) Tuesday
(D) Friday

31. Where will the speakers meet?

(A) At the woman's office
(B) At the man's office
(C) At a restaurant
(D) At a café

32. Why is the man exchanging the shirt?

(A) It's the wrong size.
(B) It's the wrong color.
(C) It has a hole.
(D) Its sleeves are too long.

33. What size shirt does the man want?

(A) 8
(B) 15
(C) 16
(D) 18

34. What color shirt does he want?

(A) White
(B) Black
(C) Green
(D) Blue

---

35. When does the man have his vacation?

(A) Spring
(B) Summer
(C) Fall
(D) Winter

36. Where does the woman suggest he go?

(A) New York
(B) Paris
(C) Florida
(D) Hawaii

37. How many weeks is the man's vacation?

(A) One
(B) Two
(C) Three
(D) Four

38. Where was the man this morning?

(A) At his desk
(B) At the store
(C) In a meeting
(D) In the supply closet

39. How many messages did he get?

(A) Four
(B) Seven
(C) Eleven
(D) Forty-two

40. What does he want the woman to do?

(A) Answer the messages
(B) Buy something
(C) Order some supplies
(D) Bring him a form

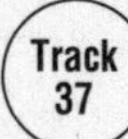

Part 4: Talks

Directions: You will hear a talk given by a single speaker. You will see three questions on each talk, each with four possible answers. Choose the best answer to each question and fill in the corresponding oval on your answer sheet.

41. What is the current temperature?

(A) 3 degrees
(B) 15 degrees
(C) 50 degrees
(D) 53 degrees

42. What should people take to work in the morning?

(A) Snow boots
(B) Luggage
(C) Sunscreen
(D) Umbrellas

43. When will the weather clear up?

(A) By 6:00 A.M
(B) By noon
(C) By late afternoon
(D) By early evening

---

44. Why is power being turned off?

(A) To reduce total demand
(B) To save money
(C) To make it cooler
(D) To make the city pay its bill

45. How long will power be off?

(A) Longer than two hours
(B) Less than two hours
(C) For one day
(D) Until the weather changes

46. How can a customer get more information?

(A) Go online
(B) Call the company
(C) Visit the company
(D) Listen to the radio

47. Where does this announcement take place?

(A) On a tour bus
(B) At the shore
(C) In a cocktail lounge
(D) On a ship

48. What is required for the first excursion?

(A) A hearty breakfast
(B) Some beautiful clothes
(C) A ticket
(D) A health report

49. What time will the first excursion begin?

(A) 4:00
(B) 7:30
(C) 9:00
(D) 9:30

---

50. What kind of subscription is being offered?

(A) Movie tickets
(B) Magazine
(C) Cable TV
(D) Video streaming

51. How long does a free subscription last?

(A) Two days
(B) Three days
(C) One month
(D) One year

52. How much does a one-year subscription cost?

(A) $50
(B) $99
(C) $150
(D) $100

ANSWER SHEET
New TOEIC
Listening Comprehension
Mini-Test

Part 1: Photographs

1. Ⓐ Ⓑ Ⓒ Ⓓ 2. Ⓐ Ⓑ Ⓒ Ⓓ 3. Ⓐ Ⓑ Ⓒ Ⓓ 4. Ⓐ Ⓑ Ⓒ Ⓓ

Part 2: Question-Response

5. Ⓐ Ⓑ Ⓒ	8. Ⓐ Ⓑ Ⓒ	11. Ⓐ Ⓑ Ⓒ	14. Ⓐ Ⓑ Ⓒ
6. Ⓐ Ⓑ Ⓒ	9. Ⓐ Ⓑ Ⓒ	12. Ⓐ Ⓑ Ⓒ	15. Ⓐ Ⓑ Ⓒ
7. Ⓐ Ⓑ Ⓒ	10. Ⓐ Ⓑ Ⓒ	13. Ⓐ Ⓑ Ⓒ	16. Ⓐ Ⓑ Ⓒ

Part 3: Conversations

17. Ⓐ Ⓑ Ⓒ Ⓓ	22. Ⓐ Ⓑ Ⓒ Ⓓ	27. Ⓐ Ⓑ Ⓒ Ⓓ	32. Ⓐ Ⓑ Ⓒ Ⓓ
18. Ⓐ Ⓑ Ⓒ Ⓓ	23. Ⓐ Ⓑ Ⓒ Ⓓ	28. Ⓐ Ⓑ Ⓒ Ⓓ	33. Ⓐ Ⓑ Ⓒ Ⓓ
19. Ⓐ Ⓑ Ⓒ Ⓓ	24. Ⓐ Ⓑ Ⓒ Ⓓ	29. Ⓐ Ⓑ Ⓒ Ⓓ	34. Ⓐ Ⓑ Ⓒ Ⓓ
20. Ⓐ Ⓑ Ⓒ Ⓓ	25. Ⓐ Ⓑ Ⓒ Ⓓ	30. Ⓐ Ⓑ Ⓒ Ⓓ	
21. Ⓐ Ⓑ Ⓒ Ⓓ	26. Ⓐ Ⓑ Ⓒ Ⓓ	31. Ⓐ Ⓑ Ⓒ Ⓓ	

Part 4: Talks

35. Ⓐ Ⓑ Ⓒ Ⓓ	39. Ⓐ Ⓑ Ⓒ Ⓓ	43. Ⓐ Ⓑ Ⓒ Ⓓ	47. Ⓐ Ⓑ Ⓒ Ⓓ
36. Ⓐ Ⓑ Ⓒ Ⓓ	40. Ⓐ Ⓑ Ⓒ Ⓓ	44. Ⓐ Ⓑ Ⓒ Ⓓ	48. Ⓐ Ⓑ Ⓒ Ⓓ
37. Ⓐ Ⓑ Ⓒ Ⓓ	41. Ⓐ Ⓑ Ⓒ Ⓓ	45. Ⓐ Ⓑ Ⓒ Ⓓ	49. Ⓐ Ⓑ Ⓒ Ⓓ
38. Ⓐ Ⓑ Ⓒ Ⓓ	42. Ⓐ Ⓑ Ⓒ Ⓓ	46. Ⓐ Ⓑ Ⓒ Ⓓ	

MINI-TEST FOR NEW TOEIC LISTENING COMPREHENSION

Part 1: Photographs

Directions: You will see a photograph. You will hear four statements about the photograph. Choose the statement that most closely matches the photograph and fill in the corresponding oval on your answer sheet.

1.

2.

3.

4.

NEW TOEIC

Part 2: Question-Response

Directions: You will hear a question and three possible responses. Choose the response that most closely answers the question and fill in the corresponding oval on your answer sheet.

5. Mark your answer on your answer sheet.
6. Mark your answer on your answer sheet.
7. Mark your answer on your answer sheet.
8. Mark your answer on your answer sheet.
9. Mark your answer on your answer sheet.
10. Mark your answer on your answer sheet.
11. Mark your answer on your answer sheet.
12. Mark your answer on your answer sheet.
13. Mark your answer on your answer sheet.
14. Mark your answer on your answer sheet.
15. Mark your answer on your answer sheet.
16. Mark your answer on your answer sheet.

Part 3: Conversations

Directions: You will hear a conversation between two or more people. You will see three questions on each conversation and four possible answers. Choose the best answer to each question and fill in the corresponding oval on your answer sheet.

17. What did the woman have at the café?

(A) Soup and a sandwich
(B) Soup and a salad
(C) A sandwich only
(D) A salad only

18. What does the man imply about the café?

(A) The food is better than the décor.
(B) The walls are in need of repair.
(C) Its menu isn't interesting.
(D) It's too far from the office.

19. What will the speakers do tomorrow?

(A) Work on a project together
(B) Look for a new place to eat
(C) Paint the walls
(D) Return to the café

---

20. Why does the second man say, "Excuse me?"

(A) He is interrupting the conversation.
(B) He wants to walk by.
(C) He can't hear what the woman is saying.
(D) He is blocking the sign.

21. How long has the woman been waiting?

(A) 5 minutes
(B) 15 minutes
(C) 50 minutes
(D) She doesn't say.

22. Look at the graphic. What time will the first man take the bus?

(A) 11:25 A.M.
(B) 11:45 A.M.
(C) 1:00 P.M.
(D) 1:45 P.M.

Bus Timetable

T14	T36
9:00 A.M.	9:15 A.M.
9:45 A.M.	10:15 A.M.
10:30 A.M.	11:25 A.M.
11:45 A.M.	12:30 P.M.
1:00 P.M.	1:45 P.M.

---

23. What does the woman want to have printed?

(A) Menus
(B) Checks
(C) Order forms
(D) Advertisements

24. What does the man agree to do?

(A) Print 24 copies
(B) Forget the rush charge
(C) Have the order ready tomorrow
(D) Print on one side of the page only

25. What does the man want the woman to do?

(A) Pick up the order at night
(B) Pay ahead of time
(C) Check the order
(D) Use a credit card

26. What do the speakers imply about the new director?

(A) He has a good background.
(B) He enjoys meeting people.
(C) He is a hard worker.
(D) He is unfriendly.

27. When did the new director begin working at this company?

(A) Today
(B) Two days ago
(C) A week ago
(D) Last Tuesday

28. What does the woman suggest?

(A) Going to a staff meeting
(B) Attending a social event
(C) Getting something to eat
(D) Calling the director at noon

---

29. What are they going to paint?

(A) The closet
(B) The office
(C) The hallway
(D) The stairwell

30. What color paint will they buy?

(A) Yellow
(B) Green
(C) White
(D) Blue

31. Look at the graphic. Which size paint will they probably buy?

(A) 1-liter can
(B) 2-liter can
(C) 5-liter can
(D) 25-liter bucket

Main Street Paints
Interior Paint Price list

Size	Coverage
1-liter can	.... up to 6 sq. meters
2-liter can	.... up to 12 sq. meters
5-liter can	.... up to 30 sq. meters
25-liter bucket	.... up to 150 sq. meters

---

32. Look at the graphic. How much of a discount will the man get?

(A) 10%
(B) 15%
(C) 20%
(D) 25%

Springer's Office Store
Store-wide sale

Discounts offered on most items throughout the store!

10% off paper and pens
15% off electronics
20% off office furniture
25% off coffeemakers

This week only!

33. What does the woman offer to do?

(A) Open the box
(B) Explain the instructions
(C) Show the man where to park
(D) Take the purchase to the cash register

34. How will the man transport his purchase to his office?

(A) He will ask a colleague to get it.
(B) He will carry it with him now.
(C) He will pick it up tomorrow.
(D) He will have it delivered.

Part 4: Talks

Track 41

Directions: You will hear a talk given by a single speaker. You will see three questions on each talk, each with four possible answers. Choose the best answer to each question and fill in the corresponding oval on your answer sheet.

35. Where would you hear this talk?
    (A) Shopping mall
    (B) Sports event
    (C) Museum
    (D) Theater

36. What are the listeners asked to do?
    (A) Buy a ticket
    (B) Watch a play
    (C) Choose a gift
    (D) Move their seats

37. Look at the graphic. Where is the gift shop?
    (A) Room A
    (B) Room B
    (C) Room C
    (D) Room D

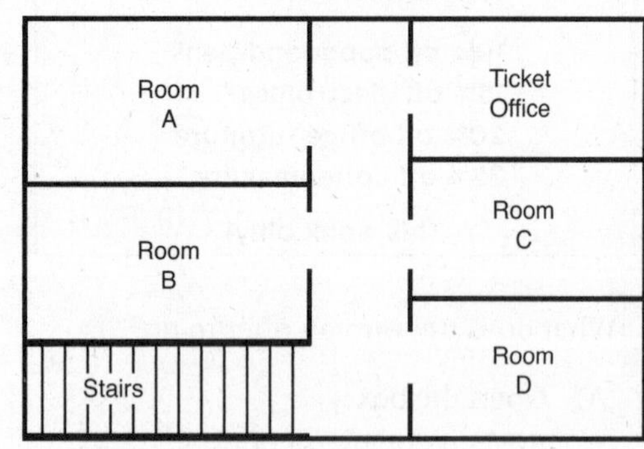

38. Why did the speaker make the call?
    (A) To make an appointment
    (B) To solicit a new client
    (C) To ask for directions
    (D) To get information

39. What does the speaker mean when he says, "It would work better for me if you came after hours"?
    (A) He prefers the cleaners to come when the office is closed.
    (B) He thinks the work will take several hours to complete.
    (C) He's at the office just a few hours a day.
    (D) He does a better job later in the day.

40. What does the speaker want the listener to do?
    (A) Come to his office next week
    (B) Wait for another call from him
    (C) Meet him downtown
    (D) Return his call soon

41. What kind of business does the speaker work in?
    (A) Hotel
    (B) Restaurant
    (C) Souvenir shop
    (D) Guided tours

42. Look at the graphic. Which month does the speaker want to focus on?
    (A) May
    (B) June
    (C) July
    (D) August

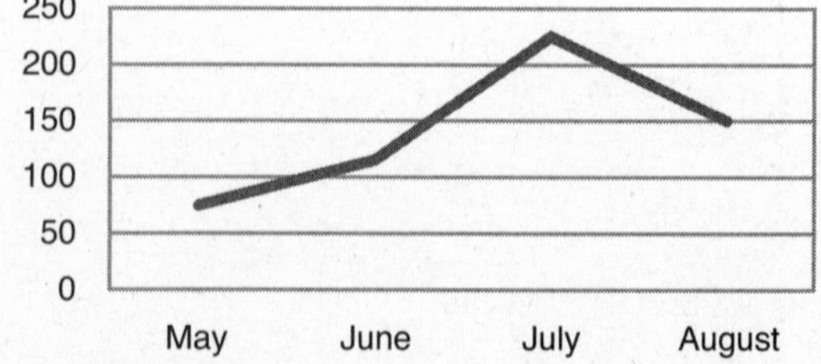

43. What does the speaker ask the listeners to do?

(A) View another graph
(B) Read a list of ideas
(C) Figure out an average
(D) Discuss something in pairs

---

44. What will happen tomorrow?

(A) Software will be installed.
(B) A new carpet will be laid.
(C) Furniture will be delivered.
(D) The hallway will be painted.

45. What does the speaker mean when he says, "They should be out of here by noon"?

(A) Staff should stay out of the office all morning.
(B) The workers will finish before 12:00.
(C) Employees can take the afternoon off.
(D) Office supplies are running low.

46. What are listeners asked to do?

(A) Arrange the new furniture
(B) Work in the front office
(C) Use the back entrance
(D) Arrive early

47. What event is the listener planning?

(A) A wedding
(B) A conference
(C) A training seminar
(D) An awards banquet

48. About how many people will attend the event?

(A) 100
(B) 125
(C) 200
(D) 225

49. Look at the graphic. Where is Ms. Jones's office located?

(A) Ground floor
(B) First floor
(C) Second floor
(D) Third floor

Hildamire Hotel
Directory

Ground floor
Lobby, Restaurant, Pool

First floor
Conference and Banquet Rooms

Third floor
Administrative Offices

Fourth–Tenth floors
Guest Rooms

ANSWER KEY FOR LISTENING COMPREHENSION SKILLS

Explanatory Answers can be found beginning on page 113.

Part 1: Photographs

SKILL 1 ASSUMPTIONS

Practice

A. T	D. T	G. F	J. PT
B. F	E. T	H. F	
C. PT	F. PT	I. T	

Exercise

Photo 1: **B** Photo 2: **C**

SKILL 2 PEOPLE

Practice

Number: There are two people in the photo.
Gender: There is one man and one woman.
Location: The man is on the right, the woman is on the left.
Description: They are elderly. They have short hair. The man has a mustache.
Activity: They are looking at a computer. The man is pointing at the computer screen. They are sitting on a bench. They have suitcases.
Occupation: They may be retired. They look like tourists.

Exercise

Photo 3: **A** Photo 4: **B**

SKILL 3 THINGS

Practice

table, chairs, glasses, plates, napkins, forks, vase, flower

Exercise

Photo 5: **A** Photo 6: **C**

SKILL 4 ACTIONS

Practice

(possible answers)
shopping, holding the fruit, picking up the fruit, looking at the fruit, pushing the cart, choosing fruit, standing in the aisle

Exercise

Photo 7: **D** Photo 8: **D**

SKILL 5 GENERAL LOCATIONS

Practice

Location: park. Context clues: benches, grass, trees, bushes, walking path, fence, lamppost

Exercise

Photo 9: **B** Photo 10: **D**

SKILL 6 SPECIFIC LOCATIONS

Practice

(possible answers)
The pen is on the notebook.
The notebook is in front of the computer.
The lamp is over the table.
The computer is between the two speakers.
The books are to the left of the speakers.
The plant is on top of the bookshelf.

Exercise

Photo 11: **A** Photo 12: **C**

Part 2: Question-Response

Skill 1 Similar Sounds	1. **A**	2. **C**	3. **A**
Skill 2 Related Words	1. **A**	2. **B**	3. **C**
Skill 3 Homonyms	1. **A**	2. **B**	3. **A**
Skill 4 Same Sound/Same Spelling but Different Meaning	1. **B**	2. **C**	3. **B**
Skill 5 Suggestions	1. **C**	2. **A**	3. **C**
Skill 6 Offers	1. **C**	2. **A**	3. **B**
Skill 7 Requests	1. **A**	2. **B**	3. **C**

Part 3: Conversations

Skill 1 People	1. **B**	2. **B**	3. **A**
Skill 2 Occupations	1. **D**	2. **D**	3. **C**
Skill 3 Place	1. **C**	2. **A**	3. **D**
Skill 4 Time	1. **C**	2. **B**	3. **D**
Skill 5 Activities	1. **D**	2. **C**	3. **D**
Skill 6 Opinions	1. **B**	2. **B**	3. **A**

Part 4: Talks

Skill 1 Events and Facts	1. **C**	2. **C**	3. **C**
Skill 2 Reasons	1. **A**	2. **A**	3. **D**
Skill 3 Numbers	1. **C**	2. **B**	3. **B**
Skill 4 Main Topics	1. **B**	2. **B**	3. **B**
Skill 5 Paraphrases	1. **B**	2. **A**	3. **D**

ANSWER KEY
Listening Comprehension Mini-Test

Explanatory Answers can be found beginning on page 118.

Part 1: Photographs

1. **C**	4. **A**	7. **A**	10. **A**
2. **D**	5. **A**	8. **B**	
3. **C**	6. **D**	9. **D**	

Part 2: Question-Response

11. **B**	15. **A**	19. **A**	23. **A**
12. **A**	16. **B**	20. **C**	24. **B**
13. **C**	17. **A**	21. **A**	25. **C**
14. **B**	18. **C**	22. **C**	

Part 3: Conversations

26. **C**	30. **C**	34. **D**	38. **C**
27. **D**	31. **B**	35. **C**	39. **B**
28. **C**	32. **A**	36. **D**	40. **D**
29. **C**	33. **D**	37. **A**	

Part 4: Talks

41. **D**	44. **A**	47. **D**	50. **D**
42. **D**	45. **B**	48. **C**	51. **C**
43. **B**	46. **A**	49. **C**	52. **C**

EXPLANATORY ANSWERS FOR LISTENING COMPREHENSION SKILLS

Part 1: Photographs

SKILL 1 ASSUMPTIONS

Photo 1

(B) In Choice (B) you can assume from the context that the people in white laboratory coats are technicians and that they could be doing experiments. Choice (A) is incorrect because the photo shows several people who could be pharmacists but none who could be customers. Choice (C) is incorrect because there are no laboratory animals pictured. Choice (D) is incorrect because the shelves contain bottles, jars, and supplies.

Photo 2

(C) The people are wearing business clothes and appear to be discussing some documents, so you can assume that they are business people having a meeting. Choice (A) correctly mentions the bottle, but no one is washing it. Choice (B) correctly mentions the computer, but the people are not in a store so no one is buying anything. Choice (D) is related to the fact that they are sitting around a table, but there is no food present, instead, there are things you might see at a business meeting—documents and a computer.

SKILL 2 PEOPLE

Photo 3

(A) Choice (A) correctly identifies the number and activity of the people. Choice (B) is incorrect because the men are in short sleeves. Choice (C) is incorrect because one woman is not as tall as the men. Choice (D) is incorrect because one of the women is pointing to the map.

Photo 4

(B) Choice (B) correctly identifies the people and their activity. Choice (A) is incorrect because it incorrectly identifies the man and woman's activity as looking for a bench rather than sitting on one. Choice (C) incorrectly describes the woman's hair. Choice (D) correctly identifies the suitcases, but no one is carrying them.

SKILL 3 THINGS

Photo 5

(A) Choice (A) correctly identifies the candles and their location—on the mantle. Choice (B) correctly identifies the piano, but there is no man in the photo. Choice (C) correctly identifies the chairs, but here are no people sitting on them. Choice (D) correctly identifies the cushions but not their location.

Photo 6

(C) Choice (C) correctly identifies the vase and its location. Choice (A) correctly identifies the flower, but not its location—it is in the vase, not in a garden. Choice (B) incorrectly identifies the location of the forks—they are on the napkins, not the plates. Choice (D) correctly identifies the table, but there is no food on it.

SKILL 4 ACTIONS

Photo 7

(D) Choice (D) correctly describes what the people (workers) are doing (laying pipeline). Choice (A) is incorrect because the men are *laying pipe*, not *smoking pipes*. Choice (B) identifies an incorrect action. Choice (C) identifies a *previous* action.

Photo 8

(D) Choice (D) correctly describes what the woman is doing. Choice (A) correctly identifies the fruit, but no one is washing it. Choice (B) is incorrect because the woman is pushing a cart, not looking for one. Choice (C) correctly identifies the oranges and the boxes, but no one is packing them.

SKILL 5 GENERAL LOCATIONS

Photo 9

(B) Choice (B) assumes that the people are passengers and are passing through a security checkpoint. Choice (A) incorrectly identifies the scene as a store. Choice (C) incorrectly identifies the scene as a bank. Choice (D) takes place on the plane, not at airport security.

Photo 10

(D) Choice (D) correctly identifies the location as a park and correctly describes the benches. Choice (A) makes an incorrect assumption about the location—there are benches at a bus stop, but everything else in the photo suggests that it is a park. Choice (B) confuses the meaning of the word *park*. Choice (C) correctly identifies the lamppost but not its location—there is no bank in the photo.

SKILL 6 SPECIFIC LOCATIONS

Photo 11

(A) Choice (A) correctly identifies the glasses and their specific location. Choice (B) correctly identifies the activity of the people but not their location—there is no window in the picture. Choice (C) correctly identifies the activity of the server but not her location—she is not near the man. Choice (D) correctly identifies the napkins but not their location—they are on a plate or under the forks.

Photo 12

(C) Choice (C) correctly identifies the location of the small clock. Choice (A) is incorrect because the plant is on top of the bookshelf, not on the desk. Choice (B) is incorrect because the pen is on the notebook, not in the cup. Choice (D) is incorrect because the speakers are next to, or on either side of, the computer, not behind it.

Part 2: Question-Response

SKILL 1 SIMILAR SOUNDS

1. **(A)** Choice (A) answers the *yes/no* question with *Yes.* Choice (B) has related words *delivery/truck* and similar sounds *letter/ladder, delivered/delivery.* Choice (C) has similar sounds *today/Tuesday, Was the/was he.* Listen for the whole meaning; note the grammar clue such as a *yes/no* question that begins with the auxiliary *was.*
2. **(C)** Choice (C) answers the *Where* question with a place: *on the next block.* Choice (A) has similar sounds *office/softest.* Choice (B) has similar sounds *fined/find.*
3. **(A)** The tag question *isn't she* asks for agreement. The question states that Mary Ann is *a nice person,* and the answer agrees by restating the idea as *she gets along well,* which has the same meaning. Choice (B) has similar sounds *nice/rice.* Choice (C) has similar sounds *person/purse.*

SKILL 2 RELATED WORDS

1. **(A)** Listen for the whole meaning; note the grammar clue: *How long* and the verb *married* suggests a length of time. Choice (A) gives the appropriate answer (ten years) to *how long.* Choice (B) has the related words *long/five feet,* but the question refers to time, not distance. Choice (C) has the related words *married/bride.*
2. **(B)** The question *When* is about time. Choice (B) answers with a time: *ten tomorrow morning.* Choice (D) relates the words *flight/ticket.* Choice (C) relates the words *flight/reservation.*
3. **(C)** The question *Where* is about a place. Choice (C) answers the question about a place to eat dinner with *restaurant.* Choice (A) relates the words *dinner/menu* and also repeats the word *like.* Choice (B) relates the words *dinner/meal.*

SKILL 3 HOMONYMS

1. **(A)** The tag question *doesn't he* requires a *yes/no* answer. Choice (A) answers the question and tells when he will leave. Choice (B) has homonyms *week/weak.* Choice (C) has homonyms *leaves* (v) / *leaves* (n).
2. **(B)** The question asks about a color of paint. Choice (B) responds with a comment about color. Choice (A) has homonyms *blue/blew.* Choice (C) has homonyms *wait (waiting room)/weight.*

3. **(A)** The embedded question *Who* asks about a person. Choice (A) responds with the name of a person, *Mr. Cho.* Choice (B) has homonyms *won/one.* Choice (C) has homonyms *do/due.*

SKILL 4 SAME SOUND/SAME SPELLING BUT DIFFERENT MEANING

1. **(B)** The phrase in (B) *Not for me* is a *no* answer to the *yes/no* question. It means, *No, the bed is not too hard for me. A hard* bed is a *firm* bed. Choice (A) incorrectly interprets *hard* to mean *difficult.* In Choice (C) *bed* means *a place for flowers.*
2. **(C)** Choice (C) is a logical response to a complaint about lack of light in the room. Choice (A) incorrectly interprets *light* in this context to mean *not heavy.* Choice (B) incorrectly interprets *room* in this context to mean *space.*
3. **(B)** In Choice (B), *I'll phone you* is a logical response to a request for a call. Choice (A) incorrectly interprets *right* in this context to mean *correct.* Choice (C) incorrectly interprets *right* in this context to mean *opposite of left.*

SKILL 5 SUGGESTIONS

1. **(C)** Choice (C) answers the *yes/no* suggestion with *Yes* and suggests a time to leave. Choice (A) has similar sounding and related word phrases *leave more time/left my watch.* Choice (B) confuses similar sounds *more/anymore.*
2. **(A)** Choice (A) answers the suggestion *Why don't we?* with *OK,* which is an agreement with the suggestion. Choice (B) confuses similar sounds *meet/meat.* Choice (C) repeats the word *three.*
3. **(C)** Choice (C) answers the suggestion *Let's* with *Good idea* and a rephrase of the suggestion. Choice (A) repeats the word *over.* Choice (B) confuses similar sounds *decision/precision.*

SKILL 6 OFFERS

1. **(C)** The other choices do not respond to the offer to accompany them out for coffee. Choice (A) uses words associated with *coffee* like *milk* and *sugar.* Choice (B) uses the location for having coffee, *a café.*
2. **(A)** Choice (A) is an appropriate way to respond to an offer. Choice (B) confuses similar-sounding words *arrives/drives.* Choice (C) confuses related words *visitors/visited.*
3. **(B)** Choice (B) thanks the speaker for the offered help and then says what help is needed. Choice (A) confuses similar-sounding words *ready/read.* Choice (C) confuses the meaning of the word *meeting.*

SKILL 7 REQUESTS

1. **(A)** The other choices do not respond to the request. Choice (B) has related words *window/door.* Choice (C) has related words *window/curtains.*
2. **(B)** Choice (B) is an appropriate way to respond to a request. Choice (A) confuses similar-sounding words *package/packed it.* Choice (C) uses related words *lunch/cafeteria.*
3. **(C)** Choice (C) is an appropriate response to a request. Choice (A) confuses similar-sounding words *collect/recollect.* Choice (B) repeats the word *town.*

Part 3: Conversations

SKILL 5 QUESTIONS ABOUT PEOPLE

1. **(B)** Listen for the context clues such as *sand, wall, first coat of paint,* and *mix the color.* Choice (A) suggests a related word for lifeguard: *sand* at the beach as opposed to the verb to *sand* a wall. Choice (C) has a word with the same sound but a different meaning: *coat of paint* (layer) and *coat* (clothing). Choice (D) has a related expression *to mix paints* (painters) and *to mix drinks* (bartenders).
2. **(B)** The man tells the woman to *sand* the wall. Choice (A) is incorrect because the man tells the woman to do the job. Choice (C) has similar sounds *boss* and *gloss.* Choice (D) confuses *helper* with *I'll help you.*
3. **(A)** The speakers talk about the kind of paint the father prefers and say they hope he will like his house when it's painted, so the house

belongs to the father. Choices (B) and (C) confuse *mother* and *brother* with the similar-sounding word *other*. Choice (D) has similar sounds *friend* and *end*.

SKILL 2 QUESTIONS ABOUT OCCUPATIONS

1. **(D)** Look for the context clues such as *put one in each room, wires along the baseboard,* and *phone rings.* Choice (A) confuses the meanings of *run wires/running* as in jogging. Choice (B) has similar sounds *baseboard/baseball.* Choice (C) has related words *phone rings/telephone operator.*
2. **(D)** The woman says the man needs a lot of phones because he has a mail order company. Choice (A) has related words *mailman* and *mail.* Choice (B) repeats the word *website.* Choice (C) has related words *employment* and *employee.*
3. **(C)** The man says, *We're all responsible for answering the phone here.* Choices (A), (B), and (D) are contradicted by the correct answer.

SKILL 3 QUESTIONS ABOUT PLACE

1. **(C)** Listen for the context clue: *I left the letter. . . .* Choice (A) is contradicted by *the stack on the desk.* Choices (B) and (D) are contradicted by *on top of these books.*
2. **(A)** The woman mentions, *the shelf by the door.* Choices (B), (C), and (D) have repeated words *computer, desk,* and *box.*
3. **(D)** The woman tells the man to put the letter on top of her computer next time. Choices (A), (B), and (C) have repeated words *printer, box,* and *folder.*

SKILL 4 QUESTIONS ABOUT TIME

1. **(C)** A half-hour is equal to 30 minutes. You may sometimes have to change hours to minutes: for example, one and a half hours is 90 minutes. Choice (A) indicates when the man had planned to leave. Choice (B) is not mentioned. Choice (D) indicates how long the woman asked him to stay.
2. **(B)** The woman says that the man's appointment is at 8:30. Choice (A) sounds similar to the correct answer. Choices (C) and (D) have similar sounds *nine* and *time.*
3. **(D)** The woman says that the man can get to his house in 45 minutes. Choices (A) and (B) have similar sounds *twenty* and *plenty.* Choice (C) sounds similar to the correct answer.

SKILL 5 QUESTIONS ABOUT ACTIVITIES

1. **(D)** Look for the context clues *turn left, one-way street,* and *map.* Choice (A) is contradicted by *one-way street.* Choice (B) has similar sounds *map/nap.* Choice (C) is contradicted by *should have bought a map.*
2. **(C)** The man mentions a restaurant, the woman mentions *dinner.* Choice (A) has similar sounds *rested/restaurant.* Choice (B) has similar sounds *snow/show.* Choice (D) has similar sounds *rent/spent* and repeats the word *movie.*
3. **(D)** They are looking for a movie theater. Choice (A) has similar sounds *read/need.* Choice (B) has similar sounds *bed/ahead.* Choice (C) associates *play* with *theater.*

SKILL 6 QUESTIONS ABOUT OPINIONS

1. **(B)** The context clues all refer to humor: *funny, laughed, jokes.* Be careful: *I never laughed so hard* means *I laughed harder than ever before.* Choice (A) has the related words *speaker/presentation.* Choice (C) is not mentioned. Choice (D) confuses similar sounds *jokes/folks.*
2. **(B)** The man says that the food is great. Choice (A) is the woman's opinion. Choice (C) has similar sounds, *seats/eat,* and confuses the meaning of *hard.* Choice (D) is incorrect because it is the portions of food that are big, not the room.
3. **(A)** The woman says, . . . *it's quite a bit on the expensive side.* Choice (B) is confused with *I'd expected it to be cheaper.* Choice (C) has similar sounds *tables/uncomfortable,* and *nice/price.* Choice (D) is how the woman feels about the price, not the hotel.

Part 4: Talks

SKILL 1 QUESTIONS ABOUT EVENTS AND FACTS

1. **(C)** The speaker says, . . . *our annual celebration of National Day is this weekend.* Choice (A) confuses the meaning of the word *book* (in *book your tickets*) and repeats the word *fair* (*food fair*). Choice (B) is confused with the mention of the conference center. Choice (D) repeats the word *international* (*international cuisine*) and confuses similar-sounding words *chance/dance.*
2. **(C)** The speaker mentions a concert at City Conference Center on Saturday evening. Choice (A) is incorrect because the parade is on Friday. Choices (B) and (D) are incorrect because both those events take place during the day on Saturday.
3. **(C)** The mayor will participate in the basketball tournament on Sunday. Choice (A) repeats the word *tickets.* Choice (B) repeats the word *crowds.* Choice (D) confuses *basketball* with *baskets.*

SKILL 2 QUESTIONS ABOUT REASONS

1. **(A)** A work slowdown is a work action. A slowdown is like a strike except workers show up, but do not work at their normal speed. They work more slowly. Choices (B), (C), and (D) do not give the reason *why.*
2. **(A)** The announcer suggests that people should eat now because the restaurants will close at midnight. Choice (B) is confused with . . . *won't reopen until tomorrow.* Choice (C) repeats the word *flight,* but no mention is made of whether or not there will be food on the flight. Choice (D) confuses *close (near)* with *close (opposite of open).*
3. **(D)** The announcer suggests listening to the announcements to hear when flights are ready for boarding. Choice (A) repeats the word *gate.* Choice (B) repeats the word *restaurants.* Choice (C) has similar sounds *bored/board.*

SKILL 3 QUESTIONS ABOUT NUMBERS

1. **(C)** If you purchase more than $100 worth of pencils, the supplier will give you a 10 percent discount. Ten percent of $200 is $20 (200 – 10%).
2. **(B)** Seasonal sales often have a 25% discount; 25% of 200 is 50. Choice (A) confuses the dollar amount of the discount with the percentage. Choice (C) is the price with a 20% discount. Choice (D) is the price with a 25 dollar, not percent, discount.
3. **(B)** Sales tax is 5%; and 5% of 200 is 10. Choice (A) confuses the dollar amount of the tax with the percentage. Choice (C) is the sales discount, not the tax. Choice (D) confuses 5 with 50.

SKILL 4 QUESTIONS ABOUT MAIN TOPICS

1. **(B)** The phrases *asked me to submit my letter of resignation* and *told me to leave by the close of business today* both indicate that the Managing Director was *fired.* Choice (A) repeats the words *Board of Directors* and *resignation.* Choice (C) is not mentioned. Choice (D) repeats the word *letter.*
2. **(B)** The speaker says, *I will no longer work as your managing director,* so he is speaking to his staff. Choice (A) has related words *clients/business.* Choice (C) confuses the meaning of *serve.* Choice (D) is the speaker's position.
3. **(B)** The speaker says that he hopes to open up a consulting business. Choice (A) has homonyms *clothes/close.* Choice (C) has similar sounds *college/colleague.* Choice (D) has similar sounds *restaurant/rest* and related words *manager/managing.*

SKILL 5 PARAPHASES

1. **(B)** The talk says the form is to track your loan application. Choices (A), (C), and (D) are not mentioned.
2. **(A)** The listener is instructed to *press firmly* when filling out the form; that is a necessity when making multiple carbon copies. Choices (B), (C), and (D) are all possible ways of making copies but are not implied in the talk.

3. **(D)** The speaker says that the listener will be contacted within *two weeks*, which is the same as fourteen days. Choice (A) repeats the word two. Choice (B) is the number of copies that will be made. Choice (C) has similar sounds *ten/then*.

EXPLANATORY ANSWERS FOR MINI-TEST FOR LISTENING COMPREHENSION

Part 1: Photographs

1. **(C)** Choice (C) identifies people (*men*) and a location (*the buffet*). Choice (B) shows negation: there are not guests in the photo. Choice (C) refers to an *officer*, whose uniform might resemble that of the waiters. Choice (D) confuses similar sounds *bus* with *busboy*.
2. **(D)** Choice (D) identifies action: *boat leaving harbor*. Choice (A) confuses similar sounds *sheep* with *ship*. Choice (B) confuses a related word *water*. Choice (C) confuses similar sounds *votes* with *boats*.
3. **(C)** Choice (C) identifies location: *large hall*. Choice (A) incorrectly identifies the location as a bank. Choice (B) confuses similar sounding *floor* with *flower*. Choice (D) is incorrect because the passengers are *at the ticket counters*, not *on the plane*.
4. **(A)** The man is looking down at the keyboard as he writes with it. Choice (B) is incorrect because the headphones are around the man's neck, not on the table. Choice (C) correctly identifies the microphone, but the man is not speaking into it. Choice (D) confuses *microphone* with *telephone*.
5. **(A)** Choice (A) identifies the occupation, *operator*, and the action, *pushing a button*. Choice (B) describes an incorrect action. Choice (C) confuses different meanings for *button* (in clothing) and *button* (on machinery). Choice (D) has the related phrase *going up*, but concerning stocks, not elevators.
6. **(D)** The men, probably construction architects, engineers, or workers, are holding building plans. Choice (A) uses the similar-sounding word *plane* for *crane*. Choice (B) uses the associated word *building* but they are building a building not entering one. Choice (C) uses the associated word *watching*. They are observing the construction, not a parade.
7. **(A)** Choice (A) identifies a thing: *electrical wires*. Choice (B) confuses the related word *poles*. Choice (C) confuses the related phrase *light fixture*. Choice (D) confuses homonyms (*polls* with *poles*) and similar sounds (*election* with *electricity*).
8. **(B)** Choice (B) identifies the action: *works with her hands*. Choice (A) cannot be assumed from the photo. Choice (C) incorrectly identifies the occupation of the woman and her action. Choice (D) is incorrect because the woman is not holding a saw.
9. **(D)** Choice (D) correctly identifies the man's action and location. Choice (A) is incorrect because no one is pushing the chair. Choice (B) correctly identifies the patient, but he isn't taking pills. Choice (C) refers to the stairs in the picture, but no one is walking down them.
10. **(A)** Choice (A) correctly identifies the location of the suitcase: *in front of her chair*. Choice (B) is incorrect because the woman is sitting in a seat, not looking for one. Choice (C) misidentifies the location of the woman: she is in the airport, not on the airplane. Choice (D) is incorrect because the bag (suitcase) is closed, not open.

Part 2: Question-Response

11. **(B)** Choice (B) is a logical response to a question about *location*. Choice (A) confuses similar sounds *live* with *five*. Choice (C) confuses similar sounds *live* with *leave* and is not a logical response to a question about *location*.
12. **(A)** Choice (A) is a logical response to a question about *time*. Choice (B) confuses similar sounds *late* with *ate*. Choice (C) confuses similar sounds *late* with *later*.
13. **(C)** Choice (C) is a logical response to a question about *who*. Choice (A) confuses similar sounds *wait* with *weight*. Choice (B) confuses similar sounds *wait* and *way*.
14. **(B)** After hearing that it will rain later, the second speaker decides to wear a raincoat. Choice

(A) confuses *letter* with the similar-sounding word *later*. Choice (C) confuses *train* with the similar-sounding word *rain*.

15. **(A)** Choice (A) is a logical response to a question about *possession*. Choice (B) confuses similar sounds *chair* with *cheer*. Choice (C) confuses similar sounds *chair* with *fair*.
16. **(B)** Choice (B) is a logical response to a question about *time*. Choice (A) has the related word *train* but answers *how*, not *when*. Choice (C) has related the word *mail* but is not a logical answer; people don't arrive by mail.
17. **(A)** Choice (A) is a logical response to a question about *duration*. Choice (B) has the related word *work* but answers *which day* not *how long*. Choice (C) confuses similar sounds *here* with *hear*, *long* with *along*.
18. **(C)** Choice (C) is a logical response to a question about *location*. Choice (A) confuses similar sounds *park* with *dark*. Choice (B) confuses different meanings *park* (leave your car) and *park* (recreational area).
19. **(A)** Choice (A) is a logical response to a question about *activity*. Choice (B) confuses similar sounds *should* with *wood*. In Choice (C), *were* (past tense) does not answer *should do now* (present tense).
20. **(C)** Choice (C) is a logical response to a question about *time*. Choice (A) confuses similar sounds *meet* with *meat*. Choice (B) confuses related words *start* (begin) with *start* (turn on, engine turn-over).
21. **(A)** Since the first speaker doesn't like the color of the walls, the second speaker suggests repainting them. Choice (B) confuses *ball* with the similar-sounding word *walls*. Choice (C) confuses *calls* with the similar-sounding word *walls*.
22. **(C)** Choice (C) is a logical response to a question about *size*. Choice (A) confuses similar sounds *large* with *inches*. Choice (B) confuses similar sounds *com(pany)* with *penny*.
23. **(A)** Choice (A) is a logical response to a question about *where*. Choice (B) confuses similar sounds *eat* with *heat*. Choice (C) confuses similar sounds *eat* with *eight*.
24. **(B)** Choice (B) is a logical response to a question about *no electricity*. Choice (A) has the related word *gas*, but it does not answer the question. Choice (C) confuses similar sounds *electricity* with *elections*.
25. **(C)** The first speaker is going to the bank, so the second speaker asks to have a check cashed. Choice (A) associates *hungry* with *lunch*. Choice (B) confuses *thank* with the similar-sounding word *bank*.

Part 3: Conversations

26. **(C)** The speakers say that they are going to see a play. Choice (A) confuses *view* with the similar-sounding word *review*. Choice (B) uses the word *play* out of context. Choice (D) associates *movie* with *review*.
27. **(D)** The woman says that the play starts at 7:00. Choice (A) confuses *two* with the similar-sounding word *too*. Choice (B) confuses *five* with the similar-sounding word *drive*. Choice (C) is the time right now.
28. **(C)** The woman mentions the rain. Choice (A) confuses *sun* with the similar-sounding word *fun*. Choice (B) confuses *ice* with the similar-sounding word *nice*. Choice (D) confuses *snow* with the similar-sounding word *slow*.
29. **(C)** The woman says she wants to discuss conference plans. Choice (A) confuses *planes* with the similar-sounding word *plans*. Choice (B) repeats the words *lunch* and *plans*. Choice (D) repeats the words *order* and *office*.
30. **(C)** The speakers finally agree to meet on Tuesday. Choices (A) and (B) are confused with the similar-sounding phrase *one day*. Choice (D) is the man's suggestion.
31. **(B)** The man says he wants to meet at his office. Choice (A) sounds similar to the correct answer. Choice (C) confuses *restaurant* with the similar-sounding word *rest*. Choice (D) is the woman's suggestion.
32. **(A)** The man says that the shirt is too small. Choice (B) is incorrect because the man asks for the same color shirt. Choice (C) confuses *hole* with the similar-sounding word *though*.

Choice (D) is confused with the description of the shirt as long-sleeved.

33. **(D)** The woman suggests size eighteen, and the man agrees. Choice (A) sounds similar to the correct answer. Choice (B) sounds similar to the size of the shirt he is returning. Choice (C) is the size of the shirt he is returning.
34. **(D)** The woman says she can give him blue, the same color as the old shirt. Choice (A) confuses *white* with the similar-sounding word *right.* Choice (B) confuses *black* with the similar-sounding word *that.* Choice (C) confuses *green* with the similar-sounding words *sixteen* and *eighteen.*
35. **(C)** The woman asks the man where he will go this fall. Choice (A) confuses *spring* with the similar-sounding word *think.* Choice (B) confuses *summer* with the similar-sounding word *some.* Choice (D) repeats the word *winter.*
36. **(D)** The woman suggests going to Hawaii because it is always warm there. Choices (A) and (B) are the places the woman asks about. Choice (C) is the man's idea.
37. **(A)** The man says he has only one week to go somewhere. Choice (B) confuses *two* with the similar-sounding word *to.* Choice (C) is the length of the woman's vacation. Choice (D) confuses *four* with the similar-sounding word *for.*
38. **(C)** The man says he was in a meeting. Choice (A) is where the woman put the phone messages. Choice (B) associates *store* with *purchase.* Choice (D) is where the purchase order forms are kept.
39. **(B)** The woman says he got seven messages. Choice (A) confuses *four* with the similar-sounding word *for.* Choice (C) sounds similar to the correct answer. Choice (D) confuses *forty-two* with the similar-sounding phrase *for you.*
40. **(D)** The man asks the woman to bring him a purchase order form. Choice (A) is incorrect because the man says he will take care of the messages. Choice (B) associates *buy* with *purchase.* Choice (C) repeats the words *purchase* and *supply.*

Part 4: Talks

41. **(D)** The announcer says that the temperature is fifty-three degrees. Choices (A), (B), and (C) sound similar to the correct answer.
42. **(D)** The speaker says, . . . *get out those umbrellas* . . . and mentions that it will rain. Choice A is incorrect because snow is not predicted—the day will be *seasonably mild.* Choice (B), *luggage,* may be associated with *National Airport.* Choice (C), *sunscreen,* is associated with *clear skies.*
43. **(B)** The speaker says, . . . *skies will be clearing up by noon.* Choice (A) is incorrect because it will be raining at 6:00 A.M. Choice (C) confuses similar-sounding words *noon/afternoon.* Choice (D) is when winds will develop.
44. **(A)** It is being turned off to *reduce total demand.* Choice (B) is incorrect because it will save *power,* not *money.* Choice (C) confuses *make cooler* with *hot weather.* Choice (D) is not mentioned.
45. **(B)** *Power will not be out longer than two hours* means it will be out *less than two hours.* Choices (A), (C), and (D) are contradicted by *not longer than two hours.*
46. **(A)** Listeners are asked to visit the company's Web site. Choice (B) confuses *call* with the similar-sounding word *all.* Choice (C) repeats the word *visit.* Choice (D) associates *radio* with *turn off.*
47. **(D)** *Cruise, at sea, ashore,* and *Main Deck* indicate the announcement is *on a ship.* Choice (A) is incorrect because tour buses are not found at sea. Choice (B) confuses *at the shore* with *ashore, shore excursion.* Choice (C) confuses *report to the lounge* (room with comfortable chairs) and *cocktail lounge.*
48. **(C)** People are requested to *report for a ticket.* Choice (A) is incorrect because *enjoy your breakfast* does not mean that breakfast is required. Choices (B) and (D) are incorrect because *clothing* and *health* are not mentioned.
49. **(C)** The announcer says that the excursion will depart at 9:00 A.M. Choice (A) confuses *four* with the similar-sounding word *shore.*

Choice (B) is the time the announcement is being made. Choice (D) sounds similar to the correct answer.

50. **(D)** The talk is an advertisement for Movie Time video streaming service. Choice (A) is associated with the mention of movies. Choice (B) is not mentioned but is something one might subscribe to. Choice (D) is associated with the mention of TV shows.
51. **(C)** The speaker says, *The first month is free.* Choice (A) is confused with the similar-sounding word *today.* Choice (B) confuses similar-sounding words *free/three.* Choice (D) is confused with the mention of a yearly subscription, but that is not free.
52. **(C)** The speaker says, *Subscriptions start at $150 annually.* Choices (A) and (D) sound similar to the correct answer. Choice (B) sounds similar to the word *sign.*

ANSWER KEY FOR NEW TOEIC LISTENING COMPREHENSION SKILLS

Explanatory answers can be found beginning on page 125.

Part 1: Photographs

1. **D**
2. **A**
3. **C**
4. **B**
5. **A**
6. **D**

Part 2: Question-Response

1. **B**
2. **A**
3. **B**
4. **A**
5. **B**
6. **A**
7. **C**
8. **C**
9. **B**
10. **A**
11. **B**
12. **C**
13. **A**
14. **B**
15. **C**
16. **B**
17. **A**
18. **C**
19. **A**
20. **B**
21. **A**
22. **C**
23. **B**
24. **B**
25. **A**

Part 3: Conversations

SKILL 1

1. **D**
2. **A**
3. **B**
4. **B**
5. **A**

SKILL 2

1. **A**
2. **B**
3. **B**
4. **A**
5. **B**

SKILL 3

1. I don't know where she went.
2. Would you like a cup of coffee?
3. We have to get it done by Friday.
4. Where did you go?
5. You can come and get it after 5.
6. Ask them to call back later.
7. Could he wait downstairs?
8. We're busy at that time of day.

SKILL 4

1. **B**
2. **A**
3. **B**
4. **A**
5. **B**

SKILL 5

1. It's very nice to meet you.
2. Can you please answer the phone?

3. I'll order some right away.
4. The reports aren't ready yet.
5. You can hang your coat in that closet.
6. It's not a very large apartment.
7. We expect them to arrive before lunch.
8. I'll see you at next week's meeting.
9. He's only just started working here.
10. I have an appointment with her next Monday.
11. Do you know when the workshop begins?
12. She's new here, isn't she?
13. Where did you work before?
14. Why is the door locked?
15. The bus stop is on the corner.
16. Would you like to wait in her office?
17. Do you prefer coffee or tea?
18. Which desk should I use?
19. We placed the order last Friday.
20. He left on the evening train.

Part 4: Talks

SKILL 1

1. **C**
2. **B**
3. **C**
4. **D**
5. **A**

SKILL 2

1. **A**
2. **B**
3. **B**
4. **A**
5. **B**

SKILL 3

1. Good evening and welcome to tonight's presentation. We are very excited to have with us tonight a world-famous journalist. I am sure you will enjoy his talk very much.
2. Here is the weather outlook for the weekend. We will have cloudy skies all day Saturday. Expect rain to begin late Saturday evening and continue through Sunday morning. The rain will clear up on Sunday afternoon.
3. Thank you for calling the Acme Company. We value your call. To check your order status, press one. For shipping information, press two. To speak with a customer service representative, press three. To repeat this menu, press four.
4. Attention shoppers. We will be closing the store in ten minutes. Please take your purchases to the checkout area at this time. If you are purchasing ten items or fewer, you may use the express checkout lane.
5. The tour will begin in just a few minutes. Please line up by the main entrance. If you don't have a ticket, you can purchase one in the gift shop.

ANSWER KEY New TOEIC Listening Comprehension Mini-Test

Explanatory Answers can be found beginning on page 128.

Part 1: Photographs

1. **B**	2. **C**	3. **A**	4. **D**

Part 2: Question-Response

5. **B**	8. **C**	11. **A**	14. **C**
6. **A**	9. **B**	12. **C**	15. **B**
7. **A**	10. **B**	13. **A**	16. **A**

Part 3: Conversations

17. **C**	22. **B**	27. **C**	32. **C**
18. **A**	23. **A**	28. **B**	33. **D**
19. **D**	24. **C**	29. **B**	34. **B**
20. **A**	25. **D**	30. **D**	
21. **B**	26. **A**	31. **C**	

Part 4: Talks

35. **C**	39. **A**	43. **D**	47. **C**
36. **A**	40. **B**	44. **B**	48. **B**
37. **C**	41. **A**	45. **B**	49. **A**
38. **D**	42. **D**	46. **C**	

EXPLANATORY ANSWERS FOR NEW TOEIC LISTENING COMPREHENSION SKILLS

Part 1: Photographs

1. **(D)** A man with a suitcase is riding up an escalator. Choice (A) confuses similar-sounding words *escalator* and *elevator.* Choice (B) correctly mentions the bag (suitcase), but the man isn't opening it. Choice (C) confuses *escalator* with *stairs* and misidentifies the man's action—he's standing not sitting.
2. **(A)** A car is parked on the street in front of a house. Choice (B) is incorrect because the garage door is closed. Choice (C) is incorrect because there are no people on the lawn. Choice (D) is incorrect because there is nothing in the driveway.
3. **(C)** Three business people are sitting around a restaurant table. Choice (A) confuses *drinking glasses* with *eyeglasses.* Choice (B) is incorrect because no one is shaking hands. Choice (D) associates the restaurant setting with the word *waiter,* but there is no waiter in the photo.
4. **(B)** A man is paying for his meal in a cafeteria. Choice (A) correctly identifies the *trays,* but there is no waiter in the photo. Choice (C) associates *cook* and *meal* with the cafeteria scene. Choice (D) associates *diners* and *menu* with the cafeteria scene.
5. **(A)** Passengers on a train station platform are boarding a train. Choice (B) is incorrect because the passengers are already at the station. Choice (C) associates *tickets* with the train station scene. Choice (D) confuses similar-sounding words *train* and *rain.*
6. **(D)** A lamp stands on a bedside table between two pictures in frames. Choice (A) is incorrect because the photos, or pictures, are on the table, not on the wall. Choice (B) is incorrect because the drawer is closed. Choice (C) is incorrect because the pillows are on the bed and there is no chair in the photo.

Part 2: Question-Response

1. **(B)** *I sent a check* is a logical response to the question about paying a bill. Choice (A) confuses similar-sounding words *pay* and *play.* Choice (C) confuses the word *bill* with the name *Bill.*
2. **(A)** *It's mine* is a logical response to the *Whose* question. Choice (B) would answer *Where.* Choice (C) would answer *Who.*
3. **(B)** This is a polite response to the polite request. Choice (A) repeats the word *report.* Choice (C) confuses similar-sounding words *report* and *sports.*
4. **(A)** This is a logical response to the *When* question. Choice (B) would answer *Where.* Choice (C) confuses similar-sounding words *ready* and *red.*
5. **(B)** This is a logical response to the *yes-no* question about the boss. Choice (A) confuses similar-sounding words *boss* and *loss.* Choice (C) would answer *When.*
6. **(A)** This is a polite response to the polite offer. Choices (A) and (C) repeat the word *wait.*
7. **(C)** *Two days* answers the *When* question Choice (A) would answer *How big.* Choice (B) would answer a *yes-no* question.
8. **(C)** This answers the *What* question. Choice (A) would answer *How long.* Choice (B) confuses similar-sounding words *meeting* and *eating.*
9. **(B)** This answers the *Where* question. Choice (A) would answer *What.* Choice (C) would answer *When.*
10. **(A)** This answers the question about a preference for a meeting time. Choice (B) confuses homonyms *week* and *weak.* Choice (C) confuses similar-sounding words *week* and *speak.*
11. **(B)** This is a logical response to the statement about running out of paper. Choice (A) confuses the meaning of the word *running* and repeats the word *printer.* Choice (C) would answer a *yes-no* question.

12. **(C)** This is a logical answer to the *What time* question. Choice (A) repeats the word *time.* Choice (B) repeats the word *bus.*
13. **(A)** *Only one* answers the *How many* question. Choice (B) would answer a *yes-no* question. Choice (C) associates *buy* with *credit card.*
14. **(B)** *Make a left* answers the question *Which direction.* Choice (A) associates *right* with *direction,* and confuses the meaning of the word, using it here to mean *correct.* Choice (C) repeats *turn* with a different meaning.
15. **(C)** This answers the *Why* question with a logical reason for being late. Choices (A) and (B) associate times (*10:30, half hour*) with *late.*
16. **(B)** This answers the *yes-no* question and adds information about the reason for being in the building. Choice (A) would answer a question about *going to* the building. Choice (C) confuses similar-sounding words *live* and *leave.*
17. **(A)** *Sydney* answers the *Where* question. Choice (B) would answer a *When* question. Choice (C) associates the topic of travel with *rental car.*
18. **(C)** This is a logical response to the comment about the coffee machine not working. Choice (A) confuses the meaning of the word *work.* Choice (B) associates *coffee* with *cup.*
19. **(A)** *10 or 15* answers the *How many* question. Choice (B) would answer *What color.* Choice (C) would be a response to an offer of help.
20. **(B)** This is a simple answer to the *yes-no* question. Choice (A) would answer a *Where* question. Choice (C) would answer a *What* question.
21. **(A)** This is a logical response to the compliment. Choice (B) repeats the word *presentation.* Choice (C), by using the word *agenda,* associates *presentation* with a meeting.
22. **(C)** *Six o'clock* answers the indirect *When* question. Choice (A) repeats the word *back.* Choice (B) repeats the word *know.*
23. **(B)** *Mary* answers the *Who* question. Choice (A) associates *message* with a phone *call.* Choice (C) repeats the word *desk.*
24. **(B)** This answers the *Where* question. Choice (A) would answer a *When* question. Choice (C) would answer a *yes-no* question.
25. **(A)** This is a logical explanation for how the door was opened. Choice (B) repeats the word *open.* Choice (C) confuses similar-sounding words *door* and *floor.*

Part 3: Conversations

SKILL 1

1. **(D)** According to the conversation, Sue will work on Jim's scheduled day, which is Thursday. Choice (A) is the day Sue was originally scheduled to work at the reception desk, but Jim is covering for her on that day. Choices (B) and (C) are days other people will work.
2. **(A)** The man says not to spend more than $150, and Choice (A) is the only model that costs less than that amount. Choices (B), (C), and (D) all cost more than the man authorized the woman to spend.
3. **(B)** The man says, *The month after we hired him, sales were up for the first time all year.* The graph shows that April was the first month sales were up, and the month before that is March. Choices (A), (C), and (D) don't agree with the man's statement.
4. **(B)** The woman asks the man to change the agenda by moving Robert's presentation to last place and starting the meeting with Maya's presentation, and Maya will talk about the sales update. Choice (A) was originally the first item on the agenda. Choices (C) and (D) are agenda items that will follow the sales update.
5. **(A)** The man says that the café is across from the book store. Choices (B), (C), and (D) don't fit this description.

SKILL 2

1. **(A)** If somethings *are starting to turn around,* they have been bad but now are changing for the better.
2. **(B)** The man says, *things are starting to pick up,* meaning *things are getting better,* and he also has a job interview scheduled, so he must be feeling optimistic.
3. **(B)** When the man questions who chose the carpet and then says, *I mean, that color,* he implies that he doesn't like the color. When the woman says that it's not a color that *would be at the top of my list,* she means it wouldn't be one of her first choices, in fact, it probably wouldn't be on her list of choices at all because she doesn't like it.
4. **(A)** The woman's statement means that the meeting felt long because it was so boring, and the man's statement means that he almost fell asleep from boredom.
5. **(B)** To be on top of something means to have it under control; the woman means that she can finish the work within the amount of time that she has.

SKILL 3

1. **I don't know where she went.** The words *don't know* are often pronounced as if they were one word, with the /t/ of *don't* dropped: *dunno.*
2. **Would you like a cup of coffee?** When *you* follows a word ending in /d/, the/d/ and /y/ sounds combine: *would you* becomes *wouldjya.* The word *of* often attaches to the word preceding it, dropping the /f/ in the process: *cup of* becomes *cuppa.*
3. **We have to get it done by Friday**. *Have to* is often pronounced *hafta. Get it* is pronounced as if it were one word: *gettit.*
4. **Where did you go?** *Where did you* combine to be pronounced as one word: *Where'djya.*
5. **You can come and get it after 5**. The words *come and* are often said as one word, with only the *n* of *and* pronounced. The words *get it* are often pronounced together as one word.
6. **Ask them to call back later**. The *th* of *them* is often dropped.
7. **Could he wait downstairs?** The *h* of *he* is often dropped following an auxiliary verb.
8. **We're busy at that time of day**. The *f* of *of* is frequently dropped.

SKILL 4

1. **(B)** *Right,* in this case, means *correct.* The man is confirming that the woman correctly understand what he said.
2. **(A)** The response is short for *It's fine with me,* with *fine* used here to mean *good.*
3. **(B)** *Get,* in this case, means *understand.* The man is confirming to the woman that he understands and has made note of her requests.
4. **(A)** *Wish I could* is short for *I wish I could join you.*
5. **(B)** *Too bad* is short for *That's too bad,* a common expression of regret. The man regrets that Ms. Chang is too busy to see him.

SKILL 5

1. It's very nice to meet you.
2. Can you please answer the phone?
3. I'll order some right away.
4. The reports aren't ready yet.
5. You can hang your coat in that closet.
6. It's not a very large apartment.
7. We expect them to arrive before lunch.
8. I'll see you at next week's meeting.
9. He's only just started working here.
10. I have an appointment with her next Monday.
11. Do you know when the workshop begins?
12. She's new here, isn't she?
13. Where did you work before?
14. Why is the door locked?
15. The bus stop is on the corner.
16. Would you like to wait in her office?
17. Do you prefer coffee or tea?
18. Which desk should I use?
19. We placed the order last Friday.
20. He left on the evening train.

Part 4: Talks

Skill 1

1. **(C)** The speaker says that her train *gets into Springfield Station at just after 11:00,* which matches the 11:02 scheduled arrival time of train no. 32. Choices (A), (B), and (D) refer to trains that arrive at other times.
2. **(B)** The speaker says, *the most logical place to start cutting is in the category where the largest percentage of our budget has been spent,* that is, *salaries,* which take up 45% of the budget. Choice (A), (C), and (D) are parts of the budget that don't fit this description.
3. **(C)** The tour starts in the Pine Grove, on the right-hand side of the river. The speaker says they will stop for lunch after crossing the footbridge, which puts them in the Rose Garden. Choices (A), (B), and (D) are other places on the map.
4. **(D)** The speaker says there was *a significant increase in sales in one part of the country,* and the graph shows the Southeast as the only region with a significant increase in sales. Choices (A), (B), and (C) are other regions shown on the graph that only had small increases in sales.
5. **(A)** The speaker expects *no more than 15* people, and the small platter serves that number. Choices (B), (C), and (D) are sizes that serve larger numbers of people.

SKILL 2

1. **(A)** The speaker says that he is rescheduling the appointment *yet again,* which implies that he has done this more than once before.
2. **(B)** The speaker says, *Could we ask for a better day? I don't think so!,* meaning that the weather on this day is very good.
3. **(B)** The speaker suggests that those who are paying cash should go to the ticket office, implying that the machine cannot accept cash.
4. **(A)** The speaker says, *It looks like we're going to have a huge turn out, certainly much more than we had a year ago.* A huge turn out means a big crowd.
5. **(B)** The man says that people should show their membership cards to the ticket seller and goes on to say that *tickets cannot be sold to non cardholders,* that is, people who aren't members.

SKILL 3

1. Good evening and welcome to tonight's presentation. We are very excited to have with us tonight a world-famous journalist. I am sure you will enjoy his talk very much.
2. Here is the weather outlook for the weekend. We will have cloudy skies all day Saturday. Expect rain to begin late Saturday evening and continue through Sunday morning. The rain will clear up on Sunday afternoon.
3. Thank you for calling the Acme Company. We value your call. To check your order status, press one. For shipping information, press two. To speak with a customer service representative, press three. To repeat this menu, press four.
4. Attention shoppers. We will be closing the store in ten minutes. Please take your purchases to the checkout area at this time. If you are purchasing ten items or fewer, you may use the express checkout lane.
5. The tour will begin in just a few minutes. Please line up by the main entrance. If you don't have a ticket, you can purchase on in the gift shop.

EXPLANATORY ANSWERS FOR MINI-TEST FOR NEW TOEIC LISTENING COMPREHENSION

Part 1: Photographs

1. **(B)** A pharmacist is wearing a white coat and holding a pill bottle and speaking with a customer. Choice (A) is incorrect because the man is wearing his coat, not hanging it up. Choice (C) correctly mentions the bottle, but the man is not opening it, and he doesn't

look like a cook. Choice (D) confuses similar-sounding words *pharmacist* and *farmer.*

2. **(C)** This choice correctly describes the location of the book. Choice (A) correctly identifies the eggs, but not their location. Choice (B) correctly identifies the pencil, but not its location. Choice (D) correctly identifies the flowers, but not their location.
3. **(A)** A man is trimming bushes in a garden. Choice (B) correctly identifies the man's action (cutting = trimming), but he is not cutting hair. Choice (C) associates *mowing* and *cutting.* Choice (D) associates *flowers* and *garden.*
4. **(D)** A woman is looking at a phone that she holds in her hand. Choice (A) correctly identifies her action, but she is reading the phone screen, not a book. Choice (B) correctly identifies her glasses, but she is not putting them on. Choice (C) correctly identifies the computer in her lap, but she is not buying it.

Part 2: Question-Response

5. **(B)** *Two days* answers the *How long* question. Choice (A) would answer *How did you like . . . ?* Choice (C) would answer a *How long* question about distance.
6. **(A)** This is a polite response to the request for help. Choice (B) would answer a *yes-no* question. Choice (C) repeats the word *desk.*
7. **(A)** This is an appropriate response to the question about possession. Choice (B) associates *package* and *mail.* Choice (C) repeats the word *door.*
8. **(C)** *25 employees* answers the *How many* question. Choice (A) repeats the words *work here.* Choice (B) confuses same-sounding words *here* and *hear.*
9. **(B)** *Ten o'clock* answers the *What time* question. Choice (A) would answer a *Where* question. Choice (C) repeats the word *close.*
10. **(B)** This is an appropriate response to a request for an appointment. Choice (A) confuses similar-sounding words *appointment* and *apartment.* Choice (C) confuses the meaning of the word *like* in this context.
11. **(A)** *At his office* answers the *Where* question. Choice (B) would answer a *When* question. Choice (C) repeats the word *meet.*
12. **(C)** This is an appropriate response to the comment about the darkness of the room. Choice (A) confuses similar-sounding words *dark* and *park.* Choice (B) repeats the word *dark.*
13. **(A)** *Two boxes* answers the *How much* question. Choice (B) repeats the word *paper.* Choice (C) confuses homonyms *buy* and *by.*
14. **(C)** This answers the *When* question. Choice (A) would answer a *How many* question. Choice (B) would answer a *Who* question.
15. **(B)** This is a logical response to a question about a preference. Choice (A) would answer a *Where* question. Choice (C) confuses similar-sounding words *later* and *waiter.*
16. **(A)** This answers the *yes-no* question. Choice (B) confuses similar-sounding words *meeting* and *reading.* Choice (C) repeats the word *yesterday.*

Part 3: Conversations

17. **(C)** The woman says that she had the sandwich of the day. Choice (A) is incorrect because the woman implies that she didn't have soup when she says, *I'd like to try the soup next time.* Choice (B) is what the man had. Choice (A) repeats the word *salad.*
18. **(A)** The man implies that he doesn't like the color of the walls when he says, *After I got past those wild colors they've painted on the walls, I actually enjoyed my lunch,* and *But those walls!* But he did say that the soup was great and the salad fresh, and he further implies that he likes the food when he says, *at least they've got the food part right.* Choice (B) repeats the word *walls,* but no repairs are mentioned. Choice (C) is incorrect because the man praises the food. Choice (D) is incorrect because the café is *down the street,* that is, nearby.
19. **(D)** The man asks the woman if she would like to try the place (that is, the café) again, and she replies saying, *tomorrow works for*

NEW TOEIC

NEW TOEIC

me, meaning that she is available tomorrow. Choice (A) confuses the meaning of the word *work* in this context. Choice (B) repeats the word *place*. Choice (C) refers to the man's dislike of the colors of the walls, but painting them is not mentioned.

20. **(A)** The first man and the woman are having a discussion about the buses, and the second man interrupts to give them some helpful information. Choices (B), (C), and (D) are plausible reasons for saying *excuse me*, but they are not the correct answer.
21. **(B)** The woman says she has been at the bus stop *for a quarter of an hour*, that is, 15 minutes. Choices (A) and (C) do not mean the same as a quarter of an hour. Choice (D) is contradicted by the correct answer.
22. **(B)** The first man is waiting for the T14, and the second man says, after checking the timetable, *you'll just catch the last one of the morning*, which is the 11:45. Choice (A) is the last T36 of the morning. Choices (C) and (D) are afternoon buses.
23. **(A)** The woman says, *This is the new menu for my restaurant*. Choice (A) repeats the word *check*, which is the way the woman wants to pay. Choice (C) repeats the word *order*. Choice (D) is plausible, but it is not mentioned.
24. **(C)** The woman asks if the order can be ready *by tomorrow morning*, and the man replies, *Sure thing*, meaning *yes*. Choice (A) repeats the number *24* (24-hour rush fee). Choice (B) mentions the rush fee, but the man implies it will be charged. Choice (D) is incorrect because the woman asks for two-sided printing and the man does not disagree.
25. **(D)** The woman offers to write a check, and the man says, *we prefer credit cards*. Choice (A) repeats the verb *pick up*. Choice (B) is what the woman wants to do. Choice (C) confuses the meaning of the word *check* and repeats the word *order*.
26. **(A)** The woman says that the new director's resume is *very impressive*, and the men mention his years of experience in the industry and his good education. Choices (B) and (C) are possible, but they are not mentioned. Choice (D) is contradicted by the second man's statement, *He seems nice*.
27. **(C)** The first man says, *Today makes a week since he started here*. Choice (A) repeats the word *today*. Choices (B) and (D) sound similar to *today*.
28. **(B)** The woman mentions a social hour, and then says, *We should all go*. Choice (A) relates *meet* and *meeting*. Choice (C) confuses similar-sounding words *meet* and *eat*. Choice (D) confuses similar-sounding words *afternoon* and *noon*.
29. **(B)** The woman mentions *this office*. Choice (A) is where they keep the paint left over from painting the hallway. Choice (C) is something they have already painted. Choice (D) is plausible but not mentioned.
30. **(D)** The woman suggests blue and the man says, *Sure. Get it*. Choice (A) is the man's suggestion. Choice (B) confuses similar-sounding words *seem* and *green*. Choice (C) confuses similar-sounding words *bright* and *white*.
31. **(C)** The man says, *We need to cover about 20 or 25 square meters*, and this size will cover that much plus a little more. Choices (A) and (B) don't have enough paint. Choice (D) has too much paint.
32. **(C)** The man is buying a computer table, which is furniture, so he will get the 20% discount. Choices (A), (B), and (D) are discounts on items he is not buying.
33. **(D)** The woman says, *I'll take it up front for you so you can pay*. Choice (A) repeats the word *box*, but she doesn't offer to open it. Choice (B) repeats the word *instructions*; the woman says they are easy to follow, but she doesn't offer to explain them. Choice (C) associates *car*, mentioned by the man, with *park*.
34. **(B)** The man says, *I'll just take it back to the office in my car*. Choices (A) and (C) are plausible, but they are not mentioned. Choice (D) is what the woman suggests.

Part 4: Talks

35. **(C)** *Gallery, painting, prints,* and *sculpture* all indicate that the location is an art museum. Choice (A) is related to the mention of shopping at the gift shop. Choices (B) and (D) are related to the mention of *tickets.*
36. **(A)** The speaker says, *If you haven't purchased a tour ticket yet, please do so now.* Choice (B) is confused with the similar-sounding word *display.* Choice (C) repeats the word *gift.* Choice (D) repeats the word *move.*
37. **(C)** Near the beginning of the talk, the speaker indicates that the group is standing by the ticket counter, and near the end she says that they will finish the tour *right next door to where we are now, at the gift shop.* Location C is the only choice that is next to the ticket counter. Choices (A), (B), and (D) are locations that don't fit the description.
38. **(D)** The caller wants to have his office cleaned and asks about prices and schedules. Choices (A), (B), and (C) are all plausible, but they are not the correct reason.
39. **(A)** The phrase, *It would work better for me,* is used to express a preference, and *after hours* refers to the time when a business is closed. Choices (B), (C), and (D) use words from the phrase, but they are not the correct meaning and do not fit the context.
40. **(B)** The speaker says, *I'll give you a ring when I get back early next week,* meaning he will call again when he returns from his trip. Choice (A) repeats the phrase *next week.* Choice (C) confuses *out of town* with *downtown.* Choice (D) is related to the topic of phone calls, but it is not the correct answer.
41. **(A)** The speaker mentions *guests* and *number of guests* per night, so she works for a hotel. Choices (B), (C), and (D) are other businesses associated with the tourist industry, but they are not the correct answer.
42. **(D)** The speaker wants to talk about the *dip,* or sudden decrease, that follows the *peak,* or high point. The peak is in July, and the dip is in August. Choices (A), (B), and (C) don't fit this description.
43. **(D)** The speaker asks the listeners to get a partner and together come up with a list of ideas. Choice (A) repeats the word *graph.* Choice (B) is what she wants listeners to write, not read. Choice (C) repeats the word *average.*
44. **(B)** The speaker says, *A team will be in tomorrow morning to install the carpet in the hallway and front office.* Choice (A) repeats the word *install.* Choice (C) happened last week. Choice (D) repeats the word *hallway.*
45. **(B)** The speaker is referring to the workers who will be laying the carpet. The expression *should be out of here* means that they will probably have left. Choices (A), (C), and (D) do not fit the context or the meaning of the expression.
46. **(C)** The speaker says that the workers *request that you enter the building through the rear doorway.* Choice (A) repeats the phrase *new furniture.* Choice (B) repeats the phrase *front office.* Choice (D) is what the workers will do.
47. **(C)** The speaker says, *You asked about renting a space for a training seminar.* Choice (A) is plausible, but it is not mentioned. Choice (B) repeats the word *conference* from the phrase *conference room,* and Choice (D) repeats the word *banquet* from the phrase *banquet room*; these are rooms mentioned by the speaker as places where the event could be held.
48. **(B)** The speaker mentions a room that *has seating for 125 people, which is just the number you are expecting.* Choices (A) and (D) sound similar to the correct answer. Choice (C) is the number of people another room can hold.
49. **(A)** The speaker says, *You'll find my office just behind the front desk in the lobby,* and the directory shows that the lobby is on the ground floor. Choices (B), (C), and (D) are floors where other facilities are located.

Reading

3

OVERVIEW—CURRENT TOEIC

There are three parts to the Reading Comprehension section of the TOEIC. You will have approximately 75 minutes to complete this section.

Part 5:	Incomplete Sentences	40 questions
Part 6:	Text Completion	12 questions
Part 7:	Reading Comprehension	
	■ Single passages	28 questions
	■ Double passages	20 questions

To prepare for the Reading Comprehension section, you must develop vocabulary, grammar, and reading comprehension skills. The grammar and vocabulary skills targeted in this chapter for Part 5 are also useful in Part 6, and vice versa.

SKILLS LIST

Part 5: Incomplete Sentences
Skill
1. Word Families
2. Similar Meanings
3. Similar Forms
4. Subject-Verb Agreement with Prepositional Phrases
5. Singular and Plural Subjects
6. Verb Tenses
7. Prepositions
8. Prepositions with Verbs and Adjectives
9. Coordinating Conjunctions
10. Parallel Structure
11. Subordinating Conjunctions
12. Future Time Clauses

Part 6: Text Completion
Skill
1. Adverbs of Frequency
2. Gerunds and Infinitives After Main Verbs
3. Gerunds and Infinitives After Prepositions and Pronouns
4. Causative Verbs
5. Real Conditionals
6. Unreal Conditionals
7. Comparisons
8. Pronouns
9. Subject Relative Pronouns
10. Object Relative Pronouns
11. Passive Voice

Part 7: Reading Comprehension
Skill
1. Advertisements
2. Forms
3. Reports
4. Letters
5. Memos
6. Tables and Charts
7. Graphs
8. Announcements
9. Notices
10. Articles
11. Schedules
12. E-mail
13. Webpages

OVERVIEW—NEW TOEIC

There are three parts to the Reading Comprehension section of the new TOEIC. You will have approximately 75 minutes to complete this section.

Part 5:	Incomplete Sentences	30 questions
Part 6:	Text Completion	16 questions
Part 7:	Reading Comprehension	
	■ Single passages	29 questions
	■ Double passages	25 questions

The following skills are directed towards preparing you for the new question types on the Reading Comprehension section of the new TOEIC. You should also study the reading skills for the current TOEIC, as those question types will also appear on the new TOEIC.

SKILLS LIST

Part 6: Text Completion
Skill
1. Understand the Context

Part 7: Reading Comprehension
Skill
1. Words in Context
2. Locating Appropriate Context

PART 5: INCOMPLETE SENTENCES

Sample Question

Directions: You will see a sentence with a missing word. Four possible answers follow the sentence. Choose the best answer to the question and fill in the corresponding oval on your answer sheet.

You will read:

1. They have decided ____________ business class.

   (A) fly
   (B) to fly
   (C) flying
   (D) flew

The best way to complete the sentence "They have decided ____________ business class" is Choice (B), "to fly." Therefore you should choose answer (B).

Word Families

Word families are created by adding endings to a word. These endings will change the word into a noun, verb, adjective, or adverb.

Common Word Endings

noun	verb	adjective	adverb
-ance	-en	-able	-ly
-ancy	-ify	-ible	-ward
-ence	-ize	-al	-wise
-ation		-ful	
-ian		-ish	
-ism		-ive	
-ist		-ous	
-ment			
-ness			
-ship			
-or			
-er			

Common Word Families

noun				
thing	person	verb	adjective	adverb
application	applicant	apply	applicable	
competition	competitor	compete	competitive	competitively
criticism	critic	criticize	critical	critically
decision		decide	decisive	decisively
economy	economist	economize	economical	economically
finale	finalist	finalize	final	finally
interpretation	interpreter	interpret	interpretive	
maintenance	maintainer	maintain	maintainable	
management	manager	manage	managerial	
mechanism	mechanic	mechanize	mechanical	mechanically
nation	nationalist	nationalize	national	nationally
negotiation	negotiator	negotiate	negotiable	
politics	politician	politicize	political	politically
production	producer	produce	productive	productively
prosperity		prosper	prosperous	prosperously
repetition	repeater	repeat	repetitious	repetitively
simplification		simplify	simple	simply
theory	theoretician	theorize	theoretical	theoretically

TIP Check the ending of the word to determine the part of speech.

➡ Examples

She is a *careful* manager.
She read the report *carefully*.

Careful is an adjective. In the example above it describes the word *manager*. It tells us *what kind* of manager she is.

Carefully is an adverb. In the example above it modifies the verb *read*. It tells us *how* she read the report.

Mr. Kim *applied* for a job at our company.
His *application* contains a lot of information about his background.

Applied is a past tense verb. In the example above, it tells us what Mr. Kim did. *Application* is a noun. In the example above it is the subject of the sentence.

EXERCISE

Choose the one word or phrase that best completes the sentence.

1. The director of purchasing can ___________ the best price.

   Ⓐ Ⓑ Ⓒ Ⓓ

   (A) negotiable
   (B) negotiate
   (C) negotiator
   (D) negotiation

2. The first day that we advertised the job on our website, there were over 700 ___________ for the position.

   Ⓐ Ⓑ Ⓒ Ⓓ

   (A) applies
   (B) applicants
   (C) appliances
   (D) applications

3. The ability to act ___________ in moments of crisis is the mark of a strong leader.

   Ⓐ Ⓑ Ⓒ Ⓓ

   (A) decide
   (B) decision
   (C) decisive
   (D) decisively

Similar Meanings

Some words have similar meanings but cannot be used interchangeably. The meanings or usage may not be exactly the same, or the grammar may be different.

Words with Similar Meanings

affect	effect	affection	effective
borrow	lend	loan	lease
develop	expand	elaborate	enhance
money	cash	currency	coin
obtain	earn	win	achieve
raise	rise	elevate	ascend
say	tell	speak	talk
travel	commute	go	journey
bill	pay	fee	cost
down	decrease	under	descent
like	similar	same	alike
soon	recent	newly	lately

TIP First try to understand the meaning of the sentence. Then determine the correct word in meaning, usage, and spelling for that sentence.

➡ Examples

Sarah *commutes* to her job in the city from the suburbs.
Sarah will *travel* to Tahiti on her vacation.

Commute and *travel* have similar meanings, however, *commute* has a very specific use. It means *travel to and from work every day. Travel* has a more general meaning.

I had to *borrow* some money in order to pay for my new car.
John *lent* me the money, and I will pay him back soon.

Borrow means to receive something as a loan. Something that is borrowed has to be returned or repaid to the owner. *Lend* means to let someone use something you own.

They will *raise* the building in order to dig a basement underneath it.
Prices have continued to *rise* throughout the first half of the year.

Raise means to lift or to increase something. It is a transitive verb—a verb with an object. In the example above, the object is *the building. Rise* means to go up or to increase. The meaning is very similar to the meaning of *raise*, but *rise* is an intransitive verb—a verb that cannot take an object.

EXERCISE

Choose the one word or phrase that best completes the sentence.

1. New employees ____________ only a small salary during the first six months.

   (A) win
   (B) gain
   (C) reach
   (D) earn

   Ⓐ Ⓑ Ⓒ Ⓓ

2. Miranda has many more responsibilities at the office now because of her ____________ promotion.

   (A) recent
   (B) lately
   (C) soon
   (D) newly

   Ⓐ Ⓑ Ⓒ Ⓓ

3. Our costs have gone down this month, but we need to ____________ them even more next month.

   (A) fall
   (B) descent
   (C) decrease
   (D) under

   Ⓐ Ⓑ Ⓒ Ⓓ

Similar Forms

Some words look similar but have different meanings. They may have the same prefix, suffix, or root, or they may simply have similar spelling but are completely unrelated.

Words with Similar Forms

reduce	produce	deduce	induce
except	expect	accept	accent
omit	emit	admit	permit
preference	inference	reference	conference
contact	contract	compact	comport
disk	desk	dusk	discus
particle	participant	participle	partition

TIP First try to understand the meaning of the sentence. Then choose the word that has the correct meaning for that sentence.

Examples

Don't *omit* any information from the form.
We *permit* our employees to work from home occasionally.

Omit and *permit* both contain the root word *mit.* However, they each have different meanings. *Omit* means to forget or leave out. *Permit* means to allow.

Please put the package on *my desk*.
They walked home *at dusk*.

Desk and *dusk* have almost the same spelling, but they are unrelated words with completely different meanings. *Desk* is a type of office furniture. *Dusk* is the time of evening right before it becomes completely dark.

EXERCISE

Choose the one word or phrase that best completes the sentence.

1. I'll need some time to read over the ____________ before I sign it.

   (A) contact
   (B) contract
   (C) comport
   (D) compact

   Ⓐ Ⓑ Ⓒ Ⓓ

2. The room is large, but we can use ____________ to divide it into smaller work areas.

   (A) partitions
   (B) participants
   (C) particles
   (D) participles

   Ⓐ Ⓑ Ⓒ Ⓓ

3. Because of low profits this quarter, we will have to ____________ the size of our staff.

   (A) produce
   (B) induce
   (C) deduce
   (D) reduce

   Ⓐ Ⓑ Ⓒ Ⓓ

Subject-Verb Agreement with Prepositional Phrases

The subject and verb of a sentence must agree. They must match in person (*I, we, he, they,* etc.) and in number (singular or plural). A prepositional phrase may come between the subject and verb of a sentence, and the phrase may contain a noun that is different in person or number from the subject. This does not change the need for subject-verb agreement.

TIP Distinguish the subject from other nouns in the sentence.

➥ Examples

The order for office supplies was on my desk.

In the example above, the subject, *order,* is singular. It agrees with the verb, *was.* The subject and verb are separated by a prepositional phrase. The plural noun *supplies* is not the subject of the sentence; it is part of the prepositional phrase *for office supplies.*

The workers in this factory receive many benefits.

In the example above, the subject, *workers,* is plural. It agrees with the verb, *receive.* The subject and verb are separated by a prepositional phrase. The singular noun *factory* is not the subject of the sentence; it is part of the prepositional phrase *in this factory.*

This group of business leaders meets with the mayor every month.

In the example above, the subject, *group,* is singular. It agrees with the verb, *meets.* The subject and verb are separated by a prepositional phrase. The plural noun *leaders* is not the subject of the sentence; it is part of the prepositional phrase *of business leaders.*

EXERCISE

Choose the one word or phrase that best completes the sentence.

1. The officers of the company __________ today at 1:00.

   (A) is meeting
   (B) meets
   (C) has met
   (D) are meeting

   Ⓐ Ⓑ Ⓒ Ⓓ

2. The owner of these buildings __________ his tenants a very reasonable rent.

   (A) charges
   (B) charge
   (C) are charging
   (D) have charged

   Ⓐ Ⓑ Ⓒ Ⓓ

3. The supplies in that closet __________ there for any staff member to use.

   (A) is
   (B) has
   (C) are
   (D) was

   Ⓐ Ⓑ Ⓒ Ⓓ

SKILL 5

Singular and Plural Subjects

Some nouns appear plural but are actually singular. Other nouns have irregular plurals that look singular. Be careful because the verb must agree with the subject.

TIP Know whether the subject is considered singular or plural.

➡ Examples

***Thirty dollars* is a low price for a nice shirt like that.**
***Five cents* is added to the price for sales tax.**

A sum of money is treated as a singular noun. Even though it may contain a plural noun such as *dollars* or *cents*, it is considered as one sum.

National Autos *owns* this factory.
***United Computers employs* most of the workers in this town.**

A company name may contain a plural noun but it is the name of one company so it is considered singular.

***Everyone wants* to have lunch now.**
***Nobody is* ready for the meeting.**

Words that begin with *every* or *no*, such as *everybody, everything, nobody,* and *nothing* are singular and take singular verbs even though they refer to a group of people or things.

Few *people understand* these laws.
***Children are* not allowed in the office without adult supervision.**

Irregular plural words may look singular because they don't end with *-s*, but they are plural and take plural verbs.

EXERCISE

Choose the one word or phrase that best completes the sentence.

1. The manager from headquarters ____________ this office at least twice a year.

   (A) visiting
   (B) to visit
   (C) visits
   (D) visit

   Ⓐ Ⓑ Ⓒ Ⓓ

2. Most people ____________ that Acme, Inc. can be relied on to consistently provide high-quality products.

   (A) agree
   (B) agrees
   (C) has agreed
   (D) is agreeing

   Ⓐ Ⓑ Ⓒ Ⓓ

3. My assistant has assured me that everything ____________ in order for the staff meeting.

   (A) have been
   (B) were
   (C) are
   (D) is

   Ⓐ Ⓑ Ⓒ Ⓓ

SKILL

Verb Tenses

The main verb of a sentence must be in the correct tense. Often, a time word or time expression indicates the verb tense.

Time Words and Expressions

Simple Present	*Present Continuous*	*Simple Past*
every day every week every year always often sometimes	now at this moment currently	an hour ago a month ago yesterday last week last year
Present Perfect since last year since Tuesday for two weeks for a long time already yet	*Future* tomorrow next month next Friday later this week	

TIP Look for a time word or expression in the sentence to help you determine the correct tense.

Examples

We *hire* an accountant to audit our books at the end of *every year*.
(simple present)

We cannot hold the meeting at our office as we *are currently redecorating*.
(present continuous)

Mr. Brown *traveled* to Japan *last month* in order to visit our branch office there.
(simple past)

Ms. Henderson *has been* a client of ours *for the last fifteen years*.
(present perfect)

The conference room *will be* ready for use *later this afternoon*.
(future)

EXERCISE

Choose the one word or phrase that best completes the sentence.

1. Mr. Cho ____________ the new budget at the staff meeting next Friday.

   (A) present
   (B) will present
   (C) is presenting
   (D) has presented

   Ⓐ Ⓑ Ⓒ Ⓓ

2. We are planning to repaint the office, but we ____________ on a color yet.

   (A) didn't decide
   (B) don't decide
   (C) haven't decided
   (D) isn't deciding

   Ⓐ Ⓑ Ⓒ Ⓓ

3. The company ____________ a picnic for all staff members at the beginning of every summer.

   (A) host
   (B) hosts
   (C) is hosting
   (D) to host

   Ⓐ Ⓑ Ⓒ Ⓓ

SKILL 7

Prepositions

Prepositions show the relationships between nouns or pronouns and other words. They can indicate time, place, movement, and so on.

TIP Learn the most common uses of prepositions.

Time

Preposition	Use	Example
at	exact time	They arrived *at* 10:30.
on	day or date	They arrived *on* Monday.
in	month or year	We began work *in* April.
from . . . to, from . . . until	beginning and end times	I lived there *from* June *to* December.
by	no later than	Please finish this report *by* noon.

Place

Preposition	Use	Example
at	exact address	He lives *at* 1267 Main Street.
on	street	He lives *on* Main Street.
in	city, country	She worked *in* London.
on	on top of	The phone is *on* my desk.
in	inside of	The pencil is *in* the drawer.
next to, beside, by	to the side of	My desk is *next to* the window.
across . . . from	on the opposite side	His house is *across* the street *from* the bank.

Movement

Preposition	Use	Example
to, toward	in the direction of	She went *to* the bank.
into	to the inside of	They walked *into* the building.
through	from one end to the other	Let's drive *through* the park.
across	from one side to the other	She walked *across* the room.

EXERCISE

Choose the one word or phrase that best completes the sentence.

1. Just put the packages __________ the table and I'll open them for you.

(A) on
(B) in
(C) to
(D) at

Ⓐ Ⓑ Ⓒ Ⓓ

2. They realized the meeting was already in progress the minute they walked __________ the room.

(A) on
(B) among
(C) until
(D) into

Ⓐ Ⓑ Ⓒ Ⓓ

3. The company cafeteria is open for lunch every day from 11:00 __________ 1:00.

(A) at
(B) for
(C) until
(D) by

Ⓐ Ⓑ Ⓒ Ⓓ

SKILL 8

Prepositions with Verbs and Adjectives

Many verbs and adjectives are commonly paired with certain prepositions.

Verb + Preposition

apologize for	insist on
agree to (something)	object to
agree with (someone)	participate in
ask for (something)	pay for
ask to (do something)	prepare for
believe in	prevent from
blame for	prohibit from
complain about	replace with
decide on	result in
depend on	think about

Adjective + Preposition

afraid of	famous for
angry about (something)	good at
angry at/with (someone)	happy about
aware of	interested in
bored with	late for
busy with	pleased with
curious about	responsible for
different from	serious about
excited about	suitable for
familiar with	tired of

TIP Learn common *verb + preposition* and *adjective + preposition* combinations.

➡ Examples

She is *thinking about* applying for a position with another company.

Everyone in the office was able to *participate in* the training session.

I'll be *busy with* some clients for the rest of the afternoon.

This city is *famous for* its wide avenues and pretty parks.

EXERCISE

Choose the one word or phrase that best completes the sentence.

1. Everyone in the office was complaining ____________ the noise from the construction site across the street.

   (A) over
   (B) about
   (C) from
   (D) with

   Ⓐ Ⓑ Ⓒ Ⓓ

2. We replaced our old copy machine ____________ a newer, more efficient model.

   (A) of
   (B) to
   (C) with
   (D) for

   Ⓐ Ⓑ Ⓒ Ⓓ

3. Ms. Chang is responsible ____________ making sure new staff members understand their duties.

   (A) for
   (B) of
   (C) in
   (D) at

   Ⓐ Ⓑ Ⓒ Ⓓ

SKILL 9

Coordinating Conjunctions

Coordinating conjunctions are used to join words, phrases, and clauses of equal importance and whose functions are grammatically similar. For example, a coordinating conjunction may join two adjectives, two prepositional phrases, or two independent clauses.

TIP Pay attention to the meaning of the coordinating conjunction.

Examples

Conjunction and
Use joins similar ideas

I need some paper *and* a pencil.
He can both dance *and* sing.

Conjunction but, yet
Use joins opposite ideas

He eats a lot *but* he never gets fat.
She speaks French fluently, *yet* I never hear her use it.

Conjunction or, either . . . or, neither . . . nor
Use joins choices

Would you like coffee *or* tea?
I can give you *either* coffee *or* tea.
I'm sorry but I drink *neither* coffee *nor* tea.

EXERCISE

Choose the one word or phrase that best completes the sentence.

1. Ms. Sam's work is both creative _______ accurate.

   (A) but
   (B) or
   (C) and
   (D) nor

   Ⓐ Ⓑ Ⓒ Ⓓ

2. George worked all night, _______ he wasn't able to finish the report on time.

   (A) yet
   (B) and
   (C) either
   (D) neither

   Ⓐ Ⓑ Ⓒ Ⓓ

3. We can either meet this afternoon _______ wait until later in the week if you prefer.

   (A) but
   (B) or
   (C) nor
   (D) neither

   Ⓐ Ⓑ Ⓒ Ⓓ

SKILL
10 Parallel Structure

The two words, phrases, or clauses joined by a coordinating conjunction must be alike: two noun forms, two verb forms, two gerunds, and so on.

TIP Learn to recognize the correct grammatical form. Learn to distinguish gerunds from infinitives, nouns from verbs, adjectives from adverbs, and so on.

Examples

Mr. Lee types quickly and accurately.
adverb adverb

I enjoy both swimming and sailing.
gerund gerund

You can either send an e-mail or write a letter.
base form base form

Neither the bus nor the subway will take you anywhere near his office.
noun noun

The manager is kind but strict.
adjective adjective

EXERCISE

Choose the one word or phrase that best completes the sentence.

1. Prompt and __________ customer service is a priority at our business.

   (A) friend
   (B) friendly
   (C) friendship
   (D) friendliness

   Ⓐ Ⓑ Ⓒ Ⓓ

2. Sharon is really good at making clients feel comfortable and __________ them interested in using our services.

   (A) get
   (B) got
   (C) gotten
   (D) getting

   Ⓐ Ⓑ Ⓒ Ⓓ

3. Focus on efficiency and __________ and you will get the job done right.

   (A) accurate
   (B) accurately
   (C) accuracy
   (D) accruing

   Ⓐ Ⓑ Ⓒ Ⓓ

Subordinating Conjunctions

Subordinating conjunctions are used to join clauses (not words or phrases) that have grammatically different functions. A subordinating conjunction together with its following clause acts like part of the main clause. The subordinate clause may come before or after the main clause.

TIP Pay attention to the meaning of the subordinating conjunction.

Examples

Common Subordinating Conjunctions

Introduce a Reason

because as since

I was late to the meeting *because* traffic was heavy.

Since Mr. Kim is out of the office today, I will be taking all his calls.

Introduce a Contradiction

though although even though

We decided to hold the conference at this hotel *even though* the rates are higher.

Although Ms. Clark is new at the company, she already knows a lot about our work.

Introduce a Time Clause

before after as soon as
when while until

I met Mr. Cho *while* I was working in New York.

As soon as the plane landed, all the passengers stood up.

EXERCISE

Choose the one word or phrase that best completes the sentence.

1. The usher allowed Ms. Sello into the concert hall __________ she was late.

   (A) because
   (B) yet
   (C) even though
   (D) before

   (A) (B) (C) (D)

2. __________ so few people showed up, we finally decided to cancel the meeting.

   (A) Since
   (B) Although
   (C) If
   (D) Until

   (A) (B) (C) (D)

3. Miranda will send a copy of the report to your office __________ it is ready.

   (A) but
   (B) so
   (C) as soon as
   (D) before

   (A) (B) (C) (D)

SKILL
12 Future Time Clauses

A time clause is a clause that tells when the action in the main clause occurs. A time clause begins with a subordinating conjunction about time, such as *when, while, before, after,* or *until.* In a sentence about the future, the main clause uses a future verb (with *will* or *going to*), but the time clause uses a present tense verb even though it is about the future.

TIP Use a present tense verb in a future time clause.

Examples

I *will show* you the report (main clause) as soon as I *finish* writing it (time clause).

When the rain *stops* (time clause), we *are going to take* a walk in the park (main clause).

He is *going to give* everyone copies of his schedule (main clause) before he *leaves* on his trip (time clause).

After they *get* to the hotel (time clause), they'*ll call* us (main clause).

EXERCISE

Choose the one word or phrase that best completes the sentence.

1. I'll let you know when the train ____________.
   (A) arrive
   (B) arrives
   (C) will arrive
   (D) arriving

   Ⓐ Ⓑ Ⓒ Ⓓ

2. We'll talk things over with our lawyer before we _________ the contract.
   (A) sign
   (B) to sign
   (C) will sign
   (D) signature

   Ⓐ Ⓑ Ⓒ Ⓓ

3. By the time the meeting _________ over, you'll know everything about our marketing plan.
   (A) will be
   (B) was
   (C) is
   (D) be

   Ⓐ Ⓑ Ⓒ Ⓓ

NEW TOEIC—PART 5: INCOMPLETE SENTENCES

There are NO changes in Part 5: Incomplete Sentences in the types of questions. The skills and strategies to prepare for Part 5 are the same for both the current and the new TOEIC.

There will be fewer questions. There are only 30 rather than 40 questions.

PRACTICE

Directions: You will see a sentence with a missing word or phrase. Four possible answers follow the sentence. Choose the best answer to the question and fill in the corresponding oval.

See page 265 for the Answer Key and pages 267–268 for the Explanatory Answers for new TOEIC practice Part 5.

1. The two sample colors are so similar that is difficult to __________ between them.

   (A) differ
   (B) difference
   (C) different
   (D) differentiate

   Ⓐ Ⓑ Ⓒ Ⓓ

2. Only __________ people have returned the questionnaire that the public relations department sent out last month.

   (A) a few
   (B) a little
   (C) any
   (D) this

   Ⓐ Ⓑ Ⓒ Ⓓ

3. Even though they __________ on that report since last week, it still isn't finished.

   (A) have been working
   (B) will be working
   (C) will work
   (D) are working

   Ⓐ Ⓑ Ⓒ Ⓓ

4. Ms. Park will be out of the office next week but can be reached __________ the day on her cell phone.

   (A) between
   (B) during
   (C) over
   (D) within

   Ⓐ Ⓑ Ⓒ Ⓓ

5. Mr. Lee will send the revised contract tomorrow and requests that you return a signed copy to __________ as soon as possible.

   (A) he
   (B) his
   (C) him
   (D) himself

   Ⓐ Ⓑ Ⓒ Ⓓ

6. Of all the designers in this department, Ms. Smith is considered to be the most _________.

(A) compete
(B) competent
(C) competence
(D) competently

Ⓐ Ⓑ Ⓒ Ⓓ

7. Our supervisor is quite flexible and _________ us telecommute from time to time.

(A) suggests
(B) permits
(C) allows
(D) lets

Ⓐ Ⓑ Ⓒ Ⓓ

8. We're hoping that the new advertising campaign will _________ many new customers to our business.

(A) attract
(B) capture
(C) seize
(D) release

Ⓐ Ⓑ Ⓒ Ⓓ

9. The new desks in the front office look very stylish, but _________ aren't very comfortable to use.

(A) their
(B) they
(C) them
(D) themselves

Ⓐ Ⓑ Ⓒ Ⓓ

10. We would like everyone in the department to _________ in the weekly planning sessions.

(A) tolerate
(B) indicate
(C) participate
(D) facilitate

Ⓐ Ⓑ Ⓒ Ⓓ

11. You must register for the course ahead of time; _________ you will not be guaranteed a place.

(A) if
(B) else
(C) unless
(D) otherwise

Ⓐ Ⓑ Ⓒ Ⓓ

12. Orientation sessions for new employees are _________ in the auditorium on the first Monday of every month.

(A) give
(B) gave
(C) given
(D) giving

Ⓐ Ⓑ Ⓒ Ⓓ

13. We expect most staff members will attend the luncheon, so we'll need to find a _________ space.

(A) largely
(B) largest
(C) larger
(D) the largest

Ⓐ Ⓑ Ⓒ Ⓓ

14. The documents in this folder _________ to be signed by both parties and returned to the attorney right away.

(A) need
(B) needs
(C) needy
(D) is needed

Ⓐ Ⓑ Ⓒ Ⓓ

15. Staff members will receive adequate _________ for any evening and weekend time they spend working on this project.

(A) inspiration
(B) compensation
(C) distribution
(D) computation

Ⓐ Ⓑ Ⓒ Ⓓ

16. Due to its growing popularity, Mr. M's Restaurant is planning to open new _________ in several neighborhoods.

(A) documents
(B) entrances
(C) avenues
(D) branches

Ⓐ Ⓑ Ⓒ Ⓓ

17. If your job requires _________ in mud and light snow, your vehicle should have all-season tires.

(A) drive
(B) drives
(C) driven
(D) driving

Ⓐ Ⓑ Ⓒ Ⓓ

18. This __________ is not large enough to hold all the documents we plan to store.

(A) contain
(B) container
(C) containment
(D) containable

Ⓐ Ⓑ Ⓒ Ⓓ

19. These toys are popular with parents because they allow children to learn __________ they play.

(A) for
(B) as
(C) from
(D) until

Ⓐ Ⓑ Ⓒ Ⓓ

20. Their offices, __________ are right in the center of the business district, are very easy to reach by public transportation.

(A) who
(B) that
(C) which
(D) whose

Ⓐ Ⓑ Ⓒ Ⓓ

21. There are a number of qualified candidates for the position, and it will be difficult to choose __________ them.

(A) because
(B) about
(C) despite
(D) among

Ⓐ Ⓑ Ⓒ Ⓓ

22. The equipment is top quality and a good value, so we shouldn't be __________ concerned about the price.

(A) overly
(B) fully
(C) hardly
(D) plentifully

Ⓐ Ⓑ Ⓒ Ⓓ

23. The company received numerous __________ about the new product as soon as it hit the market.

(A) complains
(B) complaints
(C) complainers
(D) complained

Ⓐ Ⓑ Ⓒ Ⓓ

24. We will find out the decision on salary increases after the directors __________ tomorrow.

(A) will meet Ⓐ Ⓑ Ⓒ Ⓓ
(B) to meet
(C) met
(D) meet

25. Everyone had to use the stairs __________ the elevators were out of order.

(A) however Ⓐ Ⓑ Ⓒ Ⓓ
(B) although
(C) since
(D) so

26. The bank agreed to lend us the money to expand the business, but it will take a while to repay such a __________ loan.

(A) sizeable Ⓐ Ⓑ Ⓒ Ⓓ
(B) enormity
(C) maximum
(D) miniscule

27. The meeting was __________ for a short while because the room wasn't ready on time.

(A) canceled Ⓐ Ⓑ Ⓒ Ⓓ
(B) delayed
(C) persisted
(D) lingered

28. Many local residents objected __________ the developer's plans for building a shopping mall in their neighborhood.

(A) about Ⓐ Ⓑ Ⓒ Ⓓ
(B) for
(C) on
(D) to

29. Emporium Market __________ a more successful business if it were in a better location.

(A) be Ⓐ Ⓑ Ⓒ Ⓓ
(B) was
(C) would be
(D) has been

30. Local businesses have contributed to the __________ of the city by creating many small gardens throughout the shopping district.

(A) beautify Ⓐ Ⓑ Ⓒ Ⓓ
(B) beautiful
(C) beautifully
(D) beautification

PART 6: TEXT COMPLETION

Sample Questions

> **Directions:** You will see short passages each with three blanks. Under each blank are four answer options. Choose the word or phrase that best completes the sentence.

There are three types of questions most common in Part 6.

- Vocabulary questions
- Grammar questions
- Context questions

Sometimes you will have to read just the sentence with the blank to answer the question. Usually, you will have to understand the complete passage to be able to complete the sentence.

The skills in this chapter will help you prepare to answer all three types of questions on Part 6 of the TOEIC. The skills in the chapter for Part 5 will also help you answer grammar and vocabulary questions in Part 6.

You will read this passage:

Dear Mr. Sanders,

I enjoyed ____________ you at the conference last week. I am enclosing

1. (A) met
   (B) meet
   (C) to meet
   (D) meeting

the brochures that you requested. I hope ____________ are useful to you.

2. (A) it
   (B) they
   (C) we
   (D) its

If I can be of further assistance, please let me ____________.

3. (A) know
   (B) understand
   (C) realize
   (D) learn

Sincerely,
Bertha Smith

Question 1 (Grammar)

1. (A) met
   (B) meet
   (C) to meet
   (D) meeting

The best way to complete the sentence "I enjoyed ____________ you at the conference last week" is Choice (D) "meeting." The participle *meeting* follows the verb *enjoyed*. Therefore, you should choose answer (D).

Question 2 (Context)

2. (A) it
   (B) they
   (C) we
   (D) its

The best way to complete the sentence "I hope ____________ are useful to you" is Choice (B) "they." You must read beyond this sentence to answer the question. Sometimes you have to look back; sometimes forward. In this case, you look back. The pronoun *they* refers back to the plural noun *brochures*. Therefore, you should choose answer (B).

Question 3 (Vocabulary)

3. (A) know
   (B) understand
   (C) realize
   (D) learn

The best way to complete the sentence "If I can be of further assistance, please let me ____________ " is Choice (A) "know." This is an example of a context question. All of the words have a similar meaning, but only *know* fits the context. Therefore, you should choose answer (A).

Adverbs of Frequency

Adverbs of frequency tell *when* or *how often* something happens.

TIP Pay attention to the context in order to choose the correct adverb.

Examples

Common Adverbs of Frequency

100% of the time	always
	usually
	frequently
	often
	sometimes
	occasionally
	seldom
	rarely
0% of the time	never

We *always* eat lunch at this café because it is so close to the office.

I *usually* play golf on weekends, but last Saturday I played tennis instead.

The weather is *usually* dry in the summer, but *sometimes* it rains.

Sam *rarely* works late, although last night he stayed at the office until 8:00.

I *never* drink coffee at night because it keeps me awake.

EXERCISE

Read the memo and choose the one word or phrase that best completes each sentence.

MEMO

To: All New Staff Members
Date: February 7, 20—
Re: Staff Meeting

We are holding a staff meeting on Saturday, February 9, at 2:00 P.M. for all new part-time and full-time staff. This includes anyone who joined the company after January 1. We _____________ hold staff meetings on the weekends. In fact,

1. (A) rarely
   (B) frequently
   (C) often
   (D) sometimes

I believe this is the first time we've done this, but something very important has come up. We need to address the issue immediately, and I apologize for any inconvenience this may cause.

Please note that punctuality is very important in this company. We _____________

2. (A) never
   (B) seldom
   (C) occasionally
   (D) always

begin our staff meetings on time and don't wait for late arrivals. I expect everyone to be seated and ready by 2:00 P.M.

You will get paid for attending this meeting. The payment is $20 per hour for all staff members. Our meetings _____________ last about an hour, and I expect

3. (A) usually
   (B) sometimes
   (C) rarely
   (D) never

this one will, too.

SKILL
2 Gerunds and Infinitives After Main Verbs

The main verb in a sentence can be followed immediately by a second verb. This verb can be a gerund (*-ing* form) or an infinitive (*to* + verb). The main verb determines which form is used.

TIP Pay attention to the main verb to determine whether to use a gerund or an infinitive.

➥ Examples

Common Verbs Followed by a Gerund

appreciate	I *appreciate* having the opportunity to speak.
avoid	They *avoided* looking us in the eye.
consider	We *considered* staying longer.
delay	We *delayed* writing you until we had more information.
discuss	Have you *discussed* working together on this project?
enjoy	We *enjoyed* having you for dinner.
finish	They will *finish* correcting the report soon.
mind	She didn't *mind* staying late for the meeting.
miss	We *miss* going to the movies with you.
postpone	Could we *postpone* leaving?
quit	He wants to *quit* smoking.
risk	They *risked* losing everything.
suggest	We *suggest* leaving on time.

Common Verbs Followed by an Infinitive

agree	He *agreed* to complete the project.
attempt	They *attempted* to climb Mt. Fuji.
claim	She *claims* to be an expert.
decide	We *decided* to hire her anyway.
demand	He *demanded* to know what we were doing.
fail	We *failed* to give a satisfactory answer.
hesitate	I *hesitated* to tell the truth.
hope	We *hope* to leave before dawn.
intend	She *intends* to start her own club.
learn	They will *learn* to swim at camp.
need	She *needs* to stop smoking.
offer	They *offered* to take us home.
plan	We *plan* to accept their offer.
prepare	She *prepared* to leave.
refuse	He *refused* to come with us.
seem	She *seemed* to be annoyed.
want	He didn't *want* to leave.

EXERCISE

Read the e-mail and choose the one word or phrase that best completes each sentence.

To: Sam Tyler
From: Jack Stone
Subject: Meeting with Mr. Williams

Sam,

Mr. Williams has agreed ____________ with us in order to discuss the

1. (A) met
   (B) meets
   (C) to meet
   (D) meeting

contracts. Have you had a chance to review them yet? He says he doesn't mind ____________ over to our office some time next week. Is next Tuesday

2. (A) comes
   (B) coming
   (C) to come
   (D) will come

afternoon a good time for you? If so, would right after lunch work?

Before we meet with him, I think we should take a few minutes to discuss this together. We could get together over the weekend if that would be easier for you. I've ____________ help one of our colleagues move on Saturday. We should

3. (A) offering
   (B) offered to
   (C) to offer
   (D) offered

be finished moving by 5:00 P.M. I'll be home all day Sunday.

Jack

Gerunds and Infinitives After Prepositions and Adjectives

In addition to following the main verb of a sentence or clause, gerunds and infinitives can follow other types of words, as well.

TIP Know the kinds of words that gerunds and infinitives can follow.

➡ Examples

Harry is interested *in applying* for a position with an international company.
Sara apologized *for arriving* at the meeting late.

A gerund can follow a preposition. See Skill 8 in the previous chapter for lists of common verb + preposition and adjective + preposition pairs.

They will be *happy to help* you.
He was *eager to start* working on the project.

An infinitive can follow an adjective.

He was *hungry enough to eat* three servings of rice.
They walked *too slowly to get* there in time.

An infinitive can follow phrases with the pattern adjective/adverb + *enough* or adjective/adverb + *too.*

EXERCISE

Read the advertisement and choose the one word or phrase that best completes each sentence.

Springer Lighting Systems

Let Springer Lighting Systems help you create the right atmosphere in your workplace. Do your employees complain about __________ frequent headaches or

1. (A) have
(B) having
(C) to have
(D) had

constant eye pain? With Springer Lighting Systems, these troubles will become a thing of the past. The soft, diffused light created by Springer Lighting Systems is easy on the eyes but still bright enough __________ by. Say goodbye to glare

2. (A) read
(B) reads
(C) to read
(D) reading

and stress.

The inviting atmosphere created by Springer Lighting Systems ensures that your staff will sit down at the desk ready __________ in ease and comfort. Call for a free

3. (A) to work
(B) working
(C) are working
(D) have worked

consultation today.

SKILL

Causative Verbs

Causative verbs show that one person makes another person do something. A causative is followed by another verb in either the base form or the infinitive.

> **TIP** Learn which causative verbs are followed by the base form and which are followed by the infinitive.

➥ Examples

Causative Verbs Followed by the Base Form

have	let	make

The manager had Mr. Smith demonstrate the product.
(had = causative; demonstrate = base form)

Our boss lets us leave early on Friday afternoons.
(lets = causative; leave = base form)

The driver will make you get off the bus if you don't have the exact fare.
(will make = causative; get = base form)

Causative Verbs Followed by the Infinitive Form

allow	get	require
cause	order	
force	permit	

I'll get my assistant to copy those documents.
(get = causative; to copy = infinitive form)

The company never permits employees to make public statements.
(permits = causative; to make = infinitive form)

The human resources office requires all job applicants to provide three references.
(requires = causative; to provide = infinitive form)

EXERCISE

Read the letter and choose the one word or phrase that best completes each sentence.

Fred,

Our newest staff member, John Greene, appears to have some confusion about the procedures for ordering supplies. Please make him ______________

1. (A) understand
   (B) understands
   (C) to understand
   (D) can understand

that he must have my authorization before putting in an order. We cannot permit staff ______________ anything anytime they want, or it will create

2. (A) order
   (B) to order
   (C) ordering
   (D) will order

havoc with our budget. As you know there have been major cutbacks this year due to the increase in sales tax.

Despite the cutbacks, we are still going to have the annual holiday luncheon. Therefore, it is time to get the plans for the luncheon arranged. The priority right now is getting the food ordered. Please have John Greene ______________

3. (A) call
   (B) calls
   (C) called
   (D) will call

the caterers before the end of the week. After that we can start thinking about a location and theme. Thank you.

Betty

SKILL

Real Conditionals

Conditional sentences can express two kinds of conditions: real and unreal. Conditional sentences describe a condition and a result and are made up of two clauses: an *if* clause, or condition, and a main clause, or result. Real conditionals express what is true or really possible. The *if* clause in a real conditional is always in the present tense. The main clause may be in the present or future tense or may be a command.

> **TIP** Use present tense in the *if* cause of a real conditional.

➥ Examples

Habit	*If* it rains,	I drive to work.
	if clause (real condition)	main clause
Future	*If* it rains,	I will drive to work.
	if clause (real condition)	main clause
Command	*If* it rains,	drive to work.
	if clause (real condition)	main clause

EXERCISE

Read the notice and choose the one word or phrase that best completes each sentence.

Date Posted: August 18, 20—

CLASS REGISTRATION
REMINDER

Class registration begins August 21 and classes begin August 29. If you ____________ for a class after August 28, you will have to pay a

1. (A) register
   (B) to register
   (C) will register
   (D) is going to register

$25 late registration fee. You will have to have a signed permission letter from the course instructor if you sign up for an advanced level class.

If we ____________ a class due to low enrollment, we will contact you. We

2. (A) to cancel
   (B) cancel
   (C) canceling
   (D) will cancel

recommend that you provide your phone number and e-mail address on your course selection sheet in case one of your selections is no longer available. We ____________ able to contact you if we don't have

3. (A) not be
   (B) aren't
   (C) won't be
   (D) weren't

this. Our staff is not responsible for searching for you in a directory.

Unreal Conditionals

Unreal conditions express something that is not true or is not possible. If the sentence is about a present situation, the verb in the *if* clause borrows the form of the past, but remember that it represents the present. If the situation is about the past, the verb in the *if* clause borrows the form of the past perfect. The main clause uses the auxiliary *would* + verb for a present situation and *would have* + verb for a past situation.

> **TIP** Remember that a past tense verb in the *if* clause indicates a *present* unreal conditional.

➥ Examples

Present

If George *owned* the company, he *would* accept the project.

This sentence tells us that George doesn't really own the company so he won't really accept the project.

Sarah *would get* to work on time if she *left* her house earlier every morning.

This sentence tells us that Sarah doesn't really leave her house earlier so she doesn't really get to work on time.

I *would eat* lunch with you if I *didn't have* so much work to do.

This sentence tells us that I really have a lot of work to do so I won't eat lunch with you.

Past

If I *had received* the promotion, I *would have bought* a new car.

This sentence tells us that I didn't really receive the promotion so I didn't buy a new car.

We *would have gone* skiing on our vacation if it *had snowed* in the mountains.

This sentence tells us that it didn't really snow in the mountains so we didn't go skiing.

If he *hadn't been* so busy, he *would have called* you.

This sentence tells us that he really was busy so he didn't call you.

EXERCISE

Read the letter and choose the one word or phrase that best completes each sentence.

March 15th, 20—

Dear Mr. Klugman,

I am terribly sorry about our misunderstanding yesterday. If I _______________

1. (A) knew
   (B) had known
   (C) have known
   (D) could know

that space #7 was your assigned parking space, I would never have parked there. I'm not used to the parking rules because I never drive my car to work. If you _______________ for parking elsewhere, I would have reimbursed

2. (A) have paid
   (B) had paid
   (C) pay
   (D) will pay

you. Luckily you found another free spot in the staff lot. I didn't know those spots existed until I got the message from my supervisor about this incident. I'll know to use them another time if I decide to drive again. If you _______________ here today, I would apologize in person.

3. (A) are
   (B) will be
   (C) were
   (D) had been

Sincerely,

Sophie Schmidt

Comparisons

Adjectives and adverbs can be used to show the similarities and differences among people, places, things, and actions. There are three degrees of comparison: (1) positive; (2) comparative (*-er* and *more* forms); and (3) superlative (*-est* and *most* forms).

One-syllable adjectives and two-syllable adjectives that end in *-y* have the *-er* and *-est* forms. Certain other two-syllable adjectives also have these forms. All three-syllable adjectives use *more* and *most.* Adverbs follow a similar pattern.

TIP Remember that superlative adjectives and adverbs are preceded by *the.*

Examples

Adjectives and adverbs that have the *-er/-est* forms:

Adjectives

Positive	Comparative	Superlative
pretty	prettier	the prettiest
thick	thicker	the thickest
narrow	narrower	the narrowest

I think fall is a *prettier* season *than* spring.
No one drives down that street because it is *the narrowest* in the neighborhood.
That hotel is *farther* from the airport *than* this one.

Adjectives and adverbs that have the *more/most* forms:

Adverbs

Positive	Comparative	Superlative
far	farther	the farthest
soon	sooner	the soonest
lively	livelier	the liveliest

That movie theater is *the most popular* one in town.
Shirley is a *more competent* accountant *than* her colleagues.
She works *more efficiently than* other accountants I know.

Irregular adjectives

Adjectives

Positive	Comparative	Superlative
good	better	the best
bad	worse	the worst

Adverbs

Positive	Comparative	Superlative
well	better	the best
little	less	the least

This is *the worst* weather we've had all year.

The new copier works *better than* the old one.

EXERCISE

Read the advertisement and choose the one word or phrase that best completes each sentence.

Techno Business Academy

Hone your office skills at Techno Business Academy. We guarantee to train you ___________ any other business school. We guarantee ___________

1. (A) faster than
   (B) more professionally than
   (C) longer than
   (D) more costly than

2. (A) low
   (B) lowest
   (C) lower than
   (D) the lowest

prices in town. We guarantee that when you finish our three-month course, you will be in demand at all the best offices in town. That's three guarantees. Our recent graduates earn ___________ salaries than other office professionals with years

3. (A) high
   (B) higher
   (C) highest
   (D) the highest

of experience. All other Business Academies require at least six months of training. Our professors are professionals, just like theirs.

Why study longer?

Why go anywhere else?

SKILL

8 Pronouns

Pronouns take the place of nouns. A pronoun must agree with its antecedent (the noun it replaces) in person and number. There are several different types of pronouns with different grammatical functions.

TIP **Identify the antecedent and make sure the pronoun agrees with it in person and number.**

Subject Pronouns		*Object Pronouns*		*Reflexive Pronouns*	
I	we	me	us	myself	ourselves
you	you	you	you	yourself	yourselves
he/she/it	they	him/her/it	them	himself/herself/itself	themselves
Possessive Adjectives		*Possessive Pronouns*			
my	our	mine	ours		
our	your	yours	yours		
his/her/its	their	his/hers/its	theirs		

➡ Examples

Mrs. Kim **was at the office yesterday, but I didn't see** ***her.***

The clients **will be here all day tomorrow, and** ***they*** **hope to meet with the director.**

You **should call a repairperson instead of trying to fix the machine** ***yourself.***

I **don't think this coat is** ***mine.***

Bob **will present** ***his*** **plan at the next staff meeting.**

EXERCISE

Read the letter and choose the one word or phrase that best completes each sentence.

Dear Ms. Coleman,

I would like to thank you and all ________ staff for the kind hospitality I

1. (A) yourself
   (B) yours
   (C) you
   (D) your

received while visiting the branch office last week. I was impressed with the friendliness and helpfulness of all the employees in the office. ________ all

2. (A) I
   (B) He
   (C) You
   (D) They

made my work go smoothly even though I was working in an unfamiliar setting. I would particularly like to mention your assistant, John Malstrom, who made special efforts to make sure I had everything I needed. Please tell ________

3. (A) me
   (B) him
   (C) her
   (D) them

that I appreciate all the help he gave me.

I look forward to seeing you at the regional meeting next month.

Yours,
Madeline Dubois

SKILL

Subject Relative Pronouns

A relative pronoun introduces an adjective clause. An adjective clause has the same purpose as an adjective—it modifies a noun in the main clause. The relative pronoun may be the subject or the object of the clause. The correct relative pronoun to use depends on the noun it modifies (the antecedent), on whether it is the subject or the object of the clause, and on whether the clause is restrictive or nonrestrictive.

> **TIP** Remember that the adjective clause immediately follows the noun it modifies. This will help you identify the antecedent.

Examples

A restrictive clause is one that is necessary to identify the noun it modifies. Without the restrictive clause, the identity of the noun is unclear.

Subject Relative Pronouns—Restrictive Clauses

People	*who*
	that
Things	*which*
	that
Possession	*whose*

The woman (antecedent) **who** (relative pronoun) **shares this office is very good with computers.**

The sentence above is made up of a main clause: *The woman is very good with computers,* and an adjective clause: *who shares this office.*

The packages (antecedent) **that** (relative pronoun) **arrived this morning are on your desk.**

The sentence above is made up of a main clause: *The packages are on your desk,* and an adjective clause: *that arrived this morning.*

The man (antecedent) **whose** (relative pronoun) **office is next door wants to meet you.**

The sentence above is made up of a main clause: *The man wants to meet you,* and an adjective clause: *whose office is next door.*

A nonrestrictive clause is one that is not necessary to identify the noun. It just gives some extra information. If we removed the nonrestrictive clause from the sentence, the identity of the noun would remain clear. A nonrestrictive clause is always set off from the rest of the sentence with commas.

Subject Relative Pronouns—Nonrestrictive Clauses

People	*who*
Things	*which*
Possession	*whose*

Mr. Maurice, who has worked here for a long time, will retire soon.
antecedent relative pronoun

The sentence above is made up of a main clause: *Mr. Maurice will retire soon,* and an adjective clause: *who has worked here for a long time.*

My car, which is constantly breaking down, is at the mechanic's again today.
antecedent relative pronoun

The sentence above is made up of a main clause: *My car is at the mechanic's again today,* and an adjective clause: *which is constantly breaking down.*

My assistant, whose French is excellent, will help with the clients from France.
antecedent relative pronoun

The sentence above is made up of a main clause: *My assistant will help with the clients from France,* and an adjective clause: *whose French is excellent.*

EXERCISE

Read the notice and choose the one word or phrase that best completes each sentence.

NOTICE

To: All Staff
Re: Ms. McIntyre's Visit

Ms. McIntyre, who has worked in our London offices for more than fifteen years, will be visiting us next week. As most of you have probably heard, Ms. McIntyre was recently presented with a national award of excellence for her leadership skills. Staff members ____________ wish to make an appointment to meet

1. (A) who
   (B) whom
   (C) whose
   (D which

with her and offer her congratulations are asked to contact the Human Resources office. Everyone ____________ schedule allows is invited to

2. (A) who
   (B) their
   (C) whose
   (D) they

attend a welcome luncheon on Wednesday. The luncheon will be held at Francine McKay's ranch. For directions call Mrs. McKay at 333-4989, extension 2. We are all looking forward to Ms. McIntyre's visit, ____________ will last ten

3. (A) who
   (B) that
   (C) whose
   (D) which

days. In lieu of flowers or cards, Ms. McIntyre has asked that you congratulate her by making a donation to a local youth group.

Please post on notice board.

SKILL 10

Object Relative Pronouns

An object relative pronoun is the object of the verb or a preposition in the relative clause. An object relative pronoun, except for *whose*, can be omitted from restrictive clauses.

TIP Identify the subject of the adjective clause. If the relative pronoun is the subject, use a subject relative pronoun. Otherwise, use an object relative pronoun.

Examples

Object Relative Pronouns—Restrictive Clauses

People	*whom, who, that,* nothing
Things	*which, that,* nothing
Possession	*whose*

The accountant (antecedent) **whom** (relative pronoun) **we hired last month used to work for Ibex International.**

The sentence above is made up of a main clause: *The accountant used to work for Ibex International,* and an adjective clause: *whom we hired last month.*

The office (antecedent) **that** (relative pronoun) **we rented is very close to the subway station.**

The sentence above is made up of a main clause: *The office is very close to the subway station,* and an adjective clause: *that we rented.*

The person (antecedent) **whose** (relative pronoun) **phone number you requested no longer works here.**

The sentence above is made up of a main clause: *The person no longer works here,* and an adjective clause: *whose phone number you requested.*

Object Relative Pronouns—Nonrestrictive Clauses

People	*whom, who*
Things	*which*
Possession	*whose*

My neighbor, (antecedent) **who** (relative pronoun) **I have known for many years, is moving away next month.**

The sentence above is made up of a main clause: *My neighbor is moving away next month,* and an adjective clause: *who I have known for many years.*

The City Museum, **which** **I visit almost every day, has many interesting exhibits.**
antecedent **relative pronoun**

The sentence above is made up of a main clause: *The City Museum has many interesting exhibits,* and an adjective clause: *which I visit almost every day.*

Shirley, **whose** **office you were using last week, is back at work today.**
antecedent **relative pronoun**

The sentence above is made up of a main clause: *Shirley is back at work today,* and an adjective clause: *whose office you were using last week.*

EXERCISE

Read the article and choose the one word or phrase that best completes each sentence.

Harold News — Monday, January 5, 20—
BOOK TALK-B1

The Environment Crisis

Want to know more about global warming and how you can help prevent it? Doctor Herman Friedman, ______________ many consider the foremost

1. (A) whose
   (B) which
   (C) who
   (D) him

authority on the subject, will speak at Grayson Hall next Tuesday. Friedman studied environmental science at three prestigious universities around the world before becoming a professor in the subject. He has also traveled around the world observing environmental concerns. The gradual bleaching of the Great Barrier Reef, ______________ he has been researching for several years, is the

2. (A) that
   (B) which
   (C) whom
   (D) it

subject of his latest book. Signed copies will be for sale after his talk, along with other books ______________ he has written about global warming.

3. (A) whose
   (B) that
   (C) them
   (D) who

SKILL

Passive Voice

Most sentences are in active voice—the subject performs the action. Some sentences are in passive voice—the subject receives the action. We use passive voice when the agent (the one who performs the action) is unknown or unimportant. The passive voice is formed with the verb *be* + the past participle form of the verb.

> **TIP** To identify a passive voice sentence, determine whether the subject performs or receives the action.

➡ Examples

In the passive voice, the verb *be* carries the tense and the negative. The main verb is always in the past participle form.

Simple Present

Employees are (be) paid (past participle) every Friday.

The subject of the sentence above is *employees* and the action is *pay*. The employees don't perform the action. Somebody else, probably the boss or the company, pays the employees.

Children aren't (be) allowed (past participle) in this office without adult supervision.

The subject of the sentence above is *children* and the action is *allow*. The children don't perform the action; they aren't the ones who don't allow themselves.

Simple Past

The mail was (be) delivered (past participle) at 10:00 this morning.

The subject of the sentence above is *mail* and the action is *delivered*. The mail didn't perform the action. It didn't deliver itself. The letter carrier, not mentioned in the sentence, did.

Present Perfect

The annual conference has been (be) held (past participle) in this city every year since 2005.

The subject of the sentence above is *conference* and the action is *held*. The conference doesn't perform the action; it doesn't hold itself. Some organization or group of people holds the conference.

Future

Copies of the report will be distributed at tomorrow's meeting.
be past participle

The subject of the sentence above is *copies of the report* and the action is *distributed.* The copies of the report will not perform the action; they will not distribute themselves.

Sometimes the agent, the one that performs the action, is mentioned in the sentence. In that case, we use the preposition *by.*

The letter was signed *by* everyone in the office.
All receipts are inspected *by* the accountant.

EXERCISE

Read the memo and choose the one word or phrase that best completes each sentence.

To: Office Staff
From: Office Manager
Re: Conference Room

We have just put a good deal of effort, not to mention money, into renovating the conference room. In addition to new tables and chairs, the walls ______________ painted last month.

1. (A) was
   (B) are
   (C) were
   (D) have been

We had a problem with the carpet company but we have worked that out and they have promised us that the new carpet will be ______________ before the end of this week.

2. (A) installs
   (B) installed
   (C) installing
   (D) installation

The only thing in the room that isn't new is the curtains. We determined that they are still in good shape and just needed a thorough cleaning. We sent them out to a professional cleaning facility where the stains ______________, and now the curtains look as good as new. We

3. (A) remove
   (B) removed
   (C) have removed
   (D) were removed

hope everyone will find the newly renovated conference room to be a pleasant place to work.

NEW TOEIC—PART 6: TEXT COMPLETION

The Part 6: Text Completion passages focus on memos, letters, e-mail, and other business-related texts. The skills and strategies to prepare for Part 6 are the same for both the current and the new TOEIC.

There are two changes in Part 6: Text Completion. In the new TOEIC there are more passages and more questions. There are 4 passages with 4 questions each. As on the current TOEIC, the questions focus on word choice and grammar. There is also one new question type—choosing a sentence that best fits with the context of the passage as a whole.

SKILL

Understand the Context

Some questions ask you to choose the sentence that best fits the context. The context includes both the topic and the purpose of the passage. The topic of a memo may be a staff meeting, for example, while the purpose might be to inform staff that the meeting will be held, explain the content of the meeting, or ask for evaluations of a meeting already held.

TIP Identify both the topic and the purpose of the passage.

EXERCISE

Read each group of sentences and choose the one sentence that does not belong.

1. A. There will be a meeting about our new health insurance policy next Wednesday afternoon.
   B. Attendance is not mandatory, but it is recommended.
   C. If you have questions about the new policy, this is your opportunity to get them answered.
   D. If you need a few days off work for health reasons, please inform your supervisor.
   E. We hope that the new policy will save everyone some money and will be easier to understand.

2. A. I am sending you a draft of the new contract with the XZ Company.
   B. I am meeting with the client on Thursday and would like to get your feedback before then.
   C. The XZ Company has been our client for several years now.
   D. Please review it and send me your comments by Wednesday.
   E. Your help with this matter is greatly appreciated.

3. A. The elevators in this building will undergo routine maintenance during the week of September 15.
   B. There are three elevators in the building, each with a capacity of 15 passengers.
   C. During this week, there may be one or two elevators out of service from time to time.
   D. When this occurs, please use another elevator or the stairs.
   E. We apologize for any inconvenience this may cause.

4. A. I have been unable to reach you by either phone or e-mail.
   B. Thank you for agreeing to meet with me next week.
   C. I will look for you at the Golden Café at 10:00.
   D. I look forward to the opportunity to discuss my company and the services we can offer you.
   E. We have served many satisfied clients like yourself in the past, and I feel confident we can provide you with satisfactory services, as well.

5. A. Thank you for sending your resume to us.
   B. You have exactly the kind of education and experience we are looking for.
   C. I would like you to come in for an interview soon.
   D. Please call my office to set up a time for an appointment.
   E. There are several places in the city where you can get the training you need.

NEW TOEIC

NEW TOEIC

PRACTICE

Directions: You will see short passages each with four blanks. Under each blank are four answer options. Choose the word or phrase that best completes the sentence or sentence that best completes the passage.

Questions 1–4 refer to the following letter.

Dear Client,

We ______________ invite you to attend our 3rd annual open house party on the

1. (A) cordial
   (B) cordially
   (C) cordiality
   (D) cordialness

afternoon of December 2. This is our way of showing our appreciation to our clients, as well as an opportunity for you to get to know us ______________

2. (A) any
   (B) some
   (C) a few
   (D) a little

better. Please come to our offices any time between 3:00 and 7:00 P.M. to enjoy refreshments, ______________ entertainment, and good company.

3. (A) live
   (B) alive
   (C) liven
   (D) living

____

4. (A) Please call for an appointment.
   (B) It will be charged to your account.
   (C) We look forward to seeing you.
   (D) Tickets are available at the front desk.

Questions 5–8 refer to the following e-mail.

To: Richard Simms (rsimms@acmeinc.com)
From: Ethel Burt (eburt@acmeinc.com)

Richard,

I have received ______________ request for time off during the last week of May to attend a

5. (A) you
(B) your
(C) yours
(D) you'll

training seminar. I applaud your initiative in taking advantage of this professional development opportunity. Unfortunately, the timing is a problem as your absence would occur right at the beginning of our busy ______________, when I really need to have you in the office every day. Perhaps you could take a look

6. (A) venue
(B) location
(C) season
(D) calendar

at the seminar schedule and find an appropriate one that ______________ at some time later in the year.

7. (A) give
(B) gives
(C) will give
(D) will be given

______________________________. Let me know if I can be of any further help.

8. (A) Last month's seminar was very successful.
(B) We are already making plans for the end of May.
(C) Please submit requests for time off to your supervisor.
(D) I am sorry to have to turn down your request at this time.

NEW TOEIC

Questions 9–12 refer to the following notice.

NOTICE

_______________ in this lot is for employees of the Zip Zap Company only. Cars not bearing

9. (A) Park
   (B) To park
   (C) Parking
   (D) Car park

a Zip Zap parking sticker on the lower passenger side windshield will be _______________

10. (A) towed
    (B) relocated
    (C) maintained
    (D) detailed

at the owner's expense. The Zip Zap Company will not be held responsible for any _______________ that may occur. If you are a Zip Zap employee, you can apply for a

11. (A) happenings
    (B) damages
    (C) delays
    (D) hindrances

parking sticker at the Zip Zap Human Resources Office.

____

12. (A) Cleaning the lot is the responsibility of the building manager.
    (B) The parking lot is open to the public 24 hours a day.
    (C) The front row is reserved for compact cars only.
    (D) Parking stickers are free and valid for one year.

NEW TOEIC

Questions 13–16 refer to the following announcement.

See page 265 for the Answer Key and page 268 for the Explanatory Answers for new TOEIC practice Part 6.

The Farnsworth Group announces the opening of the new Farnsworth Towers Office Center in the downtown business district.

______________________________.

13. (A) Rental space is now available for offices of all sizes.
    (B) The hallways and lobby have already been painted.
    (C) There are several other large office buildings in the area.
    (D) Investors in the project include some well-known business leaders.

We offer a prime location in the __________ of the business district, close

14. (A) edge
    (B) heart
    (C) structure
    (D) completion

to public transportation. Building amenities include a parking garage, 24-hour security, a fitness center, and more. Office sizes __________ from

15. (A) multiply
    (B) enlarge
    (C) create
    (D) range

200 sq. feet to over 2000 sq. feet. Design your office layout to suit your needs! Call now for an appointment to view __________ model offices

16. (A) your
    (B) their
    (C) our
    (D) his

and discuss your rental options.

PART 7: READING COMPREHENSION

Sample Questions

In Part 7: Reading Comprehension of the TOEIC, you will answer a total of 48 reading comprehension questions—28 based on single passages and 20 based on double passages. The questions will be about the main idea, details, or vocabulary.

PASSAGE

> **NOTICE**
>
> Please be aware that work on painting the interior of the building will begin early next month. This includes all hallways and the main lobby. Anyone who would also like their apartment painted at this time should make arrangements with me. The painting of the public areas of the building should last no more than two weeks. We apologize for any inconvenience this may cause.
>
> George Johnson
> Building Manager

Main Idea

Who is this notice for?

(A) Painters
(B) Tenants
(C) The building owner
(D) The building manager

Ⓐ ● Ⓒ Ⓓ

This is a notice for people who live in the building. Therefore, the best response is Choice (B), "Tenants."

Detail

How long will it probably take to paint the hallways and lobby?

(A) Two weeks
(B) One month
(C) Two months
(D) One year

The notice says, "The painting of the public areas of the building should last no more than two weeks." Therefore, the best response is Choice (A), "Two weeks."

Vocabulary

The word inconvenience in line 7 is closest in meaning to

(A) expense
(B) work
(C) boredom
(D) difficulty

Inconvenience means "lack of convenience" or "difficulty." Therefore, the best response is Choice (D).

THE PSRA STRATEGY

An important strategy for reading comprehension is learning to approach a passage in an organized way. First make a *Prediction* about the passage, then *Scan* it; next *Read* it, and finally *Answer* the questions. We can abbreviate this strategy to **PSRA**.

Prediction

Learning how to make predictions about what you are going to read BEFORE you read will help you establish a context for understanding the passage. This will improve your reading score.

Before you begin to read one of the reading passages, you should first look at the question introduction line. This line looks like this:

Questions 161–163 refer to the following office memo.

In the question introduction line, you will learn how many questions there are and what kind of reading passage it is (in this case an office memo). The look of the reading passage will also give you a clue: a fax will look like a fax, a phone message like a phone message, and a graph like a graph. This will help you PREDICT what the passage is about.

There are generally two or three questions for every reading passage, although there may be up to five. Look at the questions and the four answer options. This will give you a clue what to look for. These clues will help you PREDICT what the passage is about.

According to the memo, which equipment has multiple uses?

(A) Computers
(B) Fax machines
(C) Answering machines
(D) CD-players

Scan

We can predict that the memo has something to do with electronics. When we *Scan* the passage, we look for the Key Words. You may not find the exact words, but you might find words with similar meanings. Try to think of words that have meanings similar to the Key Words in the question and answer options. The Key Words for this question are:

Questions		**Answer Options**
Key words	*Similar meanings*	computers
equipment	electronic tools; hardware	fax machines
multiple uses	useful in a variety of settings	answering machines
		CD-players

Look first for the Key Words from the question; then look around the Question Key Words for the Key Words from the answer options. When you find the Answer Option Key Words, see if the words answer the question. Try to answer the question (in your head, NOT on the answer sheet). Here's a sample:

MEMORANDUM

To: Lafite, Pierre
Purchasing Department

From: Clement, Marie France
Personnel

We need **computers** for use in the office, **answering machines** for our consultants, **fax machines** for the shipping department, and **CD-players** for everyone. This **last piece of hardware** can be **used in a variety** of ways.

According to the memo, which equipment has multiple uses?

(A) Computers
(B) Fax machines
(C) Answering machines
(D) CD-players

The correct answer is (D). A CD-player is the **last** piece of hardware mentioned. *This last piece of hardware can be used in a variety of ways.*

Note how much different the answer would be if the last sentence were:

This first piece of hardware can be used in a variety of ways.

The word "first" changes the answer completely from (D) CD-players to (A) Computers. This is why you must NOT rely on Prediction and Scanning alone.

Read

You must READ the passage as well. But when you read, read quickly. Read to confirm your predictions.

You should not make any mark on your answer sheet until you have made a PREDICTION based on all of the questions, SCANNED the passage looking for key words, answered the questions in your head, and READ the passage to confirm your answer choices. The answer to the first question is found in the first part of the reading passage. The answer to the second question is found in the next part and so on. The questions follow the sequence of the passage.

Answer

Now you are ready to mark your answer sheet. ANSWER the easy questions first. If you don't know an answer, scan the passage again, look for the key words, read parts of the passage. If you still don't know, GUESS. Do NOT leave any answer blank.

Advertisements

Advertisements on the TOEIC are similar to those found in magazines or newspapers. You can find other examples in English-language newspapers and magazines and ask yourself questions about the products being advertised.

EXERCISE

Questions 1–2 refer to the following advertisement. Choose the one best answer to each question.

> **ATTENTION MANUFACTURERS!**
>
> We introduce and distribute your products to 125,000 distributors in 155 countries, FREE!
>
> For a FREE information kit call:
>
> Tel: (310) 553-4434 Ext. 105 • Fax (310) 553-5555
>
> GRAND TECHNOLOGIES LIMITED

1. Who is the advertisement written for?

   (A) Distributors
   (B) Sales representatives
   (C) Manufacturers
   (D) Information specialists

   Ⓐ Ⓑ Ⓒ Ⓓ

2. How many countries are mentioned?

   (A) 125
   (B) 155
   (C) 310
   (D) 501

   Ⓐ Ⓑ Ⓒ Ⓓ

SKILL

Forms

A form is a template: a standard form that an individual adds information to. These could include magazine subscription forms, purchase orders, immigration forms, hotel check-in forms, telephone message blanks, and so on.

EXERCISE

Questions 1–4 refer to the following form. Choose the one best answer to each question.

Special Subscription Offer

Subscribe to the journal that recently received the Editorial Excellence Award from the Society of Industrial Designers

☑ **YES!** send me INTERNATIONAL INDUSTRY for 1 year (12 issues) at just $48, a savings of 20% off the full cover price of $5.00.

☐ Payment enclosed ☑ Bill me.

Name: *Anne Kwok*
Title: *Design Specialist*
Company: *Pharmaceutical Supply Co.*
Address: *Tong Chong Street*
Quarry Bay Hong Kong

Please allow four weeks for first issue.

1. Why did Anne Kwok complete this form?
   (A) To win an award
   (B) To apply for a design job
   (C) To enroll in design school
   (D) To receive a journal

   Ⓐ Ⓑ Ⓒ Ⓓ

2. How much is the full cover price per issue?
   (A) $4
   (B) $5
   (C) $12
   (D) $48

   Ⓐ Ⓑ Ⓒ Ⓓ

3. How long will it take for the first issue to arrive?
   (A) One week
   (B) One month
   (C) One year
   (D) Unknown

   Ⓐ Ⓑ Ⓒ Ⓓ

4. The magazine comes
   (A) daily
   (B) weekly
   (C) monthly
   (D) once a year

   Ⓐ Ⓑ Ⓒ Ⓓ

SKILL 3

Reports

A report is a short paragraph containing the kind of information that might be included in a capsule summary. A report could appear in a newspaper; it could be part of a larger document such as an annual report; it could be most any kind of descriptive or narrative prose.

EXERCISE

Questions 1–3 refer to the following report. Choose the one best answer to each question.

> In October, Markel On-Line acquired Peptel Visual of Berlin, one of Europe's leading educational software companies. The deal calls for Markel (a $49 million Toronto-based company) to pay $5 million up front for Peptel and as much as $5 million more over the next few years, depending on the German company's performance. Peptel posted $4.2 million in sales last year.

1. If Peptel performs well, what is the largest total price Markel will have to pay?

   (A) $4.2 million
   (B) $5 million
   (C) $10 million
   (D) $49 million

   Ⓐ Ⓑ Ⓒ Ⓓ

2. Peptel is based in

   (A) Canada
   (B) the United States
   (C) Great Britain
   (D) Germany

   Ⓐ Ⓑ Ⓒ Ⓓ

3. What field are these companies in?

   (A) Computer software
   (B) Postal service
   (C) Visual arts
   (D) Toy manufacturing

   Ⓐ Ⓑ Ⓒ Ⓓ

Letters

The TOEIC will generally always have one letter on the test. The important information is generally contained in the body of the letter—the part between the greeting (*Dear . . .*) and the closing (*Sincerely yours*).

EXERCISE

Questions 1–3 refer to the following letter. Choose the one best answer to each question.

EUTECH, s.r.o.
Zborovská 23,150 00 Praha 5
Czech Republic
Tel: (02) 513.2343 Fax: (02) 513.2334

December 3, 20–

Post Comptoir
43 Griffith Road
Dinsdale, Hamilton
North Island, New Zealand

Dear Sir or Madam:

We are interested in becoming distributors for your software products in the Czech Republic. Would you please send us your latest catalogs, descriptive brochures, and terms?

We are a hardware company that would like to add software to our sales offerings. Our annual report is enclosed.

We look forward to hearing from you soon.

Sincerely yours,

Peter Zavel

Peter Zavel
Chairman

1. Which items were NOT requested?
   (A) Catalogs
   (B) Brochures
   (C) Samples
   (D) Pricing information

   Ⓐ Ⓑ Ⓒ Ⓓ

2. What does EUTECH sell now?
   (A) Software
   (B) Computers
   (C) Financial reports
   (D) Printing services

   Ⓐ Ⓑ Ⓒ Ⓓ

3. EUTECH wants to
   (A) distribute software
   (B) manufacture computers
   (C) purchase hardware
   (D) receive an annual report

   Ⓐ Ⓑ Ⓒ Ⓓ

SKILL 5

Memos

A memorandum (memo) is an internal form of communication that is sent from one member of a company to a member of the same company. Today these memos (memoranda) are often sent by computer as e-mail. To learn more about computer-generated language, see Skills 12 and 13 on pages 209–210.

EXERCISE

Questions 1–4 refer to the following memorandum. Choose the one best answer to each question.

MEMORANDUM

To: All Employees

From: Simon Gonzales
Personnel Officer

Date: May 15, 20—

Sub: Company Travel

Effective June 1 all personnel traveling on company business must use the most economical means possible. No flights under five hours can be booked in Business Class. No flights regardless of duration can be booked in First Class.

1. If a flight is over five hours, what class can be booked?
   (A) Economy
   (B) Economy Plus
   (C) Business
   (D) First

   Ⓐ Ⓑ Ⓒ Ⓓ

2. When will this rule go into effect?
   (A) In about two weeks
   (B) At the end of the summer
   (C) At the first of the year
   (D) In five months

   Ⓐ Ⓑ Ⓒ Ⓓ

3. Why was this memo written?
   (A) To save time
   (B) To save money
   (C) To reward the employees
   (D) To increase company travel

   Ⓐ Ⓑ Ⓒ Ⓓ

4. Who is affected by this memo?
   (A) Only the Board of Directors
   (B) Only frequent travelers
   (C) Only the personnel department
   (D) All personnel

   Ⓐ Ⓑ Ⓒ Ⓓ

SKILL
6 Tables and Charts

Tables and charts show a compilation of data that are useful for quick comparison. They can be about almost any subject. You can find examples in English-language newspapers and magazines.

EXERCISE

Questions 1–4 refer to the following table. Choose the one best answer to each question.

WORLD TEMPERATURES
January 5

	Hi (C/F)	Lo (C/F)	Weather
Amsterdam	6/41	3/37	c
Athens	13/55	8/46	sh
Bangkok	32/90	27/80	sh
Beijing	12/53	1/34	pc
Brussels	4/39	1/34	sh
Budapest	3/37	0/32	r
Frankfurt	3/37	1/34	r
Jakarta	29/84	24/75	sh
Kuala Lampur	31/88	24/75	t
Madrid	9/48	1/34	sh
Manila	33/91	21/70	pc
Seoul	9/48	–2/29	s
Taipei	21/70	14/57	c
Tokyo	9/48	–2/29	pc

Weather: s-sunny; pc-partly cloudy; c-cloudy; sh-showers; t-thunderstorms; r-rain

1. Which two cities were cloudy on January 5?
   (A) Amsterdam and Taipei
   (B) Beijing and Manila
   (C) Athens and Tokyo
   (D) Bangkok and Seoul

   Ⓐ Ⓑ Ⓒ Ⓓ

2. Which city had the highest temperature?
   (A) Athens
   (B) Bangkok
   (C) Jakarta
   (D) Manila

   Ⓐ Ⓑ Ⓒ Ⓓ

3. Which city had the closest spread between high and low temperature?
   (A) Brussels
   (B) Frankfurt
   (C) Seoul
   (D) Tokyo

   Ⓐ Ⓑ Ⓒ Ⓓ

4. Kuala Lampur had
   (A) sun
   (B) thunderstorms
   (C) rain
   (D) showers

   Ⓐ Ⓑ Ⓒ Ⓓ

Graphs

A graph is a drawing that shows the relationship between variables. On the TOEIC there can be line graphs, bar graphs, or pie graphs.

EXERCISE

Questions 1–2 refer to the following graph. Choose the one best answer to each question.

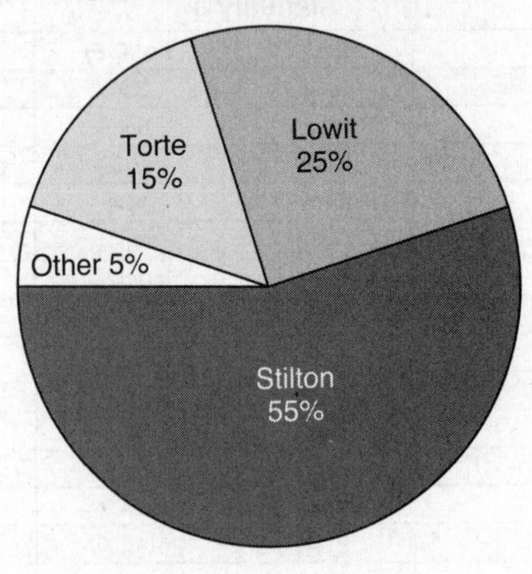

1. Who would be most interested in reading this graph?

(A) Tourists
(B) Competing hotels
(C) Landscape architects
(D) Job hunters

2. According to this graph, Lowit

(A) is the top-ranking hotel chain
(B) is only in Latin America
(C) has less of a share than Torte
(D) has one-quarter of the market

SKILL 8

Announcements

An announcement is similar to a report except it has more immediate information. There is usually an announcement on the TOEIC.

EXERCISE

Questions 1–5 refer to the following announcement. Choose the one best answer to each question.

> The Omnicable Company representatives said yesterday that John A. Kaspar, its president and chief operating officer, would resign on April 30. The announcement added to speculation that the world's third-largest cable television system could be bought within a few weeks. Mr. Kaspar, 62, said he was leaving after more than 22 years for "personal reasons." He declined to answer any questions about his future plans.

1. What is the company's world ranking?

   (A) 3 (B) 22 (C) 30 (D) 62

   Ⓐ Ⓑ Ⓒ Ⓓ

2. What might happen to the company?

   (A) It may be bought.
   (B) It may expand.
   (C) It may diversify.
   (D) It may become international.

   Ⓐ Ⓑ Ⓒ Ⓓ

3. How long has Mr. Kaspar worked for Omnicable?

   (A) For a few weeks
   (B) Since April 30
   (C) Since he was 40
   (D) 62 years

   Ⓐ Ⓑ Ⓒ Ⓓ

4. What kind of business is Omnicable?

   (A) Communications
   (B) Computer
   (C) Manufacturing
   (D) Service

   Ⓐ Ⓑ Ⓒ Ⓓ

5. The word *declined* in line 6 is closest in meaning to

   (A) fell
   (B) refused
   (C) worsened
   (D) denied

   Ⓐ Ⓑ Ⓒ Ⓓ

Notices

A notice is information that the writer feels the general public or specific product users must be made aware of. There are often notices attached to walls and public buildings or enclosed with product literature.

EXERCISE

Questions 1–2 refer to the following notice. Choose the one best answer to each question.

> ***Corporate Policy Change***
>
> *Moving Expenses. You can be reimbursed for your expenses of moving to a new home only if your new home is at least 50 miles away from your former home. In addition, expenses are limited to the costs of moving your household goods and personal effects from your former home to your new home. Meals, pre-move house-hunting expenses, and temporary-quarters expenses are no longer reimbursable.*

1. Who would be most affected by this notice?

   (A) Hotel chains 
   (B) Furniture rental companies
   (C) Real estate agents
   (D) New employees moving from another city

2. Which of the following will be reimbursed?

   (A) Lunch for the movers Ⓐ Ⓑ Ⓒ Ⓓ
   (B) Shipping household goods
   (C) Gas used looking for a house
   (D) Hotel expenses

SKILL 10 Articles

An article is a passage written for a newspaper, magazine, or newsletter. It may be about a current news item or about a topic of general or specific interest, depending on the publication where it appears.

EXERCISE

Questions 1–3 refer to the following article. Choose the one best answer to each question.

> Interns—college students or recent graduates who work for a company in exchange for the opportunity to gain work experience—can be a great asset to any company, whether large or small. Some companies complain that interns are a drain on their resources. Because of their lack of experience, interns may require close supervision and lots of support. However, the enthusiasm, energy, and creativity they bring to the workplace can more than make up for this. Really good interns can become permanent staff members, and the advantage is that they will already be familiar with the work and the company. Interns are far more than just a supply of unpaid help. They have many positive contributions to make.

1. What is this article mainly about?

   (A) How to train interns
   (B) Where to find interns
   (C) The difficulties of interns
   (D) The advantages of interns

   Ⓐ Ⓑ Ⓒ Ⓓ

2. The word *asset* in line 3 is closest in meaning to

   (A) experience
   (B) money
   (C) education
   (D) benefit

   Ⓐ Ⓑ Ⓒ Ⓓ

3. What is a disadvantage of having interns?

   (A) They lack enthusiasm.
   (B) They need a lot of help.
   (C) They require high pay.
   (D) They complain frequently.

   Ⓐ Ⓑ Ⓒ Ⓓ

SKILL

11 Schedules

A schedule is a printed form with lists of information: stock prices, train departure times, payment schedules, and so on.

EXERCISE

Questions 1–4 refer to the following schedule. Choose the one best answer to each question.

7th & Market	East Rise P&R	Tunnel	122nd East & 16th
7:11 W	**7:21**	**7:36 T**	**8:01**
7:22 W	**7:32**	**7:47 T**	**8:12**
7:30 W	**7:41**	**7:59 T**	**8:21**
7:40	**7:51**	**8:06**	8:32
8:02 W	**8:13**	**8:25**	8:53
8:25	8:35	8:49	9:14
8:51 W	9:01	9:15	9:40
9:21	9:32	9:48	10:11
9:51 W	10:10	10:24	10:40

Key:
T = Tunnel opens at 8:00 A.M. Buses prior to this time stop on 12th and Meridian.
W = Bus departs at this time. It arrives about 5 minutes earlier.
Boldface indicates peak fare.

1. What time do off-peak fares probably start?

   (A) Before 7 A.M. Ⓐ Ⓑ Ⓒ Ⓓ
   (B) 8:25 A.M.
   (C) 8:30 A.M.
   (D) 8:51 A.M.

2. What time does the 7:30 bus arrive at 7th & Market?

   (A) 7:00 Ⓐ Ⓑ Ⓒ Ⓓ
   (B) 7:22
   (C) 7:25
   (D) 7:30

3. Why doesn't the 7:30 use the tunnel?

   (A) Because it's rush hour. Ⓐ Ⓑ Ⓒ Ⓓ
   (B) Bus heights exceed limits for the tunnel.
   (C) The tunnel is closed at that time.
   (D) Early buses are rarely full enough to use the tunnel.

4. How long is the trip from 7th & Market to 122nd & 16th?

   (A) A quarter hour Ⓐ Ⓑ Ⓒ Ⓓ
   (B) A half hour
   (C) Almost an hour
   (D) An hour

E-mail

E-mail means *electronic mail* and refers to computer mail. E-mail can be used to send any type of correspondence, form, or questionnaire, so an e-mail reading item may include any type of content. One distinctive feature of e-mail is its heading, which includes information about the sender, the receiver, and the transmission. A second feature of e-mail is that its language is usually more casual than that of formal paper correspondence.

EXERCISE

Questions 1–2 refer to the following e-mail. Choose the one best answer to each question.

From: Melinda Ligos [m_ligos@hottech.com]
Sent: Tuesday, January 14, 20— 4:06 P.M.
To: Misha Polonetsky [m_polonetsky@hottech.com]
Subject: Meeting in Orlando

Misha—

The meeting went better than expected. They'll get back to us this week about the proposal.

Thanks for suggesting Sparazza's—I had dinner there on Thursday. Loved it.

Melinda

1. What is the sender's e-mail address?

   (A) m_ligos@hottech.com
   (B) m_polonetsky@hottech.com
   (C) Melinda Ligos [m_ligos@hottech.com]
   (D) Misha Polonetsky

   Ⓐ Ⓑ Ⓒ Ⓓ

2. Where was the gathering?

   (A) At Hottech
   (B) With a client of Misha Polonetsky
   (C) In Orlando
   (D) At Sparazza's

   Ⓐ Ⓑ Ⓒ Ⓓ

SKILL

13 Webpages

You may see webpages in Part 7 of the TOEIC. You can find an unlimited number of webpages on the Internet to familiarize yourself with their layout and terminology.

EXERCISE

Questions 1–2 refer to the following webpage. Choose the one best answer to each question.

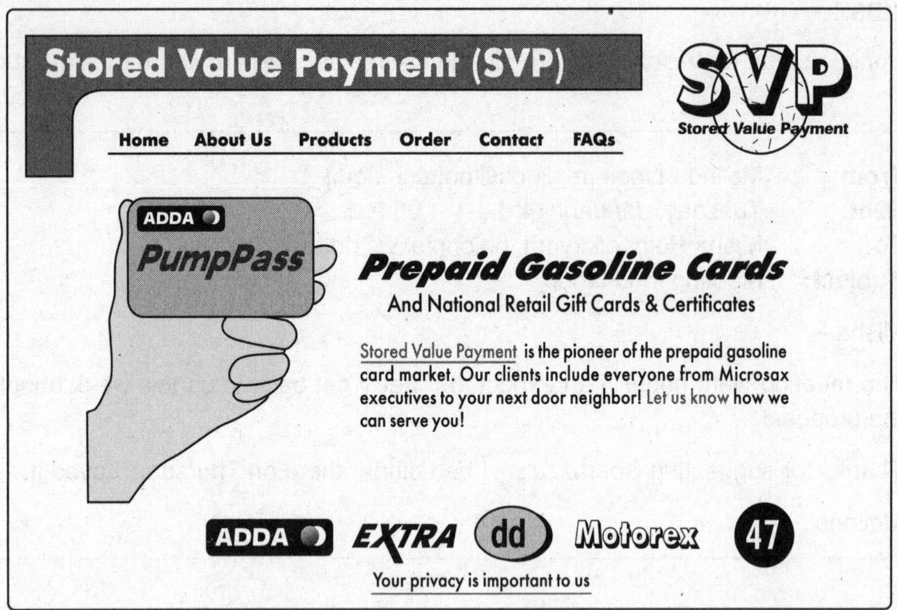

1. Where would you click to get an answer to a basic question about SVP?

   (A) Home
   (B) Products
   (C) Contact
   (D) FAQs

   Ⓐ Ⓑ Ⓒ Ⓓ

2. What is the purpose of an SVP card?

   (A) To pay for fuel in advance
   (B) To reduce costs
   (C) To ensure privacy
   (D) To store gas safely in your home

NEW TOEIC—PART 7: READING COMPREHENSION

In Part 7: Reading Comprehension there are single passages, double passages, and triple passages. There will be a small increase in the number of single and multiple passage questions. In addition, there will be new questions about the meaning of words in context and about the placement of sentences in context. There will also be some new passage types—text messages, instant messages, and online chats.

SKILL 1 Words in Context

Some questions will ask you to choose the best meaning for a word or phrase. You will have to determine the meaning according to how the word or phrase is used in the passage. Look for clues in the sentences immediately before and after the sentence that contains the word/phrase in the question.

TIP Use the context to determine the correct meaning of the word/phrase.

EXERCISE

Choose the correct meaning for the underlined words and phrases.

1. We're all ready to receive the visitors from your office. I've scheduled the meetings, made the hotel reservations, and arranged for transportation while they're here. I'm assuming you're taking care of the airline reservations <u>at your end</u>.

   A. Make the airline reservations when you finish your other tasks. Ⓐ Ⓑ
   B. Making the airline reservations is your responsibility.

2. I've had such a busy morning. I went straight from my morning meeting to the afternoon seminar and <u>had to cut</u> the client lunch. I was sorry to miss it, and hope you can fill me in on what happened.

   A. I didn't go to the lunch. Ⓐ Ⓑ
   B. I spent less time at the lunch.

3. An initial version of the report is ready for your review. It's still a bit <u>rough</u>, so I look forward to your comments. If you get them back to me soon, I can have a final version ready by the end of the week.

   A. uneven Ⓐ Ⓑ
   B. unfinished

NEW TOEIC

4. A group has been formed to develop a plan for the new project. They'll be working under the direction of Ms. Petersen.

   A. route Ⓐ Ⓑ
   B. guidance

5. We have all the information we need to get started on the report. We figure it will take about a week to write the first draft.

   A. estimate Ⓐ Ⓑ
   B. understand

SKILL

Locating Appropriate Context

Some questions will provide a sentence and ask you to choose the correct location for it in the passage. The sentence might be a topic sentence or a detail. Identify the topic of each paragraph, then determine in which paragraph the sentence fits best. Make sure the sentence matches the topic and connects logically with the details of the paragraph where you place it.

TIP Determine the main idea of each paragraph.

EXERCISE

Read the paragraph and determine where the remaining sentence belongs.

1. We are offering our staff employees a 50% discount on membership to the City Health Club. If you wish to participate, please notify personnel before the end of this month. [A] You must have been an employee in good standing for at least the past six months. In addition, you need to pay for a one-year membership in full at the time of registration. [B] We encourage everyone to take advantage of this opportunity. [C] It offers substantial savings at one of the area's most popular health clubs. [D]

   Employees who don't meet these requirements won't receive the discount.

2. Amy Ann's Bakeshop opened its doors just three months ago, but its owner is already talking about expanding. The reason? Business is booming. [A] People line up daily to buy Amy Ann's freshly baked goods. [B] Bakery owner Amy Ann Anderson is pleased but surprised at the high sales volume. [C] In fact, she has brought in close to half that amount in the first quarter alone. [D]

   She says she hoped to make $40,000 a year in profits.

3. The City of Rushworth is making plans for expanding the recreational facilities at Rushworth Park, and we are asking for citizen input. [A] A public meeting will be held at the Rushworth Park Community Center on May 21. [B] Doors will open at 6:30 and the discussion will begin promptly at 7:00. [C] The goal is to create a park that serves the recreational needs of all our citizens. [D] We hope to see you there!

   Members of the City Council will be present to hear your ideas and answer your questions.

4. If you are planning a visit to Wilmington, consider staying at the Bougainvillea Inn. [A] This charming hotel is located in the Park View neighborhood, one of the prettiest areas of the city. [B] The lobby features a mural by a local artist, and each guest room is decorated with a floral theme. The staff is friendly and helpful and have many good suggestions for sights to see and places to eat. [C] The prices are a little higher than similar hotels in the area, but the excellent service makes it well worth the cost. [D]

   The artistically designed interior is a delight to the eye.

5. A job fair will be held at the City Convention Center on March 11. [A] This is a unique opportunity to find out where the jobs are and to meet with people who are hiring now. There will also be workshops on resume writing, skills training opportunities, resources for job hunters, and more. [B] Come on down and get the information you need for a successful job search. [C] Admission is free. [D]

   Employers from all over the region and representing a variety of industries will be present.

PRACTICE

Directions: Read each passage and answer the questions.

Questions 1–2 refer to the following text message chain.

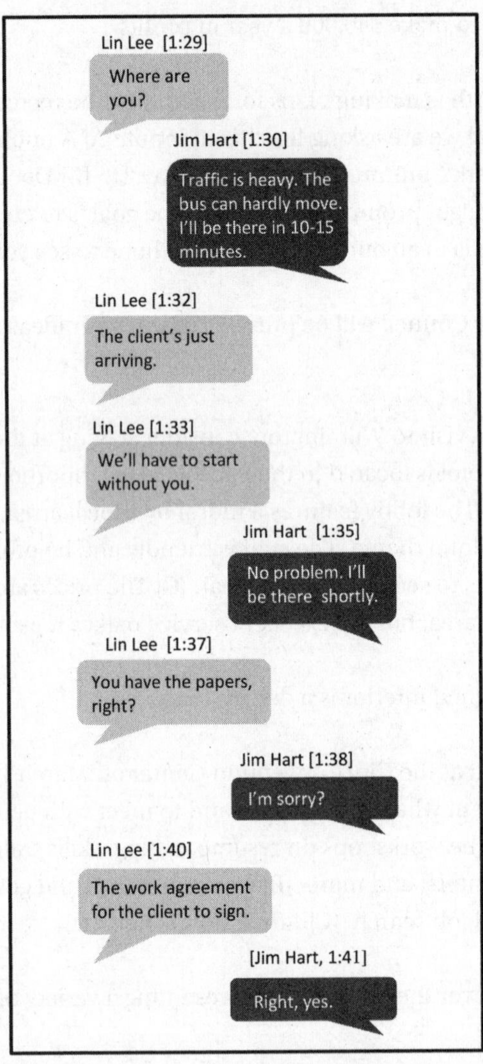

Lin Lee [1:29]
Where are you?
Jim Hart [1:30]
Traffic is heavy. The bus can hardly move. I'll be there in 10-15 minutes.
Lin Lee [1:32]
The client's just arriving.
Lin Lee [1:33]
We'll have to start without you.
Jim Hart [1:35]
No problem. I'll be there shortly.
Lin Lee [1:37]
You have the papers, right?
Jim Hart [1:38]
I'm sorry?
Lin Lee [1:40]
The work agreement for the client to sign.
[Jim Hart, 1:41]
Right, yes.

1. Why is Jim Hart late?

   (A) He missed the bus.  
   (B) His bus is slow.
   (C) His client canceled.
   (D) He forgot about the meeting.

2. What does Jim Hart mean when he writes, "I'm sorry?"

   (A) He lost the papers.  
   (B) He wants to apologize to the client.
   (C) He doesn't understand Lin Lee's text message.
   (D) He wishes he could get there more quickly.

Questions 3–5 refer to the following article.

Restaurateurs, like other business owners, are constantly seeking ways to expand their clientele and keep their restaurants filled. [1] Various types of advertising, networking, and discounts and special offers are all tried-and-true ways of attracting more business. Recently, many restaurant owners have had great success with offering cooking classes.

Customers are willing to pay to eat food prepared in your restaurant. They are also willing, it turns out, to pay to learn to prepare the meal themselves. [2] Cooking classes are most successful when they offer the opportunity to learn something unique. Classes might focus on demonstrating a specialized cooking technique or showing ways to use seasonal ingredients. [3] Classes that explain how to prepare some unusual regional dish are the ones that tend to fill up most quickly.

Cooking classes can be seen as a side line, but they are also an effective means of advertising your business. [4] Organizing cooking classes takes a little extra effort, but the costs are low and the return can be quite high.

3. What is this passage mainly about?

(A) How to organize a cooking class
(B) The costs of running a restaurant
(C) A way for restaurants to increase business
(D) Different methods of attracting customers

Ⓐ Ⓑ Ⓒ Ⓓ

4. Which cooking classes are most popular?

(A) The ones that cost the least
(B) The ones about regional cooking
(C) The ones that use seasonal ingredients
(D) The ones that explain special techniques

Ⓐ Ⓑ Ⓒ Ⓓ

5. In which of the following positions marked [1], [2], [3], and [4] does the following sentence best belong?

"Cooking class participants usually become loyal customers who recommend your restaurant to others."

(A) [1]
(B) [2]
(C) [3]
(D) [4]

Ⓐ Ⓑ Ⓒ Ⓓ

Questions 6–10 refer to the following flyer, memo, and e-mail.

Business Training Institute
Business Workshop Series
Spring Session
Sign up now for one or more of these exciting workshops.

Internet Marketing *Mondays, 3–5 pm* Learn how to use your website to attract more visitors and get more customers for your business.	**Website Design** *Mondays and Wednesdays, 2–4 pm* Learn how to design an attractive website that is easy to navigate.
Marketing through Social Media *Wednesdays, 2–4 pm* Learn how to use social media to promote your business.	**Accounting Software** *Thursdays, 3–5 pm* An introduction to accounting software that will streamline your financial record-keeping.

Fees: $250 (class meets 1x/week)
$450 (class meets 2x/week)

Registration opens April 26–May 7.
Spring session begins week of May 10.

The Markham Company
MEMO

From: Harry Roberts
To: All Staff
Re: Workshops

The Business Training Institute (BTI) is offering a series of workshops that may be of interest to many of you. The institute has an excellent reputation, and it is also conveniently located just five blocks from here. You can get professional development credits for any of the workshops on the spring schedule. In addition, you will be allowed paid time off to attend these workshops and we, as your employer, will pay the tuition in full. Please check with your supervisor before registering to make sure the class schedule is compatible with your work duties.

To: Jon Shore
From: Marissa Tompkins
Date: April 28
Subj: Re: workshops

Jon,

I fully support your interest in taking a workshop at BTI. I think any of the ones you mentioned—Internet Marketing, Website Design, Social Media—would be useful to you in your work here. Just remember that I need you here every Monday afternoon for our weekly department meetings. Otherwise, you are free to choose whichever workshop you prefer. Let me just add that you have been doing very well in this department since you started here last year. Just keep doing what you're doing, and you will go far.

Marissa

See page 265 for the Answer Key and pages 269–270 for the Explanatory Answers for new TOEIC practice Part 7.

6. Why did Harry Roberts write the memo?
   (A) To find out if there is interest in BTI
   (B) To advertise the workshops at BTI
   (C) To inform staff of an opportunity
   (D) To remind staff of a requirement

   Ⓐ Ⓑ Ⓒ Ⓓ

7. Who is Marissa Tompkins?
   (A) Jon's teacher
   (B) Jon's assistant
   (C) Jon's co-worker
   (D) Jon's supervisor

   Ⓐ Ⓑ Ⓒ Ⓓ

8. Which workshop will Jon probably take?
   (A) Internet Marketing
   (B) Website Design
   (C) Marketing through Social Media
   (D) Accounting Software

   Ⓐ Ⓑ Ⓒ Ⓓ

9. How much will Jon pay for the workshop?
   (A) $0
   (B) $200
   (C) $250
   (D) $450

   Ⓐ Ⓑ Ⓒ Ⓓ

10. In the e-mail, the word *keep* in line 8 is closest in meaning to
    (A) delay
    (B) continue
    (C) store
    (D) hold

    Ⓐ Ⓑ Ⓒ Ⓓ

Strategy Summary

Strategies to Improve Your Reading Score

The following strategies are a review of those presented in this Reading Review chapter. The more strategies you can use while reading English, the more you will be able to understand what you read.

Parts 5 and 6

- **Recognize the different parts of speech**
- **Recognize the agreement of person, number, and tense**
- **Recognize different verb forms**
- **Recognize different adjective and adverb forms**
- **Recognize singular and plural nouns**
- **Recognize different kinds of clauses**

Part 7

- **Know how to read the types of passages found on the TOEIC**
- **Know the types of reading comprehension questions found on the TOEIC**
- **Know how to use PSRA:**
  - **Predict what the passage will be about**
  - **Scan the passage and answer options for key words**
  - **Read the passage quickly**
  - **Answer the questions**

ANSWER SHEET
Reading Mini-Test

Part 5: Incomplete Sentences

1. Ⓐ Ⓑ Ⓒ Ⓓ	6. Ⓐ Ⓑ Ⓒ Ⓓ	11. Ⓐ Ⓑ Ⓒ Ⓓ	16. Ⓐ Ⓑ Ⓒ Ⓓ
2. Ⓐ Ⓑ Ⓒ Ⓓ	7. Ⓐ Ⓑ Ⓒ Ⓓ	12. Ⓐ Ⓑ Ⓒ Ⓓ	17. Ⓐ Ⓑ Ⓒ Ⓓ
3. Ⓐ Ⓑ Ⓒ Ⓓ	8. Ⓐ Ⓑ Ⓒ Ⓓ	13. Ⓐ Ⓑ Ⓒ Ⓓ	18. Ⓐ Ⓑ Ⓒ Ⓓ
4. Ⓐ Ⓑ Ⓒ Ⓓ	9. Ⓐ Ⓑ Ⓒ Ⓓ	14. Ⓐ Ⓑ Ⓒ Ⓓ	19. Ⓐ Ⓑ Ⓒ Ⓓ
5. Ⓐ Ⓑ Ⓒ Ⓓ	10. Ⓐ Ⓑ Ⓒ Ⓓ	15. Ⓐ Ⓑ Ⓒ Ⓓ	20. Ⓐ Ⓑ Ⓒ Ⓓ

Part 6: Text Completion

21. Ⓐ Ⓑ Ⓒ Ⓓ	23. Ⓐ Ⓑ Ⓒ Ⓓ	25. Ⓐ Ⓑ Ⓒ Ⓓ
22. Ⓐ Ⓑ Ⓒ Ⓓ	24. Ⓐ Ⓑ Ⓒ Ⓓ	26. Ⓐ Ⓑ Ⓒ Ⓓ

Part 7: Reading Comprehension

27. Ⓐ Ⓑ Ⓒ Ⓓ	40. Ⓐ Ⓑ Ⓒ Ⓓ	53. Ⓐ Ⓑ Ⓒ Ⓓ	66. Ⓐ Ⓑ Ⓒ Ⓓ
28. Ⓐ Ⓑ Ⓒ Ⓓ	41. Ⓐ Ⓑ Ⓒ Ⓓ	54. Ⓐ Ⓑ Ⓒ Ⓓ	67. Ⓐ Ⓑ Ⓒ Ⓓ
29. Ⓐ Ⓑ Ⓒ Ⓓ	42. Ⓐ Ⓑ Ⓒ Ⓓ	55. Ⓐ Ⓑ Ⓒ Ⓓ	68. Ⓐ Ⓑ Ⓒ Ⓓ
30. Ⓐ Ⓑ Ⓒ Ⓓ	43. Ⓐ Ⓑ Ⓒ Ⓓ	56. Ⓐ Ⓑ Ⓒ Ⓓ	69. Ⓐ Ⓑ Ⓒ Ⓓ
31. Ⓐ Ⓑ Ⓒ Ⓓ	44. Ⓐ Ⓑ Ⓒ Ⓓ	57. Ⓐ Ⓑ Ⓒ Ⓓ	70. Ⓐ Ⓑ Ⓒ Ⓓ
32. Ⓐ Ⓑ Ⓒ Ⓓ	45. Ⓐ Ⓑ Ⓒ Ⓓ	58. Ⓐ Ⓑ Ⓒ Ⓓ	71. Ⓐ Ⓑ Ⓒ Ⓓ
33. Ⓐ Ⓑ Ⓒ Ⓓ	46. Ⓐ Ⓑ Ⓒ Ⓓ	59. Ⓐ Ⓑ Ⓒ Ⓓ	72. Ⓐ Ⓑ Ⓒ Ⓓ
34. Ⓐ Ⓑ Ⓒ Ⓓ	47. Ⓐ Ⓑ Ⓒ Ⓓ	60. Ⓐ Ⓑ Ⓒ Ⓓ	73. Ⓐ Ⓑ Ⓒ Ⓓ
35. Ⓐ Ⓑ Ⓒ Ⓓ	48. Ⓐ Ⓑ Ⓒ Ⓓ	61. Ⓐ Ⓑ Ⓒ Ⓓ	74. Ⓐ Ⓑ Ⓒ Ⓓ
36. Ⓐ Ⓑ Ⓒ Ⓓ	49. Ⓐ Ⓑ Ⓒ Ⓓ	62. Ⓐ Ⓑ Ⓒ Ⓓ	75. Ⓐ Ⓑ Ⓒ Ⓓ
37. Ⓐ Ⓑ Ⓒ Ⓓ	50. Ⓐ Ⓑ Ⓒ Ⓓ	63. Ⓐ Ⓑ Ⓒ Ⓓ	76. Ⓐ Ⓑ Ⓒ Ⓓ
38. Ⓐ Ⓑ Ⓒ Ⓓ	51. Ⓐ Ⓑ Ⓒ Ⓓ	64. Ⓐ Ⓑ Ⓒ Ⓓ	
39. Ⓐ Ⓑ Ⓒ Ⓓ	52. Ⓐ Ⓑ Ⓒ Ⓓ	65. Ⓐ Ⓑ Ⓒ Ⓓ	

For the Mini-Test for New TOEIC Reading go to page 243.

MINI-TEST FOR READING

Part 5: Incomplete Sentences

TIP

See page 253 for the Answer Key and page 260 for the Explanatory Answers for this Mini-Test.

Directions: You will see a sentence with a missing word. Four possible answers follow the sentence. Choose the best answer to the question and fill in the corresponding oval on your answer sheet.

1. The pool and the fitness room ________ both available to hotel guests at no extra charge.

   (A) am
   (B) is
   (C) are
   (D) be

2. If you want your equipment to work, first attach this cable ________ the computer.

   (A) with
   (B) into
   (C) in
   (D) to

3. We won't be able to sell this product if we don't price it ________.

   (A) competitively
   (B) competitive
   (C) competition
   (D) competitor

4. Nobody expected the ________ to go on for as long as it did.

   (A) presenting
   (B) presented
   (C) present
   (D) presentation

5. Salaries must be ________ if we are to remain competitive.

   (A) ascended
   (B) increased
   (C) escalated
   (D) risen

6. We drove to the site in an open jeep ________ it was raining.

   (A) although
   (B) since
   (C) because
   (D) with

7. Since the meeting is scheduled to begin ________ noon, we will provide sandwiches and snacks for the attendees.

   (A) on
   (B) to
   (C) in
   (D) at

8. According to our records, the package was ________ to your Los Angeles address.

   (A) send
   (B) been sent
   (C) sent
   (D) sending

9. I'll show you the report when I ________ you next week.

   (A) see
   (B) saw
   (C) have seen
   (D) will see

10. Their office is located on the next block ________ the post office and the bank.

   (A) among
   (B) outside
   (C) between
   (D) through

11. All the employees at this company ________ an annual bonus.

(A) receive
(B) receives
(C) has received
(D) is receiving

12. After much deliberation, we finally decided to hold the annual conference ________ Texas.

(A) over
(B) off
(C) in
(D) beside

13. ________ the bad weather made driving difficult, few people showed up at the office yesterday.

(A) Although
(B) During
(C) Since
(D) Until

14. Immigration forms must ________ be stamped before leaving the customs area.

(A) once
(B) always
(C) still
(D) rarely

15. Neither the bus ________ the subway will get you to the airport on time.

(A) or
(B) and
(C) but
(D) nor

16. If the consultant ________ that we should hire more staff, Helen wouldn't be working here now.

(A) didn't recommend
(B) doesn't recommend
(C) hadn't recommended
(D) wasn't recommending

17. If you ________ how to use a computer, consult the manual.

(A) won't understand
(B) don't understand
(C) understood
(D) not understanding

18. If you aren't able to meet the deadline, your supervisor may make you ________ over the weekend.

(A) works
(B) work
(C) to work
(D) working

19. Although relatively young, Rheingold Consultants ________ fast becoming one of the most successful companies in the industry.

(A) were
(B) have
(C) is
(D) are

20. A friend ________ me his car while mine was at the mechanic's.

(A) borrowed
(B) belonged
(C) owed
(D) lent

Part 6: Text Completion

Directions: You will see two passages each with three blanks. Under each blank are four answer options. Choose the word or phrase that best completes the sentence.

Questions 21–23 refer to the following memorandum.

To: Edouard Fleurat
From: Maria Rotini
Subject: Client Visit

Ed,

Olga Kovacs, ____________ represents one of our most important clients,

21. (A) who
(B) whom
(C) whose
(D) which

will visit our city next week. We want to make sure she gets the best treatment possible while she is here. She will be staying at the Grand Hotel, not too far from our office. She plans ____________ our office first thing Monday morning.

22. (A) visit
(B) visits
(C) visiting
(D) to visit

Please send ____________ to her hotel by 7:30 on Monday so that she

23. (A) a greeting
(B) directions
(C) a limousine
(D) instructions

doesn't have to look for a cab. You should ride with her and make sure that she has everything she needs.

Thanks,

Maria

Questions 24–26 refer to the following newspaper article.

The Auckland Quarterly
Life Section-Health

March 1, 20—

Is Smoking the Latest Trend?

Smoking is becoming more popular among young people, and they are starting to smoke at earlier ages than before. ______ there

24. (A) Although
(B) Because
(C) When
(D) Since

have been many campaigns to discourage teenagers from smoking, more than 40% of teens say they have tried it at least once. Over 30% of these say they tried their first cigarette before the age of fourteen. This is not ______ news for public health officials, teachers,and parents.

25. (A) encourage
(B) encouraged
(C) encouraging
(D) encouragement

"We need to develop better anti-smoking campaigns that are directed at teenagers," said Dr. Howard MacDonald, director of the Center for Healthy Living. "Starting a habit like smoking during ______

26. (A) adversity
(B) addiction
(C) advertising
(D) adolescence

can mean serious health problems for the rest of one's life," he added.

Part 7: Reading Comprehension

Directions: Read the passages below and choose the one best answer, (A), (B), (C), or (D), to each question. Answer all questions following the passage based on what is *stated* or *implied* in that passage.

Questions 27–28 refer to the following advertisement.

27. What is being offered?
    (A) Translation services
    (B) Office supplies
    (C) Vacations to Africa
    (D) Books in many languages

28. What feature of the company is mentioned in this advertisement?
    (A) Its multilingual staff
    (B) Its complete service
    (C) Its fax number
    (D) Its prices

Questions 29–32 refer to the following purchase order.

PURCHASE ORDER

Ship Prepaid • Add all delivery charges on invoice

TECH 2000
44 Sankey Street
Warrington, Cheshire
WA 1 1SG ENGLAND

Tel: 0925 412 555
Fax: 0925 412 559

Vendor:
Comtex
65-67 Lowgate Hull
HU 1 1HP
England
Tel: 482-593-678
Fax: 482-593-689

Ship To: Marc Greenspan
Purchasing Department
Address above

Reference: Purchase Order 03-687-47X
Date: 12 June 20–

Invoice To: Marcia Goodall
Accounting Department
Address above

Delivery Date: ASAP

Item	Model Number	Quantity	Unit Cost	Total Cost
C180 Hard drive	M4569A	10	£675.00	£6750.00
C-52 Serial cable	C323	20	£ 12.50	£ 250.00
SE-Ethernet card	NET 0422	10	£ 50.00	£ 500.00
Sub-total				£7500.00
Shipping/Handling 10%				£ 750.00
TOTAL				£8250.00

Prepared by: Marc Greenspan
Date: 12 June 20–

cc: Accounting Department; Purchasing Department; Receiving Department

29. Who will be billed for the purchase?

(A) The Purchasing Department, TECH 2000
(B) The Accounting Department, TECH 2000
(C) The Purchasing Department, Comtex
(D) The Shipping Department, Comtex

30. Who sells hard drives and serial cables?

(A) Comtex
(B) TECH 2000
(C) Marc Greenspan
(D) Marcia Goodall

31. If the Ethernet cards were NOT ordered, what would be the subtotal?

(A) £7000
(B) £7500
(C) £7700
(D) £8250

32. Which department does NOT get a copy of the purchase order?

(A) Accounting
(B) Purchasing
(C) Receiving
(D) Personnel

Questions 33–34 refer to the following report.

> Midsize companies that want to increase their sales in international markets cannot rely on exporting their goods—not if they want to grow substantially. Customers want to be close to their suppliers. They want to provide input on design, engineering, and quality control. Also, local governments want jobs created for their citizens. This means that international companies will have to establish a manufacturing operation near their customers.

33. If international companies want to grow, they will need to

(A) improve quality control
(B) export more goods
(C) build factories close to their customers
(D) design better products

34. Who wants to provide input on design?

(A) Design consultants
(B) Customers
(C) Suppliers
(D) Engineers

Questions 35–36 refer to the following letter.

HAMBURG PAPER COMPANY
Postfach 806010
Rungerdamm 2
2050 Hamburg 80
Germany

March 10, 20–

Mr. Frank Knockaert
Crestco Inc.
26 Avenue Marnix
B-1000 Brussels
Belgium

Dear Mr. Knockaert:

In response to your letter of February 23, we apologize for the error in your shipment. We are sending immediately the additional 1000 cases of facsimile paper, model P-345X, that were not included in the shipment.

We value our relationship with your company, and we regret the inconvenience the incomplete shipment may have caused you. You can be assured that this will not happen in the future.

Sincerely yours,

Gertrude Rombach

Gertrude Rombach
Manager, Order Department

35. What is the purpose of this letter?

(A) To complain
(B) To place an order
(C) To apologize
(D) To introduce services

36. The first shipment

(A) was not complete
(B) arrived late
(C) was damaged
(D) was sent to the wrong address

Questions 37–39 refer to the following fax.

International Cargo
Place de la Concorde
45040 Orleans Cedex 1
France
Tel: (33) - 387-87445
Fax: (33) - 387-87454

FAX TRANSMISSION

To: Markus Tarasov
P.O. Box 10382 Manama, Bahrain
Fax: 973 - 213324
Tel: 973 - 213300

From: Marie Martin
Sales Representative

Date: April 18,20–

Pages: This

Ref: Your fax of April 18,20–

Messages:

Your order was received this morning and is being processed. You should expect delivery by the end of the week or at the very latest on Monday. We will fax exact time of arrival before Friday.

37. When was the order received?

(A) The end of the week
(B) Yesterday
(C) Today
(D) Friday

38. How will Ms. Martin communicate the delivery time?

(A) By phone
(B) By fax
(C) By letter
(D) By messenger

39. If the order does NOT arrive by Friday, when will it arrive?

(A) At the end of the week
(B) At the first of the month
(C) On Monday
(D) On the following Friday

Questions 40–43 refer to the following e-mail.

From: Marcello Palombo [marcello_palom@allengineering.com]

To: J. Wilson[jacob_wilson@allengineering.com]

Sent: Tuesday, October 23, 20— 4:12 P.M.

Subject: Elena Kuzikov, Ukrainian engineer

Dr. Elena Kuzikov will be visiting our company on Tuesday, March 23rd. I would like you to prepare a program for her. She will arrive in the morning before noon. Please start with lunch in the cafeteria and then show her your department. Like you, she has done research on the effects of earthquakes on bridge construction.

40. What kind of engineer is the Ukrainian?

(A) Electrical
(B) Nuclear
(C) Mechanical
(D) Railroad

41. Who will be the visitor's guide?

(A) J. Wilson
(B) Elena Kuzikov
(C) Marcello Palombo
(D) No one

42. When will she arrive?

(A) Before 12:00
(B) At noon
(C) After lunch
(D) In the evening

43. What is her chief area of interest?

(A) Designing bridges
(B) Eating lunch
(C) Touring the department
(D) Visiting

Questions 44–46 refer to the following index.

Newspaper Index

Amex Stocks	B-11
Arts	C-1
Bond Data	B-16
Commodities	B-4
World Stock Index	B-15
Economy	A-5
Editorials	A-10
Film	C-3
Foreign Exchange	B-17
International News	A-1
Legal Issues	A-6
Technology	C-4
World Markets	B-1

44. What type of features would more likely be found in the B section?

(A) Sports scores
(B) Movie reviews
(C) Market forecasts
(D) Obituaries

45. The editor's opinions are found on

(A) A-1
(B) B-4
(C) C-1
(D) A-10

46. Movie reviews would be found on

(A) B-11
(B) C-1
(C) C-3
(D) A-6

Questions 47–49 refer to the following chart.

- President
  - VP Operation
    - Mgr. Accounting
      - Payroll Clerk
    - Mgr. Personnel
    - Mgr. Shipping
  - VP Marketing
    - Mgr. Domestic
      - East staff
      - West staff
    - Mgr. Int'l
      - Europe staff
      - Pacific Rim staff
      - Latin America staff
  - VP Sales
    - Mgr. Domestic
      - East staff
      - West staff
    - Mgr. Int'l
      - Europe staff
      - Pacific Rim staff
      - Latin America staff

47. The payroll clerk reports directly to

(A) the Manager of Personnel
(B) the Vice President of Operations
(C) the Manager of Accounting
(D) the President

48. Which divisions have similar staffing patterns?

(A) Accounting and Personnel
(B) Operations and Marketing
(C) Marketing and Sales
(D) Sales and Shipping

49. The Vice President of Sales supervises

(A) the International Manager for Sales
(B) the President
(C) the Personnel Manager
(D) the Accounting Manager

Questions 50–51 refer to the following graph.

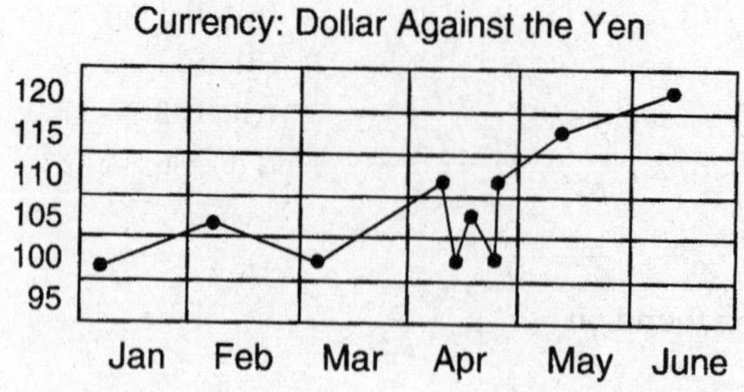

Currency: Dollar Against the Yen

120
115
110
105
100
95

Jan Feb Mar Apr May June

50. This graph shows

(A) a six-month comparison of dollar-yen conversion rates
(B) the price of Japanese commodities
(C) the value of the dollar against all currencies
(D) an annual highlight of currency rates

51. In what month were there several fluctuations?

(A) January
(B) February
(C) April
(D) June

Questions 52–53 refer to the following announcement.

> Advanced Communication Systems, Inc., of San Francisco, California, won a $250,000 contract from the Space and Naval Warfare Systems Group, Washington, D.C., for technical and management support services. The three-month contract will begin in June.

52. Where is the contractor located?

(A) Washington, D.C.
(B) San Francisco, California
(C) On the sea
(D) In space

53. About when will the contract end?

(A) January
(B) June
(C) September
(D) December

Questions 54–55 refer to the following notice in a computer manual.

> International Communication reserves the right to make improvements in the hardware and software described in this manual at any time and without notice. The information in this manual may also be revised to reflect changes in the described product without obligation to notify any person of such changes.

54. This notice gives the company the right

(A) to make changes without notice
(B) to request a refund
(C) to return software that doesn't work
(D) to start a new company

55. Where would this notice most likely be found?

(A) On an appliance warranty card
(B) In a computer manual
(C) On an airline ticket
(D) In a stock offering prospectus

Questions 56–60 refer to the following newspaper article.

September 1, Zurich: RADD, A.G., the Swiss chemical company purchased the European polypropylene business of Royal Chemical Industries, P.L.C., of Britain. No price was disclosed, but RCI said the deal represented 1 to 2 percent of its net assets and would be paid in cash. Based on net assets, the price would be between $100 million and $160 million. The acquisition includes RCI production plants in England, Denmark, Norway, and Poland. The plants alone are valued at $60 million to $80 million. Polypropylene, a tough, flexible plastic, has uses that range from rope fibers to bottles.

56. RADD is probably located in

(A) England
(B) Switzerland
(C) Denmark
(D) Poland

57. According to the article, what is used to make rope fibers?

(A) Hemp
(B) Cotton
(C) Steel
(D) Polypropylene

58. How much will RADD pay for RCI?

(A) $80 million
(B) $100 million
(C) Between $100 and $160 million
(D) Between $60 and $80 million

59. Where is RCI's head office?

(A) Norway
(B) Denmark
(C) Britain
(D) Poland

60. The word *disclosed* in line 6 is closest in meaning to

(A) announced
(B) counted
(C) agreed on
(D) calculated

Questions 61–62 refer to the following magazine article.

> Hollywood is no longer just in California. Today the entertainment industry is finding new homes in Europe, Latin America, and Asia. The American media and communications industries are looking all over the globe for new opportunities. Although many companies are investing in the fast-growing European media industry, many industry executives believe the biggest long-term opportunity is in China and other countries in Southeast Asia. The potential market is huge—over 310 million people in the European community, but over 650 million in the Pacific Rim. ■

61. Which of the following is the main topic of the article?

    (A) The media industry is expanding.
    (B) China is a big market today.
    (C) New homes are being built in Europe.
    (D) There are many opportunities in Hollywood.

62. According to the article, what does "Hollywood" represent?

    (A) All executives
    (B) American enterprise
    (C) The media industry
    (D) Big markets

Questions 63–64 refer to the following schedule.

Meeting: Conference Room C

8:30	Coffee
9:00	Opening Remarks
9:15	Introductions
9:30	Presentations
	Accounting
	Personnel
	Marketing
10:30	**BREAK**
10:45	Presentations
	CEO
	Chairman of the Board
11:30	Questions and Answers
12:00	Adjourn

63. Why was this schedule prepared?

(A) To make everyone pay attention
(B) To limit the number of coffee breaks
(C) To introduce the speakers
(D) To establish an agenda for the meeting

64. What immediately follows the presentations by the senior officers?

(A) A break
(B) Introductions
(C) A question-and-answer period
(D) Lunch

Questions 65–66 refer to the following timeline.

	Jan	Feb	Mar	Apr	May	June	July	Aug	Sept
Review budget	■								
Submit project proposal		■							
Develop prototype			■	■					
Test prototype					■	■	■		
Develop marketing plan						■	■	■	
Start production								■	
Ship to distributors									■

65. This timeline shows

(A) the number of man-hours involved in a project
(B) the stages in developing a product
(C) how long it takes to make money
(D) the changes in the seasons

66. It can be inferred that

(A) the cost will be too high
(B) the marketing plan will be more important than testing
(C) the project will be approved in February
(D) testing will slow down production

Questions 67–71 refer to the following schedule and e-mail.

Sunday 11	Monday 12	Tuesday 13	Wednesday 14	Thursday 15	Friday 16	Saturday 17
	8:15 doctor appt. 3:00 golf with Alicia	9:30 planning meeting	9:00–11:00 dept. meeting 11:30 dentist appt.	4:00 phone conference with Toronto office	8:30 train to Chicago 12:30 lunch meeting with Chicago staff	10:00 golf with Fred

To: Joe Rosen
From: Alicia Lima
Date: March 8
Subject: Golf

Hi Joe,

I'm sorry I can't make our golf date next week. It turns out I have a department meeting that starts an hour before our game is scheduled, and I'm sure it won't end before 5:00. Could we play the following day, same time, same place? Let me know, and I'll call the club to reserve the starting time.

I also wanted to let you know that Mr. Santos from our San Francisco office will be in town starting next Tuesday. I know you were eager to meet with him. Are you free Wednesday morning? If not, Thursday or Friday morning will do. I know you plan to leave for Chicago sometime Friday, but I hope you can find some time to meet with Mr. Santos before then.

Are you planning to meet Fred for golf in Chicago? If you see him, tell him I haven't forgotten that he owes me a game!

See you next week,
Alicia

67. When is Joe's dentist appointment?

(A) Monday
(B) Tuesday
(C) Wednesday
(D) Thursday

68. What will Joe do on Thursday afternoon?

(A) Go to Toronto
(B) Talk on the telephone
(C) Have a lunch meeting
(D) Go to the doctor

69. What time does Alicia's department meeting begin?

(A) 9:00
(B) 2:00
(C) 3:00
(D) 5:00

70. What day does Alicia want to play golf with Joe?

(A) Sunday
(B) Monday
(C) Tuesday
(D) Saturday

71. What will Joe probably do Thursday morning?

(A) Meet with Mr. Santos
(B) Nothing
(C) Leave for Chicago
(D) Play golf with Fred

Questions 72–76 refer to the following notice and memo.

Notice to tenants of South Ridge Office Complex   August 25, 20—

Reconstruction of the parking garage will begin at the end of next month and is scheduled to last three months. During this time there will be no parking for anyone in the building garage. The city has temporarily designated the parking spaces on the streets surrounding our building as all-day parking spaces for our use. A special pass is required to use these spaces. Since the number of parking spaces is limited, we will distribute four passes to each office in this building. Building tenants are asked to encourage their employees to use public transportation until the garage reconstruction is completed. There are also two public parking garages within five blocks of here where parking spaces can be rented on a daily, weekly, or monthly basis. Thank you for your cooperation.

South Ridge Office Complex Building Management Team

Memo

Parrot Communications, Inc.

To: All Office Personnel
From: Dena Degenaro
Office Manager
Date: August 28, 20—
Re: Parking

I am sure you have all seen the recent notice about the parking garage reconstruction by now. Since we have five times as many employees as allotted parking passes, we will reserve the parking passes for clients and ask our employees to make alternative plans. For your convenience, we have obtained subway passes that are valid for the entire amount of time that the garage reconstruction will last. They are available at a 25% discount to all Parrot Communications employees. Please see me before the end of this week if you are interested in getting one. Thank you.

72. When will the parking garage reconstruction begin?

(A) This week
(B) Next month
(C) In three months
(D) In August

73. How many employees work for Parrot Communications, Inc.?

(A) Four
(B) Five
(C) Twenty
(D) Twenty-five

74. Who can park next to the building during the garage reconstruction?

(A) Parrot Communications clients
(B) Parrot Communications employees
(C) All South Ridge tenants
(D) Dena Degenaro

75. Who should Parrot Communications employees contact to get a subway pass?

(A) The city manager
(B) Their office manager
(C) The building manager
(D) The subway station manager

76. How long are the subway passes valid?

(A) One week
(B) Three weeks
(C) One month
(D) Three months

ANSWER SHEET
New TOEIC
Reading Mini-Test

Part 5: Incomplete Sentences

1. Ⓐ Ⓑ Ⓒ Ⓓ
2. Ⓐ Ⓑ Ⓒ Ⓓ
3. Ⓐ Ⓑ Ⓒ Ⓓ
4. Ⓐ Ⓑ Ⓒ Ⓓ
5. Ⓐ Ⓑ Ⓒ Ⓓ
6. Ⓐ Ⓑ Ⓒ Ⓓ
7. Ⓐ Ⓑ Ⓒ Ⓓ
8. Ⓐ Ⓑ Ⓒ Ⓓ
9. Ⓐ Ⓑ Ⓒ Ⓓ
10. Ⓐ Ⓑ Ⓒ Ⓓ
11. Ⓐ Ⓑ Ⓒ Ⓓ
12. Ⓐ Ⓑ Ⓒ Ⓓ
13. Ⓐ Ⓑ Ⓒ Ⓓ
14. Ⓐ Ⓑ Ⓒ Ⓓ
15. Ⓐ Ⓑ Ⓒ Ⓓ

Part 6: Text Completion

16. Ⓐ Ⓑ Ⓒ Ⓓ
17. Ⓐ Ⓑ Ⓒ Ⓓ
18. Ⓐ Ⓑ Ⓒ Ⓓ
19. Ⓐ Ⓑ Ⓒ Ⓓ
20. Ⓐ Ⓑ Ⓒ Ⓓ
21. Ⓐ Ⓑ Ⓒ Ⓓ
22. Ⓐ Ⓑ Ⓒ Ⓓ
23. Ⓐ Ⓑ Ⓒ Ⓓ

Part 7: Reading Comprehension

24. Ⓐ Ⓑ Ⓒ Ⓓ
25. Ⓐ Ⓑ Ⓒ Ⓓ
26. Ⓐ Ⓑ Ⓒ Ⓓ
27. Ⓐ Ⓑ Ⓒ Ⓓ
28. Ⓐ Ⓑ Ⓒ Ⓓ
29. Ⓐ Ⓑ Ⓒ Ⓓ
30. Ⓐ Ⓑ Ⓒ Ⓓ
31. Ⓐ Ⓑ Ⓒ Ⓓ
32. Ⓐ Ⓑ Ⓒ Ⓓ
33. Ⓐ Ⓑ Ⓒ Ⓓ
34. Ⓐ Ⓑ Ⓒ Ⓓ
35. Ⓐ Ⓑ Ⓒ Ⓓ
36. Ⓐ Ⓑ Ⓒ Ⓓ

MINI-TEST FOR NEW TOEIC READING

Part 5: Incomplete Sentences

Directions: You will see a sentence with a missing word. Four possible answers follow the sentence. Choose the best answer to the question and fill in the corresponding oval on your answer sheet.

1. Rice Enterprises _________ some of the most talented design specialists in the field.

   (A) employ
   (B) employs
   (C) employees
   (D) have employed

2. The directors are happy to report that the advertising campaign has been _________ successful.

   (A) huge
   (B) huger
   (C) hugely
   (D) hugeness

3. Procom Industries has announced plans to _________ production by opening up a new manufacturing plant.

   (A) increase
   (B) enlarge
   (C) curtail
   (D) diminish

4. _________ the new restaurant has recently received a lot of attention from the press, business continues to be slow.

   (A) Because
   (B) Therefore
   (C) Although
   (D) Nevertheless

5. All information provided by clients will be kept entirely _________ and will never be shared with anyone outside the office.

   (A) professional
   (B) confidential
   (C) essential
   (D) intact

6. You may use the health club _________ you are employed by this company, but membership eligibility ends if you leave your position.

   (A) in the meantime
   (B) according to
   (C) in order to
   (D) as long as

7. Ms. Yamamoto is in charge of organizing the office party, so please let _________ know if you have any suggestions.

   (A) her
   (B) hers
   (C) she
   (D) herself

8. The sign posted just outside the front door _________ the history and architectural significance of the building.

   (A) recounts
   (B) explains
   (C) instructs
   (D) advises

9. The director had not expected to hear so much __________ to the proposed policy changes.

(A) opposition
(B) opponents
(C) opposing
(D) opposed

10. The manager asked everyone in the office __________ in the time sheets by noon on Friday.

(A) turn
(B) turns
(C) turning
(D) to turn

11. He received a job offer from this company, but we don't know __________ he will accept it or turn it down

(A) either
(B) neither
(C) whether
(D) however

12. The client is considering the offer and will give us a __________ answer by the end of the week.

(A) define
(B) definite
(C) definitely
(D) definition

13. You'll notice that the new accounting system is different __________ the old one in several ways.

(A) to
(B) for
(C) than
(D) from

14. Each table must be __________ cleaned before seating the next group of diners.

(A) thoroughly
(B) permanently
(C) directly
(D) finally

15. If the client isn't completely satisfied with the terms of the contract, some __________ can be made.

(A) introductions
(B) developments
(C) modifications
(D) permissions

Part 6: Text Completion

Directions: You will see four passages, each with three sets of blanks. Under each blank are four options. Choose the word or phrase that best completes the statement.

Questions 16–19 refer to the following flyer.

Stellar Professional Training

The following seminar ____________ in your area on April 10: **Webpage Design**.

16. (A) offers
(B) will offer
(C) will be offered
(D) will be offering

At this all-day seminar for business professionals, interns, and current business students, find out how you can create a webpage that presents your business in the most attractive way. The price ____________ lunch and materials as well as

17. (A) participates
(B) covers
(C) accounts
(D) charges

instruction. Visit us at *www.stellar.com/seminars* to sign up. ____________ ends

18. (A) Register
(B) Registrar
(C) Registered
(D) Registration

March 31. While you are there, take a look at what else we have to offer. ____.

19. (A) Stellar provides staff training, custom webpage design, and more.
(B) You can contact us any time, day or night.
(C) The seminar lasts about seven hours.
(D) Our clients have given our seminars top ratings.

We look forward to seeing you at Stellar!

NEW TOEIC

Questions 20–23 refer to the following flyer.

The Springdale Community Center offers services for all members of the Springdale community. _______ include recreational activities for children, teens, and adults,

20. (A) These
(B) There
(C) Them
(D) That

parenting workshops, arts and crafts classes, a teen drop-in center, and a daycare center. We are _______ looking for volunteers to help out with any of the above-mentioned

21. (A) lately
(B) probably
(C) currently
(D) eventually

programs. Interested people should contact our volunteer _______,

22. (A) coordinate
(B) coordinator
(C) coordinating
(D) coordination

Mabel Rivera (mrivera@commcenter.org), for further information.

_______.

23. (A) Please indicate which program you would like to work in.
(B) All our programs are free for Springdale residents.
(C) The next workshop session begins in one week.
(D) Ms. Rivera is a long-time employee of the community center.

NEW TOEIC

Part 7: Reading Comprehension

Directions: You will see single and multiple reading passages followed by several questions. Each question has four answer choices. Choose the best answer to the question and fill in the corresponding oval on your answer sheet.

Questions 24–25 refer to the following text message chain.

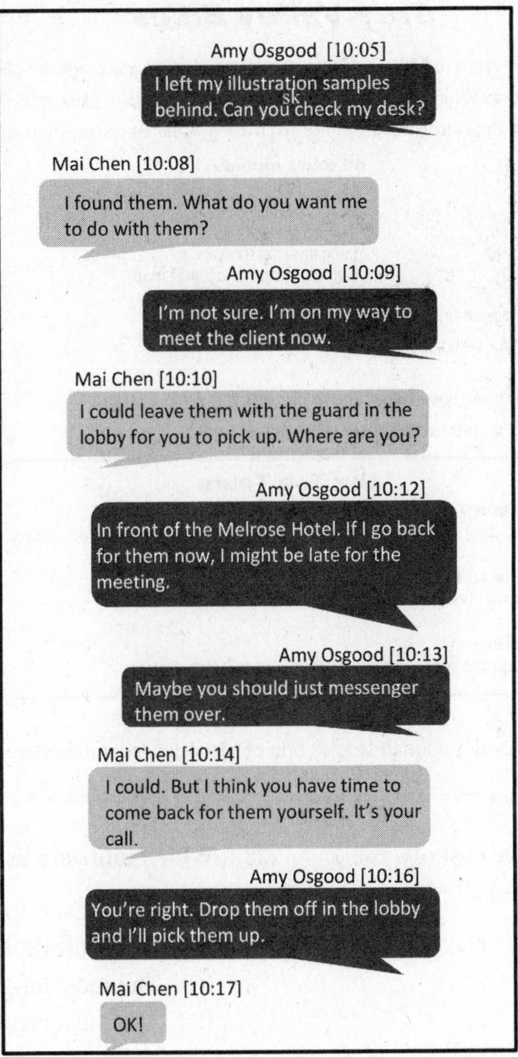

24. What is suggested about Mai Chen?
    (A) She works for Ms. Osgood's client.
    (B) She is Ms. Osgood's assistant.
    (C) She works as a messenger.
    (D) She is at the hotel.

25. What does Mai Chen mean when she writes, "It's your call"?
    (A) Ms. Osgood should phone the client right away.
    (B) Ms. Osgood should make the decision herself.
    (C) Ms. Osgood is responsible for the client.
    (D) Ms. Osgood is the owner of the samples.

NEW TOEIC

Questions 26–28 refer to the following webpage.

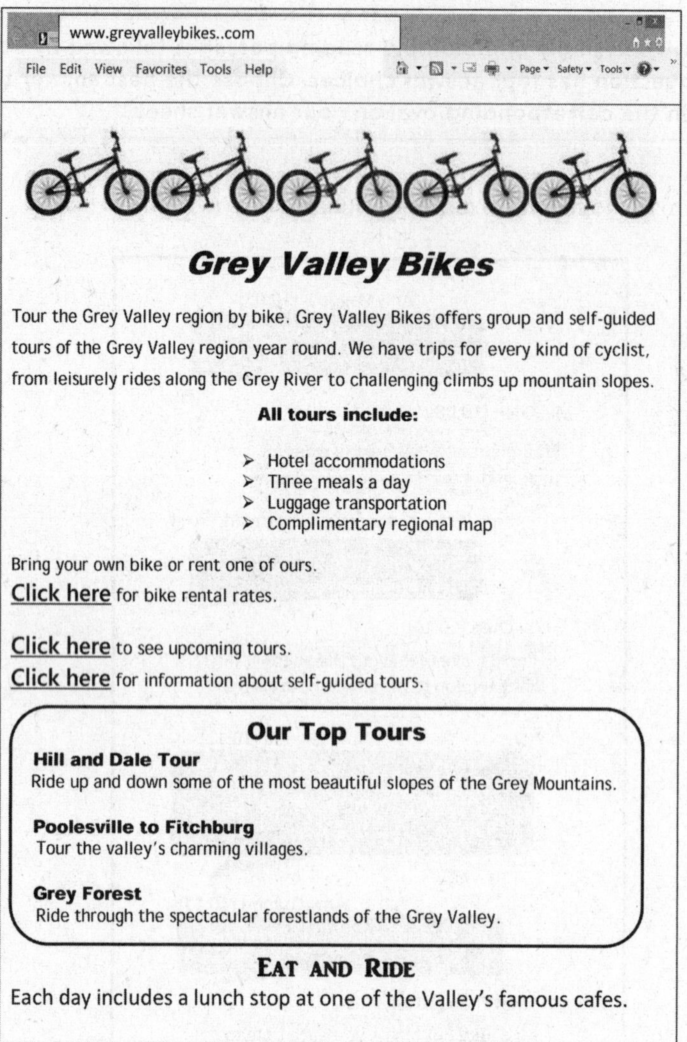
www.greyvalleybikes..com

File Edit View Favorites Tools Help

Grey Valley Bikes

Tour the Grey Valley region by bike. Grey Valley Bikes offers group and self-guided tours of the Grey Valley region year round. We have trips for every kind of cyclist, from leisurely rides along the Grey River to challenging climbs up mountain slopes.

All tours include:

- Hotel accommodations
- Three meals a day
- Luggage transportation
- Complimentary regional map

Bring your own bike or rent one of ours.
Click here for bike rental rates.

Click here to see upcoming tours.
Click here for information about self-guided tours.

Our Top Tours

Hill and Dale Tour
Ride up and down some of the most beautiful slopes of the Grey Mountains.

Poolesville to Fitchburg
Tour the valley's charming villages.

Grey Forest
Ride through the spectacular forestlands of the Grey Valley.

EAT AND RIDE
Each day includes a lunch stop at one of the Valley's famous cafes.

26. What is NOT included in the cost of a tour?

(A) Hotel
(B) Food
(C) Map
(D) Bicycle

27. What is indicated about Grey Valley Bikes tours?

(A) They last a week or more.
(B) They are only for experienced cyclists.
(C) They are for both individuals and groups.
(D) They take place in spring and summer only.

28. Which tours are listed on this webpage?

(A) The most popular
(B) The most difficult
(C) The most lengthy
(D) The most expensive

Questions 29–31 refer to the following online chat discussion.

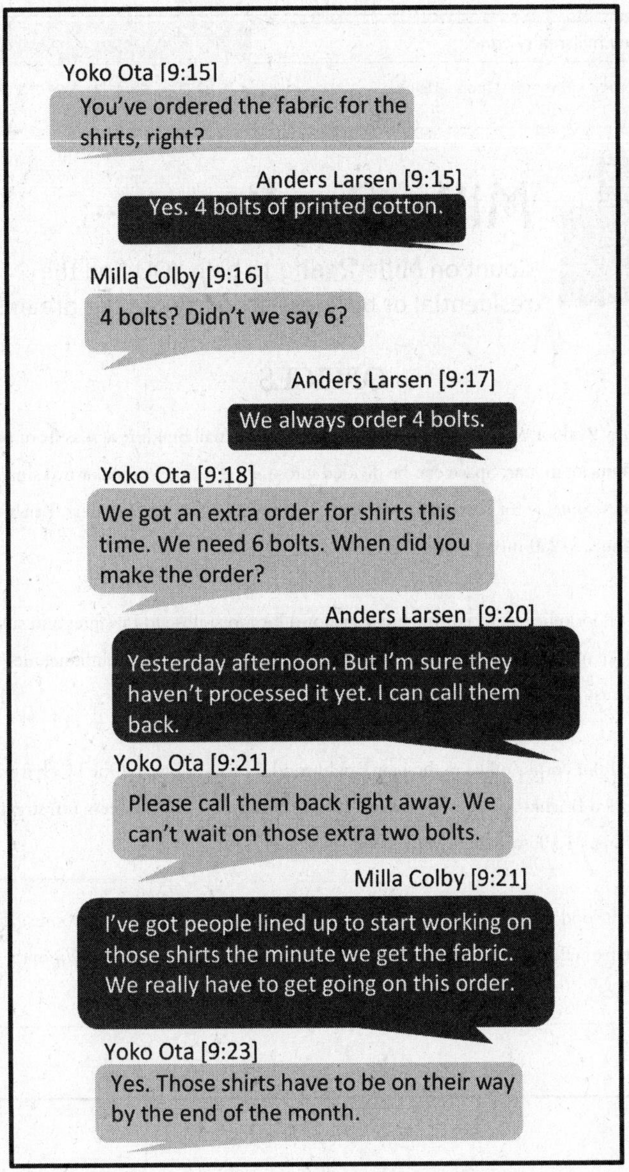

Yoko Ota [9:15]
You've ordered the fabric for the shirts, right?
Anders Larsen [9:15]
Yes. 4 bolts of printed cotton.
Milla Colby [9:16]
4 bolts? Didn't we say 6?
Anders Larsen [9:17]
We always order 4 bolts.
Yoko Ota [9:18]
We got an extra order for shirts this time. We need 6 bolts. When did you make the order?
Anders Larsen [9:20]
Yesterday afternoon. But I'm sure they haven't processed it yet. I can call them back.
Yoko Ota [9:21]
Please call them back right away. We can't wait on those extra two bolts.
Milla Colby [9:21]
I've got people lined up to start working on those shirts the minute we get the fabric. We really have to get going on this order.
Yoko Ota [9:23]
Yes. Those shirts have to be on their way by the end of the month.

29. What kind of business are they involved in?

(A) Clothing manufacturer
(B) Fabric wholesaler
(C) Shipping service
(D) Shirt retailer

30. What does Anders have to do now?

(A) Ship the order
(B) Cancel the order
(C) Add to the order
(D) Process the order

31. What does Yoko mean when she writes at 9:23, "Those shirts have to be on their way"?

(A) The fabric for making shirts has to be available.
(B) The shirts have to be shipped to the customer.
(C) The workers have to start making the shirts.
(D) The designs for the shirts have to be ready.

NEW TOEIC

Questions 32–36 refer to the following webpage, e-mail, and article.

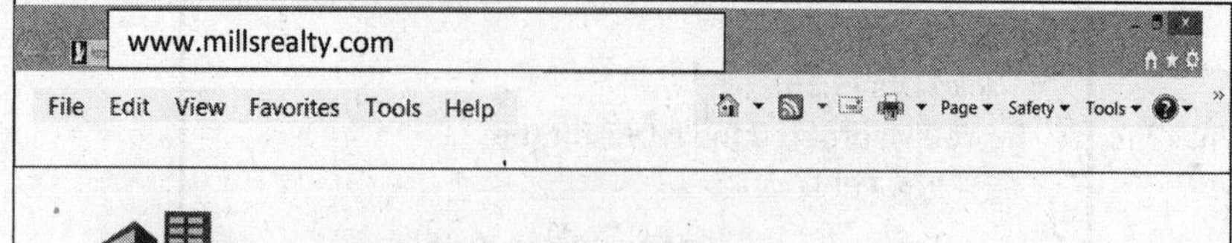

Mills Realty

Count on Mills Realty to help YOU find the residential or business property of your dreams.

OFFICES

1. Sunny 2nd floor office space, recently renovated, in small building across from park. Parking lot in rear. Space can be divided into waiting room + office or two smaller offices. Suitable for lawyers, accountants, therapists, health practitioners. Brightwood location. $1250/month + utilities.

2. First floor office suite, convenient downtown location, close to bus lines and subway. 150 sq. meters. Owner will remodel to suit your needs. $2,050/month includes utilities and customer parking.

3. Top floor corner office in the new Brightwood business district. One block from the planned Brightwood subway station. Three rooms plus small kitchen. On street parking. $1,100/month, includes utilities.

4. Brightwood office, 100 sq. meters, freshly painted and carpeted. Two rooms. Just one mile from the new Brightwood subway station. On street parking. $950/month + utilities.

To: Steve Mills
From: Elsa Roper
Date: July 25
Subject: Seeking office space

Mr. Mills,

I am interested in seeing some offices advertised on your website. I run a small accounting firm and am looking for a space of about 100–125 square meters. Unfortunately, downtown is a bit out of reach for me, but I think the Brightwood neighborhood would be very suitable. Ideally, I'd like a place with its own parking lot, but if it's close enough to the new subway station, that might not be an issue. I'd like to go no higher than $1,000/month on the rent, expecting to pay utilities on top of that. I'd like to see several of your listings this week, if possible. I am busy most mornings, but I am available any day after 1:00 PM. Please let me know when you can show me these properties.

Elsa Roper, CPA

Brightwood: Up and Coming

The new Brightwood business district is fast becoming the city's hottest new neighborhood. As rapidly rising rents are driving business owners out of the popular downtown area, many are turning to much more affordable Brightwood. This neighborhood has become even more appealing since the city announced plans to extend the subway line to its center. The new Brightwood Avenue subway station is scheduled to open early next year. Already, several offices have opened their doors along Brightwood Avenue and two new restaurants catering specifically to office workers have appeared recently, as well. The beautiful Lilac Park area of the neighborhood, with its wide streets and gardens, is also a draw. Look for a new café and several boutiques to be opening there soon.

32. What is NOT true about the advertised downtown office?
   (A) The rent covers electricity and heat.
   (B) It has recently been remodeled.
   (C) It is near public transportation.
   (D) The building has a parking lot.

33. Which advertised office will Ms. Roper probably prefer?
   (A) #1
   (B) #2
   (C) #3
   (D) #4

34. When does Ms. Roper want to look at offices?
   (A) Any afternoon
   (B) Any morning
   (C) Next week
   (D) Today

35. In the article, the word *driving* in line 2, is closest in meaning to
   (A) operating
   (B) traveling
   (C) leading
   (D) forcing

36. What is suggested about the Brightwood neighborhood?
   (A) It is less expensive than downtown.
   (B) The streets are not attractive.
   (C) It has a bad reputation.
   (D) The rents are going up.

ANSWER KEY FOR READING SKILLS

Explanatory Answers can be found beginning on page 254.

Part 5: Incomplete Sentences

Skill 1 Word Families	1. **B**	2. **B**	3. **D**
Skill 2 Similar Meanings	1. **D**	2. **A**	3. **C**
Skill 3 Similar Forms	1. **B**	2. **A**	3. **D**
Skill 4 Subject-Verb Agreement with Prepositional Phrases	1. **D**	2. **A**	3. **C**
Skill 5 Singular and Plural Subjects	1. **C**	2. **A**	3. **D**
Skill 6 Verb Tenses	1. **B**	2. **C**	3. **B**
Skill 7 Prepositions	1. **A**	2. **D**	3. **C**
Skill 8 Prepositions with Verbs and Adjectives	1. **B**	2. **C**	3. **A**
Skill 9 Coordinating Conjunctions	1. **C**	2. **A**	3. **B**
Skill 10 Parallel Structure	1. **B**	2. **D**	3. **C**
Skill 11 Subordinating Conjunctions	1. **C**	2. **A**	3. **C**
Skill 12 Future Time Clauses	1. **B**	2. **A**	3. **C**

Part 6: Text Completion

Skill 1 Adverbs of Frequency	1. **A**	2. **D**	3. **A**
Skill 2 Gerunds and Infinitives After Main Verbs	1. **C**	2. **B**	3. **B**
Skill 3 Gerunds and Infinitives After Prepositions and Adjectives	1. **B**	2. **C**	3. **A**
Skill 4 Causative Verbs	1. **A**	2. **B**	3. **A**
Skill 5 Real Conditionals	1. **A**	2. **B**	3. **C**
Skill 6 Unreal Conditionals	1. **B**	2. **B**	3. **C**
Skill 7 Comparisons	1. **A**	2. **D**	3. **B**
Skill 8 Pronouns	1. **D**	2. **D**	3. **B**
Skill 9 Subject Relative Pronouns	1. **A**	2. **C**	3. **D**
Skill 10 Object Relative Pronouns	1. **C**	2. **B**	3. **B**
Skill 11 Passive Voice	1. **C**	2. **B**	3. **D**

Part 7: Reading Comprehension

Skill 1 Advertisements	1. **C**	2. **B**			
Skill 2 Forms	1. **D**	2. **B**	3. **B**	4. **C**	
Skill 3 Reports	1. **C**	2. **D**	3. **A**		
Skill 4 Letters	1. **C**	2. **B**	3. **A**		
Skill 5 Memos	1. **C**	2. **A**	3. **B**	4. **D**	
Skill 6 Tables and Charts	1. **A**	2. **D**	3. **B**	4. **B**	
Skill 7 Graphs	1. **B**	2. **D**			
Skill 8 Announcements	1. **A**	2. **A**	3. **C**	4. **A**	5. **B**
Skill 9 Notices	1. **D**	2. **B**			
Skill 10 Articles	1. **D**	2. **D**	3. **B**		
Skill 11 Schedules	1. **C**	2. **C**	3. **C**	4. **C**	
Skill 12 E-mail	1. **A**	2. **C**			
Skill 13 Webpages	1. **D**	2. **A**			

ANSWER KEY
Reading Mini-Test

Explanatory Answers can be found beginning on page 260.

Part 5: Incomplete Sentences

1. **C**
2. **D**
3. **A**
4. **D**
5. **B**
6. **A**
7. **D**
8. **C**
9. **A**
10. **C**
11. **A**
12. **C**
13. **C**
14. **B**
15. **D**
16. **C**
17. **B**
18. **B**
19. **C**
20. **D**

Part 6: Text Completion

21. **A**
22. **D**
23. **C**
24. **A**
25. **C**
26. **D**

Part 7: Reading Comprehension

27. **D**
28. **B**
29. **B**
30. **A**
31. **A**
32. **D**
33. **C**
34. **B**
35. **C**
36. **A**
37. **C**
38. **B**
39. **C**
40. **C**
41. **A**
42. **A**
43. **A**
44. **C**
45. **D**
46. **C**
47. **C**
48. **C**
49. **A**
50. **A**
51. **C**
52. **B**
53. **C**
54. **A**
55. **B**
56. **B**
57. **D**
58. **C**
59. **C**
60. **A**
61. **A**
62. **C**
63. **D**
64. **C**
65. **B**
66. **C**
67. **C**
68. **B**
69. **B**
70. **C**
71. **A**
72. **B**
73. **C**
74. **A**
75. **B**
76. **D**

EXPLANATORY ANSWERS FOR READING SKILLS

Part 5: Incomplete Sentences

SKILL 1 WORD FAMILIES

1. **(B)** *Negotiate* is a verb. Choice (A) is an adjective. Choices (C) and (D) are nouns.
2. **(B)** *Applicants* is a noun referring to people. Choice (A) is a verb. Choice (C) is a noun that looks like it belongs to this word family, but it has a completely different meaning. Choice (D) is a noun, but it doesn't refer to people.
3. **(D)** *Decisively* is an adverb of manner modifying the verb act. Choice (A) is a verb. Choice (B) is a noun. Choice (C) is an adjective.

SKILL 2 SIMILAR MEANINGS

1. **(D)** *Earn* is often used to mean *gain money by working.* Choice (A) *win* means *be first in a competition.* Choice (B) *achieve* means *accomplish something.* Choice (C) *obtain* means *acquire something.*
2. **(A)** *Recent* is an adjective referring to something that happened a very short while ago. In this sentence, it modifies the noun *promotion.* Choices (B) and (D) are adverbs, so they cannot be used in this way. Choice (C) refers to something that will happen in the future.
3. **(C)** *Decrease* means to make smaller or less. The sentence means *We will make our costs smaller.* Choices (A) and (B) mean *go down.* They don't fit the sentence because they are intransitive verbs. Choice (D) is a preposition, but a transitive verb is needed in this sentence.

SKILL 3 SIMILAR FORMS

1. **(B)** A *contract* is a legal document. Choice (A) means *communicate with.* Choice (C) means *behave.* Choice (D) means *small* or *tightly packed.*
2. **(A)** *Partitions* are walls used to divide a room into separate areas. Choice (B) refers to people who *participate* in something. Choice (C) means *very small pieces.* Choice (D) refers to a type of verb form.
3. **(D)** *Reduce* means *make smaller or less.* Choice (A) means *make or create something.* Choice (B) means *persuade.* Choice (C) means *make a logical conclusion.*

SKILL 4 SUBJECT-VERB AGREEMENT WITH PREPOSITIONAL PHRASES

1. **(D)** This plural verb agrees with the plural subject of the sentence, *officers.* Choices (A), (B), and (C) are singular verbs.
2. **(A)** The singular verb *charges* agrees with the singular subject *owner.* Choices (B), (C), and (D) are plural verb forms.
3. **(C)** The plural verb *are* agrees with the plural subject *supplies.* Choices (A), (B), and (D) are singular verb forms.

SKILL 5 SINGULAR AND PLURAL SUBJECTS

1. **(C)** The verb *visits* agrees with the singular subject manager. Choice (A) is a gerund. Choice (B) is an infinitive verb. Choice (D) needs a plural subject.
2. **(A)** The plural verb *agree* agrees with the plural subject *people.* Choices (B), (C), and (D) are singular verb forms.
3. **(D)** The singular verb *is* agrees with the singular subject *everything.* Choices (A), (B), and (C) are plural verb forms.

SKILL 6 VERB TENSES

1. **(B)** The time expression *next Friday* indicates that a future tense verb is needed. Choice (A) is simple present. Choice (C) is present continuous. Choice (D) is simple present.
2. **(C)** The time word *yet* indicates that a present perfect verb is needed. Choice (A) is simple past. Choice (B) is simple present. Choice (D) is present continuous and doesn't agree with the plural subject.
3. **(B)** The time expression *every summer* indicates that a simple present verb is needed. Choice (A) is simple present, but it doesn't agree with the singular subject. Choice (C) is present continuous. Choice (D) is an infinitive verb, a form that can't be used as a main verb.

SKILL 7 PREPOSITIONS

1. **(A)** *On* is a preposition of place that means *on top of.* Choices (B), (C), and (D) are prepositions that do not make sense in this context.
2. **(D)** *Into* indicates movement to the inside of something. Choices (A), (B), and (C) are prepositions that don't make sense in this context.
3. **(C)** In this sentence, *until* is paired with *from* to indicate beginning and end times of an action. Choices (A), (B), and (D) are prepositions that don't make sense in this context.

SKILL 8 PREPOSITIONS WITH VERBS AND ADJECTIVES

1. **(B)** The preposition *about* correctly follows the verb *complain.* Choices (A), (B), and (C) are prepositions that are not generally used with *complain.*
2. **(C)** The preposition *with* correctly follows the verb *replace,* even when there is an object (*our old copy machine*) between. Choices (A), (B), and (D) are prepositions that are not generally used with *replace.*
3. **(A)** The preposition *for* correctly follows the verb *responsible.* Choices (B), (C), and (D) are prepositions that are not generally used with *responsible.*

SKILL 9 COORDINATING CONJUNCTIONS

1. **(C)** *And* joins two similar ideas—*creative* and *accurate*—which are both positive descriptions of Ms. Sam's work. Choice (A), *but,* joins two opposite ideas. Choice (B), *or,* joins two choices. Choice (D), *nor,* must be used together with *neither.*
2. **(A)** *Yet* joins two opposite ideas—you would expect that George would finish the report after working all night, but he didn't. Choice (B) joins two similar ideas. Choice (C) indicates a choice and must be used with *or.* Choice (D) indicates a lack of choice and must be used with *nor.*
3. **(B)** Together with *either, or* indicates a choice, in this case between two meeting times. Choice (A) joins two opposite ideas. Choice (C) must be used with *neither* to indicate a lack of choice. Choice (D) must be used with *nor.*

SKILL 10 PARALLEL STRUCTURE

1. **(B)** *Friendly* is an adjective and is parallel with the adjective *prompt.* Choices (A), (C), and (D) are nouns.
2. **(D)** The gerund *getting* is parallel with the gerund *making.* The sentence tells us that Sharon is good at two things—(1) *making clients feel comfortable* and (2) *getting them interested in our services.* Choice (A) is base form. Choice (B) is past tense. Choice (C) is a past participle.
3. **(C)** The noun *accuracy* is parallel with the noun *efficiency.* Choice (A) is an adjective. Choice (B) is an adverb. Choice (D) is a gerund and, although it looks similar, is not related in meaning to the other choices or the correct answer.

SKILL 11 SUBORDINATING CONJUNCTIONS

1. **(C)** Usually people cannot enter a concert hall after the concert has started, so this clause describes a situation that contradicts expectations. Choice (A) introduces a reason. Choice (B) is a coordinating conjunction. Choice (D) introduces a time clause.
2. **(A)** *Since* introduces a reason, and this clause describes the reason for canceling the meeting. Choice (B) introduces a contradiction. Choice (C) introduces a condition. Choice (D) introduces a time clause.
3. **(C)** *As soon as* introduces a time clause and means *immediately after.* This clause tells when Miranda will send the report. Choice (A) is a coordinating conjunction that joins opposite ideas. Choice (B) introduces a result. Choice (D) introduces a time clause, but the meaning does not make sense in this context—you cannot send a report before it is ready.

SKILL 12 FUTURE TIME CLAUSES

1. **(B)** This is a present tense verb in a future time clause, and it agrees with the subject of

the clause, *train.* Choice (A) is present tense but doesn't agree with the subject. Choice (C) is future tense. Choice (D) is a gerund.

2. **(A)** The main clause has a future verb, so a present tense verb is needed in the time clause. Choice (B) is an infinitive verb, a form that cannot be used as the main verb of a clause. Choice (C) is a future verb. Choice (D) is a noun.
3. **(C)** The main clause has a future verb, so a present tense verb is needed in the time clause. Choice (A) is future. Choice (B) is past. Choice (D) is base form.

Part 6: Text Completion

SKILL 1 ADVERBS OF FREQUENCY

1. **(A)** *Rarely* means *almost never.* The memo states that this is the first time a meeting has been held on the weekend. Choices (B), (C), and (D) indicate greater frequency.
2. **(D)** *Always* means *all the time.* The context makes it clear that meetings begin on time all the time. Choices (A), (B), and (C) indicate lesser frequency.
3. **(A)** *Usually* means *most of the time.* Choices (B), (C), and (D) indicate lesser frequency.

SKILL 2 GERUNDS AND INFINITIVES AFTER MAIN VERBS

1. **(C)** *Agree* is followed by an infinitive. Choices (A), (B), and (D) are not in the infinitive form.
2. **(B)** *Mind* is followed by a gerund. Choices (A), (C), and (D) are not gerunds.
3. **(B)** *Offer* is followed by an infinitive. Choices (A), (C), and (D) are not infinitives.

SKILL 3 GERUNDS AND INFINITIVES AFTER PREPOSITIONS AND ADJECTIVES

1. **(B)** *About* is a preposition, so it is followed by a gerund. Choices (A), (C), and (D) are not gerunds.
2. **(C)** *Bright enough* follows the adjective + enough pattern, which is followed by an infinitive verb. Choices (A), (B), and (D) are not infinitives.
3. **(A)** *Ready* is an adjective, so it is followed by an infinitive. Choices (B), (C), and (D) are not infinitives.

SKILL 4 CAUSATIVE VERBS

1. **(A)** The causative verb *make* is followed by the base form. Choices (B), (C), and (D) are not in the base form.
2. **(B)** The causative verb *permit* is followed by the infinitive form. Choices (A), (C), and (D) are not infinitives.
3. **(A)** The causative verb *have* is followed by the base form. Choices (B), (C), and (D) are not in the base form.

SKILL 5 REAL CONDITIONALS

1. **(A)** The verb in the *if* clause in a real conditional sentence must be in the present tense. Choice (B) is an infinitive verb. Choices (C) and (D) are future verbs.
2. **(B)** The verb in the *if* clause in a real conditional sentence must be in the present tense. Choice (A) is an infinitive verb. Choice (C) is a gerund. Choice (D) is future.
3. **(C)** The verb in the *if* clause in a real conditional sentence must be in the present tense. Choice (A) is base form. Choice (B) is present tense. Choice (D) is past tense.

SKILL 6 UNREAL CONDITIONALS

1. **(B)** In an unreal conditional about the past, the *if* clause uses a past perfect verb. Choice (A) is simple past. Choice (C) is present perfect. Choice (D) would be correct in an unreal conditional about the present.
2. **(B)** In an unreal conditional about the past, the *if* clause uses a past perfect verb. Choice (A) is present perfect tense. Choice (C) is present tense. Choice (D) is future tense.
3. **(C)** In an unreal condition about the present, the *if* clause uses a past tense verb. Choice (A) is present tense. Choice (B) is future. Choice (D) is past perfect.

SKILL 7 COMPARISONS

1. **(A)** *Faster than* is a correct comparative form using the *-er* ending and the word *than* and it makes sense in the context. Choice (B) is incorrect because the ad mentions that their professors are just as professional as those at other schools. Choice (C) is incorrect because Techno Business Academy has a shorter course than average. Choice (D) is incorrect because they advertise low prices.
2. **(D)** This is a correct superlative form using *the* and the *-est* ending. Choice (A) is an adjective but it is not superlative. Choice (B) is a superlative form but is missing *the.* Choice (C) is a comparative, not superlative, form.
3. **(B)** *Higher* is a correct comparative form used in a sentence that already contains *than.* Choices (A), (C), and (D) cannot be used with *than.*

SKILL 8 PRONOUNS

1. **(D)** *Your* is a possessive pronoun describing the adjective *staff,* with the antecedent *you.* Choice (A) is a reflexive pronoun. Choice (B) is a possessive pronoun. Choice (C) is a subject or object pronoun.
2. **(D)** The antecedent is *employees,* a third person plural noun, so the correct pronoun is the third person plural *they.* Choice (A) is first person singular. Choice (B) is third person singular. Choice (C) is second person singular or plural.
3. **(B)** The antecedent is *John Malstrom,* a third person singular noun, so the correct pronoun is the third person singular *him.* Choice (A) is first person singular. Choice (C) is third person singular, but it refers to a woman, not a man, and *John* is a man's name. Choice (D) is third person plural.

SKILL 9 SUBJECT RELATIVE PRONOUNS

1. **(A)** The antecedent, *staff members,* is a group of people so *who* is the correct pronoun. Choice (B) is an object relative pronoun but a subject relative pronoun is required here. Choice (C) refers to a possessive. Choice (D) refers to a thing.
2. **(C)** *Whose* is a possessive relative pronoun, referring to *everyone's schedule.* Choice (A) refers to a person, not to a possessive. Choices (B) and (D) are not relative pronouns.
3. **(D)** The antecedent, *visit,* is a thing. Choice (A) refers to a person. Choice (B) refers to a thing but cannot be used in a nonrestrictive clause. Choice (C) refers to a possessive.

SKILL 10 OBJECT RELATIVE PRONOUNS

1. **(C)** The antecedent is a person, *Dr. Herman Friedman.* Choice (A) refers to a possessive. Choice (B) refers to a thing. Choice (D) is not a relative pronoun.
2. **(B)** The antecedent is a thing, the gradual bleaching of the Great Barrier Reef. Choice (A) refers to a thing but can only be used in restrictive clauses and this is a nonrestrictive clause. Choice (C) refers to a person. Choice (D) is not a relative pronoun.
3. **(B)** The antecedent is a thing, *books,* and this is a restrictive clause. Choice (A) refers to a possessive. Choice (C) is not a relative pronoun. Choice (D) refers to a person.

SKILL 11 PASSIVE VOICE

1. **(C)** This is a passive verb in the past, *last month,* with a plural subject, *walls.* Choice (A) is singular. Choice (B) is present tense. Choice (D) is present perfect.
2. **(B)** This is passive voice. The subject, *carpet,* does not install itself. A past participle is required after the verb *be.* Choice (A) is an active form. Choice (C) is a gerund. Choice (D) is a noun.
3. **(D)** This is passive voice. The subject, *stains,* do not remove themselves. Choices (A), (B), and (C) are all active forms.

Part 7: Reading Comprehension

SKILL 1 ADVERTISEMENTS

1. **(C)** *Attention Manufacturers* indicates that the writers want manufacturers to read the

ad. Choice (A) confuses the writers of the ad with the readers. Choices (B) and (D) are not mentioned.

2. **(B)** It indicates they can distribute in 155 countries. Choice (A) is less than the number mentioned. Choices (C) and (D) are more than the number mentioned.

SKILL 2 FORMS

1. **(D)** To *subscribe* means that you will start to receive a periodical. Choices (A), (B), and (C) are contradicted by the heading *Special Subscription Offer.*
2. **(B)** The full cover price is $5 an issue ($60 divided by 12 months). Choice (A) is less than the price. Choices (C) and (D) are more than the price.
3. **(B)** *Allow four weeks for first issue* means about *one month.* Choice (A) is shorter than a month. Choices (C) and (D) are not logical.
4. **(C)** If there are 12 issues in one year, the magazine comes *monthly.* Choices (A) and (B) are more often. Choice (D) is less often.

SKILL 3 REPORTS

1. **(C)** They could pay $10 million; *$5 million up front* plus *as much as $5 million more.* Choice (A) is the amount Peptel posted in sales last year. Choice (B) is the initial price. Choice (D) is what Markel is worth.
2. **(D)** *Of Berlin* means the company is based there. Choice (A) is where Markel is based. Choices (B) and (C) are not mentioned.
3. **(A)** If Peptel is in educational software, Markel is probably in software, too. Choices (B) and (D) are not mentioned. Choice (C) confuses *visual arts* with the company name *Peptel Visual.*

SKILL 4 LETTERS

1. **(C)** *Samples* are not requested. Choices (A), (B), and (D) are explicitly requested. (*Terms* means *pricing information.*)
2. **(B)** *Hardware* includes computers. Choice (A) is contradicted by the fact that they are *adding software to their sales offerings.* Choices (C) and (D) are not mentioned.
3. **(A)** *Add software to our sales offerings* means *distribute software.* Choice (B) is not mentioned. Choice (C) confuses *selling hardware* with *purchasing hardware.* Choice (D) confuses *sending* an annual report with *receiving* an annual report.

SKILL 5 MEMOS

1. **(C)** *No flights under five hours can be booked in Business Class,* but flights over five hours can be. Choices (A) *Economy* and (B) *Economy Plus* can probably be booked. Choice (D) is contradicted by *No flights . . . can be booked in First Class.*
2. **(A)** If it is written *May 15* and goes into effect *June 1,* it goes into effect in *two weeks.* Choices (B) and (C) are contradicted by *June 1.* Choice (D) confuses *five hours* with *five months.*
3. **(B)** The memo is about using *economical means,* or *saving money.* Choices (A), (C), and (D) are not mentioned.
4. **(D)** The memo affects *all employees,* or *all personnel.* Choices (A), (B), and (C) are contradicted by *all personnel.*

SKILL 6 TABLES AND CHARTS

1. **(A)** Amsterdam and Taipei are both coded *C* for cloudy. Choice (B) cities were partly cloudy. Choices (C) and (D) had different weather but were not cloudy.
2. **(D)** Manila had a high of *33/91.* Choices (A), (B), and (C) had lower temperatures.
3. **(B)** Frankfurt had a spread from *3/37* to *1/34.* Choices (A), (C), and (D) had wider spreads.
4. **(B)** Kuala Lampur is coded for *t* thunderstorms. Choices (A), (C), and (D) are not mentioned for this city.

SKILL 7 GRAPHS

1. **(B)** Competing hotels would be most interested in market share information. Choices (A), (C), and (D) are unlikely to be interested.

2. **(D)** Lowit has 25%, or one-quarter, of the market. Choice (A) is incorrect because Stilton is the top-ranking chain. Choice (B) is incorrect because location information is not given in the graph. Choice (C) is incorrect because Torte has only 15% of the market.

SKILL 8 ANNOUNCEMENTS

1. **(A)** The world's third-largest means it has a rank of 3. Choice (B) is the number of years Mr. Kaspar has been with the company. Choice (C) confuses the rank with the date of resignation. Choice (D) is Mr. Kaspar's age.
2. **(A)** The company *could be bought.* Choices (B), (C), and (D) are contradicted by *could be bought.*
3. **(C)** If he is 62 and has been there 22 years, he has been there since he was 40. Choice (A) is contradicted by *22 years.* Choice (B) confuses the resignation date and the time he has been there. Choice (D) is his age.
4. **(A)** *Cable television systems* are communications companies. Choices (B), (C), and (D) do not include cable companies.
5. **(B)** The word *declined* means *refused.* Mr. Kaspar refused, or did not choose to, answer questions. Choices (A), (C), and (D) have meanings that do not fit the context of the reading passage.

SKILL 9 NOTICES

1. **(D)** Employees moving from other cities are most affected. Choices (A), (B), and (C) are not affected by these changes.
2. **(B)** *Moving household items* is reimbursed. Choices (A), (C), and (D) are *no longer reimbursable.*

SKILL 10 ARTICLES

1. **(D)** The article is about how interns can help a company. Choices (A) and (B) are not mentioned. Choice (C) is a detail, not the main idea.
2. **(D)** *Asset* means benefit in this context. Choices (A), (B), and (C) have meanings that do not fit the context.
3. **(B)** The article mentions that interns need supervision and support. Choice (A) is the opposite of what the article says: interns have a lot of enthusiasm. Choice (C) is also the opposite of what the article says: interns are unpaid. Choice (D) is confused with the mention of companies' complaining about interns.

SKILL 11 SCHEDULES

1. **(C)** Off-peak fares start somewhere between 8:25 and 8:32; 8:30 is a reasonable guess. Choice (A) is not mentioned. Choices (B) and (D) are times in the schedule, but neither is the start of off-peak fares.
2. **(C)** Buses marked with a *W* arrive at this stop five minutes earlier than others, so the 7:30 arrives at 7:25. Choices (A) and (B) are not mentioned. Choice (D) is the bus's departure time.
3. **(C)** The tunnel isn't open until 8:00. Choice (A) is probably true, but it isn't mentioned in the schedule. Choices (B) and (D) are not mentioned.
4. **(C)** Each trip is 50 minutes, or *almost an hour.* This question requires some quick math computation. Choice (A) means 15 minutes. Choice (B) means 30 minutes. Choice (D) is incorrect.

SKILL 12 E-MAIL

1. **(A)** The sender's address is shown in the header line: *From.* Choice (B) is the address of the receiver. Choice (C) is not an e-mail address, it is a name plus an e-mail address. Choice (D) is the name of the receiver.
2. **(C)** The gathering (or *meeting*) was in Orlando, according to the *Subject* line. Choice (A) is probably a company name, based on the e-mail addresses, but it wasn't the location of the meeting. Choice (B) repeats a name from the header. Choice (D) repeats a word from the e-mail, but this is a restaurant name, not the meeting place.

SKILL 13 WEBPAGES

1. **(D)** *FAQ* means *Frequently Asked Questions*, and is a standard option on a home page. Choices (A), (B), and (C) are all menu options, but none would be the place to go to find the response to a basic question.
2. **(A)** *Pay for fuel in advance* means *prepaid gasoline cards*. Choice (B) is not mentioned. Choice (C) repeats a line from the home page. Choice (D) repeats the word *gas* from the home page.

EXPLANATORY ANSWERS FOR MINI-TEST FOR READING

Part 5: Incomplete Sentences

1. **(C)** A compound subject requires a plural verb. Choice (A) is first person present tense. Choice (B) is singular present. Choice (D) is the simple form.
2. **(D)** *To* indicates the one-way direction of the cable. Choice (A) implies the computer is used as *a means* to attach the cable. Choices (B) and (C) would imply that the computer is opened up and the cables are "inside" the computer itself.
3. **(A)** This is an adverb of manner modifying the verb price. Choice (B) is an adjective. Choices (C) and (D) are nouns.
4. **(D)** *The* requires the noun *presentation*. Choice (A) is the gerund form, which is inappropriate here. Choice (B) is the past tense form. Choice (C) is the simple form.
5. **(B)** *Increased* means *to go up*. Choices (A) and (C) are not used with money. Choice (D) confuses *rise* and *raise*.
6. **(A)** *Although* here means *in spite of* the rain, we drove in a jeep without a roof. Choices (B) and (C) indicate cause and effect. Choice (D) is a preposition, not a conjunction.
7. **(D)** *At* is used with specific indications of time. Choice (A) is used for placement. Choice (B) is for location. Choice (C) is used for location.
8. **(C)** *Was* is followed by the past participle *sent*. Choice (A) is the simple form. Choice (B) uses *has*, not *was*. Choice (D) is the gerund form.
9. **(A)** This is a future time clause so a present tense verb is required. Choice (B) is past tense. Choice (C) is present perfect. Choice (D) is future.
10. **(C)** Choice (C) indicates position with the post office on one side and the bank on the other side. Choice (A) is used when there are three or more reference points. Choice (B) is incorrect because an office would not normally be *outside*. Choice (D) would be possible only if all three (post office, bank and office) were in one building and you had to pass through both to get to the office.
11. **(A)** The plural verb *receive* agrees with the subject employees. Choices (B), (C), and (D) are singular verbs.
12. **(C)** *In* goes with a state name, *Texas*. Choices (A), (B), and (C) are not logical.
13. **(C)** *Since*, here, shows a cause and effect relationship. Choices (A) and (D) imply contradictions. Choice (B) doesn't make sense.
14. **(B)** Adverbs of indefinite frequency occur after the auxiliary verb. Choice (A) is an adverb of definite frequency and cannot occur after the auxiliary. Choices (C) and (D) do not make sense.
15. **(D)** *Nor* is the conjunction paired with *neither*. Choices (A), (B), and (C) are not used with *neither*.
16. **(C)** We use the past perfect as the past subjunctive to show an imaginary idea, one contrary to fact, in the past. Choice (A) implies that she *always* recommends. The idea is about what happened on one occasion in the past, not what happens all the time. Choice (B) is used to make a general observation. Choice (D) means in reality that the consultant is recommending right now that we hire more staff. That's not the reality of the situation; this is something the consultant did in the past.
17. **(B)** The command form signals a real condition; use the present tense in the *if* clause. Choice (A) would be used in an unreal condition. Choice (C) is the past tense. Choice (D) is the *-ing* form.

18. **(B)** The causative verb *make* is followed by a base form verb. Choice (A) is present tense. Choice (C) is an infinitive. Choice (D) is a gerund.
19. **(C)** *Rheingold Consultants* is the name of a company; therefore it is considered singular and it takes a singular verb. Choices (A), (B), and (D) are all plural verbs.
20. **(D)** *Lend* means to let someone use something that belongs to you. Choices (A), (B), and (C) have meanings that don't fit the context of the sentence.

Part 6: Text Completion

21. **(A)** *Who* refers to a person, *Olga Kovacs*, and is the subject of the clause. Choice (B) is an object relative pronoun. Choice (C) refers to a possessive. Choice (D) refers to a person.
22. **(D)** The main verb *plan* is followed by an infinitive. Choice (A) is base form or present tense. Choice (B) is present tense. Choice (C) is a gerund.
23. **(C)** Ms. Kovacs needs a way to get to the office that is better than a cab, so Ed will send a *limousine*, or hired car, and ride in it with her. Choices (A), (B), and (D) are things one could send, but they don't fit the context of transportation.
24. **(A)** *Although* is used to introduce a situation that has an unexpected result; we don't expect so many teens to smoke when there is a campaign to discourage them. Choices (B) and (D) indicate cause and effect. Choice (C) introduces a time clause.
25. **(C)** The news causes a feeling—public health officials, teachers, and parents don't feel encouraged—so a present participle adjective is used. Choice (A) is a base form verb. Choice (B) is a past participle. Choice (D) is a noun.
26. **(D)** *Adolescence* is a stage of life, the time when one is a teenager. Choices (A), (B), and (C) look similar to the correct answer but have very different meanings.

Part 7: Reading Comprehension

27. **(D)** The ad is for an *international book supplier* who has books in many languages. Choice (A) uses *225 languages* to incorrectly suggest translation services. Choice (B) is contradicted by *book supplier.* Choice (C) is incorrectly suggested by the reference to *Zulu.*
28. **(B)** The third line says it's *full service.* Choice (A) is probably true, but it is not emphasized. Choice (C) is listed, but it is not a *feature of the company.* Choice (D) is not mentioned.
29. **(B)** The invoice goes to the *accounting department,* which pays the bill. Choice (A) receives the shipment. Choice (C) is the vendor's purchasing department. Choice (D) sent the shipment.
30. **(A)** *Vendor* means *seller.* Choice (B) bought the equipment. Choice (C) prepared the invoice. Choice (D) will get the invoice in the accounting department.
31. **(A)** Choice (A) is the subtotal without the cards. Choice (B) is the subtotal with the cards. Choice (C) is not given. Choice (D) is the total, with cards and shipping and handling.
32. **(D)** The personnel department does not get a copy of the purchase order. Choices (A), (B), and (C) are listed by *cc* which means they get copies of the order.
33. **(C)** *Establish a manufacturing operation near their customers* means *build factories close to their customers.* Choices (A) and (D) are areas that customers would like to be involved in. Choice (B) is contradicted by *cannot simply export more goods.*
34. **(B)** It says customers want *to provide input on design.* Choices (A) and (D), design consultants and engineers, would already have design input. Choice (C) is incorrect because suppliers probably do not want design input and are not mentioned.
35. **(C)** The purpose is to apologize. Choice (A) is contradicted by *we apologize* and *we regret.* Choice (B) is incorrect because the writer is *filling* an order. Choice (D) is not mentioned.
36. **(A)** *Were not included in the first shipment* means that *the shipment was incomplete.*

Choices (B), (C), and (D) are possible shipping problems, but they are not mentioned.

37. **(C)** The fax was received *this morning.* Choices (A), (B), and (D) are all contradicted by *this morning.*
38. **(B)** She will *fax exact time of delivery.* Choices (A), (C), and (D) are contradicted by *by fax.*
39. **(C)** It says, *at the end of the week, or at the very latest on Monday.* Choices (A), (B), and (D) are all contradicted by *on Monday.*
40. **(C)** A guest of the *engineering department* who has *done research on the effects of earthquakes* is probably a mechanical engineer. Choices (A), (B), and (D) are not logical.
41. **(A)** Mr. Wilson will be the Ukrainian's guide, since the memo is to him. Choice (B) is the visitor. Choice (C) is the person who wrote the memo. Choice (D) is contradicted by the memo.
42. **(A)** She will arrive before noon. Choices (B), (C), and (D) are contradicted by *before noon.*
43. **(A)** She is interested in designing bridges. Choices (B), (C), and (D) may be interesting, but they are not areas of interest within a field.
44. **(C)** Section B has other business news, so it is a likely place for market forecasts. Choices (A), (B), and (D) are not likely to be found there.
45. **(D)** Editorials contain opinions and are found on A-10. Choice (A) contains international news. Choice (B) contains commodities. Choice (C) has information on the arts.
46. **(C)** Films (movies) are found on C-3. Choice (A) is incorrect because B-11 contains information on stocks, not movies. Choice (B), page C-1, covers arts, but this choice is not as specific as Choice (C). Choice (D) is incorrect because a page covering legal issues would not contain reviews of movies.
47. **(C)** The payroll clerk reports to the Manager of Accounting. Choice (A) is not concerned with the payroll. Choices (B) and (D) do not supervise clerks.
48. **(C)** Marketing and Sales have similar staffing patterns. Choices (A), (B), and (D) do not have similar patterns.
49. **(A)** The VP of Sales supervises both the Domestic Sales Managers and International Sales Managers. Choice (B) is incorrect because the President supervises only Vice Presidents. Choices (C) and (D) are incorrect because they are not in the Sales Department.
50. **(A)** It shows a comparison of dollar-yen rates. Choices (B), (C), and (D) are not depicted by the graph.
51. **(C)** There were fluctuations in April. Choices (A), (B), and (D) did not show such fluctuations.
52. **(B)** The contractor is located in San Francisco. Choice (A) is the location of the group that awarded the contract. Choices (C) and (D) are not logical locations for a contractor.
53. **(C)** A *three-month contract beginning in June* will end sometime in September. Choices (A), (B), and (D) are contradicted by this information.
54. **(A)** *Without notice* and *without obligation to notify* mean they can change things without telling the customer. Choices (B), (C), and (D) are not the subject of the notice.
55. **(B)** *In this manual* indicates where the information is found. Choice (A) contains information about repairs and service. Choices (C) and (D) are not logical given the subject of the notice.
56. **(B)** A *Swiss chemical company* would probably be located in Switzerland. Choice (A) is the country where Royal Chemical is located. Choices (C) and (D) are places where Royal Chemical has production plants, not the place where RADD is located.
57. **(D)** *Uses that range from rope fibers to bottles* means that polypropylene is used to make ropes, bottles, and other things. Choice (A) is also used for rope, but it is not mentioned. Choice (B) is used for string. Choice (C) is used for cable.
58. **(C)** The price is *between $100 million and $160 million.* Choices (A) and (B) are lower than the purchase price given. Choice (D) gives the price for only the RCI plants.

59. **(C)** *Of Britain* means *located in Britain.* Choices (A), (B), and (D) are the locations of production plants.

60. **(A)** *Disclose* means *tell* or *announce.* Choices (B), (C), and (D) have meanings that don't fit the context of the reading passage.

61. **(A)** The article mentions many different places where the entertainment industry is expanding. Choice (B) is incorrect because China is a *potential market*; it is not a huge market now. Choice (C) confuses the meanings of *home* (house) and *home* (base of operations). Choice (D) is incorrect because the status of opportunities in Hollywood is not mentioned.

62. **(C)** *Hollywood* is used to mean *the media.* Choices (A) and (B) are incorrect because many executives and American enterprises are not part of entertainment or media. Choice (D) is incorrect because other industries also have big markets worldwide.

63. **(D)** A schedule for a meeting is an *agenda.* Choice (A) is incorrect: An agenda shows people what to expect, but it cannot make them pay attention. Choice (B) is a benefit of the agenda, but not the purpose of it. Choice (C) is incorrect because an agenda does not introduce speakers.

64. **(C)** A question-and-answer period follows the presentations. Choice (A) comes before the presentations. Choice (B) comes after opening remarks. Choice (D) probably follows the close of the meeting, but it is not part of the meeting and it is not mentioned.

65. **(B)** The items listed are stages in developing a product. Choice (A) is incorrect because the time is shown in months, not man-hours. Choices (C) and (D) are not represented by the timeline.

66. **(C)** If the proposal is submitted in February and they start work in March, the proposal will probably be approved in February. Choice (A) is incorrect because cost is not mentioned. Choice (B) is incorrect because marketing and testing are shown for the same amount of time. Choice (D) is not likely: Time is allowed for testing, so it should not slow down production.

67. **(C)** Joe's calendar shows that he has a dentist appointment at 11:30 on Wednesday. Choices (A), (B), and (D) are days that have no dentist appointment scheduled.

68. **(B)** Joe's calendar shows that he has a phone conference with the Toronto office on Thursday at 4:00. Choice (A) repeats *Toronto.* Choice (C) is what he will do on Friday afternoon. Choice (D) is what he will do on Monday morning.

69. **(B)** Alicia's meeting begins an hour before her scheduled 3:00 golf game. Choice (A) is when Joe's department meeting begins. Choice (C) is when the golf game is scheduled to begin. Choice (D) is when Alicia thinks the meeting will end.

70. **(C)** Alicia wants to play the day after their original Monday game. Choice (A) is not mentioned. Choice (B) is the day the game was originally scheduled for. Choice (D) is when Joe is scheduled to play golf with Fred.

71. **(A)** Joe is not free to meet Mr. Santos Wednesday morning, as Alicia suggested, because he has a department meeting and a dentist appointment. He is free for the meeting, however, on Thursday morning. Choice (B) is confused with the fact that he hasn't yet scheduled anything for Thursday morning, but after reading Alicia's e-mail, he will probably want to see Mr. Santos then. Choice (C) is what he will do Friday morning. Choice (D) is what he will do Saturday morning.

72. **(B)** The notice says that the work will begin *at the end of next month.* Choice (A) is confused with when employees should ask for a subway pass. Choice (C) is confused with the amount of time the work will last. Choice (D) is this month.

73. **(C)** Each office in the building will get four parking passes, and Parrot Communications has five times as many employees as that. Choice (A) is confused with the number of parking passes. Choice (B) is confused with *five times as many employees.* Choice (D) is

confused with the size of the discount on the subway passes.

74. **(A)** The parking passes allow parking on the streets around the building, and Parrot Communications will reserve its parking passes for its clients. Choice (B) is incorrect because Parrot Communications employees will not be given passes. Choice (C) is incorrect because there are only four passes allowed per office. Choice (D) is incorrect because Dena Degenaro is a Parrot Communications employee, and as such will not get a parking pass.

75. **(B)** The memo was sent by the office manager and asks employees to *see me* to ask for a subway pass. Choice (A) is confused with the city's allotting certain parking spaces for building tenants. Choice (C) is confused with the people who posted the notice. Choice (D) is a logical place to get a subway pass, but it is not mentioned.

76. **(D)** The subway passes will be valid for the entire length of the garage reconstruction, which is three months. Choices (A), (B), and (C) are not mentioned.

ANSWER KEY New TOEIC Reading Skills

Explanatory Answers can be found beginning on page 267.

Part 5: Incomplete Sentences

1. **D**
2. **A**
3. **A**
4. **B**
5. **C**
6. **B**
7. **D**
8. **A**
9. **B**
10. **C**
11. **D**
12. **C**
13. **C**
14. **A**
15. **B**
16. **D**
17. **D**
18. **B**
19. **B**
20. **C**
21. **D**
22. **A**
23. **B**
24. **D**
25. **C**
26. **A**
27. **B**
28. **D**
29. **C**
30. **D**

Part 6: Text Completion

SKILL 1

1. **D**
2. **C**
3. **B**
4. **A**
5. **E**

NEW TOEIC PRACTICE

1. **B**
2. **D**
3. **A**
4. **C**
5. **B**
6. **C**
7. **D**
8. **D**
9. **C**
10. **A**
11. **B**
12. **D**
13. **A**
14. **B**
15. **D**
16. **C**

Part 7: Reading Comprehension

SKILL 1

1. **B**
2. **A**
3. **B**
4. **B**
5. **A**

SKILL 2

1. **B**
2. **C**
3. **C**
4. **B**
5. **A**

NEW TOEIC PRACTICE

1. **B**
2. **C**
3. **C**
4. **B**
5. **D**
6. **C**
7. **D**
8. **C**
9. **A**
10. **B**

ANSWER KEY
New TOEIC
Mini-Test

Explanatory Answers can be found beginning on page 270.

Part 5: Incomplete Sentences

1. **B**
2. **C**
3. **A**
4. **C**
5. **B**
6. **D**
7. **A**
8. **B**
9. **A**
10. **D**
11. **C**
12. **B**
13. **D**
14. **A**
15. **C**

Part 6: Text Completion

16. **C**
17. **B**
18. **D**
19. **A**
20. **A**
21. **C**
22. **B**
23. **A**

Part 7: Reading Comprehension

24. **B**
25. **B**
26. **D**
27. **C**
28. **A**
29. **A**
30. **C**
31. **B**
32. **B**
33. **C**
34. **A**
35. **D**
36. **A**

EXPLANATORY ANSWERS FOR NEW TOEIC READING SKILLS

Part 5: Incomplete Sentences

1. **(D)** This is a verb meaning *distinguish.* Choice (A) is a verb meaning *be different.* Choice (B) is a noun. Choice (C) is an adjective.
2. **(A)** *A few* is correctly used before the plural count noun *people.* Choice (B) is used with noncount nouns. Choice (C) is used in negative sentences and questions. Choice (D) is used with singular count nouns or noncount nouns.
3. **(A)** The present perfect continuous tense is used to refer to an action that started in the past and is still in progress. Choices (B) and (C) are future forms. Choice (D) is present continuous.
4. **(B)** *During* is used to refer to something that occurs at any point in a period of time. Choices (A), (C), and (D) have no meaning in this context.
5. **(C)** This is an object pronoun following the preposition *to.* Choice (A) is a subject pronoun. Choice (B) is a possessive adjective. Choice (D) is a reflexive pronoun.
6. **(B)** This is an adjective referring to the noun *designer.* Choice (A) is a verb and has a completely different meaning. Choice (C) is a noun. Choice (D) is an adverb.
7. **(D)** *Lets* is the only one of the choices that is followed by a base form verb. Choice (A) does not really fit the meaning of the sentence and would require a completely different sentence structure (. . . *suggests that we telecommute* . . .). Choices (B) and (C) are followed by an infinitive verb.
8. **(A)** *Attract* means *bring to.* Choices (B), (C), and (D) have meanings that don't fit the context.
9. **(B)** This is a subject pronoun acting as the subject of the clause. Choice (A) is a possessive pronoun. Choice (A) is a possessive adjective. Choice (C) is an object pronoun. Choice (D) is a reflexive pronoun.
10. **(C)** *Participate* means *take part in.* Choices (A), (B), and (C) have meanings that don't fit the context and are words that aren't generally followed by *in.*
11. **(D)** *Otherwise* means *if not.* Choice (A) would have to be followed by *not* in order to fit the sentence. Choice (B) would have to be preceded by *or* in order to fit the sentence. Choice (C) would have to introduce the first clause of this sentence in order to make sense.
12. **(C)** This is a past participle form completing the passive verb *are given.* The sentence is passive because the subject, *orientation sessions,* does not perform the action. Choices (A) and (B) are active forms and cannot follow *are.* Choice (D) can follow *are,* but that would form an active present continuous verb.
13. **(C)** This is a comparative adjective; the idea is *a larger space than this one.* Choice (A) looks similar but has a different meaning. Choices (B) and (D) are superlative forms and cannot follow the word *a.*
14. **(A)** This verb agrees with the subject *documents.* Choices (A) and (D) don't agree with the subject. Choice (C) is an adjective.
15. **(B)** Compensation means payment. Choices (A), (C), and (D) have meanings that don't fit the context.
16. **(D)** A *branch* in this context is another location of a larger business. Because the restaurant is popular, the owners are opening up more locations. Choices (A), (B), and (C) are all things that might be *opened,* but they don't fit the context.
17. **(D)** The main verb *require* is followed by a gerund. Choice (A) is base form or present tense. Choice (B) is present tense. Choice (C) is past participle.
18. **(B)** *Container* is a noun referring an object that holds things. Choice (A) is a verb. Choice (C) is a noun, but it refers to a situation, not an object. Choice (D) is an adjective.
19. **(B)** *As* in this context means *while* or *at the same time as.* Choices (A) and (C) are prepositions, so they cannot be used to introduce a clause. Choice (D) means *up to the time.*
20. **(C)** *Which,* in this sentence, is a relative pronoun introducing a nonrestrictive adjective clause. It refers to the noun *offices.* Choice

(A) refers to a person. Choice (B) introduces a restrictive clause. Choice (D) is a possessive word.

21. **(D)** *Among* is a preposition meaning *in a group*. In this case, the group is made up of *candidates*. Choice (A) is an adverb. Choices (B) and (C) are prepositions, but they don't fit the context.
22. **(A)** *Overly* means *excessively* or *too much*. Choice (B) means *completely*. Choice (C) means *very little*. Choice (D) means *a lot*.
23. **(B)** This is a noun, the object of the verb *received*. Choices (A) and (D) are verbs. Choice (C) is a noun that refers to people.
24. **(D)** A present tense verb is required in a future time clause. Choice (A) is a future verb. Choice (B) is an infinitive. Choice (C) is past tense.
25. **(C)** *Since* introduces a cause or reason. Choices (A) and (B) introduce a contradiction. Choice (D) introduces a result.
26. **(A)** *Sizeable* is an adjective meaning *large*. Choice (B) is a noun. Choice (C) means *the most*. Choice (D) means *very small*.
27. **(B)** *Delayed* means *started late*. Choices (A), (C), and (D) have meanings that don't fit the context.
28. **(D)** The verb *object* is followed by the preposition *to*. Choices (A), (B) and (C) are prepositions that don't normally follow this verb.
29. **(C)** *Would* + base form is the correct verb form for the main clause of a present tense unreal conditional. Choice (A) is base form. Choice (B) is past tense. Choice (D) is present perfect tense.
30. **(D)** This is a noun following the main verb. Choice (A) is a verb. Choice (B) is an adjective. Choice (C) is an adverb.

Part 6: Text Completion

SKILL 1

1. **(D)** The sentences inform staff about a meeting regarding health insurance. Choice (D) is not about a meeting or about health insurance.
2. **(C)** The sentences are about asking for help with a client contract. Choice (C) mentions the client, but it is not related to the contract or the request for help.
3. **(B)** The sentences are about scheduled elevator maintenance and the disruption it might cause to elevator use. Choice (B) mentions the elevators, but it is not about maintenance or disruption of service.
4. **(A)** The sentences are about confirming an agreed-on meeting and its content. Choice (A) does not make sense because clearly the writer has been able to contact the recipient of the message.
5. **(E)** The sentences are about asking a job seeker to come in for an interview. Choice (E) is related to job seeking, but it does not make sense because the writer says that the job seeker already has the right background.

New TOEIC Practice

1. **(B)** This is an adverb modifying the verb *invite*. Choice (A) is an adjective. Choices (C) and (D) are nouns.
2. **(D)** This is an adverb modifying the adjective *better*. Choices (A) and (B) have meanings that don't fit the context. Choice (C) is not an adverb.
3. **(A)** *Live* is an adjective referring to something that is done in front of the audience rather than recorded in a studio. Choices (B) and (D) are adjectives that mean the *opposite of dead*. Choice (C) is a verb meaning *make more interesting or exciting*.
4. **(C)** The purpose of the letter is to extend an invitation to a social event, and Choice (C) is an appropriate way to conclude an invitation. Choice (A) is incorrect because appointments are not normally made for social events. Choices (B) and (D) are incorrect because guests are not normally asked to pay or get tickets for social events.
5. **(B)** This is a possessive adjective modifying the noun *request*. Choice (A) is a subject pronoun. Choice (C) is a possessive pronoun. Choice (D) is a contraction of *you will*.

6. **(C)** The request for time off is being turned down because it is at the wrong time of year; *season* means *time of year.* Choices (A) and (B) refer to a place. Choice (D) is something that shows specific dates.
7. **(D)** The implied subject of the verb is *seminar,* and a seminar does not give itself but is given by someone, so a passive voice verb is needed here. Choices (A), (B), and (C) are all active verb forms,
8. **(D)** The purpose of the e-mail is to explain the reason for turning down a request, so apologizing is appropriate near the end of the message. Choice (A) is not logical as it is a about a past seminar and the message is about future seminars. Choice (B) is out of place; it could possibly fit in with the mention of the May busy season. Choice (C) does not make sense as clearly the recipient of the message knows this as he has already done it.
9. **(C)** This is a gerund used as the subject of the sentence. Choice (A) is base form or present tense. Choice (B) is infinitive. Choice (D) is a noun that means the same as *parking lot* and doesn't make sense in the sentence.
10. **(A)** *Tow* describes a way of removing a car and taking it to another place. Choice (B) describes what will happen, but it is not usually used in the context of moving illegally parked cars. Choices (C) and (D) don't fit the context.
11. **(B)** *Damages,* or harm, may happen to a car when it is towed. Choices (A), (C), and (D) don't fit the context.
12. **(D)** The purpose of the notice is to explain that only cars with a sticker can park in the lot, so this sentence explaining how to get a sticker fits the purpose and context. Choices (A), (B), and (C) are about the parking lot, but they are not about parking stickers.
13. **(A)** The notice is directed towards people who might be interested in renting office space in a particular building, so this sentence fits the context. Choices (B), (C), and (D) are also about the building, but they are not specifically related to renting space there.
14. **(B)** *Heart* in this sentence means *center.* Choice (A) is not likely to be described as a *prime location.* Choices (C) and (D) don't make sense.
15. **(D)** *Range* refers to a series of numbers, in this case, from the smallest to the largest office sizes. Choices (A), (B), and (C) don't fit the context.
16. **(C)** *Our* refers to the owners of the building, previously referred to in the announcement as *we.* The owners are the ones who have model offices. Choice (A) would refer to the reader of the announcement. Choices (B) and (D) refer to other people.

Part 7: Reading Comprehension

SKILL 1

1. **(B)** *End* can mean *finish,* but the expression *at your end* often refers to the other person's responsibility. We know from the context that the writer is laying out the tasks that must be done and who is responsible for each.
2. **(A)** *Cut* can mean *shorten,* but it can also mean *skip entirely.* We know from the context that the writer did not attend the lunch.
3. **(B)** *Rough* can mean *the opposite of smooth,* or *uneven,* but it can also mean *unfinished* or *unpolished.* We know from the context that the writer is still working on the report.
4. **(B)** *Direction* can refer to the route one takes, but can also mean *guidance.* The people in the group will work under Ms. Petersen's guidance.
5. **(A)** *Figure* can mean understand, but in this context it means *estimate—We estimate that the work will take a week.*

SKILL 2

1. **(B)** The sentence mentions *these requirements,* referring to the two sentences prior to (B), which explain the requirements.
2. **(C)** The sentence mentions *$40,000,* which is referred to in the next sentence as *that amount.* The sentence also uses the word *she,* referring to Amy Ann Anderson, so it cannot

be placed until after that name is mentioned, that is, not in positions (A) or (B).

3. **(C)** The sentence before mentions a discussion, and this sentence describes the discussion that will take place.
4. **(B)** This sentence mentions the *artistically designed interior,* and the sentence that follows gives some examples of what this means.
5. **(A)** The first sentence states that there will be a job fair, then this sentence follows, giving a general idea of what the fair is about. The rest of the paragraph describes details of the fair.

New TOEIC Practice

1. **(B)** Jim Hart says *the bus can hardly move* due to heavy traffic. Choices (A), (B), and (C) are logical, but incorrect.
2. **(C)** *I'm sorry?,* said or written as a question, is short for *I'm sorry, but I don't understand.* Lin Lee's response, explaining which papers she is referring to, makes it clear that Jim Hart was asking for an explanation. Choice (A) is related to the mention of papers. Choice (B) is another meaning of the phrase *I'm sorry.* Choice (D) is another way of apologizing.
3. **(C)** The article talks about giving cooking classes as a way for restaurants to attract customers. Choices (A) and (B) are related to the topic, but they are not discussed. Choice (D) is mentioned, but it is not the main idea.
4. **(B)** Paragraph 2 explains that this type of cooking class usually *fills up most quickly,* that is, many people want to take it. Choice (A) is not mentioned. Choices (C) and (D) are mentioned, but not as the most popular.
5. **(D)** The sentence that precedes this explains that cooking classes are *an effective means of advertising your business,* and this sentence goes on to explain that idea in further detail. Choices (A), (B), and (C) are not logical locations for this sentence.
6. **(C)** The purpose of the memo is to give information about the workshops and encourage staff to take one. Choices (A) and (D) are plausible, but they are not correct. Choice (B) is unlikely, as Harry Roberts works at the Markham Company, not at BTI.
7. **(D)** The memo tells staff to check with supervisors before registering for a class, and the purpose of the e-mail is to give Jon permission to take time off for a workshop. Choices (A), (B), and (D) don't fit this description.
8. **(C)** Of the three workshops mentioned in the e-mail, this is the only one that does not meet on Monday afternoon, the time that Jon's supervisor wants him to stay at the office. Choices (A) and (B) meet on Monday afternoons. Choice (D) was not mentioned as a workshop Jon is interested in.
9. **(A)** The memo says the company *will pay the tuition in full,* so Jon won't have to pay anything himself. Choice (B) is not mentioned. Choice (C) is the tuition for workshops meeting once a week. Choice (D) is the tuition for workshops meeting twice a week.
10. **(B)** Marissa wants Jon to continue doing what he's doing because he has been doing so well. Choices (A), (C), and (D) are other meanings of the word *keep,* but they don't fit the context.

EXPLANATORY ANSWERS FOR MINI-TEST FOR NEW TOEIC READING

Part 5: Incomplete Sentences

1. **(B)** This third person singular verb agrees with the singular subject, *Rice Enterprises,* which is the name of a company. Choices (A) and (D) are verbs that don't agree with the subject. Choice (C) is a noun.
2. **(C)** This is an adverb modifying the adjective *successful.* Choices (A) and (B) are adjectives. Choice (D) is a noun.
3. **(A)** *Increase* means *make bigger,* and we know from the context—opening up a new manufacturing plant—that that is what the plans are about. Choice (B) also means *make bigger,* but only refers to size, not to amount or quantity. Choices (C) and (D) mean *make smaller.*
4. **(C)** *Although* introduces a contradictory cause—one would expect that press atten-

tion would cause more business, but that isn't what happened. Choice (A) introduces a cause or reason. Choice (B) introduces a result. Choice (D) introduces a contradictory result—it could be used with the second clause of this sentence.

5. **(B)** *Confidential* means *private* or *secret.* Choices (A), (C), and (D) have meanings that don't fit the context.
6. **(D)** *As long as* means *during the time.* Choices (A), (B), and (C) have meanings that don't fit the context.
7. **(A)** This is an object pronoun (follows the verb) referring to a woman, *Mrs. Yamamoto.* Choice (B) is a possessive pronoun. Choice (C) is a subject pronoun. Choice (D) is a reflexive pronoun.
8. **(B)** In this context, *explain* means *give information about.* Choices (A), (C), and (D) have meanings that don't fit the context.
9. **(A)** A noun is needed as an object of the verb *hear* and following the adjective *much.* Choice (B) is a noun but refers to people, not a situation, and as a plural noun cannot follow *much.* Choice (C) is a gerund or present participle. Choice (D) is past tense or past participle.
10. **(D)** The main verb *ask* is followed by an infinitive. Choice (A) is base form or present tense. Choice (B) is present tense. Choice (C) is a gerund or present participle.
11. **(C)** *Whether* introduces possible alternatives. Choice (A) is also used with alternatives, but it comes after the subject of the clause. Choice (B) gives a negative meaning to the sentence. Choice (D) introduces a contradiction.
12. **(B)** *Definite* is an adjective defining the noun *answer.* Choice (A) is a verb. Choice (C) is an adverb. Choice (D) is a noun.
13. **(D)** *Different* is followed by the preposition *from.* Choices (A), (B), and (C) are prepositions that don't normally follow *different.*
14. **(A)** *Thoroughly* means *completely.* Choices (B), (C), and (D) have meanings that don't fit the context.
15. **(C)** *Modifications* means *changes.* Choices (A), (B), and (D) have meanings that don't fit the context.

Part 6: Text Completion

16. **(C)** The passive form is required here because the subject, *seminar,* is not active—the seminar doesn't offer itself, it is offered by Stellar. Choices (A), (B), and (D) are all active verbs.
17. **(B)** *Covers* in this context means *includes.* In this case, the things that the price pays for are lunch and materials, as well as the seminar itself. Choices (B), (C), and (D) have meanings that don't fit the context.
18. **(D)** A noun is needed here to act as the subject of the sentence. Choices (A) and (C) are verbs. Choice (B) is a noun, but it refers to a person, not a process, which is the meaning here.
19. **(A)** The preceding sentence says, *take a look at what else we have to offer,* and Choice (A) gives examples of services that are offered. Choices (B), (C), and (D) don't fit the context.
20. **(A)** *These* is a pronoun for the plural noun *services* and is the subject of the sentence. Choice (B) is not a pronoun. Choice (C) is an object pronoun. Choice (D) is singular.
21. **(C)** *Currently* means *now.* Choice (A) means *recently,* so it refers to a past time. Choice (B) means *maybe.* Choice (D) means *at some time in the future.*
22. **(B)** *Coordinator* is a noun referring to a person. Choice (A) is a verb. Choice (C) is a gerund or present participle. Choice (D) is a noun, but it doesn't refer to a person.
23. **(A)** The previous sentence suggests contacting someone about volunteering, and this sentence mentions specific information to include related to volunteering. Choices (B), (C), and (D) are about the community center, but they are not about becoming a volunteer there.

Part 7: Reading Comprehension

24. **(B)** Ms. Osgood is texting Mai Chen to ask for assistance with something related to her work, so we can infer that Mai Chen is her assistant. Choice (A) is contradicted by the correct answer. Choice (C) is confused with the sug-

gestion to send the samples by messenger. Choice (D) is where Ms. Osgood is right now.

25. **(B)** The expression, *It's your call,* means *It's your decision to make.* Ms. Osgood has to decide for herself whether to pick up the samples or have them sent by messenger. Choice (A) confuses the meaning of the word *call* in this context. Choices (C) and (D) repeat words used in the text, but they are not the correct answer.
26. **(D)** The information states, *Bring your own bike or rent one of ours,* and then a link to rental rates is provided. Choices (A), (B), and (C) are all listed as part of a tour.
27. **(C)** Both group and self-guided (that is, an individual could take the tour without a guide) are offered. Choice (A) is incorrect because the length of the tours is not mentioned. Choice (B) is incorrect because tours are offered *for every kind of cyclist.* Choice (D) is incorrect because tours are offered *year round.*
28. **(A)** The page ends with a list of *top tours,* that is, the most popular tours. Choices (B), (C), and (D) do not have the same meaning as *top.*
29. **(A)** They are discussing ordering fabric to make shirts, so they work for a clothing manufacturer. Choice (A) is where they are buying the fabric. Choice (C) is related to the discussion of making an order. Choice (D) repeats the word *shirt.*
30. **(C)** Anders ordered 4 bolts of fabric, but they need 6, so he offers to *call them back,* in order to, we can assume, order 2 more bolts of fabric. Choices (A), (B), and (C) are related to the situation of making orders, but they are not the correct answer.
31. **(B)** Milla mentions the need to work quickly to fulfill the order, so Yoko mentions the next step—shipping it. *The expression on their way* means *traveling towards a specific place.* Choices (A), (C), and (D) don't fit the context.
32. **(B)** The ad states, *Owner will remodel to suit your needs,* so we can assume that remodeling has not been done recently. Choice (A) is true because the rent includes utilities. Choice (C) is true because the office is near bus and subway lines. Choice (D) is true because the rent includes parking.
33. **(C)** Ms. Roper wants to pay $1000 a month rent plus utilities. She also prefers a place with parking, but she could do without this if it is near the subway. Office #3 costs $1100 with utilities and is one block from the subway, so it fits her criteria. Choices (A) and (B) are too expensive. Choice (D) doesn't have parking and isn't close to the subway.
34. **(A)** Ms. Roper is available *any day after 1:00 P.M.,* that is, any afternoon. Choice (B) is incorrect because she is busy in the mornings. Choice (C) is incorrect because she wants to look this week. Choice (D) is not mentioned.
35. **(D)** Businesses are being forced out of downtown because the rents are becoming too high. Choices (A), (B), and (C) are other uses of the word *driving,* but they are not the correct answer.
36. **(A)** The article explains that businesses are leaving downtown because of high rents and then describes Brightwood as *affordable,* that is, not too expensive. Also, in the e-mail, Ms. Roper describes downtown as *a bit out of reach,* that is, more expensive than she can pay for, and goes on to say that Brightwood is suitable for her. Choice (B) is incorrect, as the article mentions wide streets, gardens, and a park as attractions. Choice (C) is incorrect because the article shows the neighborhood as a place that is enjoying increasing popularity. Choice (D) is true of downtown, not Brightwood.

TOEIC Model Tests

AUDIO AND AUDIOSCRIPTS

The MP3 files and audioscripts for all listening segments can be found online at
http://barronsbooks.com/tp/toeic/audio/

STRATEGY SUMMARY

Tips and Strategies to help you score well on the TOEIC.

***The following strategies are a review of those presented in this Listening Comprehension Review. Using these strategies will improve your score on the TOEIC.**

LISTENING

Part 1: Photographs

- When you look at the photo, analyze the people. Determine their number, gender, location, occupation, and so on.
- Look for context clues in the photo.
- Listen for the meaning of the *whole sentence* to determine which choice best matches the photo.
- Try to analyze every detail in the photograph.
- Try to describe these details in English to yourself.
- Listen to all answers until you hear the obviously correct one. Once you are sure, don't listen to the rest of the answer options. Start analyzing the next photograph.
- If you aren't sure, keep your pencil on the most likely correct answer. If you listen to all options and have no other choice, mark that answer and move on quickly.

Part 2: Question-Response

- Listen and look for context clues.
- Listen and look for the *meaning* of the statement, question, and answer choices. Do not be confused by words with similar sounds, homonyms, and related words.
- Listen carefully to the entire question and ALL the answer choices before making a final decision.

Part 3: Conversations and Part 4: Talks

- Learn to recognize types of questions. Study the common questions and common answers presented in this chapter. Remember that questions about people generally begin with *who* or *what*, questions about location generally begin with where, questions about time generally begin with *when* or *how long*, and so on.
- Read the answer choices, make assumptions about the items listed, and listen for relevant clues.
- Focus on the question. Read the three questions before you hear the talk. Don't read the answer choices. Try to listen carefully for the answer.
- As the conversations and talks start, write your potential answer choices in the exam book.
- Focusing on the details of the talk will also help you with inference and main idea questions.

READING COMPREHENSION

Part 5: Incomplete Sentences and Part 6: Text Completion

- Recognize the different parts of speech
- Recognize the agreement of person, number, and tense
- Recognize different verb forms
- Recognize different adjective and adverb forms
- Recognize singular and plural nouns
- Recognize different kinds of clauses

Part 7: Reading Comprehension

- Know how to read the types of passages found on the TOEIC
- Know the types of reading comprehension questions found on the TOEIC
- Know how to use PSRA:

  — Predict what the passage will be about
  — Scan the passage and answer options for key words
  — Read the passage quickly
  — Answer the questions

***Many thanks to my readers, especially Jean-Pierre Saint-Aimé, who have provided valuable tips on test-taking strategies.**

ANSWER SHEET
Model Test 1

LISTENING COMPREHENSION

Part 1: Photographs

1. Ⓐ Ⓑ Ⓒ Ⓓ
2. Ⓐ Ⓑ Ⓒ Ⓓ
3. Ⓐ Ⓑ Ⓒ Ⓓ
4. Ⓐ Ⓑ Ⓒ Ⓓ
5. Ⓐ Ⓑ Ⓒ Ⓓ
6. Ⓐ Ⓑ Ⓒ Ⓓ
7. Ⓐ Ⓑ Ⓒ Ⓓ
8. Ⓐ Ⓑ Ⓒ Ⓓ
9. Ⓐ Ⓑ Ⓒ Ⓓ
10. Ⓐ Ⓑ Ⓒ Ⓓ

Part 2: Question-Response

11. Ⓐ Ⓑ Ⓒ Ⓓ
12. Ⓐ Ⓑ Ⓒ Ⓓ
13. Ⓐ Ⓑ Ⓒ Ⓓ
14. Ⓐ Ⓑ Ⓒ Ⓓ
15. Ⓐ Ⓑ Ⓒ Ⓓ
16. Ⓐ Ⓑ Ⓒ Ⓓ
17. Ⓐ Ⓑ Ⓒ Ⓓ
18. Ⓐ Ⓑ Ⓒ Ⓓ
19. Ⓐ Ⓑ Ⓒ Ⓓ
20. Ⓐ Ⓑ Ⓒ Ⓓ
21. Ⓐ Ⓑ Ⓒ Ⓓ
22. Ⓐ Ⓑ Ⓒ Ⓓ
23. Ⓐ Ⓑ Ⓒ Ⓓ
24. Ⓐ Ⓑ Ⓒ Ⓓ
25. Ⓐ Ⓑ Ⓒ Ⓓ
26. Ⓐ Ⓑ Ⓒ Ⓓ
27. Ⓐ Ⓑ Ⓒ Ⓓ
28. Ⓐ Ⓑ Ⓒ Ⓓ
29. Ⓐ Ⓑ Ⓒ Ⓓ
30. Ⓐ Ⓑ Ⓒ Ⓓ
31. Ⓐ Ⓑ Ⓒ Ⓓ
32. Ⓐ Ⓑ Ⓒ Ⓓ
33. Ⓐ Ⓑ Ⓒ Ⓓ
34. Ⓐ Ⓑ Ⓒ Ⓓ
35. Ⓐ Ⓑ Ⓒ Ⓓ
36. Ⓐ Ⓑ Ⓒ Ⓓ
37. Ⓐ Ⓑ Ⓒ Ⓓ
38. Ⓐ Ⓑ Ⓒ Ⓓ
39. Ⓐ Ⓑ Ⓒ Ⓓ
40. Ⓐ Ⓑ Ⓒ Ⓓ

Part 3: Conversations

41. Ⓐ Ⓑ Ⓒ Ⓓ
42. Ⓐ Ⓑ Ⓒ Ⓓ
43. Ⓐ Ⓑ Ⓒ Ⓓ
44. Ⓐ Ⓑ Ⓒ Ⓓ
45. Ⓐ Ⓑ Ⓒ Ⓓ
46. Ⓐ Ⓑ Ⓒ Ⓓ
47. Ⓐ Ⓑ Ⓒ Ⓓ
48. Ⓐ Ⓑ Ⓒ Ⓓ
49. Ⓐ Ⓑ Ⓒ Ⓓ
50. Ⓐ Ⓑ Ⓒ Ⓓ
51. Ⓐ Ⓑ Ⓒ Ⓓ
52. Ⓐ Ⓑ Ⓒ Ⓓ
53. Ⓐ Ⓑ Ⓒ Ⓓ
54. Ⓐ Ⓑ Ⓒ Ⓓ
55. Ⓐ Ⓑ Ⓒ Ⓓ
56. Ⓐ Ⓑ Ⓒ Ⓓ
57. Ⓐ Ⓑ Ⓒ Ⓓ
58. Ⓐ Ⓑ Ⓒ Ⓓ
59. Ⓐ Ⓑ Ⓒ Ⓓ
60. Ⓐ Ⓑ Ⓒ Ⓓ
61. Ⓐ Ⓑ Ⓒ Ⓓ
62. Ⓐ Ⓑ Ⓒ Ⓓ
63. Ⓐ Ⓑ Ⓒ Ⓓ
64. Ⓐ Ⓑ Ⓒ Ⓓ
65. Ⓐ Ⓑ Ⓒ Ⓓ
66. Ⓐ Ⓑ Ⓒ Ⓓ
67. Ⓐ Ⓑ Ⓒ Ⓓ
68. Ⓐ Ⓑ Ⓒ Ⓓ
69. Ⓐ Ⓑ Ⓒ Ⓓ
70. Ⓐ Ⓑ Ⓒ Ⓓ

Part 4: Talks

71. Ⓐ Ⓑ Ⓒ Ⓓ
72. Ⓐ Ⓑ Ⓒ Ⓓ
73. Ⓐ Ⓑ Ⓒ Ⓓ
74. Ⓐ Ⓑ Ⓒ Ⓓ
75. Ⓐ Ⓑ Ⓒ Ⓓ
76. Ⓐ Ⓑ Ⓒ Ⓓ
77. Ⓐ Ⓑ Ⓒ Ⓓ
78. Ⓐ Ⓑ Ⓒ Ⓓ
79. Ⓐ Ⓑ Ⓒ Ⓓ
80. Ⓐ Ⓑ Ⓒ Ⓓ
81. Ⓐ Ⓑ Ⓒ Ⓓ
82. Ⓐ Ⓑ Ⓒ Ⓓ
83. Ⓐ Ⓑ Ⓒ Ⓓ
84. Ⓐ Ⓑ Ⓒ Ⓓ
85. Ⓐ Ⓑ Ⓒ Ⓓ
86. Ⓐ Ⓑ Ⓒ Ⓓ
87. Ⓐ Ⓑ Ⓒ Ⓓ
88. Ⓐ Ⓑ Ⓒ Ⓓ
89. Ⓐ Ⓑ Ⓒ Ⓓ
90. Ⓐ Ⓑ Ⓒ Ⓓ
91. Ⓐ Ⓑ Ⓒ Ⓓ
92. Ⓐ Ⓑ Ⓒ Ⓓ
93. Ⓐ Ⓑ Ⓒ Ⓓ
94. Ⓐ Ⓑ Ⓒ Ⓓ
95. Ⓐ Ⓑ Ⓒ Ⓓ
96. Ⓐ Ⓑ Ⓒ Ⓓ
97. Ⓐ Ⓑ Ⓒ Ⓓ
98. Ⓐ Ⓑ Ⓒ Ⓓ
99. Ⓐ Ⓑ Ⓒ Ⓓ
100. Ⓐ Ⓑ Ⓒ Ⓓ

ANSWER SHEET
Model Test 1

READING

Part 5: Incomplete Sentences

101. Ⓐ Ⓑ Ⓒ Ⓓ	111. Ⓐ Ⓑ Ⓒ Ⓓ	121. Ⓐ Ⓑ Ⓒ Ⓓ	131. Ⓐ Ⓑ Ⓒ Ⓓ
102. Ⓐ Ⓑ Ⓒ Ⓓ	112. Ⓐ Ⓑ Ⓒ Ⓓ	122. Ⓐ Ⓑ Ⓒ Ⓓ	132. Ⓐ Ⓑ Ⓒ Ⓓ
103. Ⓐ Ⓑ Ⓒ Ⓓ	113. Ⓐ Ⓑ Ⓒ Ⓓ	123. Ⓐ Ⓑ Ⓒ Ⓓ	133. Ⓐ Ⓑ Ⓒ Ⓓ
104. Ⓐ Ⓑ Ⓒ Ⓓ	114. Ⓐ Ⓑ Ⓒ Ⓓ	124. Ⓐ Ⓑ Ⓒ Ⓓ	134. Ⓐ Ⓑ Ⓒ Ⓓ
105. Ⓐ Ⓑ Ⓒ Ⓓ	115. Ⓐ Ⓑ Ⓒ Ⓓ	125. Ⓐ Ⓑ Ⓒ Ⓓ	135. Ⓐ Ⓑ Ⓒ Ⓓ
106. Ⓐ Ⓑ Ⓒ Ⓓ	116. Ⓐ Ⓑ Ⓒ Ⓓ	126. Ⓐ Ⓑ Ⓒ Ⓓ	136. Ⓐ Ⓑ Ⓒ Ⓓ
107. Ⓐ Ⓑ Ⓒ Ⓓ	117. Ⓐ Ⓑ Ⓒ Ⓓ	127. Ⓐ Ⓑ Ⓒ Ⓓ	137. Ⓐ Ⓑ Ⓒ Ⓓ
108. Ⓐ Ⓑ Ⓒ Ⓓ	118. Ⓐ Ⓑ Ⓒ Ⓓ	128. Ⓐ Ⓑ Ⓒ Ⓓ	138. Ⓐ Ⓑ Ⓒ Ⓓ
109. Ⓐ Ⓑ Ⓒ Ⓓ	119. Ⓐ Ⓑ Ⓒ Ⓓ	129. Ⓐ Ⓑ Ⓒ Ⓓ	139. Ⓐ Ⓑ Ⓒ Ⓓ
110. Ⓐ Ⓑ Ⓒ Ⓓ	120. Ⓐ Ⓑ Ⓒ Ⓓ	130. Ⓐ Ⓑ Ⓒ Ⓓ	140. Ⓐ Ⓑ Ⓒ Ⓓ

Part 6: Text Completion

141. Ⓐ Ⓑ Ⓒ Ⓓ	144. Ⓐ Ⓑ Ⓒ Ⓓ	147. Ⓐ Ⓑ Ⓒ Ⓓ	150. Ⓐ Ⓑ Ⓒ Ⓓ
142. Ⓐ Ⓑ Ⓒ Ⓓ	145. Ⓐ Ⓑ Ⓒ Ⓓ	148. Ⓐ Ⓑ Ⓒ Ⓓ	151. Ⓐ Ⓑ Ⓒ Ⓓ
143. Ⓐ Ⓑ Ⓒ Ⓓ	146. Ⓐ Ⓑ Ⓒ Ⓓ	149. Ⓐ Ⓑ Ⓒ Ⓓ	152. Ⓐ Ⓑ Ⓒ Ⓓ

Part 7: Reading Comprehension

153. Ⓐ Ⓑ Ⓒ Ⓓ	165. Ⓐ Ⓑ Ⓒ Ⓓ	177. Ⓐ Ⓑ Ⓒ Ⓓ	189. Ⓐ Ⓑ Ⓒ Ⓓ
154. Ⓐ Ⓑ Ⓒ Ⓓ	166. Ⓐ Ⓑ Ⓒ Ⓓ	178. Ⓐ Ⓑ Ⓒ Ⓓ	190. Ⓐ Ⓑ Ⓒ Ⓓ
155. Ⓐ Ⓑ Ⓒ Ⓓ	167. Ⓐ Ⓑ Ⓒ Ⓓ	179. Ⓐ Ⓑ Ⓒ Ⓓ	191. Ⓐ Ⓑ Ⓒ Ⓓ
156. Ⓐ Ⓑ Ⓒ Ⓓ	168. Ⓐ Ⓑ Ⓒ Ⓓ	180. Ⓐ Ⓑ Ⓒ Ⓓ	192. Ⓐ Ⓑ Ⓒ Ⓓ
157. Ⓐ Ⓑ Ⓒ Ⓓ	169. Ⓐ Ⓑ Ⓒ Ⓓ	181. Ⓐ Ⓑ Ⓒ Ⓓ	193. Ⓐ Ⓑ Ⓒ Ⓓ
158. Ⓐ Ⓑ Ⓒ Ⓓ	170. Ⓐ Ⓑ Ⓒ Ⓓ	182. Ⓐ Ⓑ Ⓒ Ⓓ	194. Ⓐ Ⓑ Ⓒ Ⓓ
159. Ⓐ Ⓑ Ⓒ Ⓓ	171. Ⓐ Ⓑ Ⓒ Ⓓ	183. Ⓐ Ⓑ Ⓒ Ⓓ	195. Ⓐ Ⓑ Ⓒ Ⓓ
160. Ⓐ Ⓑ Ⓒ Ⓓ	172. Ⓐ Ⓑ Ⓒ Ⓓ	184. Ⓐ Ⓑ Ⓒ Ⓓ	196. Ⓐ Ⓑ Ⓒ Ⓓ
161. Ⓐ Ⓑ Ⓒ Ⓓ	173. Ⓐ Ⓑ Ⓒ Ⓓ	185. Ⓐ Ⓑ Ⓒ Ⓓ	197. Ⓐ Ⓑ Ⓒ Ⓓ
162. Ⓐ Ⓑ Ⓒ Ⓓ	174. Ⓐ Ⓑ Ⓒ Ⓓ	186. Ⓐ Ⓑ Ⓒ Ⓓ	198. Ⓐ Ⓑ Ⓒ Ⓓ
163. Ⓐ Ⓑ Ⓒ Ⓓ	175. Ⓐ Ⓑ Ⓒ Ⓓ	187. Ⓐ Ⓑ Ⓒ Ⓓ	199. Ⓐ Ⓑ Ⓒ Ⓓ
164. Ⓐ Ⓑ Ⓒ Ⓓ	176. Ⓐ Ⓑ Ⓒ Ⓓ	188. Ⓐ Ⓑ Ⓒ Ⓓ	200. Ⓐ Ⓑ Ⓒ Ⓓ

Model Test 1

LISTENING COMPREHENSION

In this section of the test, you will have the chance to show how well you understand spoken English. There are four parts to this section, with special directions for each part. You will have approximately 45 minutes to complete the Listening Comprehension sections.

Part 1: Photographs

Directions: You will see a photograph. You will hear four statements about the photograph. Choose the statement that most closely matches the photograph and fill in the corresponding oval on your answer sheet.

1.

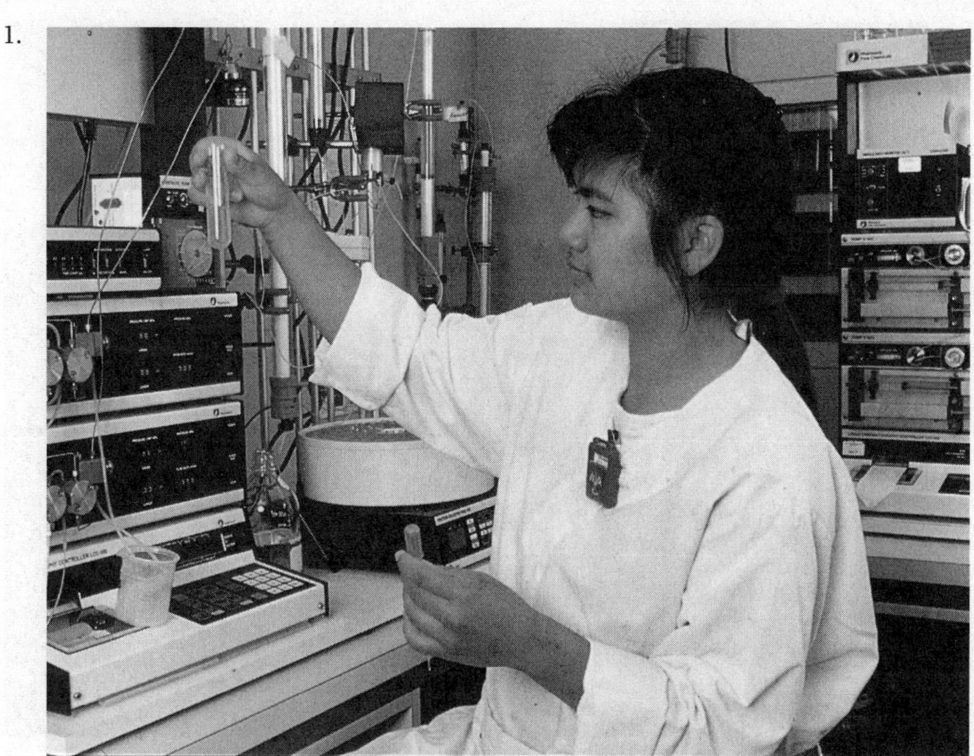

2.

3.

"PASSPORT"
ASSESSMENT
INTERESTS
VALUES
CAREERS
COLLEGES
= CAREER PLAN

4.

5.

UNION AGRICOLA REGIONAL
DE PRODUCTORES DE
FRESA Y HORTALIZAS
DEL VALLE DE ZAMORA
U.A.R.P.F.H.V.Z.

6.

7.

8.

9.

10.

Part 2: Question-Response

Directions: You will hear a question and three possible responses. Choose the response that most closely answers the question and fill in the corresponding oval on your answer sheet.

11. Mark your answer on your answer sheet.
12. Mark your answer on your answer sheet.
13. Mark your answer on your answer sheet.
14. Mark your answer on your answer sheet.
15. Mark your answer on your answer sheet.
16. Mark your answer on your answer sheet.
17. Mark your answer on your answer sheet.
18. Mark your answer on your answer sheet.
19. Mark your answer on your answer sheet.
20. Mark your answer on your answer sheet.
21. Mark your answer on your answer sheet.
22. Mark your answer on your answer sheet.
23. Mark your answer on your answer sheet.
24. Mark your answer on your answer sheet.
25. Mark your answer on your answer sheet.
26. Mark your answer on your answer sheet.
27. Mark your answer on your answer sheet.
28. Mark your answer on your answer sheet.
29. Mark your answer on your answer sheet.
30. Mark your answer on your answer sheet.
31. Mark your answer on your answer sheet.
32. Mark your answer on your answer sheet.
33. Mark your answer on your answer sheet.
34. Mark your answer on your answer sheet.
35. Mark your answer on your answer sheet.
36. Mark your answer on your answer sheet.
37. Mark your answer on your answer sheet.
38. Mark your answer on your answer sheet.
39. Mark your answer on your answer sheet.
40. Mark your answer on your answer sheet.

MODEL TEST 1

Part 3: Conversations

Directions: You will hear a conversation between two people. You will see three questions on each conversation and four possible answers. Choose the best answer to each question and fill in the corresponding oval on your answer sheet.

41. When will the speakers meet?
    (A) 3:00
    (B) 4:00
    (C) 5:00
    (D) 10:00

42. Where will they meet?
    (A) At the bus stop
    (B) At a conference
    (C) In the man's office
    (D) In the waiting room

43. What will the woman bring to the meeting?
    (A) Coffee
    (B) A letter
    (C) Photographs
    (D) Copies of a report

44. Where does the man want to go?
    (A) Cleveland
    (B) Los Angeles
    (C) Chicago
    (D) Denver

45. How will he travel?
    (A) By plane
    (B) By train
    (C) By bus
    (D) By car

46. When will he leave?
    (A) This afternoon
    (B) Tonight
    (C) Tomorrow at 1:00
    (D) Tomorrow at 10:00

47. Where does this conversation take place?
    (A) At a store
    (B) At a hotel
    (C) At a restaurant
    (D) At the man's house

48. What does the man ask for?
    (A) Keys
    (B) More soup
    (C) A better room
    (D) Towels and soap

49. When will he get what he asks for?
    (A) Right away
    (B) Later today
    (C) At 2:00
    (D) Tonight

50. When did the brochures arrive?
    (A) Yesterday afternoon
    (B) Last night
    (C) This morning
    (D) This afternoon

51. What will the woman do now?
    (A) Address the brochures
    (B) Read the brochures
    (C) Print the brochures
    (D) Copy the brochures

52. How many brochures does the woman need?
    (A) 500
    (B) 800
    (C) 1,000
    (D) 2,000

53. What kind of job is the man applying for?

(A) Waiter
(B) Caterer
(C) Advertising executive
(D) Food and beverage salesperson

54. What does the woman ask the man about?

(A) His experience
(B) His appearance
(C) His attitude
(D) His appetite

55. When does the woman want to interview the man?

(A) Today
(B) Next Sunday
(C) Next Monday
(D) Next Tuesday

---

56. Why can't the man play golf tomorrow?

(A) His wife is sick.
(B) It's going to rain.
(C) He has to take a test.
(D) He's feeling tired.

57. What time did he plan to play golf?

(A) 2:00
(B) 4:00
(C) 9:00
(D) 10:00

58. What will he do tomorrow?

(A) Talk on the phone
(B) Go to the movies
(C) Move some furniture
(D) Stay home

59. Where does the woman want to go?

(A) To a fast food restaurant
(B) To a parking lot
(C) To a bank
(D) To a park

60. Where is it?

(A) On a corner
(B) Behind a parking lot
(C) Next door to a library
(D) Across the street from a store

61. How far away is it?

(A) Five blocks away
(B) Five miles away
(C) Five minutes away
(D) Fifteen miles away

---

62. What time is it in the conversation?

(A) 8:00
(B) 8:15
(C) 9:15
(D) 9:30

63. Why is the woman angry?

(A) The man is late.
(B) The weather is bad.
(C) She had to take the bus.
(D) The man drives too fast.

64. What will the man do next time?

(A) Stay home
(B) Drive his car
(C) Leave earlier
(D) Take the train

65. When is the trip?

(A) Sunday afternoon
(B) Sunday night
(C) Monday afternoon
(D) Monday night

66. What does the man think about the woman's decision?

(A) She is being extravagant.
(B) She is being cheap.
(C) She will regret it.
(D) She waited too long.

67. How will the woman pay for the trip?

(A) Cash
(B) Check
(C) Credit card
(D) Money order

68. When does this conversation take place?

(A) In the morning
(B) At noon
(C) In the early afternoon
(D) In the evening

69. Who is the woman talking to?

(A) A butcher
(B) A waiter
(C) Her husband
(D) Her friend

70. What does the woman order?

(A) Lamb
(B) Rice
(C) Fish
(D) Vegetables

Part 4: Talks

Directions: You will hear a talk given by a single speaker. You will see three questions on each talk, each with four possible answers. Choose the best answer to each question and fill in the corresponding oval on your answer sheet.

71. Where is this train located?
    (A) In an airport
    (B) In a city
    (C) Along the coast
    (D) At an amusement park

72. Where should you stand when in a train car?
    (A) By the doors
    (B) By the windows
    (C) In the center
    (D) At either end

73. When can passengers get off the train?
    (A) When they see an exit sign
    (B) Before the bell rings
    (C) After the bell rings
    (D) After the colored light goes on

74. When on Sundays is the museum open?
    (A) In the morning
    (B) In the afternoon
    (C) In the evening
    (D) All day

75. What should be done for more information?
    (A) Go to the museum
    (B) Write a letter
    (C) Call another number
    (D) Stay on the line

76. Who doesn't have to pay to enter the museum?
    (A) Members
    (B) Adults
    (C) Children under twelve
    (D) Children under five

77. What is the first step in getting organized?
    (A) Set a timeline
    (B) Get clutter out of your life
    (C) Buy a calendar
    (D) Make a list of things to be done

78. What should you do next?
    (A) Rank the tasks by their importance
    (B) Do a little work on every task
    (C) Start working on the first task
    (D) Eliminate items and rewrite the list

79. What is the last task of the day?
    (A) Review the list
    (B) Finish uncompleted tasks
    (C) Write a new list
    (D) Throw the list away

80. What does the advertisement encourage you to do?
    (A) Take a holiday
    (B) Redecorate your office
    (C) Look at your office again
    (D) Save some money

81. Which items does the ad mention?
    (A) Decorations
    (B) Carpeting
    (C) Wallpaper
    (D) Furniture

82. When is the last day of the sale?
    (A) Sunday
    (B) Monday
    (C) Tuesday
    (D) Wednesday

83. What is this announcement for?

(A) Schoolteachers
(B) Schoolchildren
(C) Volunteer tutors
(D) Businesspeople

84. How much time does it take to participate?

(A) A minimum of 2 hours a week
(B) A maximum of 2 hours a week
(C) One week a year
(D) One day a week

85. What must people have to participate?

(A) A college degree
(B) Special training
(C) Age above eighteen
(D) Experience with children

---

86. What is today's temperature?

(A) About 15 degrees
(B) About 60 degrees
(C) About 65 degrees
(D) About 90 degrees

87. What does the speaker suggest?

(A) Stay inside
(B) Go outdoors
(C) Take sunglasses
(D) Wear a sweater

88. What will the weather be like tomorrow?

(A) Cloudy
(B) Foggy
(C) Rainy
(D) Sunny

89. What is included in the cost of the lodge?

(A) Breakfast and dinner
(B) Ski equipment
(C) Ski lift tickets
(D) Lunch on the ski slopes

90. Who can take ski lessons?

(A) Ski instructors
(B) Skiers with special abilities
(C) Beginners only
(D) Skiers of all skill levels

91. What do you get if you make a reservation before January 15th?

(A) A free book
(B) A calendar
(C) An extra night at the hotel
(D) A free ski class

---

92. Where is the train now?

(A) Leaving the Hawthorne Street Station
(B) At the Blue Line Station
(C) In between stations
(D) At the Black Avenue Station

93. What caused the problem?

(A) Weather
(B) Engine trouble
(C) Power problems
(D) Track damage

94. What should commuters do?

(A) Get on a bus
(B) Wait for the next train
(C) Get a ticket refund
(D) Stay on the train

MODEL TEST 1

95. What are Greenville residents complaining about?

(A) A new mall
(B) The cost of living
(C) Traffic regulations
(D) A construction delay

96. Where are they making their complaint?

(A) On neighborhood streets
(B) In the newspaper
(C) On TV
(D) At City Hall

97. When will the mayor meet with them?

(A) This morning
(B) This week
(C) Next weekend
(D) Next month

98. When is this talk happening?

(A) At the end of class
(B) In the middle of class
(C) At the beginning of class
(D) Before class starts

99. What should students do before the next class?

(A) Take a test
(B) Read a chapter
(C) Talk to Dr. Lyons
(D) Answer a question

100. What kind of class is this, most likely?

(A) Photography
(B) Museum studies
(C) Mathematics
(D) Drawing

This is the end of the Listening Comprehension portion of the test. Turn to Part 5 in your test book.

READING

In this section of the test, you will have the chance to show how well you understand written English. There are three parts to this section, with special directions for each part.

YOU WILL HAVE ONE HOUR AND FIFTEEN MINUTES TO COMPLETE PARTS 5, 6, AND 7 OF THE TEST.

Part 5: Incomplete Sentences

Directions: You will see a sentence with a missing word. Four possible answers follow the sentence. Choose the best answer to the question and fill in the corresponding oval on your answer sheet.

101. If the customer ——— not satisfied, please have him call the manager.

(A) am
(B) is
(C) are
(D) be

102. We ——— him to think things over carefully before agreeing to accept the new position.

(A) recommended
(B) suggested
(C) proposed
(D) advised

103. Our boss plans to ——— a party in her home for several staff members who will retire this year.

(A) entertain
(B) invite
(C) host
(D) guest

104. The seminar was canceled because the invitations were not ——— in time.

(A) printer
(B) printed
(C) printing
(D) print

105. If the waiter cannot handle your request, the captain ——— assist you.

(A) will
(B) has
(C) did
(D) is

106. Mr. Wong has been recognized by the local business community for his knowledge and ———.

(A) leading
(B) lead
(C) leadership
(D) leader

107. According to the most recent figures, our costs are expected to ——— by about five percent this year.

(A) ascend
(B) increase
(C) escalate
(D) raise

108. Any good business manager will tell you that ——— is the key to efficiency.

(A) organized
(B) organize
(C) organizer
(D) organization

109. They had to postpone the meeting with the client ——— Mr. Tan's plane was late.

(A) although
(B) while
(C) because
(D) with

110. Any information that a client provides us with will be kept completely ——— and not shared with anyone outside the office.

(A) considerable
(B) confidential
(C) constructed
(D) conferred

111. By the time Mr. Sato ——— in San Diego, the convention will have already begun.

(A) arrives
(B) arrived
(C) has arrived
(D) will arrive

112. Because Ms. Kimura has a long ———, she will always leave work at 5:30.

(A) commute
(B) commune
(C) community
(D) compost

113. You'll find the restaurant on the next block, ——— the bank and the bookstore.

(A) among
(B) outside
(C) between
(D) through

114. We hope to begin interviewing ——— applicants by the end of next week.

(A) job
(B) occupation
(C) chore
(D) positioning

115. When you need supplies, ——— a request with the office manager.

(A) filling
(B) fell
(C) fallen
(D) file

116. All cabin attendants must lock the cabin door ——— leaving the room.

(A) afterwards
(B) after
(C) later than
(D) late

117. ——— it was Mr. Guiton's birthday, his staff took him to lunch.

(A) Although
(B) During
(C) Because
(D) That

118. In order to respect our guests' privacy, employees at the Palms Hotel are ——— to knock before entering rooms for any reason.

(A) requited
(B) required
(C) requisite
(D) repulsed

119. The billing clerk was not able to find the invoice ——— the order.

(A) or
(B) and
(C) but
(D) though

120. Before he wrote the check, Jim visited his bank's website to find out his account ———.

(A) size
(B) money
(C) supply
(D) balance

MODEL TEST 1

121. Please forward a copy of the report to Mr. Maxwell as soon as it becomes ———.

(A) avail
(B) available
(C) availability
(D) availing

122. The bell captain suggested that more porters ——— hired.

(A) are
(B) have
(C) be
(D) do

123. The ——— parking spaces for company employees are located on the first level of the parking garage.

(A) signed
(B) assignment
(C) assigned
(D) significant

124. You'll find all the association members listed in the directory in ——— order.

(A) alphabet
(B) alphabetize
(C) alphabetically
(D) alphabetical

125. Raymond has been working on that account for just a few days, but he is ——— completely familiar with the client's background.

(A) yet
(B) since
(C) already
(D) soon

126. Everyone seeking entry to the premises must ——— an identification card to the security guard.

(A) showed
(B) showing
(C) shows
(D) show

127. According to several studies, ——— tasks often lead to muscular fatigue and injury.

(A) repeat
(B) repetitive
(C) repetition
(D) repetitively

128. Visitors are reminded ——— name tags at all times.

(A) to wear
(B) wear
(C) be worn
(D) is wearing

129. The position in the publicity department requires knowledge of foreign languages and ——— experience with international clients.

(A) exciting
(B) expectant
(C) exquisite
(D) extensive

130. The factory's policy is that visitors are ——— allowed to enter the manufacturing area without hard hats, for safety reasons.

(A) rare
(B) ever
(C) never
(D) no time

131. If the renovation plans had been submitted earlier, the board of directors ______ them.

(A) would approve
(B) would have approved
(C) will approve
(D) will have approved

132. Mr. Nolde called to cancel his ______.

(A) notebook
(B) calendar
(C) appointment
(D) notice

133. If Ms. Kamano leaves at 2:00, she ______ at the station on time.

(A) would have arrived
(B) will arrive
(C) arrived
(D) would arrive

134. The speaker did not leave ______ time at the end of her presentation for questions from the audience.

(A) plenty
(B) enough
(C) complete
(D) full

135. The Metropolitan Transportation Service has made service cuts, and now the last train of the evening ______ at 9:00.

(A) depart
(B) departs
(C) to depart
(D) departing

136. In order to minimize disturbances, participants are asked not to leave the room ______ the meeting.

(A) although
(B) in spite of
(C) because
(D) during

137. Due to an injury to his hand, the office assistant could not type ______.

(A) efficiently
(B) intermittently
(C) slowly
(D) gradually

138. It appears certain that the computer was damaged when it ______.

(A) was delivered
(B) has delivered
(C) was delivering
(D) had delivered

139. Mr. Green was very ______ when he learned the news about his promotion.

(A) excite
(B) exciting
(C) excited
(D) excites

140. Like many businesses in this district, that restaurant is open on weekends ______ not on holidays.

(A) either
(B) or
(C) so
(D) but

MODEL TEST 1

Part 6: Text Completion

Directions: You will see four passages each with three blanks. Under each blank are four answer options. Choose the word or phrase that best completes the sentence.

Questions 141–143 refer to the following notice.

International Airport Policy Regarding Security and Baggage

In accordance with international security regulations, passengers are not ______________ to take the following items onto a plane, either in carry-on

141. (A) permitted
(B) permitting
(C) permits
(D) permission

bags or in checked luggage: weapons of any kind, dynamite, or fireworks.

The following items may be placed in checked luggage but not in carry-on bags: Tools, including hammers, screwdrivers, and wrenches; sports equipment ______________ golf clubs, baseball bats, and skis and ski poles.

142. (A) so
(B) such as
(C) example
(D) instance

When you pass through the ______________ line, all bags will go through our

143. (A) ticket
(B) arrival
(C) security
(D) reservations

X-ray machines and some bags will be manually checked by personnel, as well. Thank you for your cooperation. Have a safe and pleasant flight.

Questions 144–146 refer to the following magazine article.

This holiday season, computer retailers hope to increase sales of tablet computers. A heavy advertising campaign began this week, with several computer ______________ placing ads on TV, radio, newspapers,

144. (A) manufacturers
(B) purchasers
(C) consumers
(D) trainers

and the Internet. The advertising campaign will continue through the holiday season.

Tablet computers are gaining popularity because of their ______________.

145. (A) fame
(B) quantity
(C) appearance
(D) convenience

They are lighter and smaller than laptops and much easier to carry around. They are filling a growing need for mobility.

The trend toward giving electronic items as holiday gifts is also growing. The old-fashioned approach to holiday celebrations is giving way to the ______________ for new technology.

146. (A) enthusiast
(B) enthusiasm
(C) enthusiastic
(D) enthusiastically

Questions 147–149 refer to the following e-mail.

To: Marguerite Michelson
From: Ambar Patel
Date: September 22, 20—
Subject: Money due

I am writing in regard to __________ payment. We sent an invoice in

147. (A) a remitted
(B) an overdue
(C) a transferrable
(D) an enclosed

July but still have not received a check. Our phone messages inquiring about the reason for the delay have gone unanswered. If we don't hear from you soon regarding this payment, we __________ to take action.

148. (A) will have
(B) have had
(C) would have
(D) going to have

Please contact me by phone before the end of the week, so we can discuss how best to resolve this matter. The details of your __________, including items and prices, are attached.

149. (A) form
(B) credit
(C) order
(D) rebate

Questions 150–152 refer to the following letter.

April 1, 20—

Richard Byron
Acme Supply Company
324 Constitution Avenue
Annandale, MD

Dear Mr. Byron,
I am writing in __________ to your ad in last Sunday's newspaper about

150. (A) response
(B) repose
(C) resort
(D) respite

the position of office manager. I have worked as an administrative assistant at several local companies for the past ten years. I thoroughly understand the operations of an office and feel that my years of experience __________ me to work as an office manager. I have taken

151. (A) qualify
(B) qualifies
(C) is qualifying
(D) has qualified

several computer courses and am familiar with most current office technology. In addition, I have good organization and people skills, and my employers have always considered me to be a responsible and reliable worker. I am enclosing my resume and two letters of reference. I look forward __________ hearing from you.

152. (A) at
(B) of
(C) to
(D) on

Sincerely,

Andrew Devon

Andrew Devon

MODEL TEST 1

Part 7: Reading Comprehension

Directions: You will see single and double reading passages followed by several questions. Each question has four answer choices. Choose the best answer to the question and fill in the corresponding oval on your answer sheet.

Questions 153–157 refer to the following newspaper article.

Job trends for the future emphasize careers in sales and marketing. Most of the growth will come in international sales, high technology, and electronic marketing. Research shows that overseas sales of high tech equipment and technology will increase 20% in the next decade.

The Internet is the primary source for advertising and marketing to these overseas customers. At the same time, however, successful marketers must find new avenues to increase consumer awareness of their products. As some clients become inundated by information on the Internet, and as others are still just learning to navigate the Web, the marketers of the future will have to be inventive.

More traditional sales skills, such as bilingualism and an agreeable character, are still useful. Willingness to travel is also a plus.

153. What kinds of careers show promise for the future?

(A) Research and development
(B) Sales and marketing
(C) High technology
(D) Travel agents

154. Why are these careers increasing in importance?

(A) Companies are trying to focus on profits.
(B) They address a neglected market segment.
(C) High-tech sales are growing.
(D) Most marketing will occur on the Internet.

155. The word *avenues* in paragraph 2, line 5, is closest in meaning to

(A) streets
(B) ways
(C) stores
(D) sales

156. The author believes that the successful marketer must be

(A) bilingual
(B) overseas
(C) abreast of research
(D) creative

157. According to the article, why isn't Internet advertising always effective?

(A) Some users see too much of it; some see too little.
(B) Many users have limited English skills.
(C) Access to the web may be limited.
(D) Consumers are unaware of products advertised on the Internet.

Questions 158–159 refer to the following announcement.

We are announcing today that we are bringing the Milestone and Ever Green brands even closer together. Effective December 5, 20—, our official name will be:

GREEN MILES WEST

The substitution of "West" in our name—replacing "California"—is the result of an agreement we reached with the California Gardening Association, following a protest over the original use of "California" in our name.

We hope this does not create any confusion among our loyal consumers. While this represents a change from our initial name introduction, it does not change the quality of products we offer our customers.

158. What was the original name of the merged companies?

(A) Milestone
(B) Green Miles California
(C) Green Miles West
(D) Milestone California

159. According to the announcement, why was the name changed?

(A) The corporate offices were relocated.
(B) There was a conflict with another organization.
(C) They did not like the initial choice.
(D) Loyal consumers were confused.

Questions 160–163 refer to the following magazine article.

Hotels are changing their wasteful habits and getting involved in the move to save the environment. At major hotels throughout the world, guests are being greeted by shampoo and mouthwash in glass dispensers instead of elaborate plastic bottles. They are discovering recycling bins in their rooms, and are encouraged to use towels more than once before they are washed.

This green movement is becoming increasingly popular among tourists who look for service providers with an environmental conscience. The business of eco-tours is increasing rapidly. Travel agents are booking clients on "Save the Rainforest" expeditions and similar trips where the emphasis is on protecting the world.

The tourists on these trips are given lectures on the effects of the loss of our planet's natural wonders and what they can do to reverse the trend. They do not need much convincing. The travelers on these excursions are already committed to environmental protection. In fact, a two-year study of litter in Antarctica found that the entire collection of litter left by visitors to the continent could be put in one small sandwich bag. Compare that amount of litter with what the average traveler finds strewn on the streets around a hotel, even an environmentally sensitive hotel.

160. What trend is currently affecting hotels and their guests?

(A) Larger rooms
(B) Better amenities
(C) Lighter foods
(D) Protecting the Earth

161. What does the article imply about glass dispensers and re-using towels?

(A) It's a marketing gimmick.
(B) It's only effective on eco-tours.
(C) It's a wise choice environmentally.
(D) Hotels can set consumer trends.

162. Which group would most likely be members of the green movement?

(A) Fashion designers
(B) First-time visitors
(C) Environmentally conscious travelers
(D) Golf course owners

163. According to the article, eco-travelers should expect to

(A) find litter
(B) hear lectures on the environment
(C) pay more than other travelers
(D) carry their own food

Questions 164–166 refer to the following press release.

VAL D' OR CATERING SUPPLY
Von-Gablenz Straße 3-7
D-50679 Köln
Germany
Telephone: (02 21) 8 25 22 00
Telefax (02 21) 8 25 22 06

FOR IMMEDIATE RELEASE

To: All Business Editors
Fm: Johann Heger
Public Relations Officer

Val D'Or is pleased to announce its purchase of Gourmet Galore, a company that specializes in specialty food products, cookware, and kitchen accessories. Gourmet Galore has profited from customers' revived interest in cooking. There are plans to expand and open five more stores across Europe. Ten of their sixteen stores were remodeled last year, and similar plans are being made for the remaining six.

The company will also open a new line of cooking schools focusing on healthful foods. Regional specialties will be included and guest cooks from all over Europe will participate in the one-week classes.

Please call us for more information.

164. What sort of products does Gourmet Galore sell?

(A) Fabric and furniture
(B) Food and cooking supplies
(C) Washing machines and dryers
(D) Clothes and shoes

165. What plans does Val D'Or have for six Gourmet Galore stores?

(A) Remodel them
(B) Buy them
(C) Sell them
(D) Relocate them

166. What will be emphasized in the cooking classes?

(A) Healthful regional foods
(B) Recipes from one region
(C) New cooking techniques
(D) Using the latest equipment

Questions 167–168 refer to the following notice.

> The company provides a benefit pension plan covering all employees. Benefits are based on years of service and on the employee's highest salary. Both the company and the employee make contributions to the plan according to government regulations. Employees eligible to receive pension funds are paid monthly through the plan.

167. What determines the benefits?

(A) Years at the company and salary
(B) Bonuses
(C) Starting wage
(D) Company profits

168. Who determines the rules of contribution?

(A) Managers of the benefit pension plan
(B) Anyone who is eligible to receive funds
(C) The company and the employee
(D) The government

Questions 169–171 refer to the following letter.

Dear Member,

The goal of Regents is to be the premier name in health care.

Since merging Royal Medical Green Shield and Jason County Medical Bureau in April, we have been working with our customers and business partners to provide more innovative health benefit plans and services, wider provider networks, and enhanced access to health care coverage.

We've been pleased to receive your suggestions for these service improvements, and we look forward to receiving your further thoughts or suggestions. Our suggestion line is open 24 hours a day at 800-998-3445.

We appreciate your patronage.

Sincerely,

Rick Nelson

Rick Nelson
President

169. What is the purpose of this note?

(A) To explain a merger
(B) To talk about Regents' plans
(C) To give a new toll-free number
(D) To describe expanded health coverage

170. What is one goal of Regents?

(A) To increase availability of health care
(B) To publish a primer for new members
(C) To reduce costs to members
(D) To work with customers and business partners

171. What does Regents request of members?

(A) To inform new potential clients of its innovations
(B) To plan for health over the long term
(C) To learn about services on the Internet
(D) To submit ideas to the company

Questions 172–173 refer to the following invoice.

Cooper & Allen, Architects
149 Bridge Street, Suite 107
Harrisville, Colorado 76521

April 5, 20__
INVOICE NUMBER 3892
PROJECT NAME Headquarters–Final Design
PROJECT NUMBER 925639

The Williams Corporation
5110 Falls Avenue
Thomaston, Colorado 76520

The following amounts for the period ending March 30 are due the end of this month.

Current period fees	$8,200.00
Unpaid prior balance	$362.00
Total due at this time	$8,562.00

We value the opportunity to service you. Your prompt payment is greatly appreciated.

172. When is the payment due?

(A) March 1
(B) March 30
(C) April 5
(D) April 30

173. What is owed in addition to current fees?

(A) Prepayment on the next project
(B) Taxes on the current fees
(C) Service charges on current fees
(D) Money not paid on a previous invoice

Questions 174–176 refer to the following memo.

FCC

FISCHER COMMUNICATIONS COMPANY

Interoffice Memorandum

To: All Department Supervisors

Fm: J. Reinhardt
Personnel Officer

Sub: Summary of 3/24 training session on improving job performance.

Date: April 1, 20__

Employees work best if they are happy. As a supervisor, there are things you can do to increase employees' job satisfaction. Make sure your employees understand what they have to do. Give them proper and thorough training so they can do it well, and give them opportunities to bring that training up to date. Make sure that employees have freedom to exercise their own judgment, to offer their suggestions, and to point out problems. Most of all, make sure that you tell them they are doing a good job, not only during special assignments but when they maintain a high standard of routine work.

174. When do employees do their best work?

(A) When they are challenged
(B) When they are happy
(C) When they are busy
(D) When they are pressured

175. Once you have trained an employee, what should you do?

(A) Provide ways to update training
(B) Make the employee train others
(C) Move the employee to a different job
(D) Control his or her chance to practice

176. What is NOT mentioned as a freedom employees should have?

(A) Exercise their own judgment
(B) Offer suggestions
(C) Make changes
(D) Point out problems

Questions 177–180 refer to the following magazine article.

Busy people don't want their vacations to be a hassle. That's why all-inclusive resorts are becoming popular. At these resorts, one price includes all meals, drinks, lodging, and sightseeing. Golf, tennis, and swimming are available for free. Other sports, such as scuba diving, deep sea fishing, and rock climbing, may require separate fees for equipment rental, but instruction and excursions are included. Many resorts also include children's activities as part of the package. Check with a travel agent to find an all-inclusive resort with activities you would enjoy.

177. The word *hassle* in line 3 is closest in meaning to

(A) adventure
(B) expense
(C) routine
(D) bother

178. What does it mean to be an "all-inclusive" resort?

(A) They're in an exclusive location.
(B) One price includes food, lodging, and activities.
(C) Only families may stay there.
(D) Room price and airfare are included.

179. What might cost extra at these resorts?

(A) Excursions and instruction
(B) Transportation for sightseeing
(C) Hotel maid service
(D) Sports equipment rental

180. What is the best way to find an all-inclusive resort?

(A) Ask a friend
(B) Read in a travel guide
(C) Consult a travel agent
(D) Call some hotels

Questions 181–185 refer to the following contract and addendum.

Contract #991YL
Hospitality Consultants Inc.

Hospitality Consultants Inc. (hereafter referred to as Contractor) agrees to perform the following duties as outlined by Cracker Barrel Winery (hereafter called the Client):

A. Statistics Analysis
1) Review the Client's wine sales over the past five years, using monthly inventory charts.
2) Review the Client's food and gift sales over the past five years.
3) Record a summary and chart for proposed sales this year, based on a five-year review.

B. Staff Review
1) Interview one staff member from each department, including the vineyards and cellar.
2) Record duties and responsibilities for each job position.
3) Suggest ways for the Client to cut staffing costs.

C. Decor
1) Meet with board members to discuss year-end renovations.
2) Research materials and costs for all indoor renovations.
3) Provide an estimate for indoor renovations by October 1st.

Any changes to this contract must be agreed upon by both parties in writing.

Contractor: Hanson Carter

Client: Julia Morris

Date: August 7th, 20—

181. What type of service does this Contractor agree to provide?

(A) Labor assistance in the vineyards
(B) Consulting related to the winery's operations
(C) Inventory on glassware and dishes
(D) Taste tests of competitors' wines

182. Which is NOT an example of a person the Contractor may need to speak with to fulfill his duties?

(A) A medical professional
(B) A wine seller
(C) A board member
(D) A part-time grape picker

183. What is the reason for the addendum to the contract?

(A) The Client is not satisfied with the Contractor's work.
(B) The Contractor can't complete the job because of illness.
(C) The Client wants to add to the Contractor's duties.
(D) The Contractor was able to complete the job ahead of schedule.

MODEL TEST 1

Addendum to Contract #991YL dated August 7, 20—
between the following parties:

Contractor: ***Hospitality Consultants Inc.***

Client: ***Cracker Barrel Winery***

The Contractor initiates the following addendum:

1) Due to unforeseen circumstances the Contractor will be unable to provide services to Cracker Barrel Winery after October 9th, 20—. The Contractor does not expect any payment for any project work that is left incomplete as of today.

2) Before December 1st, 20— the Contractor will provide the Client with the names of three alternate consulting firms capable of completing the work set out in Contract #991YL.

3) The Contractor will submit a report of all work that has been completed, including any important data collected since August 7th 20—.

4) The Client agrees to write a reference for the Contractor, stating that Contract #991YL was broken due to illness in the family, and has no reflection on the Contractor's ability to do his job.

Date: October 9th, 20—

(Contractor) Signature: ______________________________

(Client) Signature: ______________________________

184. If the Contractor honored the contract up until now, what has definitely been completed?

(A) A sales chart based on a five-year review
(B) A count of all wine bottles in the cellar
(C) A calculation of proposed renovation costs
(D) An interview with at least one staff member

185. What is the Client obliged to do in the future if he signs the addendum to the contract?

(A) Rehire the Contractor when his health returns
(B) Provide a letter that states the reasons this contract was broken
(C) Write a positive reference letter about the Contractor's personality
(D) Suggest alternative companies that may hire the Contractor in the future

Questions 186–190 refer to the following ticket and letter.

REMINDER TO OWNER

You have not yet paid the following ticket:

Parking Infraction: Exceeding a 20-minute free customer-parking limit
Location: Squires Paper Company
Vehicle Type: Minivan
License Plate Number: MG097
Owner: Tanaka Kazuya
Date of Infraction: April 1, 20—

How to pay this ticket:

A) Send a check written out to the Yokohama Parking Office. (see below for address)

OR

B) Pay online with your credit card (*www.yokogov.org/parking*). You will need your ticket number and your license plate number.

OR

C) Pay in person at the Yokohama Parking Office:

Yokohama Parking Office
145-9 Yamato-Cho, Naka-ku,
Yokohama, Japan
231-0864

To appeal this ticket contact the Parking Office and ask for form #25.

186. Why did Tanaka receive this ticket?

(A) His car was in a no-parking zone.
(B) He forgot to pay for a parking pass.
(C) His car was parked in a spot for too long.
(D) He paid for only twenty minutes.

187. Which of the following excuses can a driver legally use in order to appeal a parking ticket?

(A) I didn't notice the no-parking sign.
(B) I share the vehicle with my wife.
(C) I sold my car the day before.
(D) I didn't have any money for parking.

NOTICE OF APPEAL Page 1

STEP 1

You must submit your appeal within 28 days of receiving your parking ticket. Late appeals must be accompanied by a handwritten letter detailing the reasons for applying late. Judges will consider the following reasons:

- Medical emergencies for you or a family member
- Circumstances that caused you to be away from your residence at the time the ticket was mailed

STEP 2

Please circle the legal grounds that apply.

A: This parking infraction did not occur.

B: There was no parking attendant on duty to pay.

C: I was not the owner of this vehicle when the infraction occurred.

(D:) My vehicle was stolen on the day of the infraction.

STEP 3

Complete the personal information form on page two with your name and address, and contact information, and mail it together with this form and a photocopy of your ticket. You will hear back from the Ministry of Parking within twenty business days. If a personal appeal is granted, you will have to appear in court.

188. What would Tanaka have to do if he submitted his appeal after 28 days?

(A) Pay a double fine
(B) Appear before the judge
(C) Include a letter of explanation
(D) Give up his driver's license

189. Why was Tanaka probably unaware of the original ticket?

(A) The parking attendant forgot to write one up.
(B) Someone stole the ticket off his car at Squire's.
(C) He thought he was parked legally that day.
(D) Someone else was driving his car on April 1st.

190. What does Tanaka NOT need to include with his notice of appeal?

(A) A copy of his ticket
(B) His name and address
(C) His reason for appealing
(D) A medical note

Questions 191–195 refer to the following e-mail and schedule.

To: choisoo35@korea.net

From: leebang@theaccountants.org

Subject: Transportation to and from airport

Choi Soo,

Please confirm that you received your itinerary for your flight and hotel accommodations. I e-mailed it last week, but I haven't heard back from you. I am attaching the schedule for the free shuttle service from the airport to Yongsan Terminal. Your hotel, The Sunrise Inn, is right across the street from the bus station.

My only concern is that you will probably just miss the first shuttle of the day if your plane is delayed at all. The next shuttle isn't until early afternoon. Taxis are very expensive, but I think it will be worth it for you to take one instead of waiting several hours for the next shuttle bus. There are city buses, but they are complicated if you aren't familiar with them.

I'm sorry that nobody will be available to pick you up at the airport in a company car. We have an important meeting on that Thursday morning, and none of us can get out of it.

We look forward to meeting you next week. Have a safe flight and call me as soon as you are settled in your room.

See you soon,

Lee Bang

AIRPORT BUS SCHEDULE

The following schedule is for travel between Yongsan Bus Terminal and Incheon International Airport. This is a free bus service provided by Incheon International Airport. No tickets are necessary. Priority seating is given to those who make a reservation. Call 724-8000 to book your seat ahead of time.

Weekdays	**BUS 1-A**	**BUS 2-A**	**BUS 3-A**
Departs Incheon International Airport	9:30 A.M.	1:00 P.M.	5:30 P.M.
Arrives Yongsan Terminal	10:20 A.M.	1:59 P.M.	7:00 P.M.

Weekends	**BUS 1-B**	**BUS 2-B**	**BUS 3-B**
Departs Incheon International Airport	7:00 A.M.	3:00 P.M.	9:00 P.M.
Arrives Yongsan Terminal	8:00 A.M.	3:45 P.M.	10:50 P.M.

191. What does Lee ask Choi to do?

(A) Make a reservation at the Sunrise Inn
(B) Write back to say he received an e-mail
(C) Order a ticket for an airport shuttle
(D) Come to Thursday's meeting

192. Which bus does Lee think that Choi will probably miss?

(A) Bus 1-A
(B) Bus 2-A
(C) Bus 1-B
(D) Bus 2-B

193. What does Lee say costs a lot of money?

(A) Hotel accommodations
(B) Taxi fare
(C) Shuttle buses
(D) Plane tickets

194. On a Saturday, which shuttle bus takes the longest route to Yongsan Terminal?

(A) Bus 3-A
(B) Bus 1-B
(C) Bus 1-A
(D) Bus 3-B

195. Which transportation option is NOT available to Choi?

(A) Taxi
(B) Shuttle bus
(C) City bus
(D) Company car

Questions 196–200 refer to the following e-mail and graph.

To: v.goldsmith@placeco.com
From: gpmills@temppower.com
Subject: Your Career
Att: Temp Power employment graph

Dear Vanessa,

Thank you for attending this past week's complimentary workshop, Secretary 101 Skills, where you learned important career skills. If you're looking for a job, we want to help you. Temp Power prides itself on staffing our city's offices with top-notch administrative professionals, and we line our team up with high paying jobs and offer affordable health insurance! Many of our team go on to be hired permanently and then move up the job ladder.

Are you interested in starting your interview process? The next step is to come into our office for skills tests. You'll want to take these tests soon, while the skills you learned in our workshop tutorials are still fresh in your head.

Please click below to select a time to come to our office.

Click here to go to our Registration Page.

Please see the attached graph. We know it will convince you that you will find success as part of the Temp Power team.

Thank you,

George Mills

for Temp Power

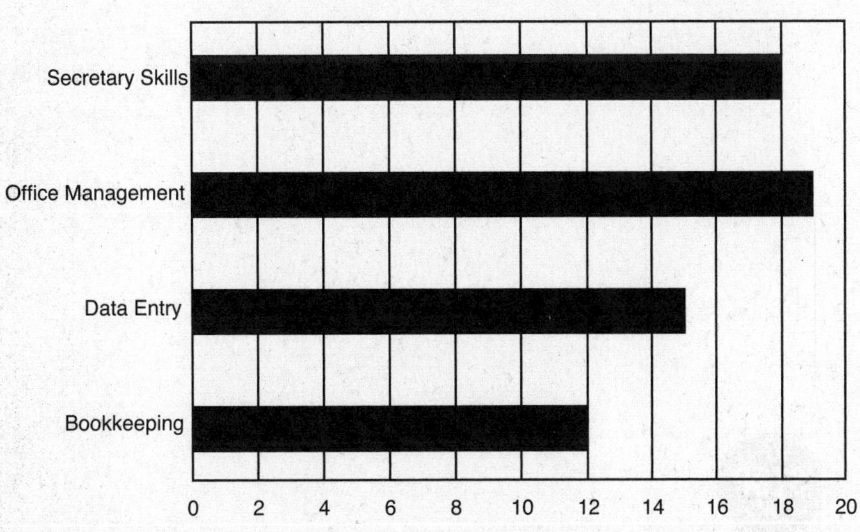

MODEL TEST 1

196. What was the ultimate purpose of the workshop?

(A) To recruit workers
(B) To find new clients
(C) To introduce a college
(D) To gather data for a graph

197. What does the message ask Vanessa to do next?

(A) Call the company
(B) Take a tutorial
(C) Send test results
(D) Sign up for a test

198. How much did Vanessa pay for the workshop?

(A) The workshop was free.
(B) It cost $20.
(C) It cost $50.
(D) The cost is unknown.

199. Which workshop led to the highest average amount of employment?

(A) Bookkeeping
(B) Data Entry
(C) Office Management
(D) Secretary Skills

200. If Vanessa signs up as a Temp Power employee, how much can she expect to work, on average?

(A) 15 days a month
(B) 18 days a month
(C) 18 days a year
(D) 12 months a year

STOP

This is the end of the test. If you finish before time is called, you may go back to Parts 5, 6, and 7 and check your work.

ANSWER KEY
Model Test 1

LISTENING COMPREHENSION

Part 1: Photographs

1. **B**
2. **A**
3. **B**
4. **A**
5. **D**
6. **A**
7. **D**
8. **C**
9. **B**
10. **A**

Part 2: Question-Response

11. **B**
12. **A**
13. **B**
14. **C**
15. **A**
16. **A**
17. **A**
18. **C**
19. **B**
20. **C**
21. **B**
22. **A**
23. **C**
24. **B**
25. **C**
26. **A**
27. **A**
28. **B**
29. **C**
30. **C**
31. **B**
32. **A**
33. **B**
34. **B**
35. **A**
36. **C**
37. **C**
38. **B**
39. **C**
40. **A**

Part 3: Conversations

41. **C**
42. **C**
43. **D**
44. **B**
45. **A**
46. **D**
47. **B**
48. **D**
49. **A**
50. **C**
51. **A**
52. **A**
53. **B**
54. **A**
55. **C**
56. **B**
57. **C**
58. **D**
59. **C**
60. **A**
61. **C**
62. **D**
63. **A**
64. **B**
65. **A**
66. **A**
67. **C**
68. **D**
69. **B**
70. **D**

Part 4: Talks

71. **A**
72. **C**
73. **C**
74. **B**
75. **C**
76. **D**
77. **D**
78. **A**
79. **A**
80. **B**
81. **D**
82. **A**
83. **C**
84. **A**
85. **C**
86. **C**
87. **B**
88. **D**
89. **A**
90. **D**
91. **C**
92. **C**
93. **D**
94. **A**
95. **A**
96. **D**
97. **B**
98. **A**
99. **B**
100. **B**

ANSWER KEY
Model Test 1

READING

Part 5: Incomplete Sentences

101. **B**	112. **A**	123. **C**	134. **B**
102. **D**	113. **C**	124. **D**	135. **B**
103. **C**	114. **A**	125. **C**	136. **D**
104. **B**	115. **D**	126. **D**	137. **A**
105. **A**	116. **B**	127. **B**	138. **A**
106. **C**	117. **C**	128. **A**	139. **C**
107. **B**	118. **B**	129. **D**	140. **D**
108. **D**	119. **A**	130. **C**	
109. **C**	120. **D**	131. **B**	
110. **B**	121. **B**	132. **C**	
111. **A**	122. **C**	133. **B**	

Part 6: Text Completion

141. **A**	144. **A**	147. **B**	150. **A**
142. **B**	145. **D**	148. **A**	151. **A**
143. **C**	146. **B**	149. **C**	152. **C**

Part 7: Reading Comprehension

153. **B**	165. **A**	177. **D**	189. **D**
154. **C**	166. **A**	178. **B**	190. **D**
155. **B**	167. **A**	179. **D**	191. **B**
156. **D**	168. **D**	180. **C**	192. **A**
157. **A**	169. **B**	181. **B**	193. **B**
158. **B**	170. **A**	182. **A**	194. **D**
159. **B**	171. **D**	183. **B**	195. **D**
160. **D**	172. **D**	184. **C**	196. **A**
161. **C**	173. **D**	185. **B**	197. **D**
162. **C**	174. **B**	186. **C**	198. **A**
163. **B**	175. **A**	187. **C**	199. **C**
164. **B**	176. **C**	188. **C**	200. **B**

TEST SCORE CONVERSION TABLE

Count your correct responses. Match the number of correct responses with the corresponding score from the Test Score Conversion Table (below). Add the two scores together. This is your Total Estimated Test Score. As you practice taking the TOEIC model tests, your scores should improve. Keep track of your Total Estimated Test Scores.

# Correct	Listening Score	Reading Score	# Correct	Listening Score	Reading Score	# Correct	Listening Score	Reading Score	# Correct	Listening Score	Reading Score
0	5	5	26	110	65	51	255	220	76	410	370
1	5	5	27	115	70	52	260	225	77	420	380
2	5	5	28	120	80	53	270	230	78	425	385
3	5	5	29	125	85	54	275	235	79	430	390
4	5	5	30	130	90	55	280	240	80	440	395
5	5	5	31	135	95	56	290	250	81	445	400
6	5	5	32	140	100	57	295	255	82	450	405
7	10	5	33	145	110	58	300	260	83	460	410
8	15	5	34	150	115	59	310	265	84	465	415
9	20	5	35	160	120	60	315	270	85	470	420
10	25	5	36	165	125	61	320	280	86	475	425
11	30	5	37	170	130	62	325	285	87	480	430
12	35	5	38	175	140	63	330	290	88	485	435
13	40	5	39	180	145	64	340	300	89	490	445
14	45	5	40	185	150	65	345	305	90	495	450
15	50	5	41	190	160	66	350	310	91	495	455
16	55	10	42	195	165	67	360	320	92	495	465
17	60	15	43	200	170	68	365	325	93	495	470
18	65	20	44	210	175	69	370	330	94	495	480
19	70	25	45	215	180	70	380	335	95	495	485
20	75	30	46	220	190	71	385	340	96	495	490
21	80	35	47	230	195	72	390	350	97	495	495
22	85	40	48	240	200	73	395	355	98	495	495
23	90	45	49	245	210	74	400	360	99	495	495
24	95	50	50	250	215	75	405	365	100	495	495
25	100	60									

Number of Correct Listening Responses ________ = Listening Score ________

Number of Correct Reading Responses ________ = Reading Score ________

Total Estimated Test Score ________

EXPLANATORY ANSWERS

Listening Comprehension

PART 1: PHOTOGRAPHS

1. **(B)** The technician is holding a test tube in her hand. Choice (A) uses the associated word *examining* for *looking* but there is no *patient* in the picture. Choice (C) uses the associated word *preparing* as in *preparing an experiment.* Choice (D) uses the associated word *watching* as in *looking at the test tube.*
2. **(A)** The participants are having a meeting and are sitting around a table. Choice (B) mentiones *glasses* that are on the table. Choice (C) suggests incorrectly that the group is having a meal. Choice (D) uses the associated word *taking* as in *taking notes.*
3. **(B)** Choice (B) identifies the action *speaker explaining a chart.* Choice (A) confuses the man's outstretched hand with handshaking. Choice (C) confuses the coffee cups on the table with a meal. Choice (D) confuses the white board with a TV.
4. **(A)** The factory worker is working on the engine of a car. Choice (B) uses the similar-sounding word *card* for *car* and the associated word *new* as in *new car.* Choice (C) uses the associated word *repairing* and the similar-sounding word *cart.* Choice (D) uses the associated words *driving* and *work.*
5. **(D)** The field workers are loading produce onto a truck. Choice (A) uses the word *fruit* that is being put onto the truck. Choice (B) uses the associated word *packing* as in *packing the boxes.* Choice (C) uses the associated word *box.*
6. **(A)** The photo shows a set of stairs leading up to the flagpole in the foreground. Choice (B) correctly identifies the roofs, but there is no soldier in the photo. Choice (C) correctly identifies the courtyard, but there are no tourists in the photo. Choice (D) is incorrect because there is no ten-story building in the photo.
7. **(D)** The woman in the photo is pushing a cart with some boxes on it. Choice (A) is incorrect because the woman is walking past the gates, not opening them. Choices (B) and (C) correctly identify the boxes but not the woman's action.
8. **(C)** Choice (C) correctly identifies the pipes and their relative position in the photo. Choices (A), (B), and (D) are incorrect because there are no mountains, cows, or trees in the photo.
9. **(B)** Choice (B) identifies the action *cleaning the floor.* Choice (A) correctly identifies the plant, but the man isn't doing anything to it. Choice (C) incorrectly identifies how he is cleaning the floor (he is vacuuming with a vacuum cleaner, not sweeping with a broom). Choice (D) is incorrect because the man is using the vacuum, so it cannot be stored.
10. **(A)** Choice (A) identifies the thing *boat* and the action *passes under the bridge.* Choice (B) is incorrect because the boat is passing through the water without any problem. Choice (C) confuses similar sounds *ridge* and *bridge.* Choice (D) confuses a *bridge over water* with a card game called *bridge.*

PART 2: QUESTION-RESPONSE

11. **(B)** Choice B answers the question about the vacation. Choices (A) and (C) answer questions about people.
12. **(A)** Choice (A) is a logical response to a question about *possession.* Choice (B) confuses similar sounds *happen* with *your pen*; *I don't know* is not a common answer for possession. Choice (C) confuses similar sounds *European* with *your pen*; *pen* uses the pronoun *it* not *he.*
13. **(B)** Choice (B) is a logical response to a question about *being late.* Choice (A) answers how long did you wait and confuses similar sounds *late* and *wait.* Choice (C) confuses similar sounds *eight* and *late.*
14. **(C)** Choice (C) is a logical response to a question about *who.* Choice (A) confuses time: *came* (past) with *is coming* (present). Choice (B) confuses the action *combing* with *coming.*

15. **(A)** Choice (A) is a logical response to the question *When*. Choice (B) answers a *Where* question. Choice (C) answers a *Why* question.
16. **(A)** Choice (A) is a logical response to a question about *food*. Choice (B) answers *Who's coming to dinner*? Choice (C) answers *When is dinner*?
17. **(A)** Choice (A) is a logical response to a question about *location*. Choice (B) confuses time: *this weekend* (present-future) and *last week* (past). Choice (C) confuses duration of time *will last a week* with past time *last week*.
18. **(C)** Choice (C) is a logical response to a question about *frequency*. Choice (A) confuses words with same sound and different meaning: *play* (verb) with *play* (performance). Choice (B) confuses similar sounds *and often* and *get off*.
19. **(B)** The second speaker thanks the first speaker for the generous offer to pay for dinner. Choice (A) confuses *thinner* with the similar-sounding word *dinner*. Choice (C) repeats the word *pay*.
20. **(C)** Choice (C) is a logical response to a question about *messages*. Choice (A) confuses massage (rubbing muscles) with message. Choice (B) confuses similar sounds *messages* with *any of us*.
21. **(B)** Choice (B) answers the question *What*. Choice (A) answers a *Where* question. Choice (C) confuses similar-sounding words *buy/goodbye*.
22. **(A)** *Ten* answers the question *How many*. Choice (B) repeats the idea of *hand out*. Choice (C) confuses the question about quantity (*how many*) with a question about price (*how much*).
23. **(C)** Choice (C) is a logical response to a question about *time*. Choice (A) identifies place (*airport*) but not time. Choice (B) has the related phrase *take off* but does not answer *when*.
24. **(B)** Choice (B) is a logical response to a question about *taking a break*. Choice (A) confuses *coffee break* with *broken (coffee) cup*. Choice (C) confuses *break* with *brakes* on a car and with *won't work* (broken).
25. **(C)** Choice (C) is a logical response to the question asking whether there is anything more that needs to be done. Choice (A) would be a logical response to an offer of cake. Choice (B) answers the question *What kind*.
26. **(A)** Choice (A) is a logical response to a question about *location*. Choice (B) gives the price of the rooms, not the location of the hotel. Choice (C) confuses similar sounds *el(evator)* with *(ho)tel*.
27. **(A)** The first speaker says there was a call, so the second speaker wants to know if the caller left a message. Choice (B) confuses *cold* with the similar-sounding word *called* and repeats the word *out*. Choice (C) confuses *file* with the similar-sounding word *while*.
28. **(B)** Choice (B) is a logical response to a question about *which*. Choice (A) confuses similar sounds *hours* with *ours*. Choice (C) has the related word *seat* but does not answer *which*.
29. **(C)** The first speaker feels cold so the second speaker offers to close the window. Choice (A) associates *winter* with *cold*. Choice (B) confuses *sold* with the similar-sounding word *cold* and *year* with the similar-sounding word *here*.
30. **(C)** Choice (C) is a logical response to a question about *location*. Choice (A) confuses similar sounds *ear* with *here*. Choice (B) confuses *closed* with *near* (*close*).
31. **(B)** Choice (B) is a logical response to a question about a meeting starting time. Choice (A) associates *meeting* and *agenda*, but it doesn't answer the question. Choice (C) confuses similar-sounding words *meeting* and *reading*.
32. **(A)** Choice (A) is a logical response to the request of a favor. Choice (B) confuses the use of the word *favor*. Choice (C) repeats the word *music*.
33. **(B)** Choice (B) is a logical response to the question about a place to hang a coat. Choice (A) confuses similar-sounding words *leave/live*. Choice (C) repeats the word *leave*.
34. **(B)** Choice (B) is a logical response to the question about the type of people at the conference. Choice (A) would answer a question

MODEL TEST 1

about the dates of the conference. Choice (C) relates the words *conference/workshop.*

35. **(A)** Choice (A) is a logical response to a question about *asking your father.* Choice (B) confuses similar sounds *far* with *father.* Choice (C) confuses similar sounds *ask* with *task.*
36. **(C)** Choice (C) is a logical response to the question about work preferences—*by myself* means the same as *alone.* Choice (A) confuses similar-sounding words *team/seem.* Choice (B) would answer a simple *yes-no* question, but this *or* question asks for a choice to be made.
37. **(C)** The second speaker agrees to eat at the restaurant that the first speaker suggests. Choice (A) confuses *rest* with the similar-sounding word *restaurant.* Choice (B) confuses *ice* with the similar-sounding word *nice.*
38. **(B)** Choice (B) is a logical response to the question about the contents of the chart. Choice (A) confuses similar-sounding words *chart/part.* Choice (C) repeats the words *page 8.*
39. **(C)** *Research and Development* answers the question about Fred's department. Choice (A) confuses similar-sounding words *department/apartment.* Choice (B) answers the question *Where.*
40. **(A)** Choice (A) answers the question *How much.* Choices (B) and (C) relate the word *account* with *money* and *check.*

PART 3: CONVERSATIONS

41. **(C)** The woman can't meet until 5:00. Choices (A) and (B) are times that the man suggests. Choice (D) confuses *ten* with the similar-sounding word *then.*
42. **(C)** The man says, *I'll wait for you in my office.* Choice (A) confuses *bus stop* with the similar-sounding word *budget.* Choice (B) is confused with where the woman will be earlier in the day. Choice (D) confuses *waiting room* with *I'll wait for you . . .*
43. **(D)** The woman says that she'll bring photocopies of the budget report. Choice (A) confuses *coffee* with the similar-sounding word *copy.* Choice (B) confuses *letter* with the similar-sounding word *better.* Choice (C) confuses *photographs* with *photocopies.*
44. **(B)** The man is traveling to Los Angeles. Choice (A) is where he is leaving from. Choices (C) and (D) are places where he might change planes.
45. **(A)** He is traveling by plane; both *plane* and *flight* are mentioned in the conversation. Choice (B) confuses *train* with the similar-sounding word *plane.* Choice (C) confuses *bus* with the similar-sounding word *but.* Choice (D) confuses *car* with the similar-sounding word *start.*
46. **(D)** The man says he wants to leave tomorrow and the woman says there is a flight at 10:00. Choice (A) confuses *afternoon* with the similar-sounding word *soon.* Choice (B) confuses *tonight* with the similar-sounding word *flight.* Choice (C) has the correct day but the wrong time.
47. **(B)** The man asks for towels and soap to be brought to his room. Choices (A) and (C) are places where a person might ask for something, but they are not the correct answer. Choice (D) is incorrect because rooms in houses don't normally have numbers.
48. **(D)** The man asks for towels and soap. Choice (A) confuses *keys* with the similar-sounding word *please.* Choice (B) confuses *soup* with the similar-sounding word *soap.* Choice (C) repeats the word *room.*
49. **(A)** The woman says *The housekeeper will bring them right away.* Choice (B) confuses *today* with the similar-sounding word *away.* Choices (C) and (D) are confused with *two towels.*
50. **(C)** The woman says that the brochures arrived this morning. Choices (A) and (D) confuse *afternoon* with the similar-sounding word *soon.* Choice (B) is not mentioned.
51. **(A)** The woman says that she will address and mail the brochures. Choice (B) is not mentioned. Choice (C) confuses *print* with *printer.* Choice (D) uses the word *copy* out of context.

52. **(A)** One thousand brochures were ordered, and that is twice the number the woman needs. Choice (B) confuses *eight* with the similar-sounding word *great.* Choice (C) is the number of brochures ordered. Choice (D) is twice the number of brochures ordered.

53. **(B)** The man says that he is calling about a catering position. Choice (A) associates *waiter* with *food and beverage.* Choice (C) is associated with *ad.* Choice (D) repeats *food and beverage.*

54. **(A)** The woman asks if the man has any experience. Choice (B) confuses *appearance* with the similar-sounding word *experience.* Choice (C) confuses *attitude* with the similar-sounding word *ad.* Choice (D) associates *appetite* with *food.*

55. **(C)** The woman asks the man to come for an interview next Monday. Choice (A) is confused with *today's paper.* Choice (B) confuses *Sunday* with the similar-sounding word *Monday.* Choice (D) confuses *Tuesday* with the similar-sounding word *today.*

56. **(B)** He can't play golf because rain is predicted. Choice (A) confuses *sick* with the similar-sounding word *predict.* Choice (C) confuses *test* with the similar-sounding word *rest.* Choice (D) uses the word *tired* out of context.

57. **(C)** He had a 9:00 golf game. Choice (A) confuses *two* with the similar-sounding word *tomorrow.* Choice (B) confuses *four* with the similar-sounding word *bore.* Choice (D) confuses *ten* with the similar-sounding word *then.*

58. **(D)** Since the man can't play golf tomorrow, he says he wants to stay home and rest. Choice (A) confuses *phone* with the similar-sounding word *home.* Choice (B) is what the woman wants him to do. Choice (C) confuses *move* with the similar-sounding word *movies.*

59. **(C)** The man is giving the woman directions to a bank. Choice (A) associates *fast food restaurant* with *drive-in window.* Choice (B) is what is next to the bank. Choice (D) is what the woman will pass on her way to the bank.

60. **(A)** The man says that the bank is on a corner. Choice (B) is confused with *a parking lot next door.* Choices (C) and (D) are confused with *across the street from the library.*

61. **(C)** The man says that the bank is only five minutes away. Choices (A), (B), and (D) sound similar to the correct answer.

62. **(D)** The woman says, *It's 9:30.* Choices (A) and (B) confuse *eight* with the similar-sounding word *late.* Choice (C) is confused with *15 minutes late.*

63. **(A)** The woman is scolding the man for arriving late. Choice (B) is mentioned but is not the reason the woman is angry. Choice (C) is what the man, not the woman, did. Choice (D) repeats the word *fast.*

64. **(B)** The man says he will drive his car because it's faster. Choice (A) repeats the word *home.* Choice (C) is what the woman suggests. Choice (D) confuses *train* with the similar-sounding word *rain.*

65. **(A)** The man asks about the woman's trip on Sunday and the woman says that she is leaving in the late afternoon. Choice (B) confuses similar-sounding words *flight* and *night.* Choices (C) and (D) confuse similar-sounding words *Sunday* and *Monday.*

66. **(A)** The man's response to the woman's decision to travel first class is, "What a luxury!" Choice (A) is confused with the woman's mention of price. Choice (C) is not mentioned. Choice (D) is related to the discussion of the timing of the trip.

67. **(C)** The woman says that she is going to put it on her credit card. Choice (A) is not mentioned. Choice (B) confuses the meaning of the word *check.* Choice (D) confuses the meaning of the word *order.*

68. **(D)** The man greets the woman, *Good evening.* Choice (A) is not mentioned. Choices (B) and (C) confuse *noon* and *afternoon* with the similar-sounding word *soon.*

69. **(B)** The woman is in a restaurant ordering from a menu, so she is talking to a waiter. Choice (A) associates *butcher* with *lamb.* Choices (C) and (D) are people one might

MODEL TEST 1

talk with in a restaurant, but they are not the people who take food orders.

70. **(D)** The woman orders the vegetable plate because she is vegetarian. Choices (A) and (B) are what the waiter recommends. Choice (C) confuses fish with the similar-sounding word dish.

PART 4: TALKS

71. **(A)** *Arrival and departure gates, baggage claims,* and *ticketing areas* all suggest an airport. Choices (B) and (C) are not specific enough. Choice (D) is incorrect because an amusement park train would not lead to *baggage claims.*
72. **(C)** The instructions say you should be in the *center of the car.* Choice (A) is contradicted by *away from the doors.* Choice (B) is incorrect because *windows* are not mentioned. Choice (D) is contradicted by *in the center.*
73. **(C)** Passengers are asked to wait until they hear a bell ring before they exit the train. Choice (A) repeats the word *sign.* Choice (B) is contradicted by the correct answer. Choice (D) repeats the word *color.*
74. **(B)** The museum is open from *one until five on Sundays*; this is afternoon. Choices (A) and (C) are not mentioned. Choice (D) contradicts the fact that the museum is open from *one until five on Sundays.*
75. **(C)** The announcement says that *lecture information can be obtained by calling our Education Office at 548-6251.* Choices (A), (B), and (D) are not mentioned.
76. **(D)** According to the message, *children under five are not charged admission.* Choice (A) are the people who get a 25% discount. Choice (B) are the people who pay $15. Choice (C) are the people who pay $10.
77. **(D)** The passage says to *start the morning by making a list.* Choices (A), (B), and (C) are not mentioned.
78. **(A)** The passage says that you should *next, rank each task . . . according to its importance.* Choice (B) is contradicted by *stay with (the task) until it is completed.* Choice (C) is contradicted by *work on the most important task first.* Choice (D) is not mentioned.
79. **(A)** According to the talk, you should review your list at the end of the day. Choice (B) is incorrect because listeners are told to leave uncompleted tasks for the next day. Choice (C) repeats the word *list,* but nothing is mentioned about writing a new one. Choice (D) confuses *away* with the similar-sounding word *day.*
80. **(B)** Since the ad is for *office furniture* and *accessories, it encourages you to redecorate your office.* Choice (A) is not mentioned. Choices (C) and (D) are part of redecorating and purchasing their furniture.
81. **(D)** The ad mentions a sale on *furniture.* Choices (A), (B), and (C) are not mentioned.
82. **(A)** According to the announcement, the sale ends on Sunday. Choice (B) sounds similar to the correct answer. Choice (C) confuses *Tuesday* with the similar-sounding word *today.* Choice (D) is not mentioned.
83. **(C)** The ad states that you can help by *serving as a volunteer tutor.* Choice (A) is not mentioned but is associated with *schoolwork, child, learning,* and *school system.* Choice (B) *school children* are the people tutors will be helping. Choice (D) *businessmen* and *businesswomen* are reading the ad.
84. **(A)** You can help for *as little as two hours a week.* Choice (B) is contradicted by *as little as.* Choices (C) and (D) are not mentioned.
85. **(C)** The announcement says that participants must be over eighteen. Choices (A) and (B) are mentioned as not necessary. Choice (D) repeats the word *children,* but experience with children is not mentioned.
86. **(C)** If temperatures are in the *mid-sixties,* it's about *65 degrees.* Choice (A) is confused with *breezes often to fifteen miles per hour.* In Choice (B), *sixty* is the first part of *sixty-five.* Choice (D) is not mentioned.
87. **(B)** The weatherman says to *spend some time outdoors.* Choice (A) is contradicted by *spend some time outdoors.* Choices (C) and (D) are possible, but they are not mentioned.

88. **(D)** The weather tomorrow will be like the weather today, which is sunny. Choices (A), (B), and (C) describe the weather later in the week.

89. **(A)** Lodge costs include *continental breakfast and gourmet dinner.* Choice (B) is contradicted by *ski equipment is available . . . for a small additional fee.* Choice (C) is not mentioned. Choice (D) is not provided.

90. **(D)** The announcement mentions ski classes for people of all ability levels. Choice (A) is confused with the people who give the lessons. Choice (B) repeats the word *abilities.* Choice (C) is contradicted by the correct answer.

91. **(C)** The announcement mentions a third night free. Choice (A) uses the word *book* out of context. Choice (B) associates *calendar* with *January.* Choice (D) repeats the word *class.*

92. **(C)** The speaker says that the train *will soon be approaching Hawthorne Street Station,* which means it is not at a station but rather in between stations. Choice (A) is confused with the correct answer—*approaching* means arriving, not leaving. Choice (B) is confused with the mention of the Blue Line trains. Choice (D) is mentioned, but it is not the current location of the train.

93. **(D)** Delays are caused by *damage to the tracks.* Choices (A), (B), and (C) are not mentioned.

94. **(A)** The speaker says *Commuters are asked to exit the train and take a bus.* Choice (B) is not mentioned. Choice (C) is confused with the mention of a free transfer ticket to ride the bus. Choice (D) is contradicted by the request to *exit the train.*

95. **(A)** Residents of the Greenville district filed a complaint protesting the construction of a shopping mall. Choice (B) repeats the word *cost,* as in *the cost of the project.* Choice (C) repeats the word *traffic,* which is what residents are afraid will be increased by the mall. Choice (D) is what the Greenville residents caused by their complaint.

96. **(D)** Greenville residents filed their complaint at City Hall. Choice (A) refers to the complaint that the mall will bring noise to neighborhood streets. Choices (B) and (C) are not mentioned.

97. **(B)** The speaker says that the mayor will meet with the protestors *later on this week.* Choices (A), (C), and (D) repeat words used in the talk.

98. **(A)** The speaker says, *Before you go,* meaning that the students are getting ready to leave but the speaker wants to tell them something first. Choices (B), (C), and (D) are contradicted by the correct answer.

99. **(B)** The speaker says to read Chapter 10 in the textbook *ahead of time.* Choice (A) is not mentioned. Choice (C) is what will happen during the class trip. Choice (D) is confused with the request to, *Come up with a few questions to ask him.*

100. **(B)** The trip is to a museum to speak with a museum manager, and the required reading is about museum management. Choice (A) is confused with the mention that photography is not allowed in the museum. Choice (C) is not mentioned. Choice (D) is confused with the suggestion to bring a sketchpad.

Reading

PART 5: INCOMPLETE SENTENCES

101. **(B)** *Customer* is singular, so it takes a singular verb; it is also third person, so it takes the third person form of *is.* Choice (A) is singular but first person. Choice (C) is plural. Choice (D) is the simple form of the verb.

102. **(D)** Although all the choices have similar meanings, choice (D), *advised,* is the only one that fits the grammatical structure of the sentence. Choices (A), (B), and (C) require a different grammatical pattern: *We ______ that he think things over . . . .*

103. **(C)** *Host* means to organize a social event. Choices (A) and (B) is what is done to the guests—you *invite* guests or *entertain* guests. Choice (D) refers to a person who is invited to

a party and does not fit the sentence because it is a noun, and a verb is needed here.

104. **(B)** *Were not* requires a past participle to complete the verb. Choice (A) is a noun. Choice (C) is in the progressive form. Choice (D) is the simple form.

105. **(A)** The present tense in the *if* clause can be matched with future tense in the second clause; *will* can also be used with *assist* to make a complete verb. Choices (B) and (C) are past tense. Choice (D) is present tense, and must be used with either the *past participle* or the *progressive form.*

106. **(C)** The noun *knowledge* followed by *and* should be joined to another noun. Choices (A) and (B) are verbs. Choice (D) is a noun, but it refers to a person rather than a thing.

107. **(B)** *Increase* is the most common verb meaning *go up* used with *costs.* Choices (A), (C), and (D) mean *go up,* but they are not used for nouns related to percentages.

108. **(D)** The subject position requires a noun. Choices (A) and (B) are verbs. Choice (C) refers to a person or thing and doesn't make sense here.

109. **(C)** *Because* establishes a logical cause and effect relationship between the two events. Choice (A) indicates contrast; it is not logical unless the plane *was on time.* Choice (B) suggests a simultaneous relationship, not possible because of present tense *is* and past tense *was.* Choice (D) is a preposition and cannot be used to join clauses.

110. **(B)** *Confidential* means *private.* Choices (A), (C), and (D) have meanings that do not fit the context.

111. **(A)** This is a future time clause, so a present tense verb is required. Choice (B) is past tense. Choice (C) is present perfect tense. Choice (D) is future tense.

112. **(A)** *Commute* means to travel from home to work. Choices (B), (C), and (D) do not fit the context of the sentence.

113. **(C)** *Between* indicates that one object has another object on each side. Choice (A) is most often used when one hard-to-count group is indicated (*among the paper clips, among the office equipment*). Choices (B) and (D) are not logical.

114. **(A)** *Job* is used here to refer to an individual position. Choice (B) implies professional standing greater than individual jobs. (*In his career (occupation) as an insurance investigator, he held jobs with several companies.*) Choice (C) implies unpleasant work smaller than an individual job. (*I like my job as a secretary, but it's a chore to sort the boss's mail.*) Choice (D) uses a related word, *position,* but in an inappropriate form.

115. **(D)** File has the same meaning here as *submit.* Choice (A) is a form of the verb *fill.* Choices (B) and (C) are forms of the verb *fall.*

116. **(B)** *After* establishes a logical time relationship between the two events. Choice (A) is an adverb, indicating a period of time after a specific event. Choice (C) indicates a comparison. (*His fax arrived later than mine.*) Choice (D) is an adjective and cannot be used to join clauses.

117. **(C)** *Because* indicates a cause and effect relationship between the two events. Choice (A) implies contrast. Choice (B) *during* cannot be followed by a sentence. Choice (D) doesn't make sense.

118. **(B)** *Required* means to be obliged. Choices (A), (C), and (D) do not fit the context of the sentence.

119. **(A)** *Or* is logical and can join two nouns. Choice (B) is not usually used in a negative relationship. Choices (C) and (D) are not logical.

120. **(D)** *Balance* refers to the amount of money left in a bank account. Choices (A), (B), and (C) are words not normally used in this context.

121. **(B)** The blank requires an adjective; *available* is the only one given. Choices (A) and (D) are verbs. Choice (C) is a noun.

122. **(C)** The causative *suggest* is followed by the simple form of the verb. Choice (A) is the plural form. Choices (B) and (D) are simple forms, but are not logical.

123. **(C)** *Spaces* must be modified by an adjective. Choices (A) and (D) are adjectives, but they are not logical. Choice (B) is a noun.

124. **(D)** *Order* must be modified by an adjective. Choice (A) is a noun. Choice (B) is a verb. Choice (C) is an adverb.

125. **(C)** *Already* can refer to something that has happened earlier than expected. In this case, Raymond learned about the clients in a very short time. Choices (A), (B), and (D) have no meaning in this context.

126. **(D)** *Must* requires the simple form of the verb. Choice (A) is the past tense. Choice (B) is the progressive form. Choice (C) is the third-person singular form.

127. **(B)** *Tasks* must be modified by an adjective. Choice (A) is a verb. Choice (C) is a noun. Choice (D) is an adverb.

128. **(A)** *Reminded* requires the infinitive form. Choice (B) is the simple form. Choice (C) is the past participle. Choice (D) is the progressive form.

129. **(D)** *Extensive* means *broad* or *a lot of.* Choices (A), (B), and (C) have meanings that do not fit the context.

130. **(C)** *Never* can come between the auxiliary and the verb. Choice (A) is an adjective and does not fit here. Choice (B) does not make sense. Choice (D) would fit if it were *at no time.*

131. **(B)** The *if* clause in the past perfect conditional tense matches with a past tense in the second clause. Choice (A) is the past conditional tense. Choice (C) is future tense. Choice (D) is future perfect tense.

132. **(C)** *Appointment* means a planned time. Choice (A), *notebook,* is not something that could be cancelled, although a cancellation could be written in a notebook. Choice (B), *calendar,* is the thing you plan schedules and appointments on. Choice (D), *notice,* is not something that could be cancelled.

133. **(B)** Present tense in the *if* clause can be matched with future tense in the second clause. Choice (A) is present perfect conditional tense. Choice (C) is past tense. Choice (D) is present tense but indicates an unreal condition.

134. **(B)** *Enough* means *a sufficient amount to meet a need.* Choice (A) has a similar meaning, but it needs to be followed by *of.* Choices (C) and (D) do not fit the context.

135. **(B)** The sentence requires a present third person singular or past tense verb; only *departs* is given. Choice (A) is present tense, but not third person singular. Choice (C) is the infinitive form. Choice (D) is an *-ing* form.

136. **(D)** *During* is logical and can immediately precede a noun phrase. Choice (A) is not logical and must be followed by a clause. Choice (B) is not logical. Choice (C) needs *of* (*because of the meeting*).

137. **(A)** *Efficiently* is logical. Choices (B), (C), and (D) are not logical; he probably does have to type more carefully, slowly, and gradually.

138. **(A)** *Was damaged* can be followed by the past tense. Choice (B) uses the present *has.* Choice (C) uses *was* but with the progressive form of *deliver.* Choice (D) is the past perfect tense.

139. **(C)** *Mr. Green* should be modified by the *-ed* form (something else caused Mr. Green to become excited). Choice (B) isn't logical because it means that Mr. Green made someone else feel excited. Choices (A) and (D) are verbs, not adjective forms.

140. **(D)** Choice (D) is logical; it implies a contrast between *weekends* and *holidays.* Choice (A) is used with *or.* Choice (B) implies a choice between items. Choice (C) indicates cause and effect.

PART 6: TEXT COMPLETION

141. **(A)** The subject, *passengers,* does not perform the action. The past participle form of the verb is needed to complete the passive verb. Choice (A) is a present participle or a gerund. Choice (C) is an active verb. Choice (D) is a noun.

142. **(B)** *such as* can begin a list of examples. Choice (A) cannot be used in this context. Choices (C) and (D) would have to be preceded by the word *for* in order to be used in this sentence.

143. **(C)** Passengers go through a security line to have their bags checked for unallowed items. Choices (A), (B), and (D) are lines that passen-

gers may have to pass through, but they don't fit the context.

144. **(A)** Computer manufacturers are companies that make and sell computers. Choices (B) and (C) mean *buyers.* Choice (D) refers to a type of person who might use computers but probably wouldn't sell them.
145. **(D)** Tablet computers are easy to carry around, and this makes them convenient. Choices (A), (B), and (C) don't fit the context.
146. **(B)** Following the article *the* a noun is required. Choice (A) is a noun, but it refers to a person, not a situation. Choice (C) is an adjective. Choice (D) is an adverb.
147. **(B)** The invoice was sent in July, it is now September, and the message is asking about a delay, so the payment is *overdue,* or *late.* Choices (A), (C), and (D) don't fit the context.
148. **(A)** This is the main clause of a future real conditional, requiring a future verb form. Choice (B) is present perfect tense. Choice (C) is an unreal conditional. Choice (D) is an incomplete future form, missing the word *are.*
149. **(C)** An order contains items and prices, as the e-mail mentions. The other choices are related to making orders but are not the correct answer.
150. **(A)** *Response* means answer; the letter answers an ad. Choices (B), (C), and (D) look similar to the correct answer but have very different meanings.
151. **(A)** The present tense verb *qualify* agrees with the plural subject *years.* Choices (B), (C), and (D) agree with singular, not plural, subjects.
152. **(C)** The expression *look forward to* means *anticipate* or *hope for.* Choices (A), (B) and (D) cannot be correctly used with this expression.

PART 7: READING COMPREHENSION

153. **(B)** Trends emphasize careers in *sales and marketing.* Choices (A), (C), and (D) repeat words from the article.
154. **(C)** *High-tech sales* are expected to grow 20% in the next decade. Choice (A) is logical but doesn't address the increasing importance. Choice (B) repeats the word *market* from the article. Choice (D) repeats words from the article, but it doesn't answer the question.
155. **(B)** Marketers must find new *ways* to get customers interested in their products. Choice (A) is a different meaning of the word *avenues,* which doesn't fit the context. Choices (C) and (D) are terms related to marketing but they don't have the correct meaning.
156. **(D)** *Creative* is synonymous with *inventive.* Choice (A) mentions a positive feature for a marketer, but not a mandatory feature. Choice (B) relates to travel. Choice (C) repeats the word *research.*
157. **(A)** Some users see too much Internet advertising (they are *inundated*), while others see too little (they're *just learning to navigate* the Web). Choices (B), (C), and (D) may be reasonable options, but none is mentioned in the article.
158. **(B)** The original name Green Miles California was changed. "California" was replaced by "West." Choice (A) is a brand name. Choice (C) is the new name. Choice (D) is a brand name combined with California.
159. **(B)** The California Gardening Association did not like the similarity of the corporations' names. Choice (A) confuses *offices* with *brands.* Choice (C) repeats the word *initial.* Choice (D) confuses the hope that they not be confused with the actual reason the names were changed.
160. **(D)** *Protecting the Earth* is the same as *saving the environment.* Choices (A), (B), and (C) are probably true, but they are not the subject of the passage.
161. **(C)** Hotels are joining the movement to save the environment. Choice (A) identifies recycling as a gimmick, but it is a trend, not a gimmick. Choice (B) implies only hotels used by Eco-Tours practice sound environmental policies. Choice (D) is true, but is not mentioned in this passage.
162. **(C)** Although the other groups could all be concerned about the environment, they are not typical of the green movement.

163. **(B)** The passage talks about *lectures* and does not mention the other options.

164. **(B)** It sells *specialty food products, cookware, and kitchen accessories.* Choices (A), (C), and (D) are not items related to the food industry.

165. **(A)** *Similar plans* refers to *remodeling.* Choices (B), (C), and (D) sound possible, but they are not mentioned. Val D'Or bought all sixteen stores so it would not buy only the remaining six.

166. **(A)** The article stresses that chefs will come from all over and that regional foods will be featured. Choice (B) contradicts the statement that chefs will come from all over Europe. Choices (C) and (D) are not mentioned.

167. **(A)** *Years of service* means *years working for the company.* Choices (B) and (D) are not considered. Choice (C) is contradicted by *highest salary.*

168. **(D)** Contributions must be made according to government regulations. Choice (A) would have to follow the government's rules. Choices (B) and (C) can contribute to the plan, but they are still obligated to follow government regulations.

169. **(B)** The note is about Regents' plans for improvements. Choices (A), (C), and (D) are mentioned, but they are not the main purpose of the letter.

170. **(A)** Regents has been working to provide enhanced access to health care coverage. Choice (B) confuses *primer* and *premier* and is not mentioned. Choice (C) is not mentioned. Choice (D) is already being done.

171. **(D)** Regents wants members to continue making suggestions. Choices (A), (B), and (C) are not mentioned.

172. **(D)** *At the end of this month* means April 30. Choice (A) is not mentioned. Choice (B) is the last day of the period covered by the invoice. Choice (C) is the date of the invoice.

173. **(D)** *Unpaid prior balance* means they owe money on the last invoice. Choice (A) is not mentioned. Choices (B) and (C) are incorrect because charges are not broken down into taxes and other charges.

174. **(B)** They *work best if they are happy.* Choice (A) is possible but not mentioned. Choices (C) and (D) are unlikely.

175. **(A)** *Bring up to date* has the same meaning as *update.* Choice (B) is unlikely. Choices (C) and (D) are not logical.

176. **(C)** It is not suggested that employees have the power to decide changes. Choices (A), (B), and (D) are explicitly mentioned.

177. **(D)** Busy people don't want to have the *bother* of planning all the details of their vacations, so they choose to go to all-inclusive resorts. Choices (A), (B), and (C) are words that could be related to the topic of vacation, but they don't have the correct meaning.

178. **(B)** *All-inclusive* means one price covers most costs. Choice (A) uses a related word, *exclusive.* Choice (C) is a service that might be provided. Choice (D) limits who may stay at the resort and does not define "all-inclusive."

179. **(D)** *Separate fees for equipment rental* means rental costs extra. Choices (A) and (B) are included at some resorts. Choice (C) is a service at all hotels.

180. **(C)** *Check with a travel agent* means to *consult a travel agent.* Choices (A), (B), and (D) are not mentioned.

181. **(B)** The Contractor will provide consulting services for different aspects of the winery's operations. Choices (A), (C), and (D) mention things that are related to a winery's business but that are not mentioned in the texts.

182. **(A)** The contract was not fulfilled because of a medical emergency, but the duties outlined in the contract have no relationship to anything medical. Choices (B) and (D) are examples of winery staff members, and the contract specifies speaking with staff members. Choice (C) is an example of someone the Contractor will speak with, mentioned in Clause C of the contract.

183. **(B)** Clause 1 states that the Contractor is unable to provide services after a certain date, and Clause 4 states the reason as being illness. Choices (A), (C), and (D) are plausible reasons, but they are not the correct answer.

184. **(C)** The contract states that an estimate of renovation costs must be completed by October 1. Choices (A), (B), and (D) are tasks that have no specific deadline assigned.
185. **(B)** This is what Clause 4 of the addendum to the contract states. Choice (A) is not mentioned. Choice (C) looks similar to the correct answer, but there is no mention made of the Contractor's personality. Choice (D) is what the Contractor must do.
186. **(C)** According to the reminder, he exceeded a twenty-minute parking limit. Choices (A) and (B) are possible reasons for getting a parking ticket but are not the correct answer. Choice (D) repeats *twenty minutes.*
187. **(C)** This choice refers to Option C under Step 2 of the Notice of Appeal: *I was not the owner of this vehicle when the infraction occurred.* Choices (A), (B), and (D) do not mean the same as any of the options listed in Step 2.
188. **(C)** The Notice of Appeal states that *late appeals must be accompanied by a handwritten letter detailing the reasons for applying late.* Choices (A), (B), and (D) are all plausible, but they are not mentioned.
189. **(D)** Option D under Step 2 is circled, so Tanaka's car was being driven by a thief on the day the ticket was issued. Choices (A), (B), and (C) are plausible reasons, but they are not mentioned in the texts.
190. **(D)** This is confused with the mention of medical emergencies as a reason for a late appeal, but there is no mention that Tanaka had a medical emergency. Choices (A), (B), and (C) are all mentioned as things that must be included as part of the appeal.
191. **(B)** Lee asks Choi to confirm that he received the itinerary. Choice (A) has already been done. Choice (C) is incorrect because Lee suggests that a taxi might be better than the shuttle. Choice (D) is confused with what Lee will have to do himself.
192. **(A)** Choi will arrive on a weekday (Thursday); Lee thinks he will miss the first bus that day, which is 1-A. Choice (B) is the second bus of that day. Choices (C) and (D) are weekend buses.
193. **(B)** Lee says that taxis are expensive. Choices (A), (C), and (D) are things Lee mentions in the e-mail, but he doesn't mention their cost.
194. **(D)** The "B" buses are the weekend buses and 3-B takes longer than the other "B" buses to get to its destination. Choices (A) and (C) are weekday buses. Choice (B) takes less time than the 3-B bus.
195. **(D)** Lee apologizes that nobody can pick up Choi with the company car because they will all be at a meeting when he arrives. Choices (A), (B), and (C) are all mentioned as transportation options.
196. **(A)** The e-mail encourages Vanessa, as a workshop participant, to start the process toward becoming an employee. Choices (B) and (C) are not mentioned. Choice (D), a graph, is mentioned, but it is included to encourage Vanessa to become an employee.
197. **(D)** The e-mail says, *The next step is to come into our office for skills tests.* Choice (A) is incorrect because Vanessa is asked to contact the company through the website, not by phone. Choice (B) is what Vanessa has already done. Choice (C) repeats the word *test.*
198. **(A)** The e-mail mentions the *complimentary,* or *free,* workshop. Choices (B), (C), and (D) are contradicted by the correct answer.
199. **(C)** Participants in the Office Management workshop worked an average of 19 days a month. Choices (A), (B), and (D) all worked less than 19 days a month on average.
200. **(B)** Vanessa took the Secretary Skills workshop, which, according to the graph, led to an average of 18 hours a week employment. Choice (A) refers to the Data Entry workshop. Choices (C) and (D) are incorrect because the graph is about a month, not days or months a year.

ANSWER SHEET
Model Test 2

LISTENING COMPREHENSION

Part 1: Photographs

1. Ⓐ Ⓑ Ⓒ Ⓓ
2. Ⓐ Ⓑ Ⓒ Ⓓ
3. Ⓐ Ⓑ Ⓒ Ⓓ
4. Ⓐ Ⓑ Ⓒ Ⓓ
5. Ⓐ Ⓑ Ⓒ Ⓓ
6. Ⓐ Ⓑ Ⓒ Ⓓ
7. Ⓐ Ⓑ Ⓒ Ⓓ
8. Ⓐ Ⓑ Ⓒ Ⓓ
9. Ⓐ Ⓑ Ⓒ Ⓓ
10. Ⓐ Ⓑ Ⓒ Ⓓ

Part 2: Question-Response

11. Ⓐ Ⓑ Ⓒ Ⓓ
12. Ⓐ Ⓑ Ⓒ Ⓓ
13. Ⓐ Ⓑ Ⓒ Ⓓ
14. Ⓐ Ⓑ Ⓒ Ⓓ
15. Ⓐ Ⓑ Ⓒ Ⓓ
16. Ⓐ Ⓑ Ⓒ Ⓓ
17. Ⓐ Ⓑ Ⓒ Ⓓ
18. Ⓐ Ⓑ Ⓒ Ⓓ
19. Ⓐ Ⓑ Ⓒ Ⓓ
20. Ⓐ Ⓑ Ⓒ Ⓓ
21. Ⓐ Ⓑ Ⓒ Ⓓ
22. Ⓐ Ⓑ Ⓒ Ⓓ
23. Ⓐ Ⓑ Ⓒ Ⓓ
24. Ⓐ Ⓑ Ⓒ Ⓓ
25. Ⓐ Ⓑ Ⓒ Ⓓ
26. Ⓐ Ⓑ Ⓒ Ⓓ
27. Ⓐ Ⓑ Ⓒ Ⓓ
28. Ⓐ Ⓑ Ⓒ Ⓓ
29. Ⓐ Ⓑ Ⓒ Ⓓ
30. Ⓐ Ⓑ Ⓒ Ⓓ
31. Ⓐ Ⓑ Ⓒ Ⓓ
32. Ⓐ Ⓑ Ⓒ Ⓓ
33. Ⓐ Ⓑ Ⓒ Ⓓ
34. Ⓐ Ⓑ Ⓒ Ⓓ
35. Ⓐ Ⓑ Ⓒ Ⓓ
36. Ⓐ Ⓑ Ⓒ Ⓓ
37. Ⓐ Ⓑ Ⓒ Ⓓ
38. Ⓐ Ⓑ Ⓒ Ⓓ
39. Ⓐ Ⓑ Ⓒ Ⓓ
40. Ⓐ Ⓑ Ⓒ Ⓓ

Part 3: Conversations

41. Ⓐ Ⓑ Ⓒ Ⓓ
42. Ⓐ Ⓑ Ⓒ Ⓓ
43. Ⓐ Ⓑ Ⓒ Ⓓ
44. Ⓐ Ⓑ Ⓒ Ⓓ
45. Ⓐ Ⓑ Ⓒ Ⓓ
46. Ⓐ Ⓑ Ⓒ Ⓓ
47. Ⓐ Ⓑ Ⓒ Ⓓ
48. Ⓐ Ⓑ Ⓒ Ⓓ
49. Ⓐ Ⓑ Ⓒ Ⓓ
50. Ⓐ Ⓑ Ⓒ Ⓓ
51. Ⓐ Ⓑ Ⓒ Ⓓ
52. Ⓐ Ⓑ Ⓒ Ⓓ
53. Ⓐ Ⓑ Ⓒ Ⓓ
54. Ⓐ Ⓑ Ⓒ Ⓓ
55. Ⓐ Ⓑ Ⓒ Ⓓ
56. Ⓐ Ⓑ Ⓒ Ⓓ
57. Ⓐ Ⓑ Ⓒ Ⓓ
58. Ⓐ Ⓑ Ⓒ Ⓓ
59. Ⓐ Ⓑ Ⓒ Ⓓ
60. Ⓐ Ⓑ Ⓒ Ⓓ
61. Ⓐ Ⓑ Ⓒ Ⓓ
62. Ⓐ Ⓑ Ⓒ Ⓓ
63. Ⓐ Ⓑ Ⓒ Ⓓ
64. Ⓐ Ⓑ Ⓒ Ⓓ
65. Ⓐ Ⓑ Ⓒ Ⓓ
66. Ⓐ Ⓑ Ⓒ Ⓓ
67. Ⓐ Ⓑ Ⓒ Ⓓ
68. Ⓐ Ⓑ Ⓒ Ⓓ
69. Ⓐ Ⓑ Ⓒ Ⓓ
70. Ⓐ Ⓑ Ⓒ Ⓓ

Part 4: Talks

71. Ⓐ Ⓑ Ⓒ Ⓓ
72. Ⓐ Ⓑ Ⓒ Ⓓ
73. Ⓐ Ⓑ Ⓒ Ⓓ
74. Ⓐ Ⓑ Ⓒ Ⓓ
75. Ⓐ Ⓑ Ⓒ Ⓓ
76. Ⓐ Ⓑ Ⓒ Ⓓ
77. Ⓐ Ⓑ Ⓒ Ⓓ
78. Ⓐ Ⓑ Ⓒ Ⓓ
79. Ⓐ Ⓑ Ⓒ Ⓓ
80. Ⓐ Ⓑ Ⓒ Ⓓ
81. Ⓐ Ⓑ Ⓒ Ⓓ
82. Ⓐ Ⓑ Ⓒ Ⓓ
83. Ⓐ Ⓑ Ⓒ Ⓓ
84. Ⓐ Ⓑ Ⓒ Ⓓ
85. Ⓐ Ⓑ Ⓒ Ⓓ
86. Ⓐ Ⓑ Ⓒ Ⓓ
87. Ⓐ Ⓑ Ⓒ Ⓓ
88. Ⓐ Ⓑ Ⓒ Ⓓ
89. Ⓐ Ⓑ Ⓒ Ⓓ
90. Ⓐ Ⓑ Ⓒ Ⓓ
91. Ⓐ Ⓑ Ⓒ Ⓓ
92. Ⓐ Ⓑ Ⓒ Ⓓ
93. Ⓐ Ⓑ Ⓒ Ⓓ
94. Ⓐ Ⓑ Ⓒ Ⓓ
95. Ⓐ Ⓑ Ⓒ Ⓓ
96. Ⓐ Ⓑ Ⓒ Ⓓ
97. Ⓐ Ⓑ Ⓒ Ⓓ
98. Ⓐ Ⓑ Ⓒ Ⓓ
99. Ⓐ Ⓑ Ⓒ Ⓓ
100. Ⓐ Ⓑ Ⓒ Ⓓ

ANSWER SHEET
Model Test 2

READING

Part 5: Incomplete Sentences

101. Ⓐ Ⓑ Ⓒ Ⓓ	111. Ⓐ Ⓑ Ⓒ Ⓓ	121. Ⓐ Ⓑ Ⓒ Ⓓ	131. Ⓐ Ⓑ Ⓒ Ⓓ
102. Ⓐ Ⓑ Ⓒ Ⓓ	112. Ⓐ Ⓑ Ⓒ Ⓓ	122. Ⓐ Ⓑ Ⓒ Ⓓ	132. Ⓐ Ⓑ Ⓒ Ⓓ
103. Ⓐ Ⓑ Ⓒ Ⓓ	113. Ⓐ Ⓑ Ⓒ Ⓓ	123. Ⓐ Ⓑ Ⓒ Ⓓ	133. Ⓐ Ⓑ Ⓒ Ⓓ
104. Ⓐ Ⓑ Ⓒ Ⓓ	114. Ⓐ Ⓑ Ⓒ Ⓓ	124. Ⓐ Ⓑ Ⓒ Ⓓ	134. Ⓐ Ⓑ Ⓒ Ⓓ
105. Ⓐ Ⓑ Ⓒ Ⓓ	115. Ⓐ Ⓑ Ⓒ Ⓓ	125. Ⓐ Ⓑ Ⓒ Ⓓ	135. Ⓐ Ⓑ Ⓒ Ⓓ
106. Ⓐ Ⓑ Ⓒ Ⓓ	116. Ⓐ Ⓑ Ⓒ Ⓓ	126. Ⓐ Ⓑ Ⓒ Ⓓ	136. Ⓐ Ⓑ Ⓒ Ⓓ
107. Ⓐ Ⓑ Ⓒ Ⓓ	117. Ⓐ Ⓑ Ⓒ Ⓓ	127. Ⓐ Ⓑ Ⓒ Ⓓ	137. Ⓐ Ⓑ Ⓒ Ⓓ
108. Ⓐ Ⓑ Ⓒ Ⓓ	118. Ⓐ Ⓑ Ⓒ Ⓓ	128. Ⓐ Ⓑ Ⓒ Ⓓ	138. Ⓐ Ⓑ Ⓒ Ⓓ
109. Ⓐ Ⓑ Ⓒ Ⓓ	119. Ⓐ Ⓑ Ⓒ Ⓓ	129. Ⓐ Ⓑ Ⓒ Ⓓ	139. Ⓐ Ⓑ Ⓒ Ⓓ
110. Ⓐ Ⓑ Ⓒ Ⓓ	120. Ⓐ Ⓑ Ⓒ Ⓓ	130. Ⓐ Ⓑ Ⓒ Ⓓ	140. Ⓐ Ⓑ Ⓒ Ⓓ

Part 6: Text Completion

141. Ⓐ Ⓑ Ⓒ Ⓓ	144. Ⓐ Ⓑ Ⓒ Ⓓ	147. Ⓐ Ⓑ Ⓒ Ⓓ	150. Ⓐ Ⓑ Ⓒ Ⓓ
142. Ⓐ Ⓑ Ⓒ Ⓓ	145. Ⓐ Ⓑ Ⓒ Ⓓ	148. Ⓐ Ⓑ Ⓒ Ⓓ	151. Ⓐ Ⓑ Ⓒ Ⓓ
143. Ⓐ Ⓑ Ⓒ Ⓓ	146. Ⓐ Ⓑ Ⓒ Ⓓ	149. Ⓐ Ⓑ Ⓒ Ⓓ	152. Ⓐ Ⓑ Ⓒ Ⓓ

Part 7: Reading Comprehension

153. Ⓐ Ⓑ Ⓒ Ⓓ	165. Ⓐ Ⓑ Ⓒ Ⓓ	177. Ⓐ Ⓑ Ⓒ Ⓓ	189. Ⓐ Ⓑ Ⓒ Ⓓ
154. Ⓐ Ⓑ Ⓒ Ⓓ	166. Ⓐ Ⓑ Ⓒ Ⓓ	178. Ⓐ Ⓑ Ⓒ Ⓓ	190. Ⓐ Ⓑ Ⓒ Ⓓ
155. Ⓐ Ⓑ Ⓒ Ⓓ	167. Ⓐ Ⓑ Ⓒ Ⓓ	179. Ⓐ Ⓑ Ⓒ Ⓓ	191. Ⓐ Ⓑ Ⓒ Ⓓ
156. Ⓐ Ⓑ Ⓒ Ⓓ	168. Ⓐ Ⓑ Ⓒ Ⓓ	180. Ⓐ Ⓑ Ⓒ Ⓓ	192. Ⓐ Ⓑ Ⓒ Ⓓ
157. Ⓐ Ⓑ Ⓒ Ⓓ	169. Ⓐ Ⓑ Ⓒ Ⓓ	181. Ⓐ Ⓑ Ⓒ Ⓓ	193. Ⓐ Ⓑ Ⓒ Ⓓ
158. Ⓐ Ⓑ Ⓒ Ⓓ	170. Ⓐ Ⓑ Ⓒ Ⓓ	182. Ⓐ Ⓑ Ⓒ Ⓓ	194. Ⓐ Ⓑ Ⓒ Ⓓ
159. Ⓐ Ⓑ Ⓒ Ⓓ	171. Ⓐ Ⓑ Ⓒ Ⓓ	183. Ⓐ Ⓑ Ⓒ Ⓓ	195. Ⓐ Ⓑ Ⓒ Ⓓ
160. Ⓐ Ⓑ Ⓒ Ⓓ	172. Ⓐ Ⓑ Ⓒ Ⓓ	184. Ⓐ Ⓑ Ⓒ Ⓓ	196. Ⓐ Ⓑ Ⓒ Ⓓ
161. Ⓐ Ⓑ Ⓒ Ⓓ	173. Ⓐ Ⓑ Ⓒ Ⓓ	185. Ⓐ Ⓑ Ⓒ Ⓓ	197. Ⓐ Ⓑ Ⓒ Ⓓ
162. Ⓐ Ⓑ Ⓒ Ⓓ	174. Ⓐ Ⓑ Ⓒ Ⓓ	186. Ⓐ Ⓑ Ⓒ Ⓓ	198. Ⓐ Ⓑ Ⓒ Ⓓ
163. Ⓐ Ⓑ Ⓒ Ⓓ	175. Ⓐ Ⓑ Ⓒ Ⓓ	187. Ⓐ Ⓑ Ⓒ Ⓓ	199. Ⓐ Ⓑ Ⓒ Ⓓ
164. Ⓐ Ⓑ Ⓒ Ⓓ	176. Ⓐ Ⓑ Ⓒ Ⓓ	188. Ⓐ Ⓑ Ⓒ Ⓓ	200. Ⓐ Ⓑ Ⓒ Ⓓ

Model Test 2

LISTENING COMPREHENSION

In this section of the test, you will have the chance to show how well you understand spoken English. There are four parts to this section, with special directions for each part. You will have approximately 45 minutes to complete the Listening Comprehension sections.

Part 1: Photographs

Directions: You will see a photograph. You will hear four statements about the photograph. Choose the statement that most closely matches the photograph and fill in the corresponding oval on your answer sheet.

1.

2.

3.

4.

5.

6.

7.

8.

9.

MODEL TEST 2

10.

Part 2: Question-Response

Directions: You will hear a question and three possible responses. Choose the response that most closely answers the question and fill in the corresponding oval on your answer sheet.

11. Mark your answer on your answer sheet.
12. Mark your answer on your answer sheet.
13. Mark your answer on your answer sheet.
14. Mark your answer on your answer sheet.
15. Mark your answer on your answer sheet.
16. Mark your answer on your answer sheet.
17. Mark your answer on your answer sheet.
18. Mark your answer on your answer sheet.
19. Mark your answer on your answer sheet.
20. Mark your answer on your answer sheet.
21. Mark your answer on your answer sheet.
22. Mark your answer on your answer sheet.
23. Mark your answer on your answer sheet.
24. Mark your answer on your answer sheet.
25. Mark your answer on your answer sheet.
26. Mark your answer on your answer sheet.
27. Mark your answer on your answer sheet.
28. Mark your answer on your answer sheet.
29. Mark your answer on your answer sheet.
30. Mark your answer on your answer sheet.
31. Mark your answer on your answer sheet.
32. Mark your answer on your answer sheet.
33. Mark your answer on your answer sheet.
34. Mark your answer on your answer sheet.
35. Mark your answer on your answer sheet.
36. Mark your answer on your answer sheet.
37. Mark your answer on your answer sheet.
38. Mark your answer on your answer sheet.
39. Mark your answer on your answer sheet.
40. Mark your answer on your answer sheet.

Part 3: Conversations

Directions: You will hear a conversation between two people. You will see three questions on each conversation and four possible answers. Choose the best answer to each question and fill in the corresponding oval on your answer sheet.

41. What does the man want the woman to do?
    - (A) Help him remember something
    - (B) Do some typing for him
    - (C) Lend him a sweater
    - (D) Read a letter

42. When does he need it done?
    - (A) This afternoon
    - (B) Before noon
    - (C) On Tuesday
    - (D) By 8:00

43. Why can't the woman help him?
    - (A) Today is her day off.
    - (B) She is leaving at noon.
    - (C) She has to help Mr. Brown.
    - (D) She's busy doing something else.

---

44. What is the woman buying?
    - (A) Shirts
    - (B) Skirts
    - (C) Shoes
    - (D) Boots

45. How much does she have to pay?
    - (A) $42.05
    - (B) $45
    - (C) $60
    - (D) $245

46. How does she want to pay?
    - (A) Check
    - (B) Cash
    - (C) Credit card
    - (D) Gift certificate

47. How many copies does the woman need to make?
    - (A) 50
    - (B) 100
    - (C) 150
    - (D) 200

48. When does she have to have them finished?
    - (A) Before 11:00
    - (B) By 2:00
    - (C) At 4:00
    - (D) Tonight

49. What will she do when the copies are made?
    - (A) Mail them
    - (B) Read them
    - (C) Show them to her boss
    - (D) Take them to a meeting

---

50. Where does this conversation take place?
    - (A) In a hotel
    - (B) In a fish store
    - (C) In a restaurant
    - (D) In someone's house

51. How long will the man have to wait?
    - (A) Eight minutes
    - (B) Nine minutes
    - (C) Fifteen minutes
    - (D) Fifty minutes

52. What will he do while he waits?
    - (A) Have a drink
    - (B) Sit and think
    - (C) Go fishing
    - (D) Wash the dishes

53. Where is Mr. Wu now?

(A) In his office
(B) Out of town
(C) At a meeting
(D) On a flight

54. What does the woman want to do?

(A) Get a massage
(B) Speak with Mr. Wu
(C) Play ball
(D) Find out Mr. Wu's phone number

55. When will the woman be in her office?

(A) 2:00
(B) 2:30
(C) 10:00
(D) 10:30

---

56. Where did the woman leave her briefcase?

(A) At a meeting
(B) In her office
(C) On her desk
(D) In a cab

57. What is in the briefcase?

(A) Notes
(B) A report
(C) A cell phone
(D) Phone numbers

58. When does she need the contents of the briefcase?

(A) This morning
(B) This afternoon
(C) Tonight
(D) Tomorrow

59. Why does the man want to wake up early?

(A) He has to catch an early train.
(B) He wants to make a phone call.
(C) He's going to take a morning plane.
(D) He wants to hear the weather report.

60. How will the weather be tomorrow?

(A) Snowy
(B) Rainy
(C) Cold
(D) Hot

61. What time will the man wake up?

(A) 5:30
(B) 6:00
(C) 6:30
(D) 8:00

---

62. Where is the woman going to see the movie?

(A) At home
(B) At the college
(C) At the theater
(D) On the train

63. What will the man do tonight?

(A) Watch the movie with the woman
(B) Buy some tires for his car
(C) Have dinner with friends
(D) Go to sleep early

64. When will they take the train tomorrow?

(A) Before breakfast
(B) After breakfast
(C) Before dinner
(D) After dinner

65. What did the man send the woman?

(A) A program schedule
(B) A personnel file
(C) A finance report
(D) A rent check

66. When did he send it?

(A) Sunday
(B) Monday
(C) Tuesday
(D) Wednesday

67. What does the woman ask the man to do?

(A) Write down her address
(B) Pick out a new dress
(C) Lend her money
(D) Resend the file

68. What sport does the man enjoy?

(A) Golf
(B) Tennis
(C) Biking
(D) Swimming

69. Where does he practice it?

(A) At the hotel
(B) At the park
(C) At the exercise club
(D) At the community center

70. How often does he practice it?

(A) Two times a week
(B) Three times a week
(C) Four times a week
(D) Five times a week

Part 4: Talks

Directions: You will hear a talk given by a single speaker. You will see three questions on each talk, each with four possible answers. Choose the best answer to each question and fill in the corresponding oval on your answer sheet.

71. Who is the audience for this advertisement?
    (A) Families
    (B) Businesspeople
    (C) Tourists
    (D) Students

72. What is the advertisement for?
    (A) Suitcases
    (B) Computers
    (C) Clothes
    (D) Travel agency

73. How can a customer get a discount?
    (A) By ordering online
    (B) By shopping at a retail store
    (C) By completing an application
    (D) By ordering next month

---

74. What best describes the weather conditions the area is facing?
    (A) Cold
    (B) Fog
    (C) Snow and ice
    (D) Wind and rain

75. What problems will this weather cause tomorrow?
    (A) People will have trouble getting to work.
    (B) People won't have enough heat.
    (C) Flights will be cancelled.
    (D) People should buy plenty of food.

76. How will the weather be tomorrow afternoon?
    (A) Icy
    (B) Clear
    (C) Warmer
    (D) Freezing

77. According to the study, who is expected to be the least fit?
    (A) A bus driver
    (B) A gardener
    (C) A waiter
    (D) An accountant

78. Which is mentioned as a way to get more exercise?
    (A) Doing aerobics after work
    (B) Riding a stationary bicycle during breaks
    (C) Walking during lunch
    (D) Stretching

79. What advice is given about eating?
    (A) Have smaller meals at night
    (B) Avoid eating at bedtime
    (C) Snack on fruits and vegetables
    (D) Eat nuts every day

---

80. Who is Lynn?
    (A) A historian
    (B) A tour guide
    (C) A guidebook writer
    (D) A property owner

81. Where does the tour take place?
    (A) A village
    (B) A school
    (C) A city
    (D) A farm

82. How many buildings are on the tour?
    (A) Three
    (B) Six
    (C) Nine
    (D) Ten

MODEL TEST 2

83. What can this company do for you?

(A) Prepare your taxes
(B) Claim your return
(C) Write your financial records
(D) Staff your accounting department

84. How does the company determine its fees?

(A) By a flat rate
(B) With a single price
(C) By a prorated amount
(D) By an hourly rate

85. What should listeners do today?

(A) Provide financial records
(B) Make an appointment
(C) Return to the office
(D) Pay their taxes

---

86. What did the airlines do to increase sales?

(A) Reduce ticket prices
(B) Provide more polite service
(C) Make partnerships with hotels
(D) Serve better meals

87. Why have these airlines lost customers?

(A) Fewer people are flying.
(B) The planes were always late.
(C) Regional airlines are competing.
(D) It's off-season.

88. What percentage of its customers did Sky King Airways lose in the past year?

(A) 15%
(B) 20%
(C) 25%
(D) 50%

89. Who would be likely to call this number?

(A) A salesperson
(B) A computer user
(C) A customer service representative
(D) An accountant

90. What will happen if the caller presses 1?

(A) She will get help.
(B) She can buy software.
(C) She will hear about new products.
(D) She can get an update.

91. What should you do if you want information not listed?

(A) Dial 10
(B) Hang up and call again
(C) Go to a local store
(D) Stay on the line

---

92. What is the destination for this flight?

(A) Dallas
(B) Houston
(C) Madison
(D) Wilmington

93. What does the captain say about the flight?

(A) It will be late.
(B) There will be turbulence.
(C) It will be smooth.
(D) The flying altitude will be low.

94. What is the weather like there?

(A) Humid
(B) Rainy
(C) Breezy
(D) Sunny

95. Who will give the keynote address?

(A) The association president
(B) A financial expert
(C) The housekeeper
(D) A wedding planner

96. What will take place in the Garden Room?

(A) A wedding
(B) A workshop
(C) A lunch
(D) A market

97. What is the audience asked to do?

(A) Speak with George Williams
(B) Leave boxes by the door
(C) Pay for lunch
(D) Complete a form

98. What will take place in seven days?

(A) The voicemail system will change.
(B) This customer will get a new telephone.
(C) This customer will get a new telephone number.
(D) The telephone company's web address will change.

99. How can a customer save a message?

(A) Press two
(B) Press four
(C) Press seven
(D) Press nine

100. How can a customer learn about all of the new codes?

(A) Press ten
(B) Press the star key
(C) Visit the company's website
(D) Listen to the entire message

STOP

This is the end of the Listening Comprehension portion of the test. Turn to Part 5 in your test book.

READING

In this section of the test, you will have the chance to show how well you understand written English. There are three parts to this section, with special directions for each part.

YOU WILL HAVE ONE HOUR AND FIFTEEN MINUTES TO COMPLETE PARTS 5, 6, AND 7 OF THE TEST.

Part 5: Incomplete Sentences

Directions: You will see a sentence with a missing word. Four possible answers follow the sentence. Choose the best answer to the question and fill in the corresponding oval on your answer sheet.

101. The Windermere Hotel offer its clients spacious accommodations suitable __________ meetings, workshops, and other business functions.

(A) for
(B) to
(C) in
(D) about

102. The planned __________ of the production process will result in significant savings for the company.

(A) simpleton
(B) simplification
(C) simplify
(D) simply

103. Following company policy, the contents were thoroughly inspected __________ the package was shipped.

(A) for
(B) that
(C) and
(D) before

104. Subscribers frequently request that we __________ the monthly journal directly to their business address.

(A) mails
(B) mailed
(C) mail
(D) mailing

105. According to the "Casual Friday" policy, employees are not required to __________ business clothes on Fridays.

(A) wear
(B) dress
(C) put
(D) attire

106. The efforts of everybody involved resulted in a very __________ project.

(A) successfully
(B) successive
(C) success
(D) successful

107. __________ you complete the job application, please leave it with the receptionist at the front desk.

(A) Before
(B) After
(C) While
(D) Later

108. The speaker has __________ his speech by three minutes in order to fit it into the allotted time slot.

(A) short
(B) shortening
(C) shortened
(D) shortage

MODEL TEST 2

109. It is customary to seat the guest of honor at the banquet _________ the chairman of the board.

(A) as
(B) by
(C) to
(D) from

110. We want to get these products into the hands of customers before the _________ date.

(A) expiration
(B) inspiration
(C) respiration
(D) perspiration

111. By Friday, twenty-five applications had been submitted _________ the position of desk clerk.

(A) at
(B) on
(C) for
(D) by

112. The deeply discounted prices offered on that line of products is sure to _________ many new customers.

(A) offer
(B) attract
(C) enjoy
(D) expect

113. Mr. Cruz needs someone to _________ him with the conference display.

(A) assume
(B) assign
(C) assent
(D) assist

114. The workshop will be repeated next week for everyone who was not able to be _________ yesterday.

(A) resent
(B) present
(C) content
(D) intent

115. One downside of living in the countryside is the long _________ to get to work.

(A) travel
(B) relay
(C) commute
(D) extension

116. The final purchase price was higher than the investors _________.

(A) had expected
(B) expect
(C) are expecting
(D) will expect

117. The new waitress made hardly any mistakes on her first day, so I imagine _________ will be hired full time.

(A) she
(B) him
(C) her
(D) they

118. The new insurance plan is especially _________ with employees who have families.

(A) popularized
(B) popular
(C) populated
(D) popularity

MODEL TEST 2

119. The provisions officer buys supplies in _________ quantities because the fishing boat is at sea for weeks at a time.

(A) largely
(B) largest
(C) larger
(D) large

120. The airline will refund your money as _________ as your travel agent cancels your reservation.

(A) well
(B) far
(C) soon
(D) little

121. Did Mr. Fisk _________ the reference guide from the company library?

(A) loan
(B) borrow
(C) lend
(D) sent

122. _________ they were ordered, the brochures and business cards were never printed.

(A) Although
(B) Even
(C) However
(D) Despite

123. The operator does not remember receiving a fax from the Madrid office _________ from the Paris office.

(A) or
(B) and
(C) either
(D) but

124. Most of our staff have not used this type of copy machine _________.

(A) before
(B) prior
(C) advance
(D) previous

125. The housekeepers will need to be paid overtime for their work over the holidays, _________ ?

(A) won't they
(B) will she
(C) aren't they
(D) they will

126. The printer in Mr. Daaka's office uses a special _________ cartridge that comes in four different colors.

(A) dye
(B) ink
(C) paper
(D) tray

127. The receptionist receives packages and _________ them until the proper department is notified.

(A) is holding
(B) held
(C) hold
(D) holds

128. The purpose of our conference is to help employees _________ our policies.

(A) understood
(B) understanding
(C) understand
(D) are understanding

129. _________ none of us were familiar with the city, Mr. Gutman drove us to the meeting.

(A) Although
(B) Because
(C) Therefore
(D) However

130. The gas station attendant suggests _________ a boat from a local to save money.

(A) rent
(B) rents
(C) rented
(D) renting

131. If this report is sent by overnight delivery, it _________ Milan by noon tomorrow.

(A) reaches
(B) will reach
(C) is reaching
(D) has reached

132. Yamamoto Sushi is across town and _________ near our hotel, so we should take a taxi.

(A) nowhere
(B) anywhere
(C) somewhere
(D) everywhere

133. Employees who _________ attending the conference can get a discount on travel arrangements.

(A) have going
(B) are going to
(C) will
(D) will be

134. Mr. Vasco has developed his _________ in electronics over many years of experience and hard work.

(A) technician
(B) professional
(C) expertise
(D) authorization

135. The city is asking for funding _________ five parks and three recreational centers.

(A) on renovating
(B) for renovation
(C) by renovating
(D) to renovate

136. The head housekeeper is going to ask Ms. Chang how much time she _________ available.

(A) will have had
(B) is having
(C) have
(D) has

137. The hotel marketing director is quite _________ about advertising in Europe.

(A) knowing
(B) knowledge
(C) knowledgeable
(D) knows

138. We _________ to know the size of the banner before we can start designing it.

(A) must
(B) need
(C) could
(D) should

139. The operator _________ Mr. Smith if she knew where to reach him.

(A) will call
(B) had called
(C) called
(D) would call

140. The trainers for the seminar had the crew _________ their equipment to the conference center.

(A) move
(B) moving
(C) mover
(D) moved

Part 6: Text Completion

Directions: You will see four passages each with three blanks. Under each blank are four answer options. Choose the word or phrase that best completes the sentence.

Questions 141–143 refer to the following letter.

Creek and Chung, Accountants
1040 Stone Way
Seattle, Washington 93108-2662

July 12, 20—

Mr. Hugh Ferrer
Unity Health Care
400 East Pine Street
Seattle, Washington 93129-2665

Dear Mr. Ferrer:

We are a mid-sized accounting firm. Our staff members have expressed dissatisfaction with our current insurance plan, so we are looking into other ______. The

141. (A) employees
(B) positions
(C) activities
(D) options

insurance company we use now has recently raised its rates, while at the same time the quality of service has gotten worse. Naturally, we are not happy about paying more and more money for poor service. ______, we are interested in learning more

142. (A) Therefore
(B) However
(C) Moreover
(D) Nevertheless

about Unity Health Care (UHC). Could you please mail a packet of information to me? Also, I would appreciate it if you could answer the following questions.

First, our employees want to choose their own doctors. Does your program allow this? Second, do your doctors have weekend and evening hours? Our employees have busy work schedules, and it is not always ______ for them to go to appointments

143. (A) enjoyable
(B) difficult
(C) convenient
(D) interesting

during regular business hours.

Thank you for your help.

Sincerely,

Felicia Braddish
Human Resources Manager

MODEL TEST 2

Questions 144–146 refer to the following e-mail.

From: Simon Yan
To: Mingmei Lee
Subject: Monday meeting

Dear Mingmei,

I have to leave town for a business trip ______ there is an emergency in our

144. (A) so
(B) if
(C) as
(D) by

Singapore office. I am sorry that I will have to miss our Monday morning meeting, especially because I am eager to see your progress on my company's new financial center. This is an important project for National Bank.

My coworker, Hugh Harrison, will ______ me. Hugh plans to look for you

145. (A) escort
(B) replace
(C) assist
(D) accompany

at the construction site at 9:00 A.M. You told me that you have some concerns about the project's budget. Please talk with Hugh about this. While we don't want to spend a lot of extra money on this building, it is going to be our company's headquarters and needs to look good. You have an excellent reputation as a Construction Project Manager, so I'm ______ that you can manage the

146. (A) doubtful
(B) positive
(C) wondering
(D) concerned

budget and build a fantastic center for us at the same time.

I will return one week from today. You can e-mail me until I return. Thank you.

Questions 147–149 refer to the following memorandum.

Memorandum

From: Belinda Beilby, Company President
To: Company Vice-Presidents
Re: Reducing electricity expenses

The electric company is ______________ its rates by 25% next month, so we need

147. (A) cutting
(B) increasing
(C) dividing
(D) improving

to look at ways to reduce our electricity usage. Below is a list of recommendations. Please distribute this list to the departments in your area.

Ways to Reduce Electricity Expenses

1. Lights: Turn off the lights in meeting rooms when your meeting ends. Turn off the lights in the offices before you leave for the day.

2. Computers: At the day's end, turn off your computer.

3. Photocopying: Don't photocopy and fax documents. Most documents can ______________ electronically.

148. (A) send
(B) sent
(C) to send
(D) be sent

4. Fans/Heaters: Using fans or heaters in the office should not be necessary. The building's temperature is set at a comfortable level. If your office is too cool or warm, please contact the maintenance staff.

5. Home Office Option: ______________ employees to work at home one or more

149. (A) Allow
(B) Allowing
(C) To allow
(D) Will allow

days a week saves money in many ways, including on electricity. Employees who are interested in this option should speak to their supervisors.

Questions 150–152 refer to the following announcement.

Sunrise Manufacturers, Inc. announced Friday that its president, Shirley Ocampo, would succeed Louis Freeland as the company's chief executive officer starting in September. Ms. Ocampo will be the first female chief executive in the company's history. Sunrise Manufacturers is ____________ manufacturer of farming

150. (A) large
(B) larger
(C) the larger
(D) the largest

equipment in the country. This is a sector that has been traditionally dominated by men, making Ms. Ocampo's appointment particularly ____________.

151. (A) signify
(B) significance
(C) significant
(D) significantly

Mr. Freeland, who will retire from Sunrise when Ms. Ocampo takes over his position next month, ____________ at the company for 25 years.

152. (A) works
(B) worked
(C) had worked
(D) has been working

MODEL TEST 2

Part 7: Reading Comprehension

> **Directions:** You will see single and double reading passages followed by several questions. Each question has four answer choices. Choose the best answer to the question and fill in the corresponding oval on your answer sheet.

Questions 153–154 refer to the following announcement.

As our company plans new products and processes, health, safety and environmental considerations are a priority. We are committed to operating our manufacturing plants and research facilities in a manner that protects the environment and safeguards the health and safety of all people. We will continue to allocate money to improve existing facilities as new safety information is brought to light.

153. What is the purpose of this announcement?

(A) To announce an expansion
(B) To report on a merger
(C) To reassure the public about safety issues
(D) To explain a new company policy

154. What will the company do with existing facilities?

(A) Make them safer
(B) Tear them down
(C) Have them inspected
(D) Renovate them

Questions 155–157 refer to the following report.

> The profits for the Wu Company more than doubled in the fourth quarter over profit levels of a year ago. This is due in part to lower operating and administrative expenses. The electronics store chain earned $42.6 million, compared with $21.1 million in the fourth quarter of last year. Total profits for the year are $122.8 million, compared with $48.5 million last year.

155. How do fourth quarter profits for this year compare to those of last year?

(A) Stayed the same
(B) Increased by twice as much
(C) Increased by more than twice as much
(D) Decreased by half

156. What contributed to the change?

(A) Reduction of operating costs
(B) Higher number of customers
(C) New and better products
(D) More expensive products

157. What kind of business is the Wu Company?

(A) Computer training
(B) Electronics manufacturer
(C) Software development
(D) Electronics retailer

Questions 158–159 refer to the following advertisement.

> **Data Entry/Clerk**
>
> Insurance firm seeks reliable, detail-oriented person for operations division. Responsibilities include data entry, filing, and word processing. Good salary and benefits. Pleasant atmosphere. Room to advance.

158. What is one responsibility of this job?

(A) Answering the phone
(B) Data entry
(C) Selling insurance
(D) Operating a division

159. What is one benefit of the position?

(A) They'll give you your own office later.
(B) You can work toward promotions.
(C) Benefits apply to dependents.
(D) You can earn commissions.

Questions 160–161 refer to the following magazine article.

When you are looking for a new job, you must talk to as many people as you can who work in your field or in related fields. This is called networking. Networking allows you to learn about new areas to pursue and to find out which companies may need someone with your skills. Networking is a fun and easy way to find out about new opportunities. And when your new job comes along, you will already know some of your colleagues.

160. What is networking?

(A) Learning your job well
(B) Meeting people in related fields
(C) Studying lots of companies
(D) Getting along with your colleagues

161. What is NOT mentioned as something you can learn from networking?

(A) New career areas
(B) Your colleagues and what they do
(C) Which companies may need you
(D) What the companies pay

Questions 162–163 refer to the following memo.

MEMORANDUM

To: All employees
Fm: Donetta Muscillo
Safety Coordinator
Date: June 5, 20–

Sub: Fire doors

Employees are reminded that doors designated as fire doors must stay closed at all times. The purpose of fire doors is to help direct smoke away from areas where people are working in case of a fire in the building. Even though the weather is hot and the repairs to the company's air conditioner are not complete, keeping the fire doors open is strictly prohibited.

162. What is the purpose of the company's fire doors?

(A) To keep smoke away from people
(B) To provide escape routes
(C) To keep fire from spreading
(D) To contain heat

163. Why were employees probably keeping the fire doors open?

(A) To get to a higher floor
(B) To look at the view
(C) To go from office to office
(D) To let in cool air

Questions 164–166 refer to the following calendar.

FEBRUARY	MARCH	APRIL	MAY
February 4–February 24 Bonn, Germany International Jewelry Trade Fair	March 11–April 15 Budapest, Hungary International Furniture Fair March 12–March 20 Milan, Italy Automobile Show March 15–March 18 Guangzhou, China International Shoe Fair March 20–March 25 Moscow, Russia International Textile Fair	April 16–April 24 Hannover, Germany Art and Antiques Fair April 14–April 21 Basel, Switzerland European Watch Fair	May 27–June 12 Bath, England International Computer Exhibit

164. What does this calendar list?

(A) Trade shows
(B) Musical events
(C) Sport competitions
(D) A tour itinerary

165. Which event does not take place in Europe?

(A) Automobile Show
(B) International Shoe Fair
(C) Art and Antiques Fair
(D) International Jewelry Trade Fair

166. If you were a buyer for a dress manufacturer, where should you go in March?

(A) Budapest
(B) Bonn
(C) Moscow
(D) Hannover

Questions 167–168 refer to the following announcement.

ESTATE AUCTION

An auction for the estate of *Raul Diega*
will be held on

Saturday, October 3, at 11:00 A.M.
(preview starts at 10:00 A.M.)

Location: 5667 North Hedge Lane

Some of the items to be auctioned
* 2004 Mercedes
* China and crystal
* Oriental rugs
* Jewelry
* Stamp collection

Questions? Please call Estate Planners at 778-0099 between noon and 5 P.M.

167. Which of the following items will be auctioned?

(A) Chinese antiques
(B) Rare books
(C) Bracelets
(D) Wall-to-wall carpeting

168. When can you start to look at things?

(A) October 3, 11:00 A.M.
(B) By appointment after calling 778-0099
(C) Any day from noon to five
(D) October 3, 10:00 A.M.

Questions 169–171 refer to the following pie chart.

First Impressions Art Gallery

Review of April Finances

Total Expenses: $75,275

Total Income: $228,566

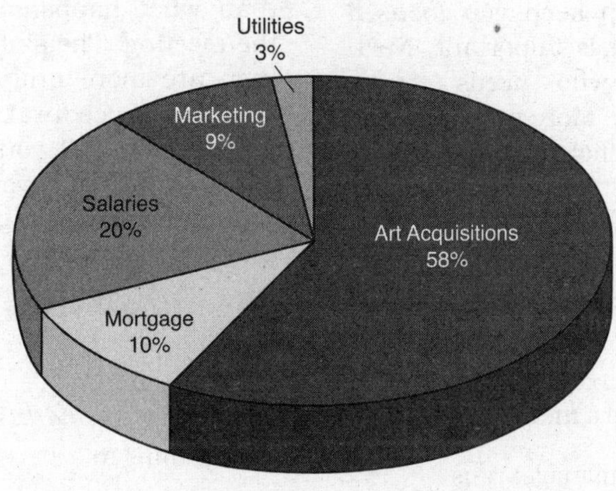

169. When was this graph created?

(A) Before April
(B) After April
(C) In early April
(D) In late April

170. What can be said about the gallery?

(A) It is earning about three times what it is spending.
(B) It is spending more than it is earning.
(C) It is spending the same amount as it is earning.
(D) It is earning half of what it is spending.

171. What is the greatest expense for the gallery?

(A) New inventory
(B) Money paid to employees
(C) Money paid to advertise
(D) Electricity and water costs

Questions 172–176 refer to the following article.

Meetings can waste a great deal of time. But you can make your meeting run more smoothly by following a few simple rules. First, have an agenda. This will help keep you focused on what is important. Next, decide who needs to be involved. More people means less efficient discussion. Finally, keep the discussion moving. Thank each speaker as he or she finishes and move on to the next speaker. This encourages people to make their remarks brief. And don't forget: What happens after a meeting is more important than what happens during the meeting. The skills used then are more professional and less procedural. So no matter how well you run a meeting, it is the work that gets done after the meeting that is important.

172. What is one way to run a meeting well?
   (A) Watch how your manager runs meetings.
   (B) Minimize the number of participants.
   (C) Let the group make decisions.
   (D) Let everyone speak.

173. What is the purpose of a meeting agenda?
   (A) To keep the speakers organized
   (B) To allow free discussion
   (C) To send to others in advance
   (D) To keep focused on important items

174. How should you receive other people's comments at a meeting?
   (A) Try to keep others from talking.
   (B) Thank them and move on.
   (C) Give them as much time as they want.
   (D) Respond in detail to all comments.

175. The word *remarks* in line 18, is closest in meaning to
   (A) meetings
   (B) questions
   (C) comments
   (D) schedules

176. The author states that
   (A) meetings should be held more frequently
   (B) all meetings should be in the morning
   (C) no one should receive credit for their work
   (D) the real work is accomplished after the meetings

Questions 177–180 refer to the following announcement.

The Hesseltine Corporation

is moving 60 technical and management-level employees to their new manufacturing plant in the western United States. Before the move, the company will prepare employees for the cultural changes they will encounter when moving from urban Europe to a small town in the American West. The employees and their families will attend special seminars on the habits of Americans. They will learn about the regional vocabulary and the daily life. Without this training, even small cultural differences could cause big misunderstandings.

177. Where is the new manufacturing plant?

(A) In an urban area
(B) In Western Europe
(C) In the western United States
(D) In a large town

178. What important part of the moving process is discussed?

(A) Completing the plant
(B) Getting the office furnishings
(C) Arranging airline tickets
(D) Teaching cultural differences

179. Who will attend the seminars in addition to the employees?

(A) Their secretaries
(B) Their families
(C) Their supervisors
(D) Their staffs

180. What do they learn in the seminars?

(A) How to make travel plans
(B) Methods of business management
(C) Characteristics of American culture
(D) Manufacturing techniques

Questions 181–185 refer to the following two e-mails.

From: "Yvonne Wu" <Yvonne@messages.com>
To: "Royal Hotel" <reservations@royal.com>
Subject: Room Reservations

I need a single room with a queen-sized bed for four nights, from March 15 until March 18. Do you have a room available then? I will be attending a conference at the Convention Center and I understand that your hotel is just two blocks from there. Please confirm this for me as I don't want to have to walk far or deal with cabs. Also, do you have a pool and a weight room? Is there a restaurant located in or near the hotel?
Thank you for your help.

From: "Royal Hotel" <reservations@royal.com>
To: "Yvonne Wu" <Yvonne@messages.com>
Subject: Re: Reservations for a Business Trip

We do have the type of room that you want. It costs $100 per night. However, for the first night of your stay only, I will have to give you a king-sized bed as there are no queens available that night. It costs an extra $25. I hope this will suit you. Starting on March 16, you can have the type of room you requested. I can confirm that we are located very close to the Convention Center, just one block further than you thought. It is a very pleasant walk through a park to the Center, and I'm sure you will enjoy it. We do have a pool, but unfortunately it is currently closed for repairs. There is a full-service restaurant, BJ's, located in the hotel. Hotel guests are entitled to a free breakfast there. Lunch and dinner are also served and can be charged to your room for your convenience. If you would like to go ahead with your reservation, please send me your credit card information as soon as possible.

181. When does Yvonne Wu want to begin her stay at the Royal Hotel?

(A) March 15
(B) March 16
(C) March 17
(D) March 18

182. What kind of room does she request?

(A) A room for one person
(B) A room with two queen-sized beds
(C) A room near the pool
(D) A room with a view of the park

183. What is the extra $25 charge for?

(A) A ride to the Convention Center
(B) A reservation cancellation fee
(C) A room with a larger bed
(D) A parking space

184. How far is the hotel from the Convention Center?

(A) One block
(B) Two blocks
(C) Three blocks
(D) Four blocks

185. What is included in the price of the hotel room?

(A) Breakfast
(B) Room service
(C) Use of the pool
(D) Use of the weight room

Questions 186–190 refer to the following agenda and e-mail message.

HORIZON OFFICE PRODUCTS, INC.
COMMITTEE MEETING ON MARKETING
THURSDAY, JUNE 15, 20– 9:30 A.M.-11:30 A.M.
PLACE: ROOM 2

AGENDA

1. REVIEW OF CURRENT STRATEGY	BEN NGUYEN
2. GOALS FOR NEW STRATEGY	BO PARK
3. FOCUS GROUPS	MARTY TAYLOR
4. PROJECTS TO BEGIN	BARBARA SPENCER
5. PLANS FOR THE YEAR	RITA PALMER

To: Max Kohler
From: Bo Park
Subject: Committee Meeting

There were serious problems at today's meeting. We began on time, but Ben wasn't there, so we had to begin with the second agenda item. Then, thirty minutes after we began, Ben finally arrived and gave his presentation. Marty never came at all. I found out later that he's been out sick, but in any case his topic was never discussed. Barbara tried to explain her topic, but it was confusing. She did the best she could, but we really needed to hear from Marty first for her presentation to make sense. We couldn't agree on our next step, so we ended the meeting early, right after Barbara's talk. When will you return from this business trip? I know none of this would have happened if you had been here.

MODEL TEST 2

186. What was the topic of the June 15 meeting?

(A) Marketing
(B) Business trips
(C) Work schedules
(D) Ordering office supplies

187. What topic was discussed first?

(A) Review of current strategy
(B) Goals for new strategy
(C) Focus groups
(D) Projects to begin

188. What time did Ben start his presentation?

(A) 9:00
(B) 9:30
(C) 10:00
(D) 11:30

189. Who gave the last presentation?

(A) Rita Palmer
(B) Barbara Spencer
(C) Marty Taylor
(D) Bo Park

190. Why didn't Max attend the meeting?

(A) He was out sick.
(B) He wasn't invited.
(C) He couldn't arrive on time.
(D) He was away on a business trip.

Questions 191–195 refer to the following e-mail and table.

From: "Aras Koca" <Aras@apex.com>
To: "Clarice Ryan" <Clarice@apex.com>
Subject: Report on Employees' Use of Time

Clarice, I agree that waste of work time is a serious issue. The Human Resources Department recently surveyed the employees. They are wasting close to two hours per day.

Here are my ideas to reduce this waste. First we need to agree on what are the most important behaviors to stop. For example, look at item #1. Many people are doing this; however, it is the most difficult to stop. I recommend that we focus on activities #2, 4, and 5.

Making phone calls shows the largest difference between men and women. Women do this much more than men. We should ask all employees to limit these calls. They should return non-urgent messages at their lunch break.

For #4, we should focus on the younger age group. We will tell them that we are going to check their work accounts for personal messages. For #5, we can ask supervisors to watch this more carefully. Perhaps activity #3 should continue. This allows employees to know each other and it can increase their motivation. The supervisors will know if someone is spending too much time talking and not enough time working.

Are you available tomorrow? I'd like to meet with you to discuss our next step.

Time Spent on Non-Work-Related Activities

Activity	Percentage of employees who do this three times per week or more: Men	Women
1. Surfing the Internet*	85%	83%
2. Making personal phone calls	65%	80%
3. Talking to coworkers**	60%	70%
4. Writing personal e-mails*	45%	45%
5. Taking long breaks	30%	20%

Key: *most common with workers 22–35; ** most common with workers 45–60

191. Why was the survey done?
   (A) To help plan a better work schedule
   (B) To find out how employees waste their work time
   (C) To learn which employees know how to use the Internet
   (D) To discover which employees are unhappy with their jobs

192. Which is the most popular activity among the employees?
   (A) Going online
   (B) Talking on the phone
   (C) Socializing with other employees
   (D) Taking breaks

193. Among which group is writing personal e-mails most common?
   (A) Younger people
   (B) Older people
   (C) Women
   (D) Men

194. Which activity does Aras Koca consider the least problematic?
   (A) Going online
   (B) Talking on the phone
   (C) Socializing with other employees
   (D) Sending e-mails

195. Which activity does Aras Koca want supervisors to monitor?
   (A) Visiting websites
   (B) Sending personal e-mails
   (C) Answering phone messages
   (D) Spending too much time on breaks

Questions 196–200 refer to the following two letters.

The Printing Press
111 Acorn Parkway
San Antonio, TX 78216-7423

April 6, 20—

Anneliese Clark
Federal Bank
8244 Centergate Street
San Antonio, TX 78217-0099

Dear Ms. Clark:

I have been a customer at your bank for more than ten years. I am a small business owner and have been renting a space for my operations. My company is now ready to expand, and I am looking into buying a small building.

I am interested in two buildings. The one I prefer is on Main Street. It would require a $200,000 loan, and I'm not sure if I qualify for that large a loan. There is another building that would suit my needs. The size is right although the location is not as good. I would need to borrow only $130,000 to purchase this building.

I have a good credit record and am carrying only two debts at this time–$5,000 on my car loan and $120,000 on my house. I am hoping to get a thirty-year loan at 5% interest.

I would like to meet with you to discuss this as soon as possible. Would Tuesday, April 21 suit you? If not, I am available any other day that week. I look forward to hearing from you.

Sincerely,

Jeremiah Hernandez

Jeremiah Hernandez

196. Why does Mr. Hernandez want to buy a building?

(A) He wants to rent it out.
(B) He needs a place to live.
(C) He is expanding his business.
(D) He just bought a new company.

197. Why does he prefer the Main Street building?

(A) It's bigger.
(B) It's cheaper.
(C) It's in a better location.
(D) It's in better condition.

198. What does Mr. Hernandez owe money for now?

(A) Business equipment
(B) Credit card debt
(C) House and car
(D) Renovations

FEDERAL BANK
8244 Centergate Street
San Antonio, TX 78217-0099

April 10, 20—

Jeremiah Hernandez
The Printing Press
111 Acorn Parkway
San Antonio, TX 78216-7423

Dear Mr. Hernandez:

Thank you for your interest in getting a loan from Federal Bank. We appreciate your business.

It is possible for us to lend you enough money for the cheaper building. We cannot give you a larger loan because you already have more than $100,000 in debt. We can offer you a loan at the interest rate and for the term you want.

I am happy to meet with you to discuss this. I am not available on the date you mentioned. Can we meet the following day? Please let me know.

Best Wishes,

Anneliese Clark

Anneliese Clark

199. How much money will the bank lend him?
    (A) $100,000
    (B) $130,000
    (C) $200,000
    (D) $330,000

200. When does Ms. Clark want to meet with Mr. Hernandez?
    (A) April 10
    (B) April 11
    (C) April 21
    (D) April 22

STOP

This is the end of the test. If you finish before time is called, you may go back to Parts 5, 6, and 7 and check your work.

ANSWER KEY
Model Test 2

LISTENING COMPREHENSION

Part 1: Photographs

1. **B**	4. **A**	7. **B**	10. **A**
2. **D**	5. **C**	8. **C**	
3. **B**	6. **A**	9. **D**	

Part 2: Question-Response

11. **A**	20. **C**	29. **C**	38. **A**
12. **C**	21. **A**	30. **B**	39. **B**
13. **A**	22. **B**	31. **A**	40. **A**
14. **B**	23. **A**	32. **B**	
15. **A**	24. **B**	33. **A**	
16. **A**	25. **A**	34. **A**	
17. **C**	26. **B**	35. **B**	
18. **A**	27. **C**	36. **B**	
19. **A**	28. **A**	37. **C**	

Part 3: Conversations

41. **B**	49. **A**	57. **A**	65. **C**
42. **B**	50. **C**	58. **D**	66. **B**
43. **D**	51. **C**	59. **C**	67. **D**
44. **A**	52. **A**	60. **B**	68. **B**
45. **B**	53. **C**	61. **A**	69. **D**
46. **D**	54. **B**	62. **B**	70. **D**
47. **C**	55. **B**	63. **D**	
48. **A**	56. **D**	64. **B**	

Part 4: Talks

71. **B**	79. **C**	87. **C**	95. **B**
72. **A**	80. **B**	88. **C**	96. **A**
73. **A**	81. **D**	89. **B**	97. **D**
74. **C**	82. **B**	90. **A**	98. **A**
75. **A**	83. **A**	91. **D**	99. **D**
76. **C**	84. **D**	92. **B**	100. **B**
77. **D**	85. **B**	93. **B**	
78. **C**	86. **A**	94. **D**	

ANSWER KEY
Model Test 2

READING

Part 5: Incomplete Sentences

101. **A**	112. **B**	123. **A**	134. **C**
102. **B**	113. **D**	124. **A**	135. **D**
103. **D**	114. **B**	125. **A**	136. **D**
104. **C**	115. **C**	126. **B**	137. **C**
105. **A**	116. **A**	127. **D**	138. **B**
106. **D**	117. **A**	128. **C**	139. **D**
107. **B**	118. **B**	129. **B**	140. **A**
108. **C**	119. **D**	130. **D**	
109. **B**	120. **C**	131. **B**	
110. **A**	121. **B**	132. **A**	
111. **C**	122. **A**	133. **D**	

Part 6: Text Completion

141. **D**	144. **C**	147. **B**	150. **D**
142. **A**	145. **B**	148. **D**	151. **C**
143. **C**	146. **B**	149. **B**	152. **D**

Part 7: Reading Comprehension

153. **C**	165. **B**	177. **C**	189. **B**
154. **A**	166. **C**	178. **D**	190. **D**
155. **C**	167. **C**	179. **B**	191. **B**
156. **A**	168. **D**	180. **C**	192. **A**
157. **D**	169. **B**	181. **A**	193. **A**
158. **B**	170. **A**	182. **A**	194. **C**
159. **B**	171. **A**	183. **C**	195. **D**
160. **B**	172. **B**	184. **C**	196. **C**
161. **D**	173. **D**	185. **A**	197. **C**
162. **A**	174. **B**	186. **A**	198. **C**
163. **D**	175. **C**	187. **B**	199. **B**
164. **A**	176. **D**	188. **C**	200. **D**

TEST SCORE CONVERSION TABLE

Count your correct responses. Match the number of correct responses with the corresponding score from the Test Score Conversion Table (below). Add the two scores together. This is your Total Estimated Test Score. As you practice taking the TOEIC model tests, your scores should improve. Keep track of your Total Estimated Test Scores.

# Correct	Listening Score	Reading Score	# Correct	Listening Score	Reading Score	# Correct	Listening Score	Reading Score	# Correct	Listening Score	Reading Score
0	5	5	26	110	65	51	255	220	76	410	370
1	5	5	27	115	70	52	260	225	77	420	380
2	5	5	28	120	80	53	270	230	78	425	385
3	5	5	29	125	85	54	275	235	79	430	390
4	5	5	30	130	90	55	280	240	80	440	395
5	5	5	31	135	95	56	290	250	81	445	400
6	5	5	32	140	100	57	295	255	82	450	405
7	10	5	33	145	110	58	300	260	83	460	410
8	15	5	34	150	115	59	310	265	84	465	415
9	20	5	35	160	120	60	315	270	85	470	420
10	25	5	36	165	125	61	320	280	86	475	425
11	30	5	37	170	130	62	325	285	87	480	430
12	35	5	38	175	140	63	330	290	88	485	435
13	40	5	39	180	145	64	340	300	89	490	445
14	45	5	40	185	150	65	345	305	90	495	450
15	50	5	41	190	160	66	350	310	91	495	455
16	55	10	42	195	165	67	360	320	92	495	465
17	60	15	43	200	170	68	365	325	93	495	470
18	65	20	44	210	175	69	370	330	94	495	480
19	70	25	45	215	180	70	380	335	95	495	485
20	75	30	46	220	190	71	385	340	96	495	490
21	80	35	47	230	195	72	390	350	97	495	495
22	85	40	48	240	200	73	395	355	98	495	495
23	90	45	49	245	210	74	400	360	99	495	495
24	95	50	50	250	215	75	405	365	100	495	495
25	100	60									

Number of Correct Listening Responses ________ = Listening Score ________

Number of Correct Reading Responses ________ = Reading Score ________

Total Estimated Test Score ________

EXPLANATORY ANSWERS

Listening Comprehension

PART 1: PHOTOGRAPHS

1. **(B)** Two men with coffee cups in their hands are sitting outside on a wall and talking. Choice (A) correctly identifies the wall, but the men are sitting on it, not leaning against it. Choice (C) correctly identifies the men's action, *sitting*, but not their location. Choice (D) confuses similar-sounding words *talking/ walking*.
2. **(D)** Choice (D) identifies the *occupation* and the *action*. The kitchen and the uniforms imply they are *cooks* engaged in their occupation. Choice (A) is incorrect because in the photo there is a man pointing, there is not a sign pointing the way. Choice (B) is incorrect because no one is chopping vegetables. Choice (C) is incorrect since no one is leaving.
3. **(B)** The man in the photo is wearing a hard hat. Choices (A) and (C) could be true in the context, but they do not correctly describe this photo. Choice (D) is the opposite of what the photo shows.
4. **(A)** Choice (A) identifies the couples' action, viewing art. Choice (B) is incorrect because some paintings are smaller than others. Choice (C) is incorrect because in the picture the *pictures are on the wall,* not *stacked on the floor.* Choice (D) correctly identifies the *gallery visitors,* but they are not resting.
5. **(C)** Choice (C) makes the assumption that the location is an *airport* and that the people waiting are *passengers.* Choice (A) misidentifies the location of the passengers—they are at the airport, not on a plane. Choice (B) is contradicted by *empty*; there are many people on the concourse. Choice (D) does not describe the location of the *bags,* which are on the *floor* not on a *truck.*
6. **(A)** Choice (A) correctly describes the action, looking at their laptop, and the background shows they are outdoors. Choice (B) confuses the action: There are two people and there is a coffee cup on the table, but they are not making the coffee. Choice (C) is incorrect because you cannot see their hands. Choice (D) is incorrect because they are already seated at a table.
7. **(B)** Choice (B) identifies the specific locations of the *trains.* Choice (A) confuses the sound of *train* with *crane* and uses the related word to *bridge, water.* Choice (C) uses words related to *train (narrow* and *tunnel),* but it does not describe the picture and confuses the sound of *cart* with *train car.* Choice (D) is incorrect because it is trains not pedestrians that are crossing the bridge.
8. **(C)** A man is holding a microphone and talking into it. Choice (A) confuses similar-sounding words *microphone* and *telephone.* Choice (B) confuses similar-sounding words *talking* and *walking* and *microphone* and *telephone.* Choice (D) mentions the man's hand, but he isn't waving it.
9. **(D)** Two men in business suits are wearing nametags. Choice (A) correctly identifies the table, but there is no waiter in the photo. Choice (B) correctly identifies the chairs, but nobody is painting them. Choice (C) correctly identifies the ties the men are wearing, but there is no salesclerk selling anything.
10. **(A)** A pharmacist is holding a bottle of pills, or medicine, and talking with a customer. Choice (B) incorrectly describes the customer's action. He is talking with the pharmacist and possibly looking at the pills, but the pills are still in the bottle and the customer doesn't appear to be counting them. Choice (C) confuses similar-sounding words *pharmacist* and *farmer.* Choice (D) mentions the shelves in the photo, but there is no one stocking them.

PART 2: QUESTION-RESPONSE

11. **(A)** Choice (A) is a logical response to the question about the trip. Choice (B) uses the vacation month *August* to confuse you. Choice (C) repeats the word *good.*
12. **(C)** Choice (C) is a logical response to the question about *length of stay.* Choice (A) gives

a time and a word with similar sounds: *stay* with *day* and answers the question *How long is a day.* Choice (B) answers *Where.*

13. **(A)** Choice (A) is a logical response to the question about *who wrote a letter.* Choice (B) confuses similar sounds *letter* with *better.* Choice (C) confuses sounds *rate* with *wrote* and *letter* with *better.*
14. **(B)** Choice (B) is a logical response to the question about *color.* Choice (A) describes the type of *shirt.* Choice (C) confuses the similar sound of *wearing* with *where I am.*
15. **(A)** Choice (A) is a logical response to the question *When.* Choice (B) confuses similar words *call* (v) and *call* (n). Choice (C) uses related words *call* (telephone) and *call* (She *said* I was lazy).
16. **(A)** Choice (A) is a logical response to the request for a hotel recommendation. Choice (B) relates *hotel* and *manager.* Choice (C) relates *Los Angeles* and *place.*
17. **(C)** Choice (C) is a logical response to the question about *family origins.* Choice (A) confuses similar sounds *family* and *famous.* Choice (B) uses related words *children* and gives an answer to a *Where* question: *at school.*
18. **(A)** Choice (A) is a logical response to the question *How soon.* Choice (B) confuses similar sounds *soon* and *son.* Choice (C) confuses similar sounds *ready* and *red.*
19. **(A)** The response agrees with the opinion about the restaurant. Choice (B) repeats the word *excellent.* Choice (C) confuses similar sounds *excellent* and *spell it.*
20. **(C)** Choice (C) is a logical response to the question about *a train departure.* Choice (A) uses the related word *stop* and the similar sound of *train* and *rain.* Choice (B) repeats the words *train* and *time.*
21. **(A)** The context is a phone call. The caller is asked to *hold,* or wait, and the caller chooses instead to *call back later.* Choice (B) uses the word *hold* in a different way. Choice (C) confuses similar-sounding words *hold/cold.*
22. **(B)** This is a logical response to the *Who* question. Choice (A) confuses similar-sounding words *shift/lift.* Choice (C) confuses similar-sounding words *working/walking* and repeats the word *night.*
23. **(A)** Choice (A) is a logical response to the question about *the date an invoice was sent.* Choice (B) confuses similar sounds *invoice* and *voice.* Choice (C) confuses similar sounds *sent* and *went,* and has a date (*in March*) but doesn't answer the question about when the *invoice* was sent.
24. **(B)** The first speaker lost a cell phone and the second speaker says that it is on a desk. Choice (A) associates *call* with *phone.* Choice (C) confuses *home* with the similar-sounding word *phone.*
25. **(A)** Choice (A) is a logical response to the *invitation for tonight.* Choice (B) uses similar sounds *tonight* and *tight.* Choice (C) also uses similar sounds *tonight* and *light.*
26. **(B)** Choice (B) is a logical response to the question of *preference.* Choice (A) confuses *tea* and *team.* Choice (C) confuses (*favo*)*rite* and *right, team* and *seem.*
27. **(C)** The second speaker says that rain is the cause of the heavy traffic mentioned by the first speaker. Choice (A) uses the word *heavy* out of context. Choice (B) repeats the word *traffic.*
28. **(A)** Choice (A) is a logical response to the question about the existence of the fax machine. Choices (B) and (C) confuse *fax* with the similar-sounding words *tax* and *facts.*
29. **(C)** Tuesday answers the question *What day.* Choice (A) confuses similar-sounding words *dentist/dent.* Choice (B) answers the question *Who.*
30. **(B)** Choice (B) is a logical response to the question about the need for a reservation. Choice (A) refers to the number of people the reservation might be for. Choice (C) confuses similar-sounding words *need/read.*
31. **(A)** Choice (A) answers the question *Where.* Choice (B) answers a *How* question. Choice (C) answers a *Why* question.

32. **(B)** The question is about time—a *deadline,* and Choice (B) answers the question with a time—*by Thursday.* Choice (A) answers a *Where* question about a project. Choice (C) confuses similar-sounding words *deadline/signed.*
33. **(A)** The second speaker thinks the first speaker is a fast reader because of having read a book in three days. Choice (B) confuses the phrase *free days* with the similar-sounding phrase *three days.* Choice (C) confuses *red* with the similar-sounding word *read.*
34. **(A)** *A client* answers the *Who* question. Choice (B) confuses similar-sounding words *standing/sanding.* Choice (C) repeats the word *door.*
35. **(B)** The second speaker thinks that the package contains something he ordered. Choice (A) confuses *packed* with the similar-sounding word *package.* Choice (C) associates *post office* with *package.*
36. **(B)** Choice (B) is a logical response to the question about *laundry service.* Choice (A) confuses similar sounds *pressed* and *depressed.* Choice (C) uses related words *pants* and *pair.*
37. **(C)** Choice (C) is a logical response to the question about *time.* Choice (A) uses related words *exercise* and *healthful.* Choice (B) confuses *exercises* (n) with *exercise* (v).
38. **(A)** Choice (A) answers the *yes/no* question. Choice (B) confuses similar-sounding words *reach/beach* and repeats the word *month.* Choice (C) confuses the usage of the word *reach.*
39. **(B)** Choice (B) is a logical response to the question about a journal article. Choice (A) confuses similar-sounding words *seen/green.* Choice (C) repeats the word *journal.*
40. **(A)** Choice (A) is a logical response to the question about *location.* Choice (B) repeats the word *go* and answers the question *When.* Choice (C) confuses *recommend* with *comment* and *go* with *memo.*

PART 3: CONVERSATIONS

41. **(B)** The man asks the woman to type a memo for him. Choice (A) confuses *remember* with the similar-sounding word *memo.* Choice (C) confuses *sweater* with the similar-sounding word *letter.* Choice (D) repeats the word *letter,* which is what the woman is typing.
42. **(B)** The man says he needs the memo before noon. Choice (A) confuses *afternoon* with *noon.* Choice (C) confuses *Tuesday* with the similar-sounding word *today.* Choice (D) confuses *eight* with the similar-sounding word *wait.*
43. **(D)** The woman is busy typing letters. Choice (A) repeats the word *today.* Choice (B) repeats the word *noon.* Choice (C) is confused with the man's asking Mr. Brown for help.
44. **(A)** The woman is buying two shirts. Choice (B) sounds similar to the correct answer. Choice (C) confuses *shoes* with the similar-sounding word *two.* Choice (D) confuses *boots* with the similar-sounding word *blue.*
45. **(B)** The man says she owes forty-five dollars. Choices (A) and (D) sound similar to the correct answer. Choice (C) confuses *sixty* with the similar-sounding word *sixteen,* which is the size of the shirts.
46. **(D)** The woman says she has a gift certificate. Choice (A) uses the word *check* out of context. Choices (B) and (C) are what the man asks.
47. **(C)** The woman needs 150 copies. Choices (A) and (B) sound similar to the correct answer. Choice (D) confuses *two* with *too.*
48. **(A)** The woman says she needs her copies *by eleven.* Choice (B) confuses *two* with *too.* Choice (C) is when the man needs his copies. Choice (D) confuses *tonight* with the similar-sounding word *right.*
49. **(A)** The woman says that she has to put the copies in the mail. Choice (B) confuses *read* with the similar-sounding word *ready.* Choice (C) repeats the word *boss.* Choice (D) is what the man will do with his copies.
50. **(C)** The man is ordering food from a waitress, so he is in a restaurant. Choice (A) is not mentioned. Choice (B) repeats the word *fish.*

Choice (D) uses the word *house* out of context.

51. **(C)** The woman says it will take fifteen minutes to cook the fish. Choice (A) confuses *eight* with the similar-sounding word *wait.* Choice (B) confuses *nine* with the similar-sounding word *mind.* Choice (D) sounds similar to the correct answer.
52. **(A)** The man says he will have a drink. Choice (B) confuses *think* with the similar-sounding word *drink.* Choice (C) associates *fishing* with *fish.* Choice (D) confuses *dish* with the similar-sounding word *fish.*
53. **(C)** The man says that Mr. Wu is at a meeting. Choice (A) is confused with *out of the office.* Choice (B) confuses *out of town* with *downtown.* Choice (D) confuses *flight* with the similar-sounding word *right.*
54. **(B)** The woman called to speak with Mr. Wu. Choice (A) confuses *massage* with the similar-sounding word *message.* Choice (C) confuses *ball* with the similar-sounding word *call.* Choice (D) is incorrect because the woman called Mr. Wu so she must know his number.
55. **(B)** The woman says she'll be in her office at 2:30. Choice (A) sounds similar to the correct answer. Choices (C) and (D) confuse *ten* with the similar-sounding word *then.*
56. **(D)** The woman says that she left her briefcase in a cab. Choices (A), (B), and (C) all repeat words used in other parts of the conversation.
57. **(A)** The woman says that her briefcase contains notes she needs for a meeting. Choice (B) uses the word *report* out of context. Choices (C) and (D) are confused with the woman's using the man's phone to call the cab company.
58. **(D)** The woman needs the notes for a meeting tomorrow. Choice (A) is when she lost the briefcase. Choice (B) confuses *afternoon* with the similar-sounding word *noon.* Choice (C) confuses *tonight* with the similar-sounding word *right.*
59. **(C)** The man says he has to catch an eight-o'clock flight. Choice (A) confuses *train* with the similar-sounding word *rain.* Choice (B) repeats the word *call.* Choice (D) repeats the word *weather.*
60. **(B)** The woman says it will rain. Choice (A) confuses *snow* with the similar-sounding word *know.* Choice (C) confuses *cold* with the similar-sounding word *call.* Choice (D) is not mentioned.
61. **(A)** The man takes the woman's advice to get up earlier and asks for a 5:30 wake up call. Choice (B) was his original request. Choice (C) sounds similar to the original request. Choice (D) is the time that the plane leaves.
62. **(B)** The woman will see the movie at the college student center. Choice (A) is where the man will go. Choice (C) confuses *theater* with the similar-sounding word *they're.* Choice (D) is where the speakers will be tomorrow.
63. **(D)** The man says that he wants to get to bed early. Choice (A) is what he decides not to do. Choice (B) confuses *tires* with the similar-sounding word *tired.* Choice (C) is what the woman will do.
64. **(B)** The man reminds the woman that they will take a train after breakfast. Choice (A) repeats the word *breakfast.* Choices (C) and (D) repeat the word *dinner.*
65. **(C)** The man sent the woman an e-mail with a finance report attached. Choice (A) confuses the usage of the word *program.* Choice (B) confuses similar-sounding words *personal/personnel.* Choice (D) confuses the usage of the word *check* and confuses similar-sounding words *sent/rent.*
66. **(B)** The woman asks the man to send it again. Choice (A) repeats the word *address.* Choice (D) confuses similar-sounding words *address/dress.* Choice (C) confuses similar sounding words *send/lend.*
67. **(D)** The woman asks the man to send the report to her home address. Choice (A) repeats the word *mail.* Choice (B) confuses *dress* with the similar-sounding word *address.* Choice (C) confuses *lend* with the similar-sounding word *send* and the word *money* with the similar-sounding word *many.*
68. **(B)** The man says, *Tennis is my sport.* Choice (A) is what the woman asks him about. Choice

(C) confuses *biking* with the similar-sounding word *like*. Choice (D) is the woman's sport.

69. **(D)** The man plays tennis with a group at the community center. Choice (A) is where the woman swims. Choice (B) is where the woman used to play tennis. Choice (C) repeats the word *club*.

70. **(D)** The man is on the tennis court five times a week. Choices (A) and (B) are how often the woman swims. Choice (C) is not mentioned.

PART 4: TALKS

71. **(B)** The ad is for people concerned about their "professional look." Choices (A), (C), and (D) are other types of people who use luggage but are not identified with the need to look professional.

72. **(A)** The speaker says the ad is for Legerton's luggage, that is, suitcases. Overnight cases, computer carriers, and garment bags—all types of luggage are also mentioned. Choice (B) repeats the word *computers*. Choice (C) is a synonym for *garment*. Choice (D) is associated with the mention of travel.

73. **(A)** Orders made through the website receive the discount. Choice (B) mentions a place where the products can be bought, but the discount is not available there. Choice (C) uses the word *apply* (application) out of context. Choice (D) is confused with *before the end of the month*, when the discount will end.

74. **(C)** The report says, *rain . . . turning to snow . . . will create ice hazards*. Choice (A) is true, but it is not complete. Choice (B) is not mentioned. Choice (D) is incorrect because wind is not mentioned.

75. **(A)** People *go to and from work* during *rush hour*. Choices (B), (C), and (D) are not mentioned.

76. **(C)** The speaker mentions warmer temperatures tomorrow afternoon. Choice (A) is how the weather will be in the morning. Choice (B) is confused with *clear the streets*. Choice (D) is confused with *temperatures above freezing*.

77. **(D)** If *office workers are less fit*, then an *accountant* would be less fit. Choices (A), (B), and (C) are not office jobs.

78. **(C)** Going for walks during lunch is a way to keep fit. Choice (A) is a good way to get more exercise, but it is not mentioned. Choice (B) confuses *riding bicycles to work* with *riding stationary bicycles during breaks*. Choice (D) is not mentioned.

79. **(C)** The talk advises bringing fruit or vegetables to work as a snack. Choice (A) confuses *night* with the similar-sounding word *right*. Choice (B) confuses *bed* with the similar-sounding word *instead*. Choice (D) confuses *nuts* with the similar-sounding word *donuts*.

80. **(B)** The speaker, Lynn, is guiding a tour of the Janteck Homestead, so she is a tour guide. Choice (A) repeats the word *historian*, which refers to the people who restored the homestead. Choice (C) is related to the context of the talk—a tour. Choice (D) repeats the word *property*.

81. **(D)** The speaker mentions that the Janteck's bought a farm outside of the city, and a homestead is a type of farm. Choice (A) is a place where a tour might go through several buildings, as this tour does. Choice (B) confuses similar-sounding words *rule/school*. Choice (C) repeats the word *city*.

82. **(B)** The speaker says that the tour will go *through six of the ten buildings*. Choice (A) repeats the word *three* (they will see *three small houses*). Choice (C) confuses similar-sounding words *time/nine*. Choice (D) repeats the word *ten*.

83. **(A)** The ad states, *if you hate to do your taxes, let us do them instead*. Choice (B) is incorrect because a company can prepare your return but cannot claim your return. Choice (C) is incorrect because you have to provide them with your financial records. Choice (D) confuses *staff your accounting department* with *staff of accountants*.

84. **(D)** The ad states, *fees are based on an hourly rate*. Choices (A), (B), and (C) are all possible

MODEL TEST 2

ways of paying for services, but they are not mentioned here.

85. **(B)** The speaker tells listeners to call today to make an appointment. Choice (A) is what would be done during an appointment. Choice (C) uses the word *return* out of context. Choice (D) is what should be done within a month.

86. **(A)** The airlines *reduced fares.* Choices (B), (C), and (D) are all possible ways to improve service, but they are not mentioned here.

87. **(C)** Airlines are trying to *win customers from competing regional airlines.* Choices (A) and (B) are possible reasons to lose customers, but they are not mentioned here. Choice (D) is not mentioned.

88. **(C)** The company lost 25% of its customer base. Choice (A) confuses *fifteen* with the similar-sounding word *fifty.* Choice (B) sounds similar to the correct answer. Choice (D) is the amount that some tickets are discounted.

89. **(B)** A computer user would call a computer helpline. Choices (A) and (C) are people you can reach by calling this number. Choice (D) might call if he or she is a computer user.

90. **(A)** The recording says to press one *if you need assistance.* Choice (B) is confused with getting assistance with software. Choices (C) and (D) are what will happen if the caller presses three.

91. **(D)** The message says, *otherwise, stay on the line.* Choices (A), (B), and (C) are not mentioned.

92. **(B)** The flight is to *Houston.* Choices (A), (C), and (D) are not mentioned.

93. **(B)** Because of the *turbulence,* passengers should remain seated with their seat belts on. We can conclude that the flight will be bumpy. Choices (A), (C), and (D) repeat words from the talk, but none of these is expected by the captain.

94. **(D)** The announcement says that the weather is *sunny.* Choices (A), (B), and (C) are all weather terms, but they are not mentioned.

95. **(B)** The speaker says that the keynote speaker is *George Williams, one of our country's top financial experts.* Choice (A) is the person giving the announcement. Choice (C) is confused with *housekeeping announcements,* which refers to conference logistics. Choice (D) repeats the word *wedding.*

96. **(A)** The speaker says that the Garden Room has been reserved for a wedding. Choice (B) is the original plan for the Garden Room. Choice (C) will take place in the Rooftop Restaurant. Choice (D) is confused with the topic of the workshop.

97. **(D)** The speaker asks listeners to fill out the evaluation form that is in their packets. Choice (A) is confused with the fact that George Williams is the *keynote speaker.* Choice (B) is confused with what listeners should do with a completed form—*leave it in the box by the door.* Choice (C) repeats the word *lunch,* but no payment is mentioned in connection with it.

98. **(A)** The message is about changes in the phone company's voicemail system. Choice (B) associates *telephone* with *voicemail.* Choice (C) repeats the phrase *new number.* Choice (D) is associated with *Web site.*

99. **(D)** A customer can save a message by pressing nine. Choice (A) confuses *two* with the similar-sounding word *new.* Choice (B) confuses *four* with the similar-sounding word *or.* Choice (C) is for deleting a message.

100. **(B)** The message instructs the listener to press the star key in order to hear the new codes. Choice (A) is confused with the number of new codes. Choice (C) repeats the name of the company, but nothing is mentioned about calling it. Choice (D) is confused with *read the entire message* on the Web site.

Reading

PART 5: INCOMPLETE SENTENCES

101. **(A)** The adjective *suitable* is commonly followed by the preposition *for.* Choices (B), (C), and (D) are prepositions that cannot be used in this context.

102. **(B)** *Simplification* is a noun and acts as the subject of this sentence. Choice (A) is also a

noun, but it has a different meaning—it refers to a person lacking in intelligence. Choice (C) is a verb. Choice (D) is an adjective.

103. **(D)** *Before* establishes a logical time relationship between the two past tense verbs. Choices (A) and (B) do not make sense. Choice (C) would establish an illogical equal relationship.

104. **(C)** *Request* is followed by the simple form of the verb when it means that one person or group (*subscribers*) made another person or group (*we*) do something. Choice (A) is a present form. Choice (B) is a past form. Choice (D) is a progressive form.

105. **(A)** *Wear* means *have clothes on.* Choices (A) and (B) have a similar meaning, but they must be followed by *in.* Choice (C) has a similar meaning when followed by *on.*

106. **(D)** *Project* must be modified by an adjective. Choice (A) is an adverb. Choice (B) is an adjective, but it means *following in order.* Choice (C) is a noun.

107. **(B)** *After* establishes a logical time relationship between the two actions—first you complete the application, then you leave it with the receptionist. Choices (A) and (C) are not logical. Choice (D) cannot be used to begin a time clause.

108. **(C)** *Has* requires the past participle *shortened* to complete the verb. Choice (A) is the simple form of the verb. Choice (B) is the progressive form. Choice (D) is a noun.

109. **(B)** A person can sit *by, beside, next to,* or *with* another at a dinner, etc. Choice (A) means *in place of.* Choice (C) indicates destination. Choice (D) indicates source.

110. **(A)** *Expiration* refers to the end of a period of time, and an *expiration date* is the date by which a product should be sold. Choices (B), (C), and (D) have meanings that don't fit the context.

111. **(C)** *For* means *with regard to.* Choices (A) and (B) illogically indicate location. Choice (D) means *through the means of.*

112. **(B)** *Attract* means to *pull in* or *get the attention of.* Choices (A), (C), and (D) have meanings that don't fit the context.

113. **(D)** *Assist* means *help.* Choice (A) means *guess.* Choice (B) means to *give a person work or responsibility.* Choice (C) means *agree* or *allow.*

114. **(B)** *Present* means at *a particular place.* Choices (A), (C), and (D) have meanings that don't fit the context.

115. **(C)** *Commute* refers to the regular trip between home and work. Choice (A) is related in meaning, but it is a verb, and a noun is needed here. Choices (B) and (D) have meanings that don't fit the context.

116. **(A)** *Was higher* is already past tense, so to establish an earlier past use the past participle *had expected.* Choice (B) is the simple form. Choice (C) is the present progressive tense. Choice (D) is the future tense.

117. **(A)** *She* is a singular subject pronoun referring to a woman, in this case, *waitress.* Choice (B) is a masculine object pronoun. Choice (C) is a possessive adjective or object pronoun. Choice (D) is a plural pronoun.

118. **(B)** The adjective *popular* can modify *plan;* the adverb *especially* can modify *popular.* Choices (A) and (C) are verbs. Choice (D) is a noun.

119. **(D)** A simple adjective is required here to modify the noun *quantities.* Choice (A) is an adverb. Choices (B) and (C) are superlative and comparative adjectives, but no comparison is being made here.

120. **(C)** *As soon as* means *immediately after.* Choices (A), (B), and (D) have no meaning in this context.

121. **(B)** *Borrow* means *to take temporarily.* Choice (A) is *what* you take (*the reference guide is a loan*). Choice (C) means *to give temporarily.* Choice (D) means *gone away.*

122. **(A)** *Although* is a subordinate conjunction that indicates that one thing *(business cards not being printed)* happened in spite of another *(ordering the cards).* Choices (B), (C), and (D) do not fit the context of the sentence.

123. **(A)** *Or* allows a choice between the items joined. Choice (B) would mean *both.* Choice (C) should be used with *or.* Choice (D) *but*

would imply a contrast (*from the Madrid office but not from the Paris office*).

124. **(A)** *Before* is an adverb and tells when the machine might have been used. Choices (B), (C), and (D) do not fit the context of the sentence.

125. **(A)** The negative tag question *won't they* matches the affirmative future sentence. Choice (B) would match a negative sentence. Choice (C) is not future tense. Choice (D) is not a tag question.

126. **(B)** *Ink* is used in a printer cartridge and comes in colors. Choice (A) comes in colors, but it is not a word used when referring to printers. Choices (C) and (D) are associated with printers, but they do not fit the meaning of the sentence.

127. **(D)** *Holds* matches *receives* (*receives and holds*). Choice (A) is present progressive tense. Choice (B) is past tense. Choice (C) is present tense, but does not match the subject.

128. **(C)** *Help* is followed by the simple form (or the infinitive) when one thing (*the conference*) helps another (*employees*) do something. Choice (A) is past tense. Choice (B) is a gerund. Choice (D) is present progressive tense.

129. **(B)** *Because* establishes a logical relationship between the two events. Choices (A) and (D) are illogical without a contrast (*Although we knew the city . . . ; We knew the city, however, . . .*). Choice (C) would belong in a result clause (*. . . therefore, Mr. Gutman drove . . .*).

130. **(D)** The verb *suggest* is followed by a gerund. Choice (A) is base form or present tense. Choice (B) is present tense. Choice (C) is past tense.

131. **(B)** Present tense in a real condition in the *if* clause requires future tense in the other clause. Choice (A) is present tense. Choice (C) is present progressive tense. Choice (D) is present perfect tense.

132. **(A)** *Nowhere* means *in no place.* Choice (B) is used in negative sentences and questions. Choice (C) means *in some place*, however, if the destination were *in some place* near the hotel, a taxi would not be required. Choice (D) means *in all places.*

133. **(D)** *Attending* forms the future progressive with *will be* (*will be attending*). Choices (A), (B), and (C) do not form logical tenses with *attending.*

134. **(C)** *Expertise* is related to the word *expert*, and the sentence means that Mr. Vasco has great abilities in electronics. Choices (A), (B), and (D) do not fit the sentence.

135. **(D)** This is an infinitive of purpose; the sentence explains the purpose of the funding. Choices (A), (B), and (C) don't fit the context.

136. **(D)** Present tense and simple future are possible; only present tense is given. *Ms. Chang* requires third person *has.* Choice (A) is future perfect tense. Choice (B) is present progressive tense. Choice (C) is plural.

137. **(C)** The adjective *knowledgeable* modifies *director; quite* modifies *knowledgeable.* Choice (A) is a gerund. Choice (B) is a noun. Choice (D) is a verb.

138. **(B)** *Need* is followed by an infinitive verb. Choices (A), (C), and (D) are modals, which are followed by a base form verb.

139. **(D)** Past tense in the *if* clause of an unreal condition requires *would + simple verb* in the other clause. Choice (A) is future tense. Choice (B) is past perfect tense. Choice (C) is past tense.

140. **(A)** *Have* requires the simple form of the second verb when one or more person(s) (trainers) *have* another (crew) do something. Choice (B) is a gerund. Choice (C) is a noun. Choice (D) is past tense.

PART 6: TEXT COMPLETION

141. **(D)** The firm doesn't like its current insurance plan, so it wants to make a different choice. Choice (A) is mentioned in the letter, but the company isn't looking for new employees. Choices (B) and (C) could be related to the work of an accounting firm, but they aren't mentioned in the text.

142. **(A)** *Therefore* introduces a result. Wanting to learn more about Unity Health Care is

the result of being unhappy with the current insurance plan. Choices (B) and (D) both have a similar meaning to *but,* introducing a contradictory idea. Choice (C) means *additionally.*

143. **(C)** It is not easy, or *convenient,* for employees to visit the doctor during their working hours. Choices (A) and (D) are not words generally used to describe doctors' appointments. Choice (B) is the opposite of the correct meaning.

144. **(C)** *As* means *because* and introduces a reason. Choice (A) introduces a result. Choice (B) introduces a condition. Choice (D) is a preposition and cannot introduce a clause.

145. **(B)** Simon Yan cannot go to the meeting, so Hugh Harrison will go in his place. Choices (A) and (D) mean *go with.* Choice (C) means *help.*

146. **(B)** Positive means *sure* or *certain.* Mr. Yan is certain that Mingmei can do the job because of her good reputation. Choices (A), (C), and (D) all give the sentence the opposite of the correct meaning.

147. **(B)** The company president wants to reduce use of electricity because the cost is *going up,* or *increasing.* Choices (A) and (C) give the sentence the opposite of the correct meaning. Choice (D) doesn't make sense in this sentence.

148. **(D)** The passive voice is necessary here because the subject of the sentence is not the actor. Choices (A), (B), and (C) are all active voice.

149. **(B)** This is a gerund form used as the subject of the sentence. Choices (A), (C), and (D) are all verb forms that cannot be used in the subject position in a sentence.

150. **(D)** *The largest* is a superlative adjective, comparing this company to all the other companies in the nation. Choice (A) is an adjective, but it is not a superlative form. Choices (B) and (C) are comparative forms.

151. **(C)** *Significant* is an adjective, modified by the adverb *particularly* and modifying the noun *appointment.* Choice (A) is a verb. Choice (B) is a noun. Choice (D) is an adverb.

152. **(D)** *Has been working* is a present perfect verb describing an action that began in the past (25 years ago) and continues into the present. Choice (A) is present tense. Choice (B) simple past tense and Choice (C) past perfect tense describe actions that are already completed.

PART 7: READING COMPREHENSION

153. **(C)** It reassures the public about safety. Choices (A) and (B) are not mentioned. Choice (D) is incorrect because the announcement doesn't say whether the policy is new or old.

154. **(A)** *Improve existing facilities with new safety information* means *make them safer.* Choice (B) is not mentioned. Choice (C) is part of improving them. Choice (D) is not mentioned.

155. **(C)** *More than doubled* means *increased by more than twice as much.* Choices (A) and (D) are contradicted by doubled. Choice (B) omits *more than.*

156. **(A)** *Reduction of operating costs* means lower operating expenses. Choices (B) and (C) are possible, but they are not mentioned. Choice (D) is unlikely.

157. **(D)** The Wu Company is described as an *electronics store chain,* that is a company that sells electronics at retail. Choices (A), (B), and (C) are businesses that involve electronics, but they are not the correct answer.

158. **(B)** *Data entry* is explicitly mentioned as a job responsibility. Choices (A), (C), and (D) are not mentioned.

159. **(B)** *Room to advance* means *opportunity for promotions.* Choices (A), (C), and (D) are all benefits, but not of this job.

160. **(B)** *Networking* means *talk to as many people as you can who work in your field or in related fields.* Choices (A), (C), and (D) are good practices, but they do not define *networking.*

161. **(D)** Discovering the salaries offered by companies is not mentioned as a benefit of networking. Choices (A), (B), and (C) are explicitly mentioned.

162. **(A)** The memo says fire doors *direct smoke away from areas where people are working.* Choices (B), (C), and (D) are not mentioned.

163. **(D)** If the weather is hot and the air conditioner is not repaired, employees were probably opening fire doors to let in cool air. Choices (A), (B), and (C) are all purposes of doors, but they do not relate to fire safety.

164. **(A)** All of the events are trade shows: shoes, furniture, autos, etc. Choices (B), (C), and (D) are not mentioned.

165. **(B)** The Shoe Fair is in Guangzhou, China. Choices (A), (C), and (D) are all held in Europe.

166. **(C)** A buyer might want to look for dress material at the International Textile Fair in Moscow. Choice (A) will have a furniture fair. Choice (B) will have a jewelry fair. Choice (D) will have an art and antiques fair.

167. **(C)** Since *jewelry* is on the list of items to be auctioned, you will probably find *bracelets* for sale. Choice (A) confuses *Chinese antiques* with *china* (dishes). Choice (B) is not mentioned, although you might relate *stamps* and *rare books.* Choice (D) confuses *wall-to-wall carpeting* and *Oriental rugs.*

168. **(D)** The preview starts at *10 A.M. on Saturday, October 3.* Choice (A) is when the auction begins. Choice (B) is not mentioned. Choice (C) is when you can call Estate Planners with questions.

169. **(B)** The graph is a review of money spent in April, so it must have been created after April. Choices (A), (C), and (D) are not possible.

170. **(A)** The gallery had an income of $228,566 and $75,275 in expenses, so it earned more than it spent. Choices (B), (C), and (D) are contradicted by the correct answer.

171. **(A)** In April, 58% of expenses went to *art acquisitions,* which is what the gallery sells, that is, it's inventory. Choice (B) refers to *salaries,* which made up 20% of expenses. Choice (C) refers to *marketing,* which made up 9% of expenses. Choice (D) refers to *utilities,* which made up 3% of expenses.

172. **(B)** Since more people mean less efficient discussion, fewer people will likely be more efficient. Choices (C) and (D) are not mentioned as ways to run meetings well.

173. **(D)** An *agenda keeps you focused.* Choices (A) and (C) may be additional advantages, but they are not mentioned. Choice (B) is incorrect; an agenda should *control* free discussion.

174. **(B)** *Thank them and move on.* Choice (A) would defeat the purpose of a meeting. Choice (C) makes the meeting inefficient. Choice (D) is not mentioned.

175. **(C)** Remarks are comments. Choices (A), (B), and (D) are related to the topic of meetings, but they don't have the correct meaning.

176. **(D)** This is the only valid option and is supported in the paragraph: *What happens after a meeting is more important . . . ; skills . . . are more professional . . . ; work that gets done after the meeting that is important.* Choices (A), (B), and (C) are not supported in the passage.

177. **(C)** The facility is in the *western United States.* Choices (A) and (D) are contradicted by *in a small town.* Choice (B) is contradicted by the *western United States.*

178. **(D)** Preparing employees for cultural changes is important. Choices (A), (B), and (C) are not the topics of the article.

179. **(B)** Their *families* will attend. Choices (A), (C), and (D) are all employees and would be attending with their families.

180. **(C)** The article mentions *cultural changes, cultural differences,* and *habits of Americans.* Choice (A) is incorrect; plans for moving are made by the company. Choices (B) and (D) are business topics.

181. **(A)** Yvonne Wu wants to stay in the hotel from March 15 until March 18. Choice (B) is when she can get the type of room she requested. Choice (C) is not mentioned. Choice (D) is when she will end her stay.

182. **(A)** She asks for a single room. Choice (B) is incorrect because she just wants one queen-sized bed. Choice (C) is confused with the fact that she asks about a pool, but she doesn't say she wants a room near it. Choice (D) is confused with the mention of the nearby park.

183. **(C)** The second e-mail offers Ms. Wu a room with a king-sized bed instead of a queen-sized bed for the first night of her stay, and states that this costs an extra $25. Choice (A) is incorrect because Ms. Wu will walk to the Convention Center. Choices (B) and (D) are not mentioned.

184. **(C)** Yvonne Wu thought that the Convention Center was two blocks from the hotel, and the hotel e-mail says that it is one block more than that. Choice (A) is confused with the one block mentioned in the hotel e-mail. Choice (B) is the distance that Yvonne Wu thought it was. Choice (D) is not mentioned.

185. **(A)** Hotel guests can have free breakfast at BJ's Restaurant. Choice (B) is associated with eating at a hotel, but it is not mentioned. Choice (C) is incorrect because the pool is closed right now. Choice (D) is what Yvonne Wu asks about, but the hotel e-mail never mentions it.

186. **(A)** According to the agenda heading, the meeting topic is marketing. Choice (B) is confused with Max's business trip. Choice (C) is confused with the discussion of the meeting schedule. Choice (D) is confused with the name of the company.

187. **(B)** Point 2 was discussed first because the first scheduled speaker didn't arrive on time. Choice (A) is the item that was scheduled to be first. Choices (C) and (D) are later items on the agenda.

188. **(C)** The meeting began at 9:30, and Ben started his presentation thirty minutes after that. Choice (A) is thirty minutes before the meeting began. Choice (B) is when the meeting began. Choice (D) is when the meeting was scheduled to end.

189. **(B)** The meeting ended after Barbara's talk. Choice (A) is the person who was scheduled to give the last presentation. Choices (C) and (D) are people who were scheduled to talk earlier in the meeting.

190. **(D)** Max is away on a business trip. Choice (A) is the reason Marty didn't attend the meeting. Choice (B) is a plausible reason, but it is not mentioned. Choice (C) is true of Ben, not Max.

191. **(B)** The survey looked into how much time employees spend on activities not related to their work, and concluded that they waste almost two hours a day. Choice (A) associates schedule with use of time. Choice (C) is just one activity mentioned in the survey. Choice (D) could be a reason why employees waste work time, but it is not mentioned.

192. **(A)** 85% of men and 83% of women spend time surfing the Internet. Choices (B), (C), and (D) refer to other activities mentioned in the survey.

193. **(A)** The key tells us that this activity is most common with workers twenty-two to thirty-five. Choice (B) is another age group mentioned in the key. Choices (C) and (D) are incorrect because there is no difference in the percentages of men and women who engage in this activity.

194. **(C)** In the e-mail, Aras Koca says that maybe #3 (talking to co-workers) should continue because it gives employees a chance to get to know each other. Choices (A), (B), and (D) refer to other activities mentioned in the survey.

195. **(D)** In the e-mail, Aras Koca suggests asking supervisors to watch #5 (taking long breaks) more carefully. The other choices refer to other activities mentioned in the survey.

196. **(C)** In the letter, Mr. Hernandez says he wants to buy a building because his company is ready to expand. Choice (A) is confused with the fact that Mr. Hernandez is currently renting space for his business. Choice (B) is incorrect because he already has a loan for his house. Choice (D) is incorrect because he is expanding his current company, not buying a new one.

197. **(C)** Mr. Hernandez says that the location of the other building is not as good as that of the Main Street building. Choice (A) is incorrect because he says the size of the other building is right. Choice (B) is incorrect because the Main Street building is more expensive.

Choice (D) is a plausible reason, but it is not mentioned.

198. **(C)** In his letter, Mr. Hernandez states that his current debts are for his car and house. Choices (A), (B), and (D) are not mentioned.

199. **(B)** The bank will lend Mr. Hernandez enough money to buy the cheaper building. Choice (A) is confused with *you already have over $100,000 in debt.* Choice (C) is the amount he would need for the Main Street building. Choice (D) is the cost of both buildings together.

200. **(D)** Mr. Hernandez suggests meeting on April 21, and Ms. Clark says she prefers to meet the day after that. Choice (A) is the date of Ms. Clark's letter. Choice (B) is the day following the date of Ms. Clark's letter. Choice (C) is the date Mr. Hernandez suggests meeting.

ANSWER SHEET
Model Test 3

LISTENING COMPREHENSION

Part 1: Photographs

1. Ⓐ Ⓑ Ⓒ Ⓓ
2. Ⓐ Ⓑ Ⓒ Ⓓ
3. Ⓐ Ⓑ Ⓒ Ⓓ
4. Ⓐ Ⓑ Ⓒ Ⓓ
5. Ⓐ Ⓑ Ⓒ Ⓓ
6. Ⓐ Ⓑ Ⓒ Ⓓ
7. Ⓐ Ⓑ Ⓒ Ⓓ
8. Ⓐ Ⓑ Ⓒ Ⓓ
9. Ⓐ Ⓑ Ⓒ Ⓓ
10. Ⓐ Ⓑ Ⓒ Ⓓ

Part 2: Question-Response

11. Ⓐ Ⓑ Ⓒ Ⓓ
12. Ⓐ Ⓑ Ⓒ Ⓓ
13. Ⓐ Ⓑ Ⓒ Ⓓ
14. Ⓐ Ⓑ Ⓒ Ⓓ
15. Ⓐ Ⓑ Ⓒ Ⓓ
16. Ⓐ Ⓑ Ⓒ Ⓓ
17. Ⓐ Ⓑ Ⓒ Ⓓ
18. Ⓐ Ⓑ Ⓒ Ⓓ
19. Ⓐ Ⓑ Ⓒ Ⓓ
20. Ⓐ Ⓑ Ⓒ Ⓓ
21. Ⓐ Ⓑ Ⓒ Ⓓ
22. Ⓐ Ⓑ Ⓒ Ⓓ
23. Ⓐ Ⓑ Ⓒ Ⓓ
24. Ⓐ Ⓑ Ⓒ Ⓓ
25. Ⓐ Ⓑ Ⓒ Ⓓ
26. Ⓐ Ⓑ Ⓒ Ⓓ
27. Ⓐ Ⓑ Ⓒ Ⓓ
28. Ⓐ Ⓑ Ⓒ Ⓓ
29. Ⓐ Ⓑ Ⓒ Ⓓ
30. Ⓐ Ⓑ Ⓒ Ⓓ
31. Ⓐ Ⓑ Ⓒ Ⓓ
32. Ⓐ Ⓑ Ⓒ Ⓓ
33. Ⓐ Ⓑ Ⓒ Ⓓ
34. Ⓐ Ⓑ Ⓒ Ⓓ
35. Ⓐ Ⓑ Ⓒ Ⓓ
36. Ⓐ Ⓑ Ⓒ Ⓓ
37. Ⓐ Ⓑ Ⓒ Ⓓ
38. Ⓐ Ⓑ Ⓒ Ⓓ
39. Ⓐ Ⓑ Ⓒ Ⓓ
40. Ⓐ Ⓑ Ⓒ Ⓓ

Part 3: Conversations

41. Ⓐ Ⓑ Ⓒ Ⓓ
42. Ⓐ Ⓑ Ⓒ Ⓓ
43. Ⓐ Ⓑ Ⓒ Ⓓ
44. Ⓐ Ⓑ Ⓒ Ⓓ
45. Ⓐ Ⓑ Ⓒ Ⓓ
46. Ⓐ Ⓑ Ⓒ Ⓓ
47. Ⓐ Ⓑ Ⓒ Ⓓ
48. Ⓐ Ⓑ Ⓒ Ⓓ
49. Ⓐ Ⓑ Ⓒ Ⓓ
50. Ⓐ Ⓑ Ⓒ Ⓓ
51. Ⓐ Ⓑ Ⓒ Ⓓ
52. Ⓐ Ⓑ Ⓒ Ⓓ
53. Ⓐ Ⓑ Ⓒ Ⓓ
54. Ⓐ Ⓑ Ⓒ Ⓓ
55. Ⓐ Ⓑ Ⓒ Ⓓ
56. Ⓐ Ⓑ Ⓒ Ⓓ
57. Ⓐ Ⓑ Ⓒ Ⓓ
58. Ⓐ Ⓑ Ⓒ Ⓓ
59. Ⓐ Ⓑ Ⓒ Ⓓ
60. Ⓐ Ⓑ Ⓒ Ⓓ
61. Ⓐ Ⓑ Ⓒ Ⓓ
62. Ⓐ Ⓑ Ⓒ Ⓓ
63. Ⓐ Ⓑ Ⓒ Ⓓ
64. Ⓐ Ⓑ Ⓒ Ⓓ
65. Ⓐ Ⓑ Ⓒ Ⓓ
66. Ⓐ Ⓑ Ⓒ Ⓓ
67. Ⓐ Ⓑ Ⓒ Ⓓ
68. Ⓐ Ⓑ Ⓒ Ⓓ
69. Ⓐ Ⓑ Ⓒ Ⓓ
70. Ⓐ Ⓑ Ⓒ Ⓓ

Part 4: Talks

71. Ⓐ Ⓑ Ⓒ Ⓓ
72. Ⓐ Ⓑ Ⓒ Ⓓ
73. Ⓐ Ⓑ Ⓒ Ⓓ
74. Ⓐ Ⓑ Ⓒ Ⓓ
75. Ⓐ Ⓑ Ⓒ Ⓓ
76. Ⓐ Ⓑ Ⓒ Ⓓ
77. Ⓐ Ⓑ Ⓒ Ⓓ
78. Ⓐ Ⓑ Ⓒ Ⓓ
79. Ⓐ Ⓑ Ⓒ Ⓓ
80. Ⓐ Ⓑ Ⓒ Ⓓ
81. Ⓐ Ⓑ Ⓒ Ⓓ
82. Ⓐ Ⓑ Ⓒ Ⓓ
83. Ⓐ Ⓑ Ⓒ Ⓓ
84. Ⓐ Ⓑ Ⓒ Ⓓ
85. Ⓐ Ⓑ Ⓒ Ⓓ
86. Ⓐ Ⓑ Ⓒ Ⓓ
87. Ⓐ Ⓑ Ⓒ Ⓓ
88. Ⓐ Ⓑ Ⓒ Ⓓ
89. Ⓐ Ⓑ Ⓒ Ⓓ
90. Ⓐ Ⓑ Ⓒ Ⓓ
91. Ⓐ Ⓑ Ⓒ Ⓓ
92. Ⓐ Ⓑ Ⓒ Ⓓ
93. Ⓐ Ⓑ Ⓒ Ⓓ
94. Ⓐ Ⓑ Ⓒ Ⓓ
95. Ⓐ Ⓑ Ⓒ Ⓓ
96. Ⓐ Ⓑ Ⓒ Ⓓ
97. Ⓐ Ⓑ Ⓒ Ⓓ
98. Ⓐ Ⓑ Ⓒ Ⓓ
99. Ⓐ Ⓑ Ⓒ Ⓓ
100. Ⓐ Ⓑ Ⓒ Ⓓ

ANSWER SHEET
Model Test 3

READING

Part 5: Incomplete Sentences

101. Ⓐ Ⓑ Ⓒ Ⓓ	111. Ⓐ Ⓑ Ⓒ Ⓓ	121. Ⓐ Ⓑ Ⓒ Ⓓ	131. Ⓐ Ⓑ Ⓒ Ⓓ
102. Ⓐ Ⓑ Ⓒ Ⓓ	112. Ⓐ Ⓑ Ⓒ Ⓓ	122. Ⓐ Ⓑ Ⓒ Ⓓ	132. Ⓐ Ⓑ Ⓒ Ⓓ
103. Ⓐ Ⓑ Ⓒ Ⓓ	113. Ⓐ Ⓑ Ⓒ Ⓓ	123. Ⓐ Ⓑ Ⓒ Ⓓ	133. Ⓐ Ⓑ Ⓒ Ⓓ
104. Ⓐ Ⓑ Ⓒ Ⓓ	114. Ⓐ Ⓑ Ⓒ Ⓓ	124. Ⓐ Ⓑ Ⓒ Ⓓ	134. Ⓐ Ⓑ Ⓒ Ⓓ
105. Ⓐ Ⓑ Ⓒ Ⓓ	115. Ⓐ Ⓑ Ⓒ Ⓓ	125. Ⓐ Ⓑ Ⓒ Ⓓ	135. Ⓐ Ⓑ Ⓒ Ⓓ
106. Ⓐ Ⓑ Ⓒ Ⓓ	116. Ⓐ Ⓑ Ⓒ Ⓓ	126. Ⓐ Ⓑ Ⓒ Ⓓ	136. Ⓐ Ⓑ Ⓒ Ⓓ
107. Ⓐ Ⓑ Ⓒ Ⓓ	117. Ⓐ Ⓑ Ⓒ Ⓓ	127. Ⓐ Ⓑ Ⓒ Ⓓ	137. Ⓐ Ⓑ Ⓒ Ⓓ
108. Ⓐ Ⓑ Ⓒ Ⓓ	118. Ⓐ Ⓑ Ⓒ Ⓓ	128. Ⓐ Ⓑ Ⓒ Ⓓ	138. Ⓐ Ⓑ Ⓒ Ⓓ
109. Ⓐ Ⓑ Ⓒ Ⓓ	119. Ⓐ Ⓑ Ⓒ Ⓓ	129. Ⓐ Ⓑ Ⓒ Ⓓ	139. Ⓐ Ⓑ Ⓒ Ⓓ
110. Ⓐ Ⓑ Ⓒ Ⓓ	120. Ⓐ Ⓑ Ⓒ Ⓓ	130. Ⓐ Ⓑ Ⓒ Ⓓ	140. Ⓐ Ⓑ Ⓒ Ⓓ

Part 6: Text Completion

141. Ⓐ Ⓑ Ⓒ Ⓓ	144. Ⓐ Ⓑ Ⓒ Ⓓ	147. Ⓐ Ⓑ Ⓒ Ⓓ	150. Ⓐ Ⓑ Ⓒ Ⓓ
142. Ⓐ Ⓑ Ⓒ Ⓓ	145. Ⓐ Ⓑ Ⓒ Ⓓ	148. Ⓐ Ⓑ Ⓒ Ⓓ	151. Ⓐ Ⓑ Ⓒ Ⓓ
143. Ⓐ Ⓑ Ⓒ Ⓓ	146. Ⓐ Ⓑ Ⓒ Ⓓ	149. Ⓐ Ⓑ Ⓒ Ⓓ	152. Ⓐ Ⓑ Ⓒ Ⓓ

Part 7: Reading Comprehension

153. Ⓐ Ⓑ Ⓒ Ⓓ	165. Ⓐ Ⓑ Ⓒ Ⓓ	177. Ⓐ Ⓑ Ⓒ Ⓓ	189. Ⓐ Ⓑ Ⓒ Ⓓ
154. Ⓐ Ⓑ Ⓒ Ⓓ	166. Ⓐ Ⓑ Ⓒ Ⓓ	178. Ⓐ Ⓑ Ⓒ Ⓓ	190. Ⓐ Ⓑ Ⓒ Ⓓ
155. Ⓐ Ⓑ Ⓒ Ⓓ	167. Ⓐ Ⓑ Ⓒ Ⓓ	179. Ⓐ Ⓑ Ⓒ Ⓓ	191. Ⓐ Ⓑ Ⓒ Ⓓ
156. Ⓐ Ⓑ Ⓒ Ⓓ	168. Ⓐ Ⓑ Ⓒ Ⓓ	180. Ⓐ Ⓑ Ⓒ Ⓓ	192. Ⓐ Ⓑ Ⓒ Ⓓ
157. Ⓐ Ⓑ Ⓒ Ⓓ	169. Ⓐ Ⓑ Ⓒ Ⓓ	181. Ⓐ Ⓑ Ⓒ Ⓓ	193. Ⓐ Ⓑ Ⓒ Ⓓ
158. Ⓐ Ⓑ Ⓒ Ⓓ	170. Ⓐ Ⓑ Ⓒ Ⓓ	182. Ⓐ Ⓑ Ⓒ Ⓓ	194. Ⓐ Ⓑ Ⓒ Ⓓ
159. Ⓐ Ⓑ Ⓒ Ⓓ	171. Ⓐ Ⓑ Ⓒ Ⓓ	183. Ⓐ Ⓑ Ⓒ Ⓓ	195. Ⓐ Ⓑ Ⓒ Ⓓ
160. Ⓐ Ⓑ Ⓒ Ⓓ	172. Ⓐ Ⓑ Ⓒ Ⓓ	184. Ⓐ Ⓑ Ⓒ Ⓓ	196. Ⓐ Ⓑ Ⓒ Ⓓ
161. Ⓐ Ⓑ Ⓒ Ⓓ	173. Ⓐ Ⓑ Ⓒ Ⓓ	185. Ⓐ Ⓑ Ⓒ Ⓓ	197. Ⓐ Ⓑ Ⓒ Ⓓ
162. Ⓐ Ⓑ Ⓒ Ⓓ	174. Ⓐ Ⓑ Ⓒ Ⓓ	186. Ⓐ Ⓑ Ⓒ Ⓓ	198. Ⓐ Ⓑ Ⓒ Ⓓ
163. Ⓐ Ⓑ Ⓒ Ⓓ	175. Ⓐ Ⓑ Ⓒ Ⓓ	187. Ⓐ Ⓑ Ⓒ Ⓓ	199. Ⓐ Ⓑ Ⓒ Ⓓ
164. Ⓐ Ⓑ Ⓒ Ⓓ	176. Ⓐ Ⓑ Ⓒ Ⓓ	188. Ⓐ Ⓑ Ⓒ Ⓓ	200. Ⓐ Ⓑ Ⓒ Ⓓ

Model Test 3

LISTENING COMPREHENSION

In this section of the test, you will have the chance to show how well you understand spoken English. There are four parts to this section, with special directions for each part. You will have approximately 45 minutes to complete the Listening Comprehension sections.

Part 1: Photographs

Directions: You will see a photograph. You will hear four statements about the photograph. Choose the statement that most closely matches the photograph and fill in the corresponding oval on your answer sheet.

1.

2.

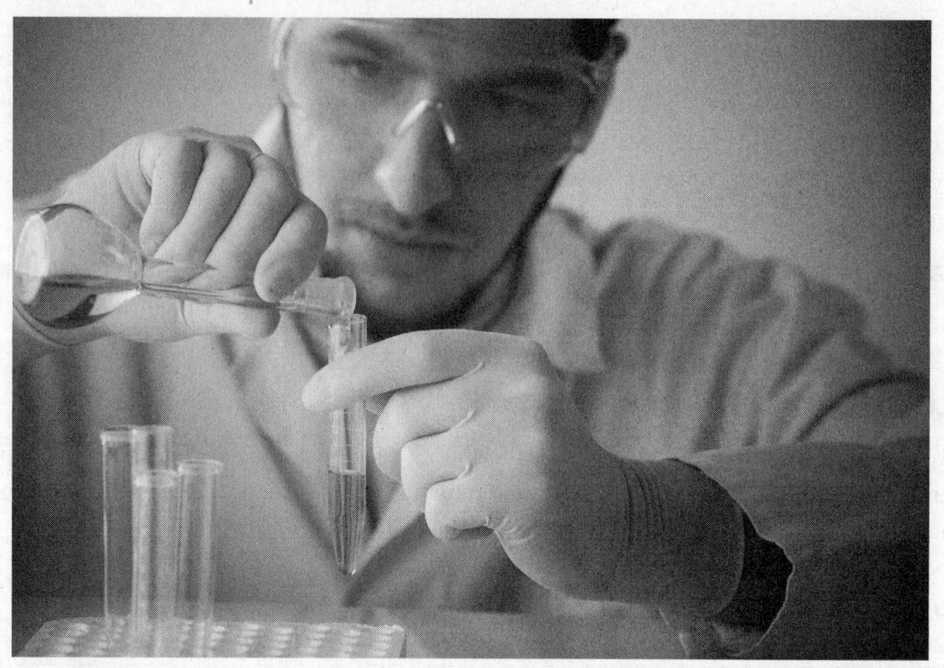

3.

4.

5.

6.

7.

8.

9.

10.

Part 2: Question-Response

Directions: You will hear a question and three possible responses. Choose the response that most closely answers the question and fill in the corresponding oval on your answer sheet.

11. Mark your answer on your answer sheet.
12. Mark your answer on your answer sheet.
13. Mark your answer on your answer sheet.
14. Mark your answer on your answer sheet.
15. Mark your answer on your answer sheet.
16. Mark your answer on your answer sheet.
17. Mark your answer on your answer sheet.
18. Mark your answer on your answer sheet.
19. Mark your answer on your answer sheet.
20. Mark your answer on your answer sheet.
21. Mark your answer on your answer sheet.
22. Mark your answer on your answer sheet.
23. Mark your answer on your answer sheet.
24. Mark your answer on your answer sheet.
25. Mark your answer on your answer sheet.
26. Mark your answer on your answer sheet.
27. Mark your answer on your answer sheet.
28. Mark your answer on your answer sheet.
29. Mark your answer on your answer sheet.
30. Mark your answer on your answer sheet.
31. Mark your answer on your answer sheet.
32. Mark your answer on your answer sheet.
33. Mark your answer on your answer sheet.
34. Mark your answer on your answer sheet.
35. Mark your answer on your answer sheet.
36. Mark your answer on your answer sheet.
37. Mark your answer on your answer sheet.
38. Mark your answer on your answer sheet.
39. Mark your answer on your answer sheet.
40. Mark your answer on your answer sheet.

MODEL TEST 3

Part 3: Conversations

Directions: You will hear a conversation between two people. You will see three questions on each conversation and four possible answers. Choose the best answer to each question and fill in the corresponding oval on your answer sheet.

41. Where did the man learn about the event?

(A) In a newspaper
(B) On the Internet
(C) From a friend
(D) On the radio

42. Why can't they go on Saturday?

(A) The man promised to help someone.
(B) The woman has plans to go to a dance.
(C) The man has to look for a new apartment.
(D) The woman has to work that day.

43. What does the woman want to do?

(A) Not go
(B) Go on Sunday
(C) Go to next year's event
(D) Wait until their friend can go

---

44. What is the appointment for?

(A) A medical checkup
(B) A sales meeting
(C) A possible presentation
(D) A job interview

45. What time is the appointment for?

(A) 8:30
(B) 9:00
(C) 10:00
(D) 10:30

46. What should the man bring?

(A) An application
(B) A finished test
(C) His resume
(D) Nothing

47. Where does this conversation take place?

(A) In a hotel
(B) In an elevator
(C) In a newsstand
(D) In an office building

48. What is the woman's room number?

(A) 15
(B) 50
(C) 215
(D) 250

49. What will be delivered to the woman tomorrow?

(A) A room key
(B) A newspaper
(C) A directory
(D) A box of stationery

---

50. Why do they need Mr. Chung?

(A) To address some letters
(B) To speak at a meeting
(C) To announce the date
(D) To show a film

51. Why is Mr. Chung late?

(A) He lost the address.
(B) He's stuck in traffic.
(C) His car broke down.
(D) He's making a phone call.

52. When will the meeting start?

(A) When Mr. Chung arrives
(B) At the scheduled time
(C) Ten minutes late
(D) At ten past nine

53. What was painted?

(A) The elevator
(B) The office
(C) The lobby
(D) The door

54. What was wrong with it before?

(A) It was out of style.
(B) It was too white.
(C) It was very light.
(D) It was too dark.

55. When will the cafeteria be painted?

(A) This afternoon
(B) On Sunday
(C) Next week
(D) After next week

---

56. What's broken?

(A) A chair
(B) A television
(C) A telephone
(D) A computer

57. When did the man talk to the company about repairs?

(A) Today
(B) On Tuesday
(C) Yesterday afternoon
(D) Last week

58. How long will the repairs take?

(A) One week
(B) Two weeks
(C) Three weeks
(D) Ten weeks

59. Why does the man need a gas station?

(A) He's out of gas.
(B) He wants a drink.
(C) He is tired.
(D) He has a flat tire.

60. How far away is the gas station?

(A) Half a mile
(B) A mile
(C) A mile and a half
(D) Two miles

61. How will the man get to the gas station?

(A) He will walk.
(B) He will take a bus.
(C) He will drive his car.
(D) He will ride with the woman.

---

62. How long is the lunch break?

(A) Fifteen minutes
(B) Thirty minutes
(C) Forty-five minutes
(D) Sixty minutes

63. What does the woman do during her lunch break?

(A) She works.
(B) She exercises.
(C) She eats lunch.
(D) She takes a walk.

64. Where does the man eat lunch?

(A) At his desk
(B) In the park
(C) At the cafeteria
(D) In the exercise room

65. Where does the man want to go?

(A) The park
(B) The post office
(C) The history museum
(D) The capitol building

66. How far away is this place?

(A) Two blocks
(B) Three blocks
(C) Nine blocks
(D) Ten blocks

67. When is this place open?

(A) Tuesday
(B) Monday–Friday
(C) Wednesday–Monday
(D) Saturday and Sunday

68. How long is the trip?

(A) Two hours
(B) Two and a half hours
(C) Five hours
(D) Five and a half hours

69. Where does the conversation take place?

(A) At an airport
(B) On a train
(C) At a mall
(D) On an airplane

70. What does the woman ask for?

(A) A ticket
(B) A newspaper
(C) A cup of coffee
(D) A gate number

Part 4: Talks

Directions: You will hear a talk given by a single speaker. You will see three questions on each talk, each with four possible answers. Choose the best answer to each question and fill in the corresponding oval on your answer sheet.

71. What is wrong with the number that was dialed?
    (A) It is the wrong number.
    (B) It is not working.
    (C) It has an answering machine.
    (D) It has a busy signal.

72. Who will help you if you stay on the line?
    (A) A repair person
    (B) An operator
    (C) A customer service representative
    (D) A telephone executive

73. How much will you have to pay for help?
    (A) Five cents a minute
    (B) Seventeen cents a minute
    (C) Seventy cents a minute
    (D) Seventy-five cents a minute

74. When will the event take place?
    (A) Next Thursday
    (B) Next week
    (C) Next weekend
    (D) Next year

75. Who is invited to the event?
    (A) Everyone
    (B) High school students only
    (C) City officials only
    (D) The mayor's family

76. How can you get a ticket for the ceremony?
    (A) Line up at the park
    (B) Pay three dollars
    (C) Order it online
    (D) Call City Hall

77. What kind of training does this school provide?
    (A) Computer training
    (B) Business management
    (C) Personnel training
    (D) Teacher training

78. How long will the training take?
    (A) Three months
    (B) Six months
    (C) Nine months
    (D) One year

79. When are the classes taught?
    (A) Daytime only
    (B) Evenings only
    (C) Daytime and evenings
    (D) Evenings and weekends

80. Who is traveling?
    (A) Ken
    (B) Dr. Phillips
    (C) Dr. Phillips' assistant
    (D) Zach Robertson

81. How will the person get to Boston?
    (A) By train
    (B) By taxi
    (C) By plane
    (D) By car

82. What is in the e-mail?
    (A) A travel ticket
    (B) An itinerary
    (C) A hotel reservation
    (D) A question list

83. When should you call back?

(A) In the evenings
(B) On Saturdays
(C) During business hours
(D) Early in the mornings

84. If you can't call back, how can you contact the company?

(A) Write them a letter
(B) Via e-mail
(C) Send them a fax
(D) Go to their office

85. What information should be included in a letter about a product?

(A) The writer's address
(B) The store's phone number
(C) The date of purchase
(D) The product serial number

---

86. How should you apply for these jobs?

(A) Send a résumé
(B) Go to the hotel
(C) Write a letter
(D) Make a phone call

87. What do the jobs offer, besides a good wage?

(A) Benefits
(B) Free food
(C) Good hours
(D) Possible promotions

88. Which of the following jobs is offered?

(A) Hotel managers
(B) Store clerks
(C) Trainers
(D) Waiters

89. What kind of ticket is being sold?

(A) Train
(B) Bus
(C) Plane
(D) Subway

90. What should the customer do first?

(A) Insert a credit card
(B) Check the ticket price
(C) Enter the travel schedule
(D) Select one-way or round trip

91. How can a customer pay cash?

(A) Show an ID card
(B) Go to the ticket office
(C) Insert dollar bills in the slot
(D) Buy the ticket from the driver

---

92. What problem can the city expect?

(A) An epidemic
(B) Extremely hot weather
(C) Flooding
(D) Infestation of insects

93. How high are the temperatures expected to be?

(A) In the seventies
(B) In the eighties
(C) In the nineties
(D) In the hundreds

94. How can citizens protect themselves?

(A) Wear dark clothing
(B) Exercise frequently
(C) Drink lots of water
(D) Swim

95. What advice is given?

(A) Take a walk
(B) Work overtime
(C) Hire an assistant
(D) Establish a quiet hour

96. According to the speaker, how can you keep others from disturbing you?

(A) Work at home
(B) Close the door
(C) Take a vacation
(D) Put up a "Do no disturb" sign

97. According to the speaker, what will help you work better?

(A) Resting your mind
(B) Training your secretary
(C) Reading business articles
(D) Learning new work techniques

98. How often does this ceremony take place?

(A) Once every five years
(B) Once every three years
(C) Once a year
(D) Three times a year

99. How many people are receiving awards today?

(A) Four
(B) Five
(C) Twenty
(D) Twenty-five

100. What are listeners asked to do?

(A) Pay their bills
(B) Give money
(C) Teach music
(D) Practice more

This is the end of the Listening Comprehension portion of the test. Turn to Part 5 in your test book.

READING

In this section of the test, you will have the chance to show how well you understand written English. There are three parts to this section, with special directions for each part.

YOU WILL HAVE ONE HOUR AND FIFTEEN MINUTES TO COMPLETE PARTS 5, 6, AND 7 OF THE TEST.

Part 5: Incomplete Sentences

Directions: You will see a sentence with a missing word. Four possible answers follow the sentence. Choose the best answer to the question and fill in the corresponding oval on your answer sheet.

101. When the contracts ________ ready, have them sent to the purchaser.

(A) am
(B) is
(C) are
(D) be

102. The recent ________ in energy costs has had a positive effect on our budget.

(A) descent
(B) decrease
(C) lower
(D) down

103. ________, the bookshelf we ordered for the front office is too tall to fit through the doorway.

(A) Unfortunately
(B) However
(C) Instead
(D) Luckily

104. ________ are three dozen cookies baking in the oven for this afternoon's event.

(A) Them
(B) They
(C) This
(D) There

105. ________ your flight is delayed, then you can relax in the airline's lounge.

(A) For
(B) So
(C) If
(D) Please

106. Sales tax and shipping charges are ________ in the price quote, so it represents your entire cost.

(A) including
(B) include
(C) been included
(D) included

107. Our attorney wants to ________ the details of the contract before the end of the week.

(A) final
(B) finalize
(C) finally
(D) finality

108. Using a washing machine is ________ than washing laundry by hand.

(A) more efficient
(B) most efficient
(C) the most efficient
(D) the more efficient

109. Mr. Flynn is the person _________ orders office supplies.

(A) which
(B) whose
(C) who
(D) whom

110. A temporary worker can be hired _________ an employee is out on maternity leave.

(A) that
(B) time
(C) which
(D) while

111. The office would look much better with a new coat of paint _________ a few pictures hanging on the walls.

(A) but
(B) and
(C) as
(D) though

112. Most people in the department are _________ that staffing cuts will have to be made.

(A) aware
(B) await
(C) awaken
(D) awe

113. The itinerary _________ the time and location of each meeting Dr. Richards has while he is visiting the department.

(A) contain
(B) contains
(C) containing
(D) have contained

114. Passengers can check in for the charter flight _________ 8:00 and 12:00 tomorrow.

(A) between
(B) with
(C) through
(D) from

115. The landscaper made several _________, including the installation of an automatic watering system.

(A) recommends
(B) recommended
(C) recommendations
(D) recommendable

116. It is _________ to transfer a document by e-mail than by fax.

(A) fast
(B) fastest
(C) the faster
(D) faster

117. You can pay your bill online, _________ you can send a check by regular mail.

(A) so
(B) or
(C) but
(D) since

118. All conference speakers need to be notified that their allowed time has been _________ from 30 minutes to 25 minutes.

(A) heightened
(B) lengthened
(C) shortened
(D) widened

119. I will ask my assistant _________ the necessary forms to you at your office.

(A) to send
(B) sending
(C) will send
(D) sends

120. Ms. Chang is very frugal and buys most of _________ business suits at large discount stores.

(A) that
(B) them
(C) our
(D) her

121. With so much light pollution in the city, it's difficult _______ many stars at night.

(A) see
(B) sees
(C) to see
(D) seeing

122. Once every three months, all stockroom employees are _______ to work overnight to do inventory.

(A) required
(B) suggested
(C) preferred
(D) appreciated

123. The variety of insurance benefits _______ very broad under this policy.

(A) are
(B) is
(C) being
(D) be

124. The purpose of the awards banquet is to _______ the many achievements of our talented staff.

(A) acknowledge
(B) determine
(C) entertain
(D) discern

125. Please leave your luggage _______ the bus for the driver to load.

(A) among
(B) between
(C) from
(D) beside

126. The hotel offers a discount for guests who stay a _______ of three nights.

(A) podium
(B) optimum
(C) minimum
(D) premium

127. If we were not certain about the safety of the product, we _______ it.

(A) had sold
(B) don't sell
(C) will sell
(D) would not sell

128. The company handbook _______ the department's policies on building customer relationships.

(A) explains
(B) is explaining
(C) explain
(D) explaining

129. Model 34 is on backorder with the _______ and probably won't be here until spring.

(A) candidate
(B) transportation
(C) manufacturer
(D) customer

130. Mr. Larsen says that he will _______ consider military veterans for the foreman position.

(A) all
(B) only
(C) some
(D) except

131. _______ we checked the budget twice, the managers found a mistake in our calculations.

(A) Unless
(B) However
(C) Since
(D) Even though

132. Everyone else left the office early, so Harry had to finish up the report by __________.

(A) alone
(B) just
(C) himself
(D) single

133. Ethel's economic predictions for the coming year __________ by her colleagues with some skepticism.

(A) were received
(B) were receiving
(C) had received
(D) received

134. Doctors __________ have recently been licensed use the medical association's website to find jobs.

(A) what
(B) who
(C) whose
(D) which

135. The only difference __________ the two flights your assistant suggested is the time of departure.

(A) with
(B) then
(C) between
(D) among

136. __________ careful planning, the caterers did not bring enough linens for the tables.

(A) During
(B) Because
(C) In spite of
(D) Although

137. The project manager is responsible for __________ every step of the project.

(A) organization
(B) organizing
(C) organized
(D) organize

138. The head of accounts __________ to sit in on the client meeting tomorrow.

(A) decisions
(B) are deciding
(C) has decided
(D) decide

139. The promotional message needs to emphasize that our product is better __________ all similar products on the market.

(A) much
(B) than
(C) off
(D) to

140. Mr. Kim spent most of the week preparing __________ his new idea to the director.

(A) present
(B) presented
(C) presenting
(D) to present

Part 6: Text Completion

Directions: You will see four passages each with three blanks. Under each blank are four answer options. Choose the word or phrase that best completes the sentence.

Questions 141–143 refer to the following letter.

Green Office Renovators
Da'an District, Taipei City 106-03
TAIWAN

Kao Su Mei, Vice President
377 Chiang An Road
Da'an District, Taipei City 106-03
TAIWAN

Dear Ms. Kao,

Thank you for considering Green Office Renovators for your upcoming office renovation project. I hope you will take the time to read through the enclosed brochure, which explains the materials we use and the measures we take to meet the highest standards for environmental protection. __________ also outlines the services we provide, as well

141. (A) You
(B) He
(C) It
(D) We

as our pricing system. Please note that Green Office Renovators __________ a minimum

142. (A) requires
(B) require
(C) have required
(D) are requiring

deposit before work can begin on any project.

Although the initial costs of installing energy-efficient systems can be high, they save money in the long run. In addition, statistics show that companies that demonstrate __________ the

143. (A) concern for
(B) happiness about
(C) placement in
(D) knowledge of

environment are more popular among customers.

I look forward to discussing the renovation needs of your company.

Sincerely,

Cai Mi

Cai Mi

Questions 144–146 refer to the following e-mail.

To: clementinebooks@learning.org
From: rep990@gaspower.net
Subject: Equal Payment Billing Plan

Dear Sheldon Murray,

It has come to my attention that your business is still paying its gas bills using our Monthly Plan. During the past year, your ______________ bill was for $400 in the

144. (A) high
(B) higher
(C) highest
(D) most high

month of January. However, your bills were as low as $23 in the summer months. The majority of your annual fees occurred in the four months of winter.

We believe that you are an excellent candidate for our Equal Billing Plan. Approximately 78% of our customers have switched to this option since it became available three years ago. Though the amount of money you spend in the year will be identical, your higher bills will be ______________ throughout the year. This

145. (A) marked down
(B) built up
(C) spread out
(D) topped off

makes it easier to budget your finances.

With the Equal Billing Plan, the amount you pay per month is based on an approximation. To do this we take an average from the bills in your previous year. After six months on the Equal Billing Plan we will adjust this amount depending on whether or not you use more or less gas than we ______________. At the end of the

146. (A) estimated
(B) permitted
(C) inquired
(D) ordered

year you will receive a debit or credit from us to balance the amount owed with the amount used.

Questions 147–149 refer to the following article.

Airport Lounge Removes Free Internet Service
By Kelly Christie

As of this Friday, passengers at Port Elizabeth Airport will no longer ____________ free Internet service in the business travelers' lounge.

147. (A) offer
(B) offered
(C) be offered
(D) be offering

Since January of last year, free Internet access has been available in the airport business lounge to travelers who have purchased a VIP card. VIP card holders enjoy numerous ____________ in the business lounge in

148. (A) utilities
(B) furniture
(C) benefits
(D) functions

addition to Internet access, including coffee, snacks, newspapers, and the use of printers. The lounges also provide an escape from crowded waiting rooms. Now users of the business lounge will need to purchase Internet access at a cost of $5 per hour, with a two-hour ____________.

149. (A) minimum
(B) minimal
(C) minimize
(D) minimally

Questions 150–152 refer to the following advertisement.

Attention Small Business Owners

Are you tired of paying too much for office supplies? It's time to stop throwing your money away on overpriced products. Meade's Paper Store offers top quality office products at ____________ prices. We supply all your paper

150. (A) easy
(B) bargain
(C) retail
(D) top

needs and also stock writing utensils, computers and computer supplies, office furniture, and more! There's ____________ reason to shop anywhere

151. (A) no one
(B) none
(C) not
(D) no

else. Meade's has it all. We have two convenient locations! Visit our main store downtown next to City Hall, or our new branch in the Valley Shopping Mall. ____________ advantage of this week's special: all paper goods are

152. (A) Take
(B) Taking
(C) To take
(D) Can take

20% off now through Saturday. When you visit, don't forget to ask about our frequent shopper program.

Part 7: Reading Comprehension

Directions: You will see single and double reading passages followed by several questions. Each question has four answer choices. Choose the best answer to the question and fill in the corresponding oval on your answer sheet.

Questions 153–155 refer to the following paragraph and table.

The research division has identified four priorities that define our work. These include: (1) improving the quality of our products; (2) lowering costs; (3) developing new products; and (4) being environmentally responsible. Please see the table below.

Research Division Priorities	
What	**How**
1. Improve product quality	Use advanced technology
2. Lower costs	Improve manufacturing processes
3. Develop new products	Expand research
4. Be environmentally responsible	Reduce waste and conserve energy

153. What is the purpose of technology for the research division?

(A) It lowers costs.
(B) It is used in research.
(C) It follows consumer trends.
(D) It increases product quality.

154. Which of the following is NOT a research priority?

(A) Improving quality
(B) Being environmentally responsible
(C) Developing new products
(D) Hiring good engineers

155. How does this division try to lower costs?

(A) By conserving energy
(B) By improving manufacturing processes
(C) By working fewer hours
(D) By limiting exploration

Questions 156–157 refer to the following advertisement.

WHY WAIT FOR A BETTER JOB?

Get a great job now!

National Air

is hiring full-time representatives for Sales & Reservations. Talk to our employees and discover why we're the best thing in the air.

Interviews on the spot!

Bring your résumé

OPEN HOUSE

National Air Headquarters

Southeast Regional Airport

Thursday, June 15 7:30 P.M.

156. What is the purpose of this ad?

(A) To meet new people
(B) To sell tickets
(C) To recruit potential employees
(D) To show off the new headquarters

157. Where will the event be held?

(A) At their headquarters
(B) At the owner's house
(C) On a plane
(D) At the regional office

Questions 158–161 refer to the following fax.

FAX TRANSMISSION FAX TRANSMISSION FAX TRANSMISSION

InterGulf Export
P.O. Box 23145
Sharjah, UAE

To: F. Omoboriowo
Head of Marketing
P.O. Box 19133
Nairobi, Kenya

Fm: Ravi Niazi
Trade Consultant

Date: 18 October, 20—
Sub: Your marketing question of October 17, 20—

We were very pleased to receive your fax of October 17. We have sent under separate cover information regarding our company and its services. This should arrive in your offices tomorrow.

In the meantime, the following addresses your immediate question:

The company sells products through a worldwide marketing network. This network operates 36 sales offices in 21 countries. Approximately 75% of company sales are direct, and 25% are through other channels. Products are shipped to customers through company distribution centers, by the method of shipment preferred by the customer whenever possible.

If you need any more information, please contact me.

158. What did the fax respond to?
   (A) A newspaper ad
   (B) A personal visit
   (C) A telephone inquiry
   (D) A faxed question

159. What was sent in addition to the fax?
   (A) A change of address
   (B) Directions to the offices
   (C) A product sample
   (D) Company information

160. Which of the following is responsible for shipping purchased goods?
   (A) The customer
   (B) The airlines
   (C) Company distribution centers
   (D) Company headquarters

161. What was probably the topic of Omoboriowo's question?
   (A) The size of the company
   (B) How goods are distributed
   (C) When the company was founded
   (D) The company's marketing plan

Questions 162–163 refer to the following notice.

ATTENTION! RIDERS

- Pay exact fare when boarding the bus. Drivers cannot make change.
- Upon boarding the bus, move toward the rear of the bus. Stand in the passenger area, not in the doorways or beside the driver.
- Allow senior citizens and disabled riders to use the priority seating area at the front of the bus.
- No music without earphones.
- Eating, drinking, and smoking are not allowed on the bus.

162. What does this passage discuss?

(A) Rules for riding buses
(B) Safety concerns
(C) Bus routes and fares
(D) Problems of the bus service

163. Who is entitled to use the priority seating area?

(A) Mothers and children
(B) Elderly and handicapped people
(C) Bus company employees
(D) Riders who pay extra

Questions 164–166 refer to the following chart.

Results of Study on Time Distribution of Tasks for Sales Managers

Training new sales personnel	15%
Identifying possible clients	10%
Reviewing monthly sales records	25%
Taking care of customer problems	5%
Making sales assignments	22%
Interacting with technical staff	10%
Administrative duties	5%
Miscellaneous	8%

164. What task do sales managers spend the most time on?

(A) Training salespeople
(B) Performing administrative tasks
(C) Reviewing sales records
(D) Making sales assignments

165. How much of their time do sales managers spend with the technical staff?

(A) 5%
(B) 8%
(C) 10%
(D) 15%

166. What can be concluded from the study?

(A) There are few customer problems.
(B) Sales are a low priority.
(C) Little time is spent on training.
(D) No time is spent on finding new customers.

Questions 167–169 refer to the following advertisement.

Summer is a great time to return to school!
If you need better business skills, let us help.

Each summer Claybourne University School of Business Administration offers special courses for experienced managers who want to sharpen their existing business skills or learn new ones. You will study with your peers in a week-long intensive session that simulates the world of international commerce. You will learn new theories and study the way business is conducted around the world. Students in previous sessions have reported that what they learned was immediately applicable to their own work situations.

Only one person from a company is accepted into this special program. All applications require three letters of recommendation and proof of employment.

For more information, call the

Summer Education Center

School of Business Administration
Claybourne University
903-477-6768 Fax: 903-477-6777

167. Who attends this center?
   (A) Professional managers
   (B) College professors changing careers
   (C) Undergraduate students in business
   (D) Office staff

168. What is required for admission?
   (A) The name of your manager
   (B) A copy of your grades
   (C) Your job title and duties
   (D) Letters of recommendation

169. How long is the course?
   (A) All summer long
   (B) One week
   (C) Three evenings a month
   (D) Two years

Questions 170–171 refer to the following announcement.

$$

OUR STORE GUARANTEE

We have the lowest prices in town. For every item we sell, we'll beat any legitimate price from any other store. Plus, if you find a lower price within 30 days of your date of purchase, we'll refund the difference. This offer is good even on our own sale prices. The item must be the same brand and style. You must present your original sales receipt. Our low price guarantee does not apply to limited quantity offers.

$$

170. What does this statement guarantee?
   (A) The lowest prices
   (B) The best service
   (C) The most convenient location
   (D) The most helpful salesclerks

171. If you buy an item at a lower price, what will the store do?
   (A) Give you a second item
   (B) Pay you the difference in price
   (C) Buy the item from you
   (D) Refund your money

Questions 172–175 refer to the following memo.

MEMO

To: All employees
From: K. Osafo
Director, Personnel

Date: November 23, 20–
Subject: Charitable Leave

The corporation is pleased to announce a new policy which will allow employees to take paid time off for volunteer activities. Employees may take up to eight hours of paid leave per month to volunteer for charity organizations. Employees are eligible for this program if they are full-time and have been employed here for at least one year. Charitable leave must be requested in advance; otherwise, employees will not be paid for that time. Charitable leave must also be approved by the employee's supervisor.

172. What does the new policy allow employees to do?

(A) Take paid leave during pregnancy
(B) Have more holidays
(C) Get paid for volunteer work
(D) Go home early

173. How much time may an employee take under this program?

(A) One hour per week
(B) Three hours per week
(C) Six hours per month
(D) Eight hours per month

174. Who can participate in the program?

(A) Full-time employees
(B) Part-time employees
(C) New employees
(D) All employees

175. What must an employee do to get paid for time off?

(A) Get the permission of the charity
(B) Leave work for one day
(C) Fill out an absence form
(D) Ask his or her supervisor in advance

Questions 176–180 refer to the following magazine article.

Are You the New Target for Hackers?

Is your company a sitting duck for hackers? When did you last change your password? How complete are your security systems? Have you ever been broken into before?

According to IANS, the International Association for Network Security, there's a new breed of hacker out there. And, there's a new target.

In the past, hackers gained notoriety from breaking into big companys' networks. In fact, the bigger the company, the bigger the success. When hackers broke into Infelmax's notoriously secure system in 2010, they made headline news around the world.

The big "successes" came with a major drawback. These headline break-ins came with international teams of investigators and serious criminal charges. Several former hackers are now sitting behind bars or working overtime to pay off hefty fines in penalties and damages.

So, hackers of the new decade have turned to a new target: smaller companies. Smaller companies often spend less on their security systems. If they have never been broken into before, they may be lulled into a feeling of security. They are often lax about changing their password frequently enough. And that spells trouble.

Also, a breached system in a smaller company may attract little public attention. Investigations may be brief and superficial, as overloaded investigators pursue bigger problems.

But if you do fall victim to hackers, it will definitely attract your own attention. These thieves can gain access to your files, destroying, copying, or altering them. They can create havoc with your data. And if they do, you'll surely wish you had changed your password once more often.

176. Which is a likely victim for the new breed of hackers?

(A) Large companies
(B) Small companies
(C) International companies
(D) Companies without a security system

177. What might have been one motive for hackers of Infelmax's network?

(A) Money
(B) Power
(C) Fame
(D) Fun

178. What has happened to some big-name hackers?

(A) They're in jail.
(B) Nothing
(C) They got better jobs.
(D) They are paying off investigators.

179. What might help hackers to succeed?

(A) They've never broken into a company before.
(B) They feel secure.
(C) Their targeted network is old.
(D) Their targets rarely change their secret code.

180. The word *havoc* in paragraph 7, line 5 is closest in meaning to

(A) order
(B) copies
(C) confusion
(D) documents

Questions 181–185 refer to the following advertisement and letter.

MARKETING REPRESENTATIVE

New Zealand's fastest-growing women's clothing company seeks a marketing representative. Position requires travel approximately one week per month, representing the company at conferences and media events.

Required qualifications

- a degree from a four-year college or university, preferably in marketing.
- at least one year of experience in sales, preferably clothing.
- excellent communication skills, including experience giving presentations.

Mail your resume and cover letter to:
Camilla Crowe
Recruiting Coordinator
NZ World
636 Simons Street
Auckland, New Zealand 6692

Camilla Crowe
NZ World
636 Simons Street
Auckland, New Zealand 6692

March 24, 20—

Akiko Sasaki
118 Hutchinson Road
Paeora, New Zealand 1230

Dear Ms. Sasaki:

Thank you for applying for the position of marketing representative. We appreciate your interest in NZ World.

Although your resume shows that you have good preparation for a career in marketing, unfortunately you don't meet all our required qualifications. You have the degree we are looking for, but not the experience. Your sales experience in an electronics store is a good background, but your time there is just half of what we ask for as a minimum. In addition, you have no experience in clothing sales.

However, your resume also shows some of your strengths. You have excellent grades and have been active in your campus' marketing club. Therefore, we would like to offer you a position as an intern.

This is a three-month, unpaid internship. Since you just graduated last month, I think this would be a great opportunity for you. It would give you some of the experience you will need to start your career. For example, your internship would give you some practice with public speaking, an important marketing skill that is lacking on your resume.

Contact me by April 1 if you are interested in accepting this position. I look forward to hearing from you.

Sincerely,

Camilla Crowe

Camilla Crowe

181. Which of the following is NOT a duty of the advertised job?
   (A) Recruiting new staff
   (B) Giving presentations
   (C) Traveling every month
   (D) Attending conferences

182. What field did Akiko get her degree in?
   (A) Electronics
   (B) Marketing
   (C) Communications
   (D) Clothing design

183. When did Akiko get her degree?
   (A) February
   (B) March
   (C) April
   (D) May

184. What type of work experience does Akiko have?
   (A) Clothing sales
   (B) Electronics sales
   (C) Career counselor
   (D) Marketing representative

185. What did Camilla Crowe offer Akiko?
   (A) A job
   (B) An interview
   (C) An internship
   (D) A club membership

Questions 186–190 refer to the following schedule and form.

Classes offered at Central Technical Institute
CATEGORY: Office Skills

Accounting

ACTG 101	Financial Accounting, Part One
ACTG 102	Financial Accounting, Part Two*
ACTG 670	Accounting for Small Businesses

Business

BUSI 100	Introduction to Business
BUSI 200	Principles of Business

Computers

COMP 104	Introduction to Microsoft Word
COMP 207	Microsoft Excel: Basics
COMP 300	Computers in the Office**

Marketing

MARK 500	Global Marketing Strategies
MARK 600	Marketing on the Internet

Classes last from January 3 until March 15. Classes at the same level are offered on the same day: 100—Monday, 200—Tuesday, 300 and 400—Wednesday, and 500 and higher—Thursday. All classes are offered from 6:00–8:00 in the evening.

The fee for each course is $300. To register, go to: *www.cti.org* and click on the "Registration" link.

*Students must take ACTG 101 and earn a grade of 75 or better before taking ACTG 102.
**This course will be offered on Tuesday evenings.

While you were out ...

To: Roberto Guzman

Jessica Moore called.

Date: Thursday, December 21, 20—

Time: 4:10 P.M.

About: Problem with online registration form

She researched your problem. You want to take ACTG 102, BUSI 100, COMP 207, and COMP 300. You can't register for ACTG 102 because you earned a grade 10% below the minimum in Part One of the course. She registered you for BUSI 100 and for COMP 207, but not COMP 300 because there is a scheduling conflict. There is also a problem with your student visa. It expires fifteen days before classes end. She recommends that you make an appointment with her to discuss these topics.

186. What time does the ACTG 101 class start?

(A) 1:00
(B) 3:00
(C) 6:00
(D) 8:00

187. What day of the week are Marketing classes offered?

(A) Monday
(B) Tuesday
(C) Wednesday
(D) Thursday

188. What was Roberto's grade in ACTG 101?

(A) Over 75
(B) 75
(C) Less than 75
(D) Exactly 10

189. How many courses is Roberto registered for?

(A) 1
(B) 2
(C) 3
(D) 4

190. What is the problem with Roberto's visa?

(A) It isn't a student visa.
(B) He hasn't applied for it yet.
(C) It will be invalid soon.
(D) He hasn't received it yet.

Questions 191–195 refer to the following advertisement and e-mail.

This year, try something different for your company's annual party. Visit the Front Street Theater.

An afternoon or evening at the Front Street Theater includes a delicious meal prepared by our Paris-trained chef, Jacques, and a show preformed by some of the region's finest actors. A tour of this historic theater is also offered before the meal. Groups of 250 or more can reserve the entire theater for their group. This option is available on Sunday afternoons only. Groups of 300–350 receive a 10% discount. Groups over 350 receive a 15% discount.

Shows are selected based on the time of the year: January–April, tragedy; May–July, drama; August–October, musical; and November–December, comedy.

Reservations are available at the following times:

Monday–Thursday:	Dinner and evening show 6–10 P.M.
Friday–Saturday	Lunch and afternoon show 12–4 P.M. Dinner and evening show 6–10 P.M.
Sunday	Only large groups renting the entire theater. Both lunch and dinner schedules are available. It is recommended to make large group reservations one month ahead of time.

Come to the Front Street Theater for food, entertainment, and fun. To make a reservation, e-mail us or call us at 216-707-2268.

To: Front Street Theater, Reservations
From: Constance Hekler, Events Coordinator
Date: October 25, 20—
Subject: Holiday party

I saw your advertisement in this week's *Business Journal.* I am interested in renting your theater for Federal Bank's annual employee party.

We have set the date for our party as Sunday, December 20. Is the theater available then? We prefer the lunch and afternoon show. There will be 325 guests.

Please fax the menu, a description of the shows, and the price list to me. And let me know about the availability of dates in December.

Thank you.

191. What is included in a visit to the theater?
    (A) Meeting the chef
    (B) Talking with the actors
    (C) Touring the theater
    (D) Selecting shows

192. When is the theater open to individuals and small groups?
    (A) Monday through Thursday only
    (B) Friday and Saturday only
    (C) Monday through Saturday only
    (D) Sunday only

193. What time does Ms. Hekler prefer the Federal Bank party to begin?
    (A) 10 A.M.
    (B) 12 P.M.
    (C) 4 P.M.
    (D) 6 P.M.

194. What type of discount will the Federal Bank get for this party?
    (A) 0%
    (B) 10%
    (C) 15%
    (D) 20%

195. What type of show will guests at the Federal Bank party see?
    (A) Tragedy
    (B) Drama
    (C) Musical
    (D) Comedy

Questions 196–200 refer to the following memorandum and form.

From: Jun Oh, Benefits Manager
To: Marcus Mains
Sent: Tuesday, July 20, 20–
Re: Early Retirement

Early Retirement Program

1. Employees must meet these requirements:
   A) Age sixty-five with twenty years of employment at this company; or
   B) Any age with twenty-five years of employment at this company; or
   C) Age fifty-five to sixty-four with twenty years of employment at this company. With this option there is a reduction in your retirement fund. It will be reduced by 2% for each year that you are under age sixty-five. For example, if you are sixty-three, it will be reduced by 4%.
2. Interested employees should apply by September 1, 20__. Supervisors with twenty years or more of employment at this company have an extra two months to apply. This gives the Benefits Office more time to work on the applications.
3. Attend a workshop. We will discuss how to invest your money. Call Suzette or Tuyen to register. Our first workshop is on August 10. All workshops will be held on Wednesdays and Fridays in Meeting Room F at 9:00 A.M.
4. We encourage you to meet with your accountant. Retiring now will influence your taxes for next year. Call our tax specialist, Geoffrey, for assistance.
5. If you have any additional questions, please contact Jun.

DATE July 21, 20– TIME 10: 30 (A.M.) P.M.

FOR Jun
RECEIVED BY Sumalee
CALLER Marcus
PHONE NUMBER ext. 9245

MESSAGE He wants to retire early. He is a supervisor with twenty years of experience at this company. First, what happened to this morning's workshop? He went to Meeting Room F at 9:00. Nobody was there. Second, how much will his funds be reduced? He is sixty-two. Third, he wants to talk to someone about his taxes. Who is the expert?

CALL BACK REQUESTED? ☑ YES ☐ NO

DATE/TIME COMPLETED _____/_____/_____ : A.M. P.M.

196. Which employee can get full retirement benefits?

(A) Age fifty with twenty years of employment
(B) Age fifty-five with twenty-five years of employment
(C) Age sixty with twenty years of employment
(D) Age sixty-five with fifteen years of employment

197. What mistake did Marcus make about the workshop?

(A) He went on the wrong day of the week.
(B) He went to the wrong room.
(C) He went to the wrong building.
(D) He went on the wrong date.

198. What is the deadline for Marcus to apply for early retirement?

(A) July 21
(B) August 10
(C) September 1
(D) November 1

199. If Marcus takes early retirement now, what will be the reduction in his retirement fund?

(A) 2%
(B) 4%
(C) 6%
(D) 8%

200. Who should Marcus talk to about his taxes?

(A) Geoffrey
(B) Suzette
(C) Tuyen
(D) Jun

STOP

This is the end of the test. If you finish before time is called, you may go back to Parts 5, 6, and 7 and check your work.

ANSWER KEY
Model Test 3

LISTENING COMPREHENSION

Part 1: Photographs

1. **C**	4. **B**	7. **D**	10. **B**
2. **D**	5. **B**	8. **A**	
3. **A**	6. **C**	9. **C**	

Part 2: Question-Response

11. **A**	19. **A**	27. **C**	35. **B**
12. **C**	20. **C**	28. **A**	36. **A**
13. **C**	21. **C**	29. **A**	37. **B**
14. **B**	22. **B**	30. **A**	38. **C**
15. **A**	23. **B**	31. **C**	39. **A**
16. **C**	24. **C**	32. **B**	40. **A**
17. **A**	25. **C**	33. **A**	
18. **C**	26. **B**	34. **C**	

Part 3: Conversations

41. **C**	49. **B**	57. **A**	65. **C**
42. **A**	50. **B**	58. **C**	66. **B**
43. **B**	51. **B**	59. **D**	67. **B**
44. **D**	52. **B**	60. **C**	68. **D**
45. **A**	53. **C**	61. **D**	69. **D**
46. **D**	54. **D**	62. **D**	70. **D**
47. **A**	55. **D**	63. **C**	
48. **C**	56. **B**	64. **A**	

Part 4: Talks

71. **B**	79. **D**	87. **D**	95. **D**
72. **C**	80. **D**	88. **D**	96. **B**
73. **D**	81. **A**	89. **B**	97. **A**
74. **C**	82. **B**	90. **C**	98. **C**
75. **A**	83. **C**	91. **B**	99. **A**
76. **D**	84. **B**	92. **B**	100. **B**
77. **A**	85. **D**	93. **D**	
78. **B**	86. **B**	94. **C**	

ANSWER KEY
Model Test 3

READING

Part 5: Incomplete Sentences

101. **C**	112. **A**	123. **B**	134. **B**
102. **B**	113. **B**	124. **A**	135. **C**
103. **A**	114. **A**	125. **D**	136. **C**
104. **D**	115. **C**	126. **C**	137. **B**
105. **C**	116. **D**	127. **D**	138. **C**
106. **D**	117. **B**	128. **A**	139. **B**
107. **B**	118. **C**	129. **C**	140. **D**
108. **A**	119. **A**	130. **B**	
109. **C**	120. **D**	131. **D**	
110. **D**	121. **C**	132. **C**	
111. **B**	122. **A**	133. **A**	

Part 6: Text Completion

141. **C**	144. **C**	147. **C**	150. **B**
142. **A**	145. **C**	148. **C**	151. **D**
143. **A**	146. **A**	149. **A**	152. **A**

Part 7: Reading Comprehension

153. **D**	167. **A**	181. **A**	195. **D**
154. **D**	168. **D**	182. **B**	196. **B**
155. **B**	169. **B**	183. **A**	197. **D**
156. **C**	170. **A**	184. **B**	198. **D**
157. **A**	171. **B**	185. **C**	199. **C**
158. **D**	172. **C**	186. **C**	200. **A**
159. **D**	173. **D**	187. **D**	
160. **C**	174. **A**	188. **C**	
161. **B**	175. **D**	189. **B**	
162. **A**	176. **B**	190. **C**	
163. **B**	177. **C**	191. **C**	
164. **C**	178. **A**	192. **C**	
165. **C**	179. **D**	193. **B**	
166. **A**	180. **C**	194. **B**	

TEST SCORE CONVERSION TABLE

Count your correct responses. Match the number of correct responses with the corresponding score from the Test Score Conversion Table (below). Add the two scores together. This is your Total Estimated Test Score. As you practice taking the TOEIC model tests, your scores should improve. Keep track of your Total Estimated Test Scores.

# Correct	Listening Score	Reading Score	# Correct	Listening Score	Reading Score	# Correct	Listening Score	Reading Score	# Correct	Listening Score	Reading Score
0	5	5	26	110	65	51	255	220	76	410	370
1	5	5	27	115	70	52	260	225	77	420	380
2	5	5	28	120	80	53	270	230	78	425	385
3	5	5	29	125	85	54	275	235	79	430	390
4	5	5	30	130	90	55	280	240	80	440	395
5	5	5	31	135	95	56	290	250	81	445	400
6	5	5	32	140	100	57	295	255	82	450	405
7	10	5	33	145	110	58	300	260	83	460	410
8	15	5	34	150	115	59	310	265	84	465	415
9	20	5	35	160	120	60	315	270	85	470	420
10	25	5	36	165	125	61	320	280	86	475	425
11	30	5	37	170	130	62	325	285	87	480	430
12	35	5	38	175	140	63	330	290	88	485	435
13	40	5	39	180	145	64	340	300	89	490	445
14	45	5	40	185	150	65	345	305	90	495	450
15	50	5	41	190	160	66	350	310	91	495	455
16	55	10	42	195	165	67	360	320	92	495	465
17	60	15	43	200	170	68	365	325	93	495	470
18	65	20	44	210	175	69	370	330	94	495	480
19	70	25	45	215	180	70	380	335	95	495	485
20	75	30	46	220	190	71	385	340	96	495	490
21	80	35	47	230	195	72	390	350	97	495	495
22	85	40	48	240	200	73	395	355	98	495	495
23	90	45	49	245	210	74	400	360	99	495	495
24	95	50	50	250	215	75	405	365	100	495	495
25	100	60									

Number of Correct Listening Responses ________ = Listening Score ________

Number of Correct Reading Responses ________ = Reading Score ________

Total Estimated Test Score ________

EXPLANATORY ANSWERS

Listening Comprehension

PART 1: PHOTOGRAPHS

1. **(C)** This identifies the *customers* in the restaurant and their action: *enjoying their meal.* Choice (A) is incorrect because there is food on the plates. Choice (B) incorrectly identifies the waiter's action—he is serving food. Choice (D) associates *menu* with the restaurant scene, but there is no menu in the photo.
2. **(D)** The scientist is wearing gloves to protect his hands while he works. Choice (A) correctly identifies the test tube, but he is pouring something into it, not washing it. Choice (B) correctly identifies his coat, but he is not taking it off. Choice (C) correctly identifies his action, *pouring,* but he is pouring something into a test tube, not into a glass or cup for drinking.
3. **(A)** The photo shows heavy traffic on a highway. Choice (B) correctly identifies the cars, but not their location. Choice (C) associates *cars* with *parking lot.* Choice (D) correctly identifies the bridge, but it goes across a highway, not a river.
4. **(B)** Choice (B) identifies *the passengers* and the action *ready to board* a train. Choice (A) confuses the similar sounds *rain* with *train.* Choice (C) confuses the similar sounds *plane* with *train.* Choice (D) confuses the similar sounds *grain* with *train.*
5. **(B)** Many trucks are pulled up to the loading docks of a large warehouse. Choice (A) confuses the similar sounds *duck* with *truck.* Choice (C) uses the associated word *ship* for *shipping,* sending things by truck. Choice (D) uses the word *shoppers,* but there are no shoppers in the photo, nor is an *aisle* visible.
6. **(C)** There is a large, open grassy field in front of the factory and the parking lot by the factory. Choice (A) assumes there are workers in the factory (plant), but none are visible in the photo. The word *plant* also means vegetation that can be seen in the field. Choice (B) uses the word *field,* but it is in a sports context. Choice (D) uses the associated word *grass* for field, but there are no mowers present.
7. **(D)** The waiters are finishing setting the table for the evening meal. Choice (A) repeats the word *chair* that the waiters are touching. It also uses the similar-sounding word *sitting* for *setting.* Choice (B) repeats the word *dishes* that are on the table. Choice (C) uses the associated word *dinner,* but no one is eating dinner.
8. **(A)** The speaker is giving an address to an audience. Choice (B) confuses the similar sound of *dressed* with *address.* Choice (C) uses the associated word *deliver* as in *deliver a talk.* Choice (D) confuses *taking a walk* for *giving a talk.*
9. **(C)** There are two men at the front of the class by the blackboard. Choices (A), (B), and (D) all use words associated with a school, but the context is not correct: *students, classroom, professor.*
10. **(B)** The highway overpasses are stacked above one another. Choice (A) uses the associated word *road.* Choice (C) uses the word *cars.* Choice (D) uses the word *bridges.*

PART 2: QUESTION-RESPONSE

11. **(A)** This is a logical response to the request to check figures. Choice (B) confuses the meaning of the word *check.* Choice (C) confuses the meaning of the word *figure.*
12. **(C)** This is a logical response to the tag question about Bob's day off. Choice (A) repeats the word *off.* Choice (B) repeats the word *day.*
13. **(C)** The first speaker complains about the coffee, so the second speaker offers to make a new cup. Choice (A) confuses *coughing* with the similar-sounding word *coffee.* Choice (B) confuses *gold* with the similar-sounding word *cold.*
14. **(B)** Choice (B) is a logical response to a question about *distance.* Choice (A) has the related words *paintings* and *modern,* but it does not give distance. Choice (C) answers a question about *When.*

15. **(A)** Choice (A) is a logical response to a question about *time.* Choice (B) tells *when they drove* by, but not *when they bought.* Choice (C) answers the question *How much,* not *When.*
16. **(C)** Choice (C) is a logical response to a question about the *subject.* Choice (A) gives the location of the book, not *its subject.* Choice (B) gives the price.
17. **(A)** The suggestion to go on Monday is a logical response to the remark that City Hall is *closed over the weekend.* Choice (B) relates *countryside* with *city.* Choice (C) implies that the speaker's sister works at City Hall, but it is not a logical response to the remark.
18. **(C)** Choice (C) is a logical response to a question about *which train.* Choice (A) confuses similar sounds *train* with *rain.* Choice (B) answers the incorrect question, *Which class should I take.*
19. **(A)** Choice (A) answers the question *Why.* Choice (B) confuses the meaning of the word *permit.* Choice (C) confuses similar-sounding words *ready/already.*
20. **(C)** Choice (C) is a logical response to a question about *When.* Choice (A) tells *How long,* not *When.* Choice (B) confuses similar sounds *is he* with *she* and related words *too long* and *when.*
21. **(C)** Choice (C) is a logical response to a question about *How much.* Choice (A) answers the question *How* you paid. Choice (B) answers the question *How many* (stories the hotel had).
22. **(B)** Since the rent is going up, the second speaker suggests looking for a cheaper place to live. Choice (A) confuses *lent* with the similar-sounding word *rent.* Choice (C) repeats the phrase *going up.*
23. **(B)** The possessive word *Robert's* answers the possessive question *Whose.* Choice (A) relates *handwriting* with *cursive.* Choice (C) relates *handwriting* with *sign.*
24. **(C)** The second speaker will arrive at the meeting in a minute. Choice (A) associates *conference room* with *meeting.* Choice (B) uses the word *meeting* out of context.
25. **(C)** Choice (C) is a logical response to a question about *winning a tennis game.* Choice (A) has related the word *smoke* to another meaning of *match.* Choice (B) confuses *ten* with *tennis.* Only Choice (C) concerns the game, *tennis.*
26. **(B)** Choice (B) is a logical response to a question about *purpose of a visit.* Choice (A) uses related words *visitors* and *visit.* Choice (C) confuses *proposal* with *purpose* and *list* with *visit.*
27. **(C)** Choice (C) is a logical response to a question about *seasonal preference.* Choice (A) confuses the related word *seasoning* with *season.* Choice (B) confuses the similar sounds *refer* and *prefer.*
28. **(A)** The first speaker mentions seeing Jim at a party, so the second speaker asks how Jim is. Choice (B) associates *dancing* with *party.* Choice (C) confuses *part* with the similar-sounding word *party.*
29. **(A)** Choice (A) is a logical response to a question about *when the mail comes.* Choice (B) confuses the similar sounds *milk* with *mail c(ome).* Choice (C) confuses the sound of *come* with *welcome.*
30. **(A)** Choice (A) is a logical response to a question about *where the bank is.* Choice (B) confuses similar-sounding words *where* and *nowhere.* Choice (C) confuses homonyms *where* and *wear.*
31. **(C)** Choice (C) is a logical response to a question about *the weather.* Choice (A) may seem close with its verb *is going* and the adverb *today.* Choice (B) confuses the sound *rain* with *complain.*
32. **(B)** Choice (B) is a logical response to a question about the *amount of a tip.* Choice (A) has related words *tip* (v) and *tip* (n). Choice (C) confuses *water* and *waded* with *waiter,* and has an answer to *How many,* not *How much.*
33. **(A)** Choice (A) is a logical response to a question about *who was the designer.* Choice (B) confuses *resign* with *design.* Choice (C) confuses *house* with *mouse.*
34. **(C)** This is a logical response to the tag question about whether or not Ken eats meat.

Choice (A) relates *meat* and *steak.* Choice (B) confuses similar-sounding words *meat* and *neat.*

35. **(B)** Choice (B) is a logical response to a question about *the fabric a shirt is made of.* Choice (A) changes the preposition from *made of* to *made in.* Choice (C) confuses similar-sounding words, *this shirt* and *dessert.*
36. **(A)** This is a logical response to the negative question about the view. Choice (B) confuses similar-sounding words *view* and *too.* Choice (C) confuses similar-sounding words *view* and *knew.*
37. **(B)** Choice (B) is a logical response to a question about *where you study English.* Choice (A) confuses the related word *students* with *study* and *England* with *English.* Choice (C) answers *How long.*
38. **(C)** Choice (C) is a logical response to a question about *which sweater fits better.* Choice (A) confuses *sweater* with *sweat pants* and the concept of *fit* with something that is *too large.* Choice (B) confuses the word *sweater* with *weather.*
39. **(A)** Choice (A) is a logical response to a question about *the time.* Choice (B) answers another *do you have* question. Choice (C) answers *what time do you have to leave.*
40. **(A)** Choice (A) is a logical response to a request *to close the window.* Choice (B) confuses the word *close* with *clothes.* Choice (C) has the related word *open.*

PART 3: CONVERSATIONS

41. **(C)** The man says that he heard it on the radio. Choice (A) is not mentioned. Choice (B) sounds similar to *I bet.* Choice (D) sounds similar to *Fred,* the person that the man is going to help.
42. **(A)** The man promised to help Fred move to his new apartment. Choice (B) confuses similar-sounding words *chance* and *dance.* Choice (C) repeats the word *apartment.* Choice (D) is not mentioned.
43. **(B)** The woman says, *Let's go on Sunday.* Choice (A) is plausible, but it is contradicted by the correct answer. Choice (C) repeats the phrase *next year.* Choice (D) confuses similar-sounding words *Fred* and *friend.*
44. **(D)** *Résumé* and *possible positions* suggest a job interview. Choices (A), (B), and (C) are all scheduled by appointment, but they would not involve a résumé.
45. **(A)** The woman suggests 8:30, and the man agrees. Choice (B) confuses *nine* with the similar-sounding word *fine.* Choices (C) and (D) confuse *ten* with the similar-sounding word *then.*
46. **(D)** The man asks if he should bring anything and the woman says no. Choice (A) is related to the word *applicant,* mentioned by the woman. Choice (B) is incorrect because the man will take the test at the time of the interview. Choice (C) is incorrect because the woman says she has already read his résumé.
47. **(A)** The man gives the woman a key, directs her to her room, and arranges to have a newspaper delivered to her; these are things that happen in a hotel. Choice (B) repeats the word *elevator.* Choice (C) associates *newsstand* with *newspaper.* Choice (D) is a place that has elevators, but it is not the correct answer.
48. **(C)** The man tells the woman that her room number is 215. Choices (A), (B), and (D) sound similar to the correct answer.
49. **(B)** The woman asks for a newspaper. Choice (A) is what the man is giving the woman now. Choice (C) confuses *directory* with the similar-sounding word *directly.* Choice (D) associates *stationery* with *paper.*
50. **(B)** The woman says, *He's due to address the meeting....* Choice (A) uses the word *address* out of context. Choice (C) confuses *date* with the similar-sounding word *late.* Choice (D) is what the speakers will do.
51. **(B)** Mr. Chung called to explain that he's stuck in traffic. Choice (A) uses the word *address* out of context. Choice (C) associates *car* with *traffic.* Choice (D) is the result of his lateness, not its cause.
52. **(B)** The man says that they'll be able to start the meeting on time. Choice (A) is wrong

because they'll start the meeting by showing a film while they wait for Mr. Chung. Choice (C) is confused with the ten minutes it will take to get the film ready. Choice (D) repeats the word *ten* and confuses *nine* with the similar-sounding word *time*.

53. **(C)** The man mentions the lobby. Choice (A) is what the woman thinks needs to be painted. Choice (B) associates *office* with *office building*. Choice (D) associates *door* with *entrance*.

54. **(D)** The man says, *It never had enough light before*. Choice (A) is not mentioned. Choices (B) and (C) are the opposite of the correct answer.

55. **(D)** The man says that the cafeteria will be painted *the week after next*. Choice (A) confuses *afternoon* with the similar-sounding word *soon*. Choice (B) confuses *Sunday* with the similar-sounding word *someday*. Choice (C) sounds similar to the correct answer.

56. **(B)** The speakers are discussing repairs to a television set. Choice (A) confuses *chair* with the similar-sounding word *repair*. Choice (C) confuses *telephone* with the similar-sounding word *television*. Choice (D) uses the word *monitor* out of context by associating it with *computer*.

57. **(A)** The man says that he called the company today. Choice (B) confuses *Tuesday* with the similar-sounding word *today*. Choice (C) confuses *afternoon* with the similar-sounding word *soon*. Choice (D) repeats the word *week*.

58. **(C)** The repairs will take a total of three weeks—two weeks to get the parts and one more week to install them. Choice (A) is confused with the one more week to install the parts. Choice (B) is the time it will take to get the parts. Choice (D) confuses *ten* with the similar-sounding word *then*.

59. **(D)** The man says that his tire is flat. Choice (A) associates *gas* with *gas station*. Choice (B) confuses *drink* with the similar-sounding word *think*. Choice (C) confuses *tired* with the similar-sounding word *tire*.

60. **(C)** The woman says that the gas station is a mile and a half away. Choices (A) and (B) sound similar to the correct answer. Choice (D) confuses *two* with the similar-sounding word *too*.

61. **(D)** The woman offers the man a ride because it is too far to walk. Choice (A) is what the man first says he will do. Choice (B) is not mentioned. Choice (C) associates *car* with *ride*.

62. **(D)** The lunch break is one hour. Choice (A) is the amount of time the man takes to eat. Choice (B) is not mentioned. Choice (C) is the amount of time the man spends walking.

63. **(C)** The woman spends her break in the cafeteria eating. Choice (A) confuses *work* with the similar-sounding word *walk*. Choice (B) is what the woman would like to do if she had the time. Choice (D) is what the man does.

64. **(A)** The man eats lunch at his desk. Choice (B) is where the man walks. Choice (C) is where the woman eats lunch. Choice (D) repeats the word *exercise*.

65. **(C)** The man asks for directions to the history museum. Choices (A), (B), and (D) are places that he will pass on the way there.

66. **(B)** The woman says that it is three blocks away. Choice (A) confuses *two* with the similar-sounding word *through*. Choice (C) confuses *nine* with the similar-sounding word *fine*. Choice (D) confuses *ten* with the similar-sounding word *then*.

67. **(B)** The museum is closed on Saturday and Sunday and open during the week. Choice (A) confuses *Tuesday* with the similar-sounding word *today*. Choice (C) makes the same confusion; these are the days the museum would be open if it were closed on Tuesday. Choice (D) are the days that the museum is closed.

68. **(D)** The man says that it is a five and a half-hour flight. Choices (A) and (B) are confused with *2:30*, the time that the plane will land. Choice (C) sounds similar to the correct answer.

69. **(D)** The speakers talk about the flight they are on and when it will land. Choice (A) is incorrect because they haven't landed at the airport yet. Choice (B) is incorrect because they are on a *flight* and they will

MODEL TEST 3

land, words that describe plane trips, not train trips. Choice (C) is confused with the man's description of the airport—you might also see newsstands and cafés at a mall.

70. **(D)** The woman asks the man whether he knows which gate her flight to Honolulu will leave from. Choice (A) is associated with travel, but it is not mentioned. Choices (B) and (C) are associated with things the man says that the woman will see at the airport—a newsstand and a café.

PART 4: TALKS

71. **(B)** *Not in service* means *not working.* Choice (A), *a wrong number,* means you misdialed. Choice (C) confuses the *recording* and an *answering machine.* Choice (D) means someone is using the phone.
72. **(C)** This is a person who helps *customers.* Choice (A) fixes broken phones. Choice (B) connects calls. Choice (D) makes decisions about the company.
73. **(D)** Callers are charged seventy-five cents a minute for assistance. Choices (A), (B), and (C) sound similar to the correct answer.
74. **(C)** The speaker says, *We'll be celebrating all next weekend....* Choice (A) is the last day to get a ticket. Choice (B) sounds similar to the correct answer. Choice (D) repeats the word *year,* which refers to the time leading up to the event.
75. **(A)** The speaker mentions activities for the whole family and says *All are welcome...* Choice (B) refers to the concert performers. Choice (C) refers to the speakers at the ceremony. Choice (D) repeats the words *mayor* and *family.*
76. **(D)** The speaker says to phone City Hall for tickets. Choice (A) confuses similar-sounding words *fine* and *line* and repeats the word *park.* Choice (B) confuses similar-sounding words *free* and *three,* and it is incorrect because the tickets are free. Choice (C) confuses similar-sounding words *fine* and *online.*
77. **(A)** A *computer school* provides *computer training.* Choice (B) is incorrect; the school trains in *business software,* not *business management.* Choice (C) confuses the ideas of *job placement* and *personnel.* Choice (D) is incorrect; the school *teaches,* it doesn't *train teachers.*
78. **(B)** The ad says, *you can train* in *six months.* Choices (A), (C), and (D) are not mentioned.
79. **(D)** Classes are taught evenings and weekends so that people who work during the day can attend. Choices (A) and (C) are incorrect because daytime is when the students work. Choice (B) is incorrect because there are also weekend classes.
80. **(D)** The message is for Zach Robinson, explaining travel arrangements that have been made for him. Choices (A) and (C) are the same person, the speaker. Choice (B) is the person the traveler will be seeing in Boston.
81. **(A)** The speaker says... *take Train 3425....* Choice (B) is how the traveler will travel after arriving in Boston. Choice (C) sounds similar to the correct answer. Choice (D) is related to the word *drive* and is how the traveler will get to the train station on the day he returns home.
82. **(B)** The speaker says, *Please check your e-mail for your complete itinerary.* Choice (A) is related to the topic of the message, but no ticket is mentioned. Choice (C) repeats the word *hotel.* Choice (D) repeats the word *question.*
83. **(C)** Those hours refer to *business hours.* Choices (A) and (B) are both contradicted; the hours given are for weekdays during the day. Choice (D) is not logical; they are not open *before 8:00.*
84. **(B)** This is what the speaker says. Choices (A), (C), and (D) are possible solutions, but they are not mentioned here.
85. **(D)** The message asks for the serial number of the product. Choices (A), (B), and (C) are confused with *the name and address of the store where it was purchased.*

86. **(B)** *Apply in person* means *go to the hotel.* Choice (A) is not required. Choices (C) and (D) are unnecessary if you apply in person.

87. **(D)** *Opportunity for advancement* means *possible promotions.* Choices (A) and (B) are not mentioned. Choice (C) is unlikely for these kinds of jobs.

88. **(D)** The announcement mentions *waiters* as one of the open positions. Choice (A) is the person to apply to. Choice (B) confuses *store clerks* with *desk clerks.* Choice (C) is confused with *we will train new employees.*

89. **(B)** The speaker mentions the *City Bus Service,* and later on mentions a *driver.* Choices (A), (C), and (D) are all things for which one might buy tickets, but they are not the correct answer.

90. **(C)** The speaker says, *To begin, enter the date and time of your travel,* that is, the travel schedule. Choices (A), (B), and (D) are later steps in the process.

91. **(B)** The speaker says, *Please approach the ticket office if you wish to pay cash.* Choice (A) is confused with the mention of a credit *card.* Choice (C) is not correct because the speaker says *the machine does not accept cash.* Choice (D) is not correct because the speaker says *drivers cannot issue tickets.*

92. **(B)** A *heat wave* means *hot weather.* Choices (A), (C), and (D) are possible problems, but they are not true here.

93. **(D)** *The report says the weather will be over one hundred degrees.* Choices (A), (B), and (C) are all under one hundred degrees.

94. **(C)** To avoid heatstroke, residents should *drink lots of water.* Choice (A) is incorrect because residents are advised to wear light, not dark, clothes. Choice (B) is contradicted by *avoid strenuous exercise.* Choice (D) is not mentioned.

95. **(D)** The speaker says, . . . *executives need to take a break,* and *It is important to set aside one hour* . . . . Choice (A) is confused with *walk away from your computer.* Choice (B) repeats the word *time.* Choice (C) repeats the word *assistant.*

96. **(B)** The speaker recommends *closing your door.* Choice (A) is related to the topic, but it is not mentioned. Choice (C) is confused with *take a break,* but it is a one-hour break that is recommended, not a vacation. Choice (D) is plausible, but it is not mentioned.

97. **(A)** The speaker recommends taking a break to relax your mind and says *A relaxed mind is ready to take on difficult tasks* . . . . Choice (B) repeats the word *secretary.* Choice (C) repeats the word *reading.* Choice (D) repeats the word *techniques.*

98. **(C)** It is an annual ceremony, so it takes place once a year. Choice (A) is confused with the size of the cash award ($5,000). Choices (B) and (D) confuse *three* with *third.*

99. **(A)** A total of $20,000 will be given out, and the size of each award is $5,000, so four people will receive awards. Choice (B) is confused with the size of each award. Choice (C) is confused with the total amount of cash given out. Choice (D) is confused with both the size of the individual awards and the total amount awarded.

100. **(B)** Listeners are asked to make donations so that awards can continue to be given in the future. Choices (A), (C), and (D) are confused with the various things winners might do with their money.

Reading

PART 5: INCOMPLETE SENTENCES

101. **(C)** The plural *contracts* requires a plural verb. Choices (A) and (B) are singular. Choice (D) is the simple form.

102. **(B)** When there is a *decrease* in costs, that means costs have become less. Choice (A) has a similar meaning, but it is not used when talking about *costs.* Choices (C) and (D) are not nouns.

103. **(A)** *Unfortunately* is used to describe a negative or disappointing situation. Choices (B), (C), and (D) have meanings that don't fit the context.

MODEL TEST 3

104. **(D)** The phrase *There are* describes the existence of something. Choices (A), (B), and (C) don't fit the context.

105. **(C)** *If* introduces a condition. Choices (A), (B), and (D) have no meaning in this context.

106. **(D)** Someone else *included* the taxes; use the past participle. Choice (A) is the present participle. Choices (B) and (C) are verbs.

107. **(B)** Complete the verb: *wants to finalize.* Choices (A) and (D) are nouns. Choice (C) is is an adverb.

108. **(A)** A comparison of two things uses *more + adjective* or the *-er* form. Choices (B) and (C) use *most.* Choice (D) uses *the.*

109. **(C)** Use *Who* to refer to people. Choice (A) refers to things. Choice (B) is possessive. Choice (D) is objective.

110. **(D)** *While* introduces the time clause and means *at the same time as.* Choices (A), (B), and (C) cannot be used to introduce a time clause.

111. **(B)** *Paint* and *pictures* are equal items joined with *and.* Choices (A), (C), and (D) join clauses, not nouns.

112. **(A)** *Aware* is the only adjective among the options. Choices (B), (C), and (D) do not fit the context of the sentence.

113. **(B)** The verb agrees with the singular third person subject *itinerary.* Choices (A) and (D) are not singular forms. Choice (C) is a gerund, so it cannot be used as a main verb.

114. **(A)** *Between* expresses beginning and ending points. Choice (B) indicates *in the company of or by means of.* Choice (C) indicates movement across something. Choice (D) indicates source.

115. **(C)** *Recommendations* is a noun, and in this sentence it acts as the object of the verb *made.* Choices (A) and (B) are verbs. Choice (D) is an adjective.

116. **(D)** The comparative form is *faster.* Choice (A) is an adjective. Choice (B) is the superlative. Choice (C) has an unnecessary article, *the.*

117. **(B)** *Or* refers to a choice between two things, in this case, two ways of paying a bill. Choice (A) introduces a result. Choice (C) introduces a contradiction. Choice (D) can introduce either a reason or a time expression.

118. **(C)** The time for the speakers has been *made shorter,* or *shortened.* Choice (A) means *make higher.* Choice (B) means *make longer.* Choice (D) means *make wider.*

119. **(A)** The causative *ask* requires a following infinitive. Choice (B) is the gerund. Choice (C) is future tense. Choice (D) is present tense.

120. **(D)** The third person singular feminine possessive adjective *her* agrees with the antecedent *Ms. Chang,* and modifies the noun *business suits.* Choices (A) and (B) are not possessive adjectives. Choice (C) doesn't agree with the antecedent.

121. **(C)** The adjective *difficult* is followed by an infinitive verb. Choices (A) and (B) are present tense verbs. Choice (D) is a gerund.

122. **(A)** This is a passive causative construction. Choices (B), (C), and (D) cannot be used as causative verbs.

123. **(B)** The subject *variety* requires a singular verb. Choice (A) is plural. Choice (C) is the gerund. Choice (D) is the simple form.

124. **(A)** *Acknowledge* means *recognize.* Choices (B), (C), and (D) have meanings that don't fit the context.

125. **(D)** *Beside* means *next to.* Choices (A) and (B) need more than one bus as a reference point. Choice (C) means *direction away*; it is not logical.

126. **(C)** *A minimum of* means *at least.* Choices (A), (B), and (D) have meanings that don't fit the context.

127. **(D)** An unreal condition requires *would* in the clause without *if.* Choice (A) is the wrong tense. Choices (B) and (C) do not use *would.*

128. **(A)** Habitual action uses present tense; *handbook* requires third person singular forms. Choice (B) is the present progressive tense. Choice (C) is the simple form. Choice (D) is the gerund.

129. **(C)** The sentence means that the manufacturer, or maker, of the product (model 34) will fulfill the order in the spring. Choices (A), (B),

and (D) are not entities from which you could order a product.

130. **(B)** *Only* is an adverb modifying the verb *consider*—Mr. Larsen will consider veterans and nobody else. Choices (A), (C), and (D) cannot be used in this position in a sentence.

131. **(D)** *Even though* establishes a logical link between clauses. Choices (A), (B), and (C) are not logical.

132. **(C)** *By himself* means *alone* or *without help.* Choices (A), (B), and (D) cannot be used following *by.*

133. **(A)** The subject of the sentence, *predictions,* does not perform the action, so a passive verb is needed. Choices (B), (C), and (D) are all active verbs.

134. **(B)** In this sentence, *who* is a subject relative pronoun with *doctors* as the antecedent. Choice (A) cannot be used as a relative pronoun. Choice (C) is possessive. Choice (D) is used as a pronoun for things, not people.

135. **(C)** Use *between* with two items. Choice (A) means *together.* Choice (B) indicates time. Choice (D) is used with three or more items.

136. **(C)** *In spite of* means *despite.* It is a prepositional phrase, so it must be followed by a noun or a gerund. Choice (A) doesn't make sense in this context. Choices (B) and (D) must introduce a clause.

137. **(B)** *Organizing* is a gerund, the object of the preposition *for.* Choice (A) is a noun. Choices (C) and (D) are verbs.

138. **(C)** This third person singular verb agrees with the subject *head of accounts.* Choice (A) is a noun, not a verb. Choices (B) and (D) are plural verbs, so they don't agree with the subject.

139. **(B)** *Than* completes the comparative adjective *better.* Choice (A) could precede the adjective, but it cannot follow it. Choices (C) and (D) are not used to form comparisons.

140. **(D)** *Prepare* as a main verb is followed by an infinitive. Choice (A) is base form or present tense. Choice (B) is past tense. Choice (C) is a gerund.

PART 6: TEXT COMPLETION

141. **(C)** The pronoun *it* agrees with the verb *outlines* and has the antecedent *brochure.* Choices (A) and (D) don't agree with the verb. Choice (B) refers to a person.

142. **(A)** The verb *requires* agrees with the singular subject, *Green Office Renovators,* the name of a single company. Choices (B), (C), and (D) don't agree with the subject.

143. **(A)** To *demonstrate concern* for something means to *care* about it. Choices (B), (C), and (D) have meanings that do not fit the context.

144. **(C)** This is the correct superlative form for a one-syllable adjective. Choice (A) is not a superlative adjective. Choice (B) is the comparative form. Choice (D) is an incorrect form for a one-syllable adjective.

145. **(C)** *Spread out* can mean divided up; the customer will not pay the highest bills at one time of the year, but instead divide the bills into smaller pieces and pay them throughout the year. Choice (A) means *reduced in price.* Choice (B) means *increased.* Choice (D) means *added to.*

146. **(A)** The company *estimates,* or *guesses,* how much gas the customer will use in a year based on use in past years. Choice (B) means *allowed.* Choice (C) means *asked about.* Choice (D) means *asked for.*

147. **(C)** A passive voice form is needed because the subject, *passengers,* is not active. It is the airport that offers the Internet service. Choices (A), (B), and (D) are all active voice forms.

148. **(C)** VIP card holders receive *benefits,* that is, special *advantages* or *favors* because they have purchased the card. Choices (A), (B), and (D) don't fit the context.

149. **(A)** A noun is needed here. Choice (B) is an adjective. Choice (C) is a verb. Choice (D) is an adverb.

150. **(B)** A *bargain* price is a *good* or *low* price, and the point of the ad is that this store offers lower prices than other stores. Choice (A) is a word that is not normally used to describe prices. Choice (C) describes prices that cus-

MODEL TEST 3

tomers generally pay to stores. Choice (D) means *high.*

151. **(D)** *No* is the correct word to use to make a noun negative. Choices (A) and (B) are pronouns. Choice (C) is used to make a verb negative.

152. **(A)** Since there is no subject, the imperative form is required here, telling the reader what to do. Choice (B) is a gerund. Choice (C) is an infinitive. Choice (D) is a modal plus base form verb and requires a subject.

PART 7: READING COMPREHENSION

153. **(D)** Product quality is improved by improvements in technology. The other options are not explicitly mentioned.

154. **(D)** *Hiring practices* are not mentioned. Choices (A), (B), and (C) are explicitly mentioned.

155. **(B)** It is *lowering costs by improving manufacturing processes.* Choice (A) is not linked to lowering costs. Choices (C) and (D) are not logical ways to lower costs.

156. **(C)** To find people to apply for jobs. Choice (A) is incorrect; they want to meet job applicants, not *new people.* Choices (B) and (D) might encourage people, but they do not describe the purpose of the ad.

157. **(A)** National Headquarters is mentioned with the *time* and *date,* so it must be the place. Choice (B) is not mentioned. Choice (C) is not a logical location for an open house. Choice (D) is incorrect; the airport is regional, not the office.

158. **(D)** The first line of the letter gives the answer: *pleased to receive your fax.* The other choices are not mentioned.

159. **(D)** The fax states, *We have sent under separate cover information regarding our company and its services.* Choice (A) confuses the meaning of the word *address.* Choice (B) repeats the word *offices.* Choice (C) repeats the word *product.*

160. **(C)** *Company distribution centers* ship goods. Choice (A) suggests the shipping method, but it does not ship. Choice (B) is incorrect; the distribution centers may *use* airlines. Choice (D) is incorrect; *headquarters* does not ship goods.

161. **(B)** The details in the fax answer the question about the company's distribution network. The other questions are not answered in the fax.

162. **(A)** It gives *etiquette rules for bus riders.* Choices (B), (C), and (D) are not the subjects of the notice.

163. **(B)** *Senior citizens and disabled riders* means *elderly people and handicapped people.* Choices (A), (C), and (D) are not designated for priority seats.

164. **(C)** *Reviewing sales records* makes up 25%. Choice (A) makes up 15%. Choice (B) makes up 5%. Choice (D) makes up 22%.

165. **(C)** They spend *10%* of their time with the technical staff. Choice (A) is spent in *administrative duties.* Choice (B) is spent in *miscellaneous tasks.* Choice (D) is spent *training new salespeople.*

166. **(A)** If only 5% of each manager's time is spent dealing with customer problems, it can be assumed that there are few problems. Choice (B) is contradicted in the passage: *training sales personnel* (15%), *reviewing records* (25%), and *making sales assignments* (22%) show that sales are the highest priority. Choices (C) and (D) are also contradicted.

167. **(A)** The ad states, *You will study with your peers. Peers* are defined here as *other experienced managers.* The other choices are not mentioned.

168. **(D)** The application must be accompanied by *three letters of recommendation.* The other choices are not specifically mentioned.

169. **(B)** The course is a *week-long* intensive one. The other periods of time are not mentioned.

170. **(A)** It guarantees the *lowest prices.* Choices (B), (C), and (D) are not mentioned.

171. **(B)** They will *refund the difference,* which means *pay you the difference in price.* Choices (A) and (C) are not given as resolutions to the problem. Choice (D) is incorrect; the store will *refund the difference,* not refund all of your money.

172. **(C)** It *allows employees to take paid time off for volunteer activities.* Choices (A), (B), and (D) concern other types of *time off.*

173. **(D)** They may take *up to eight hours of paid leave per month.* Choices (A) and (C) are all less than the allowed time. Choice (B) is more than the allowed time.

174. **(A)** The memo says that to be eligible, employees must be full time and employed at the company for at least one year. Choices (B), (C), and (D) are contradicted by the correct answer.

175. **(D)** Volunteer leave must be *requested in advance* and *approved by the supervisor.* Choices (A), (B), and (C) are not mentioned as requirements.

176. **(B)** Smaller companies are a likely *victim,* or *target.* Choice (A) refers to the common target of the past. Choice (C) is not mentioned. Choice (D) repeats the words *security system* from the article.

177. **(C)** *Notoriety* means *fame.* Choices (A), (B), and (D) are likely reasons for a hacker to do his work, but none is mentioned in the article.

178. **(A)** *Sitting behind bars* means *in jail.* Choice (B) is not mentioned in the reading. Choice (C) refers to *working overtime.* Choice (D) repeats *pay off* from the article.

179. **(D)** A *password* is a *secret code.* Choices (A) and (B) refer to characteristics of smaller companies that are likely to be attacked. Choice (C) repeats the word *network* from the article.

180. **(C)** When thieves steal data, they can create *confusion* with it. Choice (A) is the opposite of the correct answer. Choices (B) and (D) are things that could be done with data, but they don't have the correct meaning.

181. **(A)** This is confused with Camilla Crowe's title of *Recruiting Coordinator,* but is not mentioned as part of the advertised job. Choices (B), (C), and (D) are all mentioned in the ad as duties of the job.

182. **(B)** Camilla Crow says that Akiko has the degree they are looking for, which, according to the ad, is a degree in marketing. Choice (A) is confused with the store where Akiko worked. Choice (C) is confused with the communications skills asked for in the ad. Choice (D) is confused with the conferences mentioned in the ad as a job duty.

183. **(A)** Camilla Crowe mentions that Akiko graduated last month; since the letter has a March date, last month was February. Choice (B) is the month the letter was written. Choice (C) is confused with the date by which Akiko must contact Camilla about the internship. Choice (D) is not mentioned.

184. **(B)** The letter mentions Akiko's *sales experience in an electronics store.* Choice (A) is the type of experience the company is looking for. Choice (C) is not mentioned. Choice (D) is the job Akiko applied for.

185. **(C)** Camilla offered Akiko a three-month unpaid internship. Choice (A) is what Akiko applied for, but Camilla says she is not experienced enough. Choice (B) is associated with a job application, but it is not mentioned. Choice (D) is confused with the Marketing Club.

186. **(C)** All the classes start at 6:00. Choices (A) and (B) are confused with the course level numbers. Choice (D) is the time that classes end.

187. **(D)** Both the Marketing classes are 500 level and above; classes at these levels are offered on Thursday. Choices (A), (B), and (C) are days that classes at other levels are offered.

188. **(C)** A grade of 75% or higher is required in ACTG 101 in order to take the 102 level; this is the reason Roberto can't register for ACTG 102. Choices (A) and (B) are confused with the correct answer. Choice (D) is the amount by which Roberto failed the course.

189. **(B)** According to the message, Jessica registered Roberto for two courses—BUSI 100 and COMP 207. Choices (A), (C) and (D) are contradicted by the correct answer.

190. **(C)** According to the message, Roberto's student visa will expire, or be invalid, fifteen days before classes end. Choice (A) is incorrect because the message states that it is a

student visa. Choices (B) and (D) are incorrect because Roberto already has a visa.

191. **(C)** The ad says that a tour of the theater is included. Choice (A) is confused with the mention of the French chef. Choice (B) is confused with the mention of the region's finest actors. Choice (D) is done by the theater, not the guests.

192. **(C)** Sundays are for large groups only, so it follows that all the other days are for individuals and small groups. Choice (A) are the days when only evening shows are available. Choice (B) are the days that both afternoon and evening shows are available. Choice (D) is the day reserved for large groups.

193. **(B)** In her e-mail, Ms. Hekler says she prefers the lunch and afternoon show, which runs from 12–4 P.M. Choice (A) is not mentioned. Choice (C) is the time the event will end. Choice (D) is the time the evening events begin.

194. **(B)** The group from the Federal Bank is 325 people, so they will get the 10% discount. Choice (A) applies to groups smaller than 300. Choice (C) applies to groups larger than 350. Choice (D) is confused with the date of the party.

195. **(D)** The Federal Bank party is in December, so they will see a comedy. Choice (A) is the type of show available January–April. Choice (B) is the type of show available May–July. Choice (C) is the type of show available August–October.

196. **(B)** An employee of any age with twenty-five years' experience can take early retirement with full retirement benefits. Choice (A) describes a person who doesn't qualify for early retirement. Choices (C) and (D) describe people who would get reduced benefits.

197. **(D)** The first workshop is on August 10; Marcus went this morning, which is July. Choice (A) is incorrect because workshops are on Wednesdays and Fridays, and today is Wednesday. Choice (B) is incorrect because he went to the right room. Choice (C) is incorrect because no building is mentioned.

198. **(D)** Marcus is a supervisor, so he has two months more than other employees to apply. Choice (A) is the date of the phone message. Choice (B) is the date of the first workshop. Choice (C) is the deadline for most employees.

199. **(C)** Marcus is sixty-two, and the reduction is 2% for every year under age sixty-five. Choice (A) is the reduction for one year. Choice (B) is the reduction for two years. Choice (D) is the reduction for four years.

200. **(A)** Geoffrey is the tax specialist. Choices (B) and (C) are the people to talk to about registering for a workshop. Choice (D) is the benefits manager.

ANSWER SHEET
Model Test 4

LISTENING COMPREHENSION

Part 1: Photographs

1. Ⓐ Ⓑ Ⓒ Ⓓ	4. Ⓐ Ⓑ Ⓒ Ⓓ	7. Ⓐ Ⓑ Ⓒ Ⓓ	10. Ⓐ Ⓑ Ⓒ Ⓓ
2. Ⓐ Ⓑ Ⓒ Ⓓ	5. Ⓐ Ⓑ Ⓒ Ⓓ	8. Ⓐ Ⓑ Ⓒ Ⓓ	
3. Ⓐ Ⓑ Ⓒ Ⓓ	6. Ⓐ Ⓑ Ⓒ Ⓓ	9. Ⓐ Ⓑ Ⓒ Ⓓ	

Part 2: Question-Response

11. Ⓐ Ⓑ Ⓒ Ⓓ	19. Ⓐ Ⓑ Ⓒ Ⓓ	27. Ⓐ Ⓑ Ⓒ Ⓓ	35. Ⓐ Ⓑ Ⓒ Ⓓ
12. Ⓐ Ⓑ Ⓒ Ⓓ	20. Ⓐ Ⓑ Ⓒ Ⓓ	28. Ⓐ Ⓑ Ⓒ Ⓓ	36. Ⓐ Ⓑ Ⓒ Ⓓ
13. Ⓐ Ⓑ Ⓒ Ⓓ	21. Ⓐ Ⓑ Ⓒ Ⓓ	29. Ⓐ Ⓑ Ⓒ Ⓓ	37. Ⓐ Ⓑ Ⓒ Ⓓ
14. Ⓐ Ⓑ Ⓒ Ⓓ	22. Ⓐ Ⓑ Ⓒ Ⓓ	30. Ⓐ Ⓑ Ⓒ Ⓓ	38. Ⓐ Ⓑ Ⓒ Ⓓ
15. Ⓐ Ⓑ Ⓒ Ⓓ	23. Ⓐ Ⓑ Ⓒ Ⓓ	31. Ⓐ Ⓑ Ⓒ Ⓓ	39. Ⓐ Ⓑ Ⓒ Ⓓ
16. Ⓐ Ⓑ Ⓒ Ⓓ	24. Ⓐ Ⓑ Ⓒ Ⓓ	32. Ⓐ Ⓑ Ⓒ Ⓓ	40. Ⓐ Ⓑ Ⓒ Ⓓ
17. Ⓐ Ⓑ Ⓒ Ⓓ	25. Ⓐ Ⓑ Ⓒ Ⓓ	33. Ⓐ Ⓑ Ⓒ Ⓓ	
18. Ⓐ Ⓑ Ⓒ Ⓓ	26. Ⓐ Ⓑ Ⓒ Ⓓ	34. Ⓐ Ⓑ Ⓒ Ⓓ	

Part 3: Conversations

41. Ⓐ Ⓑ Ⓒ Ⓓ	49. Ⓐ Ⓑ Ⓒ Ⓓ	57. Ⓐ Ⓑ Ⓒ Ⓓ	65. Ⓐ Ⓑ Ⓒ Ⓓ
42. Ⓐ Ⓑ Ⓒ Ⓓ	50. Ⓐ Ⓑ Ⓒ Ⓓ	58. Ⓐ Ⓑ Ⓒ Ⓓ	66. Ⓐ Ⓑ Ⓒ Ⓓ
43. Ⓐ Ⓑ Ⓒ Ⓓ	51. Ⓐ Ⓑ Ⓒ Ⓓ	59. Ⓐ Ⓑ Ⓒ Ⓓ	67. Ⓐ Ⓑ Ⓒ Ⓓ
44. Ⓐ Ⓑ Ⓒ Ⓓ	52. Ⓐ Ⓑ Ⓒ Ⓓ	60. Ⓐ Ⓑ Ⓒ Ⓓ	68. Ⓐ Ⓑ Ⓒ Ⓓ
45. Ⓐ Ⓑ Ⓒ Ⓓ	53. Ⓐ Ⓑ Ⓒ Ⓓ	61. Ⓐ Ⓑ Ⓒ Ⓓ	69. Ⓐ Ⓑ Ⓒ Ⓓ
46. Ⓐ Ⓑ Ⓒ Ⓓ	54. Ⓐ Ⓑ Ⓒ Ⓓ	62. Ⓐ Ⓑ Ⓒ Ⓓ	70. Ⓐ Ⓑ Ⓒ Ⓓ
47. Ⓐ Ⓑ Ⓒ Ⓓ	55. Ⓐ Ⓑ Ⓒ Ⓓ	63. Ⓐ Ⓑ Ⓒ Ⓓ	
48. Ⓐ Ⓑ Ⓒ Ⓓ	56. Ⓐ Ⓑ Ⓒ Ⓓ	64. Ⓐ Ⓑ Ⓒ Ⓓ	

Part 4: Talks

71. Ⓐ Ⓑ Ⓒ Ⓓ	79. Ⓐ Ⓑ Ⓒ Ⓓ	87. Ⓐ Ⓑ Ⓒ Ⓓ	95. Ⓐ Ⓑ Ⓒ Ⓓ
72. Ⓐ Ⓑ Ⓒ Ⓓ	80. Ⓐ Ⓑ Ⓒ Ⓓ	88. Ⓐ Ⓑ Ⓒ Ⓓ	96. Ⓐ Ⓑ Ⓒ Ⓓ
73. Ⓐ Ⓑ Ⓒ Ⓓ	81. Ⓐ Ⓑ Ⓒ Ⓓ	89. Ⓐ Ⓑ Ⓒ Ⓓ	97. Ⓐ Ⓑ Ⓒ Ⓓ
74. Ⓐ Ⓑ Ⓒ Ⓓ	82. Ⓐ Ⓑ Ⓒ Ⓓ	90. Ⓐ Ⓑ Ⓒ Ⓓ	98. Ⓐ Ⓑ Ⓒ Ⓓ
75. Ⓐ Ⓑ Ⓒ Ⓓ	83. Ⓐ Ⓑ Ⓒ Ⓓ	91. Ⓐ Ⓑ Ⓒ Ⓓ	99. Ⓐ Ⓑ Ⓒ Ⓓ
76. Ⓐ Ⓑ Ⓒ Ⓓ	84. Ⓐ Ⓑ Ⓒ Ⓓ	92. Ⓐ Ⓑ Ⓒ Ⓓ	100. Ⓐ Ⓑ Ⓒ Ⓓ
77. Ⓐ Ⓑ Ⓒ Ⓓ	85. Ⓐ Ⓑ Ⓒ Ⓓ	93. Ⓐ Ⓑ Ⓒ Ⓓ	
78. Ⓐ Ⓑ Ⓒ Ⓓ	86. Ⓐ Ⓑ Ⓒ Ⓓ	94. Ⓐ Ⓑ Ⓒ Ⓓ	

ANSWER SHEET
Model Test 4

READING

Part 5: Incomplete Sentences

101. Ⓐ Ⓑ Ⓒ Ⓓ	111. Ⓐ Ⓑ Ⓒ Ⓓ	121. Ⓐ Ⓑ Ⓒ Ⓓ	131. Ⓐ Ⓑ Ⓒ Ⓓ
102. Ⓐ Ⓑ Ⓒ Ⓓ	112. Ⓐ Ⓑ Ⓒ Ⓓ	122. Ⓐ Ⓑ Ⓒ Ⓓ	132. Ⓐ Ⓑ Ⓒ Ⓓ
103. Ⓐ Ⓑ Ⓒ Ⓓ	113. Ⓐ Ⓑ Ⓒ Ⓓ	123. Ⓐ Ⓑ Ⓒ Ⓓ	133. Ⓐ Ⓑ Ⓒ Ⓓ
104. Ⓐ Ⓑ Ⓒ Ⓓ	114. Ⓐ Ⓑ Ⓒ Ⓓ	124. Ⓐ Ⓑ Ⓒ Ⓓ	134. Ⓐ Ⓑ Ⓒ Ⓓ
105. Ⓐ Ⓑ Ⓒ Ⓓ	115. Ⓐ Ⓑ Ⓒ Ⓓ	125. Ⓐ Ⓑ Ⓒ Ⓓ	135. Ⓐ Ⓑ Ⓒ Ⓓ
106. Ⓐ Ⓑ Ⓒ Ⓓ	116. Ⓐ Ⓑ Ⓒ Ⓓ	126. Ⓐ Ⓑ Ⓒ Ⓓ	136. Ⓐ Ⓑ Ⓒ Ⓓ
107. Ⓐ Ⓑ Ⓒ Ⓓ	117. Ⓐ Ⓑ Ⓒ Ⓓ	127. Ⓐ Ⓑ Ⓒ Ⓓ	137. Ⓐ Ⓑ Ⓒ Ⓓ
108. Ⓐ Ⓑ Ⓒ Ⓓ	118. Ⓐ Ⓑ Ⓒ Ⓓ	128. Ⓐ Ⓑ Ⓒ Ⓓ	138. Ⓐ Ⓑ Ⓒ Ⓓ
109. Ⓐ Ⓑ Ⓒ Ⓓ	119. Ⓐ Ⓑ Ⓒ Ⓓ	129. Ⓐ Ⓑ Ⓒ Ⓓ	139. Ⓐ Ⓑ Ⓒ Ⓓ
110. Ⓐ Ⓑ Ⓒ Ⓓ	120. Ⓐ Ⓑ Ⓒ Ⓓ	130. Ⓐ Ⓑ Ⓒ Ⓓ	140. Ⓐ Ⓑ Ⓒ Ⓓ

Part 6: Text Completion

141. Ⓐ Ⓑ Ⓒ Ⓓ	144. Ⓐ Ⓑ Ⓒ Ⓓ	147. Ⓐ Ⓑ Ⓒ Ⓓ	150. Ⓐ Ⓑ Ⓒ Ⓓ
142. Ⓐ Ⓑ Ⓒ Ⓓ	145. Ⓐ Ⓑ Ⓒ Ⓓ	148. Ⓐ Ⓑ Ⓒ Ⓓ	151. Ⓐ Ⓑ Ⓒ Ⓓ
143. Ⓐ Ⓑ Ⓒ Ⓓ	146. Ⓐ Ⓑ Ⓒ Ⓓ	149. Ⓐ Ⓑ Ⓒ Ⓓ	152. Ⓐ Ⓑ Ⓒ Ⓓ

Part 7: Reading Comprehension

153. Ⓐ Ⓑ Ⓒ Ⓓ	165. Ⓐ Ⓑ Ⓒ Ⓓ	177. Ⓐ Ⓑ Ⓒ Ⓓ	189. Ⓐ Ⓑ Ⓒ Ⓓ
154. Ⓐ Ⓑ Ⓒ Ⓓ	166. Ⓐ Ⓑ Ⓒ Ⓓ	178. Ⓐ Ⓑ Ⓒ Ⓓ	190. Ⓐ Ⓑ Ⓒ Ⓓ
155. Ⓐ Ⓑ Ⓒ Ⓓ	167. Ⓐ Ⓑ Ⓒ Ⓓ	179. Ⓐ Ⓑ Ⓒ Ⓓ	191. Ⓐ Ⓑ Ⓒ Ⓓ
156. Ⓐ Ⓑ Ⓒ Ⓓ	168. Ⓐ Ⓑ Ⓒ Ⓓ	180. Ⓐ Ⓑ Ⓒ Ⓓ	192. Ⓐ Ⓑ Ⓒ Ⓓ
157. Ⓐ Ⓑ Ⓒ Ⓓ	169. Ⓐ Ⓑ Ⓒ Ⓓ	181. Ⓐ Ⓑ Ⓒ Ⓓ	193. Ⓐ Ⓑ Ⓒ Ⓓ
158. Ⓐ Ⓑ Ⓒ Ⓓ	170. Ⓐ Ⓑ Ⓒ Ⓓ	182. Ⓐ Ⓑ Ⓒ Ⓓ	194. Ⓐ Ⓑ Ⓒ Ⓓ
159. Ⓐ Ⓑ Ⓒ Ⓓ	171. Ⓐ Ⓑ Ⓒ Ⓓ	183. Ⓐ Ⓑ Ⓒ Ⓓ	195. Ⓐ Ⓑ Ⓒ Ⓓ
160. Ⓐ Ⓑ Ⓒ Ⓓ	172. Ⓐ Ⓑ Ⓒ Ⓓ	184. Ⓐ Ⓑ Ⓒ Ⓓ	196. Ⓐ Ⓑ Ⓒ Ⓓ
161. Ⓐ Ⓑ Ⓒ Ⓓ	173. Ⓐ Ⓑ Ⓒ Ⓓ	185. Ⓐ Ⓑ Ⓒ Ⓓ	197. Ⓐ Ⓑ Ⓒ Ⓓ
162. Ⓐ Ⓑ Ⓒ Ⓓ	174. Ⓐ Ⓑ Ⓒ Ⓓ	186. Ⓐ Ⓑ Ⓒ Ⓓ	198. Ⓐ Ⓑ Ⓒ Ⓓ
163. Ⓐ Ⓑ Ⓒ Ⓓ	175. Ⓐ Ⓑ Ⓒ Ⓓ	187. Ⓐ Ⓑ Ⓒ Ⓓ	199. Ⓐ Ⓑ Ⓒ Ⓓ
164. Ⓐ Ⓑ Ⓒ Ⓓ	176. Ⓐ Ⓑ Ⓒ Ⓓ	188. Ⓐ Ⓑ Ⓒ Ⓓ	200. Ⓐ Ⓑ Ⓒ Ⓓ

Model Test 4

LISTENING COMPREHENSION

In this section of the test, you will have the chance to show how well you understand spoken English. There are four parts to this section, with special directions for each part. You will have approximately 45 minutes to complete the Listening Comprehension sections.

Part 1: Photographs

Track 54

Directions: You will see a photograph. You will hear four statements about the photograph. Choose the statement that most closely matches the photograph and fill in the corresponding oval on your answer sheet.

1.

2.

3.

4.

5.

6. 

7. 

8. 

9. 

10.

Part 2: Question-Response

Directions: You will hear a question and three possible responses. Choose the response that most closely answers the question and fill in the corresponding oval on your answer sheet.

11. Mark your answer on your answer sheet.
12. Mark your answer on your answer sheet.
13. Mark your answer on your answer sheet.
14. Mark your answer on your answer sheet.
15. Mark your answer on your answer sheet.
16. Mark your answer on your answer sheet.
17. Mark your answer on your answer sheet.
18. Mark your answer on your answer sheet.
19. Mark your answer on your answer sheet.
20. Mark your answer on your answer sheet.
21. Mark your answer on your answer sheet.
22. Mark your answer on your answer sheet.
23. Mark your answer on your answer sheet.
24. Mark your answer on your answer sheet.
25. Mark your answer on your answer sheet.
26. Mark your answer on your answer sheet.
27. Mark your answer on your answer sheet.
28. Mark your answer on your answer sheet.
29. Mark your answer on your answer sheet.
30. Mark your answer on your answer sheet.
31. Mark your answer on your answer sheet.
32. Mark your answer on your answer sheet.
33. Mark your answer on your answer sheet.
34. Mark your answer on your answer sheet.
35. Mark your answer on your answer sheet.
36. Mark your answer on your answer sheet.
37. Mark your answer on your answer sheet.
38. Mark your answer on your answer sheet.
39. Mark your answer on your answer sheet.
40. Mark your answer on your answer sheet.

Part 3: Conversations

Directions: You will hear a conversation between two people. You will see three questions on each conversation and four possible answers. Choose the best answer to each question and fill in the corresponding oval on your answer sheet.

41. What time did the man call the woman?
    (A) 2:00
    (B) 7:00
    (C) 8:00
    (D) 10:00

42. Why didn't the woman hear the phone?
    (A) She was out.
    (B) She was singing.
    (C) She was sleeping.
    (D) She was watching TV.

43. Why did the man call the woman?
    (A) To ask her to go to a party
    (B) To ask her to see a movie
    (C) To ask her to go on a walk
    (D) To ask her to help him with work

44. What kind of room does the man want?
    (A) Small
    (B) Quiet
    (C) Large
    (D) Noisy

45. What room does the woman give him?
    (A) 355
    (B) 365
    (C) 517
    (D) 570

46. What will the man do now?
    (A) Put on his sweater
    (B) Swim in the pool
    (C) Have dinner
    (D) Take a rest

47. What is the problem?
    (A) A door is locked.
    (B) A car was stolen.
    (C) An alarm went off.
    (D) A man is lost.

48. Who is Jerry?
    (A) An ambulance driver
    (B) A firefighter
    (C) A thief
    (D) A coworker

49. What will the man do?
    (A) Check the time
    (B) Fix his phone
    (C) Call Jerry
    (D) Take a break

50. What is the man's complaint?
    (A) The tour was too fast.
    (B) They didn't see any paintings.
    (C) His back hurt.
    (D) He didn't like the paintings.

51. What does the woman suggest to the man?
    (A) Take another tour
    (B) Hurry up
    (C) Return to the museum alone
    (D) Get a painting of his own

52. When will the speakers leave the city?
    (A) This afternoon
    (B) Tomorrow afternoon
    (C) Next week
    (D) Next weekend

53. How are the speakers traveling?

(A) By car
(B) By plane
(C) By train
(D) By walking

54. What is the weather like?

(A) Cloudy
(B) Sunny
(C) Rainy
(D) Snowy

55. When will the speakers arrive at their destination?

(A) 2:00
(B) 5:00
(C) 6:00
(D) 9:00

---

56. Why does the man take the train?

(A) Driving is too expensive.
(B) He sometimes needs his car.
(C) The train is faster than driving.
(D) He doesn't like to park in the city.

57. Where does the woman keep her car all day?

(A) At the park
(B) In a garage
(C) On the street
(D) At the train station

58. How much does she pay to keep her car there every day?

(A) $3.00
(B) $4.00
(C) $7.00
(D) $11.00

59. Why is the man disappointed?

(A) The post office is closed.
(B) The post office isn't close.
(C) The post office is hard to find.
(D) The post office is underground.

60. How does the woman recommend getting to the post office?

(A) By car
(B) By bus
(C) By foot
(D) By taxi

61. How long does it take to get to the post office?

(A) Two minutes
(B) Five minutes
(C) Nine minutes
(D) Ten minutes

---

62. Who is the woman talking to?

(A) Her manager
(B) Her assistant
(C) A travel agent
(D) A new employee

63. How often do employees at this company get paid?

(A) Once a week
(B) Twice a week
(C) Once a month
(D) Twice a month

64. What is NOT a benefit of the job?

(A) Individual health insurance
(B) Family health insurance
(C) Life insurance
(D) Vacation time

65. Where are the speakers going?

(A) Home
(B) To the store
(C) To the airport
(D) To the train station

66. What time does the man want to leave?

(A) At noon
(B) At 2:00
(C) At 3:00
(D) At 10:00

67. Why does he want to leave at this time?

(A) He likes to arrive early.
(B) He doesn't like to hurry.
(C) He's afraid traffic will be bad.
(D) He wants to try a new way of getting there.

68. What will the woman drink?

(A) Lemonade
(B) Coffee
(C) Water
(D) Tea

69. Why doesn't she want pie?

(A) She isn't hungry.
(B) The pie is too hot.
(C) She doesn't like pie.
(D) She hasn't had lunch yet.

70. What will the man do?

(A) Have some pie
(B) Bake some buns
(C) Buy some bacon
(D) Make some toast

Part 4: Talks

Track 57

Directions: You will hear a talk given by a single speaker. You will see three questions on each talk, each with four possible answers. Choose the best answer to each question and fill in the corresponding oval on your answer sheet.

71. Who should get on the plane during priority boarding?
    (A) People with connecting flights
    (B) Large groups
    (C) Elderly people
    (D) Airline personnel

72. If someone needs help, who should they ask?
    (A) The security officer
    (B) A flight attendant
    (C) The pilot
    (D) The gate agent

73. What are other passengers asked to do?
    (A) Stand near the door
    (B) Assist the flight attendants
    (C) Make their phone calls now
    (D) Listen for their row number

---

74. What kind of books does this store carry?
    (A) Novels
    (B) Children's books
    (C) Professional books
    (D) Textbooks

75. If the store doesn't have the book in stock, what will it do?
    (A) Refer you to another store
    (B) Look it up in the master list
    (C) Give you a different book at a discount
    (D) Order it

76. What else does this store sell?
    (A) Newspapers
    (B) Carry-alls
    (C) Journals
    (D) CDs

77. When can we expect it to get cloudy?
    (A) In the morning
    (B) In the afternoon
    (C) In the evening
    (D) At night

78. How long will the rain last?
    (A) All weekend
    (B) All day
    (C) All afternoon
    (D) All morning

79. What will the weather be like on Monday?
    (A) Hot
    (B) Cold
    (C) Rainy
    (D) Sunny

---

80. How long do most colds last?
    (A) 1 day
    (B) 1–2 days
    (C) 3 days
    (D) 3–5 days

81. How can you speed recovery?
    (A) Stay warm
    (B) Drink fluids
    (C) Take medication
    (D) Avoid caffeine

82. According to the talk, what is true about colds?
    (A) They are common.
    (B) They are easy to cure.
    (C) They require a lot of tests.
    (D) They rarely affect healthy people.

83. Who should hear this advertisement?

(A) Homemakers
(B) Business people
(C) Mail clerks
(D) Receptionists

84. What does this company provide?

(A) Conference planning
(B) Furniture rentals
(C) Food for business occasions
(D) Maid service

85. What is the largest group size the company can handle?

(A) 200
(B) 400
(C) 500
(D) 800

89. Why are these closings taking place?

(A) It's Sunday.
(B) There is no transportation.
(C) It's a federal holiday.
(D) The weather is bad.

90. What service is the transportation system eliminating for the day?

(A) Rush hour service
(B) Weekend service
(C) Service into the city
(D) Service to recreation areas

91. Where is parking free today?

(A) In public garages
(B) In private garages
(C) On downtown streets
(D) At the bus stations

---

86. Where is this train going?

(A) Into the city
(B) To the hospital
(C) To the business district
(D) To the shopping mall

87. Which subway line goes to the airport?

(A) The gray line
(B) The green line
(C) The red line
(D) The blue line

88. How often do airport trains leave?

(A) Every two minutes
(B) Every five minutes
(C) Every fifteen minutes
(D) Every sixteen minutes

92. Who participated in this survey?

(A) Hotel owners
(B) Secretaries
(C) Housekeepers
(D) Business travelers

93. Where would travelers prefer to have hotels located?

(A) In the business district
(B) Close to parks and museums
(C) Near shopping and entertainment
(D) Beside the airport

94. What additional service should the hotels provide at night?

(A) Access to exercise and recreation rooms
(B) Movies in the rooms
(C) Light snacks in the lobby
(D) Transportation services

95. What does this service do?

(A) Provide visitors with maps
(B) Tell you which buses and subways to take
(C) Sell you tickets for transportation
(D) Tell you what you should see

96. What information is necessary to get help?

(A) Your ticket number
(B) Your budget
(C) How you would like to get there
(D) The day and time of travel

97. What should you have ready by the phone?

(A) An address book
(B) A list of tourist attractions
(C) A pencil and some paper
(D) A guidebook

98. What is the first step in packing?

(A) Get your suitcase
(B) Wash your clothes
(C) Choose your outfits
(D) Check your medicine

99. What should go into the suitcase first?

(A) Underwear
(B) Heavy items
(C) Smaller items
(D) Jeans and slacks

100. What should you use to help airport security?

(A) Travel guides
(B) Light items
(C) Plastic bags
(D) Slip-on shoes

STOP

This is the end of the Listening Comprehension portion of the test. Turn to Part 5 in your test book.

READING

In this section of the test, you will have the chance to show how well you understand written English. There are three parts to this section, with special directions for each part.

YOU WILL HAVE ONE HOUR AND FIFTEEN MINUTES TO COMPLETE PARTS 5, 6, AND 7 OF THE TEST.

Part 5: Incomplete Sentences

Directions: You will see a sentence with a missing word. Four possible answers follow the sentence. Choose the best answer to the question and fill in the corresponding oval on your answer sheet.

101. If the weather is any worse tomorrow, we _________ the client lunch.

(A) canceled
(B) will cancel
(C) have canceled
(D) are canceling

102. We cannot process the order _________ we get a copy of the purchase order.

(A) because
(B) that
(C) until
(D) when

103. Although he met many new people at the party, William was able to _________ all their names.

(A) recall
(B) remind
(C) review
(D) remark

104. After completing the questionnaire, use the _________ envelope to return it to our office.

(A) is enclosed
(B) enclose
(C) enclosing
(D) enclosed

105. When buying a home, a licensed realtor is your best source for _________.

(A) guide
(B) consultant
(C) advice
(D) lawyer

106. Check the delivery service's website to _________ out when the package will be delivered.

(A) bring
(B) find
(C) get
(D) point

107. Because of the drop in oil prices, the cost of our raw materials is expected to _________.

(A) increase
(B) decrease
(C) escalate
(D) even out

108. Using a checklist is an _________ way to make plans.

(A) effective
(B) effect
(C) effectiveness
(D) effectively

109. Lunch has been ordered, __________ the delivery person has not arrived yet.

(A) or
(B) since
(C) because
(D) but

110. It is almost impossible to schedule an appointment with Ms. Grimm at this time of year because she is busy __________ the annual report.

(A) in
(B) for
(C) with
(D) from

111. The head of operations __________ to the convention and will be away from the factory all week long.

(A) going
(B) are going
(C) go
(D) is going

112. Customers can speak with a sales __________ by calling our 1-800 number.

(A) representation
(B) representative
(C) represented
(D) represents

113. Guests can find a telephone directory and a binder with information about local attractions __________ their rooms.

(A) around
(B) below
(C) in
(D) on

114. __________ smoking nor flash photography is allowed inside the museum.

(A) Either
(B) Neither
(C) But
(D) Or

115. As part of her annual evaluation, the supervisor had Ms. Balla __________ down her job responsibilities.

(A) to write
(B) wrote
(C) written
(D) write

116. State law __________ that residents change the address on their driver's license within 30 days of moving.

(A) submits
(B) ignores
(C) mandates
(D) requests

117. Glenda __________ to arrive at work late, but she makes up the time by staying late or working over the weekend.

(A) tends
(B) is scheduled
(C) is supposed
(D) attempts

118. We hope that the new marketing __________ for the county's recycling program will encourage residents to participate.

(A) competence
(B) candidate
(C) collusion
(D) campaign

MODEL TEST 4

119. Mr. and Mrs. Xiao decided to stay at the hotel that ________ travel agent suggested.

(A) their
(B) they
(C) them
(D) they're

120. The YRTL-32 is our most reliable model, mostly because it is hardly every brought in for ________.

(A) despair
(B) compares
(C) impairs
(D) repairs

121. The ________ to get into the building is 4-5-2-6.

(A) reason
(B) method
(C) code
(D) dial

122. Mr. Phelps suggested ________ a committee to research which kind of trucks we should add to our fleet.

(A) formed
(B) forming
(C) form
(D) to form

123. Human resources asks employees ________ one months' notice when leaving their job.

(A) to give
(B) will give
(C) giving
(D) gave

124. This list of contributors is more ________ the one on the computer server.

(A) current
(B) currently
(C) current than
(D) current as

125. Stuart isn't able to use his corporate credit card ________ it was stolen along with his wallet while he was in London.

(A) until
(B) because
(C) although
(D) once

126. The ship's captain requests that all passengers ________ emergency procedures.

(A) reviewing
(B) reviews
(C) review
(D) to review

127. The person ________ lost a briefcase may claim it in the lobby.

(A) whose
(B) which
(C) whom
(D) who

128. This memo about the new schedule is ________ the one you prepared yesterday.

(A) as confusing
(B) confusing as
(C) as confusing as
(D) as confused as

129. Ms. Friel ________ about her promotion before it was announced.

(A) knew
(B) known
(C) is knowing
(D) has known

130. Please ________ me at any time if you have any questions at all about the software.

(A) are calling
(B) call
(C) calls
(D) will call

MODEL TEST 4

131. After the presentation at the staff meeting, the director and I __________ the budget proposal at length.

(A) discussed
(B) mentioned
(C) talked
(D) recount

132. What __________ will changing to a new trucking company have on the contract?

(A) effect
(B) effective
(C) effectively
(D) effectiveness

133. Please confirm that Mr. Dimitri's hotel __________ is for a room with a king-sized bed.

(A) rumination
(B) reservation
(C) trepidation
(D) motivation

134. Our latest advertising package includes videos __________ brochures.

(A) but
(B) or
(C) and
(D) either

135. The merger, __________ will be announced today, should be extremely profitable.

(A) when
(B) whose
(C) it
(D) which

136. The receptionist should ______ a message if a manager does not answer his or her office phone.

(A) take
(B) takes
(C) to take
(D) taking

137. She ______ a file when she lost her Internet connection.

(A) downloaded
(B) is downloading
(C) was downloading
(D) downloads

138. The books __________ by an outside consultant at the end of last year.

(A) were audited
(B) was auditing
(C) audited
(D) audit

139. Content for the company's blog should be written by a ______ writer, not an intern.

(A) struggling
(B) professional
(C) potential
(D) fledgling

140. The IT department works ______ the clock, even over the weekends.

(A) near
(B) beside
(C) outside
(D) around

Part 6: Text Completion

Directions: You will see four passages each with three blanks. Under each blank are four answer options. Choose the word or phrase that best completes the sentence.

Questions 141–143 refer to the following letter.

Modern Tech Inc.
St. No 2, Sector H 1/6, Hunter Complex
Islamabad, Pakistan

April 13th, 20—

Vaqas Mahmood
21, Sharah-e-Iran, Clifton
Karachi, Pakistan

Dear Mr. Mahmood,

Thank you for purchasing the XY40 USB digital speakers. We received your mail-in rebate card this week. Unfortunately, we will not be able to honor it because the rebate offer had already __________ when you mailed it.

141. (A) launched
(B) initiated
(C) expired
(D) transferred

Rebates must be mailed within three days of purchase. However, you sent yours in almost two weeks after your purchase was made. Please understand that we value your business, and in place of the rebate, we would like __________ you a book of

142. (A) to offer
(B) offering
(C) offered
(D) will offer

coupons that can be used toward other Modern Tech, Inc. products. You will find great __________ on many of our products, including our new speaker phone with

143. (A) explanations
(B) discounts
(C) packages
(D) instructions

improved sound quality.

Thank you for choosing Modern Tech, Inc. for all your technology needs.

Sincerely,

Tarik Khan

Tarik Khan
President

MODEL TEST 4

Questions 144–146 refer to the following e-mail.

To: benlivingston@accountantsgroup.ca
Copy: Kyle; Cheryl; Leslie
From: ryanedison@accountantsgroup.ca
Subject: Golf Tournament

Hi Everyone,

I'm starting the planning for the __________ company golf tournament in

144. (A) daily
(B) weekly
(C) monthly
(D) annual

May. I know it's more than two months away, but I wanted to get going early this year. I'd like to get everyone's input, so I am drawing up a list of points to discuss. I will hand it __________ at our next staff meeting so we can go

145. (A) in
(B) out
(C) over
(D) down

over it together. Last year's tournament was a great success. We __________

146. (A) spent
(B) saved
(C) raised
(D) invested

over $7000 for charity. This year we are aiming for $10,000. With your support, we can do it.

Thanks,
Ryan

MODEL TEST 4

Questions 147–149 refer to the following article.

Indoor Air Pollution

New studies on air quality inside office buildings show that the indoor air quality is __________ to human health

147. (A) hazardous
(B) more hazardous
(C) most hazardous
(D) the most hazardous

than the polluted air outside. According to the Committee on the Environment, the air quality in approximately 30% of buildings __________ unsafe.

148. (A) is
(B) are
(C) seem
(D) are becoming

The most common reason for Sick Building Syndrome, a medical condition that has been blamed on poor indoor air quality, is the __________ opening of businesses.

149. (A) premeditated
(B) premature
(C) premium
(D) prevented

When a building opens too early, paint fumes and cleaning products don't have enough time to disperse.

MODEL TEST 4

Questions 150–152 refer to the following announcement.

To: Bill O'Hara
From: Edie Saunders
Subject: Workshop

Bill,

I am trying to finalize plans for next Friday's workshop. Please let me ____________ how

150. (A) know
(B) knows
(C) to know
(D) knowing

many people you expect to attend so that I can know how much food to order. Also, how long do you expect the workshop to last? In addition to lunch, should I order afternoon coffee and snacks ____________? If a workshop goes all day,

151. (A) moreover
(B) instead
(C) furthermore
(D) as well

people usually expect some sort of mid-afternoon refreshment. I also need to know expected numbers so I can decide which conference room to reserve. Conference Room 2 is ____________ than Conference Room 1, but it might not be big enough.

152. (A) pleasant
(B) pleasanter
(C) pleasantly
(D) pleasantest

Please get back to me as soon as possible because I need to take care of this soon. Thanks.

Edie

Part 7: Reading Comprehension

Directions: You will see single and double reading passages followed by several questions. Each question has four answer choices. Choose the best answer to the question and fill in the corresponding oval on your answer sheet.

Questions 153–155 refer to the following announcement.

Trust Line cordially invites you to attend a morning seminar to learn how you can predict the trends that will assist your clients with the success of their investments.

To reserve a seat, fill out the attached card and mail it with your registration fee.

Don't miss this chance to learn about the resources that drive successful fiduciary service management firms.

For further information, please call 676-9980.

153. Who would be likely to attend the seminar?
   (A) A private investor
   (B) A manager in a not-for-profit organization
   (C) A stockbroker
   (D) A newspaper publisher

154. What will be discussed at the seminar?
   (A) Building client relationships
   (B) Fiduciary service management firms
   (C) How to foresee good investments
   (D) How to get new clients

155. How can you join the seminar?
   (A) Present this letter
   (B) Send a short form and payment
   (C) Send your business card and request
   (D) Call 676-9980

Questions 156–159 refer to the following magazine article.

NewTech Equipment Company announced that it expects to cut 4,000 jobs within the next six months in Brazil as part of its strategy to reorganize its money-losing business. NewTech has been struggling to make a profit after two years of losses worldwide.

The reduction in its labor force comes as a surprise to business analysts, who had been impressed with the performance of the company in recent months. Although its revenues have not matched those of its first two years of business, they had been increasing steadily since June.

New competition was blamed for this loss of revenue, but sources close to the company place the blame on the lack of direction from the chairman of the company, Pierre Reinartz. Mr. Reinartz has been with the company for only a year, and he will probably resign soon.

It is expected that Elizabeth Strube, the current V. P. of the company, will succeed him. Ms. Strube was responsible for opening the international offices, which have been more profitable than those in Brazil. NewTech employs about 25,000 people in Brazil, another 20,000 in Asia, and 10,000 in Europe. The international offices will not be affected by the staff reductions.

156. Why will NewTech cut jobs locally?

(A) To be more profitable
(B) Because it is moving overseas
(C) Because labor costs have gone up
(D) Because Chairman Reinartz directed it

157. How long has NewTech been losing money?

(A) Six months
(B) One year
(C) A year and a half
(D) Two years

158. What is the current NewTech chairman likely to do?

(A) Sell the company
(B) Quit his job
(C) Increase profits
(D) Open new offices

159. What describes the international branches of NewTech?

(A) They earn more money than the Brazilian office.
(B) They are less cost-effective.
(C) They are older than the Brazilian branch.
(D) They will be closed within six months.

Questions 160–162 refer to the following schedule.

BUS FARES

		Peak	Off Peak
Effective March 1, 20__	Any one zone	1.00	.75
Peak hours,	Between zones 1 and 2	1.35	1.00
Weekdays 5:30–9:30 A.M.	zones 1 and 3	1.70	1.35
and 3:00–7:00 P.M.	zones 2 and 3	1.35	1.00

160. When do these bus fares take effect?

(A) Immediately
(B) On March 1
(C) On February 28
(D) Next week

161. Which time is off-peak?

(A) 7:00 A.M. Monday
(B) 9:00 A.M. Wednesday
(C) 8:00 P.M. Thursday
(D) 5:00 P.M. Friday

162. What is the peak fare between zones 1 and 3?

(A) $.75
(B) $1.00
(C) $1.35
(D) $1.70

Questions 163–165 refer to the following advertisement.

Leading TV-Advertising

company with broadcast interests worldwide seeks a Specialist in Audience Research. The Specialist will design studies to determine consumer preferences and write reports for use within the company. Candidates must have a college degree with courses in research. Must also have experience in advertising. Outstanding oral, written, and computer skills are necessary. Downtown location. Excellent benefits.

163. What does this job involve?

(A) Making TV commercials
(B) Discovering what consumers like
(C) Advertising products
(D) Testing products

164. Who will use the reports the Specialist writes?

(A) The consumer
(B) The television station
(C) The manufacturers
(D) The TV-advertising company

165. What qualifications should the candidate have?

(A) Education in research and experience in advertising
(B) Experience in television audiences
(C) Ability in accounting
(D) A degree in broadcasting

Questions 166–170 refer to the following report.

Peru is reforming its maritime transportation system. New regulations designed to reduce port costs and increase efficiency have already had encouraging results. Because of these reforms, Peru has established itself as the gateway for exports to Pacific Rim markets like Japan, Korea, and China. These reforms have been in three areas: labor, regulations, and custom clearances.

High labor costs had sabotaged Peru's import and export businesses. Where 80% of all goods had previously been transported by ship, ports in recent years have been moving only half of their capacity. Shipping companies took their business to Chilean ports where costs averaged one-sixth of those of Peru. Reform in this area was needed quickly. Consequently, agreements with port workers now allow shippers and receivers to make their prices competitive with other ports in Latin America. The port workers benefit as well, since many have formed limited partnerships or cooperatives.

Prior to the reforms, 60% of all exports had to be shipped on Peruvian flag-carriers. That regulation has been abolished and has opened the ports to ships from around the world. This increase in traffic has caused dock procedures to be streamlined. Accordingly, customs regulations have become more efficient and commercial processing can be accomplished more quickly.

166. Why were reforms necessary?

(A) The industry was outdated.
(B) Corruption was the norm.
(C) Labor regulations were being violated.
(D) The shipping industry was inefficient and costly.

167. What markets are most important to Peru?

(A) All Latin America
(B) Asian
(C) European
(D) Only Chilean

168. Prior to the reforms, at what percentage capacity did the ports operate?

(A) 20%
(B) 50%
(C) 60%
(D) 80%

169. The word *abolished* in paragraph 3, line 4, is closest in meaning to

(A) passed
(B) stopped
(C) renewed
(D) continued

170. According to the report, why were dock procedures streamlined?

(A) To make them easier to read
(B) To handle increased traffic
(C) To reduce labor costs
(D) To satisfy the dock workers

Questions 171–174 refer to the following fax.

Starling Brothers Investment Firm
145 East 45th Street
New York NY 10019

To: All airline investors
Fm: Alfonso O'Reilly
Broker

BY FAX
Pages: 1 of 1

Stock Alert *Stock Alert* *Stock Alert* *Stock Alert*

Southern Regional Airlines earned $9.8 million in the fourth quarter, compared with a loss of $584.1 million the previous year. The profit was due to reduced costs and an increase in profitable routes. This year, the airline lost $112.4 million in total, compared with a loss of $1 billion last year.

If the present management does not change, we assume that the cost-reduction measures and their choice of routes will continue to have a positive effect on earnings. By eliminating even more routes across the Atlantic, the airline should be able to focus on the short-haul markets where it has built its strong base.

We suggest keeping Southern Regional stock at this time. If there is any change in this forecast, we will advise you.

171. What is the purpose of this notice?
(A) To warn investors of poor stock performance
(B) To suggest a change in management
(C) To explain recent success to investors
(D) To encourage investors to hold on to their stock

172. Why are airline profits up?
(A) New marketing strategies
(B) Lower cost and better routes
(C) Greater ticket sales
(D) Changes in the competition

173. How much did the airline lose this year?
(A) $1 million
(B) $9.8 million
(C) $112.4 million
(D) $1 billion

174. Which routes have been most profitable for the airline?
(A) Cross-Atlantic routes
(B) International routes
(C) Shorter routes
(D) Freight routes

Questions 175–176 refer to the following notice.

The Griffith Hotel

Charleston, South Carolina
803-349-7204

Reservations will be held until 4:00 p.m. unless guaranteed by advance deposit or credit card.

Cancellations must be made 24 hours prior to scheduled arrival in order to avoid the first night's room charge.

175. Why would you guarantee your reservation by credit card?

(A) So you can cancel your room
(B) So you can arrive after 4:00
(C) So you can arrive before 4:00
(D) So you don't have to check in

176. What happens if you do not cancel 24 hours in advance?

(A) You must pay for one night.
(B) You get first choice of rooms.
(C) You can schedule your arrival.
(D) You can get an advance deposit.

Questions 177–180 refer to the following memo.

From: Mazola Sawarani
Sent: Thursday, June 03, 20__ 9:30 A.M.

To: All Employees

Sub: Vacation

Supervisors must approve any and all vacation periods longer than one week. Approval is not automatic. If (1) your absence would create a heavy workload for your team, or cause your team to miss deadlines; (2) you fail to give at least one week's advance notice; (3) there are problems with your job performance; or (4) you have had other frequent absences, your request could be denied. In that case, please contact the Personnel Review Board.

177. What is this memo about?

(A) Work shortage
(B) Vacation time
(C) Sick leave
(D) Starting hours

178. Which of the following vacation periods requires a supervisor's approval?

(A) One hour
(B) One day
(C) One week
(D) One month

179. What might influence a supervisor's decision?

(A) You are a new employee.
(B) You are poorly paid.
(C) You are a team leader.
(D) You often miss work.

180. If approval is not given, the employee can

(A) ask another supervisor
(B) stay at work
(C) take a different vacation
(D) ask the Personnel Review Board

Questions 181–185 refer to the following fax and notice.

FAX

To: Management
From: Unhappy customer
Date: Friday, February 4th

To Whom It May Concern:

I'm sending this complaint by fax because I haven't been able to reach anyone at your company by telephone. I am extremely disappointed with the service that Concord's call center provides. I called yesterday at 10: 30 A.M. for help with my new dishwasher. I was immediately put on hold. I listened to some annoying music for 35 minutes before I finally hung up and called again. The same person, he said his name was Kazuki, told me that he was with another caller and that my call was important to him. If my call was important, someone would have been available to help me.

The worst part is, my call really was important. I had a major flood yesterday after I turned my new dishwasher on, and I couldn't figure out how to get the water to stop running. There is a lot of damage to my kitchen floor. I would appreciate a personal phone call explaining why nobody was available to answer my call. I will not be purchasing from your store in the future.

Suzuki Kana

NOTICE

Date: February 7, 20—
For: Call center employees
Re: Weekly meetings

As of March 1, call center employees will no longer be required to attend weekly Concord staff meetings. The minutes from each meeting will be posted in the staff room for all employees to view after the Thursday morning meetings.

There are two reasons for this change:

1) Our current arrangement of using one employee to cover all ten phones during the meeting hour is not working. We have had numerous complaints from customers saying that they wait up to half an hour to have a call answered on Thursday mornings.

2) We are losing up to $300 in sales every Thursday morning because we don't have all the phones working. Call center representatives generate extra sales while handling help line calls. You are also losing money, because commission is lost when you have to take time out for meetings.

If you have any questions regarding these changes, please contact Itou Saki at manager3@concord.org.

181. Which of the following is NOT true about the caller?

(A) She recently purchased an appliance from Concord.
(B) She was calling for advice about how to clean up a flood.
(C) She was upset with the length of time she waited on the phone.
(D) She disliked the music that played while she was on hold.

182. Why are call center employees no longer required to attend weekly staff meetings?

(A) The content of the meetings is not relevant to them.
(B) They need to be available to answer the help line.
(C) They complained about the frequency of staff meetings.
(D) They are worried about the loss of sales commissions during meeting time.

183. How many people were working the phones when Suzuki called this company?

(A) None
(B) One
(C) Nine
(D) Ten

184. How will call center employees learn about what happened at the weekly meetings?

(A) A memo will be delivered two days later.
(B) There will be one call center representative taking notes.
(C) A summary will be available in the staff room.
(D) Itou Saki will send out an e-mail with the details.

185. How did management handle this complaint?

(A) By putting the customer on hold
(B) By phoning the call center employees
(C) By changing the company procedures
(D) By sending a notice to the customer

MODEL TEST 4

Questions 186–190 refer to the following advertisement and e-mail.

www.busybusinessworkers.com

It's time to take a break, relax, and enjoy some time away from the office. This month we're offering three holiday packages especially for busy business workers like you. May is the best month for travel. While students are busy with their exams, you can enjoy beaches and resorts in peace. Book a vacation this month and receive 25% off the regular price. Packages do not include tax. Cancellation insurance is recommended.

Click on any packages for full details. Prices are per person.
Package A: twelve nights. fivestar hotel in Portugal. includes all meals. $1,650
Package B: five nights. Caribbean Cruise. $1,400
Package C: Angelino's Spa and Golf Getaway. from $600.
Package D: Sorry. No longer available.

Don't wait until the end of the year. Take a break now. You deserve it.

To: manager@marketpro.org
From: francogerard@marketpro.org
Subject: Vacation

Hi Alain,

It looks like I'll be working all weekend to meet this deadline. Milan will help me on Saturday. He'll check my numbers, but I'll still need you to review everything before I submit it because he is so new at his job.

Anyway, the real reason I'm writing is that I'd like to take a vacation soon. I wanted to check the dates with you. I'm looking at the first week of May. I found an ad for 25% off a Caribbean cruise. My wife and I are having our first wedding anniversary so I'd like to surprise her. It will be nice for her to have someone do all of the cooking. Too bad there won't be anywhere to golf, though!

Please let me know if you think it will work out. I would be gone May 2nd through May 8th. I'd love to go for two weeks, but will need to use my other vacation week in the fall when my brother gets married.

Thanks,
Franco

186. Who is the intended audience of this ad?

(A) Golfers
(B) Students on a budget
(C) Travelers on business
(D) Tired business workers

187. According to the ad, when is the best time to travel?

(A) At the beginning of the year
(B) During student exams
(C) While students are on break
(D) At the end of the year

188. What is the total amount Franco will pay for the trip before taxes?

(A) $1,400
(B) $1,650
(C) $2,800
(D) $3,300

189. Who is Milan?

(A) Franco's travel agent
(B) Franco's brother
(C) Franco's manager
(D) Franco's new coworker

190. Why would Franco NOT choose Package A?

(A) He wants to use only one week of his vacation now.
(B) His wife will want to make her own meals.
(C) He wants to receive 25% off his trip.
(D) His wife has specifically requested a cruise.

Questions 191–195 refer to the following two e-mails.

To: Operator 7, Operator 9, Operator 11
Sender: Park Gi
Subject: Recorded names and titles

I have recently discovered that a number of you have reprogrammed your telephones and changed the information on your answering machines. You have replaced the generic title, *systems operator*, with your own name, or worse for at least one of you, a nickname. Not only is this unprofessional, it is against the rules set out in your manual. The original recordings were set up with generic names and titles for a good reason. Your supervisor may ask you to change stations or departments at any time in order for you to learn a new position at the office. New interns will take your desk and the duties that go along with it.

Please refer to page 14 of your manual, which starts, "As temporary employees, you do not have the right to reprogram the telephone on your desk or the settings on your computer."

Thank you,
Park Gi

To: parkgi@financialguide.net
From: student7@financialguide.net
Subject: Answering machines

Dear Mr. Park,

I want to apologize for reprogramming the answering machine at desk 12. After being referred to as Operator 7 several times by repeat customers, I decided to change the recorded name to my own. I don't believe the message I recorded was unprofessional in any way. I simply gave my full name and my title, *student intern*.

I changed the recording because I got a message from a customer who said, "It would be nice to know your name. It feels impersonal to say thank you to a number."

Would you like me to change the message back to a generic one, or do you plan to do this yourself? I know how to do it, but I don't want to break the rule again.

Finally, I didn't realize that we would be moving to other stations, but I look forward to trying new positions. I am enjoying my internship so far.

All the best,
Chong Dae

191. Who was the first e-mail written to?
   (A) All temporary employees
   (B) Three student trainers
   (C) Selected student interns
   (D) All systems operators

192. How does Park Gi suggest interns find out the rules about answering machines?
   (A) By reading their manuals
   (B) By asking their supervisors
   (C) By e-mailing Park Gi
   (D) By talking with other temporary employees

193. What did Chong Dae record on her answering machine?
   (A) Her nickname
   (B) Her telephone number
   (C) Her name and job title
   (D) Her desk number

194. What excuse does Chong use to defend her actions?
   (A) Her own name is easy to pronounce.
   (B) She thought she would be offered full-time work.
   (C) A customer commented on her telephone's recording.
   (D) She didn't read the training package manual.

195. What does Park forget to mention in his e-mail?
   (A) Where the rule for interns was written
   (B) If interns should change the recordings back
   (C) Whether or not interns are temporary employees
   (D) Why the policy was made in the first place

Questions 196–200 refer to the following article and telephone message.

Popular Opera Company in Jeonju
March 7, 20—

The hit ballet *Starfish* had its last performance yesterday; however, the new Encore Theater immediately welcomed another group of performers. The Valley Opera Group, composed of twenty-five members ranging in age from 11–65, is donating all of the profits from tonight's opening performance of *Floria* to the new theater. "We have been waiting for an adequate concert hall to open in Jeonju for more than five years. We are happy to be able to perform here," said director Hwang Chae-ku.

Hwang says the group often donates profits from performances to local charities. "We are in it for the love of music, not to make a profit. Any money we earn goes toward advertising and costumes." Though they sound like professionals, the singers from The Valley Opera Group don't earn a salary. Despite this, it is one of the foremost opera companies in Korea. *Floria* will run through March 30. Tickets for the 60-minute show run from 25, 000 won to 80, 000. Only single seats are available. See the new theater's website: encoreart@korea.net for details.

Telephone Message

For: Lee Chang
From: Kim Arum
Date: March 7, 20—
Time: 8:30 A.M.
Call back: ☑ YES ☐ NO
Message taken by: Park Sun

Arum called. The opera group you like will be performing at the new theater next week. If you want to take some clients to see a show, he can get you a group rate. Also, there is a new Italian restaurant, Antonio's, near the theater. He thinks your clients would really like it. You would need to make a reservation very soon, though. It is a very busy restaurant, and people wait up to two hours to eat there.

I thought I should mention that I ate at that restaurant last week and the service was terribly slow. It took two hours to order and eat our meal. The new theater is really nice, though. I saw the ballet, but I've heard that the opera is even better. Tickets seem expensive for such a short show, so it must be really good. –Sunny

196. What is *Floria*?

(A) An opera company
(B) A ballet
(C) An opera title
(D) A new concert hall

197. Which of the following is true about the Valley Opera Group?

(A) Its members earn a good salary.
(B) It has never played in Jeonju before.
(C) It is only holding one show at the new hall.
(D) Its singers are well respected in Korea.

198. What does Kim not realize?

(A) The ballet is already finished.
(B) The group seating is sold out.
(C) The opera singers are only amateurs.
(D) The opera closes tonight.

199. According to Park, which is true about the new Italian restaurant?

(A) A meal there takes twice as long as the opera.
(B) It doesn't honor its reservations.
(C) It's located just inside the new theater.
(D) The menu is a bit too expensive.

200. What will Park likely suggest if she talks to Lee?

(A) Going to the ballet instead of the opera
(B) Choosing a restaurant other than Antonio's
(C) Calling ahead to book a table
(D) Taking the clients to dinner before the show

STOP

This is the end of the test. If you finish before time is called, you may go back to Parts 5, 6, and 7 and check your work.

ANSWER KEY
Model Test 4

LISTENING COMPREHENSION

Part 1: Photographs

1. **C**	4. **A**	7. **A**	10. **B**
2. **B**	5. **C**	8. **C**	
3. **D**	6. **D**	9. **C**	

Part 2: Question-Response

11. **C**	20. **A**	29. **A**	38. **A**
12. **B**	21. **B**	30. **A**	39. **A**
13. **A**	22. **B**	31. **C**	40. **C**
14. **A**	23. **A**	32. **B**	
15. **B**	24. **B**	33. **A**	
16. **B**	25. **A**	34. **B**	
17. **A**	26. **C**	35. **A**	
18. **C**	27. **A**	36. **C**	
19. **C**	28. **C**	37. **B**	

Part 3: Conversations

41. **B**	49. **C**	57. **B**	65. **C**
42. **D**	50. **A**	58. **D**	66. **C**
43. **A**	51. **C**	59. **B**	67. **C**
44. **B**	52. **D**	60. **B**	68. **D**
45. **C**	53. **A**	61. **B**	69. **A**
46. **D**	54. **B**	62. **D**	70. **A**
47. **C**	55. **C**	63. **D**	
48. **D**	56. **D**	64. **B**	

Part 4: Talks

71. **C**	79. **B**	87. **A**	95. **B**
72. **B**	80. **D**	88. **C**	96. **D**
73. **D**	81. **B**	89. **C**	97. **C**
74. **C**	82. **A**	90. **A**	98. **C**
75. **D**	83. **B**	91. **C**	99. **B**
76. **C**	84. **C**	92. **D**	100. **C**
77. **B**	85. **C**	93. **C**	
78. **A**	86. **D**	94. **A**	

ANSWER KEY
Model Test 4

READING

Part 5: Incomplete Sentences

101. **B**
102. **C**
103. **A**
104. **D**
105. **C**
106. **B**
107. **B**
108. **A**
109. **D**
110. **C**
111. **D**
112. **B**
113. **C**
114. **B**
115. **D**
116. **C**
117. **A**
118. **D**
119. **A**
120. **D**
121. **C**
122. **B**
123. **A**
124. **C**
125. **B**
126. **C**
127. **D**
128. **C**
129. **A**
130. **B**
131. **A**
132. **A**
133. **B**
134. **C**
135. **D**
136. **A**
137. **C**
138. **A**
139. **B**
140. **D**

Part 6: Text Completion

141. **C**
142. **A**
143. **B**
144. **D**
145. **B**
146. **C**
147. **B**
148. **A**
149. **B**
150. **A**
151. **D**
152. **B**

Part 7: Reading Comprehension

153. **C**
154. **C**
155. **B**
156. **A**
157. **D**
158. **B**
159. **A**
160. **B**
161. **C**
162. **D**
163. **B**
164. **D**
165. **A**
166. **D**
167. **B**
168. **B**
169. **B**
170. **B**
171. **D**
172. **B**
173. **C**
174. **C**
175. **B**
176. **A**
177. **B**
178. **D**
179. **D**
180. **D**
181. **B**
182. **B**
183. **B**
184. **C**
185. **C**
186. **D**
187. **B**
188. **C**
189. **D**
190. **A**
191. **C**
192. **A**
193. **C**
194. **C**
195. **B**
196. **C**
197. **D**
198. **B**
199. **A**
200. **B**

TEST SCORE CONVERSION TABLE

Count your correct responses. Match the number of correct responses with the corresponding score from the Test Score Conversion Table (below). Add the two scores together. This is your Total Estimated Test Score. As you practice taking the TOEIC model tests, your scores should improve. Keep track of your Total Estimated Test Scores.

# Correct	Listening Score	Reading Score	# Correct	Listening Score	Reading Score	# Correct	Listening Score	Reading Score	# Correct	Listening Score	Reading Score
0	5	5	26	110	65	51	255	220	76	410	370
1	5	5	27	115	70	52	260	225	77	420	380
2	5	5	28	120	80	53	270	230	78	425	385
3	5	5	29	125	85	54	275	235	79	430	390
4	5	5	30	130	90	55	280	240	80	440	395
5	5	5	31	135	95	56	290	250	81	445	400
6	5	5	32	140	100	57	295	255	82	450	405
7	10	5	33	145	110	58	300	260	83	460	410
8	15	5	34	150	115	59	310	265	84	465	415
9	20	5	35	160	120	60	315	270	85	470	420
10	25	5	36	165	125	61	320	280	86	475	425
11	30	5	37	170	130	62	325	285	87	480	430
12	35	5	38	175	140	63	330	290	88	485	435
13	40	5	39	180	145	64	340	300	89	490	445
14	45	5	40	185	150	65	345	305	90	495	450
15	50	5	41	190	160	66	350	310	91	495	455
16	55	10	42	195	165	67	360	320	92	495	465
17	60	15	43	200	170	68	365	325	93	495	470
18	65	20	44	210	175	69	370	330	94	495	480
19	70	25	45	215	180	70	380	335	95	495	485
20	75	30	46	220	190	71	385	340	96	495	490
21	80	35	47	230	195	72	390	350	97	495	495
22	85	40	48	240	200	73	395	355	98	495	495
23	90	45	49	245	210	74	400	360	99	495	495
24	95	50	50	250	215	75	405	365	100	495	495
25	100	60									

Number of Correct Listening Responses ________ = Listening Score ________

Number of Correct Reading Responses ________ = Reading Score ________

Total Estimated Test Score ________

EXPLANATORY ANSWERS

Listening Comprehension

PART 1: PHOTOGRAPHS

1. **(C)** Choice (C) correctly identifies the location of the table. Choice (A) is incorrect because the lamps are on the wall, not on the table. Choice (B) is incorrect because there is no picture on the wall in the photo. Choice (D) is incorrect because both pillows are on, not next to, the beds.
2. **(B)** Choice (B) correctly identifies the pipeline and its location. Choice (A) is incorrect because the land is hilly or mountainous, not flat. Choice (C) is incorrect because there are no trees in the photo. Choice (D) is incorrect because there is no crack in the tube or pipe.
3. **(D)** Choice (D) identifies the thing, *X rays,* and their location, *behind the doctor.* Choice (A) incorrectly identifies the people and their clothing. Choice (B) confuses related word *examine* and gives an incorrect action. Choice (C) gives the incorrect action and misidentifies the doctor.
4. **(A)** Choice (A) makes assumptions: *it looks like a restaurant,* so *the customers must be holding a menu* and *ordering food.* Choice (B) confuses *reading a menu* and *learning to read.* Choice (C) is incorrect because the waiter has already approached the customer. Choice (D) is incorrect because the guest is ordering, not waiting to order.
5. **(C)** Choice (C) identifies the correct action: A woman is putting a suitcase into the trunk of the car. Choice (A) correctly identifies the luggage but not the woman's location. Choices (B) and (D) correctly identify the bag/baggage, but not the woman's action.
6. **(D)** Choice (D) correctly identifies the condition of the gate—all the doors are shut. Choice (A) correctly identifies the gate, but there is no car in the photo. Choice (B) correctly identifies the lamps, but not their location. Choice (C) relates *gate* with *lock,* but there is no man in the photo.
7. **(A)** Choice (A) correctly describes the man's action. Choice (B) associates *writing* with the pen the man has in his hand, but he is not writing with it. Choice (C) correctly identifies the man's glasses, but he is not adjusting them. Choice (D) uses *chart* as a synonym for *map,* but the man is not rolling it up.
8. **(C)** The delivery person is knocking on a door in order to deliver a package. Choice (A) correctly identifies the boxes, but the man is not opening them. Choice (B) correctly identifies the glass in the doors, but the man is not washing it. Choice (D) correctly identifies the man's action, but not the object he is delivering—he is delivering boxes or packages, not his hat.
9. **(C)** Choice (C) identifies the action *unloading cargo.* Choices (A) and (B) misidentify the cargo (*shopping bags, pillows*). Choice (D) does not match the photo.
10. **(B)** A young man is sitting at a table in a café turning the page in a book that he is reading. Choice (A) confuses similar-sounding words *book* and *cook.* Choice (C) is incorrect because the man's glasses are on the table in front of him. Choice (D) correctly identifies the table, but the man is not wiping it.

PART 2: QUESTION-RESPONSE

11. **(C)** Choice (C) is a logical response to a *Who* question. Choice (A) confuses similar-sounding words *door* and *floor.* Choice (B) relates *door* and *exit.*
12. **(B)** The speakers will use the stairs because the elevator is broken. Choice (A) confuses *spoken* with the similar-sounding word *broken.* Choice (C) repeats the word *elevator.*
13. **(A)** Choice (A) is a logical response to a question about *time.* Choice (B) confuses different meanings *leave* (v) and *leaves* (n). Choice (C) would answer *Where,* but the speaker asks *When.*
14. **(A)** Choice (A) is a logical response to the *yes-no* question about a guest bedroom. Choice (B) repeats the word *guest.* Choice (C) relates *guest bedroom* and *bed.*

15. **(B)** Choice (B) is a logical response to the question about the way to reach, or contact, someone. Choice (A) confuses the usage of the word *reach.* Choice (C) confuses similar-sounding words *reach* and *beach.*
16. **(B)** Choice (B) is a logical response to the question about packing for a camping trip. Choice (A) relates *camping trip* with *light a fire.* Choice (C) relates *camping trip* with *backpack.*
17. **(A)** Choice (A) is a logical response to a question about *weather.* Choice (B) contains the same verb *was* and might be related to *weather* (bad weather causes some people to wear hats), but it does not describe the weather. Choice (B) also confuses similar sounds *weather* and *wearing.* Choice (C) confuses similar sounds *weather* and *wet.*
18. **(C)** Choice (C) is a logical response to a question about *coffee.* Choice (A) confuses similar sounds *coffee* and *cough.* Choice (B) confuses similar sounds *coffee* and *fee.*
19. **(C)** Choice (C) is a logical response to the *yes-no* question about paying a bill—*I took care of it* means *I paid it.* Choice (A), *I opened it,* refers to something you might do with a bill that comes in the mail. Choice (B) confuses similar-sounding words *paid* and *pain.*
20. **(A)** Since the first speaker doesn't want cake, the second speaker offers fruit in its place. Choice (B) associates *baking* with cake. Choice (C) confuses the phrase *buy it* with the similar-sounding word *diet.*
21. **(B)** Choice (B) is a logical response to a question about *time.* Choice (A) confuses related words *time* and *watch.* Choice (C) confuses related words *morning* and *get up.*
22. **(B)** Choice (B) is a logical response to a question about *duration of time.* Choice (A) confuses similar sounds *ride* and *bride* and related words *long* with *tall.* Choice (C) describes *how long the train is* (ten cars), not *how long the ride is* (two hours).
23. **(A)** Choice (A) is a logical response to a question about *occupation.* Choice (B) confuses similar sounds *occupation* and *attention.* Choice (C) confuses similar sounds *occupied* with *occupation.*
24. **(B)** Choice (B) is a logical response to a question about *coming:* Choice (A) confuses *not coming* with *are coming* or *not* (coming) and does not match the subject (*you–he*). Choice (C) confuses *didn't come* with *are coming* or *not* (coming) and does not match subject (*you–they*) or tense.
25. **(A)** Choice (A) is a logical response to a question about *seat location.* Choice (B) confuses similar sounds *sitting* and *city.* Choice (C) confuses similar sounds *sitting* and *sitter.*
26. **(C)** The first speaker wants to take a walk, so the second speaker suggests going to the park. Choice (A) confuses *work* with the similar-sounding word *walk.* Choice (B) confuses *talk* with the similar-sounding word *walk.*
27. **(A)** Choice (A) is a logical response to the question about a relative. Choice (B) confuses similar-sounding words *brother* and *bother.* Choice (D) confuses similar-sounding words *busy* and *isn't he.*
28. **(C)** Choice (C) is a logical response to the negative question about the length of the meeting. Choice (A) confuses similar-sounding words *meeting* and *seating.* Choice (B) confuses the meaning of the word *rather.*
29. **(A)** The second speaker suggests leaving at 6:00 in order to get to the airport on time. Choice (B) associates *plane tickets* with *airport.* Choice (C) confuses *court* with the similar-sounding word *airport.*
30. **(A)** Choice (A) is a logical response to a question about *what color.* Choice (B) confuses similar sounds *hall* and *tall.* Choice (C) confuses related words *paint* and *painting* and similar sounds *wall* with *hall.*
31. **(C)** Choice (C) is a logical response to a question about *Which.* Choice (A) confuses similar sounds *my gray* and *migraine.* Choice (B) confuses similar sounds *tie* and *tried* and *suit* and *do it.*
32. **(B)** Choice (B) is a logical response to the *How* question. Choice (A) repeats the word *visitor.* Choice (C) would be an answer to a *yes-no* question.

33. **(A)** Choice (A) is a logical response to a question about *When*. Choice (B) is incorrect; *finished* (past tense) does not match the tense of the question—*will be finished* (future). Choice (C) is incorrect; *thought* (past tense) does not match the tense of the question—*think* (present tense).

34. **(B)** Choice (B) is a logical response to a question about *not coming with us*. Choice (A) has the related word *go*, but it does not answer *Why*. Choice (C) is incorrect; *didn't come* (past tense) does not match *aren't coming* (present tense) and does not answer *Why*.

35. **(A)** Choice (A) answers the tag question about possession of a key. Choice (B) confuses the meaning of the word *key*. Choice (C) would be a response to a remark about not having a key.

36. **(C)** Choice (C) is a logical response to a tag question about *what page*. Choice (A) answers *when*, not *what page*. Choice (B) confuses *on* with *under* and does not answer *what page*.

37. **(B)** Choice (B) is a logical response to a question about *Where*. Choice (A) confuses similar sounds *wait* and *weigh*. Choice (C) is incorrect; *waited* (past tense) does not match *should wait* (present-future) and answers *How long* (an hour) but not *Where*.

38. **(A)** Choice (A) answers the *How long* question. Choice (B) confuses similar-sounding words *cord* and *card*. Choice (C) would answer a *When* question.

39. **(A)** Choice (A) is a logical response to a question about *sending a memo*. Choice (B) confuses sending with *shipping department* (any department can send and receive memos). Choice (C) confuses related words *departments* with *department store*.

40. **(C)** The second speaker offers to give the first speaker money for the bus. Choice (A) confuses *rush* with the similar-sounding word *bus*. Choice (B) uses the word *change* out of context.

PART 3: CONVERSATIONS

41. **(B)** The man says that he called at 7:00. Choice (A) is the time that the man got home. Choice (C) confuses *eight* with the similar-sounding word *great*. Choice (D) is the time that the woman went to bed.

42. **(D)** The woman says she didn't hear the phone because she had the TV on. Choice (A) is the man's guess. Choice (B) confuses *singing* with the similar-sounding word *ringing*. Choice (C) is what the woman did later on.

43. **(A)** The man says that he wanted to invite the woman to a party. Choice (B) is what the woman was watching on TV. Choice (C) confuses *walk* with the similar-sounding word *work*. Choice (D) repeats the word *work*.

44. **(B)** The man says he prefers a quiet room. Choice (A) describes the room he gets, but it's not the reason he asked for it. Choices (C) and (D) describe the first room he is offered.

45. **(C)** The woman gives him room 517. Choice (A) sounds similar to the number of the first room offered. Choice (B) is the first room offered. Choice (D) sounds similar to the correct answer.

46. **(D)** The man says he wants to get some rest. Choice (A) confuses *sweater* with the similar-sounding word *better*. Choice (B) repeats the word *pool*. Choice (C) is what he will do later.

47. **(C)** The man says he needs someone to turn off the alarm on the emergency exit door. Choice (A) is incorrect because the door was opened. Choice (B) is related to *alarm*. Choice (D) is confused with the fact that they are looking for Jerry, but he isn't lost.

48. **(D)** The speakers are responsible for getting the alarm turned off, and Jerry will help them, so they must all work together. Choices (A) and (B) are related to *accident* and *emergency*. Choice (C) could be a reason for an alarm going off, but it is not the cause here.

49. **(C)** The man says he will try to contact Jerry on his cell phone. Choice (A) repeats the word *time*. Choice (B) repeats the word *phone*. Choice (D) is what Jerry is doing now.

50. **(A)** The man complains that the tour guide was in a hurry. Choice (B) confuses *any* with

the similar-sounding word *many*. Choice (C) uses the word *back* out of context. Choice (D) repeats the word *paintings*.

51. **(C)** The woman suggests that the man go back on his own. Choice (A) repeats the word *tour*. Choice (B) repeats the word *hurry*. Choice (D) uses the word *own* out of context.

52. **(D)** The woman says that they are leaving next weekend. Choice (A) is when the tour took place. Choice (B) repeats the word *afternoon*. Choice (C) sounds similar to the correct answer.

53. **(A)** The speakers are discussing how glad they are that they decided to drive. Choice (B) is incorrect because they say they are glad they decided not to fly. Choice (C) confuses *train* with the similar-sounding word *rain*. Choice (D) confuses *walk* with the similar-sounding word *week*.

54. **(B)** The man mentions the sunny skies. Choice (A) is incorrect because the man says that there are no clouds. Choice (C) is how the weather was last week. Choice (D) confuses *snow* with the similar-sounding word *know*.

55. **(C)** The man says they will get there by 6:00. Choice (A) confuses *two* with the similar-sounding word *too*. Choice (B) confuses *five* with the similar-sounding word *drive*. Choice (D) confuses *nine* with the similar-sounding word *time*.

56. **(D)** The man says that he doesn't like to park in the city. Choice (A) is associated with the fact that the woman pays a lot for parking, but the man doesn't give it as a reason. Choice (B) is the reason the woman drives. Choice (C) repeats the word *train*.

57. **(B)** The woman parks in the garage downstairs. Choice (A) uses the word *park* out of context. Choice (C) is the man's guess. Choice (D) repeats the word *train*.

58. **(D)** The woman says she pays $11.00. Choice (A) confuses *three* with the similar-sounding word *street*. Choice (B) confuses *four* with the similar-sounding word *for*. Choice (C) sounds similar to the correct answer.

59. **(B)** The man was looking for a post office close enough to walk to. Choice (A) confuses *closed* with the similar-sounding word *close*. Choice (C) is incorrect because the woman says *You can't miss it*. Choice (D) confuses *underground* with the similar-sounding word *around*.

60. **(B)** The woman tells the man to take the bus. Choice (A) confuses *car* with the similar-sounding word *far*. Choice (C) is how the man wanted to go. Choice (D) is not mentioned.

61. **(B)** The woman says it takes five minutes. Choice (A) is confused with the number of bus stops. Choice (C) confuses *nine* with the similar-sounding word *time*. Choice (D) confuses *ten* with the similar-sounding word *then*.

62. **(D)** The woman is explaining company benefits to a new employee. Choice (A) repeats the word *manager*. Choice (B) repeats the word *assistant*. Choice (C) associates *travel agent* with *vacation*.

63. **(D)** Employees get paid *every two weeks*, which amounts to twice a month. Choice (A) repeats the word *once*. Choice (B) confuses *twice a week* with *every two weeks*. Choice (C) is what the man says he doesn't prefer.

64. **(B)** There is health insurance for the employee but not for his family. Choices (A), (C), and (D) are all mentioned as job benefits.

65. **(C)** The man says they will leave for the airport. Choice (A) is where they will leave from. Choice (B) confuses *store* with the similar-sounding word *more*. Choice (D) confuses *train* with the similar-sounding word *rain*.

66. **(C)** The man says he wants to leave at 3:00. Choice (A) confuses *noon* with the similar-sounding word *soon*. Choice (B) confuses *two* with the similar-sounding word *too*. Choice (D) confuses *ten* with the similar-sounding word *then*.

67. **(C)** The man mentions the *heavy traffic*. Choice (A) repeats the word *early*. Choice (B) confuses *hurry* with the similar-sounding word *worry*. Choice (D) uses the word *way* out of context.

68. **(D)** The woman says she prefers hot tea. Choice (A) associates *lemonade* with *lemon*. Choice (B) is what the woman says she doesn't

want. Choice (C) is what the man will use to make tea.

69. **(A)** The woman says she had a big lunch and can't eat any more. Choice (B) repeats the word *hot.* Choice (C) is not mentioned. Choice (D) repeats the word *lunch.*

70. **(A)** The man says he'll have a piece of pie. Choice (B) repeats the word *bake* and confuses *buns* with the similar-sounding word *one.* Choice (C) confuses *bacon* with the similar-sounding word *baked.* Choice (D) repeats the word *toast.*

PART 4: TALKS

71. **(C)** *Senior citizens* means *elderly people.* Choices (A), (B), and (D) are not mentioned.

72. **(B)** People may *request assistance from a flight attendant.* Choices (A), (C), and (D) are airline personnel but have other duties.

73. **(D)** The other passengers are asked to stay away from the door until they hear their row numbers called. Choice (A) is the opposite of the correct answer. Choice (B) is confused with *request assistance from a flight attendant.* Choice (C) uses the word *call* out of context.

74. **(C)** This ad is for *professional* books. Choices (A) and (B) would not be sold at such a store. Choice (D) is incorrect; textbooks are for students who are not yet professionals.

75. **(D)** They will *order it.* Choice (A) is unnecessary if they can order it. Choice (B) would not help in getting the book. Choice (C) is not logical.

76. **(C)** The store sells scientific and technical journals. Choice (A) confuses *newspapers* with the similar-sounding word *newest.* Choice (B) confuses *carry-alls* with *carry all.* Choice (D) is not mentioned.

77. **(B)** It says *cloudiness is expected this afternoon.* Choice (A) is contradicted by *this morning will be partly sunny.* Choices (C) and (D) are incorrect; it will already be cloudy by evening and night.

78. **(A)** *Continue through the weekend* means *all weekend.* Choices (B), (C), and (D) are not logical ways to express *all weekend.*

79. **(B)** There will be unusually cold temperatures on Monday. Choice (A) confuses *hot* with the similar-sounding word *not.* Choice (C) is how the weather will be over the weekend. Choice (D) is how the weather is this morning.

80. **(D)** *3–5 days* is explicitly mentioned. Choices (A), (B), and (C) are all shorter periods of time.

81. **(B)** Drink plenty of *water* and *fruit juices,* which are *fluids.* Choices (A), (C), and (D) may help but are not mentioned.

82. **(A)** *Everyone* catches colds during this season, so colds are common. Choice (B) is incorrect because the talk says there is no cure for colds. Choice (C) confuses *tests* with the similar-sounding word *rest.* Choice (D) repeats the word healthy.

83. **(B)** Since the ad concentrates on *meetings,* it is for businesspeople. Choice (A) is incorrect; *homemakers* do not have business meetings. Choices (C) and (D) do not set up business meetings.

84. **(C)** The advertisement discusses *food for business occasions.* Choice (A) confuses *conference planning* and *conference room.* Choices (B) and (D) are not provided by catering companies.

85. **(C)** The largest group size mentioned in the ad is five-hundred. Choice (A) confuses *two* with the similar-sounding word *too.* Choice (B) confuses *four* with the similar-sounding word *for.* Choice (D) confuses *eight* with the similar-sounding word *wait.*

86. **(D)** The subway is *to the shopping mall and suburbs.* Choices (A) and (C) are contradicted by *to the northern suburbs.* Choice (B) is not mentioned.

87. **(A)** The announcement says to catch *the gray line to the airport.* Choice (B) is the current line. Choices (C) and (D) are not mentioned.

88. **(C)** The announcer says that airport trains leave every fifteen minutes. Choices (A) and (B) are confused with *2:05,* the time that the

MODEL TEST 4

next train is due. Choice (D) sounds similar to the correct answer.

89. **(C)** *Things will close* because of *the federal holiday.* Choice (A) is incorrectly suggested by *weekend schedule.* Choice (B) is contradicted by *public transportation will operate.* Choice (D) is not mentioned.
90. **(A)** The announcement says there will be *no additional buses or trains for rush hour service.* Choice (B) is confused with *operate on a weekend schedule.* Choices (C) and (D) are unlikely if transportation follows weekend service.
91. **(C)** The announcer says that parking is free downtown. Choice (A) is incorrect because public garages are closed today. Choice (B) is incorrect because some of them will be charging weekend rates. Choice (D) is associated with *buses.*
92. **(D)** This was a *survey of business travelers.* Choices (A), (B), and (C) do not travel much on business.
93. **(C)** Hotels should be located close to *shopping and entertainment facilities.* Choice (A) is where they don't want hotels located. Choices (B) and (D) are not mentioned.
94. **(A)** *To provide access* means that *facilities should be open.* Choice (B) is not mentioned. Choice (C) confuses *light snacks* and serving *lighter meals.* Choice (D) is not mentioned.
95. **(B)** The service helps people *find their way around the city by public transportation.* Choice (A) is not mentioned. Choice (C) is incorrect; they tell you how to use transportation but do not sell tickets. Choice (D) is incorrect; they tell you how to use transportation but do not tell you what to see.
96. **(D)** You should have the day and time of travel available in order to get help. Choices (A), (B), and (C) are not mentioned.
97. **(C)** The announcement tells you to have *a pencil and paper ready to write down information.* Choice (A) is not needed for this information service. Choices (B) and (D) might give you destinations but are not necessary or mentioned.
98. **(C)** The speaker says, *Select your clothes.* Choice (A) repeats the word *suitcase.* Choice (B) repeats the word *clothes.* Choice (D) repeats the word *medicine.*
99. **(B)** The speaker suggests packing heavier items first. Choices (A), (C), and (D) are other things mentioned by the speaker.
100. **(C)** The speaker suggests that clear plastic bags let security officers see what's inside them. Choices (A) and (B) are other things mentioned by the speaker. Choice (D), shoes, are mentioned, but slip-on shoes are not.

Reading

PART 5: INCOMPLETE SENTENCES

101. **(B)** The present tense in the *if* clause of a real condition can use future tense in the other clause. Choice (A) is past tense. Choice (C) is past perfect tense. Choice (D) is present progressive tense.
102. **(C)** *Until* joins the clauses; it is logical. Choices (A) and (D) are not logical. Choice (B) is used in relative clauses or in time clauses.
103. **(A)** *Recall* means *remember.* Choices (B), (C), and (D) have meanings that don't fit the context.
104. **(D)** Someone else *enclosed* the envelope; use the past participle. Choice (A) has an unnecessary *is.* Choice (B) is the simple form of the verb. Choice (C) is the present participle.
105. **(C)** *Advice* is something a realtor (a professional who helps people buy and sell houses) can provide. Choices (A), (B), and (D) all refer to a person, not something a realtor can provide.
106. **(B)** The phrasal verb *find out* means *learn* or *discover.* Choices (A), (C), and (D) can also be used with *out,* but they have meanings that don't fit the context.
107. **(B)** *Decrease* means *go down.* It is logical to expect that when oil prices drop, or go down, the overall cost of raw materials will also go down. Choices (A) and (C) both mean *go up* or *get bigger.* Choice (D) means *flatten* or *become balanced.*

108. **(A)** The adjective *effective* modifies *way.* Choices (B) and (C) are nouns. Choice (D) is an adverb.

109. **(D)** Join contrasting clauses with *but.* Choices (A), (B), and (C) are not logical.

110. **(C)** The adjective *busy* is generally used with the preposition *with.* Choices (A), (B), and (D) are prepositions, but they are not generally used with *busy.*

111. **(D)** *Head of operations* requires a singular verb. Choice (A) is a gerund. Choice (B) is plural. Choice (C) is the simple form.

112. **(B)** *Representative* is a noun referring to a person. Choice (A) is a noun, but it does not refer to a person. Choices (C) and (D) are verbs.

113. **(C)** *In* means *inside.* Choices (A), (B), and (D) do not fit the context.

114. **(B)** *Neither* pairs with *nor* to refer to a negative choice. Choices (A), (C), and (D) cannot be used with *nor.*

115. **(D)** The causative *had* is followed by the simple form. Choice (A) is the infinitive. Choice (B) is past tense. Choice (C) is the past participle.

116. **(C)** *Mandates* means *demands* and is often used when talking about a law. Choices (A), (B), and (C) have meanings that don't fit the context.

117. **(A)** *Tends* means *has the habit of.* Choices (B), (C), and (D) have meanings that don't fit the context.

118. **(D)** A marketing *campaign* is a planned course of action designed to sell a product. Choices (A), (B), and (C) have meanings that don't fit the context.

119. **(A)** *Their* is a possessive adjective with the antecedent *Mr. and Mrs. Xiao.* Choice (B) is a subject pronoun. Choice (C) is an object pronoun. Choice (D) is a contraction with a subject pronoun.

120. **(D)** *Repairs* is the only noun among the options. Choices (A), (B), and (C) do not fit the context of the sentence.

121. **(C)** In this sentence, a *code* is a set of numbers used to unlock a door. Choices (A), (B), and (D) do not fit the context.

122. **(B)** The causative *suggest* is followed by the gerund. Choice (A) is the past tense. Choice (C) is present tense. Choice (D) is the infinitive.

123. **(A)** The main verb *ask* is followed by an infinitive. Choice (B) is future tense. Choice (C) is a gerund. Choice (D) is past tense.

124. **(C)** The comparative *more* is followed by an adjective and *than.* Choice (A) omits *than.* Choice (B) is an adverb. Choice (D) is an incomplete *as-as* comparison.

125. **(B)** *Because* establishes a cause-and-effect relationship. Choices (A), (C), and (D) are not logical.

126. **(C)** The causative *request* is followed by the simple form of the verb. Choice (A) is the gerund. Choice (B) is the present tense. Choice (D) is the infinitive.

127. **(D)** *Who* refers to the subject *person.* Choice (A) is possessive. Choice (B) refers to things. Choice (C) is objective.

128. **(C)** Equal comparisons use *as* + adjective + *as*; *the memo* is causing people to become confused, so the adjective must be the present participle. Choice (A) omits the second *as.* Choice (B) omits the first *as.* Choice (D) uses the past participle.

129. **(A)** Since *know* happened before *was,* it must also be past tense. Choice (B) is the past participle. Choice (C) is the present progressive tense. Choice (D) is the past perfect tense.

130. **(B)** Commands are in the simple form of the verb. Choice (A) is the present progressive tense. Choice (C) is the present tense. Choice (D) is the future tense.

131. **(A)** *Discussed* means *talked about.* Choice (A) means talk about briefly, not *at length.* Choice (C) needs to be followed by *about* or *over.* Choice (D) means *tell a story.*

132. **(A)** *Effect* is a logical noun. Choice (B) is an adjective. Choice (C) is an adverb. Choice (D) is a noun, but it doesn't fit here.

133. **(B)** *Reservation* is the only noun among the options that matches a hotel context. Choices (A), (C), and (D) do not fit the context of the sentence.

134. **(C)** *And* joins equal terms. Choice (A) implies a contrast. Choice (B) implies a choice. Choice (D) is used with *or.*

135. **(D)** *Which* refers to *merger.* Choice (A) refers to time. Choice (B) is possessive. Choice (C) repeats the subject *merger.*

136. **(A)** *Should* is a modal, and modals are followed by base form. Choice (B) is present tense. Choice (C) is an infinitive. Choice (D) is a gerund.

137. **(C)** This is a past continuous verb that refers to an action that was in progress in the past when it was interrupted by another action. The loss of the Internet connection interrupted the downloading. Choice (A) is simple past, which would make this sentence mean: *First she lost the Internet connection, then she downloaded the file.* That is impossible. Choice (B) is present continuous tense. Choice (D) is simple present tense.

138. **(A)** A passive verb is needed here because the subject, *books,* did not perform the action. Choices (B), (C) and (D) are all active verbs.

139. **(B)** A *professional* writer is trained and experienced, as opposed to an *intern,* who is still learning. Choices (A), (C), and (D) have meanings that don't fit the context.

140. **(D)** *Around the clock* means *24 hours a day.* Choices (B), (C), and (D) cannot be used in this context.

PART 6: TEXT COMPLETION

141. **(C)** The date for using the rebate card had passed; this is the meaning of *expired.* Choices (A), (B), and (D) don't fit the context.

142. **(A)** *Would like* is followed by an infinitive verb. Choice (B) is a gerund. Choice (C) is simple past tense. Choice (D) is a future form.

143. **(B)** The company is sending the customer a page of coupons; coupons are a form of *discount.* Choices (A), (C), and (D) are words that are related to *products,* but they don't have the correct meaning.

144. **(D)** This is probably a yearly, or *annual,* tournament. Since the tournament is two months away, Choices (A), (B), and (C) are not likely.

145. **(B)** *Hand out* means to *distribute* or *give away.* Choice (A) creates a word that means *submit.* Choice (C) creates a word that means *give up possession.* Choice (D) creates a word that means *give away something no longer useful.*

146. **(C)** During the tournament, the company *raised,* or *collected money that it needed* to give to charity. Choices (A), (B), and (D) are all words that are related to money, but they don't fit the context.

147. **(B)** This is a comparison using the word *than,* so an adjective with *more* is needed. Choice (A) is an adjective, but it is not a comparative form. Choices (C) and (D) are superlative adjectives, which are not used with *than.*

148. **(A)** The verb must agree with the singular subject *air quality.* Choices (B), (C), and (D) are verbs that agree with a plural subject.

149. **(B)** Premature means *too early.* Choices (A), (C), and (D) look similar to the correct answer but have very different meanings.

150. **(A)** The verb *let* is followed by the base form of a verb. Choice (B) is simple present tense. Choice (C) is an infinitive. Choice (D) is a gerund.

151. **(D)** *As well* means also. Choices (A) and (C) are used to introduce additional information to a paragraph. Choice (B) means *in place of.*

152. **(B)** The sentence compares Conference Room 2 to Conference Room 1, so a comparative adjective is used. Choice (A) is a simple adjective. Choice (C) is an adverb. Choice (D) is a superlative form.

PART 7: READING COMPREHENSION

153. **(C)** A stockbroker is likely to attend to learn how he/she can better assist clients. Choice (A) is contradicted by *clients.* Choice (B) confuses *manager* and *management firm.* Choice (D) is not likely.

154. **(C)** The seminar will help you learn about how you can predict trends for successful investments. Choices (A) and (B) are mentioned, but they are not what will

be discussed. Choice (D) repeats the word *clients.*

155. **(B)** To reserve a seat, fill out the card and mail it with your registration fee. Choices (A) and (C) are not mentioned. Choice (D) is what you do to get more information.
156. **(A)** New Tech has cut jobs as part of its strategy to reorganize its money-losing business and become more profitable. Choice (B) is incorrect because the international offices are already opened and are more cost-effective. Choices (C) and (D) are not mentioned.
157. **(D)** The company has had *two years of losses.* Choices (A), (B), and (C) are contradicted by *two years.*
158. **(B)** The article states that Mr. Reinartz, the chairman, *will probably resign soon.* Choice (A) is not likely as the article mentions job cuts and the probability of a new chairman. Choice (C) is exactly what the chairman has been unable to do. Choice (D) is confused with the international offices that were opened by the current vice president.
159. **(A)** Ms. Strube has made the international branches more profitable. The other choices are not mentioned in the passage.
160. **(B)** The new fares are *effective March 1.* Choices (A), (C), and (D) are contradicted by *March 1.*
161. **(C)** *8:00 P.M. Thursday* is off-peak. Choices (A), (B), and (D) are peak hours when everyone is traveling to or from work.
162. **(D)** The peak fare is *$1.70.* Choice (A) is the off-peak fare within one zone. Choice (B) is the peak fare within one zone. Choice (C) is the peak fare between zones 1 and 2, the off-peak fare between zones 1 and 3, and the peak fare between zones 2 and 3.
163. **(B)** *Consumer preferences* means *what consumers like.* Choices (A) and (C) are likely uses for this information, but they are not the duties of the Specialist. Choice (D) is incorrect; product testing is a way to discover consumer preferences, but it is not explicitly mentioned.
164. **(D)** The Specialist will write reports *for use within the company.* Choice (A) is incorrect; the reports will be *about* the consumer. Choices (B) and (C) are contradicted by *within the company.*
165. **(A)** The qualifications are *a college degree in research and experience in advertising.* Choice (B) is not logical. Choice (C) is not mentioned. Choice (D) is related, but not necessary.
166. **(D)** The new regulations *reduced port costs* and *increased efficiency.* Choices (A), (B), and (C) are not mentioned.
167. **(B)** The *Pacific Rim* refers to *Asian markets.* Choices (A), (C), and (D) are not mentioned.
168. **(B)** Ports in recent years have been moving only half of their capacity. Choices (A), (C), and (D) refer to other statistics in the passage.
169. **(B)** A regulation was *stopped* in order to help the port run more efficiently. Choices (A), (C), and (D) have the opposite of the correct meaning.
170. **(B)** This is the best choice and is directly stated in the passage: *increase in traffic.* Choices (A), (C), and (D) may be true, but they are not stated in the passages.
171. **(D)** The purpose of this notice is to encourage investors to keep their Southern Regional stock. Choice (A) associates *warning* with *alert.* Choice (B) confuses *suggesting a change in management* and *if present management does not change.* Choice (C) is mentioned, but it is not the purpose of the notice.
172. **(B)** *Reduced costs* and *lowered costs* have the same meaning; they also had a higher number of *profitable routes.* Choices (A), (C), and (D) are not mentioned.
173. **(C)** The airline lost *$112.4 million for all of this year.* Choices (A) and (D) are contradicted by the figure given. Choice (B) is the amount earned in the fourth quarter.
174. **(C)** The fax describes the improved routes as *short-haul markets where it [the airline] has built its strong base.* This means that the company already has many customers on its shorter routes. Choice (A) is the routes the company is cutting out. Choices (B) and (D) are not mentioned.
175. **(B)** Guaranteed arrival allows you to get a room after check-in time. Choice (A) is not

logical. Choice (C) is incorrect; you must arrive before 4:00 if you did *not* guarantee arrival. Choice (D) is incorrect because you still have to check in.

176. **(A)** You must pay for the *first night's room charge.* Choice (B) confuses *first choice* and *first night's charge.* Choices (C) and (D) are not logical.

177. **(B)** The memo is about *vacation time.* Choices (A), (C), and (D) are not mentioned. Also Choice (C) is a different kind of time off.

178. **(D)** The supervisor has to approve *vacation periods longer than one week.* Choices (A), (B), and (C) are one week or less.

179. **(D)** If you have frequent absences, your request could be denied. Choices (A), (B), and (C) are not mentioned.

180. **(D)** The Personnel Review Board can examine the vacation request. Choice (A) is incorrect; supervisors can approve vacations only for their own employees. Choices (B) and (C) may not be possible.

181. **(B)** The caller wanted advice for turning off the water to stop the flood, not for cleaning up. Choice (A) is true because a problem with a new dishwasher was the reason for the call. Choices (C) and (D) are both things the caller mentioned as upsetting her.

182. **(B)** The meeting policy was changed because of problems with handling the help line calls. Choice (A) is not true; the minutes of each meeting will be posted, probably because all employees will want to be able to see them. Choice (C) is also not true. Customers have complained about having to wait to get help but there is no mention of staff members complaining. Choice (D) is mentioned in the memo as a disadvantage of attending meetings, but this comes from management, not from the employees themselves and is mentioned as a side effect, not as the main reason.

183. **(B)** She called on a Thursday morning, which, according to the notice is when staff meetings are held and therefore only one person is available to work the phones. Choice (A) is not true because somebody answered the phone even though they immediately put the caller on hold. Choice (C) is the number of unattended phones. Choice (D) is the number of phones normally in operation.

184. **(C)** The meeting minutes will be posted in the staff room. Choices (A), (B) and (D) are not mentioned.

185. **(C)** The company handled the problem by releasing call center employees from the weekly meetings so that there would be enough people to answer the phones. Choice (A) was a complaint made in the customer's fax. Choice (B) uses words from the texts but is not mentioned. Choice (D) confuses a notice for the customer with the notice for call center employees.

186. **(D)** The ad tells *busy business workers* to take a vacation and relax. Choice (A) is incorrect because only one of the vacations includes golf. Choice (B) is mentioned as people who normally travel at a different time. Choice (C) is incorrect because the ad is about vacations, not business trips.

187. **(B)** While students are in school taking exams, vacation places are quieter. Choice (A) is incorrect because the ad promotes May vacations. Choice (C) is the opposite of the correct answer. Choice (D) is incorrect because the ad says, *Don't wait until the end of the year.*

188. **(C)** Franco will take the Caribbean Cruise, which costs $1400 per person. Choice (A) looks similar to the correct answer. Choice (B) is the cost of the golf vacation. Choice (D) is the cost of the Portugal vacation.

189. **(D)** Milan is Franco's co-worker who will help him with work over the weekend. Choice (A) is associated with booking a vacation. Choice (B) is the person who will get married next fall. Choice (C) is the person to whom the e-mail is addressed.

190. **(A)** This vacation lasts more than a week, and Franco needs to save a week of vacation to go to his brother's wedding. Choice (B) is incorrect because Franco says his wife would like a break from cooking. Choice (C) is incorrect because a discount is offered on all the vacations. Choice (D) is not mentioned.

191. **(C)** The operators are all student interns. Choice (A) is incorrect because the e-mail is addressed to three people only. Choice (B) is incorrect because the operators are interns, or trainees, not trainers. Choice (D) is incorrect because the e-mail is addressed to three operators only.

192. **(A)** Park Gi refers the interns to a page in their manuals that states the rules. Choices (B), (C), and (D) are all people mentioned in the texts, but Park Gi does not refer the interns to them.

193. **(C)** Chong Dae says that she changed the message to include her own name and her job title. Choice (A) is what another intern put on her answering machine. Choice (B) is associated with the *answering machine*, but it is not mentioned. Choice (D) is mentioned, but she didn't put this information on the answering machine.

194. **(C)** Chong Dae changed the recording after a customer said that calling a person by a number instead of a name was impersonal. Choices (A), (B), and (D) are related to the topic, but they are not mentioned.

195. **(B)** Chong Dae says she hasn't changed the recording back to the original one because she wasn't sure if this was allowed. Choice (A) is mentioned; the rule is in the manual. Choice (C) is implied by the wording of the rule in the manual. Choice (D) is explained very clearly—the interns may be asked to move to a new department at any time, leaving their phone and answering machine to be used by another person.

196. **(C)** *Floria* is the name of an opera being performed by the Valley Opera Group. Choice (A) is the Valley Opera Group. Choice (B) is the type of performance that closed at the theater yesterday. Choice (D) is the Encore Theater.

197. **(D)** According to the article, the Valley Opera Group is a leading Korean opera company. Choice (A) is incorrect because the article says that the members don't earn any salary. Choice (B) is incorrect because the company has been wanting a better theater in Jeonju. Choice (C) is incorrect because the show will run from March 7 to March 30.

198. **(B)** Kim offers to get group tickets, but the article says only individual seats are available. Choices (A) and (C) are incorrect because Kim makes no reference to these facts. Choice (D) is not true.

199. **(A)** The opera lasts one hour, and Park's meal at the restaurant took two hours. Choice (B) is not mentioned. Choice (C) is not true; the restaurant is near, not in, the theater. Choice (D) is incorrect because it is the opera tickets, not the restaurant, that are expensive.

200. **(B)** Park clearly didn't like the restaurant. Choice (A) is wrong because she thinks the opera will be very good. Choices (C) and (D) are what Kim suggests.

ANSWER SHEET
New TOEIC—Model Test 5

LISTENING COMPREHENSION

Part 1: Photographs

1. Ⓐ Ⓑ Ⓒ Ⓓ
2. Ⓐ Ⓑ Ⓒ Ⓓ
3. Ⓐ Ⓑ Ⓒ Ⓓ
4. Ⓐ Ⓑ Ⓒ Ⓓ
5. Ⓐ Ⓑ Ⓒ Ⓓ
6. Ⓐ Ⓑ Ⓒ Ⓓ

Part 2: Question-Response

7. Ⓐ Ⓑ Ⓒ Ⓓ
8. Ⓐ Ⓑ Ⓒ Ⓓ
9. Ⓐ Ⓑ Ⓒ Ⓓ
10. Ⓐ Ⓑ Ⓒ Ⓓ
11. Ⓐ Ⓑ Ⓒ Ⓓ
12. Ⓐ Ⓑ Ⓒ Ⓓ
13. Ⓐ Ⓑ Ⓒ Ⓓ
14. Ⓐ Ⓑ Ⓒ Ⓓ
15. Ⓐ Ⓑ Ⓒ Ⓓ
16. Ⓐ Ⓑ Ⓒ Ⓓ
17. Ⓐ Ⓑ Ⓒ Ⓓ
18. Ⓐ Ⓑ Ⓒ Ⓓ
19. Ⓐ Ⓑ Ⓒ Ⓓ
20. Ⓐ Ⓑ Ⓒ Ⓓ
21. Ⓐ Ⓑ Ⓒ Ⓓ
22. Ⓐ Ⓑ Ⓒ Ⓓ
23. Ⓐ Ⓑ Ⓒ Ⓓ
24. Ⓐ Ⓑ Ⓒ Ⓓ
25. Ⓐ Ⓑ Ⓒ Ⓓ
26. Ⓐ Ⓑ Ⓒ Ⓓ
27. Ⓐ Ⓑ Ⓒ Ⓓ
28. Ⓐ Ⓑ Ⓒ Ⓓ
29. Ⓐ Ⓑ Ⓒ Ⓓ
30. Ⓐ Ⓑ Ⓒ Ⓓ
31. Ⓐ Ⓑ Ⓒ Ⓓ

Part 3: Conversations

32. Ⓐ Ⓑ Ⓒ Ⓓ
33. Ⓐ Ⓑ Ⓒ Ⓓ
34. Ⓐ Ⓑ Ⓒ Ⓓ
35. Ⓐ Ⓑ Ⓒ Ⓓ
36. Ⓐ Ⓑ Ⓒ Ⓓ
37. Ⓐ Ⓑ Ⓒ Ⓓ
38. Ⓐ Ⓑ Ⓒ Ⓓ
39. Ⓐ Ⓑ Ⓒ Ⓓ
40. Ⓐ Ⓑ Ⓒ Ⓓ
41. Ⓐ Ⓑ Ⓒ Ⓓ
42. Ⓐ Ⓑ Ⓒ Ⓓ
43. Ⓐ Ⓑ Ⓒ Ⓓ
44. Ⓐ Ⓑ Ⓒ Ⓓ
45. Ⓐ Ⓑ Ⓒ Ⓓ
46. Ⓐ Ⓑ Ⓒ Ⓓ
47. Ⓐ Ⓑ Ⓒ Ⓓ
48. Ⓐ Ⓑ Ⓒ Ⓓ
49. Ⓐ Ⓑ Ⓒ Ⓓ
50. Ⓐ Ⓑ Ⓒ Ⓓ
51. Ⓐ Ⓑ Ⓒ Ⓓ
52. Ⓐ Ⓑ Ⓒ Ⓓ
53. Ⓐ Ⓑ Ⓒ Ⓓ
54. Ⓐ Ⓑ Ⓒ Ⓓ
55. Ⓐ Ⓑ Ⓒ Ⓓ
56. Ⓐ Ⓑ Ⓒ Ⓓ
57. Ⓐ Ⓑ Ⓒ Ⓓ
58. Ⓐ Ⓑ Ⓒ Ⓓ
59. Ⓐ Ⓑ Ⓒ Ⓓ
60. Ⓐ Ⓑ Ⓒ Ⓓ
61. Ⓐ Ⓑ Ⓒ Ⓓ
62. Ⓐ Ⓑ Ⓒ Ⓓ
63. Ⓐ Ⓑ Ⓒ Ⓓ
64. Ⓐ Ⓑ Ⓒ Ⓓ
65. Ⓐ Ⓑ Ⓒ Ⓓ
66. Ⓐ Ⓑ Ⓒ Ⓓ
67. Ⓐ Ⓑ Ⓒ Ⓓ
68. Ⓐ Ⓑ Ⓒ Ⓓ
69. Ⓐ Ⓑ Ⓒ Ⓓ
70. Ⓐ Ⓑ Ⓒ Ⓓ

Part 4: Talks

71. Ⓐ Ⓑ Ⓒ Ⓓ
72. Ⓐ Ⓑ Ⓒ Ⓓ
73. Ⓐ Ⓑ Ⓒ Ⓓ
74. Ⓐ Ⓑ Ⓒ Ⓓ
75. Ⓐ Ⓑ Ⓒ Ⓓ
76. Ⓐ Ⓑ Ⓒ Ⓓ
77. Ⓐ Ⓑ Ⓒ Ⓓ
78. Ⓐ Ⓑ Ⓒ Ⓓ
79. Ⓐ Ⓑ Ⓒ Ⓓ
80. Ⓐ Ⓑ Ⓒ Ⓓ
81. Ⓐ Ⓑ Ⓒ Ⓓ
82. Ⓐ Ⓑ Ⓒ Ⓓ
83. Ⓐ Ⓑ Ⓒ Ⓓ
84. Ⓐ Ⓑ Ⓒ Ⓓ
85. Ⓐ Ⓑ Ⓒ Ⓓ
86. Ⓐ Ⓑ Ⓒ Ⓓ
87. Ⓐ Ⓑ Ⓒ Ⓓ
88. Ⓐ Ⓑ Ⓒ Ⓓ
89. Ⓐ Ⓑ Ⓒ Ⓓ
90. Ⓐ Ⓑ Ⓒ Ⓓ
91. Ⓐ Ⓑ Ⓒ Ⓓ
92. Ⓐ Ⓑ Ⓒ Ⓓ
93. Ⓐ Ⓑ Ⓒ Ⓓ
94. Ⓐ Ⓑ Ⓒ Ⓓ
95. Ⓐ Ⓑ Ⓒ Ⓓ
96. Ⓐ Ⓑ Ⓒ Ⓓ
97. Ⓐ Ⓑ Ⓒ Ⓓ
98. Ⓐ Ⓑ Ⓒ Ⓓ
99. Ⓐ Ⓑ Ⓒ Ⓓ
100. Ⓐ Ⓑ Ⓒ Ⓓ

ANSWER SHEET
New TOEIC—Model Test 5

READING

Part 5: Incomplete Sentences

101. Ⓐ Ⓑ Ⓒ Ⓓ	109. Ⓐ Ⓑ Ⓒ Ⓓ	117. Ⓐ Ⓑ Ⓒ Ⓓ	125. Ⓐ Ⓑ Ⓒ Ⓓ
102. Ⓐ Ⓑ Ⓒ Ⓓ	110. Ⓐ Ⓑ Ⓒ Ⓓ	118. Ⓐ Ⓑ Ⓒ Ⓓ	126. Ⓐ Ⓑ Ⓒ Ⓓ
103. Ⓐ Ⓑ Ⓒ Ⓓ	111. Ⓐ Ⓑ Ⓒ Ⓓ	119. Ⓐ Ⓑ Ⓒ Ⓓ	127. Ⓐ Ⓑ Ⓒ Ⓓ
104. Ⓐ Ⓑ Ⓒ Ⓓ	112. Ⓐ Ⓑ Ⓒ Ⓓ	120. Ⓐ Ⓑ Ⓒ Ⓓ	128. Ⓐ Ⓑ Ⓒ Ⓓ
105. Ⓐ Ⓑ Ⓒ Ⓓ	113. Ⓐ Ⓑ Ⓒ Ⓓ	121. Ⓐ Ⓑ Ⓒ Ⓓ	129. Ⓐ Ⓑ Ⓒ Ⓓ
106. Ⓐ Ⓑ Ⓒ Ⓓ	114. Ⓐ Ⓑ Ⓒ Ⓓ	122. Ⓐ Ⓑ Ⓒ Ⓓ	130. Ⓐ Ⓑ Ⓒ Ⓓ
107. Ⓐ Ⓑ Ⓒ Ⓓ	115. Ⓐ Ⓑ Ⓒ Ⓓ	123. Ⓐ Ⓑ Ⓒ Ⓓ	
108. Ⓐ Ⓑ Ⓒ Ⓓ	116. Ⓐ Ⓑ Ⓒ Ⓓ	124. Ⓐ Ⓑ Ⓒ Ⓓ	

Part 6: Text Completion

131. Ⓐ Ⓑ Ⓒ Ⓓ	135. Ⓐ Ⓑ Ⓒ Ⓓ	139. Ⓐ Ⓑ Ⓒ Ⓓ	143. Ⓐ Ⓑ Ⓒ Ⓓ
132. Ⓐ Ⓑ Ⓒ Ⓓ	136. Ⓐ Ⓑ Ⓒ Ⓓ	140. Ⓐ Ⓑ Ⓒ Ⓓ	144. Ⓐ Ⓑ Ⓒ Ⓓ
133. Ⓐ Ⓑ Ⓒ Ⓓ	137. Ⓐ Ⓑ Ⓒ Ⓓ	141. Ⓐ Ⓑ Ⓒ Ⓓ	145. Ⓐ Ⓑ Ⓒ Ⓓ
134. Ⓐ Ⓑ Ⓒ Ⓓ	138. Ⓐ Ⓑ Ⓒ Ⓓ	142. Ⓐ Ⓑ Ⓒ Ⓓ	146. Ⓐ Ⓑ Ⓒ Ⓓ

Part 7: Reading Comprehension

147. Ⓐ Ⓑ Ⓒ Ⓓ	161. Ⓐ Ⓑ Ⓒ Ⓓ	175. Ⓐ Ⓑ Ⓒ Ⓓ	189. Ⓐ Ⓑ Ⓒ Ⓓ
148. Ⓐ Ⓑ Ⓒ Ⓓ	162. Ⓐ Ⓑ Ⓒ Ⓓ	176. Ⓐ Ⓑ Ⓒ Ⓓ	190. Ⓐ Ⓑ Ⓒ Ⓓ
149. Ⓐ Ⓑ Ⓒ Ⓓ	163. Ⓐ Ⓑ Ⓒ Ⓓ	177. Ⓐ Ⓑ Ⓒ Ⓓ	191. Ⓐ Ⓑ Ⓒ Ⓓ
150. Ⓐ Ⓑ Ⓒ Ⓓ	164. Ⓐ Ⓑ Ⓒ Ⓓ	178. Ⓐ Ⓑ Ⓒ Ⓓ	192. Ⓐ Ⓑ Ⓒ Ⓓ
151. Ⓐ Ⓑ Ⓒ Ⓓ	165. Ⓐ Ⓑ Ⓒ Ⓓ	179. Ⓐ Ⓑ Ⓒ Ⓓ	193. Ⓐ Ⓑ Ⓒ Ⓓ
152. Ⓐ Ⓑ Ⓒ Ⓓ	166. Ⓐ Ⓑ Ⓒ Ⓓ	180. Ⓐ Ⓑ Ⓒ Ⓓ	194. Ⓐ Ⓑ Ⓒ Ⓓ
153. Ⓐ Ⓑ Ⓒ Ⓓ	167. Ⓐ Ⓑ Ⓒ Ⓓ	181. Ⓐ Ⓑ Ⓒ Ⓓ	195. Ⓐ Ⓑ Ⓒ Ⓓ
154. Ⓐ Ⓑ Ⓒ Ⓓ	168. Ⓐ Ⓑ Ⓒ Ⓓ	182. Ⓐ Ⓑ Ⓒ Ⓓ	196. Ⓐ Ⓑ Ⓒ Ⓓ
155. Ⓐ Ⓑ Ⓒ Ⓓ	169. Ⓐ Ⓑ Ⓒ Ⓓ	183. Ⓐ Ⓑ Ⓒ Ⓓ	197. Ⓐ Ⓑ Ⓒ Ⓓ
156. Ⓐ Ⓑ Ⓒ Ⓓ	170. Ⓐ Ⓑ Ⓒ Ⓓ	184. Ⓐ Ⓑ Ⓒ Ⓓ	198. Ⓐ Ⓑ Ⓒ Ⓓ
157. Ⓐ Ⓑ Ⓒ Ⓓ	171. Ⓐ Ⓑ Ⓒ Ⓓ	185. Ⓐ Ⓑ Ⓒ Ⓓ	199. Ⓐ Ⓑ Ⓒ Ⓓ
158. Ⓐ Ⓑ Ⓒ Ⓓ	172. Ⓐ Ⓑ Ⓒ Ⓓ	186. Ⓐ Ⓑ Ⓒ Ⓓ	200. Ⓐ Ⓑ Ⓒ Ⓓ
159. Ⓐ Ⓑ Ⓒ Ⓓ	173. Ⓐ Ⓑ Ⓒ Ⓓ	187. Ⓐ Ⓑ Ⓒ Ⓓ	
160. Ⓐ Ⓑ Ⓒ Ⓓ	174. Ⓐ Ⓑ Ⓒ Ⓓ	188. Ⓐ Ⓑ Ⓒ Ⓓ	

New TOEIC—Model Test 5

LISTENING COMPREHENSION

In this section of the test, you will have the chance to show how well you understand spoken English. There are four parts to this section, with special directions for each part. You will have approximately 45 minutes to complete the Listening Comprehension sections.

Part 1: Photographs

Directions: You will see a photograph. You will hear four statements about the photograph. Choose the statement that most closely matches the photograph and fill in the corresponding oval on your answer sheet.

1.

2.

3.

4.

5.

6.

Part 2: Question-Response

Directions: You will hear a question and three possible responses. Choose the response that most closely answers the question and fill in the corresponding oval on your answer sheet.

7. Mark your answer on your answer sheet.
8. Mark your answer on your answer sheet.
9. Mark your answer on your answer sheet.
10. Mark your answer on your answer sheet.
11. Mark your answer on your answer sheet.
12. Mark your answer on your answer sheet.
13. Mark your answer on your answer sheet.
14. Mark your answer on your answer sheet.
15. Mark your answer on your answer sheet.
16. Mark your answer on your answer sheet.
17. Mark your answer on your answer sheet.
18. Mark your answer on your answer sheet.
19. Mark your answer on your answer sheet.
20. Mark your answer on your answer sheet.
21. Mark your answer on your answer sheet.
22. Mark your answer on your answer sheet.
23. Mark your answer on your answer sheet.
24. Mark your answer on your answer sheet.
25. Mark your answer on your answer sheet.
26. Mark your answer on your answer sheet.
27. Mark your answer on your answer sheet.
28. Mark your answer on your answer sheet.
29. Mark your answer on your answer sheet.
30. Mark your answer on your answer sheet.
31. Mark your answer on your answer sheet.

Part 3: Conversations

Directions: You will hear a conversation between two or more people. You will see three questions on each conversation and four possible answers. Choose the best answer to each question and fill in the corresponding oval on your answer sheet.

32. Why did the man call Mr. Wilson's office?
    (A) To make an appointment
    (B) To cancel an appointment
    (C) To ask for directions
    (D) To speak with Mr. Wilson

33. What does the woman mean when she says, "Nothing easier"?
    (A) The office isn't close to the subway station.
    (B) The streets are pleasant to walk along.
    (C) The directions are difficult to explain.
    (D) The office isn't hard to find.

34. Where is Mr. Wilson's office?
    (A) On Main Street
    (B) On Green Street
    (C) On the corner
    (D) Next to the subway station

---

35. What is the conversation mainly about?
    (A) An apartment
    (B) A plane ticket
    (C) A hotel room
    (D) An office

36. What is the man's problem about?
    (A) The view
    (B) The price
    (C) The size
    (D) The location

37. What does the woman suggest that the man do?
    (A) Call back later
    (B) Choose another date
    (C) Make a payment now
    (D) Look elsewhere

38. What is the purpose of the man's trip?
    (A) To take a vacation
    (B) To attend a meeting
    (C) To go to a job interview
    (D) To see a sports event

39. How is he traveling?
    (A) By plane
    (B) By train
    (C) By car
    (D) By bus

40. What does the woman imply about the man's method of travel?
    (A) It's uncomfortable.
    (B) It's expensive.
    (C) It's boring.
    (D) It's slow.

---

41. Where is the man going tonight?
    (A) To a dinner
    (B) To a party
    (C) To a meeting
    (D) To the office

42. Why doesn't the woman like the suit?
    (A) It isn't clean.
    (B) It is too dark.
    (C) It doesn't fit.
    (D) It has a rip in it.

43. What will the man do next?
    (A) Send the suit to the cleaner's
    (B) Ask for another opinion
    (C) Change into a new suit
    (D) Put on another tie

44. What does the woman invite the man to do?

(A) Take a walk
(B) Go to a play
(C) Play golf
(D) Have lunch

45. When does she want to do it?

(A) Sunday
(B) Monday
(C) Tuesday
(D) Saturday

46. What will the woman do tonight?

(A) Change the meeting time
(B) Visit her friends
(C) Go to bed early
(D) Call the club

---

47. What does the man ask the woman to help with?

(A) Finding a bus schedule
(B) Making photocopies
(C) Finishing a report
(D) Reviewing a record

48. What problem does the man mention?

(A) The photocopier needs replacement.
(B) The office has too few employees.
(C) The woman usually arrives late.
(D) The bus station is too far away.

49. Look at the graphic. What time will the woman get on the bus?

(A) 8:10
(B) 8:30
(C) 8:40
(D) 9:30

Evening Bus Schedule

Lv. Winwood Street	Arr. Berksville
7:10	8:00
7:40	8:30
8:10	9:00
8:40	9:30

---

50. What are the speakers discussing?

(A) A place to meet
(B) A time to meet
(C) A client appointment
(D) The weekly schedule

51. What does the woman mean when she says, "That's no good"?

(A) She can't meet at that time.
(B) The presentation has problems.
(C) She doesn't like her office.
(D) The work is too difficult.

52. What do the men imply about the presentation?

(A) It will be well received by the client.
(B) It will take a long time to prepare.
(C) It is going very well so far.
(D) It has to be finished soon.

---

53. What does the woman want to do?

(A) Buy a new car
(B) Mail a package
(C) Order business cards
(D) Make an appointment

54. What does the man recommend?
(A) Increasing the order
(B) Using only one color
(C) Returning on Tuesday
(D) Consulting an expert

55. What does the woman ask the man to do?
(A) Look up an address
(B) Pick up something
(C) Make a delivery
(D) Call her up

---

56. Who is the woman?
(A) A bank officer
(B) A real estate agent
(C) A financial advisor
(D) A business owner

57. What does the man want to do?
(A) Buy a house
(B) Borrow money
(C) Start a business
(D) Get a credit card

58. What is the man's complaint?
(A) The forms are too long.
(B) The situation is too risky.
(C) He needs more information.
(D) His accountant is not available.

---

59. What is the new parking policy?
(A) Employees can't park in the garage.
(B) Employees are charged a fee to park.
(C) Employees must park in assigned spaces.
(D) Employees aren't allowed to park in the lot.

60. Why do the women like the policy?
(A) Public transportation is quicker.
(B) The parking lot is too crowded.
(C) Traffic is a problem in the city.
(D) They don't like driving.

61. What does the man mean when he says, "This idea isn't going to go over"?
(A) The parking policy won't be popular.
(B) The parking policy won't get city approval.
(C) The parking policy won't be in effect very long.
(D) The parking policy won't be adopted by other companies.

---

62. What is the conversation mainly about?
(A) A luncheon
(B) A trip to Tokyo
(C) A conference
(D) A staff meeting

63. When will Ms. Yamamoto arrive?
(A) At noon
(B) At 4:00
(C) Next week
(D) In a month

64. Look at the graphic. Where will Ms. Yamamoto sit?

(A) Table A
(B) Table B
(C) Table C
(D) Table D

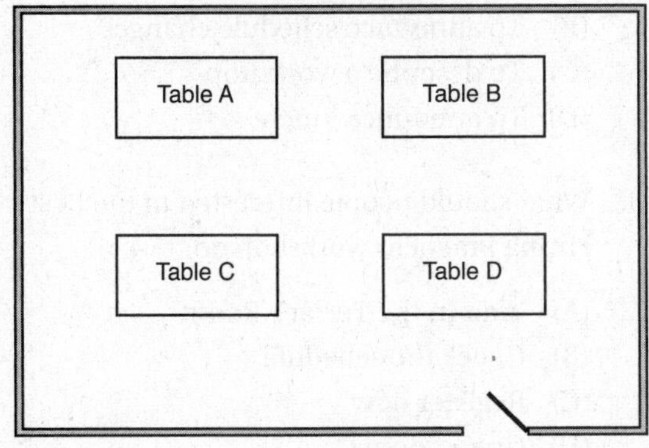

65. What is the woman hiring the man to do?

(A) Rearrange furniture
(B) Clean the office
(C) Paint the walls
(D) Lay a carpet

66. When will the job be done?

(A) This afternoon
(B) Tomorrow
(C) Thursday
(D) Tuesday

67. What will the woman do now?

(A) Check her calendar
(B) Finish her work
(C) Greet a client
(D) Pay the man

68. What is the man looking for?

(A) A new job
(B) A place to live
(C) A business suit
(D) An office to rent

69. What do the speakers imply about the café?

(A) It's too noisy for conversation.
(B) The prices are very high.
(C) The food tastes bad.
(D) It's too far away.

70. What does the man suggest?

(A) Taking a walk
(B) Going to his house
(C) Meeting at his office
(D) Chatting on the phone

Part 4: Talks

Directions: You will hear a talk given by a single speaker. You will see three questions on each talk, each with four possible answers. Choose the best answer to each question and fill in the corresponding oval on your answer sheet.

71. What will the guest speak about?
    (A) Mountain climbing
    (B) Novel writing
    (C) Photography
    (D) Sales

72. How long will the program last?
    (A) 15 minutes
    (B) 50 minutes
    (C) One hour
    (D) One and a half hours

73. What will happen after the program?
    (A) The speaker will read from her book.
    (B) There will be a photography exhibit.
    (C) Refreshments will be served.
    (D) Signs will be removed.

---

74. What was the cause of the delay?
    (A) An accident
    (B) Equipment repair
    (C) Crowds on the train
    (D) Construction in the station

75. What are passengers asked to do now?
    (A) Sit in the boarding area
    (B) Travel with a group
    (C) Buy their tickets
    (D) Line up at the gate

76. Where should passengers put large suitcases?
    (A) At the luggage counter
    (B) At the gate
    (C) In the boarding area
    (D) Under their seats

77. What is the purpose of this talk?
    (A) To explain registration procedures
    (B) To announce schedule changes
    (C) To describe a workshop
    (D) To announce lunch

78. What should people interested in the Best Hiring Practices workshop do?
    (A) Wait in the Terrace Room
    (B) Check the schedule
    (C) Register now
    (D) Go to Room C

79. What does the speaker mean when she says, "I wouldn't miss that event"?
    (A) She plans to be there.
    (B) She wants to go but can't.
    (C) She recommends attending.
    (D) She expects it to be crowded.

---

80. Where would you hear this talk?
    (A) On a tour bus
    (B) At a theater
    (C) At a museum
    (D) In a private home

81. What is everyone asked to do now?
    (A) Save questions for later
    (B) Pay for their tickets
    (C) Stop talking
    (D) Sit down

82. What will happen at noon?
    (A) A talk will be heard.
    (B) Lunch will be served.
    (C) A tour will be given.
    (D) The schedule will be reviewed.

83. What is being advertised?

(A) A school
(B) Bank loans
(C) An employment agency
(D) Financial planning services

84. Who would be interested in this announcement?

(A) Small business owners
(B) Bank employees
(C) Business assistants
(D) Police officers

85. How can someone get more information?

(A) Make a phone call
(B) Visit the office
(C) Take a workshop
(D) Read a brochure

---

86. What is the purpose of this talk?

(A) To organize an event
(B) To choose a location
(C) To get ideas for an event
(D) To decide who will get awards

87. Look at the graphic. When will the speaker arrive at the banquet?

(A) 6:30
(B) 7:30
(C) 8:30
(D) 9:30

Awards Banquet
March 17 – Winchester Hotel

Social hour	*6:30–7:30*
Dinner	*7:30–8:30*
Awards Ceremony	*8:30–9:30*
Music and Dancing	*9:30–11:30*

88. What will happen next?

(A) The speaker will call the hotel.
(B) The guests will receive invitations.
(C) People will volunteer for different jobs.
(D) Someone will check the sound system.

---

89. What does the speaker mean when he says, "Things are finally looking up"?

(A) His predictions are based on research.
(B) Temperatures were higher yesterday.
(C) The condition of the sky is changing.
(D) The bad weather is now improving.

90. What will the weather be like today?

(A) It will be rainy.
(B) It will cool down.
(C) It will get warmer.
(D) It will get cloudier.

91. What does the speaker suggest listeners do on Saturday?

(A) Carry an umbrella in case of rain
(B) Dress for cold temperatures
(C) Go out to enjoy the weather
(D) Notice the spring flowers

---

92. Who is Joe Roberts?

(A) A banker
(B) A doctor
(C) An assistant
(D) An accountant

93. What is the purpose of the message?

(A) To ask for information
(B) To explain a procedure
(C) To make an appointment
(D) To change an appointment

94. What does the speaker want the listener to do?
   (A) Return the call
   (B) Explain some concerns
   (C) Provide an office address
   (D) Submit a financial statement

95. What has been found?
   (A) A large package
   (B) A piece of clothing
   (C) A train ticket
   (D) A blue bag

96. Where was it found?
   (A) On the track
   (B) By a door
   (C) In a waiting room
   (D) Outside the station

97. Look at the graphic. Where is the station manager's office?
   (A) A
   (B) B
   (C) C
   (D) D

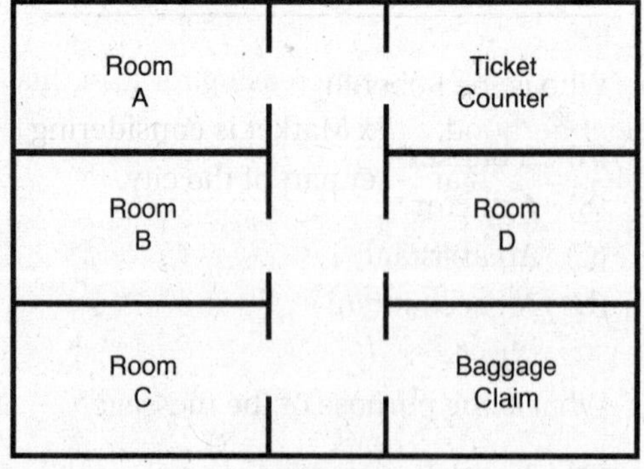

98. Where would you hear this announcement?
   (A) At a farm
   (B) At a bank
   (C) At a clothing store
   (D) At a grocery store

99. How long will the special offer last?
   (A) One day
   (B) Two days
   (C) All week
   (D) Until Tuesday

100. What does the speaker suggest shoppers do?
   (A) Write a check
   (B) Return next week
   (C) Count their change
   (D) Go to the checkout counter

STOP

This is the end of the Listening Comprehension portion of the test. Turn to Part 5 in your test book.

READING COMPREHENSION

In this section of the test, you will have the chance to show how well you understand written English. There are three parts to this section, with special directions for each part.

YOU WILL HAVE ONE HOUR AND FIFTEEN MINUTES TO COMPLETE PARTS 5, 6, AND 7 OF THE TEST.

Part 5: Incomplete Sentences

Directions: You will see a sentence with a missing word. Four possible answers follow the sentence. Choose the best answer to the question and fill in the corresponding oval on your answer sheet.

101. Registration for the computer training workshops _________ the first week of April.

(A) begin
(B) begins
(C) beginning
(D) have begun

102. ColPro, Inc. announced yesterday that Priscilla Perkins has _________ from her position as Chief Financial Officer after fifteen years with the company.

(A) contracted
(B) resigned
(C) dismissed
(D) retreated

103. It is your responsibility to let your supervisor know _________ you will be unable to attend next week's staff meeting.

(A) if
(B) so
(C) then
(D) but

104. I don't plan to _________ my contract with the company next year unless they are willing to discuss a raise.

(A) subscribe
(B) affirm
(C) renew
(D) employ

105. The agreement must _________ by both parties before work on the project can proceed.

(A) sign
(B) signed
(C) to sign
(D) be signed

106. The office manager has decided to buy a new printer for the marketing department and _________ for the front office.

(A) either
(B) any
(C) another
(D) this

107. _________ of the increasing rents in this neighborhood, Apex Market is considering relocating to another part of the city.

(A) Because
(B) Instead
(C) Despite
(D) Due

108. Staff members plan to _________ in the lobby at 5:00 for a small party in honor of Martha's retirement.

(A) join
(B) gather
(C) attend
(D) combine

109. You should always __________ your work carefully before turning it in to your supervisor.

(A) review
(B) reviewing
(C) to review
(D) reviewed

110. The directors are expecting to hear an answer __________ the client before the end of the week.

(A) of
(B) to
(C) from
(D) over

111. A sound __________ in improving manufacturing facilities now will result in increased profits over the next few years.

(A) invest
(B) investor
(C) investiture
(D) investment

112. Rising fuel costs have __________ many companies to seek alternative sources of energy for their facilities.

(A) desired
(B) expected
(C) motivated
(D) generated

113. An ad posted on the company's website resulted __________ hundreds of applicants for the vacant position.

(A) on
(B) in
(C) of
(D) about

114. The low attendance at the business conference last month was __________ due to the bad weather conditions affecting that part of the country.

(A) largely
(B) almost
(C) because
(D) usually

115. According to economic forecasters, a significant increase in transportation costs is __________ to occur in the next quarter.

(A) like
(B) likely
(C) likeable
(D) dislike

116. You should take the time to talk the matter over with your colleagues before __________ a final decision.

(A) make
(B) made
(C) making
(D) had made

117. This is a part-time position, but it requires __________ during evening hours as well as on occasional weekends.

(A) avail
(B) availing
(C) available
(D) availability

118. There is a __________ chance that the company will increase salaries this year, but it is not probable.

(A) slight
(B) normal
(C) good
(D) huge

119. __________ we have hired several new workers at the factory, we are still not able to meet our weekly quotas.

(A) Since
(B) Following
(C) Although
(D) Therefore

120. The board meeting had to be cancelled at the last minute because so few people __________ for it.

(A) turned in
(B) showed up
(C) stood by
(D) took over

121. We will need to __________ in several areas if we want to stay within the budget.

(A) economy
(B) economize
(C) economist
(D) economics

122. We have been assured that the person __________ is giving the workshop is an expert in international finance.

(A) who
(B) whom
(C) whose
(D) which

123. If you accept a job offer from another company, please __________ the personnel director as soon as possible.

(A) signify
(B) testify
(C) notify
(D) dignify

124. Everybody __________ to find out whether an agreement about the new contract has been reached.

(A) have waited
(B) are waiting
(C) is waiting
(D) wait

125. You don't have to accept an initial salary offer because it is almost always __________.

(A) negotiate
(B) negotiation
(C) negotiator
(D) negotiable

126. I would have signed up for that workshop if I __________ it on the schedule.

(A) saw
(B) had seen
(C) would see
(D) would have seen

127. Everyone in the department __________ Mr. Hammersmith was present at last night's awards banquet.

(A) expect
(B) accept
(C) except
(D) accent

128. We chose this photocopier because it is a good deal __________ the one it is replacing.

(A) fast
(B) faster
(C) the fastest
(D) faster than

129. Ms. Soto would like you to call __________ back before 5:00 this afternoon.

(A) her
(B) she
(C) hers
(D) herself

130. We asked the designer to come up with several options so that we could __________ the best one.

(A) select
(B) selective
(C) selectively
(D) selection

Part 6: Text Completion

Directions: You will see four passages each with three blanks. Under each blank are four answer options. Choose the word or phrase that best completes the sentence.

Questions 131–134 refer to the following e-mail.

To: "Stevens, Dan"
From: "Markston, Phil"
Date: June 12
Subject: Changes to Registration Form

We have a problem with our e-mail mailing list. The problem isn't with the list ________,

131. (A) its
(B) it's
(C) itself
(D) its self

but with how people can sign up. Our sign up form is buried so far down on our website that it is impossible to find. We need ________ it easier for people to subscribe.

132. (A) make
(B) to make
(C) making
(D) will make

________________________________.

133. (A) One option might be to move the registration form to the home page.
(B) Most people don't mind taking a few minutes to complete the form.
(C) The number of subscribers is growing faster than we expected.
(D) Our newsletter is enjoying widespread popularity.

While we are making this change, I want to edit the form slightly. There are five questions on the form, and each must be answered to submit the form. I think these should be optional—only ________ name and e-mail address fields should be required to subscribe.

134. (A) a
(B) an
(C) the
(D) this

Let's talk about this tomorrow. Come to my office when you have a moment.

Phil

Questions 135–138 refer to the following notice.

NOTICE TO MOVERS

While picking up and lifting furniture from a client's home to the moving van is often ________ quickest option, I am asking that movers also consider pushing

135. (A) their
(B) her
(C) his
(D) our

furniture when possible. ________________________________.

136. (A) Speed and efficiency are the company's top priorities
(B) This will reduce your risk of injury and save you energy
(C) The ability to lift heavy items is a requirement of this job
(D) We are fully insured for any damage done to a client's property

Please use hand carts to move stacks of boxes and furniture with a ________

137. (A) solid
(B) solidly
(C) solidify
(D) solidity

base. Alternatively, a piece of cardboard can be placed under heavy furniture so that you can more easily slide it along the floor. ________ option you choose,

138. (A) However
(B) Whenever
(C) Whichever
(D) Whomever

remember not to track dirt into a client's home and not to damage the client's valuables.

Questions 139–142 refer to the following letter.

Dear Ms. Thompson,

We have received your job __________ and resume. Thank you for your

139. (A) request
(B) solicitation
(C) application
(D) petition

interest in working with us here at the Amet Corporation. Unfortunately, we do not currently have any __________ positions for which you would

140. (A) vacate
(B) vacant
(C) vacancy
(D) vacated

be qualified. __________, we will keep your information on file and will

141. (A) However
(B) While
(C) As long as
(D) Even though

contact you when a suitable position becomes available.

____.

142. (A) Please call my assistant this week to make an appointment
(B) We are looking for someone with your exact training and background
(C) Job application forms are available on the careers page of our website
(D) If you have not heard from us in six months, you may resubmit your résumé

In the meantime, if you have any questions, please contact Ms. Garcia, our Human Resources Manager.

Again, thank you for your interest.

Sincerely,
Michel Boudreau

Questions 143–146 refer to the following e-mail.

From: Vanessa Holden
To: All department staff
Subject: Away next week
cc: Kyle Rogers

I will be out of the office for all of next week, attending a conference in Rome. During my __________, my assistant, Kyle Rogers, will be handling

143. (A) tenure
(B) absence
(C) pursuit
(D) engagement

all my correspondence. He will also be available __________ with any issues

144. (A) will help
(B) can help
(C) to help
(D) help

that may arise while I am away. I understand that some of you wish to meet with me to discuss your annual evaluation. I will be happy to do this when I __________ from the conference.

145. (A) go over
(B) get back
(C) come up
(D) turn in

____.

146. (A) The evaluations will be ready for your review next week
(B) I plan to do some sightseeing after the conference is over
(C) There will be many worthwhile workshops at the conference
(D) I will be available for appointments the week after I return

Vanessa Holden

Part 7: Reading Comprehension

Directions: You will see single and multiple reading passages followed by several questions. Each question has four answer choices. Choose the best answer to the question and fill in the corresponding oval on your answer sheet.

Questions 147–148 refer to the following advertisement.

ATTENTION JOB SEEKERS

Businesses throughout the region are hiring computer programmers every day.

You could be one of them.

Start a new career as a computer programmer by enrolling in the Computer School at City College.

Complete the program in as little as two years.

Day, evening, and weekend classes are available.

Why wait?

Call now to find out how you can become a computer programmer.

- Open to all high school graduates.
- No previous experience necessary!

147. What is being advertised?

(A) A job opening
(B) A training course
(C) An employment agency
(D) A computer programming business

148. What is a requirement?

(A) A college degree
(B) Computer training
(C) Previous experience
(D) A high school diploma

Questions 149–150 refer to the following text message chain.

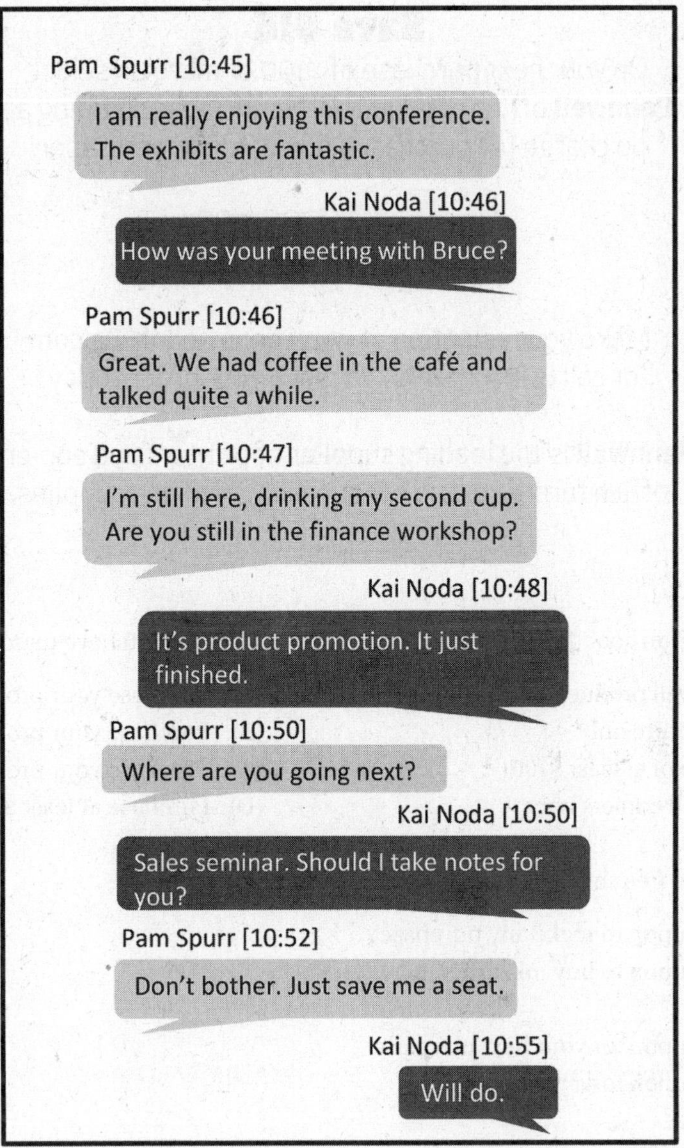

Pam Spurr [10:45]
I am really enjoying this conference. The exhibits are fantastic.
Kai Noda [10:46]
How was your meeting with Bruce?
Pam Spurr [10:46]
Great. We had coffee in the café and talked quite a while.
Pam Spurr [10:47]
I'm still here, drinking my second cup. Are you still in the finance workshop?
Kai Noda [10:48]
It's product promotion. It just finished.
Pam Spurr [10:50]
Where are you going next?
Kai Noda [10:50]
Sales seminar. Should I take notes for you?
Pam Spurr [10:52]
Don't bother. Just save me a seat.
Kai Noda [10:55]
Will do.

149. Where is Ms. Spurr now?

(A) In a meeting
(B) In the café
(C) In a workshop
(D) In the exhibit hall

150. What does Ms. Spurr imply about her plans?

(A) She is on her way to a meeting.
(B) She will wait for her friend in the café.
(C) She is going back to the exhibit hall.
(D) She will attend the Sales Seminar.

NEW TOEIC—MODEL TEST 5

Questions 151–153 refer to the following coupon.

Save $15

On your next purchase of $100 or more on select **Pennwell** office products. Offer includes shipping at no charge for purchases of ink, toner, and paper.

Coupon code: POS97865
Expires April 30

Make your selection at www.pennwelloffice.com or call 800-123-4567 to place your order today.

Pennwell is *the* leading supplier of printers and copiers, office furniture, and other essential office supplies.

151. What is the coupon good for?
   (A) Any Pennwell product
   (B) Office furniture only
   (C) A purchase of at least $100
   (D) Printers and copiers only

152. How can you get free shipping?
   (A) Use the coupon to make any purchase
   (B) Use the coupon to buy ink, toner, or paper
   (C) Use the coupon for your next purchase
   (D) Use the coupon for a printer or photocopier

153. What do you have to do to get the discount?
   (A) Purchase your products by April 30
   (B) Purchase your products on online
   (C) Purchase your products by phone
   (D) Purchase at least $15 worth of products

Questions 154–156 refer to the following form.

Dorchester Towers
Tenant Application

Name Howard Danes

Address 113 Fordham Road
Winesburg, OH

Apartment type

____ studio X one-bedroom ____ two-bedroom ____ three-bedroom

Number of occupants 2

Desired move-in date November 15

Application fee	$100
First month's rent*	$800
Security deposit	$600
Total due on signing of lease	$1500

All apartments will be cleaned, repainted, and re-carpeted prior to move in. Return of security deposit upon termination of the lease is contingent upon an apartment inspection. Questions and repair requests should be directed by phone or e-mail to the building manager:

Michael Lee
548-9982
michaell@redbird.com

*Rent does not include parking. A limited number of parking spaces are available in the garage for a fee. Please contact the manager for further information.

154. What is this purpose of this form?
(A) To ask for repairs
(B) To make a payment
(C) To request an apartment
(D) To give notification of lease termination

155. What is the monthly rent for a one-bedroom apartment?
(A) $100
(B) $600
(C) $800
(D) $1500

156. What is included with all apartments?
(A) A parking space
(B) A repair
(C) A phone
(D) A new carpet

Questions 157–159 refer to the following invoice.

Invoice

SMITHFIELD KITCHEN SUPPLIES

Supplying restaurants and offices for over 50 years!

Order # 40291 Date: April 10

Your customer service representative: Pamela Jones
Thank you for your order. Please keep this invoice for your records.

Ship to:
Mark Gillman
Park House Restaurant
85 South Street
Greensboro, NH

Bill to:
The Hubert Restaurant Group
Attn: Rita Spofford
74 Belt Avenue
Hudson, MA

Payment due upon receipt of order

157. Who will pay the invoice?
   (A) Mark Gillman
   (B) Pamela Jones
   (C) Park House Restaurant
   (D) The Hubert Restaurant Group

158. What is the $20 charge for?
   (A) Holiday and weekend delivery
   (B) Sending the order quickly
   (C) Shipping heavy items
   (D) Special packaging

159. When should the invoice be paid?
   (A) By the date on the invoice
   (B) When the order is made
   (C) When the order is delivered
   (D) Before the end of the month

Questions 160–162 refer to the following webpage.

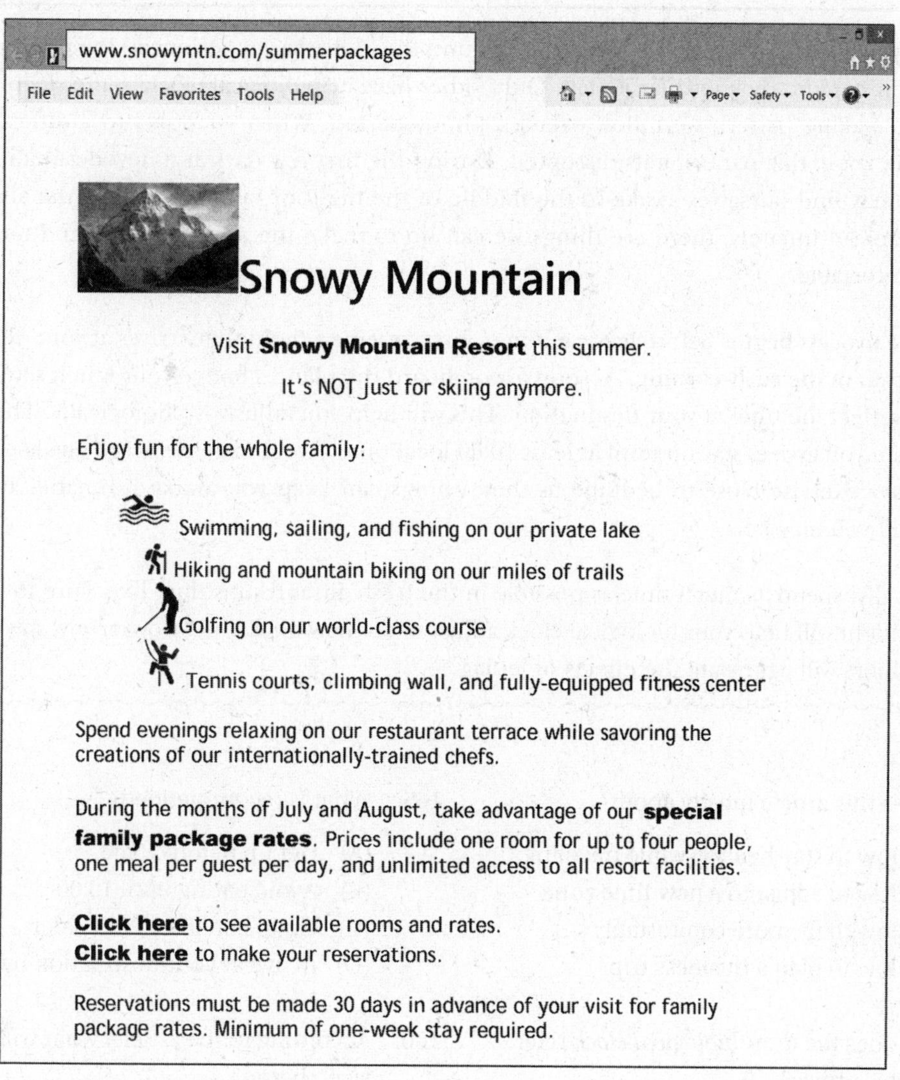

www.snowymtn.com/summerpackages

File Edit View Favorites Tools Help

Snowy Mountain

Visit **Snowy Mountain Resort** this summer.

It's NOT just for skiing anymore.

Enjoy fun for the whole family:

- Swimming, sailing, and fishing on our private lake
- Hiking and mountain biking on our miles of trails
- Golfing on our world-class course
- Tennis courts, climbing wall, and fully-equipped fitness center

Spend evenings relaxing on our restaurant terrace while savoring the creations of our internationally-trained chefs.

During the months of July and August, take advantage of our **special family package rates**. Prices include one room for up to four people, one meal per guest per day, and unlimited access to all resort facilities.

Click here to see available rooms and rates.
Click here to make your reservations.

Reservations must be made 30 days in advance of your visit for family package rates. Minimum of one-week stay required.

160. What is suggested about Snowy Mountain Resort?

(A) It is known as a ski resort.
(B) It is only open in the summer.
(C) It has luxurious accommodations.
(D) It is less expensive than other resorts.

161. Which of the following is NOT mentioned as a resort activity?

(A) Dining
(B) Cycling
(C) Water sports
(D) Horseback riding

162. When must reservations be made to get the special rate?

(A) A week ahead of time
(B) A month ahead of time
(C) In July or August
(D) Any time

Questions 163–166 refer to the following article.

Any business person who has traveled around the globe has experienced the phenomenon commonly known as jet lag. Our bodies have a "biological clock"—the sleeping and waking pattern we follow over a 24-hour period. When we travel to a different time zone, this pattern gets disrupted. During the first few days at a new destination, we may find ourselves awake in the middle of the night or falling asleep in the afternoon. Fortunately, there are things we can do to make the adjustment period more comfortable.

The process begins before leaving home. First, reserve a flight that arrives at your destination in the early evening. As soon as you board the plane, change your watch setting to reflect the time at your destination. This will help you adjust psychologically. Then, when you arrive, stay up until at least 10:00 local time. Avoid caffeine, large meals, and heavy exercise close to bedtime as these things can keep you awake no matter how tired you may be.

Finally, spend as much time as possible in the fresh air and sunshine. Exposure to the sunlight will help your biological clock adjust to the new time zone. Conversely, staying indoors will aggravate the effects of jet lag.

163. What is this article mostly about?

(A) How to stay healthy while traveling
(B) How to adjust to a new time zone
(C) How to fly more comfortably
(D) How to plan a business trip

164. What does the term *biological clock* refer to in this article?

(A) A special watch for travelers
(B) The body's usual sleep schedule
(C) A clock that shows 24 hours
(D) The natural aging process

165. What is recommended?

(A) Get up before 10:00
(B) Avoid eating until 10:00
(C) Go to bed at 10:00 or later
(D) Arrive at your destination by 10:00

166. According to the article, what will help you sleep better?

(A) Going outside
(B) Avoiding the sun
(C) Getting enough exercise
(D) Adjusting your mealtimes

Questions 167–170 refer to the following letter.

ROGERS, MILTON, & COLE, PC
17 Willow Avenue
Moltonsburgh

May 10, 20—

To Whom It May Concern:

This is a letter regarding Ms. Amelia Spark, a former employee at Rogers, Milton, & Cole, PC. Ms. Spark began with our company as an intern soon after she graduated from university. At the end of her internship, we hired her on as a full-time legal assistant. [1] At the same time, she continued to take classes at the university, I understand with the goal of eventually going for an advanced degree. [2]

As well as being reliable and hardworking, we could always count on Ms. Sparks to be pleasant and helpful to everyone in the office. [3] These characteristics were especially helpful in Ms. Spark's dealings with clients. In fact, clients often specifically asked to work with her. [4]

We were sorry to lose Ms. Spark when she left us last month, but wish her much success with her decision to move to New York and in all her future professional endeavors. We know she will be a great asset to any firm she works with. Please don't hesitate to contact me if you require any further information.

Sincerely,

Stephen Cole

Stephen Cole

167. What will Ms. Spark use this letter for?

(A) To hire someone
(B) To get a new a job
(C) To get new clients
(D) To apply to university

168. What profession does Ms. Spark work in?

(A) Law
(B) Education
(C) Accounting
(D) Business

169. Why did Ms. Spark leave her job?

(A) She was fired.
(B) She became ill.
(C) She moved to a new city.
(D) She returned to school.

170. In which of the following positions marked [1], [2], [3], and [4] does the following sentence best belong?

"She worked diligently at that job, proving herself always eager to learn and willing to put in whatever time and effort a project required."

(A) [1]
(B) [2]
(C) [3]
(D) [4]

Questions 171–175 are based on the following article.

The Rockville Development Group (RDG) announced today a proposal for a mixed-use complex on the outskirts of Bingchester, close to Highway 10. The proposed complex includes 1,000 square meters of office space, 50,000 square meters of retail space, a parking garage, and several hectares of outdoor parking.

The announcement got a mixed reception. Bingchester City Council members hailed it as a boost to the local economy. "It will bring jobs. People will come here to spend money. What could be better?" proclaimed Council Member Miriam Hodges. But local business owners had a different opinion. "Its location can only hurt our businesses," said Bill Smithers, president of the Bingchester Business Owner's Association. "Look at the distance from the downtown shopping district. People driving down Highway 10 may stop at the mall, but they won't then drive the extra mile to spend money at our local shops." Environmental groups also expressed opposition to the proposal. "In addition to destroying acres of valuable agricultural land, water run-off from the pavement will dirty our local streams and rivers and damage natural habitats."

A spokesperson for RDG dismissed the opposition, saying, "This development has been five years in the planning. We have received all the necessary permits and are closely following government regulations. When it is completed, this project will be one of Bingchester's greatest assets. We expect to break ground before the end of the year." Construction will take close to two years to complete.

171. What is this article mostly about?

(A) Local business regulations
(B) The grand opening of a mall
(C) A plan to build stores and offices
(D) The revival of a downtown shopping district

172. The word *boost* in paragraph 2, line 2 is closest in meaning to

(A) problem
(B) explanation
(C) reflection
(D) improvement

173. What is a complaint about the project?

(A) It is too big.
(B) It harms farm land.
(C) It is too close to downtown.
(D) It will create parking problems.

174. Who is Miriam Hodges?

(A) A politician
(B) A shopper
(C) A builder
(D) A retailer

175. When will work on the project begin?

(A) By December 31
(B) Next January
(C) In two years
(D) In five years

Questions 176–180 refer to the following e-mail and survey.

To: Elizabeth Simons
From: Rosemount Hotel
Subject: Guest Satisfaction Survey

Dear Ms. Simons,

Thank you for choosing the Rosemount Hotel during your recent visit to Springfield.

Please visit the Internet link below. It will take you to our Guest Satisfaction Survey. We appreciate the time you take to fill out this survey as it enables us to provide you with the best possible experience at the Rosemount. Please follow this link to take the survey. We are sorry but we are unable to respond directly to feedback as the survey is conducted by a third party.

We hope your stay at the Rosemount was pleasant, and that we will see you here again soon.
For billing or future stay assistance, please contact the following:
Billing inquiries—Mr. Perez: rperez@rosemounthotel.com
Future stay inquiries—Ms. Lee: klee@rosemounthotel.com

If you wish to opt out of future e-mails from the Rosemount Hotel, please follow this link to be removed from our list.

Again, thank you.

Harold Custer for the Rosemount Hotel

Rosemount Hotel
Guest Satisfaction Survey

Please rate the hotel staff:

Please rate your room:

Please rate the fitness center:*

If you experienced any problems during your stay, please explain:

I had to wait several minutes before someone was available to check me in. Then, the clerk had problems with the credit card machine. One other thing, I tried to use the fitness center, but by the time I got there (10:00 PM), it was closed.

Comments:

I thoroughly enjoyed my stay at the Rosemount. I was here this time for a client meeting but hope to return soon with my family for some sightseeing.

Your name: Elizabeth Simons

Date of stay: April 10–11

*Please leave this section blank if you did not visit our fitness center.

176. What is the purpose of the e-mail?

(A) To ask for feedback
(B) To explain a bill
(C) To advertise the hotel
(D) To confirm a reservation

177. Why should someone contact Ms. Lee?

(A) To ask about a bill
(B) To submit a survey
(C) To make a hotel reservation
(D) To be removed from the e-mail list

178. What problem did Ms. Simons have with the hotel?

(A) The room cost
(B) The comfort of the bed
(C) The cleanliness of the room
(D) The registration process

179. Why didn't Ms. Simons use the fitness center?

(A) It was closed.
(B) It wasn't clean.
(C) She never exercises.
(D) The equipment was in poor condition.

180. What was the purpose of Ms. Simons' trip to Springfield?

(A) A family visit
(B) A business meeting
(C) A sightseeing tour
(D) A conference

Questions 181–185 refer to the following schedule and e-mail.

BOA
TENTH ANNUAL CONFERENCE
HALISTON HOTEL

SCHEDULE

8:30–9:45	CONTINENTAL BREAKFAST (MAIN LOBBY)
10:00 – 12:00	WORKSHOP SESSION 1 A: FINANCING YOUR BUSINESS (GARDEN ROOM) B: MARKETING IN THE DIGITAL AGE (ROOM 3)
12:15–1:15	LUNCH (DINING ROOM)
1:30–3:30	WORKSHOP SESSION 2 C: SMALL BUSINESS HIRING PRACTICES (ROOM 2) D: TRAINING YOUR PERSONNEL (MEZZANINE)
4:00–5:00	SOCIAL HOUR (MAIN LOBBY)

To: Bob Schumacher
From: Anne Kemp
Date: November 10
Subject: BOA Conference

Hi Bob,

I am attaching the conference schedule as you requested. I am really looking forward to it, especially since this is the first year I will be attending without being a presenter. Without that pressure, I will really have a chance to enjoy everything the conference has to offer.

I hope we can get together sometime during the day. I'd like to take the opportunity to discuss with you a loan I hope to get for expanding my business. I would really appreciate your advice on this matter as you have so much experience in this area and with the particular lender I hope to work with. Also I know you are active in the local Finance Educators Association and could perhaps point me to further resources. I plan to attend workshops A and C. I don't know whether you will be at either one of those, but we should make another time to get together to really have a chance to talk. I have a meeting with a colleague at noon, so I won't be at the conference lunch, but what about the social hour? Let's plan to look for each other there.

Anne

181. Who is this conference for?
   - (A) Marketing specialists
   - (B) Business owners
   - (C) Personnel managers
   - (D) Money lenders

182. Why did Ms. Kemp write the e-mail to Mr. Schumacher?
   - (A) To invite him to go to the conference
   - (B) To tell him about a workshop she will present
   - (C) To make plans to meet with him
   - (D) To suggest which workshops he should attend

183. Where will Ms. Kemp be at 1:30?
   - (A) Main lobby
   - (B) Dining room
   - (C) Room 2
   - (D) Mezzanine

184. In the e-mail, the word *active* in paragraph 2, line 4, is closest in meaning to
   - (A) busy
   - (B) ready
   - (C) energetic
   - (D) involved

185. What does Ms. Kemp want to discuss with Mr. Schumacher?
   - (A) Borrowing money
   - (B) Presenting a workshop
   - (C) Organizing the conference
   - (D) Arranging a social hour

Questions 186–190 refer to the following schedule, newspaper announcement, and e-mail.

Torryton 150th Annual National Day Celebration
Schedule of Events
Saturday

CRAFTS FAIR
Time: All Day **Location: Torryton Park, Oak Walk**
Enjoy the shade of our city's famous old oak trees as you shop for hand-made items by local, national, and international crafters.

HISTORY EXHIBITS
Time: 10 AM–7 PM **Location: History Museum**
Bring the whole family to see special National Day exhibits, inside the newly renovated History Museum. Special activities for the little ones include craft making and a film.

INTERNATIONAL FOOD FESTIVAL
Time: Noon–8 PM **Location: Main and Maple Sts.**
Sample delights from all around the world as you stroll along the sidewalks of Main and Maple Streets.

SOCCER GAME
Time: 6 PM **Location: Torryton High School Soccer Field**
Watch local teams compete for the coveted National Day Trophy.

CONCERT
Time: 8:30 PM **Location: Torryton Park, East Field**
Relax under the stars while listening to music from local bands.

ANNOUNCEMENT
National Day Celebration

Due to the predicted bad weather, the City Council has announced several changes to this weekend's National Day celebration. All outdoor activities have been canceled, with the exception of the evening concert. This has been moved to the Torryton Theater. Like all the weekend's events, there is no charge for the concert. However, due to limited seating, tickets must be obtained ahead of time. Contact the City Arts Council to reserve your tickets. All indoor activities will proceed as scheduled.

To: patr@ztown.com
From: timrogers@river.com
Date: June 11
Subject: Torryton trip

Hi Pat,

Thanks for recommending the Torryton National Day celebration. I had a great time despite the weather. I guess you heard about that storm. Anyhow, there were still lots of celebration events going on. I was really sorry to miss the food festival, but maybe I can catch it next year. I saw the history exhibits early in the day, then I was lucky enough to get a ticket to the concert. It was fantastic. I'll give you a full account when I see you next week.

Tim

186. What is NOT true about the celebration?

(A) It takes place once a year.
(B) It includes a sports event.
(C) It costs money to attend.
(D) It is an old tradition.

187. Which activity is especially for children?

(A) A movie
(B) A crafts sale
(C) An international meal
(D) A walk on Main Street

188. Why didn't Tim go to the food festival?

(A) It was canceled.
(B) He wasn't hungry.
(C) He didn't feel well.
(D) It was too early in the day.

189. Where was Tim in the evening?

(A) At the park
(B) At the theater
(C) At the museum
(D) At the soccer game

190. In the e-mail, the word *account* in line 5 is closest in meaning to

(A) bill
(B) money
(C) reason
(D) description

Questions 191–195 refer to the following ad, review, and article.

Come to the new

Beeline Bistro

Use these coupons to take advantage of special offers when you visit us this month.

Beeline Bistro

***** *2 for 1 Special* *****

Choose any 2 entrees from our dinner menu for the price of one.

Offer expires March 31

One coupon per customer

Beeline Bistro

***** *Free Dessert* *****

Enjoy one free dessert with any lunch entree

Offer expires March 31

One coupon per customer

Beeline Bistro

*** *Sandwich Special* ***

Choose selected sandwiches from our lunch menu for just $6.99 each.

Offer expires March 31

One coupon per customer

Beeline Bistro

***** *Appetizer Tray* *****

Get 25% off our Appetizer Tray when you come in for dinner before 6:00 P.M.

Offer expires March 31

One coupon per customer

Beeline Bistro

113 Riverside Avenue

Serving 3 meals a day, seven days a week

Beeline Bistro

My husband and I tried out the new Beeline Bistro last week, and it did not disappoint! What a great dinner. It's still pricy, but we used a coupon and that made a big difference. They offer the same great selection as always. We skipped the appetizers and went straight to the entrees, and of course, couldn't pass up the great desserts. If you enjoy the old Beeline as much as we do, you're sure to like the Riverside version, too.

Penny Barlow

RIVERSIDE
Revival of a Neighborhood

The new restaurant and shopping district in the Riverside section of town is booming. Specialty clothing, book, and gift stores have popped up around the neighborhood. At the same time, numerous new eating places have appeared, and some old favorites have opened new locations there as well. The latter include the ever-popular Beeline Bistro. This is a wise move on the part of Beeline's owners, as the contemporary menu will surely appeal to the youthful residents of the neighborhood. The newcomer Café Cookie Cutter, just next door, is already *the* place to go for home-baked pastries.

In general, the concentration of restaurants in the area is a draw for other businesses as well, and on weekend evenings the streets are alive with shoppers, sightseers, and, most of all, people with money to spend. All in all, Riverside businesses are taking off.

191. What is suggested about the Beeline Bistro restaurant?
   (A) It is a new business.
   (B) It will be remodeled.
   (C) It has changed the menu.
   (D) It has opened a new branch.

192. Which coupon did Ms. Barlow use?
   (A) Free dessert
   (B) Appetizer tray
   (C) 2 for 1 special
   (D) Sandwich special

193. What criticism does Ms. Barlow have of the Beeline Bistro?
   (A) It is expensive.
   (B) It is too busy.
   (C) The menu is short.
   (D) The appetizers aren't good.

194. In the article, the word *concentration* in paragraph 2, line 1, is closest in meaning to
   (A) thinking
   (B) attention
   (C) crowding
   (D) shrinkage

195. What is suggested about Riverside businesses?
   (A) They are prosperous.
   (B) They are in a bad location.
   (C) They need more publicity.
   (D) They appeal only to young people.

Questions 196–200 refer to the following sign, e-mail, and notice.

AIRPORT TRANSPORTATION

All transportation services leave from the front of the East Terminal.

	Schedule	**Destinations**	**Cost**
City Bus #46	Every hour	Downtown, Parkview, Business District	$3.50
Train Station Shuttle	Every 30 min.	Central Train Station	$5.00
Hotel Shuttles	Varies	Neighborhood hotels	None
Taxi	Varies	Any	Varies

To: m.reed@company.com
From: s.chang@company.com
Date: Friday, September 15
Subject: travel

Melinda,

Thanks for doing such a great job organizing my trip. Everything has gone smoothly so far except for one little glitch at the airport. I was all set to take the downtown bus, as you suggested, because it stops right across the street from the hotel, but unfortunately it didn't work out because of the mess at the terminal, what with all the work going on, and then, of course, Friday is such a heavy travel day. I ended up having to pay for a taxi, which cost a good deal more, and I doubt whether it saved me any time. The traffic around here is horrendous. At any rate, I'm settled into the hotel now and getting ready for tomorrow's meetings. I'll let you know how everything goes.

Sam

NOTICE to Airport Users

The following changes to airport transportation have been put in place due to renovations and repairs being carried out at the East Terminal:

- o All shuttle and taxi services now leave from the front of the West Terminal.
- o Service from City Bus #46 is temporarily suspended. Those desiring to connect with other City Bus lines can take a shuttle or taxi to Central Train Station, which is serviced by buses #32, #57, and #75.

Please direct any questions or concerns to the Airport Office of Public Relations.

This notice is in effect from August 30 to October 15.

196. Which type of transportation is free to use?

(A) City Bus
(B) Train Station Shuttle
(C) Hotel Shuttles
(D) Taxi

197. Why didn't Sam take the bus?

(A) It doesn't go to his destination.
(B) It isn't in operation right now.
(C) It takes too long.
(D) It costs too much.

198. What does Sam suggest about the airport?

(A) It is crowded on Fridays.
(B) It is not cleaned regularly.
(C) It is far from downtown.
(D) It is close to his hotel.

199. What is happening at the airport from August to October?

(A) Construction of a new terminal
(B) Changes in shuttle schedules
(C) Reorganization of bus routes
(D) Remodeling of a building

200. In the notice, the word *direct* in line 10 is closest in meaning to

(A) advise
(B) manage
(C) express
(D) instruct

STOP

This is the end of the test. If you finish before time is called, you may go back to Parts 5, 6, and 7 and check your work.

ANSWER KEY
New TOEIC—Model Test 5

LISTENING COMPREHENSION

Part 1: Photographs

1. **A**	3. **C**	5. **B**
2. **D**	4. **A**	6. **C**

Part 2: Question-Response

7. **B**	14. **C**	21. **C**	28. **A**
8. **B**	15. **A**	22. **A**	29. **B**
9. **C**	16. **B**	23. **B**	30. **C**
10. **A**	17. **C**	24. **C**	31. **B**
11. **A**	18. **A**	25. **C**	
12. **C**	19. **C**	26. **A**	
13. **B**	20. **B**	27. **B**	

Part 3: Conversations

32. **C**	42. **B**	52. **D**	62. **A**
33. **D**	43. **D**	53. **C**	63. **C**
34. **A**	44. **C**	54. **A**	64. **D**
35. **C**	45. **D**	55. **D**	65. **B**
36. **B**	46. **A**	56. **A**	66. **B**
37. **C**	47. **C**	57. **B**	67. **D**
38. **A**	48. **B**	58. **A**	68. **B**
39. **B**	49. **C**	59. **B**	69. **A**
40. **D**	50. **B**	60. **C**	70. **C**
41. **B**	51. **A**	61. **A**	

Part 4: Talks

71. **A**	79. **C**	87. **C**	95. **B**
72. **D**	80. **A**	88. **C**	96. **C**
73. **C**	81. **D**	89. **D**	97. **A**
74. **B**	82. **B**	90. **C**	98. **D**
75. **D**	83. **B**	91. **A**	99. **A**
76. **A**	84. **A**	92. **D**	100. **B**
77. **B**	85. **C**	93. **C**	
78. **C**	86. **A**	94. **A**	

ANSWER KEY
New TOEIC—Model Test 5

READING

Part 5: Incomplete Sentences

101. **B**
102. **B**
103. **A**
104. **C**
105. **D**
106. **C**
107. **A**
108. **B**
109. **A**
110. **C**
111. **D**
112. **C**
113. **B**
114. **A**
115. **B**
116. **C**
117. **D**
118. **A**
119. **C**
120. **B**
121. **B**
122. **A**
123. **C**
124. **C**
125. **D**
126. **B**
127. **C**
128. **D**
129. **A**
130. **A**

Part 6: Text Completion

131. **C**
132. **B**
133. **A**
134. **C**
135. **D**
136. **B**
137. **A**
138. **C**
139. **C**
140. **B**
141. **A**
142. **D**
143. **B**
144. **C**
145. **B**
146. **D**

Part 7: Reading Comprehension

147. **B**
148. **D**
149. **B**
150. **D**
151. **C**
152. **B**
153. **A**
154. **A**
155. **C**
156. **D**
157. **D**
158. **B**
159. **C**
160. **A**
161. **D**
162. **B**
163. **B**
164. **B**
165. **C**
166. **A**
167. **B**
168. **A**
169. **C**
170. **A**
171. **C**
172. **D**
173. **B**
174. **A**
175. **A**
176. **A**
177. **C**
178. **D**
179. **A**
180. **B**
181. **B**
182. **C**
183. **C**
184. **D**
185. **A**
186. **C**
187. **A**
188. **A**
189. **B**
190. **C**
191. **D**
192. **C**
193. **A**
194. **C**
195. **A**
196. **C**
197. **B**
198. **A**
199. **D**
200. **C**

TEST SCORE CONVERSION TABLE

Count your correct responses. Match the number of correct responses with the corresponding score from the Test Score Conversion Table (below). Add the two scores together. This is your Total Estimated Test Score. As you practice taking the TOEIC model tests, your scores should improve. Keep track of your Total Estimated Test Scores.

# Correct	Listening Score	Reading Score	# Correct	Listening Score	Reading Score	# Correct	Listening Score	Reading Score	# Correct	Listening Score	Reading Score
0	5	5	26	110	65	51	255	220	76	410	370
1	5	5	27	115	70	52	260	225	77	420	380
2	5	5	28	120	80	53	270	230	78	425	385
3	5	5	29	125	85	54	275	235	79	430	390
4	5	5	30	130	90	55	280	240	80	440	395
5	5	5	31	135	95	56	290	250	81	445	400
6	5	5	32	140	100	57	295	255	82	450	405
7	10	5	33	145	110	58	300	260	83	460	410
8	15	5	34	150	115	59	310	265	84	465	415
9	20	5	35	160	120	60	315	270	85	470	420
10	25	5	36	165	125	61	320	280	86	475	425
11	30	5	37	170	130	62	325	285	87	480	430
12	35	5	38	175	140	63	330	290	88	485	435
13	40	5	39	180	145	64	340	300	89	490	445
14	45	5	40	185	150	65	345	305	90	495	450
15	50	5	41	190	160	66	350	310	91	495	455
16	55	10	42	195	165	67	360	320	92	495	465
17	60	15	43	200	170	68	365	325	93	495	470
18	65	20	44	210	175	69	370	330	94	495	480
19	70	25	45	215	180	70	380	335	95	495	485
20	75	30	46	220	190	71	385	340	96	495	490
21	80	35	47	230	195	72	390	350	97	495	495
22	85	40	48	240	200	73	395	355	98	495	495
23	90	45	49	245	210	74	400	360	99	495	495
24	95	50	50	250	215	75	405	365	100	495	495
25	100	60									

Number of Correct Listening Responses ________ = Listening Score ________

Number of Correct Reading Responses ________ = Reading Score ________

Total Estimated Test Score ________

EXPLANATORY ANSWERS

Listening Comprehension

PART 1: PHOTOGRAPHS

1. **(A)** A woman is looking at her wristwatch. Choices (B) and (D) correctly identify the bus in the background, but the woman is not watching it or riding on it. Choice (C) correctly identifies the tree in the background, but the woman is not planting it.
2. **(D)** The photo shows empty tables and chairs in front of some houses. Choice (A) is incorrect because the doors are closed. Choice (B) correctly identifies the benches, but there are no people on them. Choice (C) is incorrect because there is nothing on the tables.
3. **(C)** A man is standing in a grocery store aisle reading the label on a jar. Choice (A) correctly identifies the jar, but not the man's activity. Choice (B) relates *grocery store* and *food.* Choice (D) correctly identifies the shelves, but not the man's activity.
4. **(A)** A train stands in a station. Choice (B) is incorrect because there are no passengers in the photo. Choice (C) is incorrect because the platform is empty of people. Choice (D) confuses similar-sounding words *train* and *rain.*
5. **(B)** This statement correctly describes the woman. Choice (A) is incorrect because the man is not wearing a tie. Choice (C) is incorrect because the shelves are filled with books. Choice (D) confuses the *coffee cup* with a *coffee pot.*
6. **(C)** A chef stands in a kitchen. Choice (A) confuses similar-sounding words *kitchen* and *chicken.* Choice (B) correctly identifies the vegetables, but not their location. Choice (D) correctly identifies the plates, but not their location.

PART 2: QUESTION-RESPONSE

7. **(B)** This answers the question *Which.* Choice (A) repeats the verb *live.* Choice (C) confuses similar-sounding words *which* and *wish.*
8. **(B)** This answers the *yes-no* question with additional information about the time of the appointment. Choice (A) confuses similar-sounding words *appointment* and *disappointing.* Choice (C) relates the words *appointment and calendar.*
9. **(C)** *Susan* answers the question *Who.* Choice (A) repeats the name *Mr. Jenkins.* Choice (B) repeats the word *phone.*
10. **(A)** *Two months ago* answers the question *When.* Choice (B) confuses homonyms *here* and *hear.* Choice (C) repeats the word *here.*
11. **(A)** This answers the *yes-no* question about attending the conference. Choice (B) uses the related word *conferring.* Choice (C) confuses the meaning of the word *last* and repeats the word *month.*
12. **(C)** This is an appropriate response to the offer of a cup of coffee. Choice (A) confuses homonyms *wait* and *weight.* Choice (B) confuses similar-sounding words *coffee* and *coughing.*
13. **(B)** This is an appropriate response to the request to carry a box. Choice (A) would answer a *yes-no* question that is not a request. Choice (C) repeats the word *box.*
14. **(C)** This answers the *yes-no* question about the visitors' arrival. Choice (A) uses the related word *visit.* Choice (B) would answer a question about the arrival of something, but not of people.
15. **(A)** This answers the question about a preference. Choice (B) confuses similar-sounding words *train* and *rain.* Choice (C) confuses the meaning of the word *train.*
16. **(B)** This answers the *How long* question about time. Choice (A) relates *meeting* and *agenda.* Choice (C) would answer a *How long* question about size.
17. **(C)** The word *belongs* is the clue that this is the correct answer to the *Whose* question about possession. Choice (A) confuses similar-sounding words *closet* and *closest.* Choice (B) uses a plural pronoun, *they,* for the singular word *coat.*
18. **(A)** This answers the *Why* question with a logical reason. Choice (B) relates *bus* and *fares.* Choice (C) repeats the word *work.*

19. **(C)** This is a logical response to the invitation to play tennis. Choice (A) relates the words *tennis* and *racket.* Choice (B) confuses similar-sounds *tennis* and *ten of us.*
20. **(B)** This answers the question *What.* Choices (A) and (C) confuse *weekend* with similar-sounding words *weakened* and *week.*
21. **(C)** This is a logical response to the comment about the short cord. Choice (A) repeats the word *cord.* Choice (B) confuses similar-sounding words *cord* and *bored.*
22. **(A)** This answers the *yes-no* question about possession of a car. Choice (B) would answer a *Which* question. Choice (C) would answer a *Where* question.
23. **(B)** *Noon* answers the *When* question. Choice (C) would answer a *Where* question. Choice (A) relates *arrive* and *time,* but it does not answer the question.
24. **(C)** The speaker responds to the comment about enjoying the play by agreeing. Choice (A) confuses the meaning of the word *play.* Choice (B) repeats *play,* but it does not answer the question.
25. **(C)** Behind my desk answers the *Where* question. Choice (A) would answer a *What* question. Choice (B) uses *left,* related to *leave. Where can I leave my bags?*
26. **(A)** This answers the *yes-no* question about John's presence at the party. Choice (B) is future tense, but the question is about the past. Choice (C) is not an answer to a *yes-no* question.
27. **(B)** *Fifteen* answers the *How many* question. Choice (A) repeats the word *many.* Choice (C) confuses similar-sounding words *fit* and *sit.*
28. **(A)** This answers the negative *yes-no* question about an office key. Choice (B) relates *key and lock.* Choice (C) confuses the meaning of *key.*
29 **(B)** This answers the *What* question. Choice (A) confuses similar-sounding words *talking* and *walking.* Choice (C) repeats the word *talking.*
30. **(C)** This answers the *Which* question. Choice (A) repeats the word *office.* Choice (B) would answer a *yes-no* question.
31. **(B)** This is a logical response to the suggestion to take a walk. Choice (A) repeats the word *take.* Choice (C) confuses similar-sounding words *take* and *make.*

PART 3: CONVERSATIONS

32. **(C)** The man says he is calling to ask how to get to the office from the subway. Choice (A) is incorrect because the man already has an appointment. Choice (B) is what the woman asks about. Choice (D) repeats the name *Mr. Wilson.*
33. **(D)** *Nothing easier* means that there is nothing easier than finding Mr. Wilson's office. Choices (A), (B), and (C) do not correctly explain the meaning of this expression.
34. **(A)** According to the woman's directions, the man will see the office building after taking a left onto Main Street. Choices (B) and (C) are other places mentioned in the directions. Choice (D) is incorrect because the man has to walk to another street after leaving the subway station.
35. **(C)** The man and woman both mention a room, and the woman quotes a price per night, so they are talking about a hotel room. Choices (A), (B), and (D) are things one might pay a deposit for, but they are not paid for per night.
36. **(B)** The man says, *That's more than I expected to pay,* and asks for something that costs less. Choices (A), (C), and (D) are all mentioned, but the man doesn't express any problems about them.
37. **(C)** The woman advises the man to *put a deposit down now.* Choice (A) repeats the word *later.* Choice (B) repeats the word *date.* Choice (D) is plausible, but it is not mentioned.
38. **(A)** The man states that he will be on vacation. Choice (B) repeats the word *meeting.* Choice (C) is not mentioned. Choice (D) confuses similar-sounding words *reports* and *sports.*
39. **(B)** The man states that he bought a train ticket. Choice (A) confuses similar-sounding

words *train* and *plane* and is confused with the woman's mention of *flying*. Choice (C) confuses similar-sounding words *far* and *car*. Choice (D) is not mentioned.

40. **(D)** The woman says, *It'll take you forever to get there* and *I wouldn't have the patience*, which imply that she thinks the train is slow. Choices (A) and (B) are what the man says train travel is not. Choice (C) is related to the idea of slowness, but it is not mentioned.
41. **(B)** The woman mentions that the man is going to a party. Choice (A) confuses similar-sounding words *thinner* and *dinner*. Choice (C) relates *suit* with *meeting*. Choice (D) relates *suit* with *office*.
42. **(B)** The woman says *you should wear a lighter color*. Choice (A) uses related words *cleaner's/clean*. Choice (C) repeats the word *fit*. Choice (D) confuses similar-sounding words *fit* and *rip*.
43. **(D)** The man says, *I think I'll change my tie*. Choice (A) is what the man has already done. Choice (B) repeats the word *opinion*. Choice (C) is what the woman wants the man to do, but he doesn't agree.
44. **(C)** The woman is playing golf with some friends and invites the man to join them. Choice (A) confuses similar-sounding words *work* and *walk*. Choice (B) confuses the meaning of the word *play*. Choice (D) repeats the word *lunch*.
45. **(D)** The woman says that the golf game is on Saturday morning. Choices (A) and (B) are confused with the similar-sounding word *fun*. Choice (C) is confused with the similar-sounding word *two*.
46. **(A)** The woman will call her friends tonight and tell them to meet at two instead of seven. Choice (B) is incorrect because she will call her friends, not visit them. Choice (C) is not mentioned. Choice (D) repeats the word *call* and confuses the meaning of the word *club*—the man mentions his golf clubs.
47. **(C)** The man asks the woman to *help me get this report done*. Choice (A) is related to the discussion about which bus the woman will take. Choice (B) is incorrect because it is the assistant who will make copies. Choice (D) confuses similar-sounding words *report* and *record*.
48. **(B)** The man says that the office is *short staffed*, that is, there aren't enough employees. Choice (A) relates *copies* and *photocopier*, but there is no need to replace it. Choice (C) repeats the word *late*, which refers to the discussion of when the woman will leave, not when she arrives. Choice (D) is related to the discussion of the bus schedule.
49. **(C)** The woman says that she can *make the last bus leaving from Winwood Street*. Choice (A) is when the second-to-last bus leaves. Choice (B) is a time when a bus arrives in Berksville and is also the time that the woman will probably leave the office. Choice (D) is when the last bus arrives at its destination.
50. **(B)** The first man says, *We need to get together to work on the presentation*, and then the speakers discuss a day and time to do this. Choice (A) is incorrect because the speakers quickly agree on a place; it is the time that they discuss. Choice (C) repeats the word *appointment*, which is what prevents the woman from agreeing to the first suggested time. Choice (D) is related to the mention of different times and days, but it is not the topic of discussion.
51. **(A)** In this context, *That's no good* means *I can't do that*, and it is the woman's response to the first suggested meeting time. Choices (B), (C), and (D) don't fit the meaning of this expression in the context.
52. **(D)** One man says, *We really have to get going on this*, meaning *We have to start working on this very soon*. The other agrees, mentioning the due date: *Monday's coming up soon*. Choices (A), (B), and (C) are not mentioned.
53. **(C)** The woman says, *I'd like to get some business cards . . . .* Choice (A) confuses similar-sounding words *card* and *car*. Choice (B) relates *address* (which the woman wants to include on her cards) and *mail*. Choice (D) relates *Tuesday* (which is when the woman wants the cards to be ready) and *appointment*.

54. **(A)** The woman wants to order 250 cards, and the man says she will save money by ordering 500. Choice (B) refers to the description of the logo the woman wants on her card. Choice (C) repeats the word *Tuesday.* Choice (D) is related to the woman's *consulting* business.

55. **(D)** The woman asks the man to phone her when the cards are ready for pick up. Choice (A) repeats the word *address.* Choice (B) repeats *pick up.* Choice (C) relates *address* and *delivery.*

56. **(A)** The man is applying for a loan, so she is a bank officer. Choice (B) relates *house* and *real estate.* Choice (C) repeats the word *financial.* Choice (D) is who the man is.

57. **(B)** The man is interested in *taking out a loan,* that is, borrowing money. Choice (A) repeats the word *house.* Choice (C) is incorrect because the man already has a business; he wants to expand it. Choice (D) repeats the word *credit.*

58. **(A)** The man says, *That's a lot of paper. Do I really need to complete all those pages?* Choice (B) relates *risk* and *risky.* The man says he is a good risk, that is, he will surely repay the loan. Choice (C) repeats the word *information.* Choice (D) relates *account* and *accountant.*

59. **(B)** The man describes the parking policy as the one where employees *have to pay to park in the lot.* Choice (A) is not mentioned. Choice (C) is incorrect because employees lose assigned spaces as part of the policy. Choice (D) is contradicted by the correct answer.

60. **(C)** The women agree that people need to be encouraged to use public transportation instead of driving because the streets are too crowded with traffic. Choice (A) repeats the phrase *public transportation,* but no mention is made of whether or not it is quicker. Choice (B) repeats the word *crowded.* Choice (D) is related to the discussion of parking and driving, but it is not mentioned.

61. **(A)** If a plan doesn't *go over,* it means it won't be liked or accepted. Choices (B), (C), and (D) don't fit the meaning of the expression in this context.

62. **(A)** The speakers are discussing plans for a luncheon for a visitor from Tokyo. Choice (B) repeats *Tokyo.* Choice (C) is confused with *conference room,* the location of the luncheon. Choice (D) confuses similar-sounding words *seating* and *meeting.*

63. **(C)** The woman refers to next week's luncheon for Ms. Yamamoto. Choice (A) confuses similar-sounding words *soon* and *noon.* Choice (B) confuses similar-sounding words *door* and *four.* Choice (D) is not mentioned.

64. **(D)** The speakers agree that Ms. Yamamoto should sit near the door. Choices (A), (B), and (C) are not near the door.

65. **(B)** The woman asks the man to shampoo the carpets, wash the walls, and polish the furniture, that is, to clean the office. Choice (A) repeats the word *furniture.* Choice (C) repeats the word *walls.* Choice (D) repeats the word *carpet.*

66. **(B)** The man says, *We can have it all done by tomorrow afternoon at 5.* Choice (A) repeats the word *afternoon.* Choice (C) is when the woman has a meeting with a client. Choice (D) is not mentioned.

67. **(D)** The woman is going to write a check for the deposit. Choice (A) confuses the meaning of the word *check.* Choice (B) repeats the word *work.* Choice (C) repeats the word *client.*

68. **(B)** The woman asks the man about his *house hunting,* so he is looking for a house to live in. Choices (A) and (D) are related to the mention of an *office.* Choice (C) confuses the meaning of the word *suit.*

69. **(A)** When the woman suggests going to the café, the man says he would prefer *some place quieter* and the woman agrees, saying, *It's not really suited for talking.* Choice (B) is incorrect because the man says the café *is not expensive.* Choice (C) is incorrect because the woman says, *The food there's not bad.* Choice (D) is not mentioned.

70. **(C)** The man says, *So why don't you come to my office around noon tomorrow. . . .* Choice (A) confuses similar sounds *talk* and *walk.* Choice (B) repeats the words *house* and *going.*

Choice (D) is incorrect because the man suggests chatting in his office, not on the phone.

PART 4: TALKS

71. **(A)** The guest will speak about climbing in the Andes. Choices (B) and (C) are mentioned as things she does, but they are not the topic of the talk. Choice (D) is not mentioned.
72. **(D)** The speaker says the program will last *about an hour and a half total.* Choice (A) is the length of the film that will be shown. Choice (B) sounds similar to *15 minutes.* Choice (C) sounds similar to the correct answer.
73. **(C)** The speaker says that *coffee, tea, and snacks will be available in the lobby.* Choice (A) is confused with the *book signing.* Choice (B) is confused with the mention of the guest's interest in photography. Choice (D) confuses the meaning of the word *sign.*
74. **(B)** The speaker apologizes for the delay that was caused by *maintenance work on the engine.* Choice (A) is related to the word *emergency.* Choices (C) and (D) are mentioned, but they are not the cause of the delay.
75. **(D)** The speaker says, *Please approach Gate 9 and line up single file.* Choice (A) is not possible, as the speaker says, *there is no seating in the boarding area.* Choices (B) and (C) are mentioned, but they are not what passengers are being asked to do.
76. **(A)** The speaker asks passengers to *check any large suitcases at the luggage counter before boarding.* Choices (B), (C), and (D) are all mentioned, but not as places to leave luggage.
77. **(B)** The speakers says, *you need to be aware of a few minor adjustments to the schedule,* and that is mostly what she talks about. Choice (A) is confused with the mention of registering for one of the workshops. Choice (C) repeats the word *workshop,* but none are described, just named. Choice (D) is incorrect because lunch is over.
78. **(C)** The speaker says about that workshop, *anyone interested in attending it should visit the registration desk now.* Choice (A) is where the social hour will take place. Choice (B) repeats the word *schedule.* Choice (D) is incorrect because the workshop has been moved to Room D.
79. **(C)** *I wouldn't miss that* can be a way of recommending something, meaning that it is too good to miss. The speaker is recommending that listeners go to the social hour. Choices (A), (B), and (D) don't fit the context.
80. **(A)** The speaker is speaking to tourists on a bus explaining all the places the bus will take them to. Choice (B) is not mentioned. Choices (C) and (D) are places they will visit.
81. **(D)** The speaker says, *please take your seats now.* Choice (A) repeats the word *questions.* Choice (B) fits the context, but it is not mentioned. Choice (C) repeats the word *talk.*
82. **(B)** The speakers says that at noon *we are scheduled for lunch at the Blue Moon Restaurant.* Choice (A) will happen after the noontime lunch. Choice (B) is the entire context. Choice (D) is what the speaker is doing now.
83. **(B)** The speaker mentions *financial assistance, loans,* and *the money you need to start or grow your business.* Choice (A) is confused with the mention of workshops, Choice (C) repeats the word employment. Choice (D) is related to the topic, but it is not what is being advertised.
84. **(A)** The name of the loan program is *Small Business Assistance Program,* and the speaker also says, *We believe in supporting local businesses.* Choices (B), (C), and (D) repeat words mentioned in the talk.
85. **(C)** The speaker says, *Find out more about what we have to offer by attending one of our monthly workshops.* Choices (A), (B), and (D) are all plausible, but they are not mentioned.
86. **(A)** The speaker begins by saying, *Let's go over the plans,* and the rest of the talk is about tasks that need to be done and who will do them. Choices (B) and (C) are incorrect because from the context, we can assume they have already happened. Choice (D) uses the word *awards,* but there is no discussion about who will receive them.

87. **(C)** The speaker says that she *won't arrive until the ceremony begins,* which, according to the schedule, is 8:30. Choices (A), (B), and (D) are other times on the schedule.

88. **(C)** After describing the tasks to be done, the speaker ends by saying, *Who would like to do what?* Choice (A) repeats the word *hotel,* but calling the hotel is not mentioned. Choice (B) repeats the word *guests,* but sending them invitations is not mentioned. Choice (D) is mentioned as one of the tasks, but it is not what will be done next.

89. **(D)** *Things are looking up* means that things are improving. The speaker goes on to describe clearing skies and warmer temperatures, which are improvements in the weather. Choice (A) uses another meaning of *look up—research.* Choices (B) and (C) associate *higher* and *sky* with *up.*

90. **(C)** The speaker mentions *rising temperatures.* Choice (A) is the weather on Saturday. Choice (B) is the weather on Sunday. Choice (D) is the opposite of what the speaker says will happen—cloudy skies will clear up.

91. **(A)** The speaker says, *bring along that umbrella if you venture out on Saturday as occasional showers are expected.* Choice (B) is confused with the colder temperatures on Sunday. Choice (C) repeats the words *enjoy* and *out.* Choice (D) confuses similar-sounding words *showers* and *flowers.*

92. **(D)** The speaker says that Joe Roberts is an accountant. Choice (A) is related to the mention of a *financial statement.* Choice (B) is related to the topic of appointments. Choice (C) is who the speaker is.

93. **(C)** The speaker says that Joe Roberts would like to meet with the listener and suggests a day and time. Choices (A) and (B) are plausible, but they are not the correct answer. Choice (D) cannot be correct because no previous appointment is mentioned.

94. **(A)** The speaker wants to know when the listener can meet with Mr. Roberts and leaves a phone number. Choice (B) is what Mr. Roberts wants to do at the appointment. Choice (C) repeats the word *office.* Choice (D) has already been done.

95. **(B)** The found item is a jacket, that is, a piece of clothing. Choice (A) confuses similar-sounding words *jacket* and *package.* Choice (C) repeats the word *ticket.* Choice (D)repeats the word *blue.*

96. **(C)** The speaker says that the item was found in *the Track 10 waiting area.* Choice (A) repeats the word *track.* Choice (B) confuses similar-sounding words *floor* and *door.* Choice (D) is incorrect because we can assume the waiting area is inside, not outside, the station.

97. **(A)** The speaker says that the station manager's office is *across from the ticket counter.* Choices (B), (C), and (D) don't fit this description.

98. **(D)** There is a sale in the *produce section,* so it is a grocery store. Choice (A) associates *fruit* with *farm.* Choice (B) associates *bank* with *savings.* Choice (C) confuses similar-sounding words *closing* and *clothing.*

99. **(A)** The sale is for today only. Choices (B) and (D) confuse *today* with similar-sounding words *two days* and *Tuesday.* Choice (C) repeats the word *week.*

100. **(B)** The speaker says to *come back next week* for the weekly sale. Choice (A) confuses the usage of the word *check.* Choice (C) confuses the usage of the word *change.* Choice (D) confuses the usage of *check out.*

Reading

PART 5: INCOMPLETE SENTENCES

101. **(B)** This is a present tense verb that agrees with the subject *Registration.* Choices (A) and (D) do not agree with the subject. Choice (C) is a gerund or present participle and cannot act as a main verb.

102. **(B)** *Resign* means *leave a job.* Choices (A), (C), and (D) have meanings that don't fit the context.

103. **(A)** *If* introduces a condition. Choice (B) introduces a result. Choice (C) shows sequence in time, or introduces the result

of a condition. Choice (D) introduces a contradiction.

104. **(C)** To *renew* a contract means to *continue* or *extend* it. Choices (A), (B), and (D) have meanings that don't fit the context.

105. **(D)** The subject, *agreement,* receives the action rather than performs it, so a passive verb is required. Choices (A), (B), and (C) are all active verbs.

106. **(C)** *Another* in this sentence is a pronoun that refers to *another printer.* Either a noun or a pronoun is needed here as an object of the verb *buy,* and Choices (A) and (B) are not pronouns. Choice (D) is sometimes used as a pronoun, but it does not make sense in this context.

107. **(A)** *Because of* introduces a cause. Choice (B) introduces an alternative. Choice (C) introduces a contradiction and cannot be used with *of.* Choice (D) introduces a cause, but it cannot be used with *of.*

108. **(B)** *Gather* means *collect,* and can be used, as it is here, as an intransitive verb (a verb with no object). Choices (A) and (C) are transitive verbs—they need objects. Choice (D) doesn't fit the context.

109. **(A)** This is a base form verb following the modal *should.* Choices (B), (C), and (D) are not base form verbs.

110. **(C)** *From* is a preposition indicating the place where something starts, in this case, *the answer* from *the client.* Choices (A), (B), and (D) don't fit the context.

111. **(D)** *Investment* is a noun referring to money paid into something with the hope of future profit. Choice (A) is a verb. Choice (B) is a noun, but it refers to a person. Choice (C) is a noun, but it has a completely different meaning that does not fit the context.

112. **(C)** *Motivate* means to make someone want to do something. Choices (A), (B), and (D) don't fit the context.

113. **(B)** The verb *result* is followed by the preposition *in.* Choices (A), (C), and (D) can't follow *result.*

114. **(A)** *Largely* means *mostly.* Choices (B), (C), and (D) don't fit the context.

115. **(B)** *Likely* is an adjective meaning *probable.* Choice (A), when used as an adjective, means *similar.* Choice (C) means *nice* or *easily liked.* Choice (D) is a verb.

116. **(C)** *Before* is followed by a gerund. Choices (A), (B), and (D) are not gerunds.

117. **(D)** This is a noun used in this sentence as the object of the verb *requires.* Choice (A) is a verb. Choice (B) is a gerund. Choice (C) is an adjective.

118. **(A)** *Slight* means *very small.* Choices (B), (C), and (D) do not fit the context.

119. **(C)** *Although* introduces a contradiction. Choices (A) and (B) introduce a cause. Choice (D) introduces a result.

120. **(B)** *Showed up* means *appeared.* Choices (A), (C), and (D) do not fit the context.

121. **(B)** *Economize* is a verb, in this sentence, an infinitive verb following the main verb *need.* Choices (A), (C), and (D) are all nouns.

122. **(A)** *Who* is a subject relative pronoun with the antecedent *person.* Choice (B) is an object relative pronoun. Choice (C) is possessive. Choice (D), when used as a relative pronoun, refers to a thing, not a person.

123. **(C)** *Notify* means *inform.* Choices (A), (B), and (D) have meanings that don't fit the context.

124. **(C)** This singular verb agrees with the singular subject *Everybody.* Choices (A), (B), and (D) all need plural subjects.

125. **(D)** This is an adjective modifying the noun *offer.* Choice (A) is a verb. Choices (B) and (C) are nouns.

126. **(B)** This is the correct form for the verb in the *if* clause of a past tense unreal conditional sentence. Choice (A) is simple past tense. Choice (C) is a present tense conditional main clause form. Choice (D) is a past unreal conditional, but the form for the main clause verb.

127. **(C)** *Except* means *but* or *excluding.* Choices (A), (B), and (D) do not fit the context.

128. **(D)** *Faster than* is a comparative form. Choice (A) is not comparative. Choice (B) omits *than.* Choice (C) is superlative.

129. **(A)** *Her* is an object pronoun (follows the verb). Choice (B) is a subject pronoun. Choice (C) is a possessive pronoun. Choice (D) is a reflexive pronoun.

130. **(A)** This is a base form verb following the modal *could.* Choice (B) is an adjective. Choice (C) is an adverb. Choice (D) is a noun.

PART 6: TEXT COMPLETION

131. **(C)** This is a reflexive pronoun used to place emphasis on its antecedent (*list*). Choice (A) is a possessive pronoun or adjective. Choice (B) is a contraction of *it is.* Choice (D) is two separate words, not a correct reflexive pronoun form.

132. **(B)** The verb *need* is followed by an infinitive verb. Choice (A) is base form. Choice (C) is a gerund. Choice (D) is a future verb.

133. **(A)** The preceding sentence expresses a need to make registration easier, and this sentence explains one way that might be done. Choices (B), (C), and (D) are related to the topic of subscribing to an e-mail list, but they don't fit the passage in this place.

134. **(C)** *The* is a definite article referring to something that has been defined (the reader knows that the name and address fields referred to are the ones on the registration form). Choices (A) and (B) are indefinite articles and are used with singular nouns only. Choice (D) is used with singular nouns only.

135. **(D)** *Our* in this case refers to people who work for the moving company, including the writer of the notice. Choices (A), (B), and (C) would refer to groups or individuals that do not include either the writer or the readers of this notice.

136. **(B)** This is a logical reason for the suggestion to push rather than lift furniture. Choices (A), (C), and (D) do not fit the context.

137. **(A)** This is an adjective modifying the noun *base.* Choice (B) is an adverb. Choice (C) is a verb. Choice (D) is a noun.

138. **(C)** *Whichever* implies a choice among two or more things, in this case, among different options. Choice (A) refers to the manner of doing something. Choice (B) refers to time. Choice (D) refers to people.

139. **(C)** A job *application* refers to the process of seeking a job by submitting information. Choices (A), (B), and (D) have meanings related to the idea of asking for something, but they are not correctly used in this context.

140. **(B)** This is an adjective modifying the noun *positions.* Choices (A) and (D) are verbs. Choice (C) is a noun.

141. **(A)** *However* introduces a contrast and is similar in meaning and use to *but*—there are no job positions, but they will keep the applicant's information. Choices (B), (C) and (D) have uses that don't fit the context.

142. **(D)** After stating that there are currently no positions available, the applicant is invited to re-apply at a later date. Choice (A) is illogical—there is no reason to make an appointment since there are no current job openings. Choice (B) contradicts what was stated earlier in the letter. Choice (C) is irrelevant because the application has already been made.

143. **(B)** *Absence* refers to the state of being away from a place—the writer will be away from the office next week. Choices (A), (C), and (D) have meanings that don't fit the context.

144. **(C)** The adjective *available* is followed by an infinitive verb. Choice (A) is a future verb. Choice (B) is a modal + verb. Choice (D) is base form.

145. **(B)** *Get back* means return. The other choices have meanings that don't fit the context.

146. **(D)** The writer of the e-mail mentions that people might want to meet with her, so it is logical to follow that with the mention of availability for appointments. Choices (A), (B), and (C) are related to other things mentioned in the e-mail, but they don't fit the passage in this place.

PART 7: READING COMPREHENSION

147. **(B)** The ad is for a computer training course at a college. Choices (A) and (C) are confused with the headline for job seekers. Choice (D) is confused with the correct answer, but the

ad is clearly about a school, not a programming business.

148. **(D)** The ad states that the course is open to high school graduates. Choice (A) is confused with the location of the course—at City College. Choice (B) is the content of the course. Choice (C) is exactly what the ad says is not required.

149. **(B)** After mentioning her meeting in the café, she writes, "I'm still here." Choices (A) and (C) are other places she was earlier. Choice (D) is where Mr. Noda is.

150. **(D)** She writes to Mr. Noda, *Save me a seat,* meaning she will attend the same seminar that he will be at. Choice (A) refers to her mention of the meeting with Bruce, but that was in the past. Choice (B) refers to the fact that she is in the café, but she makes no mention of waiting for her friend there. Choice (C) is incorrect because even though she says the exhibits are good, she makes no mention of looking at them again.

151. **(C)** The coupon is good for a *purchase of $100 or more.* Choice (A) is incorrect because the coupon mentions *select,* or designated, products. Choices (B) and (D) are incorrect because other types of products are mentioned.

152. **(B)** The coupon says, *Offer includes shipping at no charge for purchases of ink, toner, and paper.* Choices (A) and (D) are contradicted by the correct answer. Choice (C) repeats the phrase *your next purchase,* but just use of the coupon itself does not guarantee free shipping.

153. **(A)** The coupon expires on April 30. Choice (B) and (C) are confused with the provided contact information. Choice (D) is confused with the size of the discount.

154. **(A)** The application form mentions a move-in date, rent, and lease, so it is an application for an apartment. Choices (B), (C), and (D) repeat words from details on the form, but they are not the correct answer.

155. **(C)** The form shows that the applicant owes $800 for the first month's rent. Choice (A) is the application fee. Choice (B) is the security deposit. Choice (D) is the total of all the fees.

156. **(D)** The form states that all apartments will be *re-carpeted prior to move in.* Choices (A) and (B) are things that can be requested. Choice (C) is confused with the provided contact information.

157. **(D)** This is the name listed under *Bill to.* Choice (A) is the person who will receive the order. Choice (B) is the customer service representative. Choice (C) is the place the order will be sent to.

158. **(B)** This is the fee for *expedited,* or rushed, shipping. Choices (A), (C), and (D) are all plausible, but they are not correct.

159. **(C)** The invoice states, *Payment due upon receipt of order.* Choices (A), (B), and (D) are all plausible, but they are not correct.

160. **(A)** The phrase, *It's not just for skiing anymore,* suggests that most people know the place as a ski resort, and that the resort is now introducing new types of activities. Choice (B) is incorrect because it is a ski resort, so it must be open in the winter, as well. Choice (C) is incorrect because the quality of the accommodations is not mentioned. Choice (D) is incorrect because a price comparison with other resorts is not mentioned.

161. **(D)** This activity is not mentioned at all. Choice (A) refers to the mention of the *restaurant* and *chefs.* Choice (B) refers to the mention of *mountain biking.* Choice (C) refers to the mention of *swimming, sailing, and fishing.*

162. **(B)** The information states, *Reservations must be made 30 days in advance of your visit.* Choice (A) refers to the minimum stay length. Choice (C) refers to the months when the special rates are available. Choice (D) is contradicted by the correct answer.

163. **(B)** The article talks about how to adjust sleeping patterns to a new time zone. Choice (C) refers to the mention of jet lag and plane travel. Choice (A) refers to the mention of meals, exercise, and caffeine, but they are mentioned here specifically in terms of managing sleep, not health in general. Choice (D)

refers to the context of business travel, but planning the trip is only mentioned in terms of managing sleep patterns.

164. **(B)** The article defines this term as *the sleeping and waking pattern we follow over a 24-hour period.* Choice (A) uses a synonym for *clock.* Choice (C) repeats the phrase *24 hours.* Choice (D) relates *natural process* and *biological.*

165. **(C)** The article recommends to *stay up until at least 10:00.* Choices (A), (B), and (D) all mention *10:00,* but they are not what is recommended.

166. **(A)** The article says to spend time *in the fresh air and sunshine.* Choice (B) is the opposite of what is recommended. Choice (C) is confused with the mention of avoiding exercise close to bedtime. Choice (D) is confused with the mention of avoiding large meals close to bedtime.

167. **(B)** This is a letter of reference, so it will be used to get a new job. Choice (A) is what the recipient of the letter will use it for. Choices (C) and (D) repeat words used elsewhere in the letter.

168. **(A)** Ms. Spark was hired as a *legal assistant,* so her profession is law. Choice (B) is related the mention of *university.* Choices (C) and (D) are not mentioned.

169. **(C)** The last paragraph mentions Ms. Spark's *decision to move to New York.* Choices (A) and (B) are plausible reasons, but they are not mentioned. Choice (D) is incorrect because Ms. Spark continued at her job while taking classes.

170. **(A)** The phrase *that job,* refers back to the position of *legal assistant* mentioned in the previous sentence. Choices (B), (C), and (D) are not logical locations for this sentence.

171. **(C)** It is about *a proposal for a mixed-use complex* that will include both *office* and *retail* space. Choice (A) is related to the topic, but it is not the correct answer. Choice (B) relates *retail space* and *mall,* but there is no grand opening as nothing has been built yet. Choice (D) is related to the mention of *downtown* and *local shops.*

172. **(D)** Council members like the project because it will be a boost, or improvement, to the local economy. Choices (A), (B), and (C) do not mean the same as *boost.*

173. **(B)** Environmental groups oppose the project because it will destroy *acres of valuable agricultural land.* Choice (A) is related to the mention of the size of the project, but no one complained about it. Choice (C) is the opposite of the business owners' complaint—they think it is too far away to attract business to their shops. Choice (D) is related to the mention of parking, but no problems with it are mentioned.

174. **(A)** Ms. Hodges is a City Council member and, therefore, a politician. Choices (B) and (D) are related to the mention of retail space. Choice (C) refers to the Rockville Development Group.

175. **(A)** The RDG spokesperson says that they will *break ground,* that is, begin construction, *before the end of the year,* that is, by December 31. Choice (B) is the beginning of next year. Choice (C) is related to the amount of time it will take to complete the project. Choice (D) is related to the amount of time it took to plan the project.

176. **(A)** The e-mail asks the hotel guest to complete a *Guest Satisfaction Survey.* Choices (B), (C), and (D) are related to the hotel business, but they are not the purpose of the e-mail.

177. **(C)** The e-mail says to contact Ms. Lee for *future stay inquiries,* that is, to make plans to stay at the hotel. Choice (A) requires contacting Mr. Perez. Choices (B) and (D) are done by clicking on a link.

178. **(D)** In the survey, Ms. Simmons describes problems with *check in,* that is, registration. Choice (A) is not mentioned. Choices (B) and (C) are things she rated as excellent.

179. **(A)** Ms. Simmons says of the fitness center *by the time I got there (10:00 P.M.) it was closed.* Choices (B) and (D) are things she didn't rate because she didn't use the center. Choice (C) is incorrect because she wanted to use the center.

180. **(B)** Ms. Simons states the purpose of her trip as a *client meeting*. Choices (A) and (C) are things she plans for the future. Choice (D) is not mentioned.
181. **(B)** The topics of the workshop sessions relate to different aspects of running a business. Choices (A), (C), and (D) each refer to specific workshop topics, but not to the overall theme of the conference.
182. **(C)** At the beginning paragraph 2 of the e-mail, Ms. Kemp writes, *I hope we can get together sometime during the day*, and making arrangements to do that is main topic of the rest of her message. Choice (A) is incorrect because Mr. Schumacher already has plans to go to the conference. Choice (B) is incorrect because she states that she won't be a presenter. Choice (A) is incorrect because Ms. Kemp mentions which workshops she will attend, but she makes no suggestions for Mr. Schumacher.
183. **(C)** Ms. Kemp writes that she will attend Workshop C, which takes place at 1:30 in Room 2. Choices (A), (B), and (D) are locations of other events.
184. **(D)** Because of Mr. Schumacher's involvement in the local Finance Educators Association, Ms. Kemp thinks he might know of useful resources for her in her search for a loan. Choices (A), (B), and (C) are other meanings of *active* that don't fit the context.
185. **(A)** Ms. Kemp wants to discuss a loan. Choices (B), (C), and (D) all repeat words from the e-mail, but they are not the correct answer.
186. **(C)** The announcement states, *Like all the weekend's events, there is no charge for the concert*, meaning none of the events cost money. Choice (A) is a true statement because the schedule describes the celebration as *annual*. Choice (B) is a true statement because one of the events on the schedule is a soccer game. Choice (D) is a true statement because this the 150th celebration.
187. **(A)** On the schedule, under History Exhibits, the schedule mentions a *film* (movie) for *the little ones* (children). Choices (B), (C), and (D) are all activities that are not mentioned as being specifically for children.
188. **(A)** Tim wanted to attend this event but, according to the announcement, most outdoor events were canceled due to weather, and on the schedule we can see that the food festival was an outdoor event. Choices (B), (C), and (D) are all plausible, but they are incorrect reasons.
189. **(B)** Tim attended the concert, which took place in the evening and was moved from its outdoor location to the theater. Choice (A) is where the concert was originally scheduled to take place. Choice (D) is incorrect because everything that would take place outdoors was canceled. Choice (C) is where Tim was *early in the day*.
190. **(C)** Tim means he will give Pat a complete description of the celebration when they meet. Choices (A), (B), and (D) are other meanings of *account*, but they don't fit the context.
191. **(D)** It is referred to as *new* in the review, but the article makes it clear that this is a new location for an old business, not a new business entirely. Choice (B) is not mentioned. Choice (C) is incorrect because the reviewer mentions *the same great selection*, that is, *the same great menu*.
192. **(C)** She used it for dinner, which eliminates Choices (A) and (D), good for lunch only, and she says they didn't have appetizers, which eliminates Choice (B).
193. **(A)** She says the restaurant is *pricy*. Choice (B) is not mentioned. Choice (C) is incorrect because she describes the menu (selection) as *great*. Choice (D) is incorrect—she didn't have the appetizers, but she does not mention a reason or say anything more about them.
194. **(C)** The article is about the many new restaurants in the area, so from the context we know that the idea here is *crowding*. Choices (A), (B), and (D) are other uses of the word *concentration*, but they don't fit the context.

195. **(A)** The article says that businesses are *booming* and *taking off*, that is, fast becoming successful. Choices (B) and (C) are incorrect because the article suggests the opposite. Choice (D) is confused with the mention of the appeal of the menu to young people.
196. **(C)** The cost of the Hotel Shuttles is listed as *none*. Choices (A), (B), and (D) all have a cost.
197. **(B)** According to the notice, bus service to the airport is *temporarily suspended* because of work on renovations. Sam also says that he didn't take the bus because of the *mess at the terminal*, referring, in part, to the disruption caused by the renovation work. Choices (A), (C), and (D) are all plausible, but they are incorrect answers.
198. **(A)** Sam mentions that *Friday is such a heavy travel day*, implying that there were a lot of travelers at the airport. Choice (B) confuses the meaning of the word *mess* in this context. Choices (C) and (D) are not mentioned.
199. **(D)** The notice mentions *renovations and repairs being carried out at the East Terminal*. Choice (A) is confused with the correct answer, but it is an already-existing building that is being worked on, not a new one being built. Choice (B) is confused with the change in the location of the shuttles, but no schedule changes are mentioned. Choice (C) is confused with the mention of different bus routes, but no reorganization of them is mentioned.
200. **(C)** The idea is that people can *express*, or *talk about*, their questions and concerns with the PR Office. Choices (A), (B), and (D) are other uses of the word *direct*, but they don't fit the context.

ANSWER SHEET
New TOEIC—Model Test 6

LISTENING COMPREHENSION

Part 1: Photographs

1. Ⓐ Ⓑ Ⓒ Ⓓ	3. Ⓐ Ⓑ Ⓒ Ⓓ	5. Ⓐ Ⓑ Ⓒ Ⓓ
2. Ⓐ Ⓑ Ⓒ Ⓓ	4. Ⓐ Ⓑ Ⓒ Ⓓ	6. Ⓐ Ⓑ Ⓒ Ⓓ

Part 2: Question-Response

7. Ⓐ Ⓑ Ⓒ Ⓓ	14. Ⓐ Ⓑ Ⓒ Ⓓ	21. Ⓐ Ⓑ Ⓒ Ⓓ	28. Ⓐ Ⓑ Ⓒ Ⓓ
8. Ⓐ Ⓑ Ⓒ Ⓓ	15. Ⓐ Ⓑ Ⓒ Ⓓ	22. Ⓐ Ⓑ Ⓒ Ⓓ	29. Ⓐ Ⓑ Ⓒ Ⓓ
9. Ⓐ Ⓑ Ⓒ Ⓓ	16. Ⓐ Ⓑ Ⓒ Ⓓ	23. Ⓐ Ⓑ Ⓒ Ⓓ	30. Ⓐ Ⓑ Ⓒ Ⓓ
10. Ⓐ Ⓑ Ⓒ Ⓓ	17. Ⓐ Ⓑ Ⓒ Ⓓ	24. Ⓐ Ⓑ Ⓒ Ⓓ	31. Ⓐ Ⓑ Ⓒ Ⓓ
11. Ⓐ Ⓑ Ⓒ Ⓓ	18. Ⓐ Ⓑ Ⓒ Ⓓ	25. Ⓐ Ⓑ Ⓒ Ⓓ	
12. Ⓐ Ⓑ Ⓒ Ⓓ	19. Ⓐ Ⓑ Ⓒ Ⓓ	26. Ⓐ Ⓑ Ⓒ Ⓓ	
13. Ⓐ Ⓑ Ⓒ Ⓓ	20. Ⓐ Ⓑ Ⓒ Ⓓ	27. Ⓐ Ⓑ Ⓒ Ⓓ	

Part 3: Conversations

32. Ⓐ Ⓑ Ⓒ Ⓓ	42. Ⓐ Ⓑ Ⓒ Ⓓ	52. Ⓐ Ⓑ Ⓒ Ⓓ	62. Ⓐ Ⓑ Ⓒ Ⓓ
33. Ⓐ Ⓑ Ⓒ Ⓓ	43. Ⓐ Ⓑ Ⓒ Ⓓ	53. Ⓐ Ⓑ Ⓒ Ⓓ	63. Ⓐ Ⓑ Ⓒ Ⓓ
34. Ⓐ Ⓑ Ⓒ Ⓓ	44. Ⓐ Ⓑ Ⓒ Ⓓ	54. Ⓐ Ⓑ Ⓒ Ⓓ	64. Ⓐ Ⓑ Ⓒ Ⓓ
35. Ⓐ Ⓑ Ⓒ Ⓓ	45. Ⓐ Ⓑ Ⓒ Ⓓ	55. Ⓐ Ⓑ Ⓒ Ⓓ	65. Ⓐ Ⓑ Ⓒ Ⓓ
36. Ⓐ Ⓑ Ⓒ Ⓓ	46. Ⓐ Ⓑ Ⓒ Ⓓ	56. Ⓐ Ⓑ Ⓒ Ⓓ	66. Ⓐ Ⓑ Ⓒ Ⓓ
37. Ⓐ Ⓑ Ⓒ Ⓓ	47. Ⓐ Ⓑ Ⓒ Ⓓ	57. Ⓐ Ⓑ Ⓒ Ⓓ	67. Ⓐ Ⓑ Ⓒ Ⓓ
38. Ⓐ Ⓑ Ⓒ Ⓓ	48. Ⓐ Ⓑ Ⓒ Ⓓ	58. Ⓐ Ⓑ Ⓒ Ⓓ	68. Ⓐ Ⓑ Ⓒ Ⓓ
39. Ⓐ Ⓑ Ⓒ Ⓓ	49. Ⓐ Ⓑ Ⓒ Ⓓ	59. Ⓐ Ⓑ Ⓒ Ⓓ	69. Ⓐ Ⓑ Ⓒ Ⓓ
40. Ⓐ Ⓑ Ⓒ Ⓓ	50. Ⓐ Ⓑ Ⓒ Ⓓ	60. Ⓐ Ⓑ Ⓒ Ⓓ	70. Ⓐ Ⓑ Ⓒ Ⓓ
41. Ⓐ Ⓑ Ⓒ Ⓓ	51. Ⓐ Ⓑ Ⓒ Ⓓ	61. Ⓐ Ⓑ Ⓒ Ⓓ	

Part 4: Talks

71. Ⓐ Ⓑ Ⓒ Ⓓ	79. Ⓐ Ⓑ Ⓒ Ⓓ	87. Ⓐ Ⓑ Ⓒ Ⓓ	95. Ⓐ Ⓑ Ⓒ Ⓓ
72. Ⓐ Ⓑ Ⓒ Ⓓ	80. Ⓐ Ⓑ Ⓒ Ⓓ	88. Ⓐ Ⓑ Ⓒ Ⓓ	96. Ⓐ Ⓑ Ⓒ Ⓓ
73. Ⓐ Ⓑ Ⓒ Ⓓ	81. Ⓐ Ⓑ Ⓒ Ⓓ	89. Ⓐ Ⓑ Ⓒ Ⓓ	97. Ⓐ Ⓑ Ⓒ Ⓓ
74. Ⓐ Ⓑ Ⓒ Ⓓ	82. Ⓐ Ⓑ Ⓒ Ⓓ	90. Ⓐ Ⓑ Ⓒ Ⓓ	98. Ⓐ Ⓑ Ⓒ Ⓓ
75. Ⓐ Ⓑ Ⓒ Ⓓ	83. Ⓐ Ⓑ Ⓒ Ⓓ	91. Ⓐ Ⓑ Ⓒ Ⓓ	99. Ⓐ Ⓑ Ⓒ Ⓓ
76. Ⓐ Ⓑ Ⓒ Ⓓ	84. Ⓐ Ⓑ Ⓒ Ⓓ	92. Ⓐ Ⓑ Ⓒ Ⓓ	100. Ⓐ Ⓑ Ⓒ Ⓓ
77. Ⓐ Ⓑ Ⓒ Ⓓ	85. Ⓐ Ⓑ Ⓒ Ⓓ	93. Ⓐ Ⓑ Ⓒ Ⓓ	
78. Ⓐ Ⓑ Ⓒ Ⓓ	86. Ⓐ Ⓑ Ⓒ Ⓓ	94. Ⓐ Ⓑ Ⓒ Ⓓ	

ANSWER SHEET
New TOEIC—Model Test 6

READING

Part 5: Incomplete Sentences

101. Ⓐ Ⓑ Ⓒ Ⓓ	109. Ⓐ Ⓑ Ⓒ Ⓓ	117. Ⓐ Ⓑ Ⓒ Ⓓ	125. Ⓐ Ⓑ Ⓒ Ⓓ
102. Ⓐ Ⓑ Ⓒ Ⓓ	110. Ⓐ Ⓑ Ⓒ Ⓓ	118. Ⓐ Ⓑ Ⓒ Ⓓ	126. Ⓐ Ⓑ Ⓒ Ⓓ
103. Ⓐ Ⓑ Ⓒ Ⓓ	111. Ⓐ Ⓑ Ⓒ Ⓓ	119. Ⓐ Ⓑ Ⓒ Ⓓ	127. Ⓐ Ⓑ Ⓒ Ⓓ
104. Ⓐ Ⓑ Ⓒ Ⓓ	112. Ⓐ Ⓑ Ⓒ Ⓓ	120. Ⓐ Ⓑ Ⓒ Ⓓ	128. Ⓐ Ⓑ Ⓒ Ⓓ
105. Ⓐ Ⓑ Ⓒ Ⓓ	113. Ⓐ Ⓑ Ⓒ Ⓓ	121. Ⓐ Ⓑ Ⓒ Ⓓ	129. Ⓐ Ⓑ Ⓒ Ⓓ
106. Ⓐ Ⓑ Ⓒ Ⓓ	114. Ⓐ Ⓑ Ⓒ Ⓓ	122. Ⓐ Ⓑ Ⓒ Ⓓ	130. Ⓐ Ⓑ Ⓒ Ⓓ
107. Ⓐ Ⓑ Ⓒ Ⓓ	115. Ⓐ Ⓑ Ⓒ Ⓓ	123. Ⓐ Ⓑ Ⓒ Ⓓ	
108. Ⓐ Ⓑ Ⓒ Ⓓ	116. Ⓐ Ⓑ Ⓒ Ⓓ	124. Ⓐ Ⓑ Ⓒ Ⓓ	

Part 6: Text Completion

131. Ⓐ Ⓑ Ⓒ Ⓓ	135. Ⓐ Ⓑ Ⓒ Ⓓ	139. Ⓐ Ⓑ Ⓒ Ⓓ	143. Ⓐ Ⓑ Ⓒ Ⓓ
132. Ⓐ Ⓑ Ⓒ Ⓓ	136. Ⓐ Ⓑ Ⓒ Ⓓ	140. Ⓐ Ⓑ Ⓒ Ⓓ	144. Ⓐ Ⓑ Ⓒ Ⓓ
133. Ⓐ Ⓑ Ⓒ Ⓓ	137. Ⓐ Ⓑ Ⓒ Ⓓ	141. Ⓐ Ⓑ Ⓒ Ⓓ	145. Ⓐ Ⓑ Ⓒ Ⓓ
134. Ⓐ Ⓑ Ⓒ Ⓓ	138. Ⓐ Ⓑ Ⓒ Ⓓ	142. Ⓐ Ⓑ Ⓒ Ⓓ	146. Ⓐ Ⓑ Ⓒ Ⓓ

Part 7: Reading Comprehension

147. Ⓐ Ⓑ Ⓒ Ⓓ	161. Ⓐ Ⓑ Ⓒ Ⓓ	175. Ⓐ Ⓑ Ⓒ Ⓓ	189. Ⓐ Ⓑ Ⓒ Ⓓ
148. Ⓐ Ⓑ Ⓒ Ⓓ	162. Ⓐ Ⓑ Ⓒ Ⓓ	176. Ⓐ Ⓑ Ⓒ Ⓓ	190. Ⓐ Ⓑ Ⓒ Ⓓ
149. Ⓐ Ⓑ Ⓒ Ⓓ	163. Ⓐ Ⓑ Ⓒ Ⓓ	177. Ⓐ Ⓑ Ⓒ Ⓓ	191. Ⓐ Ⓑ Ⓒ Ⓓ
150. Ⓐ Ⓑ Ⓒ Ⓓ	164. Ⓐ Ⓑ Ⓒ Ⓓ	178. Ⓐ Ⓑ Ⓒ Ⓓ	192. Ⓐ Ⓑ Ⓒ Ⓓ
151. Ⓐ Ⓑ Ⓒ Ⓓ	165. Ⓐ Ⓑ Ⓒ Ⓓ	179. Ⓐ Ⓑ Ⓒ Ⓓ	193. Ⓐ Ⓑ Ⓒ Ⓓ
152. Ⓐ Ⓑ Ⓒ Ⓓ	166. Ⓐ Ⓑ Ⓒ Ⓓ	180. Ⓐ Ⓑ Ⓒ Ⓓ	194. Ⓐ Ⓑ Ⓒ Ⓓ
153. Ⓐ Ⓑ Ⓒ Ⓓ	167. Ⓐ Ⓑ Ⓒ Ⓓ	181. Ⓐ Ⓑ Ⓒ Ⓓ	195. Ⓐ Ⓑ Ⓒ Ⓓ
154. Ⓐ Ⓑ Ⓒ Ⓓ	168. Ⓐ Ⓑ Ⓒ Ⓓ	182. Ⓐ Ⓑ Ⓒ Ⓓ	196. Ⓐ Ⓑ Ⓒ Ⓓ
155. Ⓐ Ⓑ Ⓒ Ⓓ	169. Ⓐ Ⓑ Ⓒ Ⓓ	183. Ⓐ Ⓑ Ⓒ Ⓓ	197. Ⓐ Ⓑ Ⓒ Ⓓ
156. Ⓐ Ⓑ Ⓒ Ⓓ	170. Ⓐ Ⓑ Ⓒ Ⓓ	184. Ⓐ Ⓑ Ⓒ Ⓓ	198. Ⓐ Ⓑ Ⓒ Ⓓ
157. Ⓐ Ⓑ Ⓒ Ⓓ	171. Ⓐ Ⓑ Ⓒ Ⓓ	185. Ⓐ Ⓑ Ⓒ Ⓓ	199. Ⓐ Ⓑ Ⓒ Ⓓ
158. Ⓐ Ⓑ Ⓒ Ⓓ	172. Ⓐ Ⓑ Ⓒ Ⓓ	186. Ⓐ Ⓑ Ⓒ Ⓓ	200. Ⓐ Ⓑ Ⓒ Ⓓ
159. Ⓐ Ⓑ Ⓒ Ⓓ	173. Ⓐ Ⓑ Ⓒ Ⓓ	187. Ⓐ Ⓑ Ⓒ Ⓓ	
160. Ⓐ Ⓑ Ⓒ Ⓓ	174. Ⓐ Ⓑ Ⓒ Ⓓ	188. Ⓐ Ⓑ Ⓒ Ⓓ	

New TOEIC—Model Test 6

LISTENING COMPREHENSION

In this section of the test, you will have the chance to show how well you understand spoken English. There are four parts to this section, with special directions for each part. You will have approximately 45 minutes to complete the Listening Comprehension sections.

Part 1: Photographs

Track 62

Directions: You will see a photograph. You will hear four statements about the photograph. Choose the statement that most closely matches the photograph and fill in the corresponding oval on your answer sheet.

1.

2.

3.

4.

5.

6. 

Part 2: Question-Response

Directions: You will hear a question and three possible responses. Choose the response that most closely answers the question and fill in the corresponding oval on your answer sheet.

7. Mark your answer on your answer sheet.
8. Mark your answer on your answer sheet.
9. Mark your answer on your answer sheet.
10. Mark your answer on your answer sheet.
11. Mark your answer on your answer sheet.
12. Mark your answer on your answer sheet.
13. Mark your answer on your answer sheet.
14. Mark your answer on your answer sheet.
15. Mark your answer on your answer sheet.
16. Mark your answer on your answer sheet.
17. Mark your answer on your answer sheet.
18. Mark your answer on your answer sheet.
19. Mark your answer on your answer sheet.
20. Mark your answer on your answer sheet.
21. Mark your answer on your answer sheet.
22. Mark your answer on your answer sheet.
23. Mark your answer on your answer sheet.
24. Mark your answer on your answer sheet.
25. Mark your answer on your answer sheet.
26. Mark your answer on your answer sheet.
27. Mark your answer on your answer sheet.
28. Mark your answer on your answer sheet.
29. Mark your answer on your answer sheet.
30. Mark your answer on your answer sheet.
31. Mark your answer on your answer sheet.

Part 3: Conversations

Directions: You will hear a conversation between two people. You will see three questions on each conversation and four possible answers. Choose the best answer to each question and fill in the corresponding oval on your answer sheet.

32. What does the woman ask the man to do?
    (A) Give her a ride to work
    (B) Lift something heavy
    (C) Take her shopping
    (D) Fix her car

33. Why does the man want to be at the office early?
    (A) To repair some office equipment
    (B) To get ready for a client meeting
    (C) To wrap some presents
    (D) To finish a report

34. What does the woman suggest doing?
    (A) Leaving later
    (B) Calling a client
    (C) Stopping at the library
    (D) Asking someone for help

---

35. What are the speakers discussing?
    (A) Getting the office cleaned
    (B) Renting an apartment
    (C) Buying furniture
    (D) Going out to eat

36. What problem do they have?
    (A) They lost the contact information.
    (B) They think the price is too high.
    (C) They can't find anyone to hire.
    (D) They don't like the schedule.

37. What does the man suggest they do?
    (A) Leave earlier
    (B) Offer to pay less
    (C) Meet somewhere else
    (D) Buy new furniture

38. Why is the woman talking to the man?
    (A) To invite him somewhere
    (B) To make a suggestion
    (C) To discuss a problem
    (D) To ask for advice

39. What is the man doing?
    (A) Watching sports
    (B) Writing a report
    (C) Cleaning his desk
    (D) Making a phone call

40. What does the man ask the woman to do?
    (A) Give him directions to the restaurant
    (B) Come back to talk with him later
    (C) Help him with his work
    (D) Wait for him at 7:00

---

41. What is the man renting?
    (A) Some furniture
    (B) An apartment
    (C) A heater
    (D) A car

42. What does the woman suggest the man do?
    (A) Request something larger
    (B) Look at other options
    (C) Rent for more time
    (D) Reread the agreement

43. What will the man do next?
    (A) Fill the tank
    (B) Sign a document
    (C) Go away for the weekend
    (D) Go to another rental agency

44. Why did the man make the call?

(A) To report a problem
(B) To make a complaint
(C) To order a product
(D) To ask for information

45. What costs $20?

(A) Standard shipping
(B) Express shipping
(C) Special packaging
(D) Guaranteed delivery

46. What does the man mean when he says, "That's it"?

(A) He's decided which products to buy.
(B) His questions have been answered
(C) He's chosen his shipping method.
(D) His order is completed.

---

47. What best describes this conversation?

(A) An introduction
(B) A staff meeting
(C) An interview
(D) A sales pitch

48. What does the man like most about his job?

(A) The pay
(B) The events
(C) The benefits
(D) The schedule

49. What will probably happen next?

(A) The man will answer the woman's last question.
(B) The woman will speak with Mrs. Patterson.
(C) The man will leave for the weekend.
(D) The woman will go home.

---

50. What is likely the purpose of the man's trip?

(A) To meet a client
(B) To take a vacation
(C) To take photographs
(D) To attend a conference

51. What do the women imply about the hotel?

(A) It is in a bad location.
(B) It is uncomfortable.
(C) It is too expensive.
(D) It is very noisy.

52. What will the man do next?

(A) Research other hotels
(B) Reserve a room
(C) Cancel his trip
(D) Take a nap

---

53. What kind of work are they hiring contractors for?

(A) Construction
(B) Decorating
(C) Transportation
(D) Editing

54. What will happen at the meeting tomorrow?

(A) They will write a quote for the project.
(B) They will meet the contractor.
(C) They will talk about the schedule.
(D) They will review the submitted quotes.

55. What was the problem with the last contractor?

(A) He didn't finish the work.
(B) He left the job site a mess.
(C) He was located too far away.
(D) He tore up the contract.

---

56. Where does this conversation take place?

(A) Clothing store
(B) Restaurant
(C) Paint store
(D) Bank

57. Why is the man there?

(A) To apply for a job
(B) To return an item
(C) To order something
(D) To make a complaint

58. Why does the man say, "The selection certainly could be better"?

(A) He wants more time to make his choice.
(B) He doesn't like the offered choices.
(C) He hasn't ever seen better choices.
(D) He needs help making his choice.

59. What are the speakers discussing?

(A) A play
(B) A concert
(C) A business trip
(D) A boxing match

60. What is the woman's problem?

(A) She has to go out of town.
(B) She doesn't like her seat.
(C) She is busy tomorrow.
(D) She can't get tickets.

61. What does the second man offer to do?

(A) Plan a trip
(B) Call his cousin
(C) Buy some tickets
(D) Go to the box office

62. Look at the graphic. What floor will the woman go to?

(A) First floor
(B) Second Floor
(C) Third Floor
(D) Fourth Floor

Building Directory

1st floor:	Woolman & Fox, PC
2nd floor:	Gilchrist, Inc.
3rd floor:	Zenith Enterprises
4th floor:	HCR Company

63. Why is she going there?

(A) To start a new job
(B) For a job interview
(C) To look at an apartment
(D) For a doctor's appointment

64. What does the man imply about his relationship with Mr. Gill?

(A) He works near Mr. Gill.
(B) He is a client of Mr. Gill's.
(C) He has never met Mr. Gill.
(D) He wants to work for Mr. Gill.

65. What does the woman want to buy?

(A) Skis
(B) Shoes
(C) Boots
(D) Books

66. Look at the graphic. Why did the woman have a problem with the coupon?

(A) It has expired.
(B) She used the wrong code.
(C) She didn't spend enough money.
(D) It is not valid for online purchases.

www.sportstown.com

Sports Town

Discount Coupon

Take 25% off of any purchase of $150 or more

Coupon good for online or in-store purchases.

Coupon expires June 30.
Type in code: A106

67. What does the man mean when he says, "Tell you what"?

(A) He's going to tell a story.
(B) He's going to ask a question.
(C) He's going to explain something.
(D) He's going to offer to do something.

---

68. Why has there been a delay?

(A) The chef arrived late.
(B) There aren't enough servers.
(C) The restaurant is very crowded.
(D) There are some new staff working.

69. What does the woman imply about the restaurant?

(A) It has a good reputation.
(B) It is not well known.
(C) It is not very popular.
(D) It always has slow service.

70. Look at the graphic. What will the woman eat?

(A) Tuna fish salad
(B) Vegetable salad
(C) Baked fish
(D) Sautéed vegetables

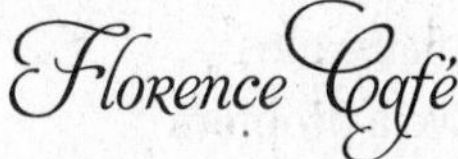

Lunch Specials

1. Tuna fish salad plate $13
2. Mixed vegetable salad............... $12
3. Baked fish with rice.................. $16
4. Sautéed vegetables with rice...... $15

NEW TOEIC—MODEL TEST 6

Part 4: Talks

Directions: You will hear a talk given by a single speaker. You will see three questions on each talk, each with four possible answers. Choose the best answer to each question and fill in the corresponding oval on your answer sheet.

71. What is the purpose of this message?
    (A) To explain rules
    (B) To solve a problem
    (C) To describe a schedule
    (D) To introduce a special offer

72. What happens once a year?
    (A) The park stays open late.
    (B) There is a movie night.
    (C) A discount is offered.
    (D) A concert is performed.

73. Who can the listener talk to by pressing one?
    (A) A musician
    (B) An operator
    (C) A sales agent
    (D) A park manager

---

74. What is the topic of the workshop?
    (A) Budgets
    (B) Computers
    (C) Investments
    (D) Software

75. What does the speaker give each participant?
    (A) A schedule
    (B) A laptop
    (C) A snack
    (D) A chair

76. How many breaks will there be?
    (A) 1
    (B) 2
    (C) 3
    (D) 4

77. Where is this talk happening?
    (A) On a plane
    (B) On a boat
    (C) At a hotel
    (D) On a bus

78. What is the problem?
    (A) Storage compartments are full.
    (B) There are not enough seats.
    (C) There is bad weather.
    (D) Bags have been lost.

79. What has been delayed?
    (A) Serving drinks
    (B) The arrival time
    (C) Showing a movie
    (D) The departure time

---

80. What problem does the speaker have with the product?
    (A) It doesn't have a cover.
    (B) The fan doesn't blow.
    (C) She can't turn it on.
    (D) It doesn't heat.

81. When did the speaker buy the product?
    (A) This morning
    (B) Two days ago
    (C) Last Tuesday
    (D) Nine days ago

82. What does the speaker ask the listener to do?
    (A) Replace the product
    (B) Provide a refund
    (C) Return the call
    (D) Send a manual

83. What is the focus of the tour?

(A) Architecture
(B) Gardens
(C) History
(D) Parks

84. How will the group travel?

(A) Bus
(B) Van
(C) Foot
(D) Bike

85. What will the group do first?

(A) Have lunch
(B) Look at a map
(C) Visit City Hall
(D) Buy their tickets

---

86. Where would this product be used?

(A) In an office
(B) At a restaurant
(C) On an airplane
(D) In a private home

87. How many cups of coffee does the product make?

(A) 20
(B) 24
(C) 28
(D) 29

88. What are listeners asked to do?

(A) Place an order
(B) Try other products
(C) Ask for a free sample
(D) Look for information

---

89. What event is the speaker reporting?

(A) Approval of bridge plans
(B) Completion of a bridge
(C) Repainting of an old bridge
(D) Repair work on all city bridges

90. What are people waiting to do?

(A) Photograph the bridge
(B) Talk with the reporter
(C) Cross the bridge
(D) See the mayor

91. What does the speaker mean when she says, "Hard to believe, but final costs came in well under budget"?

(A) She doesn't understand the budget.
(B) She's surprised the project cost so little.
(C) She thinks incorrect numbers have been given.
(D) She isn't certain what the total cost of the project is.

---

92. What is the book about?

(A) History
(B) Cooking
(C) Travel
(D) Memoir

93. What does the speaker mean when he says, "He jumped at the chance"?

(A) Roger decided not to take a risk.
(B) Roger immediately accepted a job offer.
(C) Roger was surprised to hear about the job.
(D) Roger looked for other work opportunities.

94. What will Roger do tomorrow?

(A) Cook a meal
(B) Eat at a restaurant
(C) Read from his book
(D) Travel to the Caribbean

---

95. What type of product does this company sell?

(A) Shoes
(B) Clothes
(C) Sports equipment
(D) Construction materials

96. Look at the graphic. Which age group does the speaker want to focus on?

(A) 13–20
(B) 21–40
(C) 41–60
(D) 61+

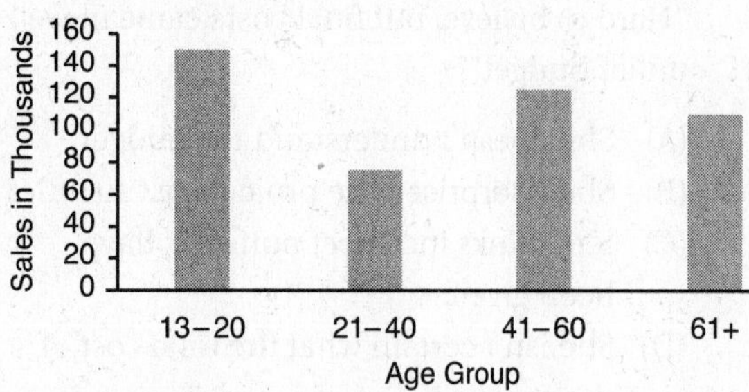

97. What will the listeners do next?

(A) Read a sales report
(B) Work in groups
(C) Have a discussion
(D) Look at another slide

98. Who is Marc, most likely?

(A) A ticket agent
(B) A hotel manager
(C) The speaker's boss
(D) The speaker's assistant

99. Why does the speaker want to change her travel plans?

(A) To go to a seminar
(B) To add more meetings
(C) To stay at a better hotel
(D) To use a different form of transportation

100. Look at the graphic. Which hotel will the speaker prefer?

(A) Richmond
(B) Golden
(C) Asterly
(D) Montshire

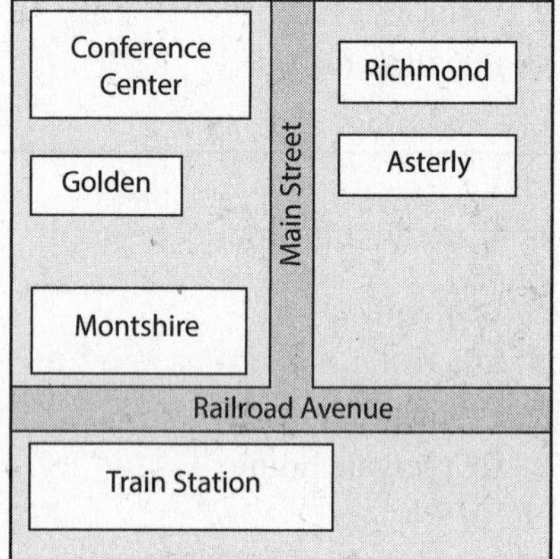

This is the end of the Listening Comprehension portion of the test. Turn to Part 5 in your test book.

READING COMPREHENSION

In this section of the test, you will have the chance to show how well you understand written English. There are three parts to this section, with special directions for each part.

YOU WILL HAVE ONE HOUR AND FIFTEEN MINUTES TO COMPLETE PARTS 5, 6, AND 7 OF THE TEST.

Part 5: Incomplete Sentences

Directions: You will see a sentence with a missing word. Four possible answers follow the sentence. Choose the best answer to the question and fill in the corresponding oval on your answer sheet.

101. Earn a good salary while building _________ job skills when you enroll in the City Tech carpentry program.

(A) value
(B) valued
(C) valuably
(D) valuable

102. The Whip cargo van can haul _________ to 5,350 pounds and comes with a rear back-up camera and security alarm.

(A) over
(B) up
(C) before
(D) in

103. The course is _________ for working professionals, so the class meets two evenings a week.

(A) barely
(B) rapidly
(C) primarily
(D) slightly

104. Greg Trist opens his art studio to the public on the first Monday of the month, which coincides _________ the city's monthly Art Walk event.

(A) between
(B) by
(C) through
(D) with

105. The executive team decided to use the pink and orange color _________ for the new laundry detergent logo.

(A) appearance
(B) photo
(C) scheme
(D) line

106. I strongly recommend _________ a contract with LL Logistics to handle our domestic deliveries.

(A) sign
(B) signed
(C) signing
(D) will sign

107. The landscaper said he _________ the hedges around the office when he comes next week.

(A) trims
(B) will trim
(C) has trimmed
(D) has been trimming

108. If you can wait a few minutes, Ms. Sato will attend _________ your problem as soon as she is free.

(A) to
(B) for
(C) beside
(D) in

109. Zasels' weekly coupon is good for 40% off items store-wide __________ custom framing, furniture, and electronics.

(A) exempt
(B) having
(C) without
(D) except

110. Visitors to the factory must leave their personal __________ at the security desk and put on a protective coat and a pair of goggles.

(A) belongings
(B) costumes
(C) experiences
(D) appearances

111. While he is a team player and always on time, Daniel doesn't have the skills to do __________ job.

(A) he
(B) him
(C) his
(D) her

112. By signing this form, you __________ KM Recovery Group to act as your agent.

(A) authorizing
(B) authorization
(C) authority
(D) authorize

113. Full-time employees __________ attend the RSTLC annual conference at their department's expense with approval from their supervisor.

(A) be
(B) don't
(C) can
(D) won't

114. Unfortunately, the kitchen needs __________ repairs that have to be made by a trained plumber.

(A) marginal
(B) extensive
(C) minimal
(D) common

115. __________ budget reductions, the company will not be filling the currently available Marketing Supervisor position.

(A) Due to
(B) However
(C) Because
(D) In that

116. The remote control __________ programmed to work with the television in the lobby but not the break room.

(A) has
(B) be
(C) been
(D) is

117. The person __________ signature appears on the document is the one ultimately responsible for the deal.

(A) who
(B) who's
(C) whose
(D) whom

118. __________ until the last minute to turn in work is definitely not encouraged in this department.

(A) Wait
(B) Waiting
(C) To wait
(D) Wait for

NEW TOEIC—MODEL TEST 6

119. You can sign up for the online training at your convenience _________ attend the next week's onsite training session in person.

(A) or
(B) so
(C) if
(D) as

120. The budget report had to be rewritten because some of the figures it contained were _________.

(A) acceptable
(B) inaccurate
(C) comprehensive
(D) calculating

121. The company has plans to _________ several neighboring properties, which will be used for expanding the manufacturing plant.

(A) inquire
(B) require
(C) expire
(D) acquire

122. _________ the client accepts the plan, the team has one month to complete the final design.

(A) Before
(B) After
(C) While
(D) Then

123. The best way to ________ approval from your supervisor is to consistently complete your projects on time.

(A) earn
(B) collect
(C) grant
(D) incur

124. When the renovations _________ complete, we will have a much more attractive and spacious office.

(A) are
(B) is
(C) be
(D) will be

125. The production team can _________ the photos if the client thinks they are too large.

(A) size
(B) resize
(C) sizeable
(D) sizing

126. _________ the shipment went out later than promised, the client decided to make another order.

(A) Because
(B) Therefore
(C) Despite
(D) Although

127. The prices quoted on the website _________ materials as well as labor, but not shipping and handling costs.

(A) include
(B) including
(C) inclusive
(D) inclusively

128. The Human Resources Department requires all applicants to provide references from their _________ employers.

(A) before
(B) advanced
(C) previous
(D) precede

129. You can choose to receive your paycheck by mail or opt for direct deposit into your back account _________.

(A) either
(B) instead
(C) alternative
(D) in addition

130. Last quarter's sales would have been better if the company _________ more in advertising.

(A) had invested
(B) has invested
(C) has been investing
(D) would have invested

Part 6: Text Completion

Directions: You will see four passages each with three blanks. Under each blank are four answer options. Choose the word or phrase that best completes the sentence.

Questions 131–134 refer to the following letter.

Dear Business Owner,

We are writing to let you __________ about our new company, Executive Dining,

131. (A) know
(B) knows
(C) to know
(D) will know

which provides catering services to local businesses. We cater everything from elegant banquets to informal refreshments for meetings and workshops. We have a variety of menus from which you can choose, and we can also tailor our offerings to meet __________ specific needs. We do everything from set up to

132. (A) its
(B) our
(C) your
(D) their

serving to clean up, and we can provide table settings, decorations, and chairs and tables as needed. As the company's __________, we have a combined 25 years of

133. (A) auditors
(B) backers
(C) clients
(D) founders

experience in food service and are both graduates of the National Culinary School.

____.

134. (A) We believe you will enjoy the meal we have planned for you
(B) We hope you will contact us to discuss your catering needs
(C) We have put your next company banquet on our schedule
(D) We look forward to meeting you at the end of the week

Sincerely,

Elaine Mayfield and Georgina Simms

Questions 135–138 refer to the following notice.

NOTICE TO RIDERS OF RED LINE BUSES

_____________________.

135. (A) Buses are undergoing routine maintenance
(B) Bus fares are scheduled to go up next month
(C) The number of buses serving this line will increase
(D) Renovations on selected bus shelters will begin soon

Therefore, Red Line service will be temporarily suspended at the Main Street stop as of June 1. Passengers can use the Oakland Avenue or River Street stops __________. Please check the City Transport Services (CTS)

136. (A) also
(B) despite
(C) instead
(D) nevertheless

website for schedule information for those stops. We apologize for any inconvenience this situation may cause. It is part of the mayor's initiative to __________ bus service for all users. Please __________ the CTS Public

137. (A) approve
(B) improve
(C) disprove
(D) reprove

138. (A) contact
(B) to contact
(C) can contact
(D) you will contact

Relations office with any questions or comments.

NEW TOEIC—MODEL TEST 6

Questions 139–142 refer to the following memo.

To: All employees
From: Arthur Ivers
Date: February 10
Re: Annual leave policy

We have revised the company's annual leave policy.

____.

139. (A) Revisions need approval from the HR office
(B) Please follow the guidelines in the handbook
(C) Annual leave can be taken at any time of year
(D) Here is the policy as it looks with the changes

- Leave requests must __________ a minimum of one month in advance.

140. (A) submit
(B) to submit
(C) be submitted
(D) be submitting

- To request time off, please complete Form 54 and make one copy for your supervisor and __________ for the HR office.

141. (A) another
(B) that one
(C) some
(D) this

- You may take no more than two weeks of leave at a time. If special circumstances require that you take more, please discuss with your supervisor.

I will be happy to answer any questions you may have __________ the

142. (A) pertaining
(B) regarding
(C) concerns
(D) relative

policy revisions.

Please stop by my office any time.

NEW TOEIC—MODEL TEST 6

Questions 143–146 refer to the following letter.

Hotel Comar

April 3

Dear Mr. Warren,

We have received your letter describing your stay at the Hotel Comar last week. ______________________.

143. (A) Thank you for choosing to stay at the Comar during your visit to this city
(B) We were very sorry to hear that you had such an unpleasant experience
(C) We regret that we have no rooms available at that time
(D) Our hotel is known as one of the finest in the city

We pride ourselves __________ our excellent customer service and strive

144. (A) on
(B) in
(C) of
(D) due

to make all our guests feel welcome and comfortable. Unfortunately, we did not meet this goal during your __________ stay. It was an unusually

145. (A) upcoming
(B) final
(C) lately
(D) recent

busy time for us as we were hosting two conferences, and it was also the height of the tourist season. However, that is not an excuse for neglecting the comfort of all our guests.

We hope you will consider __________ to the Hotel Comar the next time

146. (A) return
(B) returns
(C) returning
(D) to return

you are in town. We offer a prime location, fully-equipped gym, and a five-star restaurant. I am enclosing a coupon for twenty percent off the cost of your next stay with us.

Sincerely,

Amalia Knight
Manager

Part 7: Reading Comprehension

> **Directions:** You will see single and multiple reading passages followed by several questions. Each question has four answer choices. Choose the best answer to the question and fill in the corresponding oval on your answer sheet.

Questions 147–148 refer to the following webpage.

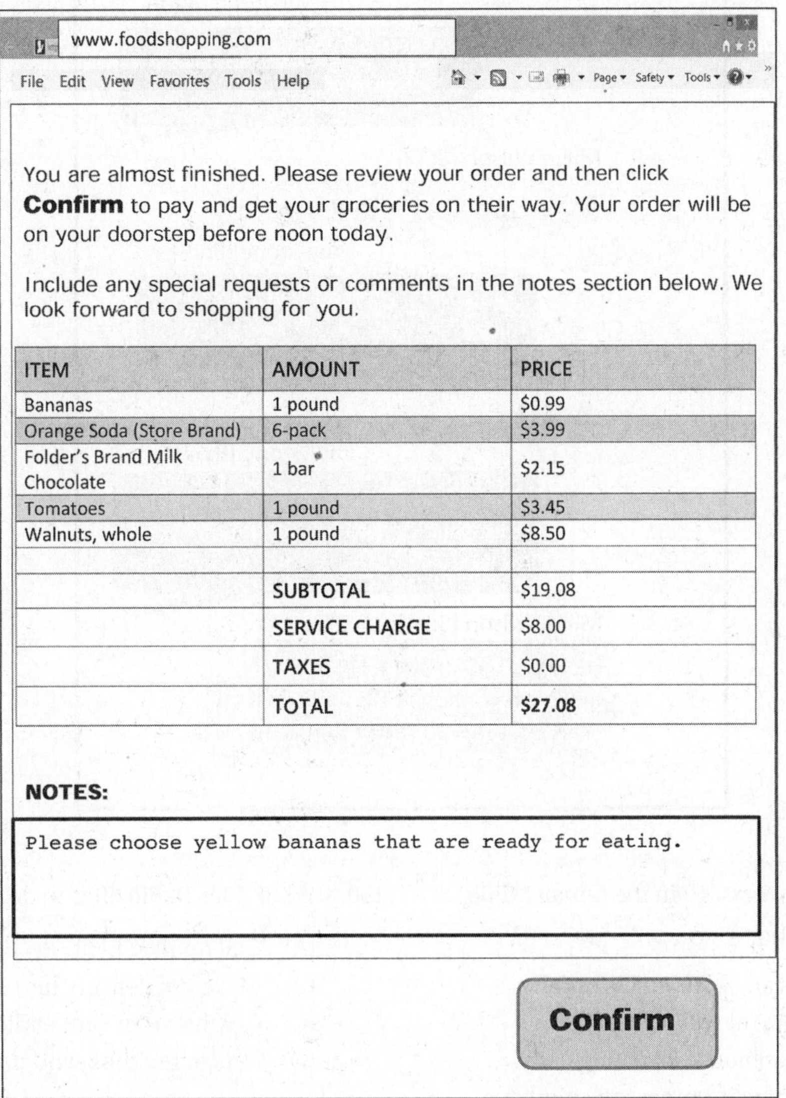

www.foodshopping.com

File Edit View Favorites Tools Help

You are almost finished. Please review your order and then click **Confirm** to pay and get your groceries on their way. Your order will be on your doorstep before noon today.

Include any special requests or comments in the notes section below. We look forward to shopping for you.

ITEM	AMOUNT	PRICE
Bananas	1 pound	$0.99
Orange Soda (Store Brand)	6-pack	$3.99
Folder's Brand Milk Chocolate	1 bar	$2.15
Tomatoes	1 pound	$3.45
Walnuts, whole	1 pound	$8.50
	SUBTOTAL	$19.08
	SERVICE CHARGE	$8.00
	TAXES	$0.00
	TOTAL	**$27.08**

NOTES:

Please choose yellow bananas that are ready for eating.

Confirm

147. When will the order be delivered?

(A) This morning
(B) This afternoon
(C) Tomorrow morning
(D) Tomorrow afternoon

148. What does the customer request?

(A) Cold soda
(B) Yellow tomatoes
(C) Ripe bananas
(D) Chopped walnuts

Questions 149–150 refer to the following text message chain.

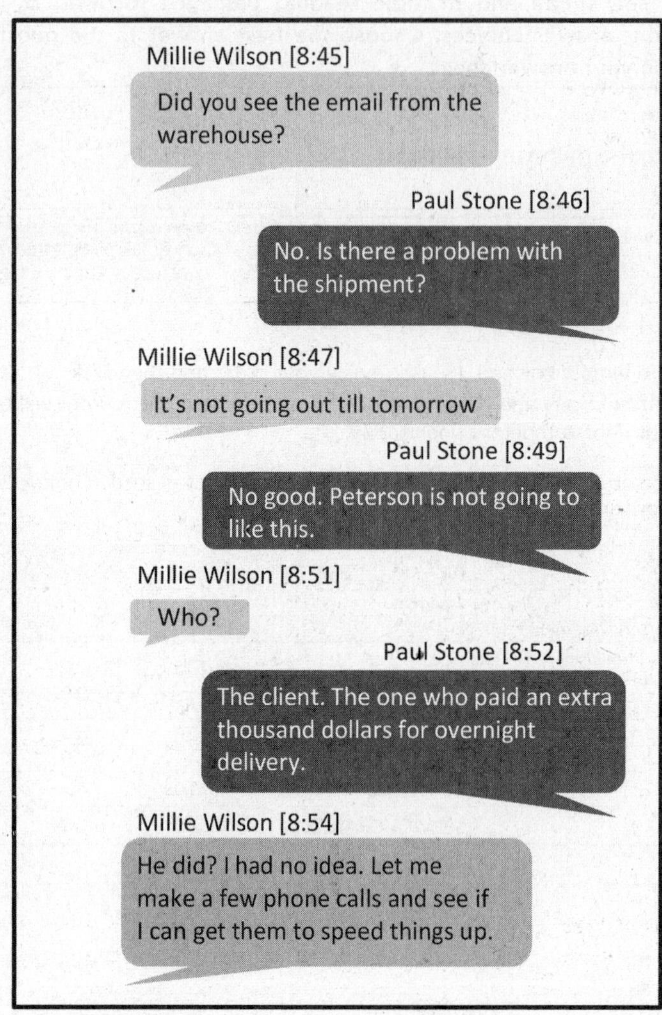

Millie Wilson [8:45]
Did you see the email from the warehouse?
Paul Stone [8:46]
No. Is there a problem with the shipment?
Millie Wilson [8:47]
It's not going out till tomorrow
Paul Stone [8:49]
No good. Peterson is not going to like this.
Millie Wilson [8:51]
Who?
Paul Stone [8:52]
The client. The one who paid an extra thousand dollars for overnight delivery.
Millie Wilson [8:54]
He did? I had no idea. Let me make a few phone calls and see if I can get them to speed things up.

149. What is the message in the e-mail Millie received?

(A) Paul is angry about his order.
(B) A shipment will be delayed.
(C) The warehouse is closing early.
(D) Paul forgot to process a shipment.

150. What does Millie offer to do?

(A) Call up the client
(B) Make the delivery herself
(C) Get the order sent earlier
(D) Return the thousand dollars

Questions 151–152 refer to the following expense report.

	Asterix, Inc. Expense Authorization Employee: Roland Webb Purpose: Wilmont office training seminar			
Category	**Date**	**Description**	**Notes**	**Amount**
Airfare	Sept. 16, Sept. 21	Round trip, business class.	Seminar originally planned for week of Sept. 9. Amount includes $200 change fee.	$885.
Hotel	Sept. 16–Sept. 20	$110/night x 5, at Atrium Hotel, Wilmont		$550
Car Rental	Sept. 16–Sept. 21	Zippo Rental Agency		$275

151. What fee is included in the cost of the airfare?

(A) Special meal
(B) Extra baggage
(C) First class upgrade
(D) Rescheduling charge

152. How many nights did the employee stay at the hotel?

(A) 1
(B) 5
(C) 6
(D) 10

Questions 153–154 refer to the following employment ad.

Part-time office assistant needed for small accounting firm. Will be trained in all aspects of the job including computer data entry, file management, and appointment scheduling. Must have pleasant manner and ability to provide excellent customer service. Must be proficient with word processing functions and able to learn software programs used in the office. Apply in person to Estelle Fox, 110 Grayson Avenue, Suite 10. No phone calls.

153. What is a requirement of the job?

(A) Proficiency in data entry
(B) Ability to program computers
(C) Knowledge of word processing
(D) Experience with appointment scheduling

154. How can someone apply for the job?

(A) Visit the office
(B) Send an e-mail
(C) Mail a résumé
(D) Call Ms. Fox

Questions 155–157 refer to the following article.

Richard Wenger, director of the Metropolitan Area Public Transportation System (MPTA), has announced that as of February 1 conductors on the MPTA's commuter rail lines will start accepting e-tickets on passengers' smartphones. Passengers can go to the MPTA website to purchase single-ride and round-trip tickets as well as weekly and annual passes, which are then sent by e-mail to the purchaser. Train conductors can scan the ticket or pass directly from the passenger's smartphones. Passengers can also choose to print their tickets, and the conductor will scan the printed copy. As an incentive to start using the new system, e-ticket purchasers will receive a 15 percent discount on all tickets and passes purchased during the month of February. Traditional paper tickets are still available for sale at ticket machines in most commuter rail stations. However, these tickets are being phased out and will no longer be available as of January 1st of next year. Mr. Wenger commented that surveys of commuter rail riders showed overwhelming enthusiasm for the new system.

155. What is this passage mostly about?

(A) A special discount
(B) A passenger survey
(C) A new kind of train ticket
(D) An increase in train fares

156. How are traditional tickets sold?

(A) On the web
(B) By machine
(C) From conductors
(D) At the MPTA office

157. The phrase *phased out* in line 21 is closest in meaning to

(A) displayed
(B) discovered
(C) distributed
(D) discontinued

Questions 158–160 refer to the following description

Professional Certification

The Southeastern Interior Design Association's professional certification program offers three levels of certification for professional interior designers. The program is open to anyone who has been a member in good standing for at least one year. The Southeastern Interior Design Association's professional certificates are recognized by most interior design businesses and training programs in the country.

Certificates are awarded upon successful completion of a test. To take the test for any one level of certification except Level One, you must have passed the previous level test. While no coursework is required, we do offer classes and reading materials to help you prepare for the test.

Currently, certification tests are administered every six months at the association's headquarters in Savannah. A web-based test will be available by the end of next year. For information on certification levels, test preparation classes, or test registration, please request an information packet from our office: *info@sidassn.org*. Don't forget to include your member number in your message.

158. What is required to take a test?
   (A) Membership in the association
   (B) Completion of certain classes
   (C) Experience in interior design
   (D) Graduation from a training program

159. How often are the tests given?
   (A) Six times a month
   (B) Six times a year
   (C) Once a year
   (D) Twice a year

160. What should someone do who wants to take the test?
   (A) Enroll in a class
   (B) E-mail the office
   (C) Visit the website
   (D) Speak with an advisor

Questions 161–163 refer to the following flier.

Lightning Car Rentals

NEW: Damage Fee Waiver offer

Your standard rental agreement includes comprehensive insurance. However, if your rented vehicle is involved in an incident during your rental period, you could be responsible for a $500 damage fee that is not covered by insurance.

Renters who are aged 21 or over and haven't been involved in an accident in the past 12 months have the option to purchase a Damage Fee Waiver. These waivers are not a substitute for insurance coverage; they offer extra peace of mind against unexpected costs. The waiver must be added to the rental agreement at the time of signing.

Two Damage Fee Waivers are available.

- Half Waiver: For $10 per day of rental period, reduce your damage fee to $250
- Full Waiver: For $15 per day of rental period, reduce your damage fee to $0

Ask your rental agent to add this waiver to your rental agreement now.

161. Who can get a waiver?

(A) Any agency customer
(B) Drivers who pass a road test
(C) Customers who rent for a week
(D) People with a safe driving record

162. What is the waiver for?

(A) To extend coverage to 12 months
(B) To remove the age requirement
(C) To reduce or eliminate a charge
(D) To replace regular insurance

163. When should a waiver be purchased?

(A) When signing the rental agreement
(B) When making a reservation
(C) When reporting an accident
(D) When insurance is purchased

Questions 164–167 refer to the following online chat discussion.

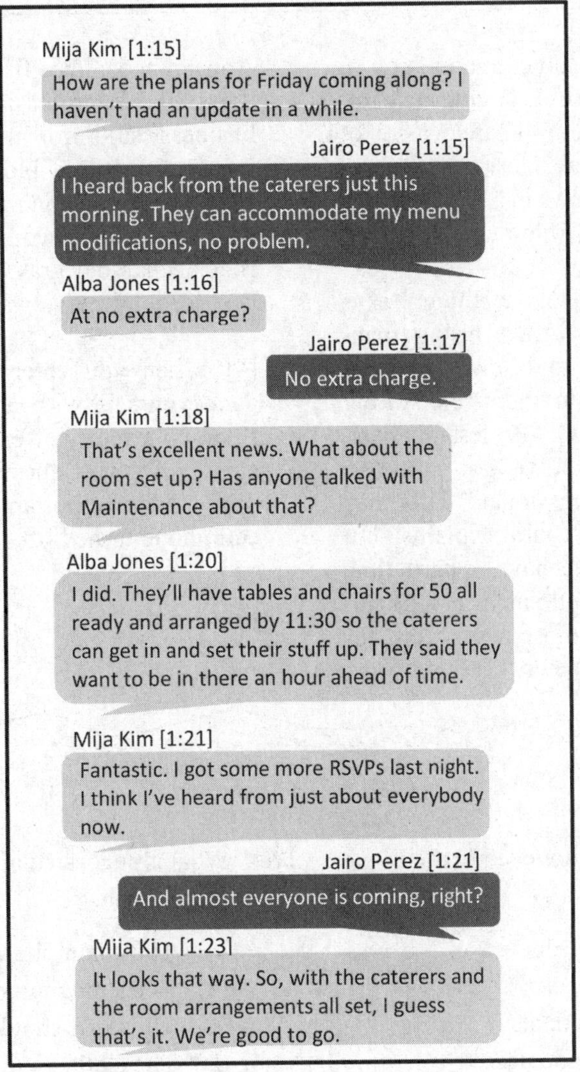
Mija Kim [1:15]
How are the plans for Friday coming along? I haven't had an update in a while.

Jairo Perez [1:15]
I heard back from the caterers just this morning. They can accommodate my menu modifications, no problem.

Alba Jones [1:16]
At no extra charge?

Jairo Perez [1:17]
No extra charge.

Mija Kim [1:18]
That's excellent news. What about the room set up? Has anyone talked with Maintenance about that?

Alba Jones [1:20]
I did. They'll have tables and chairs for 50 all ready and arranged by 11:30 so the caterers can get in and set their stuff up. They said they want to be in there an hour ahead of time.

Mija Kim [1:21]
Fantastic. I got some more RSVPs last night. I think I've heard from just about everybody now.

Jairo Perez [1:21]
And almost everyone is coming, right?

Mija Kim [1:23]
It looks that way. So, with the caterers and the room arrangements all set, I guess that's it. We're good to go.

164. What is being planned?

(A) A workshop
(B) A staff meeting
(C) A demonstration
(D) A luncheon

165. What did Jairo change?

(A) The menu
(B) The schedule
(C) The number of guests
(D) The room arrangement

166. What did Mija receive last night?

(A) A guest list
(B) Invitation responses
(C) Room arrangement plans
(D) A message from the caterers

167. At 1:23, what does Mija mean when she writes, "We're good to go"?

(A) The guests are happy to be invited.
(B) It's time to set up the room.
(C) Everything is ready.
(D) She has to leave.

Questions 168–171 refer to the following excerpt from an article.

The question is all too common. You're new to the job market, having just finished your education. There's a lot of competition out there. How can you prepare for job interviews in a way that will help you stand out from the crowd? [1]

"It all boils down to one thing," says Evelyn Pritchard, former hiring manager at XQ, Inc. and now president of her own employment consulting firm, Pritchard, LLC. "Professionalism. That's the key. You've got to dress, talk, act like a professional." This may seem obvious, Pritchard explains, but many young people have a hard time grasping this concept. She offers the following advice for those setting out for their first job interviews. [2]

Appearance comes first. [3] You should dress like a professional. This means business suits for men and business suits or skirt and blouse combinations for women. Keep in mind that you don't want the color of your clothes to shout. Black, charcoal gray, or deep blue are best for job interviews.

[4] When you enter the room, introduce yourself with a firm handshake. Look your interviewer in the eye as you speak. Answer questions with confidence. Most important of all, keep your cell phone turned off.

168. Who would be most interested in this article?

(A) Hiring managers
(B) Employment agencies
(C) Mid-level professionals
(D) Recent college graduates

169. What does Ms. Pritchard mean in paragraph 2, line 1, when she is quoted as saying, "It all boils down to one thing"?

(A) It is important to stand out from the crowd.
(B) Her advice can be summarized in one word.
(C) People must work hard to look professional.
(D) Interviews are a key part of the hiring process.

170. What is suggested about clothes worn for job interviews?

(A) The colors should be dark.
(B) The suits should be clean.
(C) The skirts should be long.
(D) The clothes should be new.

171. In which of the positions marked [1], [2], [3], and [4] does the following sentence best belong?

"Acting like a professional is as important as looking like one."

(A) [1]
(B) [2]
(C) [3]
(D) [4]

Questions 172–175 refer to the following letter.

August 22

Stephanie Jackson
PO Box 110
Marston, NH

Dear Ms. Jackson,

I heard you speak last week when you were a guest on our local radio show, Green Energy Talk. I was very impressed with the depth of your knowledge about solar energy. I know a little bit about this subject myself. I belong to a small local organization called Sun Power that has the goal of bringing more solar power to our community. I have some familiarity with the different types of solar panels and have installed some on the roof of my house. They provide my family with most of our domestic hot water needs throughout the year.

As you are well aware, replacing fossil fuels with alternative forms of energy is crucial to our future, and I believe we need to spread the word and get more people on board with this. To that end, we are having an alternative energy fair in our community toward the end of next month. We would be very grateful if you would consider being one of our speakers. We wouldn't be able to pay you, but you would have the chance to sell your books there. If you plan to attend, I will need to hear back from you before the end of two weeks so that I can put you on the schedule. Thank you for considering my request, and I hope to see you in September.

Sincerely,

Fred Marquez

Fred Marquez

172. Why did Mr. Marquez write the letter to Ms. Jackson?

(A) To tell her about his organization
(B) To sell her some solar panels
(C) To invite her to an event
(D) To ask her for a job

173. What is indicated about Mr. Marquez?

(A) He is the president of the Sun Power organization.
(B) He wants to get people interested in his cause.
(C) He makes a living installing solar panels.
(D) He is an expert on solar energy.

174. What is suggested about Ms. Jackson?

(A) She has written some books.
(B) She is a friend of Mr. Marquez.
(C) She hosts a radio show.
(D) She travels frequently.

175. When does Mr. Marquez need to have Ms. Jackson's reply?

(A) In one week
(B) In two weeks
(C) Before September
(D) Before next month

Questions 176–180 refer to the following webpage and e-mail.

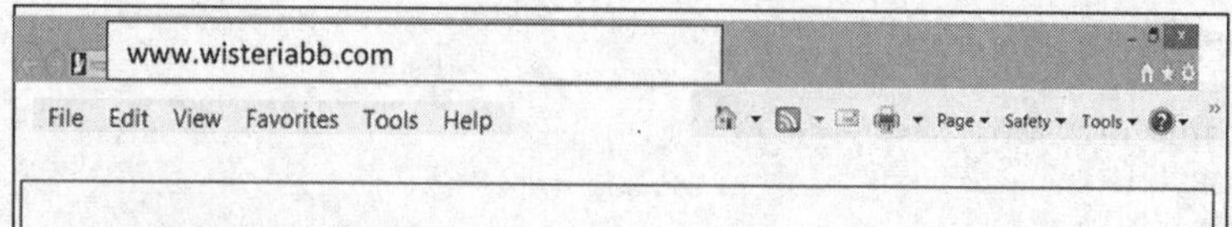

Wisteria Bed and Breakfast

Come stay with us at the Wisteria Bed and Breakfast, a historical converted farmhouse. Each one of our six guest rooms is decorated with period furnishings and artifacts. Enjoy peace and quite while relaxing on our wisteria-covered porch with views of pastures and hills. Take a guided horseback ride through nearby wooded trails. Enjoy the many exciting cultural and sports activities available in our area.

Our spacious refurbished barn is the perfect setting for your wedding or family reunion.

Click here for information about holding your event at Wisteria Bed and Breakfast.

All rooms include breakfast of homemade pastries and seasonal dishes carefully crafted from the finest local ingredients.

Rooms start at $99/night.

Two-night minimum required for weekend stays.

Click here to see rooms and check availability.

Book your room before April 30 and receive 20% off the usual price.

From: lsimmonsherbs@simmons.com
To: info@wisteriabb.com
Subject: introducing myself
Date: April 1

Hi,

I just saw your bed and breakfast website. It looks lovely. I noticed that you include local ingredients in your breakfast dishes. I am a local grower of herbs and flowers. I sell my products at local farmer's markets and also have a number of regular customers among the area's hotels and restaurants.

I would be happy to provide your business with fresh herbs and flowers on either a regular or as-needed basis. I can supply fresh herbs for your breakfasts and floral decorations for weddings that you host. In addition, you may want to consider providing your guests with fragrant herbal bouquets in their rooms.

I can come by your place any time next week to talk it over. In the meantime, I am attaching a list of herbs and flowers I have available, by season. Prices vary but are always competitive.

I look forward to hearing from you.

Lucinda Simmons

176. What is suggested about the Wisteria?

(A) It is a large hotel.
(B) It is in a rural setting.
(C) It has a flower garden.
(D) It has a modern design.

177. What can guests do at the Wisteria?

(A) Buy crafts
(B) Have lunch
(C) Host a party
(D) Work in the barn

178. How can a guest get a discount?

(A) Hold an event in the barn
(B) Stay at the Wisteria in April
(C) Stay for two weekend nights
(D) Make a reservation before April 30

179. Why did Ms. Simmons write the e-mail?

(A) To offer products for sale
(B) To make a room reservation
(C) To ask about buying the business
(D) To find out about holding an event

180. What kind of business does Ms. Simmons have?

(A) Farm
(B) Hotel
(C) Restaurant
(D) Event planning

Questions 181–185 refer to the following e-mail and flier.

From: drosen@mycompany.com
To: customerservice@marvelclean.com
Subject: cleaning
Date: December 15

Dear Marvel Cleaning Service,

I am interested in finding out about your cleaning services. I am currently located at the Octagon Towers, but plan to be leaving next month. According to the terms of the lease here, tenants must leave everything in good condition or be charged a penalty by the landlord. So, I need a service to come in and clean up after I have left, and a colleague at work suggested I contact you. I am contacting several services at this time, so that I can compare costs. Could you let me know how much you would charge to clean my place? Would you need to visit it first, or can you tell me the price based on size? It is an efficiency apartment, so it consists of just one large room.

Thank you.

David Rosen

Marvel Cleaning Service

"Big or small, we clean it all."

Leave the housekeeping to us. Whether you live in a palatial mansion or an efficiency apartment, we will make your home sparkle and shine.

Up to 3 rooms	.... $75
4–5 rooms	.... $125
6–7 rooms	.... $175
8 rooms	.... $200
over 8 rooms	.... Contact us

If your space is larger than 8 rooms, a customer service representative will discuss your needs with you and provide you with an estimate. We guarantee that our prices are always competitive. Call us when you need us, or arrange for regular weekly or monthly service.

Book your cleaning today.
customerservice@marvelclean.com
303-555-1212

181. Why does Mr. Rosen need to have his apartment cleaned?

(A) He is looking for a tenant.
(B) He is expecting visitors.
(C) He is moving away.
(D) He is hosting a party.

182. How did Mr. Rosen hear about Marvel?

(A) A co-worker recommended it.
(B) He found it on the Internet.
(C) His landlord suggested it.
(D) He saw the flier.

183. How much will it cost to clean Mr. Rosen's apartment?

(A) $75
(B) $125
(C) $175
(D) $200

184. What is suggested about Marvel Cleaning Service?

(A) It charges more than other cleaners.
(B) It cleans residences only.
(C) It doesn't serve one-time customers.
(D) It rarely cleans spaces larger than 8 rooms.

185. In the flier, the word *estimate* in paragraph 2, line 3, is closest in meaning to

(A) guess
(B) value
(C) analysis
(D) approximation

Questions 186–190 refer to the following webpage, e-mail, and review.

www.lannons.com

File Edit View Favorites Tools Help

LANNON'S OFFICE SUPPLY

✱Special Promotions✱

E-Z Folding Table

Need extra work space? Holding a large meeting or luncheon? Desk too small? The E-Z Folding Table expands your space in just seconds. It quickly unfolds to accommodate up to 8 people. When you no longer need it, it folds back up to a compact size that fits easily in most closets. Black table top with chrome legs.

Buy now and save!

Small (seats 4)	$65
Medium (seats 6)	$85
Large (seats 8)	$110
Set of 3 (1 of each size)	$230

(Prices good though March 30.)

First-time customer? Use coupon code **Z54** at checkout for a 15% discount.

Click here to calculate shipping costs.

Free shipping on all orders of $100 or more.

From: noreply@lannon.com
To: miker@trex.com
Subject: your order

The following item(s) shipped today.

Item	Quantity	Price
E-Z Folding Table	1	$110.00
Tax		$6.50
Shipping		$0
Total		$116.50

Tracking no. 1205039299919111
You can track your order at *www.lannons.com/tracking*

By Mike Rivera on June 14, 2016

I received my Lannon's E-Z Folding Table last week. Everything was great until I went to put it away. It unfolds easily and is very sturdy and also attractive, but when I first folded it up to put away, I realized the clips were missing. These are needed because without them, the table doesn't stay folded and you can't store it. I originally gave this product 3 stars because of this. However, I contacted customer service and they sent me the clips right away. The customer service person was very polite, and now that I have the clips, the table perfectly suits my needs. We use it in our office for our weekly staff meetings and everybody says it is very comfortable and convenient to use. Highly recommended.

186. What is suggested about the folding table?

(A) It is currently on sale.
(B) It is available only in March.
(C) It is comes in a variety of colors.
(D) It is the website's most popular item.

187. Which table did Mr. Rivera order?

(A) Small
(B) Medium
(C) Large
(D) Set of 3

188. Why didn't Mr. Rivera pay shipping costs?

(A) He had a coupon for free shipping.
(B) His order cost more than $100.
(C) The company never charges for shipping.
(D) He forgot to include this on his order form.

189. Why did Mr. Rivera order the table?

(A) For client consultations
(B) For extra desk space
(C) For guests at a lunch
(D) For use at meetings

190. Why did Mr. Rivera change his original product rating?

(A) His use of the product changed.
(B) His co-workers liked the product.
(C) The company corrected a mistake.
(D) He listened to other reviewers' opinions.

Questions 191–195 refer to the following flier and e-mails.

Stoneybrook Dinner Theater

presents

Romeo and Juliet
by William Shakespeare
June 12, 13, 14, 19, 20, and 21

Enjoy a three-course meal followed by our own specially-choreographed version of Shakespeare's classic tale.

Reserve your place now! Visit us online at *www.stoneybrookdt.com* or call us at 493-555-2121.

	Show only	Dinner and Show
per person	$50	$80
per couple	$90	$135

Dinner begins at 6:30, show begins at 8:00.

Three-course meal includes:

- Choice of soup or salad
- Entrée—beef, chicken, or vegetarian
- Dessert

From: estherwilson@acme.com
To: bobcharles@workplace.com
Subject: dinner theater
Date: June 12

Bob,

Are you interested in seeing Romeo and Juliet? My sister gave me some tickets that she can't use. They're for that Stoneybrook Dinner Theater place, so we'd have dinner first and then see the play. I've heard the food there is only mediocre, but the play got fantastic reviews.

The tickets are for June 21st. I won't be able to leave the office that day until a little after 6:00, and I really don't want to be late for the dinner, so I think the best plan would be for me to take a cab and meet you there. I hope you can come. I know it will be fun.

Esther

From: bobcharles@workplace.com

To: estherwilson@acme.com

Subject: re: dinner theater

Date: June 12

Hi Esther,

Yes, I would love to join you at the dinner theater. It sounds like a lot of fun, and it will my first time seeing this particular play. I'll have my car with me, so I'll plan to pick you up. Then you won't have to worry about a cab. It only takes 15 minutes to get to the dinner theater from your office, so I think we'll make it just in time.

I know what you mean about the food. I've actually eaten there before. I suppose we could just skip the dinner and see the show only, but you already have the tickets, so we might as well enjoy it as much as we can. And I am really looking forward to seeing the play.

See you June 21st.

Bob

191. What is suggested about the meal at the dinner theater?

(A) It is served after the show.
(B) It includes dishes without meat.
(C) It can be bought apart from show tickets.
(D) It is highly-rated by restaurant reviewers

192. How much did Esther pay for the dinner theater tickets?

(A) $0
(B) $80
(C) $90
(D) $135

193. How will Esther probably get to the dinner theater?

(A) She will drive.
(B) She will take a cab.
(C) She will ride the bus.
(D) She will get a ride with Bob.

194. What is suggested about Bob?

(A) He doesn't like to see plays.
(B) He has never seen Romeo and Juliet.
(C) He thinks the play won't be very good.
(D) He has not been to the dinner theater before.

195. In the second e-mail, the word *skip* in paragraph 2, line 2, is closest in meaning to

(A) consume
(B) improve
(C) omit
(D) jump

Questions 196–200 refer to the following itinerary, flier, and e-mail.

HR Manufacturers
Itinerary for: Siri Hakim
Wiltshire/Montague trip
April 10–April 15

Sunday, April 10	lv. 2:30 P.M. Breezeways Flight 23 arr Wiltshire 8:30 P.M. Rivera Hotel, Wiltshire
Monday, April 11	10 A.M. – 5 P.M. Meetings with Product Development Team
Tuesday, April 12	8:00 A.M. Train to Montague, tour of HR Manufacturers Plant Hotel Pine, Montague
Wednesday, April 13	9:15 A.M. Train to Wiltshire 2:00 P.M. Meeting with Marketing Department Riviera Hotel, Wiltshire
Thursday, April 14	8:00 A.M. Breakfast meeting with John Andrews 10:00 A.M. Tour of Wiltshire. 1:30 pm. Presentation to Wiltshire staff
Friday, April 15	lv. 9:45 A.M. Breezeways Flight 567

Don't miss the 3rd annual Wiltshire

Business Expo!

Exhibits by businesses from all over the region

✔ See new products and innovations
✔ Find out about current best business practices

Workshops by renowned business experts

✔ Learn from some of the country's most respected business professionals.

(See other side for a list of workshop topics and a complete schedule.)

Bring your resume!

✔ Recruiters from major companies will be available to meet with job seekers and discuss employment opportunities.

Wiltshire Conference Center

April 15–17

From: shakim@hrmanufacturersinc
To: kkato@hrmanufacturersinc
Subject: April trip
Date: March 29

Ken,

Thanks for putting together the itinerary for my trip next month. It all looks great. I'm really looking forward to finally having the chance to meet the Wiltshire team. Just one thing. I've learned that there will be a business expo in Wiltshire that weekend, and I'd like to take the opportunity to see it. It would be a chance to meet up with some former colleagues and possibly make some valuable connections. So if you could just change my return date to Saturday, that would be great. I guess that'll mean another night at the hotel as well as rescheduling the flight.

Thanks.

Siri

196. When will Ms. Hakim visit a factory?

(A) April 10
(B) April 11
(C) April 12
(D) April13

197. What can people do at the business expo?

(A) Buy products
(B) Interview for jobs
(C) Learn to write resumes
(D) Find out about business loans

198. In the flier, the word *renowned* in line 6 is closest in meaning to

(A) trained
(B) famous
(C) experienced
(D) knowledgeable

199. What change does Ms. Hakim want to make to her itinerary?

(A) Add a day to her trip
(B) Move to a different hotel
(C) Have another staff meeting
(D) Stay in Wiltshire for the weekend

200. What is suggested about Ms. Hakim?

(A) She has never been to the Wiltshire office.
(B) She takes frequent business trips.
(C) She is looking for people to hire.
(D) She used to work in Wiltshire.

STOP

This is the end of the test. If you finish before time is called, you may go back to Parts 5, 6, and 7 and check your work.

ANSWER KEY
New TOEIC—Model Test 6

LISTENING COMPREHENSION

Part 1: Photographs

1. **C**
2. **A**
3. **D**
4. **A**
5. **B**
6. **D**

Part 2: Question-Response

7. **B**
8. **A**
9. **C**
10. **A**
11. **C**
12. **A**
13. **B**
14. **B**
15. **A**
16. **C**
17. **C**
18. **B**
19. **A**
20. **B**
21. **B**
22. **A**
23. **C**
24. **C**
25. **B**
26. **A**
27. **A**
28. **C**
29. **B**
30. **A**
31. **A**

Part 3: Conversations

32. **A**
33. **B**
34. **A**
35. **A**
36. **D**
37. **C**
38. **A**
39. **B**
40. **C**
41. **D**
42. **C**
43. **B**
44. **D**
45. **B**
46. **B**
47. **C**
48. **D**
49. **B**
50. **D**
51. **B**
52. **A**
53. **A**
54. **D**
55. **C**
56. **D**
57. **C**
58. **B**
59. **A**
60. **D**
61. **B**
62. **C**
63. **B**
64. **A**
65. **C**
66. **A**
67. **D**
68. **B**
69. **A**
70. **B**

Part 4: Talks

71. **D**
72. **A**
73. **C**
74. **C**
75. **A**
76. **B**
77. **A**
78. **C**
79. **A**
80. **D**
81. **B**
82. **C**
83. **A**
84. **C**
85. **B**
86. **A**
87. **B**
88. **D**
89. **B**
90. **C**
91. **B**
92. **B**
93. **B**
94. **C**
95. **A**
96. **B**
97. **C**
98. **D**
99. **A**
100. **D**

ANSWER KEY
New TOEIC—Model Test 6

READING

Part 5: Incomplete Sentences

101. **D**
102. **B**
103. **C**
104. **D**
105. **C**
106. **C**
107. **B**
108. **A**
109. **D**
110. **A**
111. **C**
112. **D**
113. **C**
114. **B**
115. **A**
116. **D**
117. **C**
118. **B**
119. **A**
120. **B**
121. **D**
122. **B**
123. **A**
124. **A**
125. **B**
126. **D**
127. **A**
128. **C**
129. **B**
130. **A**

Part 6: Text Completion

131. **A**
132. **C**
133. **D**
134. **B**
135. **D**
136. **C**
137. **B**
138. **A**
139. **D**
140. **C**
141. **A**
142. **B**
143. **B**
144. **A**
145. **D**
146. **C**

Part 7: Reading Comprehension

147. **A**
148. **C**
149. **B**
150. **C**
151. **D**
152. **B**
153. **C**
154. **A**
155. **C**
156. **B**
157. **D**
158. **A**
159. **D**
160. **B**
161. **D**
162. **C**
163. **A**
164. **D**
165. **A**
166. **B**
167. **C**
168. **D**
169. **B**
170. **A**
171. **D**
172. **C**
173. **B**
174. **A**
175. **B**
176. **B**
177. **C**
178. **D**
179. **A**
180. **A**
181. **C**
182. **A**
183. **A**
184. **B**
185. **D**
186. **A**
187. **C**
188. **B**
189. **D**
190. **C**
191. **B**
192. **A**
193. **D**
194. **B**
195. **C**
196. **C**
197. **B**
198. **B**
199. **A**
200. **A**

TEST SCORE CONVERSION TABLE

Count your correct responses. Match the number of correct responses with the corresponding score from the Test Score Conversion Table (below). Add the two scores together. This is your Total Estimated Test Score. As you practice taking the TOEIC model tests, your scores should improve. Keep track of your Total Estimated Test Scores.

# Correct	Listening Score	Reading Score	# Correct	Listening Score	Reading Score	# Correct	Listening Score	Reading Score	# Correct	Listening Score	Reading Score
0	5	5	26	110	65	51	255	220	76	410	370
1	5	5	27	115	70	52	260	225	77	420	380
2	5	5	28	120	80	53	270	230	78	425	385
3	5	5	29	125	85	54	275	235	79	430	390
4	5	5	30	130	90	55	280	240	80	440	395
5	5	5	31	135	95	56	290	250	81	445	400
6	5	5	32	140	100	57	295	255	82	450	405
7	10	5	33	145	110	58	300	260	83	460	410
8	15	5	34	150	115	59	310	265	84	465	415
9	20	5	35	160	120	60	315	270	85	470	420
10	25	5	36	165	125	61	320	280	86	475	425
11	30	5	37	170	130	62	325	285	87	480	430
12	35	5	38	175	140	63	330	290	88	485	435
13	40	5	39	180	145	64	340	300	89	490	445
14	45	5	40	185	150	65	345	305	90	495	450
15	50	5	41	190	160	66	350	310	91	495	455
16	55	10	42	195	165	67	360	320	92	495	465
17	60	15	43	200	170	68	365	325	93	495	470
18	65	20	44	210	175	69	370	330	94	495	480
19	70	25	45	215	180	70	380	335	95	495	485
20	75	30	46	220	190	71	385	340	96	495	490
21	80	35	47	230	195	72	390	350	97	495	495
22	85	40	48	240	200	73	395	355	98	495	495
23	90	45	49	245	210	74	400	360	99	495	495
24	95	50	50	250	215	75	405	365	100	495	495
25	100	60									

Number of Correct Listening Responses ________ = Listening Score ________

Number of Correct Reading Responses ________ = Reading Score ________

Total Estimated Test Score ________.

EXPLANATORY ANSWERS

Listening Comprehension

PART 1: PHOTOGRAPHS

1. **(C)** A woman is standing at a podium speaking into a microphone. Choice (A) confuses similar-sounding words *microphone* and *cell phone.* Choice (B) correctly identifies the action of standing, but there is no store in the picture. Choice (D) refers to the woman's hands, which are visible, but she is not shaking hands with anyone.
2. **(A)** A man in a business suit is looking at a computer and writing notes with a pen. Choice (B) correctly identifies the glass of water on the table, but there is no waiter. Choice (C) correctly identifies the computer, but there is no salesman and the scene doesn't appear to be in a store. Choice (D) is incorrect because the man is reading from a computer, not a book.
3. **(D)** The photo shows teacups, a teapot, and a vase of flowers on a tray. Choices (A), (B), and (C) correctly identify objects in the photo, but not their locations.
4. **(A)** The photo shows a man and a woman looking at items in a store; the types of items make it appear to be a hardware store. Choice (B) refers to the rake the man is holding, but he is not raking anything. Choice (C) refers to the store location, but it incorrectly identifies the woman's action. Choice (D) correctly identifies the broom, but no one is sweeping.
5. **(B)** Two men are crossing the street. Choice (A) refers to the coffee cup in one man's hand, but no one is ordering coffee. Choice (C) confuses *suitcase* with the *briefcase* in one man's hand. Choice (D) associates traffic with the street scene, but there are no policemen in the photo.
6. **(D)** A freight train is seen in a country setting. Choice (A) refers to the water seen in the photo, but it is not a city scene. Choice (B) associates *train* and *conductor.* Choice (C) associates *train* and *railroad.*

PART 2: QUESTION-RESPONSE

7. **(B)** This answers the *yes-no* question about Sam's arrival. Choice (A) confuses similar-sounding words *yet* and *set.* Choice (C) repeats the name *Sam.*
8. **(A)** *A shop right across the street* answers the *Where* question. Choice (B) associates *coffee* and *cup.* Choice (C) would be a response to an offer of a cup of coffee.
9. **(C)** This is an appropriate response to a request for help. Choice (A) confuses the meaning of the word *show* in this context. Choice (B) confuses related words *printer* and *print.*
10. **(A)** This answers the *Why* question with a plausible reason. Choice (B) associates *lunch* and *sandwich.* Choice (C) repeats the word *desk.*
11. **(C)** *Fifteen* answers the *How many* question. Choice (A) confuses similar-sounding words *dinner* and *winner.* Choice (B) would answer a *When* question.
12. **(A)** This is an appropriate response to the remark about the lamp not working. Choice (B) would answer a *Why* question. Choice (C) confuses similar-sounding words *lamp* and *damp.*
13. **(B)** *Half an hour ago* answers the *When* question. Choice (A) relates *meeting* and *agenda.* Choice (C) repeats the word *start.*
14. **(B)** This is an appropriate response to the *yes-no* question about living in the neighborhood. Choice (A) repeats the word *neighborhood.* Choice (C) confuses similar-sounding words *neighborhood* and *good.*
15. **(A)** This is an appropriate response to the question about weekend plans. Choice (B) confuses similar-sounding words *plans* and *plants.* Choice (C) repeats the word *weekend.*
16. **(C)** *Fifteen minutes* answers the *How much time* question. Choice (A) confuses the meaning of the word *left* in this context. Choice (B) confuses similar-sounding words *much time* and *lunchtime.*
17. **(C)** This answers the indirect *Why* question with a plausible reason. Choices (A) and (B) repeat the word *open.*

18. **(B)** This is an appropriate response to the offer of help. Choice (A) associates *phone* and *message.* Choice (C) confuses similar-sounding words *phone* and *fun.*

19. **(A)** This is a logical response to the comment about the museum's opening time. Choice (B) uses a number, but it is not in the context of time. Choice (C) uses related word *opener.*

20. **(B)** *The leather one* answers the *Which* question. Choice (A) would answer a *Who* question. Choice (C) uses relate words *decided* and *decision.*

21. **(B)** *A biography* answers the question about reading. Choice (A) would answer a question about *eating,* not *reading.* Choice (C) confuses similar-sounding words *read* and *need.*

22. **(A)** This answers the *Where* question. Choice (B) would answer a *When* question. Choice (C) repeats the word *credit.*

23. **(C)** This answers the *yes-no* question. Choices (A) and (B) would answer a *When* question.

24. **(C)** This answers the *yes-no* question. Choice (A) confuses similar-sounding words *class* and *glass.* Choice (B) uses the word *sign* with a different meaning.

25. **(B)** This answers the *How much* question about cost. Choice (A) associates *air conditioner* and *degrees.* Choice (C) would answer a *How many* question.

26. **(A)** This answers the question *When will you be leaving.* Choice (B) would answer a *Why* question. Choice (C) would answer *When is your appointment.*

27. **(A)** This answers the *yes-no* question. Choice (B) uses the word *watch* with a different meaning. Choice (C) would be a response to *Thank you.*

28. **(C)** *Henry* responds to the comment about something *someone* did. Choice (A) associates *lights* with *turn on.* Choice (B) associates *lights* with *electrician.*

29. **(B)** The *Clinton project* answers the *What* question. Choice (A) would answer a *Where* question. Choice (C) associates *talking* with *sound.*

30. **(A)** The comment *You look nervous* is answered with a reason. Choice (B) uses the word *look* with a different meaning. Choice (C) confuses similar-sounding words *nervous* and *service.*

31. **(A)** This is a logical response to the *yes-no* question about a phone number. Choice (B) repeats the word *phone.* Choice (C) associates *number* and *five.*

PART 3: CONVERSATIONS

32. **(A)** The woman asks for a *lift,* meaning a *ride,* and the man talks about getting to the office, so the ride is to work. Choice (B) confuses the meaning of the word *lift.* Choice (C) confuses the meaning of the word *shop* (her car is in the shop, that is, at the mechanic's). Choice (D) is related to the fact that her car is in the shop, but it is not what she asks the man to do.

33. **(B)** The man says he has to give a presentation to a client and needs time to prepare. Choice (A) confuses similar-sounding words *prepare* and *repair.* Choice (C) confuses similar-sounding words *presentation* and *present.* Choice (D) repeats the word *finish.*

34. **(A)** The man wants to leave at 7:00, and the woman says, *Why don't you pick me up at 8:00.* Choice (B) repeats the word *client.* Choice (C) repeats the word *library,* the place where they will meet. Choice (D) repeats the word *help*—the woman offers to help the man, but she doesn't suggest asking someone else to do so.

35. **(A)** The woman says that she contacted the cleaning company, and later she mentions the good job they do on the floors, windows, and furniture. Choice (B) is associated with the mention of *floors, windows,* and *furniture.* Choice (C) repeats the word *furniture.* Choice (D) is associated with the mention of a *restaurant.*

36. **(D)** The man wants the office cleaned before his client meeting, but the cleaners can't come until Monday, which is after the meeting. Choice (A) is incorrect because

the woman says she contacted the cleaning company. Choice (B) is incorrect because they say the price is reasonable. Choice (C) is incorrect because they are hiring the cleaning company.

37. **(C)** The man says, *Why don't we plan to meet the clients at a restaurant instead of here?* Choice (A) repeats the word *earlier.* Choice (B) associates *pay* with *price.* Choice (D) repeats the word *furniture*

38. **(A)** The woman is going to a restaurant with a group of friends and asks the man to go with them. Choices (B), (C), and (D) are all plausible reasons, but they are not the correct answers.

39. **(B)** The man says, *I still have this report to finish.* Choice (A) confuses similar-sounding words *report* and *sports.* Choice (C) repeats the word *desk.* Choice (D) confuses similar-sounding words *all* and *call.*

40. **(C)** The man asks the woman to *work on the last part of it with me, it* meaning *report,* so he can finish on time to go to the restaurant. Choice (A) repeats the word *restaurant.* Choice (B) is not mentioned. Choice (D) repeats the time they will go to the restaurant.

41. **(D)** The woman mentions a *vehicle,* and the man mentions *GPS* and a *tank of gas,* so they are talking about a car. Choice (A) is related to the mention of *seats.* Choice (B) is incorrect because it is not something that someone can *bring back.* Choice (C) is related to the mention of *heated seats.*

42. **(C)** The woman says, *you can keep it over the weekend, if you want it for a little longer.* Choice (A) is related to the man's request for a large vehicle. Choice (B) is plausible, but it is not mentioned. Choice (D) repeats the word *agreement.*

43. **(B)** The woman has shown the man a rental agreement, and the man requests a pen. Choice (A) is what he will do when he returns the car. Choice (C) repeats the word *weekend.* Choice (D) is related to the topic, but it is not mentioned.

44. **(D)** The man called to ask about shipping options. Choices (A), (B), and (C) are all plausible reasons, but they are not the correct answers.

45. **(B)** The woman says, *there is a $20 surcharge for express shipping.* Choice (A) costs $10. Choice (C) is not mentioned. Choice (D) is part of standard shipping.

46. **(B)** The woman asks, *Is there anything else,* meaning *Is there anything else you want to know,* and the man replies, *That's it,* meaning there is nothing else. Choices (A), (C), and (D) are plausible in the context, but they are not the correct answers.

47. **(C)** The woman asks about work and benefits and says, *If I'm hired....* Choices (A), (B), and (D) are all plausible, but they are not the correct answers.

48. **(D)** The man says, *the hours are great.* Choices (A), (B), and (C) are all things someone might like about a job, but they are not the correct answers.

49. **(B)** The woman asks a question about benefits and the man says he will take her to see Mrs. Patterson, who can answer that question. Choice (A) is incorrect because the man says that Mrs. Patterson is the one who can answer the question. Choice (C) repeats the word *weekend,* related to the mention of the work schedule. Choice (D) is contradicted by the correct answer.

50. **(D)** The man mentions that the hotel where he plans to stay is next to the conference center. Choices (A) and (B) are plausible, but they are incorrect answers. Choice (C) is confused with the photos the man says he saw on the hotel website.

51. **(B)** One woman says she couldn't sleep and then mentions the beds. The other woman agrees about the beds and adds that the rooms are small. All this adds up to an uncomfortable hotel. Choice (A) is incorrect because all the speakers agree that the price is *reasonable,* that is, *fair.* Choice (C) is incorrect because they say the hotel is *well located.* Choice (D) is a plausible reason for not sleeping, but it is not mentioned.

52. **(A)** The man says, *I'll look into some other possibilities,* meaning he'll research other

possible places to stay. Choice (B) is contradicted by the correct answer. Choice (C) is plausible in the context, but it is not mentioned. Choice (D) relates *sleep* and *nap.*

53. **(A)** The speakers are talking about a *renovation* project, and the contractor's trucks are mentioned. Choice (B) is related to renovation. Choice (C) is related to the mention of trucks. Choice (D) is something contractors might be hired for.
54. **(D)** The woman says, *Three contractors have submitted quotes, and the team is meeting tomorrow to review them.* Choice (A) repeats the word *quotes.* Choice (B) repeats the word *contractor.* Choice (C) repeats the word *schedule.*
55. **(C)** The man says, *we need a contractor that's based within 30 miles of the job site,* and the woman says that the last contractor *complained about the distance.* Choices (A), (B), and (D) are plausible in the context, but they are not the correct answer.
56. **(D)** The man is ordering checks at a place where he has an account, so he is at a bank. Choices (A) and (C) are associated with the mention of *colors and styles.* Choice (B) is associated with *order* and *check* (with a different meaning—at a restaurant *check* means *bill*).
57. **(C)** The man is ordering checks—he says he wants more checks and the woman shows him styles and colors he can order and says the order will arrive in two weeks. Choices (A), (B), and (D) are plausible, but not the correct answers.
58. **(B)** *Selection* refers to the variety of choices; when the man says it *could be better,* he means it is not good enough. Choices (A), (C), and (D) don't fit the context or the meaning of the phrase.
59. **(A)** They are talking about a show at a theater that has great acting and for which you need tickets, so it is a play. Choice (B) is an event that could take place at a theater and requires tickets. Choices (C) and (D) are things that require tickets.
60. **(D)** The woman called the box office and found out the show was sold out, that is, all the tickets had been sold. Choice (A) is what one of the man's cousins is doing. Choice (B) repeats the word *seat.* Choice (C) repeats the word *tomorrow*—the day that the cousin is going out of town.
61. **(B)** The man offers to call his cousin to find out if the cousin will give his tickets to the woman. Choice (A) repeats the word *trip,* but there is no mention of planning. Choice (C) is incorrect because he only offers to find out if the tickets are available, he does not offer to pay for them. Choice (D) repeats the words *box office*—where the woman called to try to buy tickets.
62. **(C)** The woman is going to see Mr. Gill at Zenith Enterprises, which is on the 3rd floor. Choices (A), (B), and (D) are the locations of other offices.
63. **(B)** The woman says she hopes to work with Mr. Gill and is going to see him for a job interview. Choice (A) is related to the discussion of work. Choice (C) confuses similar-sounding words *appointment* and *apartment.* Choice (D) repeats the word *appointment.*
64. **(A)** The man says that Mr. Gill's office is on the way to his own office and also that he hasn't seen the woman there before, both of which imply he works near Mr. Gill. Choices (B), (C), and (D) are contradicted by the correct answer.
65. **(C)** The woman says she was trying to order *ski boots.* Choices (A) and (D) sound similar to the correct answer. Choice (B) is not mentioned.
66. **(A)** The coupon expires June 30 and the man says, *Today's July 3rd.* Choice (B) is incorrect because the code that the woman gives the man is the same as the code on the coupon. Choice (C) is incorrect because the charge for the order is $175, and the coupon is good, for purchases over $150. Choice (D) is incorrect because the coupon states it is good for online purchases.
67. **(D)** After the man says, *Tell you what,* he offers the woman a discount on her next pur-

chase. Choices (A), (B), and (C) are different ways the word *tell* could be used, but they do not fit the context or the meaning of the expression.

68. **(B)** The man says, *We're a bit understaffed today,* meaning there aren't enough staff members at work. Since the speakers are in a restaurant, that means there aren't enough servers. Choice (A) repeats the word *chef.* Choice (C) is plausible, but it is not mentioned. Choice (D) uses the related word *staff.*
69. **(A)** The woman says, *Everybody knows the food here is worth waiting for,* meaning most people have a good opinion of the restaurant. Choice (B) is not mentioned. Choice (C) repeats the word *popular.* Choice (D) is related to the fact that there was a delay.
70. **(B)** The woman says, *I'll try the number 2.* Choices (A) and (C) include fish, which the woman says she doesn't like. Choice (D) includes vegetables, which the woman says she wants, but it isn't what she ordered.

PART 4: TALKS

71. **(D)** The message offers a discount on annual passes and explains the benefits of having a pass. Choices (A) and (B) are plausible, but they are not mentioned. Choice (C) is associated with the description of the different activities that take place at the park.
72. **(A)** The speaker mentions the annual Evening Extravaganza, when the park stays open until midnight. Choices (B) and (D) refer to activities that are mentioned, but there is no mention of how often they take place. Choice (C) is the topic of the message, but there is no mention of how often a discount is offered.
73. **(C)** The listener can *talk to a representative about purchasing annual passes,* that is, a person who will sell them something. Choice (A) is associated with the mention of concerts. Choice (B) is associated with the context of talking on the phone. Choice (D) is associated with the topic of a park.
74. **(C)** The workshop will cover *stocks and bonds,* how to *help your money grow,* and *places you can put your money.* Choice (A) associates *money* and *budgets.* Choice (B) associates *laptops* and *computers.* Choice (D) repeats the word *software.*
75. **(A)** The speaker mentions *the schedule I'm passing out.* Choice (B) is what the participants were asked to bring. Choice (C) is what the participants might have later during the break. Choice (D) associates *seat* and *chair.*
76. **(B)** The speaker says, *We'll take one break after the first hour and then another at around eleven.* Choice (A) is confused with *one break.* Choices (C) and (D) are not mentioned.
77. **(A)** The speaker is talking to passengers, mentions a storm, and then says, *We cannot fly over or around it.* If they are flying, they must be on a plane. Choice (B) has passengers and a captain, but it does not fly. Choice (C) is associated with the mention of bags. Choice (D) has passengers, but it does not fly.
78. **(C)** The problem is a storm. Choice (A) repeats the phrase *storage compartments.* Choice (B) repeats the word *seats.* Choice (D) repeats the word *bags.*
79. **(A)** The speaker says, *beverage service will be suspended until further notice.* Choices (B), (C), and (D) are plausible in the context of plane travel, but they are not mentioned.
80. **(D)** The product is a heater, and the speaker says, *I haven't been able to get it to heat again.* Choice (A) is confused with the mention of the manual cover. Choice (B) is incorrect because the woman says that the fan blows. Choice (C) is incorrect because the woman says she can turn it on, and when she does, the fan blows.
81. **(B)** The speaker says, *I've had the heater for two days.* Choice (A) repeats the word *morning.* Choice (C) sounds similar to the correct answer. Choice (D) confuses similar-sounding words *fine* and *nine.*
82. **(C)** The speaker asks the listener to *phone me* to let her know if there is a way to fix the heater. Choice (A) is plausible in the context, but it is not mentioned. Choice (B) is what the

speaker says she doesn't want. Choice (D) is incorrect because she already has a manual.

83. **(A)** The speaker mentions visiting buildings and looking at building styles. Choices (B) and (D) are things they will see, but they are not the focus of the tour. Choice (C) is related to the *historic district*, the part of the city they are touring, but it is not the focus.

84. **(C)** The speaker mentions that they will *stroll* and *walk*. Choices (A), (B), and (D) are all plausible in the context, but they are not the correct answers.

85. **(B)** The speaker says she will show the group a map; this will happen before they set off on the tour. Choice (A) is the last thing they will do. Choice (C) is the first stop on the tour; they will do this after looking at the map. Choice (D) has already been done because the speaker says she has everyone's tickets.

86. **(A)** The speaker mentions using this product in a *break room* and with *colleagues*, so it is being marketed to office workers. Choices (B), (C), and (D) are all places where coffeemakers are used, but they are not the correct answers.

87. **(B)** The speaker says that the product *can make 24 cups at a time.* Choice (A) sounds similar to the correct answer. Choice (C) is confused with how long the coffee stays warm (*8 hours*). Choice (D) confuses similar-sounding words *time* and *nine*.

88. **(D)** The speaker tells listeners to visit the company's website *to find out about this and other fine Stenson's products*, that is, to look for more information. Choices (A) and (C) are other things a customer might do on a website. Choice (B) repeats the word *products*.

89. **(B)** The speaker is talking about an *opening ceremony* for a new bridge. Choice (A) is confused with the mention that the plans met with approval from city residents. Choices (C) and (D) are plausible in the context, but they are not mentioned.

90. **(C)** The speaker says, *there is a long line of drivers waiting to be among the first to go across the new bridge.* Choices (A) and (B) are plausible, but they are not mentioned. Choice (D) repeats the word *mayor*.

91. **(B)** *It's hard to believe* is a phrase used to express surprise at an occurrence, and Choices (A), (C), and (D) do not correctly interpret the meaning of this phrase.

92. **(B)** The word *cuisine* is included in the title. Roger has a career as a chef, and the book contains recipes. Choices (A) and (C) are mentioned. Choice (D) is plausible in the context.

93. **(B)** To *jump at a chance* means to *take advantage of a good opportunity*; Roger was offered a job as a chef, and he accepted it. Choices (A), (C), and (D) do not fit the meaning of the phrase or the context.

94. **(C)** The speaker says that Roger will be at a restaurant where he will *share excerpts from his book*. Choices (A) and (B) are associated with the place where Roger will be. Choice (D) is what Roger has done in the past.

95. **(A)** The speaker mentions *footwear*, which refers to shoes in general, and *sandals*, *slippers*, and *running shoes*, which are types of shoes. Choice (B) is associated with *footwear*. Choice (C) is associated with *running shoes*. Choice (D) is confused with *brick-and-mortar store*, which actually refers to a physical store as opposed to an online store.

96. **(B)** The speaker is concerned about the group with the *noticeably lower sales*. Choices (A), (C), and (D) all had higher sales, and there were no large differences among them.

97. **(C)** The speaker says, *I'd like to take a few minutes to talk over any ideas you might have*. Choice (A) relates *reported* and *report*. Choice (B) repeats the word *groups*. Choice (D) repeats the word *slide*.

98. **(D)** Marc is arranging the details of the speaker's trip, so he is her assistant. Choices (A) and (B) are incorrect because Marc is responsible for arranging more than just train tickets or hotels; he is responsible for both those things as well as meeting schedules. Choice (C) is related to the context, but it is unlikely that a boss would arrange trip details.

99. **(A)** The speaker wants to add time to her trip in order to attend Professor Obard's seminar. Choice (B) repeats the word *meetings*, but adding more is not mentioned. Choice (C) repeats the word *hotel*, but getting a better one is not mentioned. Choice (D) repeats the word *transportation*.

100. **(D)** The speaker says she wants a hotel that is as close to the train station as possible, and the Montshire is the closest. Choices (A), (B), and (C) don't fit this description.

Reading

PART 5: INCOMPLETE SENTENCES

101. **(D)** *Valuable* is an adjective describing the noun *skills*. Choice (A) is a verb or a noun. Choice (B) is a past tense or past participle verb. Choice (C) is an adverb.

102. **(B)** *Up to* means *as much as*. Choices (A), (C), and (D) have no meaning in this context.

103. **(C)** *Primarily* means *mainly*. Choices (A), (B), and (D) have meanings that don't fit the context.

104. **(D)** The verb *coincide* is followed by the preposition *with*. Choices (A), (B), and (C) are prepositions that don't normally follow *coincide*.

105. **(C)** *Color scheme* refers to a combination or arrangement of colors. Choices (A), (B) and (D) don't fit the context.

106. **(C)** The main verb *recommend* is followed by a gerund. Choice (A) is present tense or base form. Choice (B) is past tense. Choice (D) is future tense.

107. **(B)** The time expression *next week* indicates that a future verb is required here. Choice (A) is present tense. Choice (C) is present perfect tense. Choice (D) is present perfect continuous tense.

108. **(A)** The verb *attend* is followed by the preposition *to*. Choices (B), (C), and (D) are prepositions that don't normally follow *attend*.

109. **(D)** *Except* is a preposition meaning *not including*. Choices (A) and (B) are not prepositions. Choice (C) does not fit the context.

110. **(A)** *Belongings* means *possessions*. People are not allowed to take their possessions into the factory with them. Choices (B), (C), and (D) have meanings that don't fit the context.

111. **(C)** *His* is a possessive adjective, in this case, meaning *Daniel's* and modifying the noun *job*. Choice (A) is a subject pronoun. Choice (B) is an object pronoun. Choice (D) refers to a woman.

112. **(D)** A verb is needed here to act as the main verb of the clause. Choice (A) is a gerund or present participle. Choices (B) and (C) are nouns.

113. **(C)** *Can* is a modal, in this case, preceding the base form verb *attend* and meaning *are allowed to*. Choice (A) is grammatically incorrect. Choices (B) and (D) don't make sense in this sentence.

114. **(B)** *Extensive*, in this case, means *a lot of*. Choices (A), (C), and (D) have meanings that don't fit the context.

115. **(A)** *Due to* introduces a cause. Choices (B) and (C) need to introduce a clause, not a phrase. Choice (D) introduces a contradiction.

116. **(D)** This is a passive verb made up of the present tense form of the verb *be* and the past participle of the main verb. Choice (A) is not a form of the verb *be*. Choices (B) and (C) are forms of the verb *be* but don't have any verb tense.

117. **(C)** This is a possessive relative pronoun. The meaning is *the person's signature*. Choices (A) and (D) can be used as relative pronouns, but they are not possessive. Choice (B) is a contraction for *who is*.

118. **(B)** This is a gerund in the position of subject of the sentence. Choices (A) and (D) are base form or present tense. Choice (C) is an infinitive verb.

119. **(A)** *Or* introduces a choice. Choice (B) introduces a result. Choice (C) introduces a condition. Choice (D) introduces a cause or a comparison.

120. **(B)** *Inaccurate* means *not correct*, so *inaccurate figures* would be a reason for rewriting a

budget report. Choices (A), (C), and (D) have meanings that don't fit the context.

121. **(D)** *Acquire* means *get* or *obtain.* Choices (A), (B), and (C) have meanings that don't fit the context.

122. **(B)** *After* introduces a time clause that describes the action that happened first, in this case, first the client accepts the plan, then the team has one month to complete the design. Choices (A) and (D) would introduce the action that happens second. Choice (C) introduces an action that happens at the same time as another action.

123. **(A)** To *earn* approval means *to get approval* as a result of your actions. Choices (B), (C), and (D) have meanings that don't fit the context.

124. **(A)** This is a future time clause, so a present tense verb is needed. Choice (B) is present tense, but it doesn't agree with the plural subject, *renovations.* Choice (C) is base form. Choice (D) is future tense.

125. **(B)** *Resize* is a verb following the modal *can.* Choice (A) is a noun. Choice (C) is an adjective. Choice (D) is a noun or a gerund.

126. **(D)** *Although* introduces a dependent clause that describes a contradiction. Choice (A) introduces a cause. Choice (B) introduces a result. Choice (C) is a preposition and is not used to introduce a clause.

127. **(A)** *Include* is the main verb of the sentence. Choice (B) is a gerund or present participle. Choice (C) is an adjective. Choice (D) is an adverb.

128. **(C)** *Previous* is an adjective describing something from before, in this case, the noun *employers.* Choice (A) is a preposition, not an adjective. Choice (B) refers to something that is forward or ahead. Choice (D) is a verb, not an adjective.

129. **(B)** *Instead* is an adverb meaning *as a substitute.* Choice (A) would be correctly used in the clause that precedes *or.* Choice (A) is not an adverb. Choice (D) has the wrong meaning.

130. **(A)** The past perfect form of the verb is used for an unreal past conditional. Choice (B) is present perfect tense. Choice (C) is present perfect continuous tense. Choice (D) is the correct form for the main clause, not the *if* clause.

PART 6: TEXT COMPLETION

131. **(A)** A verb following *let* is in the base form. Choice (B) is present tense. Choice (C) is an infinitive. Choice (D) is a future verb.

132. **(C)** This possessive adjective modifies the noun *needs,* referring to the needs of the person addressed in the letter, so the second person form is required. Choices (A) and (D) are third person forms. Choice (C) is a first person form.

133. **(D)** The company founders are the people who started the company; they are the people writing the letter to introduce their new business. Choices (A), (B), and (C) have meanings that don't fit the context.

134. **(B)** This is a logical way to end a letter that introduces a new business. Choices (A), (C), and (D) all imply that there already has been contact between the writers and the recipient of the letter, and that is illogical since it is a letter of introduction.

135. **(D)** This is a logical reason for temporarily suspending service at a bus stop. Choices (A), (B), and (C) are about buses, but they don't fit the context.

136. **(C)** *Instead* means *in place of.* Passengers can use these stops in place of the Main Street stop. Choices (A), (B), and (D) have meanings that don't fit the context.

137. **(B)** *Improve* means *make better.* Renovating bus shelters is one way of making bus service better. Choices (A), (C), and (D) have meanings that don't fit the context.

138. **(A)** This is an imperative verb suggesting something that readers can do. Choice (B) is an infinitive verb. Choice (C) would require mention of a subject. Choice (D) is a command and would not be used on a notice of this sort.

139. **(D)** This sentence introduces the bulleted list that follows. Choices (A), (B), and (C) are

related to the topic of company policy, but they do not fit the context.

140. **(C)** A passive verb is required here because the subject, *requests,* is not active. The requests don't submit themselves. Choices (A), (B), and (D) are reactive verb forms.

141. **(A)** In this sentence, *another* is a pronoun for *another copy.* The meaning *is one copy for your supervisor and one copy for the HR office.* Choices (B) and (D) don't make sense in this context. Choice (C) is incorrect because *some* refers to a plural noun, but a singular word is needed here.

142. **(B)** *Regarding* in this context means *about.* Choices (A), (C), and (D) have similar meanings, but they require the use of prepositions or adverbs. Choices (A) and (B) are followed by *to.* Choice (C) is preceded by *as.*

143. **(B)** The purpose of the letter is to apologize for a guest's bad experience, and this sentence introduces that idea. Choices (A), (C), and (D) are related to the topic of a hotel, but they do not fit the context.

144. **(A)** *On* is the correct preposition to use with the expression *to pride oneself on.* Choices (B), (C), and (D) cannot be used in this context.

145. **(D)** *Recent* refers to something that happened just a short while ago, and the first sentence of the letter tells us that this guest's stay happened *last week.* Choice (A) describes something that will happen in the near future. Choice (B) means *last.* Choice (C) is an adverb, so it cannot be used to describe a noun.

146. **(C)** The verb *consider* is followed by a gerund. Choice (A) is present tense or base form. Choice (B) is present tense. Choice (D) is an infinitive verb.

PART 7: READING COMPREHENSION

147. **(A)** The order will be delivered *before noon today,* that is, this morning. Choices (B), (C), and (D) don't fit this description.

148. **(C)** In the notes section, the customer asks for *yellow bananas that are ready for eating,* that is, ripe bananas. Choice (A) is incorrect because the customer didn't specify a temperature for the soda. Choice (B) repeats the word *yellow,* but it was not used in relation to tomatoes. Choice (D) is incorrect because the customer specified *whole walnuts.*

149. **(B)** Paul asks if there is a problem with the shipment and Millie replies, *It's not going out till tomorrow.* This is a problem because the client paid for overnight delivery. Choices (A), (C), and (D) are related to the topic of shipments, but they are not the correct answer.

150. **(C)** Millie writes that she will try to *get them to speed things up,* that is, to get the shipment sent sooner. Choice (A) refers to the phone calls Millie will make, but they are to the warehouse, not the client. Choice (B) is not mentioned. Choice (D) refers to the payment made by the client for overnight delivery, but there is no mention of returning it.

151. **(D)** According to the notes column, the change fee is because the date of the trip was rescheduled from September 9 to September 16. Choices (A), (B), and (C) are all plausible reasons for an extra fee, but they are not the correct answers.

152. **(B)** The description of the hotel charge is *\$110/night × 5,* which means the \$110 nightly fee was charged five times. Choices (A), (C), and (D) are not mentioned.

153. **(C)** The ad states, *Must be proficient with word processing functions.* Choices (A) and (D) are what the assistant will be trained to do. Choice (B) repeats the words *program* and *computers,* but programming computers is not mentioned.

154. **(A)** The ad states, *Apply in person,* and then gives the address of the office. Choices (B) and (C) are not mentioned. Choice (D) is incorrect because the ad specifically states *no phone calls.*

155. **(C)** The article is about e-tickets on commuter trains. Choices (A) and (B) are mentioned, but they are not the main topic. Choice (D) is not mentioned.

156. **(B)** The article states that traditional tickets are for sale by machine. Choice (A) is how to

buy e-tickets. Choice (C) is mentioned but not as a way to buy tickets. Choice (D) is not mentioned.

157. **(D)** *Phased out* means *discontinued.* Traditional tickets will be discontinued soon because e-tickets are being used. Choices (A), (B), and (C) have meanings that don't fit the context.

158. **(A)** The passage states, *The program is open to anyone who has been a member in good standing for at least one year.* Choice (B) is mentioned as an option, not a requirement. Choice (C) is plausible in the context, but it is not mentioned. Choice (D) repeats the phrase *training program*, which is mentioned as something that recognizes the certificates.

159. **(D)** The tests are given *every six months*, that is, twice a year. Choices (A) and (B) repeat *six.* Choice (C) is an incorrect interpretation of *every six months.*

160. **(B)** An e-mail address is provided for requesting information about test registration. Choice (A) is mentioned as an option for preparing for the test. Choices (C) and (D) are plausible in the context, but they are not mentioned.

161. **(D)** The requirements for purchasing a waiver are to be over 21 and to not have *been involved in an accident in the past 12 months.* Choice (A) is contradicted by the correct answer. Choices (B) and (C) are plausible in the context, but they are not mentioned.

162. **(C)** A waiver can reduce the damage fee from $500 to $250 or to $0. Choice (A) repeats the phrase 12 months. Choice (B) refers to the age requirement for purchasing a waiver. Choice (D) contradicts the information in the passage: *These waivers are not a substitute for insurance coverage.*

163. **(A)** According to the passage, *The waiver must be added to the rental agreement at the time of signing.* Choices (B), (C), and (D) are related to the topic, but they are not the correct answers.

164. **(D)** *Caterers, menu, tables,* and *chairs* all indicate that food will be served, and this is the only choice that is a food event. Choices (A), (B), and (C) are events that colleagues might plan together, but they are not the correct answers.

165. **(A)** Jairo mentions *my menu modifications.* Choices (B), (C), and (D) are all mentioned, but they are not things Jairo changed.

166. **(B)** Mija writes that she got *RSVPs*, that is, responses to invitations, and she and Jairo go on to discuss the people that are coming, that is the people who have been invited. Choice (A) is related, but it is not mentioned. Choice (C) is discussed, but it is not what Mija received. Choice (D) is what Jairo got this morning.

167. **(C)** The expression, *We're good to go,* means *We're ready to get started,* and Mija mentions the things that have been all arranged—the caterers and the room. Choices (A), (B), and (D) don't fit the meaning of the phrase or the context.

168. **(D)** The article is directed at people who are *new to the job market* and have *just finished your education,* and who are described as *young people.* Choices (A) and (B) are incorrect because the article is for people who are seeking jobs, not people who are involved with hiring. Choice (C) is incorrect because the article is not for experienced people.

169. **(B)** The expression, *It all boils down to . . .* means *It can be summarized as . . .*, and the word that summarizes Ms. Pritchard's advice—*professionalism*—soon follows. Choices (A), (C), and (D) don't fit the meaning of the expression or the paragraph.

170. **(A)** The article states, *Keep in mind that you don't want the color of your clothes to shout. Black, charcoal gray, or deep blue are best for job interviews,* which suggests dark colors. Choices (B), (C), and (D) are plausible in the context, but they are not mentioned.

171. **(D)** This sentence introduces the topic of the paragraph—how to act like a professional. Choices (A), (B), and (C) are not the right context for this sentence.

172. **(C)** He wrote the letter to ask her to speak at an alternative energy affair, that is, to invite her to an event. Choice (A) is mentioned, but it is not the main topic of the letter. Choice (B) is incorrect because there is no mention of his selling anything. Choice (D) is a plausible reason to write a letter, but it is not mentioned.

173. **(B)** Mr. Marquez writes, about alternative energy: *I believe we need to spread the word and get more people on board with this,* that is, he wants to inform people and persuade them of his point of view. Choice (A) refers to the organization Mr. Marquez belongs to, but there is no mention of whether or not he is president of it. Choice (C) is incorrect because the implication is that he has done this for his own family only. Choice (D) describes Ms. Jackson; Mr. Marquez has some knowledge but probably not an expert level.

174. **(A)** Mr. Marquez tells Ms. Jackson that she can sell her books at the fair, which implies that she has written some. Choice (B) is incorrect because it is implied that Mr. Marquez has never met her, or only heard her speak on the radio. Choice (C) is incorrect because she was a guest, not the host. Choice (D) is plausible, but there is nothing that implies this.

175. **(B)** Mr. Marquez writes *I will need to hear back from you before the end of two weeks.* Choice (A) is not mentioned. Choices (C) and (D) are incorrect because the letter is dated August 22, so September will begin sooner than two weeks.

176. **(B)** The Wisteria is in a converted farmhouse with views of pastures and hills and nearby horseback trails through the woods, so it is in a rural setting. Choice (A) is incorrect because there are only six guest rooms. Choice (C) is plausible, but it is not mentioned. Choice (D) is incorrect because it is in an historical farmhouse.

177. **(C)** Guests can rent the barn for a wedding or family reunion. Choice (A) confuses the use of the word craft. Choice (B) is incorrect because only breakfast is mentioned. Choice (D) repeats the word barn, but it is only mentioned in the text as a place for parties, not as a working barn.

178. **(D)** The information on the webpage states, *Book your room before April 30 and receive 20% off,* that is, make a reservation before April 30 to get a discount. Choice (A) is mentioned, but not in connection with a discount. Choice (B) is confused with when the reservation must be made. Choice (C) is mentioned, but it is not in connection with a discount.

179. **(A)** Ms. Simmons writes, *I would be happy to provide your business with fresh herbs and flowers.* Choices (B) and (D) would be reasons to contact the Wisteria, but they are not the purpose of the e-mail. Choice (C) repeats the word *business.*

180. **(A)** Ms. Simmons is a grower of herbs and flowers, that is, a farmer. Choices (B) and (C) are mentioned as the types of customers Ms. Simmons deals with. Choice (D) is related to the mention on the webpage of holding events in the barn.

181. **(C)** Mr. Rosen writes that he is *leaving next month* and must leave his apartment in good condition to avoid a penalty. Choice (A) repeats the word *tenants.* Choice (B) confuses the word *visitors* with Mr. Rosen's asking whether someone from the service needs to *visit* his apartment. Choice (D) is a plausible reason, but it is not the correct answer.

182. **(A)** Mr. Rosen writes, *a colleague at work suggested I contact you.* Choice (A) is plausible, but it is not the correct answer. Choice (C) repeats the word *landlord.* Choice (D) is incorrect because Mr. Rosen asks for information (prices) that is on the flier, so it is unlikely that he has seen it.

183. **(A)** Mr. Rosen states that his apartment has just one room, and this is the price quoted on the flier for an apartment of 1–3 rooms. Choices (B), (C), and (D) are the costs to clean larger apartments.

184. **(B)** The flier mentions *mansion, apartment,* and *home,* which all refer to residences, and no other type of place is mentioned. Choice (A) is incorrect because the flier describes the prices as *competitive,* meaning they are

similar to those of it competitors. Choice (C) is incorrect because the flier states, *Call us when you need us, or arrange for regular weekly or monthly service,* implying that customers are invited to hire the service for either one-time or regular service. Choice (D) is incorrect because there is information on pricing for larger spaces with no indication that this is rare.

185. **(D)** This refers to a price estimate, or an approximate price. Choices (A), (B), and (C) don't fit the context.

186. **(A)** It is on the website's *special promotions* page, and the listed prices are described as *good through March 30,* so they will change after that date. Choice (B) is incorrect because it is the current prices, not the product itself, that are available only through March. Choice (C) is incorrect because only one color combination—black with chrome—is mentioned. Choice (D) is not mentioned.

187. **(C)** According to the e-mail, Mr. Rivera is paying $110 for his table, and this is the price listed on the webpage for the large table. Choices (A), (B), and (D) have other prices, according to the webpage.

188. **(B)** The webpage states, *Free shipping on all orders of $100 or more,* and Mr. Rivera is paying $110 for his table. Choice (A) is confused with the discount coupon mentioned on the webpage. Choice (C) is incorrect because the webpage has a link for calculating shipping costs. Choice (D) is contradicted by the correct answer.

189. **(D)** In his review, Mr. Rivera mentions using the table for weekly staff meetings. Choice (A) is not mentioned. Choices (B) and (C) are uses suggested on the webpage.

190. **(C)** Mr. Rivera explains that a part (the clips) was missing and says that he originally gave a 3-star rating because of this, but then the company sent him some clips, and now he is happy with the product. Choices (A) and (D) are plausible, but they are not mentioned. Choice (B) is mentioned in the review, but it is not as a reason for changing the rating.

191. **(B)** The menu description includes the word *vegetarian* as one of the entrees. Choice (A) is incorrect because the flier states the dinner will be *followed* by the show. Choice (C) is incorrect—there are prices listed for *show only* but none for dinner only. Choice (D) is incorrect as Esther writes that the food is *mediocre,* and Bob agrees with her.

192. **(A)** Esther did not pay anything for the tickets; her sister gave them to her. Choices (B), (C), and (D) are prices listed in the flier.

193. **(D)** In his e-mail, Bob offers to pick up Esther with his car. Choice (A) is incorrect because it is Bob, not Esther, who will drive. Choice (B) is what Esther suggests. Choice (C) is not mentioned.

194. **(B)** Bob writes, *it will my first time seeing this particular play.* Choices (A) and (C) are incorrect because Bob writes that he is *looking forward to seeing the play.* Choice (D) is incorrect because Bob writes, *I've actually eaten there before,* referring to the dinner theater.

195. **(C)** Bob means that they could *omit* the dinner, that is, not eat it because it is not likely to be good. Choices (A), (B), and (D) don't fit the context.

196. **(C)** According to the itinerary, Ms. Hakim will take a *tour of HR Manufacturers Plant* on April 12. Choices (A), (B), and (D) are other dates on the itinerary when she has other activities scheduled.

197. **(B)** The information on the flier states, *Recruiters from major companies will be available to meet with job seekers to discuss employment opportunities.* Choice (A) refers to the products that will be exhibited, but there is no mention of sales. Choice (C) repeats the word *résumé,* which is suggested that people bring with them. Choice (D) is not mentioned.

198. **(B)** *Renowned* means *famous.* Choices (A), (C), and (D) are not the correct meaning for this word.

199. **(A)** Ms. Hakim wants to change her return day from Friday to Saturday, so she can attend the business expo. Choices (B), (C),

and (D) are plausible in the context, but they are not the correct answers.

200. **(A)** Ms. Hakim writes, *I'm really looking forward to finally having the chance to meet the Wiltshire team,* which implies that she has not been to the Wiltshire office before. Choice (B) is related to the topic of the e-mail, but it is not mentioned. Choice (C) is something she might do at the business expo, but she doesn't mention it. Choice (D) is contradicted by the correct answer.

MP3 TRACK LIST

Track 1 Introduction

Listening Comprehension

Part 1: Photographs

Track 2	Skill 1—Assumptions
Track 3	Skill 2—People
Track 4	Skill 3—Things
Track 5	Skill 4—Actions
Track 6	Skill 5—General Locations
Track 7	Skill 6—Specific Locations
Track 8	Part 1—Photographs

Part 2: Question-Response

Track 9	Skill 1—Similar Sounds
Track 10	Skill 2—Related Words
Track 11	Skill 3—Homonyms
Track 12	Skill 4—Same Sound/Same Spelling but Different Meaning
Track 13	Skill 5—Suggestions
Track 14	Skill 6—Offers
Track 15	Skill 7—Requests
Track 16	Part 2—Question-Response

Part 3: Conversations

Track 17	Skill 1—Questions About People
Track 18	Skill 2—Questions About Occupations
Track 19	Skill 3—Questions About Place
Track 20	Skill 4—Questions About Time
Track 21	Skill 5—Questions About Activities
Track 22	Skill 6—Questions About Opinions

New TOEIC—Part 3: Conversations

Track 23	Skill 1—Graphic
Track 24	Skill 3—Deleted Sounds
Track 25	Skill 5—Multiple Accents

Part 4: Talks

Track 26	Skill 1—Questions About Events and Facts
Track 27	Skill 2—Questions About Reasons
Track 28	Skill 3—Questions About Numbers
Track 29	Skill 4—Questions About Main Topics
Track 30	Skill 5—Paraphrases

New TOEIC—Part 4: Talks

Track 31	Skill 1—Graphic
Track 32	Skill 2—Implied Meaning
Track 33	Skill 3—Multiple Accents

Mini-Test for Listening Comprehension

Track 34	Part 1—Photographs
Track 35	Part 2—Question-Response
Track 36	Part 3—Conversations
Track 37	Part 4—Talks

Mini-Test for New TOEIC Listening Comprehension

Track 38	Part 1—Photographs
Track 39	Part 2—Question-Response
Track 40	Part 3—Conversations
Track 41	Part 4—Talks

Model Test 1

Track 42	Part 1—Photographs
Track 43	Part 2—Question-Response
Track 44	Part 3—Conversations
Track 45	Part 4—Talks

Model Test 2

Track 46	Part 1—Photographs
Track 47	Part 2—Question-Response
Track 48	Part 3—Conversations
Track 49	Part 4—Talks

Model Test 3

Track 50	Part 1—Photographs
Track 51	Part 2—Question-Response
Track 52	Part 3—Conversations
Track 53	Part 4—Talks

Model Test 4

Track 54	Part 1—Photographs
Track 55	Part 2—Question-Response
Track 56	Part 3—Conversations
Track 57	Part 4—Talks

New TOEIC—Model Test 5

Track 58	Part 1—Photographs
Track 59	Part 2—Question-Response
Track 60	Part 3—Conversations
Track 61	Part 4—Talks

New TOEIC—Model Test 6

Track 62	Part 1—Photographs
Track 63	Part 2—Question-Response
Track 64	Part 3—Conversations
Track 65	Part 4—Talks

u can also download the files and audioscripts online http://barronsbooks.com/ tp/toeic/audio/